THE
MEMOIRS OF
MARSHAL FOCH

FOCH CARRIES THE BATON OF A MARSHAL OF FRANCE, IMMEDIATELY AFTER ITS PRESENTATION TO HIM ON AUGUST 23RD, 1918, BY M. POINCARÉ

THE MEMOIRS OF MARSHAL FOCH

TRANSLATED BY

COLONEL T. BENTLEY MOTT

The Naval & Military Press Ltd

Published by

The Naval & Military Press Ltd
Unit 5 Riverside, Brambleside
Bellbrook Industrial Estate
Uckfield, East Sussex
TN22 1QQ England

Tel: +44 (0)1825 749494

www.naval-military-press.com
www.nmarchive.com

In reprinting in facsimile from the original, any imperfections are inevitably reproduced and the quality may fall short of modern type and cartographic standards.

CONTENTS

	PAGE
Translator's Introductory Note	xi
Note	xvi
Foreword	xviii
Preface	xxxvii

BOOK I

PART I
THE XX ARMY CORPS

Chapter   I The XX Corps as part of the Covering Forces   3

II The XX Corps in the Lorraine offensive and Battle of Morhange   11

III The XX Corps during the retreat from the Meurthe and the counter-attack   34

PART II
IN COMMAND OF THE NINTH ARMY

Chapter   I The Retreat   47

II The Battle of the Marne   68

III The End of the Battle, and the Pursuit   98

IV The Halt   112

PART III
THE BATTLE OF FLANDERS

Chapter   I The Movement North   131

II The Battle of the Yser   157

CONTENTS

			PAGE
Chapter	III	The Battle of Ypres	165
	IV	The Events on the Remainder of the Front of the Armies in the North	191
	V	A General Survey of the Battle	195
	VI	First Allied Attempts against the German Front. Regrouping of the Allied Forces in Flanders	212

BOOK II

IN COMMAND OF THE ALLIED ARMIES

Preface to Book II		231
I In Command of the Armies of the North		233
II In Disfavour		251
III Chief of the General Staff		254

Chapter	I	The German Offensive of March 21st, 1918, and the Doullens Agreement	281
	II	The First Acts of the Allied Commander-in-Chief	301
	III	The Beauvais Agreement	312
	IV	The Restoration of the Allied situation on the Somme and the German effort in Flanders	319
	V	The Question of the strength of the Allied Armies in France	347
	VI	The German attack from Rheims to Montdidier	355
	VII	The Period of Waiting	380
	VIII	The Second Battle of the Marne	404
	IX	The Memorandum of July 24th	425

CONTENTS

			PAGE
Chapter	X	Partial Allied Offensives	433
	XI	The General Offensive of the Allied Armies, September 26th to October 15th—Breaking of the Hindenburg Line	467
	XII	The Problem of Effectives, Communications, and Manufacture of Munitions in the Autumn of 1918	489
	XIII	General Offensive of the Allied Armies from October 15th to November 11th, 1918	496
	XIV	The Armistice	525
	XV	The March to the Rhine	573

ILLUSTRATIONS

FOCH CARRIES THE BATON OF A MARSHAL OF FRANCE	*frontispiece*
	FACING PAGE
THE FIVE FACSIMILES OF THE FIRST PAGE OF MARSHAL FOCH'S PREFACE AND THE FOUR TYPED COPIES FOR CORRECTIONS	xl
FOCH AS A TWELVE-YEAR-OLD SCHOOLBOY	xli
THE FUTURE MARSHAL AS A CAPTAIN OF ARTILLERY	xli
"L'ECOLE SUPERIEURE DE GUERRE," WHERE FOCH ONCE LECTURED ON TACTICS, AND OF WHICH HE WAS LATER COMMANDANT	xli
ALGERIAN TROOPS ANSWER THE CALL TO THE COLOURS	54
"ONE MUST EAT!"	70
A LETTER WRITTEN BY MARSHAL FOCH TO HIS OLD FRIEND GENERAL MILLET AFTER THE BATTLE OF THE MARNE	102
JOFFRE AND FOCH, AS COMMANDER-IN-CHIEF AND ASSISTANT COMMANDER-IN-CHIEF, CONFER TOGETHER DURING THE AUTUMN OF 1914	118
GENERALS JOFFRE, FOCH, D'URBAL AND BALFOURIER INSPECTING TROOPS ON THE MARCH BEFORE THE FIRST BATTLE OF YPRES	166
FIELD-MARSHAL SIR JOHN FRENCH, GENERAL FOCH AND GENERAL WILSON AT THE CHATEAU DE BRYAS, MAY 22ND, 1915	182
JOFFRE AND FOCH AT AN INSTRUCTION CAMP BEHIND THE FRENCH FRONT	183

ILLUSTRATIONS

	FACING PAGE
FLOWERS FOR BRITISH SOLDIERS ALONG THE ROADS OF FRANCE	222
SAPPERS IN GAS MASKS LAY LINES TO THE TRENCHES	222
A COUNTRY CHURCH BECOMES A HOSPITAL FOR THE FRENCH WOUNDED	222
GENERALS JOFFRE, FOCH AND WIRBEL, IN 1915	223
A FRENCH INFANTRY REGIMENT ADVANCING TO THE FIRING LINE	223
GENERAL PERSHING ARRIVES IN FRANCE	262
DEEP TRENCHES AND DUG-OUTS, WITH SAND-BAG REVETMENTS	278
A HEAVY NAVAL BATTERY MOUNTED ON RAILS	310
FOCH WITH HIS CHIEF OF STAFF, GENERAL WEYGAND, AT SARCUS, 1918	326
GENERAL FOCH AND THE INTER-ALLIED STAFF AT SARCUS, IN APRIL, 1918	342
M. TARDIEU, GENERALS WEYGAND AND PERSHING, M. CLEMENCEAU AND MARSHAL FOCH AT PERSHING'S HEADQUARTERS AT CHAUMONT IN JUNE, 1918	358
THE ALLIED COMMANDERS-IN-CHIEF ON THE FRENCH FRONT, WITH THEIR AUTOGRAPHS	430
A CAPTURED GERMAN BATTERY	454
FOCH AND H.M. KING ALBERT OF THE BELGIANS	470
THE FIRST BRITISH PATROL ENTERS THE STREETS OF CAMBRAI	482
M. POINCARE SALUTES FOCH AFTER PRESENTING HIM WITH THE BATON OF A MARSHAL OF FRANCE	486
MR. LLOYD GEORGE, M. BRIAND AND MARSHAL FOCH	502
THE LAST PAGE OF THE ARMISTICE AGREEMENT	558
FOCH'S OFFICE IN HIS HEADQUARTERS AT SENLIS IN OCTOBER, 1918	558

ILLUSTRATIONS

FACING PAGE

THE TABLE AT WHICH THE ARMISTICE WAS SIGNED IN MARSHAL FOCH'S CAR	558
MARSHAL FOCH HOLDS IN HIS HAND THE SIGNED COPY OF THE ARMISTICE, AS HE LEAVES HIS TRAIN AT 7 A.M. ON NOVEMBER 11TH, 1918	559
LORRAINE WELCOMES THE FRENCH ARMIES, NOVEMBER 10TH, 1918	559
FOCH'S ARRIVAL AT JULIERS, IN THE RHINELAND, MAY, 1919	566
FOCH LEADING THE FRENCH TROOPS PAST THE ROYAL STAND IN THE LONDON " VICTORY PARADE " OF JULY 19TH, 1919	567
FOCH AT HIS COUNTRY PLACE " TRENFEUNTINION," IN BRITTANY, WITH HIS GRANDCHILDREN	582
THE FUNERAL OF MARSHAL FOCH, AN IMPOSING PAGEANT WATCHED BY THOUSANDS IN THE CHAMPS ELYSEE	583
THE PAPAL NUNCIO, CARDINAL DUBOIS, AND CARDINAL BINET IN FOCH'S FUNERAL PROCESSION	583

MAPS

	FACING PAGE
THE RETREAT—AUG. 30-SEPT. 5, 1914	50
THE BATTLE OF THE MARNE—SEPT. 6-10, 1914	78
THE PURSUIT—SEPT. 9-15, 1914	114
STABILIZATION OF THE FRONT—SEPT. 15-25, 1914	119
SITUATION—OCT. 5, 1914	130
SITUATION—OCT. 17, 1914	131
THE BATTLE OF THE YSER (OCT. 18-30) AND THE BATTLE OF YPRES (OCT. 21-NOV. 12, 1914)—SITUATION OCT. 23, 1914	162
GENERAL DISPOSITION OF THE ALLIED FORCES IN THE NORTH, IN APRIL, 1915	228
SITUATION OF THE ALLIED FORCES IN FRONT OF AMIENS ON MARCH 26	254
GERMAN OFFENSIVES OF MAR. 21-JULY 15, 1918	286
ALLIED OFFENSIVES—JULY 18-OCT. 15, 1918	438
THE MARCH TO THE RHINE—NOV. 11-DEC. 12, 1918	574

TRANSLATOR'S INTRODUCTORY NOTE

DURING all the time that Marshal Foch commanded the Allied Armies I served at his Headquarters, having been appointed by General Pershing as liaison officer between him and the Marshal. General Weygand was Chief of Staff, Captain Boutal was Aide-de-Camp and Captain Pupier attended to the non-military matters in the Marshal's ever-increasing correspondence. These and a few other officers took their meals with the Marshal, while the rest of the Staff, about a dozen in number, had a Mess of their own, to which were invited the Italian, Belgian and American liaison officers. The British mission, headed by that admirable soldier, Lieutenant-General Sir John Du Cane, being quite numerous, messed in their own house.

Headquarters were first established during April, 1918, in the tiny village of Sarcus, north of Beauvais; from there we moved to the Château de Mouchy and then to Bombon, not far from Provins, the Headquarters of General Pétain. Bombon was also within easy reach of Chaumont, where General Pershing was installed. In October we were at Senlis, thirty miles north of Paris, and here the Armistice found us. All of these changes were dictated by the necessities or conveniences of the operations; but the first two relieved us of the annoyance of incessant bombardment by German aeroplanes.

A peculiar requirement always dictated the choice of the house in which to establish the Marshal, steam heat. He lived and worked in an atmosphere that was stifling

TRANSLATOR'S INTRODUCTORY NOTE

even to an American, and if we saw Major Bontemps in a particularly bad humour we knew that the temperature of Headquarters had fallen below eighty and the Marshal had told him in vigorous terms of his feelings on the subject.

It can well be imagined that I have no thought of making an estimate of Marshal Foch's powers or of describing his processes; but as the characteristics of his person are less known in English-speaking countries than in France, it may not be out of place to indicate some of them.

A good deal has been said about the ties which united the Marshal and General Weygand. The two men constituted the most efficient team for the conduct of a great war that history has reported; moreover, confidence and affection bound them as closely together as did community of ideas. It was not so much that Foch conceived and Weygand executed, as was the case with Lee and Stonewall Jackson, but rather that the two minds seemed to constitute a single entity whose capacity was double that which any man working alone could furnish.

General Weygand once said to me: " The Marshal is the locomotive; I am the tender that furnishes him with coal and water." I do not think this image gives a true idea of their relationship. It was more like a chemical union, whereby two distinct elements produce a substance having characteristic qualities of its own. I doubt if General Weygand ever paid the Marshal a compliment, and probably the Marshal at no time ever expressed in words to the General what he thought about him. It would have been like saying handsome things to oneself.

The Marshal certainly felt a profound satisfaction

when success crowned one of his plans, but if at any time he spoke of such matters to one of us, we seemed to be listening to some impersonal force expressing itself rather than to a man telling about what he had done.

He was instinctively distrustful of three categories of men : orators, politicians and journalists, for he believed that they all did more harm in the world than good. He listened attentively if one spoke to the point, but he stopped you if you left it. He was brief in matters of business and he liked others to be so. It was not so much that he was silent by nature as that he preferred to talk in images or complete his thought by gestures significantly his own. Those about him learned to interpret this peculiarity with ready accuracy.

During the perilous events that succeeded each other so rapidly in the spring of 1918, at moments when we at the mess table were green with apprehension, no external sign of anxiety was ever seen to mark his countenance or his gait ; but he wore his cap set squarely on his head. In August and September, when nearly every day brought some piece of good news, you would see him swinging down the deserted little street of Bombon, stick over shoulder and his cap settled well over toward his right ear. No need to ask him how the battle was going.

I met him almost every morning that summer, I on my way from Headquarters, he returning from the village church where he had been to say his prayers. One day as I saluted him, he paused as though inviting me to speak, and I ventured the remark that the Germans seemed to be getting more than they could stand. He came up close to me, took a firm hold on my belt with his left hand and with his right fist delivered a punch at my chin, a hook under my ribs and another drive at my ear; he then shouldered his stick and without a single word marched on to the château, his straight back and horseman's legs presenting as gallant a sight as one would wish to look upon.

M. Clemenceau came to Bombon unexpectedly one morning and asked to be shown to the Marshal. Captain Boutal told him that he was at church, adding, " I will go at once and tell him you are here." " Do not interrupt him for anything in the world—it agrees with him too well," answered the witty old heathen, quite willing to take a chance even with the Almighty if France could be benefited.

On another occasion, in the midst of our Argonne offensive, I had been directed by General Pershing to present certain matters of a grave and rather delicate nature to the Marshal. He listened to all I had to say and then beckoned me over to the billiard table on which he always kept spread out a huge map of the Western Front. "Look at this," he said, waving his hand along the marked positions; " I am the leader of an orchestra. Here are the English basses, here the American baritones, and there the French tenors. When I raise my baton, every man must play or else he must not come to my concert."

This might seem a strange way of answering the presentation of a serious question; but I knew exactly what he meant and also that no amount of conversation would elicit a more definite reply.

The Marshal was a kindly man but he was not gentle. He had no pose of any kind, and in all the intimate chatter which naturally marked a year's close association with his Staff and other Staffs, I never heard a phrase which suggested some little evidence of personal vanity or anything implying favouritism or injustice on his part. Those who served immediately around him admired, respected and loved him, but he made no effort to induce their enthusiastic personal attachment. During the war he represented to them a sort of prodigious impersonal force, but in the years succeeding its close, when immense responsibilities no longer intensified relationships, he became more like a father in his attitude toward all of us who had been with him.

I once asked the Marshal how he accounted for the fact that so many of the professors at the *Ecole de Guerre* had won distinction as great leaders in the War.

" To teach a doctrine successfully," he answered, " you have got to be absolutely sure it is right. This means profound study and a long meditation upon all the objections advanced against it. Once sure, you can proceed with confidence and you carry conviction with your pupils. The men who had taught at the *Ecole de Guerre* went through this process. The early disasters of the conflict could not shake their faith in our doctrine. They continued to apply it and we finally won."

As Marshal Foch's memoirs will undoubtedly reach a wide circle of non-military readers, I have used as few technical military terms as possible in the translation, always giving preference to a rendering which will make the meaning clear to those unacquainted with military terminology.

T. BENTLEY MOTT.

NOTE

IN the course of the year 1920, Marshal Foch, yielding to the insistence of those about him, decided to write his reminiscences of the war. He directed his Staff officers to collect the necessary documents and to draw up a strictly objective recital of the events in which he had taken part during the hostilities. This recital was used by the Marshal as a frame-work which he considerably altered and enlarged, and into which he built his personal judgments, recollections and reflections.

The Marshal pursued this task during his spare moments between 1921 and 1928, but without devoting himself to it with any continuity. It was above all in the summer, when he was at his country-place in Brittany, that he did his writing, and he would constantly go over pages that he had already finished and introduce new reflections that had occurred to him.

This habit left its mark upon some of the chapters, where certain repetitions will be observed ; and while they do no injury to the value of the work—indeed they often serve to accentuate its sincerity—such a method certainly delayed its completion. Indeed, the Marshal was able to finish only the account of events in which he participated during 1914 and 1918. This forms the subject of the present work.

Before being handed to the publishers, the Memoirs were gone over by the Marshal's family and by his immediate collaborators. The accounts of military operations appeared in certain places to be too long ;

NOTE

cuts were therefore made in them, but these apply only to the relation, more or less anonymous, which the Marshal's staff officers had prepared to facilitate his work. Everything which came direct from his pen, his personal recollections, his reflections, his judgments, his teachings, have been scrupulously respected, both in form and substance : they go to the public exactly as he wrote them.

The Memoirs were intended to appear only after the lapse of several years ; certain recent and painful controversies have brought about their earlier publication. During his lifetime, Marshal Foch was in the habit of saying that he accepted the responsibility for only what he had signed. He would certainly have disavowed the polemics which were stirred up after his death, just as he disavowed, when alive, words and intentions which were gratuitously ascribed to him.

Faced by posthumous quarrels and desiring to continue this line of conduct faithfully, the Marshal's family very justly decided that it was best to let him speak for himself. In the pages which follow, the reader will have before him the thoughts of the War's great victor exactly as he set them down.

FOREWORD

In the course of the recent war I was appointed successively to various posts in the French Army. First, as Commander of the XX Corps, I took part in the operations in Lorraine up to the end of August, 1914. I then commanded the Ninth Army during the battle of the Marne. Subsequently, as assistant to the Commander-in-Chief, I was entrusted with the task of co-ordinating the action of French troops with that of our Allies, British and Belgian, in the north of France. This period comprised the Battles of the Yser and of Ypres, the Artois attacks and the Battle of the Somme. This brings us up to the end of 1916.

In 1917, as Chief of the General Staff, I performed the duties of military adviser to the French Government. For the Government had decided to participate in the conduct of the war. Amongst other tasks entrusted to me at this time was that of French co-operation in Italy, beginning in the month of April. I personally directed this work during the last part of October and all of November. Finally, I assisted in establishing the American Army in France.

In 1918, first as president of the Versailles Military Executive Committee and afterwards as Commander-in-Chief of the Allied Armies, I prepared and led the Allied forces on the Western Front.

I am now in all sincerity writing my memoirs. They do not form a history of the War; they merely give the story of the events in which I took part. From what has just been said it follows that only during the last year of the conflict will this narration bear upon the operations on the western front taken as a whole. What I have written is based upon the impressions felt at the moment of action and also upon the information we had or the hypotheses we made concerning the enemy; these at the time were necessarily full of uncertainty.

To enable the reader better to understand the way I saw and interpreted the events to be described, it may be useful to turn back to the past and tell something of the person who is writing. Indeed, the way a man of middle age looks upon events, and what he does under their influence, depends upon how his intellect and character have been formed; when this is known his reactions are easily understood. They are also the result of certain special circumstances which have so stamped themselves upon his life as to have guided its course and constantly fixed its conduct.

I was born at Tarbes, at the foot of the Pyrenees, in October, 1851, of a family coming entirely from that region. I went to school successively at Tarbes, at Rodez, at the little seminary of Polignan in the department of the Haute-Garonne, and then at the College of the Jesuits of St. Michael at Saint-Etienne. My father was a civil servant of the Government and his duties successively led him, and with him his family, to these places. My preparatory studies for the degree of Bachelor of Arts were concluded at Saint-Etienne, where one of my school-mates was the future Marshal Fayolle. Although I had early conceived the idea of going to the Polytechnic, as had my illustrious fellow-student whom I have just mentioned, our families and our masters did not think it advisable for us to omit these literary studies, in spite of the fact that they were bound to delay our preparation for that school.* Thus it was that after the course in philosophy we took our degree of B.A. before beginning our scientific studies.

If the object of the latter, and of mathematics especially, is to accustom the mind to consider objects and forms as materially defined, fix with precision one's ideas upon those subjects, link them up by inexorable processes and so mould the brain to a method of the strictest reasoning, it is the essential of letters, philosophy and history—above all of history—to quit the domain of abstract observation and direct our thoughts towards the world in which we live. This renders the intelligence broad and supple; it keeps it awake, active and creative in the presence of that land of the indefinite which life opens up to us. Standing in the midst of this vast horizon, which, indeed, is a reality, one must, in order to advance, first attentively survey the whole, then, choosing a goal, march resolutely toward it, seizing each point of vantage, surmounting or turning every difficulty. It is at this moment that the dual preparation furnished by general knowledge and special studies brings its aid to those who wish not only to learn a trade, but also, if need be, to develop and apply it successively to new purposes.

In what concerns especially the army officer, the future probably will merely accentuate this need of general culture combined with professional knowledge. As the sphere of war extends, so should the minds of those waging it broaden out. An officer of first-rate ability can no longer be satisfied with mere professional attainments, such as the technique of leading troops and supplying their material wants; nor must he be content

* The *Ecole Polytechnique* is a Government military school in Paris whose graduates enter the Engineers, Artillery and certain Civil Services.—T. B. M.

to live in a little world of his own. Soldiers in time of peace form the young and manly element of the country; in time of war they constitute the nation in arms. How then, can an officer who is not in constant touch with the spirit of his people hope to turn such resources to good account? How can he comprehend and direct the social phenomena which characterise great national wars unless he has some acquaintance with moral and political sciences and possesses that knowledge of history which alone can explain to him the life of nations in the past and in the present? Here again technical acquirements are no longer sufficient; he must complete them with a large addition furnished by other faculties.

Moreover, as any officer can readily perceive, his mind and character will be far better prepared for a coming war, and even his career will be advanced in time of peace, if he keeps himself—always with a loyal sense of discipline—constantly abreast of the events and problems of his time, instead of confining his interest solely to garrison life, obsessed by thoughts of promotion and careless of developing his higher capacities.

Without this conception, the regular officer, when war arrives, runs the risk of seeing himself outdistanced by the reserve officer, who can bring to his work—in addition to an indispensable military equipment—faculties and knowledge which a wider life has maintained in fruitful activity.

In 1869, having completed my literary studies at Saint-Michael's College, I went to Saint-Clement's, at Metz, where I continued my preparation for the Polytechnic School. Saint-Clement's was a very well-managed college, then at the height of its development. Its students came mainly from Alsace and Lorraine, and many of them took advantage of its excellent courses to prepare themselves for state schools such as the Polytechnic, Saint-Cyr and the School of Forestry. Two of the professors stood out most prominently by reason of their ability and their whole-hearted devotion to the instruction of their pupils : Father Saussié and Father Causson. Living on the borders of that ever-threatened eastern frontier, their patriotism was constantly stimulated to a burning glow, and they easily communicated this sentiment to their disciples, receiving in return a lively satisfaction from the successes obtained by the latter in the competitive examinations for admission to the state schools.

It was while engaged in this absorbing work that the events of 1870 found us ; they were to leave us with imperishable memories.

In July of that year a large part of the French Army was assembled around Metz. Its spirit was excellent but organization was almost wholly lacking. Late one evening we saw the Emperor Napoleon III arrive to assume his duties as Commander-in-Chief. As he drove up the Rue Serpenoise in an open carriage accompanied by the Prince Imperial, gazing about him curiously and uneasily, he produced the impression of a man utterly worn out. The magnificent " Cent Gardes " escorted them through a crowd of anxious townspeople, who were in no way reassured by this picture of lassitude.

The Emperor's Headquarters were established in the Prefecture, and here we caught glimpses of magnificent uniforms and the bearers of many great names. Then came the decisive days of August 4th, 5th and 6th, and while France was tottering to her ruin on the battlefields we were busy with our examinations for entrance into the Polytechnic School. The windows of the High School of Metz were wide open and we wrote to the sound of

FOREWORD

the distant cannon. The last paper was on French composition, and the prophetic nature of its title might have given the candidates pause. It was : " Develop this thought of Kléber's : 'The young must train their faculties.' "

On the morning of August 7th the Emperor intended to go by rail to Forbach ; he arrived at the station of Metz only to be told by the station master that, following the loss of a battle, Forbach had been evacuated the night before, and that trains no longer went to that place. The Emperor returned to the Prefecture, which was immediately closed, taking on the aspect of a headquarters overwhelmed by disaster.

The Metz population now became excited, saw spies on every corner and wanted to fling them into the Moselle. Then came the Emperor's first proclamation, telling France of her defeat in three battles. Even here the truth was distorted by his punctuation : " Marshal MacMahon telegraphs me that he has lost a big battle on the Sarre. Frossard attacked by superior numbers," etc. ; instead of—" Marshal MacMahon telegraphs me that he has lost a big battle. On the Sarre, Frossard, attacked by superior numbers. . . ." etc.

Dismay was everywhere. During the afternoon, the inhabitants of the invaded and threatened districts flocked toward the town, giving us our first vision of the consequences of defeat, with its sorrowful exodus of families driven from their homes and marching wearily into the unknown : old men, women and children, carrying off some few belongings, cattle or furniture, despair in their hearts and misery staring them in the face.

The students of St. Clement's left Metz a few days later to rejoin their families. All along the line to

Paris we saw troop trains moving in every direction; these were carrying the VI Corps which had been started from Châlons for Metz only to be returned to the place of departure because it was feared that the railway line had been cut near the latter place. On the outskirts of Paris we passed the troops of the VII Corps which had been recalled from Belfort; then those of the I Corps, brought up from Charmes after Froeschwiller and directed on the entrenched camp of Châlons. Later we met train loads of village firemen wearing their traditional helmets and armed with flint-lock muskets. These had been called by the Government to the defence of the Capital; but their ill-assorted and antiquated organization soon convinced the authorities of their unsuitability for the task in view, and these willing citizens, in no way prepared for war, were sent back to their villages. Everywhere there reigned that spirit of " error and confusion, dire precursor of the fall of kings."

The State was crumbling. For its Government, having lulled the country to sleep during a long period of peace, prosperity and luxury, which diverted the eyes of all from the approaching danger, had not only itself neglected to take the elementary precautions suggested by the situation but had also failed to ensure the moral and material efficiency of its army. Had this force been carefully and intelligently administered, it might at least have delayed and diminished the disaster.

This journey to Paris, through such evidences of a general breakdown, following as it did upon the spectacle of the first effects of defeat, naturally made an indelible impression upon our youthful minds. Shortly afterwards, I enlisted in the 4th Infantry for the duration of the War, but before I could take any active part in it, the struggle came to an end. On being demobilized in

FOREWORD

March, 1871, I returned to Metz for the purpose of resuming with my old professor, Father Saussié, my interrupted course in higher mathematics; for in spite of the fact that the normal period of study had been so seriously shortened, I had determined to try for the Polytechnic that same year.

At St. Clement's we had to share quarters with German troops passing through Metz and also with a battalion of the 37th Pomeranian Regiment that was permanently garrisoned in the college buildings. From this propinquity many incidents inevitably resulted, for the Germans were quite determined to make us feel the weight of their victory. By their violence and brutality, without even the smallest pretext, they showed us that they considered it as giving them the right to do whatever they pleased.

Three times in the summer of 1871 I went to Nancy to take my qualifying examinations for the Polytechnic. First came the written exams. and then the final oral tests for admission. General von Manteuffel was the governor of Lorraine, and commanded the army of occupation of that province. He resided in the government palace on the Place Carrière, the very house where the year 1914 found me in command of the XX Army Corps. Many distinguished German princes, generals and high officials were received there while on their way through Nancy. Each arrival was greeted by the same noisy outbursts of enthusiasm, the same military parades and ceremonies, in honour of generals who had led the German armies to victory or of statesmen who, in spite of the unanimous protests of the populations concerned, had torn Alsace and Lorraine from France. Many a time did I witness these scenes, and it was with the memory of all they meant fresh in my mind that I left Nancy in October, 1871, to enter the Polytechnic School, in a Paris whose ruins were still smoking from the fires lit by the Commune. Here, indeed, there was rebuilding to be done.

When the question of my going to the Polytechnic had first been discussed, my family had in view my adoption of one of the civil careers to which this school gives access. The disastrous war from which we had just emerged, however, imposed upon all of us, and especially upon the youth of the nation, the sacred task of building up our country, now dismembered and constantly menaced with complete destruction. Accordingly, without hesitation, I joined those students who were volunteering for the artillery, known by the sobriquet of " the little hats." After spending fifteen months at the Polytechnic, we entered the School of Application at Fontainebleau, from which, in September, 1874, we proceeded to join our regiments as officers.

Following her defeat, and as a result of the compulsory surrender of her war material, France had found herself completely disarmed. Nevertheless, in spite of the large indemnity she had to pay, she succeeded in not only rapidly reforming her military institutions but also in replenishing her armament. She made haste to put herself in a position to resist, if need should arise, the constant threats of an adversary who was strangely surprised to see this quick recovery and who, more than once, notably in 1875, was on the point of reopening the war in order to consummate his rival's destruction.

It was during this period of hasty reorganization with gravely insufficient means that I began my career in the 24th Regiment of Artillery at Tarbes. Fortunately, everybody was imbued with a wonderful spirit of enthusiasm and activity. No praise can ever be too high for the noble work of the vanquished officers of 1870, and their successors, in re-creating our army and preparing it for war. They have this merit also, that they set themselves the task of studying and comprehending the great operations of war on a Continental scale, the notion of which had been completely lost by the army of the Second Empire, absorbed as it had been by small expeditions outside of Europe and an easy campaign in Italy, having limited objectives and pursued with very restricted means of action.

At each of the military schools which I attended, the Polytechnic, the Artillery School of Application and the Cavalry School, we were given an excellent instruction; our faculties were developed logically and we were furnished with real food for reflection. But the *Ecole de Guerre*, which I entered in 1885, was an absolute revelation to me. The natural gifts and knowledge already possessed by an officer of average capacity were here improved by a more or less theoretical instruction based on the lessons of history, while his mind was trained to approach the problems of war on a great scale, to study and discuss them and to search intelligently for their solution.

A remarkable body of instructors constituted the staff of the school at this time; men such as Cardot, Maillard, Millet, Langlois and Cherfils, all characterised by wide experience, sound judgment and an impassioned conscientiousness. Their painstaking studies in history had enabled them to comprehend and define War's far-reaching moral aspects and, by deduction, to arrive at the material factors upon which its success depended. In this way, they not only gave us solid instruction along normal lines, but they showed us how we ourselves should approach the problems of the future.

One of these instructors, Major Millet, was good

enough to take a special interest in my work and to continue that interest throughout my career. He was subsequently called to some of the highest posts in our service, commanding first a corps and then an army, and I served him in both of these positions as Chief of Staff. He continually expounded to me the conclusions he had drawn from his experience during the war of 1870 and from his unremitting study of the methods applicable to the conduct of military operations in the future. In this way, he had a marked influence upon the ideas I formed regarding the approaching struggle.

In his opinion fire-power had become, since 1870, the dominating factor on the field of battle, and this to such a degree that the advance of any body of troops not possessing an unquestionable superiority of fire would be paralysed. He held that fire action, by reason of the improvement in arms, would assume even greater importance in the next war, and that it was essential for us to study this question with the double purpose of increasing, by the use of more powerful weapons, the effect of our own fire and of securing better protection from that of the enemy. The means we were then using, such as the formations prescribed for infantry, were notoriously insufficient and could not fail to result in severe losses for the troops. Once fire superiority has been established, it must, of course, be followed by an assault which alone could drive the enemy from his position; but that was only one phase of the battle. Forcing back the enemy at a single point might be a costly operation and very limited in effect; if it was not to remain sterile, a new attack must be made rapidly and in considerable force.

This operation ought to be prepared beforehand and launched at the exact moment that would complete the confusion already produced in the enemy's formations and bring about his destruction ; only in this way could all the advantages of the previously successful but costly effort be reaped. This meant that when the commander of any considerable body of troops organised an attack, he must not content himself with making the dispositions necessary for the immediate tactical success he had in view, but he should, in his preliminary plans, study the probable development of the action and make preparations for moving forward the forces necessary to follow it up. The effect of the initial thrust must be succeeded by fresh attacks, the value of which would lie not so much in their number and violence as in their rapidity and precision.

Modern armament rendered it comparatively easy for an adversary to recover from a first onset ; the means of preventing it consisted in exploiting that partial success by repeated blows. This requires that a second operation, carefully organized beforehand, be held ready to be put into immediate effect. In this way only could an initial success be consolidated and extended sufficiently to create widespread disorganization in the enemy's ranks and thereby lead to victory.

The three years that I spent in the Operations Bureau of the General Staff (of which General de Miribel was the head), gave me a knowledge of the plans which had been drawn up for the mobilisation, concentration and supply of the French armies in time of war, as well as the ideas which then constituted our war doctrine.

The German army was superior to ours in numbers, in training and in equipment. General de Miribel, consequently, made a complete study of the terrain on our eastern frontier, with the object of selecting broad defensive positions against which the flood of the wide invasion he anticipated would spend itself. He brought great energy and undoubted ability to this task, but, as is the case in all solely defensive strategy, this employment of the terrain for parrying or delaying enemy attacks did not include any provision for counter-strokes. Moreover, during this period our army was proceeding on the theory that the choice of the time and place for launching a counter-offensive was the function of the Commander-in-Chief of the French armies; as if changing in the face of the enemy from the defensive to the offensive was not one of the most delicate of all decisions, presenting, in view of the vast effectives of modern armies, a most exceptional difficulty of execution. Such a change, if it is to be successfully initiated and then followed by that forward movement without which there can be no victory, requires minute preparation. Before he reached the problem of the counter-offensive and the best method of employing the troops which such action involved, General de Miribel died. It was at this very moment, it may be remarked in passing, that the German General Staff was strengthening its field armies by the addition of a heavy artillery which, up to that time, had been used solely in siege warfare.

Towards the end of 1895 I was assigned to duty at the War College as instructor in general tactics, for which work my chief equipment consisted of the fundamental ideas taught me by General Millet. During six years of intense labour I strove to extend my comprehension of them and to complete their application.

Nothing could be more stimulating to a man who has consecrated himself to the search for the essential truth of war than this task of instructing those who will be called upon to apply it on the battlefield, where the lives of their soldiers and the fate of their country are at stake.

FOREWORD

But if, when found, he expects to instil that truth into minds, open indeed, but which the influences of practical military life have rendered somewhat sceptical toward school studies, the search must never be relaxed until at last he has seized it and made it his very own.

The obligation placed upon a man through having to instruct officers in the higher precepts of military science leads him to ask himself many questions concerning war, its causes as well as its purposes, and to examine the phenomena which accompany all great conflicts. In this way, with his mind no longer limited to the domain of mere military pedagogy, he is free to study the philosophy of war, seek what wants it fulfils and to what hopes it corresponds in the life of a nation, and estimate the sacrifices it will entail. The development of civilization in times of peace, notably in the domain of education and of industry, places ever new resources at the command of a nation making war, and it is the essential function of a professor to estimate at their true value the profound transformations which these may induce in the practice of the military art.

Napoleon declared that an army should alter its tactics every ten years. How important, then, were the changes to be anticipated thirty or forty years after 1870, on the part of an adversary who, since the days of Frederick II, had never ceased his search for more efficient methods of conducting war. During this period, Germany's industrial development had been altogether extraordinary, while the national pride of her people had been raised to the highest pitch. Her military writers, notably Falkenhausen and Bernhardi, to mention only two, had left no doubts as to the huge proportions which her newly modelled military organizations would attain or the wide interpretation which she would give to the laws of war as applied to hostile populations—that is to say, the law of the strongest.

In the face of this disquieting outlook, it is not surprising that our *Ecole de Guerre*, where the dangers threatening our country were studied in all their aspects, should have furnished from among its professors, selected from every arm and already tested, such a large number of the leaders who achieved high distinction in the Great War, to say nothing of the remarkable body of staff officers it produced. Such were Pétain, Fayolle, Maistre, Debeney, and de Maud'huy.

The years I spent at the *Ecole de Guerre* had already left an indelible mark on my mind, when I was relieved and sent to a regiment. This was done in pursuance of a plan inspired by party politics and which had for its avowed purpose the advancement of officers whose opinions were supposed to coincide with those of the cabinet in power, and one of whose unfortunate results was to divide France into two distinct camps. At the *Ecole de Guerre*, however, I had learned to look the problems of the coming struggle squarely in the face, examine them dispassionately and seek for their solution.

I put in the next four years as a regimental officer, first as lieutenant-colonel of the 29th Artillery, under a particularly painstaking colonel, and subsequently as colonel commanding the 35th Artillery. During this service with my regiment I was continually confronted with the difficulties which attend the practical execution of any plan, however satisfactory it seems to be in theory.

To command troops is certainly the greatest pleasure of military life, but above all is this the case when one is a captain or a colonel. For the captain, by reason of his immediate contact with the rank and file, which in

FOREWORD

the French Army is intelligent, active and devoted; for the colonel, because of the influence he exerts on a body of officers imbued with the noblest sentiments, competent in their trade and of proved devotion. It is through his officers that a colonel moulds his regiment so that it becomes in time the very image of its commander.

But a colonel must also give his officers a clear picture of the tasks which will confront them in action, their duty toward subordinates, equals and superiors, at the moment when communication between all ranks becomes more and more difficult and decisions are hampered by the fog of battle. In modern war, all ranks have their allotted part to play, for which something more than bravery and discipline are required. Leaders must not only know their business thoroughly, they must be capable of exercising initiative. Those years in command of a regiment left me with the feeling that our young army was capable of any effort, and that it would be victorious if properly directed and adequately armed. This was the affair of the High Command, a matter of organization.

Since 1890 our neighbours beyond the Rhine had been increasing in a marked degree the number and calibres of the guns they destined for field operations, and they were working diligently to improve their instruments of communication and observation. There was danger of our finding ourselves left behind.

It was during this period of my career that I served as Chief of Staff of an army corps and later as commander of the artillery of this same corps; here the ideas I had pondered so deeply at the *Ecole de Guerre* continued, with little change, to guide my conceptions of what the next war would hold in store.

In 1908, I was appointed to the command of the *Ecole*

FOREWORD

de Guerre. My own experience as a student in this school had fortified my opinion that, in view of the great extension made in the art of war, two years were not sufficient for a comprehensive study of military science, and I suggested that a third year be added for certain officers.

In 1911 I was placed at the head of the 13th Division which, composed of most excellent material, was designated as part of the covering troops for the concentration which precedes active operations. In 1912, I was given command of the VIII Army Corps and, in August 1913, that of the XX Corps at Nancy. At that time a corps commander had under him not only the fighting troops but also the administrative services and military establishments of the army corps region. It can be seen that the duties were heavy and required the display of a constant activity.

I had hardly taken over the VIII Corps, when I was transferred to the XX Corps, consisting of two infantry divisions and one cavalry division. The strength of all three of these divisions had been reinforced in order that they could be rapidly placed on a war footing. At the moment of my arrival, the law extending military service to three years was coming into effect, so that all the organizations would soon be composed of three classes of conscripts instead of two. For these increased effectives, barracks had to be built and provision made for additional accommodation in the hospitals and other military services. At the same time the construction of defensive works around Nancy was being started and pressed forward.

It will be seen that my successive changes of station during the years immediately preceding the War imposed upon me the need of an ever-increasing activity, if I was to be fully equal to the situation. Not only did the training of troops have to be intensified, but many other matters had to be attended to without delay, for the adversary was becoming each day both more threatening and more powerful. Far from being able to think of taking a rest, though well past my sixtieth year, I was obliged to redouble all my energies; for war was approaching.

While I was in command of the *Ecole de Guerre*, I came into relations with officers of note belonging to several foreign armies. Amongst the British the one I knew best was the Commandant of the Staff College at Camberley, a Brigadier-General who later was to prove himself one of the most active minds of the Imperial General Staff and become the chief of that staff. This was Field-Marshal Sir Henry Wilson. For many a long year, especially during the war, we worked together. His remarkable intelligence, tireless activity and perfect uprightness destined him to become one of the moving spirits of the British Army, and one of the most faithful servants of the common cause.

I had also on several occasions received Russian missions sent from the Nicholas Academy, headed by General Tcherbatcheff. This fact led to my being invited by the Emperor Nicholas to attend the Russian manœuvres of 1910. Aside from the cordial relations which these visits established between the two armies, they afforded me an excellent opportunity to estimate the extent of the support which our future allies might furnish in a war against Germany, supposing that our respective governments were in agreement.

At the time of my visit to that country in 1910, Russia seemed a gigantic empire with a social code still crude and a government wholly concentrated, even as regards spiritual matters, in the hands of one man, the Czar.

FOREWORD

Disquieting thoughts naturally arose when I viewed at close range this sovereign's task and the extraordinary capacities required of him if he was to keep his people in the path of progress. Such an undertaking would have required a Peter the Great. And if to the natural difficulties resulting from the existing system there should come to be added the shock which a great war always brings to test the solidity of any state, what resistance would such a government be capable of offering, what help could be expected from a people that had been so systematically prevented from sharing in the management of their own affairs as to be utterly unprepared to take charge of them? Was it not possible that Russia, deprived of the moral and social principles which fortified the nations of western and central Europe, would, in the face of a great conflict, crash to earth, a veritable colossus made with feet of clay?

In any case, and most happily for us, his French Allies, the Emperor Nicholas II was a sovereign of unshakable integrity. There could be no doubt as to the use he would make of the army at his disposal, and fortunately it was very large. Such was the clear impression left in my mind by the numerous conversations I had with him. Throughout the entire period of the manœuvres he kept me constantly at his side, and as field exercises are always very long for those who like myself were only spectators, we had ample opportunity for talk. I could not help being struck by the anxiety with which he regarded the future, conscious as he seemed to be even then of the perils which lay in wait for his vast Empire. I left Russia feeling that it was only prudent for us to base our calculations upon the things we could be sure of rather than the intentions he affirmed.

PREFACE

FULLY launched upon her Weltpolitik, the Germany of 1914 would never have resorted to war if she had properly estimated her own interests. No appeal to arms was necessary; she had only to continue an economic development that already was penetrating every country in the world. Who would have dared to oppose her?

The power of her army and navy was acknowledged by all; her commercial travellers and engineers, supported by a formidable propaganda, in their search for business or concessions, were assured of a favourable reception all over the globe, thus opening the way to unusual facilities for penetration and acquisition. Her trade and commerce were moving forward with steady strides that left other nations far behind. In 1914 there was no need for Germany to have recourse to the instrument of war in order to conquer the world. If a day should come when, awaking from their old habits, peoples sought to measure the diminution of their liberties and all the possibilities which this involved, they would find themselves confronted with men of German origin, established in every country and in every form of activity, remaining always German (thanks to their dual nationality) and taking orders from Berlin.

In the face of this German hegemony marching ever onward, no government, above all no democratic government, would have dared to take effective measures of protection, lest it incur the ultimate disaster of domination by its own German population. Before the discussion and the struggle that would have been precipitated with a state as powerfully armed as was Germany, such a government would inevitably have recoiled, dreading lest its actions might provoke hostilities, and appalled by the horrors which a modern conflict between great nations would surely involve. With twenty more years of peace, the world would have found itself Germanized and humanity in shackles.

But the Berlin Government, drunk with power and driven forward by the blind pan-German party, fully confident, moreover, in the superiority of its army over any other, did not hesitate to have recourse to arms and open an era of perilous adventures leading over mountains of dead, in order to hasten that domination of the world which, to its mind, was Germany's heritage.

Indeed, the German people of 1914 rushed to arms in support of their government's vast and crazy aspirations with genuine enthusiasm, never stopping to measure the immensity of the crimes for which they were assuming responsibility before the eyes of a startled humanity; for Germany had become one vast Prussia.

Home of the Junker and cradle of a militarism and of a philosophy both marked by rabid positivism, Prussia, from the earliest times, had cultivated war as a national industry. Directed by a conception of politics especially dear to the Hohenzollerns, this industry had fashioned the German Empire out of the Electorate of Brandenburg.

After excluding Austria, because she represented different ideals and might have opposed her, Prussia united Germany for her own profit. In this amalgamation were to be found many populations which were peaceful by nature and purely Christian in their moral conceptions. But the iron hand of Prussia, working in

THE FIVE FACSIMILES OF THE FIRST PAGE OF MARSHAL FOCH'S PREFACE WHICH FOLLOW SHOW HIS HANDWRITING AND THE FOUR TYPED COPIES FOR CORRECTIONS.

Préface

L'Allemagne de 1914, lancée dans la Welpolitik, n'eut pas déclaré la guerre, si elle avait largement compris son intérêt. Elle pouvait, sans faire appel aux armes, poursuivre dans le monde son développement économique. Formidable déjà, et soutenue d'ailleurs par une active propagande comme aussi par une puissance militaire reconnue tant sur terre que sur mer, qui garantissait à ses voyageurs de commerce, comme à ses ingénieurs en quête de concessions à l'étranger un accueil des plus avantageux et par là une capacité de pénétration et d'acquisition incomparable, le développement allemand dans une marche soutenue *constante* distançait grandement celui des autres nations. Sans faire de guerre nouvelle, l'Allemagne conquérait le monde. L'humanité, en quelques vingt ans, se fut trouvée ligotée et aux mains des éléments allemands établis dans les différents pays sous toutes les formes, mais restés toujours citoyens allemands, grâce à leur double nationalité, et recevant le mot d'ordre de Berlin, le jour où il se serait reveillé de ses vieilles habitudes pour mesurer l'étendue de ses libertés et de ses possibilités. Dans le camp opposé, pas un gouvernement, surtout d'essence démocratique, n'aurait eu le courage, devant cette hégémonie allemande en marche, et, en vue d'éviter le désastre final, la domination de son pays par l'élément allemand, de prendre des dispositions de protection. Il aurait reculé devant la discussion avec un Etat si fortement armé que l'Allemagne. Loin de paraître chercher la guerre, encore plus éloigné de la déclarer, il aurait même craint de la provoquer - tant il redoutait de déchaîner les ~~sacrifices~~ (horreurs qu'allait coûter un conflit moderne entre de grandes nations.

Si l'Allemagne de 1914 a couru aux armes pour appuyer ses aspirations ambitieuses, c'est qu'elle était devenue une Grande Prusse.

PREFACE.
-o-o-o-o-o-o-o-o-o-o-o-o-

L'Allemagne de 1914, lancée dans la Weltpolitik, n'eut pas déclaré la guerre si elle avait *justement* compris son intérêt. Elle pouvait, sans faire appel aux armes, poursuivre dans le monde son développement économique. Formidable déjà, et soutenue d'ailleurs par une active propagande comme aussi par une puissance militaire reconnue tant sur terre que sur mer, qui garantissait à ses voyageurs de commerce comme à ses ingénieurs en quête de concessions à l'étranger un accueil des plus avantageux et par là une capacité de pénétration et d'acquisition incomparable, le développement allemand dans une marche constante distançait grandement celui des autres nations. Sans faire de guerre nouvelle, l'Allemagne conquérait le monde. L'humanité, en quelques vingt ans, se fût trouvée ligotée aux mains des éléments allemands établis dans les différents pays sous toutes les formes, mais restés toujours citoyens allemands grâce à leur double nationalité, et recevant le mot d'ordre de BERLIN, le jour où elle se serait réveillée de ses vieilles habitudes pour mesurer l'étendue de ses libertés et de ses possibilités. De toute façon, pas un gouvernement, surtout d'essence démocratique, n'aurait eu le courage, devant cette hégémonie allemande en marche, et, en vue d'éviter le désastre final, la domination de son pays par l'élément allemand, de prendre des dispositions de protection. Il aurait reculé devant la discussion avec un Etat si fortement armé que l'Allemagne. Loin de paraître chercher la guerre, encore plus éloigné de la déclarer, il aurait même craint de la provoquer tant il redoutait de déchaîner les horreurs qu'allait coûter un conflit moderne entre de grandes nations.

....

PRÉFACE
-o-o-o-o-o-o-o-o-o-o-

L'Allemagne de 1914, lancée dans la Weltpolitik, n'eût jamais déclaré la guerre si elle avait pleinement compris son intérêt. Elle pouvait, sans faire appel aux armes, *qui eut osé se mettre en travers ?* poursuivre dans le monde son développement économique, formidable déjà, et soutenu d'ailleurs par une active propagande ce ne aussi par une puissance militaire reconnue sur terre et sur mer, qui garantissait à ses voyageurs de commerce comme à ses ingénieurs en quête de concessions à l'étranger un accueil des plus avantageux et par là une capacité de pénétration et d'acquisition incomparable, le développement allemand dans une marche constante distançait grandement celui des autres nations. Sans faire de guerre nouvelle, l'Allemagne conquérait le monde. L'humanité, en quelques vingt ans, se fût trouvée ligotée. Le jour où elle se serait réveillée de ses vieilles habitudes pour mesurer *la réduction* de ses libertés et de ses possibilités, elle se serait trouvée tenue par les mains des éléments allemands établis dans les différents pays sous toutes les formes, mais restés toujours citoyens allemands grâce à leur double nationalité, et recevant le mot d'ordre de Berlin. *De son côté*, pas un gouvernement, surtout d'essence démocratique, n'aurait pris la décision, devant cette hégémonie allemande en marche, et en vue d'éviter le désastre final, la domination de son pays par l'élément allemand, de prendre des dispositions particulières de protection. Il aurait reculé devant la discussion avec un état si fortement armé que l'Allemagne. Loin de paraître chercher la guerre, encore plus éloigné de la déclarer, il *eut* même craint de la provoquer, tant il redoutât de déchaîner les horreurs qu'allait coûter un conflit moderne entre de grandes nations.

Mais le Gouvernement de Berlin, grisé par la situation, emporté par un parti pangermaniste aveugle, pleinement confiant d'ailleurs en son armée supérieure à toute autre, ne craignait pas de recourir aux armes et d'ouvrir une ère de lourdes

....

PRÉFACE

L'Allemagne de 1914, lancée dans la weltpolitik, n'eût jamais déclaré la guerre si elle avait posément compris son intérêt. Elle pouvait, sans faire appel aux armes, poursuivre dans le monde son développement économique. Qui eut osé se mettre en travers ? Formidable déjà, et soutenu d'ailleurs par une active propagande comme aussi par une puissance militaire reconnue sur terre et sur mer, qui garantissait à ses voyageurs de commerce comme à ses ingénieurs en quête de concessions à l'étranger un accueil des plus avantageux et par là une capacité de pénétration et d'acquisition incomparable, le développement allemand dans une marche constante distançait grandement celui des autres nations. Sans faire de guerre nouvelle, l'Allemagne conquérait le monde. L'humanité ~~en quelques vingt ans, se fût trouvé ligotée~~. Le jour où elle se serait réveillée de ses vieilles habitudes pour mesurer la réduction de ses libertés et de ses possibilités, elle se serait trouvée tenue par les ~~mains des~~ éléments allemands établis dans les différents pays sous toutes les formes, mais restés toujours citoyens allemands grâce à leur double nationalité, et recevant le mot d'ordre de Berlin. ~~D~~'ailleurs, pas un gouvernement, surtout d'essence démocratique, n'aurait pris la décision, devant cette hégémonie allemande en marche, et en vue d'éviter le désastre final, la domination de son pays par l'élément allemand, de prendre des dispositions particulières de protection. Il aurait reculé devant la discussion et la lutte ~~économique~~ avec un état si fortement armé que l'Allemagne. Loin de paraître chercher la guerre, encore plus éloigné de la déclarer, il aurait même craint de la provoquer, tant il eut redouté de déchaîner les horreurs qu'allait coûter un conflit moderne entre de grandes nations. En quelques vingt ans de paix le monde se fut trouvé germanisé, l'humanité ligotée.

Mais le gouvernement de Berlin, grisé par la puissance, emporté par un parti pangermaniste aveugle, pleinement confiant d'ailleurs en son armée supérieure à toute autre, ne craignait pas de recourir aux armes et d'ouvrir une ère de lourdes hécatombes

FOCH AS A TWELVE-YEAR-OLD SCHOOLBOY.

THE FUTURE MARSHAL AS A CAPTAIN OF ARTILLERY.

"L'ECOLE SUPERIEURE DE GUERRE," WHERE FOCH ONCE LECTURED ON TACTICS, AND OF WHICH HE WAS LATER COMMANDANT.

PREFACE

the spiritual domain as well as in the material, through government officials, school teachers and army officers, all directed by an administration that was Prussian by necessity when not by conviction, gradually bent these people to her own ideas and institutions. Moreover, the Government of Berlin, through its world-wide military prestige, had brought them an economic development and a material prosperity they had never known before. By 1914 all Germany had become completely Prussified and every German held that might makes right.

The foundation of the national edifice rested on the army. It had been carefully organized and lavishly supported, while its development had been kept fully abreast of the economic advance of the country. Thus Germany had at her disposal a military force superior to any other in numbers, armament and instruction, upon which she could count for realizing and justifying that dominant rôle in the world to which the German race, by reason of its superiority, considered itself entitled.

The idea of an appeal to force was also supported by the argument that it would inevitably facilitate the realization of Germany's world-hegemony. This plan presented the advantage of hastening the course of events as well as of extending and consolidating their results. Once Germany had defeated the great powers of Europe, she would be the uncontested mistress of the ancient continent; and strongly established along the coasts of the North Sea and the English Channel, she would hold in her grasp the great naval power of England and thereby become the ruler of the seas.

Who could then set a limit to her power? Would not the future of her Weltpolitik be assured beyond the possibility of doubt? Who dared set against such benefits for Germany the seas of blood which they might

PREFACE

entail? It was with blood that Prussia had cemented Germany and widened her boundaries; with blood, therefore, let her still further enlarge this dominion.

Such was the philosophy of the conquering Junker, adopted now by every true German. What mattered the rights of other nations or the lives of their citizens? Victory was certain, and victory made all things legitimate. To allow moral considerations to upset the plans of those who had force on their side would be preposterous weakness.

And so, driven by the rod of Prussia, a blinded Germany started off to war in the midst of general enthusiasm. Deutschland über Alles!

* * * * *

The France of 1914, far from desiring war and still farther from seeking it, did everything possible to avoid it; and toward the end of July, when the struggle seemed imminent, the French Government made every possible effort to stave it off. But if her Allies were attacked, France, resolved to honour her signature, would come to their aid.

Such was the policy which the Government of the Republic had consistently practised for more than forty years. While never forgetting her lost provinces and trying by every means to heal the wounds their amputation had caused her, France had replied with dignity and resignation to the virulent provocations that accompanied the successive incidents of Schnœbele, Tangier, Agadir and Saverne. She had reduced the term of military service first from five to three years, then from three to two years, and it was only in face of the menace presented by the continual reinforcement of the German Army and under the force of most legitimate anxiety and evident danger, that she hurriedly returned, in 1913, to the three years service plan. It was high time.

France was fully determined not to resort to force unless her existence and her liberty were put in peril by some German aggression ; nothing short of such a danger could have driven a democratic government into war, fully alive to the immensity of the sacrifices and the stupendousness of the cataclysm which a European conflict would bring upon the peoples involved.

Although the month of July, 1914, found the Franco-German sky still charged with clouds, France, full of confidence in her sagacity, so little believed a storm to be imminent, that the President of the Republic and the Prime Minister, immediately after the national holiday of July 14th, set out for a stay of several weeks in Russia. The vacation season for Members of Parliament and government officials had begun, and I myself left Nancy on July 18th with the intention of spending a fortnight's leave in Brittany.

Suddenly, on July 23rd, Austria's ultimatum to Serbia came like a stroke of lightning in the political sky. In spite of Serbia's acceptance of Austria's demands, subject to two unimportant reservations suggesting that the issue be submitted to the judgment of the Great Powers and of the Hague Tribunal, Austria's representative at Belgrade, declaring the reply unsatisfactory, broke off relations and quit the capital. This act made evident Austria's clear intention to go to war without more discussion. Furthermore, the close alliance existing between the two Central Empires gave rise to the fear that the action of the " faithful second " was simply the prelude to the carefully prepared entrance of Germany upon the scene, and that the conflict deliberately precipitated in the East was merely the precurser of one to be pursued in the West. The rapid development of events soon proved that such was the case.

On July 28th Austria declared war against Serbia; on the 29th she bombarded Belgrade, the Serbian capital; on the 31st she ordered the general mobilization of her army. In vain the British Government proposed that the quarrel be submitted to the arbitration of four disinterested great powers, France, England, Germany and Italy; in vain Russia agreed to this suggestion. Germany refused to support any effort to arrange the difficulty. Already, on July 26th, she had menaced Russia with the threat of mobilizing her army, " and," added the German ambassador at Petrograd, " mobilization means war." Russia, in fact, had replied to the Austrian mobilization of July 31st by a measure of the same order, whereupon the German Emperor proclaimed the " kriegsgefahrzustand," which consists in making the more important dispositions for putting the German Army on a war footing. At the same time he demanded of the French Government a declaration of neutrality, to be guaranteed by the surrender of the fortresses of Toul and Verdun to German troops for the duration of the war.

While on this same day Austria was manifesting some desire to bring about an arrangement, Germany addressed an ultimatum to Russia, and on August 1st she decreed the remaining measures of mobilization which were intended to group her forces on the eastern and western fronts. She then declared war on Russia. France replied by ordering the general mobilization of her army.

It may be here pointed out that the starting of this conflict by the Central Empires against a Slavonic

PREFACE

nation had the effect of bringing all the Russian forces into action at the earliest possible moment. Had these Powers raised the dispute over some question affecting the West, Russia might not have acted with such resolution, and the aid which she brought to France might have been appreciably delayed. But the German Government did not look at matters too closely when it came to the details of its policy. It felt not the shadow of a doubt as to the triumph of its arms, as long as it acted with boldness and despatch. It had an absolute confidence in its military machine, so vastly superior as it was to anything of the kind ever seen before by reason of the number of its mobilized units, the degree of their instruction, the power of their armament, the care with which their operations had been prepared, the spirit which animated them, and the science which directed them.

With no less overwhelming confidence and in contempt of the most elementary notions of right, an ultimatum was addressed on the 2nd of August to Belgium, demanding free passage across her territory for the German Armies. These had already and with even less formality violated the neutrality of Luxemburg. Such actions overcame the last lingering hesitations of London and brought into the allied ranks the armies of Great Britain and Belgium.

Whether the Germans had here made a mistake or met with a surprise seemed to make little difference to them. They believed that a wide offensive movement rapidly executed in accordance with a carefully laid plan would overcome any resistance that could be offered by a coalition that was only just being organized and which, besides, was showing itself curiously restrained by sentiments of honour and scruples of conscience. Hampered by such weaknesses, delayed by such niceties, how could it hope to arrest the movement of the most formidable war machine the world had ever seen, and which at that very moment was already launched in full operation?

Moreover, in case the Allied Governments attempted to resist the designs of Germany, was not her army strong enough to crush the opposition of any invaded people by sowing terror amongst them on a scale and by methods which the necessities of the conflict would be invoked to justify? Would not the expression "We are at war," whether spoken by general or private, serve as the excuse for utterly unnecessary atrocities and the most blatant violations of the rights of humanity? No, in the eyes of the German Government, victory would justify every excess, decide every dispute; and victory was certain to reward an immediate and audacious offensive. No foolish scruples must be allowed to delay it! What difference did it make if the rigours of war were to fall with unheard-of violence upon inoffensive populations? One course alone ensured success, and that was for the German Armies to march forward resolutely and rapidly, spreading devastation and terror in front of them.

The struggle that was about to begin found the French Army animated by the same spirit as that of the entire nation. This Army of the Republic had been carefully reconstituted after our disasters of 1870 and was now recruited for the first time under the régime of obligatory military service. It gave many evidences of an extraordinary regeneration. If, during the period which followed 1870, our people by their many sacrifices had affirmed their determination to survive as a nation and maintain their country's rank amongst the European

PREFACE

powers, the army had no less shown that by admirable endeavour it was preparing itself successfully to resist any new aggression on the part of its powerful neighbour. To that end our officers had been studying and the army had been diligently trained in military operations on a grand scale, the notion of which had been lost by the Army of the Second Empire, as the two incomparable disasters of Metz and Sedan had fully proved.

The next step was to make sure that our troops possessed those qualities which form the elements of victory : high morale, physical endurance and professional knowledge. With these provided, the army could be counted upon for the successful prosecution of a European war.

Manœuvres of all sorts, repeated and prolonged under every condition of fatigue, had brought out not only the excellent spirit that animated all ranks, but their ardent desire to learn. The men also displayed an endurance and discipline such as the armies of the Second Empire had never known. Large units such as divisions, army corps and armies, had been assembled for autumn exercises and operations had been conducted with perfect order and precision. Certain classes of reservists took part in this training. The ready handling of these forces and of the numerous auxiliary services they involve, combined with a wide utilization of railways, had become familiar to commanders and their staffs, and the ease displayed in their manipulation had spread confidence throughout all ranks. Reservists, momentarily taken from the occupations of civil life, came regularly to resume their places in the regiment and imbibe anew its spirit. Officers, whether complementary, or belonging to the Reserves or the Territorials, were carefully selected and tested, thus insuring to us the most

PREFACE

precious resources for the future.*

With their eyes turned ever in the direction of the frontier, yet never allowing themselves to become distracted from their patriotic task, our regular officers had passed through the numerous crises which marked our political life in silent dignity, though not without experiencing serious loss. Periods of diminished patriotism, wilful pacifism or official sectarianism, various forms of a sort of national abdication which were taken advantage of by certain parties for the advancement of personal interests (and not the most legitimate), all these had at times served to reduce the military value of the corps of officers. But in spite of such vicissitudes, they had preserved to France her army. For those of us especially who had known the military system of the Second Empire, the army of Republican France was seen to have become, through the unremitting work of all, a superior instrument of war, animated by a fine sense of duty, and resolved at all costs to protect the life of the nation. Its final test came on the battlefields of 1914.

As regards the moral qualities it would there display, no one had any doubts. The existence of the country was in the balance and to save it the Army recoiled before no effort or sacrifice. From the highest leader to the humblest, there was one continual rivalry of abnegation and devotion, and merit alone opened the way to advancement. Nevertheless, it was fair to ask would these virtues alone suffice in the face of modern weapons?

* Note.—The French Army, before the war, was composed of three categories: the Active or Regular army, the Reserve and the Territorial forces. Each of these had its own cadres of officers. In addition to these, a fourth group of officers, such as regular officers who had resigned, retired from the service before their time, or who were on indefinite leave, constituted the "officiers de complément."—TRANSLATOR.

PREFACE

The Army Commands, with their staffs and services, had long been methodically organized. At their head were many chiefs of the highest military reputation, aided by subordinates perfectly trained for their functions. In the lesser units, such as army corps, divisions and brigades, the command still suffered from the part that politics had played, under certain ministries, in the advancement of officers. The presence at the head of the army since 1911 of a Commander-in-Chief, highly endowed and enjoying the full confidence of the Government, had made it possible to reduce, but not entirely eliminate, the number of inefficient general officers whose political opinions had won them their commands. The harm had not been fully repaired.

It may be remarked in passing that the very position of an officer should prohibit him, whether in time of peace or of war, from mixing up in the struggles and quarrels of politics. His professional value can reveal itself only on the field of action before men of the same trade, his peers or his superiors; it cannot be estimated by political men. Whenever these find themselves the object of solicitation on the part of soldiers, they have only to display a little discernment and sincerity to be convinced that they generally have before them officers who have utterly failed on the manœuvre ground. Such officers flatter those in power and, discarding the dictates of uprightness and high character, bring forth their quasi-philosophical ideas and their temporary political opinions for the purpose of justifying military ambitions which are unsupported by military virtues. Politics bring to the choice of Army officers nothing but error and injustice, two causes which more than anything else tend to enfeeble that body of public servants.

Taken as a whole, our Army of 1914 had the defects

PREFACE

of its qualities. Above all, the doctrine of the offensive, through having been so greatly accentuated and generalized, tended to impose an invariable rule leading too often to tactics that were blind and brutal, and for that very reason dangerous. It also induced a strategy that was bare and uniform, easily sterile, unproductive of results and costly. A doctrine as restricted as this was sure to bring surprises during the first contacts with the enemy.

Our army had emerged from an unbroken peace of forty years. During that period the field exercises in which it had taken part had naturally furnished no picture of the rigours of a modern battlefield nor of the violence of the fire action that sweeps it. A study based especially upon what took place in 1870, and consecrated in Field Service Regulations, might have given the Army some notion of the destructive power of modern weapons and the consequences to be deduced from it. But as a matter of fact, the recommendations contained in our service regulations of 1875 were already of ancient date and had been largely lost to view. Many of our officers since then had taken part in colonial wars in which they had never faced any such weapons, wielded by an adversary capable of making full use of them.

In this way there had been deduced from our Autumn Manœuvres and Colonial wars a single formula for success, a single combative doctrine, namely the decisive power of offensive action undertaken with the resolute determination to march on the enemy, reach and destroy him. To carry out this idea, formations of attack had been devised that would constantly enable reinforcements to reach the line. Nothing had been so persistently preached to General and Regimental officers as well as to private soldiers as the power of morale, and above all, of the will to conquer; and this had been done with a total absence of either qualification or discernment.

From this teaching it was found, when the time of application arrived, that the battle developed rapidly and in force, but often blindly, without sufficient preparation by fire action and notably by the artillery, since the latter took more time to get into position. In this way too many troops were put into action at once; they were feebly supported by artillery fire, and being preoccupied chiefly with the idea of getting forward quickly and together, they soon found themselves exposed and impotent in the face of a fire poured upon them from every direction by invisible weapons, so that, in spite of all their efforts, they could not reach the enemy.

The attack now had to be recommenced by fire action. Thus the troops, already tired and suffering from severe losses, had to be halted while the still distant artillery was given time to break down the obstacles, or silence the guns that had checked the infantry. Being well forward and often too closely grouped, casualties multiplied, and finally, checked and powerless, the enterprise came to an end because it was insufficiently prepared. And yet, it had been undertaken with ample forces and prosecuted with admirable dash by infantrymen who thought their valour alone could overcome the obstacle which the enemy's artillery and machine-guns suddenly erected in front of them.

If the idea of offensive action, first, last and all the time, might be sufficient for the private soldier's catechism, it could hardly suffice, as we have seen, for a general leading a considerable body of troops to battle. He must precede and accompany their advance by every aid and precaution. Without disregarding the indispensable principle of movement, he must be sure to

PREFACE

apply it only in the light of information carefully sought and under cover of liaisons previously established. His forces should be pushed forward and engaged progressively, never reassembling in attack formation until the right moment arrives. This only occurs when the objective can be clearly indicated and when artillery fire has broken down the opposing obstacles.

If the engagement of more important forces is being considered, turn to our " Provisional Instructions " and the subsequent " Regulations for the Conduct of Large Units," dated 1912 and 1913. These, it will be seen, flatly proclaim the dogma of the offensive as applicable to such cases.

" The teachings of the past have borne their fruit," we read. " The French Army, reviving its old traditions, no longer admits for the conduct of operations any other law than that of the offensive."

In 1870, our High Command perished through its attachment to the defensive, and a passive defensive at that. In 1914 it was destined to meet with useless repulses and cruel losses as a consequence of its exclusive passion for the offensive and its ignorance of all save its usual methods, which were applied to every situation. What is really essential is that for each case, the respective advantages and weaknesses of the offensive and defensive be thoroughly studied, and the possibility of their employment decided upon. As a rule it is only by judiciously combining and applying the two systems that a powerful offensive can be brought to bear upon the desired point. The necessity of making this combination increases with the number of troops engaged.

The commander of a large unit must be the last to content himself with being merely " a gallant soldier," satisfied with ordering the attack and rigidly

PREFACE

following the rules prescribed for lesser organizations. He can prepare an offensive with a good chance of reaching the enemy only when the ground is practicable for the action of a strong infantry force and favourable for the use of a powerful artillery. On any ground that does not fulfil these conditions, the terrain itself makes it imperative that demonstration or even the defensive be resorted to. In such a case a commander must reduce the scope of his plans.

A Divisional Commander, still more a Corps Commander, and above all a Commander-in-Chief, must be governed by the nature of the ground in deciding upon the use he is going to make of his forces, the tasks he assigns to each unit, and the method of action each should employ. He should prescribe the offensive at certain points, demonstration or the defensive at others, and constantly combine all three, realizing that the spirit of the offensive becomes blind and therefore dangerous when systematically generalized.

On many occasions during the war we suffered from this abuse of a correct idea, that of the offensive, because it was applied without discernment.

During the years when our officers were thus absorbed in the study of the offensive, and were indeed getting over-excited about it, and convincing themselves that it dominated every other consideration, forgetting for the moment the prodigious power which fire action had recently developed, they were giving too little attention to the matter of armament, and in this way it came about that fewer machine-guns were assigned to the service of our infantry than was the case in Germany.

Our army corps had only 120 guns, all of 75-millimetre calibre, while the German corps, though less strong in infantry, had 160 pieces, some of them 150-mm. and

105-mm. howitzers. The same situation was presented by the heavy artillery allotted to our armies, which, both in number and calibre, was inferior to the German. In spite of all its virtues, our excellent *soixante-quinze* could not compensate, especially on the offensive, for these deficiencies in number and calibre; moreover, it was not adapted to high-angle fire. On the defensive, the powerful barrage it was able to lay down rendered us the greatest service by implacably breaking up the formidable attacks of the enemy. But in order to carry out these tactics advantageously, our guns ought to have been furnished with a large supply of ammunition. Unfortunately there were only 1,500 rounds per piece, and the manufacture of cartridges had not been prepared on a sufficient scale.

In the matter of aviation, field telephones and telegraphs we were notably deficient. The speech made in the summer of 1914 by M. Charles Humbert aroused the country to these dangers, but it arrived too late to be followed by any improvement, and it doubtless gave the enemy precious information.

In reality our Government was so fully decided on a policy of peace and was so little impressed by the possibility of having to defend the country that for years it had refused to appropriate sufficient money for military preparation. In this way we greatly lacked those material means for successfully carrying on a battle which had become more and more necessary with the rising importance of armament in modern war.

This was another reason why the offensive, as the invariable form of our action, was bound to meet with grave difficulties in execution. Politics and the conduct of war are so closely united that the latter may be said to be only the continuation of the former. However ardent he may be, however anxious to achieve victory by the only route that leads to it—vigorous offensive action—the man who is placed at the head of a nation's army in war is often obliged to begin by the defensive, owing to the situation which politics have created for him.

The more his machinery for attack has been reduced, the more his strategy is forced to prescribe a defensive rôle along a large part of his front, in order that he may concentrate the limited offensive means at his disposal in other places, and attack under good conditions. Let us point out once more that the idea, the technique and the practise of the defensive should all be familiar to every commanding officer. Has it not held true in all wars, that in order to get the better of a capable adversary one must know how to parry as well as to strike? The uniform doctrine of the offensive, which during this war led our soldiers into so many blind and sterile attacks, was no less insufficient as a guiding principle for the High Command. It was bound to lead, as we have seen, to an ineffectual strategy unless there were available superior forces strong enough and mobile enough to envelop the enemy on at least one of his wings, after having parried his blows directed elsewhere. The strength of the French Army in 1914, even augmented by the British forces (which at the beginning were very small) could not justify any such enterprise.

Our war doctrine was thus too summary, limited as it was for all ranks to one magnificent formula: the offensive.

To compensate for our doctrinal weakness, we had a first class General Staff whose officers thoroughly understood their business. It comprised, moreover, some men of remarkable intelligence. The *Ecole de Guerre* and the Course in Higher Military Studies had developed in our

PREFACE

officers a passion for work while at the same time training and widening their faculties. Those whom nature had endowed with a good mental equipment were destined to prove the extent to which they had profited by what they had learned at these schools, and the degree to which their intelligence had been broadened and sharpened there. During the war they rendered most eminent service by quickly adapting themselves to circumstances, however new they might be.

But they had to be commanded and guided, for the majority were young and not yet mentally mature ; that is, they lacked experience which alone can develop judgment, and the habit of authority which alone can ensure to an officer the calm confidence that leads to wise as well as vigorous decisions.

In any case, from the very start the operations of requisition and mobilization, the transport of troops and supplies, as well as the enormous expansion of the services behind the battle area, were all carried out with perfect precision.

* * * * *

The outbreak of war found me commanding the XX Corps at Nancy. The inhabitants of this town, like those of all Lorraine, manifested in a particularly high degree the patriotic sentiments which animated everybody in France. For more than forty years their hands had been stretched across the frontier to captive Metz and their brothers in annexed Lorraine, and now they asked themselves whether at last the day might not be dawning which would see their destinies once more blended. The reports that arrived in the town recounting the successive steps which the Germans on the frontier were taking, such as stoppage of all communication, trains and travellers, was received in perfect calm. Then came the announcement of the French Government's decisions; finally mobilization began, and the requisition of horses and vehicles got under way. There was no sign of disorder or alarm, but everywhere evidence of a quiet resolution to be ready for any eventuality. In a few days, perhaps, battle would be raging at the city's gates, but no one thought of leaving. All were confident in the justice of their cause and the valour of their soldiers.

The XX Corps consisted of the 11th and 39th Infantry Divisions and the 2nd Cavalry Division. Its artillery was a model of excellence. No finer troops could be imagined, and their natural ardour had been intensified by service along this eastern frontier that cut like a scar across the breast of their country.

This intensity of patriotic sentiment had greatly aided in the training and instruction of the men, and they stood ever impatient for the final trial. Every regiment was fortified by an *esprit-de-corps* and stirred by emulation of its fellows that gave rich promise for the day of battle. Indeed, so strong were the traditions which had been created, and which were maintained throughout all the War's cruel experiences, that in 1918 these regiments were still amongst the very best in the French Army, although they had lost nearly every man that had started out with them in 1914. To command such troops was an intense satisfaction, and our most industrious and energetic officers, especially amongst the Field Officers, considered it a high privilege to be assigned to them.

It was in this way that a geographical influence and the attractions of the soldiers' career combined to give to the officers and men of the XX Corps an extraordinary professional and moral value. Their passionate eagerness to measure themselves with the enemy was accompanied by such a contempt of danger that my only fear was lest they should rush upon it too inconsiderately.

During the period preceding the war my efforts with the officers had aimed solely towards enlightening and calming this magnificent ardour, the fountain of their energy, and hence the basis of our hopes ; any effort to stimulate it would have been quite superfluous. However, it was my duty to show them the difficulties of their task, to warn them against precipitation and to point out the peril that would follow any lack of co-operation between the different arms in action. How happy the lot of a Commander called to be the guide of such determined spirits !

PART I

THE XX ARMY CORPS

(July 25th—August 28th, 1914)

CHAPTER I

THE XX ARMY CORPS AS PART OF THE COVERING FORCES

(July 25th—August 13th, 1914)

Early dispositions, July 26th-31st—General mobilization, August 1st—The XX Army Corps covers the concentration of the Second Army, August 1st to 10th—The G.O.C. Second Army assumes command, August 6th—The Second Army Assembles: the XV and XVI Corps move into line August 10th; the IX Corps, August 12th.

By July 26th events had assumed so serious an aspect that I was recalled from leave in Brittany, and on the morning of July 27th I arrived at my Headquarters at Nancy. The same day orders were sent out by the Minister of War directing all officers and men on leave to rejoin their units, and the precautionary measures of security affecting the civil population were put into effect.

The dispositions prescribed for the surveillance of the frontier came into force on the 28th, and on the 29th we began to construct the field works east of Nancy which had been planned for its protection. The object of these works was to complete the defences at La Rochette, the Grand Mont d'Amance and Rambétant* which had been begun during the winter of 1913—14 but which in July, 1914, were still unfinished.

The first task which devolved upon the XX Corps was to establish itself where it could play the part of sentinel

* North of Dombales; key to the eastern defences of the Grand Couronné de Nancy.

and watch the enemy during the period of political tension; the next was to provide a screen in front of the Basse Meurthe sector behind which the French Second Army could complete its mobilization and concentration, should subsequent events require these preliminary dispositions for war to be taken.

On the evening of the 30th the covering troops of the XX Corps moved out by route march and took up positions intended for guarding against any surprise attack. It was ordered, however, that no patrols were to advance beyond a line running six miles inside the frontier. The exact trace of this line had been furnished by the War Department. It can thus be seen that the protective measures prescribed by the Government were restricted both in extent and importance, since the advance of our troops was definitely limited to the line laid down and no reservists were to be called up until further orders.

These steps were fully justified by the Intelligence reports telling of the activity reigning on the other side of the frontier. At Nancy, especially, it was known that the entrenched camp of Metz had been partly mobilized and put in a state of defence and that the forts were heavily occupied.

Although none of the classes of German reservists had yet been mobilized, the strength of all units had been increased by the arrival of men called individually to the colours. Measures had been taken to screen the whole frontier of Alsace and Lorraine; all roads crossing it had been closed and were guarded by the military; troops were detraining north of Metz. A sudden attack in considerable force was therefore to be feared at any moment. The XX Corps was ready to meet it.

In the plan drawn up by our General Staff, the XX

Corps was not expected to employ more than the equivalent of a division for carrying out the measures of protection assigned to it. By bringing up the leading troops of the 39th Division (which would otherwise have remained far in rear) and by forming the advanced line from regiments of this division and of the 11th Division, I would not be exceeding this limit, while at the same time the main body of the 11th Division would continue to garrison Nancy, which would thus retain its normal aspect. The remainder of the two Divisions would constitute the second line at and to the south of Nancy. This would concentrate the whole corps in the hands of its commander.*

In order to carry out this plan, the 39th Division left Toul at 5 A.M. on the 31st and took up its quarters the same afternoon south of Nancy. The 11th Division occupied the heights to the north and north-east of the Grand Couronné, and began work at once on the defences which had been studied and sketched out during the preceding days.

Political developments soon brought about an extension of these preparatory dispositions. On July 31st orders were received from Paris to " send forward the covering troops," but the requirement that they were not to advance beyond the line laid down in the telegram of the previous day was maintained. When an hour later these instructions were transmitted to the 11th and 39th Divisions, they were already in position and practically ready to begin operations. All that remained was for their reservists to join and for the Corps Commander to issue his detailed instructions relative to covering operations to these Divisions and to the 2nd Cavalry

---

* General Dantant commanded the 39th Division at Toul ; General Balfourier the 11th Division at Nancy ; General Lescot the Division of Cavalry.

Division, which had been placed under his orders.

The order for general mobilization was despatched from Paris on August 1st and arrived at Nancy on the same day at 3.55 P.M. Shortly afterwards I received a telegram from the Minister of War repeating the order not to advance beyond the line fixed on July 30th, except in the case of a definite attack. On July 31st, however, I had already given instructions to the Divisional Commanders to push their advanced units beyond that line, so as to secure positions of the highest importance, such as Mont d'Amance, Mont St. Jean and the heights of La Rochette, the real keys to Nancy. If we had taken up a line more in rear, we could not have secured these heights which, undefended, would have been easily seized by the enemy. There could be no question as to that. Therefore, on August 1st I obtained authority to maintain my troops on the line I had fixed. However, by the afternoon of August 2nd the frontier had been several times violated by the Germans, and the French Government decided to cancel the provisional order regarding the six mile line, thus leaving the Commander-in-Chief of its Armies entire freedom of action.

At 5.30 P.M., August 2nd, General Joffre telephoned this news to the officers responsible for the covering movement. He added that " for national reasons of a moral nature and for urgent reasons of diplomacy " it was indispensable that " the entire responsibility for hostilities should be left to the Germans." Consequently, we were to avoid crossing the frontier at all costs and we were to limit ourselves to resisting enemy attacks vigorously without in any way provoking them.

Shortly after receiving this message, a cipher telegram arrived from the Commander-in-Chief conveying his "secret instructions for covering troops." It informed us amongst other things that:

"The Commander-in-Chief does not propose to launch any general offensive movement until all his forces are concentrated. The covering troops, in addition to their task of screening the mobilization and concentration, will conform to what follows. . . .

"The XX Army Corps—to press forward the preparation of defences now in course of organization to the east of Nancy so as to ensure the passage of the Meurthe.

"General Headquarters will be established at Vitry-le-François as from 6 A.M., August 5th."

The instructions of the Commander-in-Chief were fully covered by the orders I had already issued. The mobilization of the XX Corps proceeded rapidly and in excellent order. The front-line troops were working strenuously, and the rain which fell on the afternoon of August 2nd did not succeed in damping their ardour. The efforts of all were directed to ensuring the occupation of the prescribed front with the minimum of forces. The troops were in excellent spirits, full of confidence and eager to advance.

Our orders, however, were formal; moreover, they were repeated at 10.30 A.M. on August 3rd in a telephone message from the Commander-in-Chief, saying: "It is of the utmost importance not to cross the frontier." Nevertheless, authority was obtained for the front line troops to make a reconnaissance a mile in front of their positions.

Intelligence reports showed that heavy German concentrations were taking place around and to the north of Metz, and that large numbers of troops were detraining along the Metz-Sarrebourg railway. The line of the frontier was occupied in force and the construction of field works was in active progress.

Bodies of enemy cavalry continued their incursions on to French ground and some of our customs posts were forced to withdraw. These patrols provoked several skirmishes with our cavalry, after which they would retire across the frontier in the evening. On the night of August 3rd-4th a more serious alarm occurred in the neighbourhood of Noményé; according to one source of information worthy of reliance, an attack was threatened along the whole front.

Contact with the enemy was thus becoming closer and closer and our troops, continually on the alert, getting little sleep and exposed to frequent downpours of rain, were beginning to feel the strain. It was now learned that the Germans had invaded the Grand Duchy of Luxemburg on August 2nd and had violated Belgian neutrality on the 4th. This last news was received only a short time before that of Germany's declaration of war against France, which was immediately published to the troops of the XX Corps.

On August 5th the G.O.C. the Second Army* informed me from his Headquarters at Neufchâteau that he would assume command of his Army and of the Basse Meurthe covering sector the following day; meantime, and until further instructions, I was to keep under my orders all the units, and especially the 2nd Cavalry Division, which had been detailed to the sector. War being now declared, all restrictions were withdrawn from covering operations, " which will be executed in such manner as best to fulfil the mission assigned to the various sectors."

* General de Castelnau.

The XX Corps at once took advantage of this freedom of action by sending the cavalry forward to the river Seille and executing air reconnaissances on the line Delme-Château-Salins-Dieuze. No important concentration was reported and we gathered that the enemy on the XX Corps front was waiting upon events and that only comparatively weak bodies of infantry, widely dispersed, were in the front line facing us.

However, on August 6th, I decided to send troops of all arms as far as the Seille. These met with only small detachments of cavalry and cyclists, which they easily drove back. On the contrary, at Vic and Moyenvic they ran against German infantry and artillery and were obliged to retire. The following day a false alarm indicated the necessity of reinforcing the flanks of the covering troops. With this object in view I sent a strong detachment of all arms to the region of Mont St. Jean, with instructions to cover the left of the corps, while on the right wing I supported the 2nd Cavalry Division by the 10th,* which had just been placed under my command. Very little activity, however, was manifested on the part of the enemy. Information coming in tended to show that he was occupied in organizing his troops which, after a hurried mobilization, had been rapidly distributed along the frontier. In order to gain the necessary time for this work he strengthened his defences by cutting the dam which held the Lake of Lindre, thus flooding the valley of the Seille as far as Moyenvic. He did not destroy the bridges over the river, however, as he would need them in case he decided to take the offensive. It looked as though our rapid mobilization and concentration had forestalled him.

The troops of the XX Corps had been continually on

* General Conneau.

the alert for ten days, when the arrival, on August 8th, of the XVI* and XV† Army Corps in Lorraine made it possible to give them some rest.

The G.O.C. Second Army now ordered the Basse Meurthe covering sector to be divided into three zones : the XX Corps on the left, the XVI Corps in the centre, and the XV Corps on the right. Then, on August 12th, the IX Corps‡ began to arrive, enabling a still larger reduction to be made in the front held by the XX Corps, which now settled down comfortably into its positions.

It was in this situation that our period of waiting came to an end. The XX Corps had covered the assembling of the Second Army. This meant that, until that Army was fully formed, we were to prevent any hostile operations on our territory, while at the same time taking care neither to be drawn into an action nor to force one, even for the purpose of gaining intelligence of the enemy's movements. During these two weeks the nearness of two opposing masses and frequent contact with hostile detachments created an excitement amongst the men which might have led to serious and annoying incidents. Any engagement would have been premature and contrary to the intentions of the Commander-in-Chief. Every effort was therefore made to prevent being taken unawares and to confine all fighting within the strictest limits. These preliminary results obtained, the XX Corps thenceforward constituted one of the units of the Second Army and operated under its orders on the same footing as the other corps of that army, the IX, XV, XVI and XVIII.

This Army was preparing to take the offensive. We will now indicate its objectives.

* General Taverna.   † General Espinasse.   ‡ General Dubois.

CHAPTER II

THE XX CORPS IN THE LORRAINE OFFENSIVE

BATTLE OF MORHANGE

(August 14th—20th, 1914)

Conditions governing an offensive in Lorraine—Attack of the right wing of the XX Corps in support of the XV and XVI Corps—The German artillery, August 14th—Extensive German withdrawal, August 16th—Re-alignment of the Second Army and preparations for an offensive in a northerly direction, August 17th and 18th—The Battle of Morhange, August 19th and 20th.

A FRENCH offensive on a large scale in Lorraine might be justified as a demonstration having for its object the retention in that region of the important German forces known to be assembled there. The invasion of Belgium and Luxemburg, now in full swing, indicated that by far the strongest portion of the hostile armies would be drawn to and retained in the North ; therefore an offensive in Lorraine, pursued in a divergent direction and far removed from the principal theatre of operations could not hope to achieve any success important enough to affect the main issue seriously. This would be fought out in a separate and distant region between the bulk of our forces and those of the enemy. Such an enterprise, moreover, would be attended by great difficulties and grave risks.

Lorraine, considered as a theatre of operations, was isolated and accessible only through one door, while its peculiar physical features had been greatly strengthened by artificial means. In shape it was a triangle whose base, constituted by the common frontier, was open. Its sides were closed by two serious obstacles, the Moselle on the west and the Sarre on the east. It was separated from the main theatre of operations by the Moselle, whose banks were commanded and protected for a considerable distance by the fortified region of Metz-Thionville. This greatly increased the importance of the river as an obstacle, strengthened the barrier which already divided Lorraine from the northern theatre of operations and provided an excellent base for a counter-attack by the strong reserves which the enemy could at any moment detach from his other armies. These reserves could be easily and rapidly brought up by the numerous railways converging on Metz and Thionville. Under the protection of the artillery of these fortresses they could be concentrated in a well-sheltered area and from there, if it became advantageous, they could easily be thrown into a battle engaged in Lorraine.

On the east and north, the Sarre likewise formed a strong line of resistance, supported in rear and to the south by the fortress of Strasbourg, the line of the Bruche and the defences of Molsheim. Reserves from almost any region of Germany could be assembled here in perfect safety. The Sarre, therefore, constituted yet another base of manœuvre for launching counter-attacks. Towards the centre of the triangle, between the two rivers, the line of the Rotte-Albe, prolonging that of the German Nied, had been organized for several years past and its defences joined up to Thionville. This constituted a strong transversal position between the line of resistance and the manœuvre base which could be easily used in combination with them.

The only ground favourable to a French offensive

extended for thirty miles from the Delme hill (which marked the limit of the advanced fortifications of Metz) to the Sarre at Sarrebourg. A large portion of this ground (Sarrebourg-Dieuze, ten miles) was extensively wooded and much cut up by canals and large ponds. Its defence, therefore, presented little difficulty to the enemy. On another portion, which was comparatively open (Dieuze-Delme, about fifteen miles) numerous artificial aiming points had been erected in the last few years. These extended many miles back from the frontier, showing that this ground had been specially prepared for the action of artillery.

The Lorraine theatre, as can be seen, was not only a mass of natural obstacles, but its already limited breadth had been further contracted by fortification. With its flank positions and lateral lines of defence resting on the great fortresses of Strasbourg and Metz-Thionville, and provided as it was with a complete network of railways, it furnished the Germans with a field of battle admirably suited for stopping the adversary with small numbers and then, as occasion arose, inflicting upon him a severe defeat by containing him in front and counter-attacking from the flanks. At the same time, it provided a strong pivotal position for an extensive manœuvre of German armies seeking to bring on a great battle in the comparatively open plains of northern France. This region did not seem indicated as the starting point of an important offensive, for it would have to be undertaken over extremely difficult ground with no prospect of attaining a decisive objective.

Therefore a French advance in Lorraine with the purpose of bringing the enemy to battle was an idea to be approached with the utmost reserve. About the only ground favourable for it was that lying between Delme and Dieuze, about twelve miles in extent, and there the mysterious aiming points would have to be taken into account. The country to the east of Dieuze, as far as the Sarre, was wooded and intersected by ponds and canals. Consequently the right flank would be threatened by the possibility of the enemy debouching from the upper Sarre and the Bruche.

A further advance of a French offensive in Lorraine would bring its left flank into contact with the enemy forces of the Metz and Moselle regions. Having only a very narrow front at its disposal, many obstacles would be certain to delay its progress. Such a movement, with both flanks constantly threatened, would present small prospects of success, especially as the further it advanced the more serious would become the danger. Then again, there would be no means of estimating beforehand at what moment or at what place this growing danger might be definitely averted by a tactical victory, for the position of the Germans was strategically sound and well organized in depth and they were capable of nullifying at any moment such initial tactical successes as we might have obtained.

Indeed, with this German snare spread before us as it was in August 1914, how could we hope that even the most vigorous thrust would succeed in penetrating an organized defensive position, forty miles in depth, and in obtaining decisive results before the enemy had time to reply? It was more than hazardous to count upon such a possibility. On the other hand, by making repeated demonstrations in force against the trap, we could keep it set, maintain in front of us the hostile forces which constituted it, and thus bring our help to the great battle which was to be fought elsewhere.

On August 12th the General commanding the Second

Army issued his orders for the operations to be effected on the 14th. These prescribed that the Second Army, while covering itself on the north, was to extend its line eastwards in the direction of Avricourt; then, after affecting a junction with the First Army, it was to attack in a north-easterly direction on the left of that army. The operation was to be carried out by the XV and XVI Corps and the main body of the XX Corps, the whole disposed in echelon from the right. The remainder of the army was to support the attack.

The special task of the XX Corps was to advance against the ridge Donnelay-Juvelize. On its right the XV Corps was to move in the direction of Avricourt, while on its left the IX Corps would cover the attack from Moncel up to the Moselle. In rear, the units of the 2nd Group of Reserve Divisions (59th and 68th)* then detraining, were to occupy, as they arrived, the positions prepared east of Nancy.

To comply with these instructions, I issued orders to my command to move at 7 A.M., the 11th Division on the right, the 39th on the left. A detachment under the command of General Wirbel was to cover the advance, operating on both sides of the Moncel road and keeping in touch with the IX Corps. Information gathered by our aviation showed that the Germans were actively building defensive works in the immediate neighbourhood of the frontier between Delme and Maizières, on the Metz-Strasbourg road.

As a matter of fact, the G.O.C. Second Army was fully aware of the difficulties accompanying an offensive operation in this area, and which I have described above. He therefore impressed upon his corps commanders the necessity of methodically organizing their attacks by

* General Léon Durand.

preceding and strongly supporting each advance of the infantry with artillery fire. In addition, he fixed a line beyond which the advance was not to go that day.

At the outset, no serious difficulties attended the carrying out of this programme for August 14th. During the morning the divisions of the XX Corps had no trouble in occupying the heights which dominated the frontier ridge, the enemy outposts on this front falling back without resistance. But in the afternoon the advance became as hard as in the morning it had been easy. Upon nearing the ridge, our men met with little opposition on the part of infantry, but came under intense artillery fire, including that of heavy pieces accurately ranged on the conspicuous points which stand out along the frontier. Thanks to their long range, these guns were able to select emplacements which our field artillery could not reach. However, in spite of this fire and the losses it caused, the Corps succeeded in reaching its objectives. The front-line troops, although bombarded all day long, dug in on their positions, as much to protect themselves against counter-attack as to be ready to resume the advance the following morning. Headquarters of the XX Corps were established at Serres.

The superiority of the enemy's armament had already been demonstrated, likewise the advantage he derived from having previously prepared the ground on his side of the frontier. In addition to being numerous, his heavy guns had a longer range than our artillery and could therefore support his troops at a distance impossible for us; moreover, their fire having been ranged beforehand on selected aiming points was extremely accurate. From this moment on it was evident that artillery was to be the dominant factor in the opening phase of any battle, and long before the infantry could take any part in it. Only small detachments could move across this shell-swept area, and however determined the infantry might be, the hostile artillery would, from the outset, hold up its advance and prevent it from approaching near enough to overwhelm the opposing line by its fire and then take it by assault. The hostile artillery had to be silenced or neutralized by our own guns before these could be employed to support the infantry attack.

This meeting of two great armies after forty years of peace was bringing to light astonishing changes in the practice of war. As time went on our tactics became adapted to the new conditions, but even now our General Officers could not fail to be impressed by the necessity of restraining the impetuosity of their troops and of organizing their operations with the greatest care.

The attack was to be resumed the next day, August 15th, at 4 A.M. The task of the XX Corps was to hold fast at all costs along its northern front and support the advance of the XV Corps toward Maizières by attacking Donnelay with its remaining troops. We were not to move out until the XV Corps had come up in line with us. As a matter of fact, the XV Corps was unable to advance all day. During the morning it reported that, by reason of its losses the day before and the necessity of relieving its front-line division, it would not be able to renew the attack before the 16th.

The XX Corps, therefore, had to remain stationary for the entire day, which was all the more unpleasant as it lay exposed to a persistent and well regulated fire from the German heavy artillery. Notwithstanding this painful experience and the losses resulting from it, the Corps was ready to renew the attack ordered for the whole of the Second Army the following day, August 16th.

The first reports of the engagements of August 14th and 15th had led the General Officer Commanding the Second Army to issue a memorandum to his Corps Commanders " on the methods to be adopted in the attack of defensive positions." The advance was to be carried out methodically " up to the moment when combined infantry and artillery attacks on the objectives selected for assault would be rendered possible by a solid organization of ground already won and by careful artillery preparation." In my turn, I impressed on my subordinates the vital importance of artillery action, urging special attention to this point during the operations of August 16th. However, that day was going to develop quite differently from the previous ones.

The right of the XX Corps moved forward shortly before 7 A.M. Not a shot from rifle or cannon was fired at us. The inhabitants reported that the Germans had begun the previous morning to withdraw in the direction of Dieuze and that this movement had continued during the whole of the night of August 15th-16th. Every one of the few prisoners we captured acknowledged the demoralizing effect of our field artillery (75's). Stranger still, in places we saw signs of a hasty retreat, and an officer's patrol of the 5th Hussars reported the discovery of quantities of abandoned equipment and shells.

I accordingly ordered my troops to push forward along the whole front, gain contact with the enemy and seize Donnelay-Juvelize as quickly as possible. At the end of the day, the XX Corps was firmly established on this line, with its left holding the Seille in the neighbourhood of Château-Salins.

On August 17th the Second Army started to effect a change of front toward the north with the view of attacking in that direction. The XX Corps had only to establish itself facing north, closing in on its left, its right resting on the heights south of Marsal.

These movements were carried out during the 17th, although they were greatly hampered by the rain which had been falling without pause since the morning before. By nightfall the leading troops of the XX Corps, which had closed in to the left, were established facing north on the heights south of the Seille, between Marsal and Chambrey. The 5th Hussars had occupied Morville-les-Vic and Château-Salins during the day, after a skirmish with a body of Germans. By the evening of the 18th, the Second Army had completed its change of front and was getting ready to advance in a northerly direction. Once these preliminaries were completed, the offensive was to be resumed on August 19th and vigorously pushed as prescribed for a pursuit. Instruction No. 3 from H.Q. Second Army, dated August 18th, read as follows:

" The enemy is retiring on our front and has abandoned Sarrebourg and Château-Salins.

" He must be pursued with the utmost vigour and rapidity.

" The G.O.C. Second Army relies on the energy of all to achieve this result.

" He expects Corps Commanders to instil into their troops the necessary dash, which differs from that required for a methodical advance against prepared positions.

" With the same end in view, all heavy units likely to slow down the advance will march at the rear of the columns until required for action."

The following operation orders were issued on the same day:

"The Army will continue its advance to-morrow, August 19th, with the object of reaching the line Sarrebourg—Pont-à-Mousson.

"Leading units of main bodies will cross the line Seille—Salines Canal at 8 A.M. and will not advance beyond the line marked by the River Albe below Lening and continued by the line Virmingen—Morhange—Baronville.

"The XVI Corps, covering the eastern flank of the army, will move in the general direction Lening—St. Avold. . . .

"The XV Corps will attack in the general direction Rodalbe—Pont Pierre.

"The XX Corps, moving to the west of Marsal, inclusive, will have as its general direction the line Château—Salins—Faulquemont. . . .

"The Group of Reserve Divisions will cover the left flank of the army from the direction of Metz. It will take up successive positions facing north-west, in order to resist any attack from that quarter.

"The XVIII Corps, as from the 17th, has ceased to form part of the Second Army.

"The IX Corps has been placed at the disposal of the Commander-in-Chief."

The departure of the IX and XVIII Corps greatly reduced the strength of the army, and consequently its striking power. To protect the left flank, in particular, only the Group of Reserve Divisions would be available, and these, as the army advanced, would become stretched out over more than thirty miles. The protection afforded would be so precarious as to be virtually negligible.

On reading these instructions, my first thought was

that the General in command must have received some very reliable intelligence which caused him to feel justified in ordering this rapid advance with objectives assigned as far off as the road from Pont-à-Mousson to Sarrebrück. As I saw it, the operations thus far carried out by the Second Army had not constituted an encounter with the enemy so serious in its nature as to have compelled his retreat and much less to have created disorganization in his ranks. What had taken place had been little more than artillery engagements. Nevertheless, on the very day that it had been deprived of two of its corps and was therefore more weakly protected from the direction of Metz than ever before, this army was ordered to undertake an advance on distant objectives through a country whose dangers have already been described. I presumed that special information from very high sources justifying the enterprise must have been received.

However that might be, following my instructions, I issued orders to the XX Corps to advance on the line Baronville—Morhange, the 11th Division on the line Morhange—Signal de Baronville, and the 39th Division on the line Baronville—Signal de Marthil. General Wirbel's detachment was to continue to cover the left flank of the Corps and to maintain touch with the 68th Reserve Division.

Shortly after 8 A.M. on the 19th, I established my advanced headquarters on the road from Vic to Château-Salins. In the course of the morning, on the right, the wooded country considerably delayed the advance of the 11th Division, but it encountered no other difficulties. On the left, the 39th Division and General Wirbel's detachment made much easier progress. Reports from the inhabitants indicated the withdrawal of the enemy from the country around Delme and the presence of strong hostile forces in the neighbourhood of Baronville.

At 2 P.M., as it debouched on the far side of the Petite Seille, the 11th Division came under heavy and accurate artillery and machine-gun fire and suffered considerable loss. Taking advantage of the hollow ground on its left, the division pushed forward to Révange, where at nightfall it dug itself in. It did not advance any further that day.

In the meantime, the 39th Division had directed one regiment on Baronville and another on Marthil and the Signal de Marthil. Although these regiments soon became the target for heavy artillery fire, they pushed forward and, by 4.30 P.M., the 160th had reached the ground to the south of Baronville, while the 153rd had occupied Marthil and the Signal de Marthil. General Wirbel's detachment had advanced considerably beyond the Château-Salins forest.

I did not consider it possible for the XX Corps to reach all of its allotted objectives that day. Before launching an attack on the strong position of Morhange—Baronville, it would be necessary to reorganize the infantry, which had suffered heavily from the enemy's bombardment, and also to precede the assault by a serious artillery preparation. The remaining daylight did not give sufficient time for these operations. Moreover, the 11th Division, which would have to make the main attack, had been obliged to detach some of its troops to guard its unprotected flank, a situation which resulted from the XV Corps not having advanced nearly as far as the XX Corps; its left in particular had not succeeded in debouching from Köking and the Forest of Bride. It was necessary, therefore, for me to order the 11th Division to occupy the Haut-de-Köking in strength in order to safeguard its right flank, which I did at 4.30 P.M.

This move anticipated the special order which I received at 5.20 P.M. from the G.O.C. Second Army :

" The G.O.C. Second Army desires the G.O.C. XX Corps to support the troops of the 30th Division which are trying to debouch to the north from Köking and the Forest of Bride.

" The XX Corps will to-night hold the road from Conthil to Dieuze."

It was under these conditions that the day came to an end. Before leaving my command post at Berlioncourt, I indicated the positions to be taken up during the evening and the attitude to be assumed until the following day. I then returned to my Headquarters at Château-Salins, while the troops reorganized on the captured ground.

To sum up, the Corps had executed without difficulty the greater part of the prescribed advance and had pushed forward some twelve miles from its starting point, the Seille. It had come under heavy artillery and machine-gun fire from the heights of Marthil, Baronville and Morhange, but in spite of serious losses it had, with unshaken determination, proceeded to occupy Marthil and the Signal de Marthil.

At the end of the day it still had six battalions in reserve and was in a position for attacking with every chance of success the heights which remained to be conquered. Strong artillery support would, of course, be necessary for this purpose. It was also essential that the right flank of the Corps be covered by a parallel advance of the XV Corps and that its left flank be fully protected.

The latter task had been entrusted to the Group of Reserve Divisions, which did not come under my orders. The most advanced Division of this Group was far in rear of the left wing of the XX Corps.

As I received neither orders nor information from the Second Army during the evening of August 19th—20th, I confined myself to carrying out the spirit of the instructions sent me on the 18th. Accordingly, late in the night, I issued orders from Château-Salins for my Corps to renew its attack at 6 o'clock the following morning. However, when this hour arrived the situation had so changed that the operation was not undertaken.

As a matter of fact, the movements of August 19th, instead of being merely the pursuit of a retiring enemy, had developed into a general battle along the whole front of the Second Army and against a well-posted enemy.

The advance on the right had been less pronounced than that of the XX Corps. The XVI Corps had been unable to debouch north of the Salines Canal and the left of the XV Corps, as has been seen, had been held up in the southern part of the Forest of Köking. These two corps were therefore a long way short of the line which the orders of the 18th contemplated they would reach by the evening of the 19th.

The General Officer Commanding the Second Army had in consequence issued fresh orders* for August 20th, instructing the XV and XVI Corps, closely co-ordinating their action, to advance at 5 A.M. with the object of forcing the enemy back from the Bensdorff—Sarrebourg

* These orders did not reach either the XX Corps or the 68th Reserve Division. It was only during the morning of the 20th, at my advanced headquarters at Berlioncourt, that I was informed of these new instructions, and even then I did not receive the actual text. By that time, the initiative had passed to the enemy, bringing about a radical change in the general situation of the army.

railway. The XX Corps was to take position on the ground won and the Group of Reserve Divisions was to guard against any movement coming from the direction of Metz. There could be no doubt that these divisions, weak as they were and particularly so in artillery, would find it extremely difficult to carry out such a task.

The dangers attending an advance in the neighbourhood of the fortified region of Metz now began to be manifest ; for not only was the area thoroughly organized for defence and perfectly equipped with facilities in the matter of railways and detraining platforms, but every inch of it was familiar ground to the Germans.

At 5.15 A.M. on the 20th, I informed Second Army Headquarters that the XX Corps had passed the night on its positions and would renew the attack at 6 A.M.

I was continually preoccupied by my right flank and the support we were expected to give the XV Corps. I therefore at 6 A.M. ordered the 11th Division to reinforce the detachment holding the Köking heights, so as to ensure their possession. I added : " One of the essential tasks of the XX Corps is to support the left of the XV Corps. If your detachment can make itself felt at once, as it should do, this task can be most effectively carried out by opening fire in the direction of Bourgaltroff."

But by this time the action decided upon by the enemy was beginning to have its effect. All night long the movement of trains in the direction of Han-sur-Nied had been heard, a sure sign that large enemy reinforcements were arriving. A general attack on our front and flanks was to be the outcome. Before dawn on the 20th, General Wirbel's outposts had been driven in and his position attacked by strong forces. A heavy bombardment of the front and flanks of the 39th Division was added to that already coming from the heights of Marthil and Baronville, and General Wirbel's detachment was forced to fall back to the edge of the Château-Salins forest.

The German attack, preceded by intense artillery fire, was not long in developing along the whole front of the 39th Division. Powerful assaults launched about 5.30 A.M. drove this division from Marthil and the Signal. Two groups of its artillery were put out of action and the division was obliged to withdraw to the line Château-Bréhain—Bréhain.

This made it impossible for the 11th Division to carry out the intended attack on Morhange. Moreover, this Division since daybreak had been subjected to severe assaults in the course of which Conthil was lost. However, our troops stood their ground and the advance of the enemy's infantry was stopped by our artillery fire.

Further to the right the detachment on the Haut-de-Köking likewise had been attacked by a force of all arms which advanced about 5 A.M. from the east as well as from the northern edges of the Forests of Bride and Köking. Some ground was lost, but the detachment held fast.

To sum up. By 7 A.M. the enemy had forced the 39th Division to fall back and take up new positions; but the 11th Division had held its ground along the whole of its front and stood ready to support the XV Corps with its right.

This Corps had been heavily attacked all along its front and its position had become critical. At 7.15 A.M. I received the following order from the General Officer Commanding the Second Army :—

" A strong enemy offensive is debouching from Köking and the Forest of Bride against the flank of the 30th

Division. Attack at once in the direction of Lidrezing in order to break up this offensive and extricate the XV Corps."

To cope with the general situation and at the same time carry out this order, I directed my troops to hold fast to their present defensive positions. Meanwhile I prepared a line of resistance in rear along the front Château Bréhain—Dalhain—Haboudange wood—Haut-de-Köking, to which I directed my reserves. At the same time, I ordered the Haut-de-Köking detachment, which I had reinforced, to attack at once in aid of the XV Corps.

Meanwhile important events were happening on my left. The enemy had outflanked General Wirbel's detachment and penetrated into the Viviers wood. Towards 10 A.M. the 68th Reserve Division in its turn was forced to abandon Faxe and Viviers and to withdraw on Laneuveville-en-Saulnois. The attack soon spread to the Delme—Château-Salins road, having Château-Salins as its objective. This threatened not only the flank but the communications of the XX Corps.

Events even more critical were taking place on the front of the XV and XVI Corps as the result of a general attack by the enemy in that part of the field. These led the General Officer Commanding the Second Army to order, at 7.15 A.M., the rear Division of the XVI Corps to fall back. The left of the XV Corps, assailed by a powerful offensive debouching from the Forests of Bride and Köking, was now driven in, carrying with it the right of that corps and the left of the XVI, already badly cut up. Under these conditions, at 10.10 A.M., the commander of the Second Army ordered a general retreat as follows :—

"XV Corps to establish itself on the line Marsal—Marimont.

"XVI Corps to retire in the direction of Maizières and Réchicourt-le-Château.

"XX Corps to refuse its right flank so as to rest it on the Seille at Marsal, and to hold the line Marsal—Hampont — Amelécourt — Fresnes-en-Saulnois — Jallacourt."

This order on reaching me caused me the greatest surprise, as I was unaware at that time of the extent of the difficulties which the XVI and XV Corps on my right had encountered, as also of the progress of the enemy attack on my left, on the Delme road. I knew that at the end of the morning my XX Corps was firmly established on the northern edge of the Forest of Château-Salins, that it was successfully holding its own north of the line of resistance occupied by its reserves and that its right was preparing an attack for the purpose of extricating the XV Corps. Along the whole of its front the increased ranges at which they were now firing had caused the enemy guns, both field and heavy, posted on the heights of Morhange, Baronville and Marthil, to lose much of their effect. This artillery could only move down from its positions with great difficulty and the enemy's attack was making no further progress. I felt no doubts as to my Corps being able to maintain its present positions, in spite of the ten miles of front it occupied.

My intention was to hold on firmly to the present line, then to bring the enemy to a halt in front of the positions which were being methodically organized in rear, and finally renew the attack, after having assured my contact with the XV Corps on my right and provided for the security of my left flank. It was in the midst of these preparations that the order just quoted arrived. It was dated from Maizières; another order dated from Arracourt at 11.45 A.M. soon followed. This prescribed:

" If the Second Army is forced to retreat, it will retire along the following lines :
" XVI Corps in the general direction of Lunéville, resting on the Manonviller fort and the Forest of Parroy ;
" XV Corps in the general direction of Dombasle ;
" XX Corps in the general direction of St. Nicolas—Laneuveville ;
" The Group of Reserve Divisions will occupy the fortified works of the Couronné de Nancy. All transport, parks and convoys will move by the left bank of the Meurthe."

It was evident that a more complete knowledge of the general situation of the army than I possessed (and especially in what concerned the other Corps) had inspired these two orders. Both of the other Corps had been very heavily attacked and forced to fall back a considerable distance south of the lake region. At 11.45 A.M., in compliance with the order of 10.10 A.M., I directed my divisions to take up their march toward the line indicated. At the moment these instructions reached them a new order from Army Headquarters was brought to me. It read :

" The task of the XX Corps is, in general, to cover the retirement of the Second Army by holding the Château-Salins bridgehead as long as possible. The 68th Reserve Division is placed at the disposal of the XX Corps."

The orders I had already issued to my Corps, and which were in course of being carried out, required no change. I merely supplemented them by the despatch of a special order to the 68th Reserve Division.*

Thanks to the detailed measures prescribed by their commanders, the successive retirement of the 11th and 39th Divisions was carried out in good order and without difficulty, covered as it was on the left by General Wirbel's detachment.

At 4.50 P.M. the Army Commander ordered the 68th Reserve Division to rejoin the Group of Reserve Divisions in order to aid in the defence of the fortified area of Nancy.

About 2 P.M. I moved my advanced headquarters to the west of the Géline Wood, where I had already posted the heavy artillery of the Corps. I remained there until nightfall. Before leaving for my headquarters at Moyenvic, I issued the following orders :

" 1. The XX Corps by the end of the day should be established on the line Marsal—Herraucourt-sur-Seille—northern edge of the Géline Wood—Château-Salins—Amelécourt, maintaining contact on its right with the XV Corps which holds Moncey, and on its left with the 68th Reserve Division which holds Fresnes-en-Saulnois and Jallaucourt.

" 2. As from this evening, the above line will be strongly occupied and held against any counter-attack which may be pronounced to-night or to-morrow."

These orders had hardly been written and sent out when I received the following from Army Headquarters dated Arraucourt, 4 P.M. :

* General Brun d'Antignosc.

"The Second Army will withdraw during the night under cover of rear-guards established on the general line Maizières—Donnelay—Juvelize—Marsal—Hampont—Fresnes-en-Saulnois, in order to reorganize the units which have suffered most.

Each Corps will take up the positions indicated for it in Army Order No. 28. Preparations will be made for receiving the rear-guards, when withdrawn, on the line Moussay—Garenne Wood—Haut de la Croix Wood—Juvrecourt Hill—northern edge of the Bezange Forest—left bank of the Seille.

"The XX Corps will blow up the bridges over the Seille as soon as its last troops have passed.

"Main bodies will move to the following areas:

"XVI Corps—Manonviller Fort—Crion—Sionviller.

"XV Corps—Harraucourt.

"XX Corps—Cercueil—Pulnoy."

The XX Corps anticipated no difficulty in maintaining its rear-guards and outposts in their existing positions. The ease with which the withdrawal had been carried out and the feebleness of the pursuit proved that it was possible to hold on that night and if necessary the following day. The troops proceeded to take up positions for the night which would conform to the mission assigned to the Corps, namely, to hold the Château-Salins bridge-head as long as possible and cover the retreat of the Second Army. However, at 9.45 P.M., I received from Army Headquarters, which had been established at Nancy, the following message:

"It appears that the XV Corps, which has suffered very heavily, will not be able to maintain its positions on your right. I consider it advisable, therefore, that you profit by the darkness and fall back to-night."

Evidently, as time passed and information regarding the situation of certain regiments reached the Army Commander, he was confirmed in his determination to effect a general withdrawal. Indeed, the dangers and difficulties of a French offensive in Lorraine were made only too evident to him when, on the morning of August 20th, he saw that the Second Army could not advance and he learned that the First Army had been halted at Sarrebourg. He then realized the necessity of changing his attitude and acting on the defensive; therefore he abruptly broke off the action and proceeded to establish his reorganized army behind a strong defensive line. From this position he was later on to undertake a task which the means at his disposal justified.

I now made my arrangements for moving my Corps to the south of the Seille. My instructions reached the troops just as they were installing themselves in the billets which had been allotted to them during the afternoon of the 20th. They immediately resumed their march and despite a long and exhausting night march, following on two days of heavy fighting, the main bodies arrived south of the Forest of Bezange about 4 A.M. on the 21st, and by 5 A.M. the outposts were in position and ready to defend the front assigned to the Corps.

The history of these operations since published by the Germans shows that their attack of August 20th was carried out in the following manner:

Attack on the XX Corps and Group of Reserve Divisions.

By the Metz garrison (33rd Reserve Division and 53rd Landwehr Brigade) in the direction of Nomény.

By the 10th Ersatz Division, moving from Romilly on the Delme ridge.

By the III Bavarian Corps, moving from Han-sur-

Nied—Vatimont—Lesse (covered by the 8th Cavalry Division and the Bavarian Cavalry Division) on Hannocourt—Oron—Château-Bréhain.

By the II Bavarian Corps, moving from Baronville and Morhange on Hampont—Wuisse.

Attack on the XV and XVI Corps.
By the XXI Corps, moving from Nesdorff on Dieuze—Rohrbach.
By the Bavarian I Reserve Corps on Bisping.
By the Bavarian I Corps on Langatte.

The shock could not be other than very severe on the Second Army, which had launched its three corps upon a very difficult and strongly defended country. Facing Metz, this army was protected only by a flank guard composed of units from three reserve divisions, partly immobilized and in any case very widely extended.

By the morning of August 20th the General Officer Commanding the Second Army had correctly appreciated the situation and estimated all its dangers. There was nothing for him to do but to halt his offensive.

CHAPTER III

THE XX CORPS DURING THE RETREAT FROM THE MEURTHE AND THE COUNTER-ATTACK

(August 21st—28th, 1914)

The retreat behind the Meurthe, August 21st to 23rd—The attack of the XX Corps to the north and south of the Sanon, August 24th and 25th—The attack of the whole Second Army on the enemy's communications, August 26th—I leave the XX Corps to take over another command, August 28th—Comments on the operations in Lorraine.

THE excellent behaviour of the XX Corps during the battle and the retreat which followed had left me quite confident of being able to carry out the mission entrusted to me. Moreover, not only did the enemy undertake no pursuit on the 20th, but our rear-guards had lost all contact with him during the morning of the 21st. However, on that morning the General Officer Commanding the Second Army decided to withdraw the main portion of his forces behind the Meurthe, the XV and XVI Corps holding the front line, with outposts on the east bank of the river; the XX Corps in reserve in the region of Saint Nicolas. The left of the Army would be covered by the Grand Couronné position, held by the 59th and 70th Reserve Divisions, reinforced by a part of the IX Corps.

These movements were made in perfect order and without being interfered with in any way by the Germans.

During the evening I went to see the Army Commander at his Headquarters in Nancy and after having reported to him the excellent morale of my Corps, I returned to Saint Nicolas.

On the morning of August 22nd the XX Corps was concentrated in the vicinity of the Meurthe, the 11th Division at Saint Nicolas—Varangéville and the 39th Division at Art-sur-Meurthe—Lenoncourt. No move was anticipated for the 22nd but, as we constituted the reserve of the army, arrangements had to be made to carry out any order which might be received.

As it happened, the XV Corps reported at 5.30 A.M. that its troops were so exhausted that they could not be counted upon to resist an attack which the enemy might make on the right bank of the Meurthe. The General Officer Commanding the Second Army therefore instructed me to send outposts from the XX Corps to Flainval and Anthelupt to replace those of the XV Corps. I accordingly ordered the 11th Division to detach immediately one infantry brigade supported by artillery for that purpose.

This brigade took up its position shortly before midday. In the evening it was attacked from the direction of Crévic by a Bavarian brigade, which four times attempted to seize the Flainval heights; but our brigade stood firm and enabled the XV Corps to withdraw its troops. At 11 P.M. his task having been completed, orders were given to the Brigade Commander* to withdraw and blow up the bridges over the Meurthe. This action was taken as a result of the decision of the General Officer Commanding the Second Army to retire all his troops to the left bank of the Meurthe and prolong in that region the line of resistance of the Grand Couronné of Nancy.

* General Ferry.

By 3 A.M., August 23rd, all the units of the XX Corps had crossed to the west bank of the river. Corps Headquarters were established at Manoncourt-en-Vernois.

The retreat of the Second Army stopped at the Meurthe and the position of the Grand Couronné of Nancy. Behind this exceedingly strong line the troops were able to rest and reorganize; at the same time the Army was reinforced by two new reserve divisions. As a consequence of our abruptly breaking off the fight on the morning of the 20th, and of the adversary's failure to push the pursuit on that or the following day, no decisive result had been achieved by the enemy and we had suffered no disorganization. Our check had therefore not entailed anything irreparable and we could look forward to renewing under more favourable conditions our interrupted operations. The moment for undertaking these, as well as their nature, would be mainly determined by the movements of the enemy.

Opposite the XX Corps, he had reached the high ground on the right bank of the Meurthe. He spent the 30th in establishing his batteries and digging himself in. The only activity he showed on that day was to launch two small attacks, which crumpled up under the fire of the XX Corps artillery.

The 23rd of August had not been a wasted day for the Second Army. All its units had been able to reorganize and establish themselves on their new positions. General de Castelnau now had at his disposal a mass of manœuvre whose employment was soon to be determined by events.

On the evening of the 23rd, he issued orders for the left of his army to be ready to attack if necessary. About noon on the 24th he learnt that a hostile force, estimated at not less than two army corps, was passing from north to south toward Lunéville, thus exposing its right flank in the direction of Nancy. He therefore ordered the XX Corps and the Group of Reserve Divisions to attack this flank. The movement of the XX Corps was well supported by artillery and, by 6 P.M., progressing without difficulty, it had reached the ridges of Flainval and the Crévic Wood, where I halted it.

These movements during August 24th clearly indicated the enemy's intention. His main body having been directed on Lunéville, he was now evidently pushing towards the gap at Charmes. In order to frustrate this plan, the General Officer Commanding the Second Army decided that on the 25th he would vigorously attack with his left while maintaining his actual front, the object being to seize the Arracourt—Einville—Lunéville road, which seemed to be the enemy's line of communication. The right of the army was to act in conjunction with the First Army ; the attack on the left was to be carried out by the XX Corps and the Group of Reserve Divisions.

Early in the morning, the 39th Division, in touch with the 70th Reserve Division, attacked to the north of the Sanon and forced the enemy back from the high ground west of the Einville Wood. Towards midday I ordered the 11th Division in its turn to attack to the south of the Sanon, as the XV Corps had by then made considerable progress. The four regiments of the 11th Division, after a violent action, gained possession of the Anthelupt and Vitrimont ridges.

During this time the enemy stiffened his resistance to the north of the Sanon, where his communications were directly threatened, by concentrating strong forces in this vicinity. To the west of the Einville Wood, the 39th Division was heavily engaged. Its right was forced back on the Crévic Wood which, after a succession of desperate fights, was captured by the enemy about 5 P.M. Its left found itself in a still more critical situation owing to the losses suffered by the 70th Reserve Division. With its right flank exposed by the loss of the Crévic Wood and its left by the forcing back of the 70th Reserve Division, at 6 P.M. it retired, though slightly and in good order.

August 25th had been a very hard day for the XX Corps. With varying fortunes it had fought a long and serious battle ; but it had given the death blow to the enemy's projects. Although it had not accomplished any great advance on the whole of its front, it had drawn against itself a large part of the enemy's forces and had held them in check. Their absence may have prevented his succeeding in his main design, which was to break through on the road to Charmes. Although my Corps had obtained no decisive result, its action might lead to important developments for the operations of the Second Army, " provided its troops hold the enemy under the threat of a fresh attack and stand constantly ready to take up the pursuit now begun on the right of the army and the Cavalry Corps."

It was in these terms that I expressed my ideas on the evening of August 25th, after I learned what had been accomplished along the whole front of the Second Army, whose right wing had effected so important an advance.

The orders of the Army for the 26th were drawn up with a view to exploiting the success gained by the right wing the day before. General de Castelnau prescribed that the pursuit be pushed " to the extreme limit of endurance." The general line of direction for the XX Corps was Valhey—Bezange-la-Petite. " In spite of the violent effort already sustained and the losses suffered, the General commanding counts upon his men to strike a final blow which will ensure victory."

At 5.30 A.M. on the 26th, I issued orders from my advanced headquarters for the two infantry divisions to move forward " as soon as the enemy makes it possible," the 11th Division toward Einville and the 39th Division on the Crévic Woods—Valhey.

At 7 A.M. the Division Commanders gave the order to attack. The 11th Division was to operate between the Nancy road and the river Sanon, directing its principal effort on the Friscati heights which command Lunéville. Owing to delay in the artillery preparations, the attack could not be launched until 12.15 P.M. It made good progress at first and passed Vitrimont. The 69th Regiment advanced steadily towards the Signal de Friscati and obtained a footing on its slopes. But at this moment, 1.45 P.M., when the regiment tried to gain ground beyond the Signal, it was met by heavy infantry and artillery fire which the guns of the 11th Division could not silence. For three hours the troops of the division were subjected to a bombardment by the German heavy batteries and no progress was possible.

The situation of the 69th Regiment on the Signal de Friscati became, in consequence, critical, but it succeeded in holding on.

While the 11th Division was fighting these actions to the south of the Sanon, the 39th Division, whose troops had been greatly fatigued by the work of the previous days, advanced only very slowly. By nightfall, it had not been able to do more than establish itself to the east of the Crévic Woods, its right resting on the Sanon.

The XV and XVI Corps, also, owing to fatigue and previous losses, were not in a condition to take up a vigorous pursuit. Indeed, the effects of incessant effort and loss of sleep were being seriously felt. In spite of this fatigue, the morale of the XX Corps remained high, and its conduct under fire during the whole of the 26th of August had been exemplary from every point of view.

The battle had now lasted several days along the whole front of the Second Army and the culminating point of the German advance from Charmes to the Moselle had been reached. The enemy's thrust toward the southeast had been stopped and he had been forced to fight a serious action to protect his communications—and particularly those formed by the Lunéville—Einville road—from the attacks of the XX Corps. This turn of fortune must be seized, notwithstanding the fatigue of our troops. That was to be the work of the following days.

The Second Army had now advanced beyond the left of the First Army, and this enabled General de Castelnau to make a halt of twenty-four hours to give his troops some rest. He therefore issued orders for the 27th to be spent in consolidating the ground won and in reorganizing the units, with a view to making a fresh effort during the following days.

The Second Army was to resume its offensive in a northerly direction on August 28th. The task of the XX Corps was to support the attack of the XV Corps on Lunéville and to ensure its being able to debouch to the north of that town. Accordingly, the right of the 11th Division was ordered to advance at 8 A.M. on the Friscati heights and throw the enemy back to the north. Some delay occurred at the crossing of the Meurthe, so that it was only at noon that the attack could be started. Before the day closed the Signal de Friscati was captured, but when that happened I had already left the XX

Corps, as orders had come from the Commander-in-Chief directing me to report at General Headquarters in order to receive a new command. At midday I left my advanced post at Hudiviller, turning over the command of the Corps to General Balfourier, who was at the head of the 11th Division.

I took with me Lieutenant-Colonel Weygand, 5th Hussars. During the whole of the war, in the various commands which I was called upon to fill, he was to serve as my Chief of Staff.

It was not without considerable emotion that I left the gallant regiments of the XX Corps. In my farewell order I recalled to them the glorious achievements of the preceding days, during which they had never once given ground except in obedience to formal instructions from higher authority. I arrived at Vitry-le-François at 6 P.M. Here I found General Joffre.

The impressions left upon me by this first month of fighting in Lorraine were quite definite.

The flood of invasion had been checked and even forced back, in spite of an undeniable superiority in numbers and *matériel*, especially heavy artillery, possessed by the enemy. The impetus of the German offensive had been broken. It was solely due to the high moral qualities of our men and our officers that we had everywhere met the enemy with calm resolution and handled him severely. If our efforts had not been crowned with a Saalfeld or a Jena, we had at least escaped a Wissembourg or a Froeschwiller. And we were beginning to forge ahead. Although we had not defeated the left wing of the German armies we had broken their force and obliged them to retire.

Our adversary was dangerously superior to us in the modern war material which he had been preparing for many years and was now using with great effect. In spite of that and of the exceptional nature of the ground here in Lorraine, his first dash had been checked and he had failed to obtain a decisive result. He had not been able to bring about that rapid and victorious march of events which his undoubted superiority in men and armament had led him to expect. He had seen his undertakings fail and a retreat imposed upon him. He realized that the victory he had counted upon must be postponed to another day.

The question which arose in my mind was this: Could we, by judiciously exploiting the undoubted qualities possessed by our army, now undertake first to halt the enemy along the whole of our front, and then prevent his achieving immediate victory through his temporary superiority in weapons and men, by ourselves assuming a rapid and vigorous offensive?

Was it possible for us even now to anticipate the day when fortune would turn definitely in our favour, through the accession of strength which not only our own reserves and our industries but also our powerful allies would bring us?

For the German Command had evinced an undoubted hesitancy in the conduct of the war in Lorraine. If he had let us penetrate deeply into the country and had then counter-attacked us with all his forces united, he might have engaged a defensive battle having decisive results. He did not attempt this, notwithstanding the thorough preparation of this whole theatre of operations and his superior numbers.

Our rapid break-off on August 20th was followed by only a feeble pursuit. When the enemy did decide to undertake a vigorous offensive, it was confined to the sole idea of forcing the gap of Charmes; and this operation was pursued in total disregard of our forces on the Meurthe and the Grand Couronné. Our flank attacks made it impossible for him to continue his advance, much less to penetrate. He retired. What had happened to us at Morhange had fallen upon him in double measure at the Couronné.

Generally speaking, it seemed proved that the new means of action furnished by automatic weapons and long-range guns enabled the defence to hold up any attempt at breaking through long enough for a counter-attack to be launched with saving effect. The " pockets," which resulted from partial attacks which were successful and seemingly even decisive, could not be maintained, in spite of very costly losses, long enough to ensure a definite rupture of the adversary's line. They could be too quickly rendered uninhabitable and useless for the assailant.

When a defensive front has been forced by superior numbers to fall back, it has not thereby been broken. Counter-attacks on the assailant's flank have often consumed the latter's reserves and threatened his communications, to the extent of eventually stopping his partial advance and causing him to retire.

Many new subjects for reflection are offered when we examine the limitations and the weaknesses of an offensive which, while tactically successful at first, is continued in violation of the principles which modern weapons have now imposed ; we see that it is more than ever necessary to study the situation created by the circumstances of the moment and to make sure of the possibilities to which they may give rise.

Because he had checked us at Morhange without having defeated us or even disorganized our forces, the German Command, discounting a success which was purely negative, launched his army southward toward the Moselle, heedless of the resistance which Nancy could offer on the west and the Vosges on the east. He was obliged to retire without having reached the Moselle at Charmes.

His superior strength had inspired him with contempt for his adversary and had given him a confidence which could not be long enough sustained for victory to crown it. This début was a fit harbinger of the battle of the Marne.

PART II

IN COMMAND OF THE NINTH ARMY

(August 29th—October 4th, 1914)

CHAPTER I

THE RETREAT

Arrival at General Headquarters—The situation from the Somme to the Vosges—The Commander-in-Chief assigns me to my new post, August 28th to 29th—I take command of the "Army Detachment," August 29th to 30th—Retreat and re-grouping of forces on the Retourne, on the Suippe, and as far as Rheims, August 31st to September 2nd—The troops of the Regular and Reserve Divisions—The retreat continues—The reinforced "Army Detachment" becomes the Ninth Army, September 3rd—The About Turn; orders and plans for the Battle of the Marne, September 5th—The Field of Battle.

WHEN I gave up command of the XX Corps I took Lieutenant-Colonel Weygand with me, and on my way through Second Army headquarters at Neuves-Maisons I picked up Lieutenant-Colonel Devaux. A special countersign being in use in the entrenched camp of Toul, we had some difficulty in passing certain of the posts. This caused considerable delay.

That matters were progressing favourably in Lorraine, we, of course, knew, but our journey to General Headquarters was made in entire ignorance of what had happened to the other armies.

When we arrived at Vitry, however, and read the morning *communiqué*, we had a rude awakening. This said : " The front of the invasion now reaches from the Somme to the Vosges," which meant that Belgium and all the north of France up to the River Somme were in the hands of the enemy. He was advancing on Paris, the heart of the country, at furious speed. Our general offensive on the frontier had been thrown back and our armies in the centre and on the left wing, (the Third,

Fourth, Fifth and the British), were in full retreat, closely pursued and constantly threatened by envelopment on the west. Moreover, the touch between these armies had been endangered.

The country on our line of retreat did not lend itself to defence. The river valleys, such as the Oise and the Aisne on the west and the Meuse on the east, led straight to the region of Paris. In consequence, it was difficult to see where there could be found a continuous line of defence facing north, behind which our vast front might be re-established, thus giving us at least a few days in which to reorganize our forces and put them in order. Where could the retreat be definitely halted and the offensive resumed with a fair chance of success? Fortunately, during this time of danger and uncertainty, the Commander-in-Chief never for a moment lost his wonderful calm.

The magnitude and impetuosity of the German sweep through Belgium had impelled his decision to withdraw his forces behind the following line:

Third Army: Verdun.

Fourth Army: The Aisne, from Vouziers to Guignicourt.

Fifth Army: Craonne—Laon—La Fère.

British Army: Behind the Somme from Ham to Bray.

At the same time, he had ordered the formation of the Sixth Army, in the neighbourhood of Amiens, for the purpose of checking the enemy's advance by operating well out beyond the western flank of the French formation.

Once our front had been re-formed behind the above-described general line, the offensive was to be resumed. The attack was to be executed by the Fifth Army concentrated behind the Oise in the area Moy—Saint

Quentin—Vermand, by the British Army assembled behind the Somme between Ham and Bray, and by the Sixth Army, which was to be formed in the Amiens area not later than September 2nd.

The Commander-in-Chief counted on gaining the time necessary to put this plan into operation by the action of rear-guards; these, taking advantage of every obstacle on the enemy's march, would deliver short and violent counter-attacks, using artillery fire for this purpose whenever possible.

I arrived at General Headquarters on August 28th, just after these instructions had been sent out. The rapid pursuit of our forces by the enemy, however, was making it difficult to put the plan into execution.

On August 25th the Fifth Army had begun to retire from the general line Rocroi—Chimay—Avesnes, towards the upper waters of the Oise, where it arrived on August 28th. In spite of a brilliant success at Guise on the morning of the 29th, in the course of which the exhausted British Army on its left was extricated, the Fifth Army was not quite able to restore the situation.

The British Army had already fallen back from the Somme, and its retreat behind the Oise, between Noyon and La Fère, had caused a gap in the Allied front. Farther to the west, the enemy had already crossed the Somme, so that it remained to be seen whether it would be possible to form the Sixth Army as planned. Some of its units were still detraining near Amiens, while others had already been severely engaged between Amiens and Péronne.

Towards the right, the Third and Fourth Armies had retired on August 26th to the left bank of the Meuse. On the 27th and 28th the Third Army continued its retirement unmolested, and on the morning of the 29th the main body of the Fourth Army also fell back, pursuant to the general plan to the high ground south-west of the Meuse, although its brilliant counter-attacks on the 27th and 28th had effectively held the enemy to the line of that river.

From the outset, an essentially offensive rôle had been assigned to the Fourth Army, for the fulfilment of which it had been given unusual strength. For the operations that were now in view its size and the wide extent of its front made it too unwieldy to be manœuvred efficiently by one man. Moreover, the chief danger at present threatening this army lay on its left, where contact with the Fifth Army had been lost. The formation of some of its units into a separate command, therefore, would have the double advantage of reducing its size and of providing a strong detachment whose mission would be to cover it on the west and to regain contact with the Fifth Army.

By the evening of the 28th the Commander-in-Chief had not yet defined my future task, but since my arrival I had been gathering full information as to the general situation, and I had formed the beginnings of a staff by adding Major Naulin and Interpreter-Officer Tardieu to the two lieutenant-colonels and the aide-de-camp I had brought from Lorraine.

In spite of the bad news that continued to reach General Headquarters, especially since August 20th, no signs of agitation or confusion, much less of panic, were to be observed there. The new minister of war, M. Millerand, who arrived on the 27th, was struck by this atmosphere of calm, order and decision, and upon taking his departure the following morning, he announced his approval of the attitude and line of conduct adopted by the Commander-in-Chief. When I arrived that night

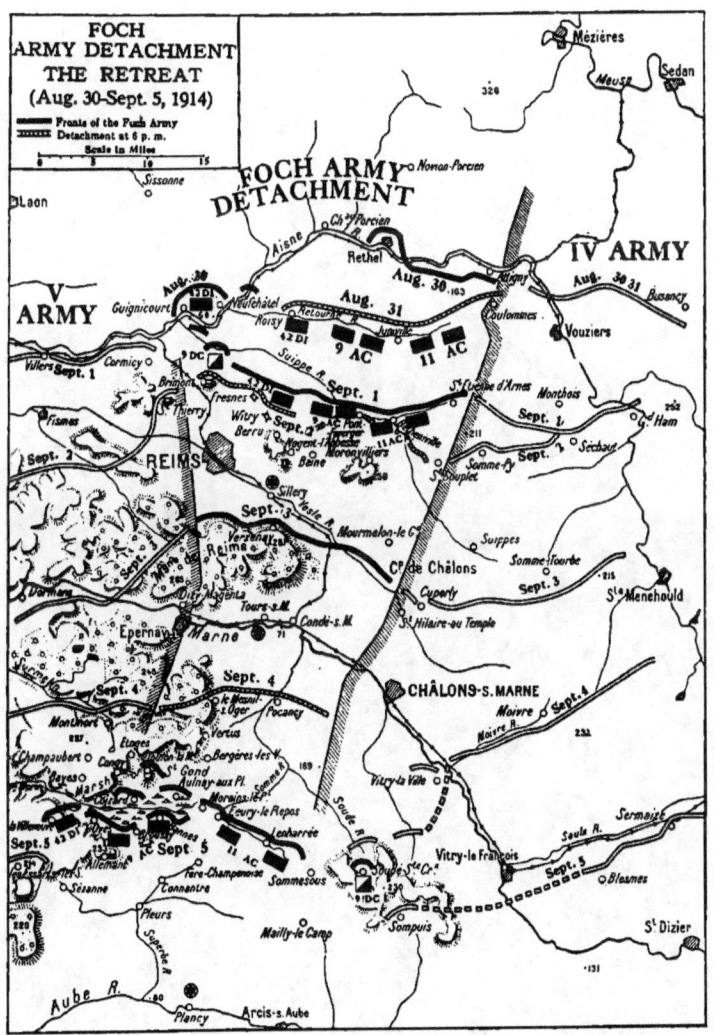

(August 28th) I was assigned the quarters he had just vacated. The Commander-in-Chief departed the next morning to visit the Fifth Army, which was about to engage the Battle of Guise. Before leaving he directed me to take command of an "Army Detachment" which he had constituted on the left of the Fourth Army. He called my attention especially to movements of the enemy that might start from the direction Rocroy-Philippeville. For the execution of my task, I was to come to an understanding with General de Langle de Cary, then commanding the Fourth Army, with headquarters at Machault.

My command consisted of the following troops:
The IX Corps* (Moroccan and 17th Infantry Divisions).
The XI Corps† (21st and 22nd Infantry Divisions).
The 52nd and 60th Reserve Divisions and the 9th Cavalry Division‡ taken from the Fourth Army.
The 42nd Infantry Division,§ taken from the Third Army and at that moment detraining near Guignicourt.
I was to act under the orders of the General commanding the Fourth Army. My mission was to protect the operations of that army against hostile movements from the direction of Rocroy. I was assigned Saint Erme —Guignicourt as my general direction in case of retreat.

Being clear as to my mission and the extent of my powers, and with full information touching past events as well as regarding the plan of operations for the Allied armies, I left the Headquarters of the Fourth Army at Machault in order to supervise the formation of my command. The Chief of Staff was to be Lieutenant-

* General Dubois.   ‡ General de l'Espée.
† General Eydoux.   § General Grossetti.

Colonel Weygand ; the Assistant Chief, Lieutenant-Colonel Devaux, while Major Naulin and Interpreter-Officer Tardieu were to form the nucleus of a staff that would gradually be completed.

When I arrived at Machault, about 2.0 P.M., General de Langle de Cary was in the midst of an interview with the Prefect of the Department of the Ardennes, who was explaining the needs of the crowd of refugees whom the enemy's advance had driven down from that Department and from Belgium. The General's greeting to me was: " You have been sent by Providence."

I found that communications between Fourth Army's Headquarters and the units that were to come under my command were not good, so that nothing definite as to their situation was known. I learned, however, that they had been greatly tried during the preceding days ; order was lacking, and if they were to be counted upon for effective action, it was essential that they be taken closely in hand and a new spirit infused into them. Furthermore, the General Officer Commanding the Fourth Army informed me that on the next day, August 30th, he purposed to interrupt his retreat, so as to be in a position to support the Third Army in an attack that it intended to carry out on his right. A delaying action of this description agreed entirely with the general plan laid down for the centre armies. The rear-guards of the Fourth Army therefore were to maintain their positions during the day of the 30th and I was instructed to cover that Army's left.

During the 29th, however, the enemy had forced back the IX Corps, forming the left of my army detachment, to the south-west of the Mézières—Rethel road. Its retreat uncovered the bridges at Rethel and left them at the enemy's mercy ; worse still, the 42nd Infantry

Division was not yet capable of intervening in this direction. If the situation was not quickly re-established the safety of the whole Fourth Army would be imperilled. I accordingly gave orders at once for my detachment to retake the heights north of the Aisne between Attigny and Rethel and to hold them so as to deny to the enemy during the day of the 30th the Mézières—Rethel and the Mézières—Attigny roads.

On the morning of the 30th news reached my advanced headquarters, established at the Mairie of Attigny, that these orders had not been carried out, owing either to delay in their transmission or to the closeness of the enemy's pursuit. In any case, two things were evident, namely, that there was confusion in our channels of command and that the enemy was following us vigorously. Moreover, violent enveloping attacks on both my flanks forced me at 4.30 P.M. to withdraw all my troops south of the Aisne between Rethel and Attigny. In spite of the men's exhaustion the retreat was carried out with comparative ease.

The French Fourth Army, during its passage through the Ardennes, had been opposed by the German Fourth Army and forced to retreat to the Meuse, where it halted in an effort to dispute the crossing of the river. Now it found itself outflanked by another German army, the Third, that had crossed the Meuse at Dinant and, on August 28th, had delivered an attack against the French left at Signy l'Abbaye.

Moreover, during the past few days, the space between the French Fourth Army and the Fifth Army, which was manœuvring on its left as it fell back on the Oise, had become greater and greater; by August 29th, it amounted to about twenty-five miles. In consequence of this gap, the German Third Army had encountered no opposition during its march forward and it was seriously beginning to outflank our Fourth Army's left.

This was the danger which my detachment was called upon to guard against. But the right of the German Fourth Army was pressing us from the direction of Mézières where it had debouched, while at the same time strong bodies of the German Third Army had out-distanced us at Novion Porcien. We were thus in danger of being cut off from the Aisne at Rethel.

It was in the midst of these difficulties that I took command of the Army Detachment which had been formed on August 30th under the very guns of the enemy. That evening, very tired but in good order, it crossed the Aisne, and was now well placed to cover the left of the Fourth Army. As the Fifth Army had reached the Oise many miles away, there still existed the danger of being outflanked and turned on our left.

I now had to see about re-establishing order and cohesion in my force. The regiments had lost a large number of their officers and a re-assignment of those remaining, especially of the company commanders, was most urgent. Some of the bravest of these troops, such as the Bretons of the XI Corps, were wandering about, incapable of accomplishing any useful result from lack of proper direction.

The Reserve Divisions had shown a lack of steadiness, owing no doubt to their having been but recently formed and thrown so abruptly into action. I decided therefore to withdraw them from the front line and to place them in reserve. They could there be taken in hand and shaken down into organizations capable of looking after themselves; with discipline and order restored and material wants regularly supplied, cohesion

ALGERIAN TROOPS ANSWER THE CALL TO THE COLOURS.

and confidence would return to the men and the habit of authority to the officers.

At the same time, I took steps to regulate the movements of supply trains and convoys for all the troops. On the 30th I instructed Commanders of Army Corps and Reserve Divisions to send out detachments of gendarmes, cavalry or other reliable troops, to round up stragglers and return them to their units.

The General Officer Commanding the Fourth Army intended to resume his offensive toward the north on August 31st, with the object of assailing the hostile forces that had crossed the Meuse above Stenay. He was to be supported on his right by the Third Army. For my part, informed by the events of the previous day, I decided to withdraw my detachment south of the Retourne. By so doing, I would still be in a position to cover the left flank of the Fourth Army, I would avoid being too closely pressed by the enemy, and I would escape the danger of having him outflank me. My left would be extended by the early entrance into line of the 42nd Infantry Division, which, in its turn, would be covered in the direction of the Aisne by the 9th Cavalry Division.

On the morning of the 31st my advanced headquarters were established at Bétheniville. Here I learned that during the night a considerable amount of disorder had been caused in the 52nd and 60th Reserve Divisions by returning stragglers. I at once decided, therefore, to withdraw these divisions behind the Suippe in order to get them firmly in hand.

The enemy showed little activity during the morning, and I counted upon this respite and the imminent concentration of my detachment in the valley of the

Retourne for organizing a line of resistance along that river. In the afternoon, three German Divisions crossed to the south bank of the Aisne but they did not trouble our line of defence. In spite of this calm on our front, the detachment remained continually threatened by envelopment on its left flank, as contact with the Fifth Army had not yet been established. It also risked being separated from the Fourth Army on its right, if that army should delay too long on the east bank of the Aisne.

The Commander-in-Chief appreciated the dangerous situation which this might precipitate, and, at 6.15 P.M., he telephoned as follows to the G.O.C. Fourth Army:

" I wish to have General Foch's personal estimate of the situation arising from the enemy's dispositions on his front. Can he hold on and hope for a successful issue? Forward this message to him and request him to reply at once."

I received this note about 7.30 P.M., and immediately proceeded to Fourth Army Headquarters at Monthois, so that my answer might be forwarded to the Commander-in-Chief. It was given in the following terms:

" The Army Detachment will have trouble in holding on for two, let alone three days, in the face of hostile forces already identified as two corps, and which may be increased. I base my reasons upon:

" 1. The nature of the ground in the Champagne area, which facilitates the enemy's advance. There are no strong supporting positions for the defence, the woods are easily penetrated and no important streams afford us lines of resistance.

" 2. The weakness of the IX Corps in artillery.

" 3. The fatigue of the men.

"The only way the detachment could hold out would be by manœuvring in retreat, and this over a depth which, without doubt, would endanger the Fourth Army."

The Commander-in-Chief agreed with my view and ordered the Fourth Army to fall back, covered by the detachment. He added:

"All ranks must be made to understand that this retirement is being effected with a view to future operations, and that it is not being forced upon us by the enemy."

In order to carry out my task of covering the withdrawal of the Fourth Army, I decided to hold on firmly to the line of the Retourne during September 1st, and at the same time to make the reserve divisions prepare a second position on the line Arnes—Suippe.

The morning of September 1st was comparatively quiet. The enemy had not yet made any serious attack when I received information from the Fourth Army that, in conformity with instructions from General Headquarters, it would continue its retirement after passing to the south of the Aisne. Accordingly, I issued orders for all my forces to reach the south bank of the rivers Arnes and Suippe by evening, with the reserve divisions south of the line Beine—Moronvilliers. The 9th Cavalry Division was to continue to cover my left and to delay as much as possible any hostile forces that might cross the Aisne in the neighbourhood of Neufchâtel.

When the front line units received this order, they were fighting on the Retourne. Nevertheless, the withdrawal from action was effected under the cover of strong rear-guards without too much difficulty, and the detachment reached its new positions during the night.

The hostile forces on my front were identified from captured prisoners as being the Prussian XI and VIII Corps and the Saxon XIX and XII Reserve Corps ; the whole forming the German Third Army under General von Hausen.

I now established my Headquarters at Sillery. The Fourth Army spent September 2nd in establishing its troops in good order behind the line Séchaut—Somme Py, while my force executed only the slight movements necessary to bring the main body south of the line Moronvilliers—Rheims. Touch was regained on the left with the Fifth Army and Fort St-Thierry. It was also in communication with the Commandants of the forts north of Rheims, Berry, Fresnes and Brimont ; we would consequently be able to make use of these forts for our infantry and field artillery if occasion arose. The 9th Cavalry Division being no longer required on the west, I moved it over to the east to assure our touch with the Fourth Army.

As the days went by I got to know my troops better. I had not been with them during the battles they had fought in Belgium, but I now began to comprehend the impression this severe experience had left on the men.

The Moroccan Division* of the IX Corps had been engaged in violent fighting for several days and had suffered heavily. It remained full of spirit but needed reinforcements. The 17th Division† of that Corps had been less tried.

The severe ordeals experienced by the XI Corps,

* General Humbert.
† General Guignabaudet.

especially at Maissin, had left their mark on the men. Many officers had been killed, especially in the Breton regiments. The men were constantly asking for officers to be sent to lead them against the enemy once more.

The 42nd Division was in excellent shape. It had only recently arrived, was very well commanded and had not been through any costly experiences. The Reserve Divisions, immediately upon their arrival, had been plunged into a battle lasting several days, and this had considerably shaken them. Many of their officers were inexperienced or too old. The consequence was that the men of these Divisions needed encouragement and their officers new blood.

Our methodical retreat of the last few days had enabled us not only to elude the enemy's grasp, but also to tighten up discipline and re-infuse order in the ranks. The arrival of reinforcements had also made it possible to re-group and reorganize the Reserve Divisions, keeping them during this process removed from the excitement of the forward line. Our front was now firmly and continuously established, and contact with the Fifth and Fourth Armies on the left and right had been regained. The result was a considerable improvement in the tactical situation, and this in its turn engendered a feeling of confidence. The severity of the fighting, the sleepless nights and exhausting marches, intensified the inevitable depression that accompanies a retreat, and all ranks were in a state of serious fatigue. But it was already possible to predict that, with a few more days of rest and reorganization, the troops would be ready to turn about and attack again with fair chances of success. The hope, however, at one time entertained, of being able to resume a general offensive on or about September 2nd had now to be definitely abandoned.

Such was the situation when September opened.

* * * *

On September 1st, the Commander-in-Chief issued the following instructions to Army Commanders:

"In spite of the tactical victories gained by the Third, Fourth and Fifth Armies on the Meuse and at Guise, the enemy's attempt to envelop the left flank of the Fifth Army has been insufficiently blocked by the Sixth Army and the British, thus making it necessary for the Allied forces to effect a change of front, pivoting on their right.

"*The whole of the Third, Fourth and Fifth Armies will renew the offensive as soon as the Fifth Army is freed from the danger of being outflanked.*

"This movement may oblige the armies to continue falling back in a general north-south direction for some little time.

"The Fifth Army, on the marching wing, must, at any cost, prevent the enemy from outflanking it on its left. The other armies, not faced by a similar danger and less pressed in their movements, must seize every favourable occasion to halt, attack and delay the enemy."

The instructions then proceeded to define the limit that the retirement might attain, without in any way presupposing that such a limit would be reached. The limit indicated for the Fourth Army was the rivers Ornain and Aube, in the region of Arcis-sur-Aube.

As can be seen, the Commander-in-Chief still thought it advisable, on September 1st, to continue the retreat.

We, of course, had only to comply with his views, profiting meanwhile by the breathing spell allowed us, to prepare our troops for the coming battle. During the next few days the retreat southwards continued without any interference on the part of the enemy.

By the evening of September 3rd the forces of the Army Detachment were in echelon between the Marne and the Vesle, with Headquarters at Tours-sur-Marne. On the 4th the main body was on the general line of the Châlons—Bergères—Etoges highway, with Headquarters at Fère-Champenoise.

That morning, crowds of refugees, which were being continually augmented by the inhabitants of the abandoned districts, had greatly impeded the movements of troops and supply trains. On passing through Vertus, about noon, I gave orders that, except between the hours of 3.0 P.M. and midnight, the refugees on our line of march were to be kept clear of the roads, so as to prevent any recurrence of this trouble and to ensure the movement of our trains.

On September 5th the normal services of supply etc. appropriate to an army were assigned to my detachment, thus enabling it to function independently of the Fourth Army, and my force was then formally constituted as the Ninth Army. It was reinforced by the 18th Infantry Division* (IX Corps), which after August 20th, had been temporarily left in Lorraine.

The movements prescribed for the day of September 5th anticipated that the advanced guards of the Ninth Army would reach the line Sommesous—Fère-Champenoise—Sézanne, but early in the morning of that day new instructions arrived from General Headquarters which were to bring our retreat to an end.

* General Lefèvre.

These were as follows :

" The time has come to take advantage of the hazardous situation in which the German First Army now finds itself and bring to bear upon it the concentrated efforts of the Allied Armies on our extreme left.

" The necessary dispositions will be taken during September 5th for launching an attack on the 6th. By the evening of the 5th, the following movements must have been effected :

. . . . .

" (c) The Fifth Army, closing slightly on its left, will be established on the general front Courtaçon—Esternay—Sézanne, ready to attack in a general south-north direction.

" (d) The Ninth Army (General Foch) will cover the right of the Fifth Army, holding the southern exits of the Saint-Gond Marshes and moving a portion of its forces on to the plateau north of Sézanne.

" The various armies will take the offensive on the morning of September 6th."

This order I received during the night of the 4th and 5th. To prevent my troops from marching too far south and thus finding themselves too far from the field of battle now prescribed for them, it was urgent to stop their retirement. I therefore issued, at 5 A.M. on September 5th, the following orders :

" The main body of the XI Corps will halt south of the Somme. Contact will be maintained on its left with the IX Corps, whose advanced guards will be established on the line Aulnay-aux-Planches—Morains-le-Petit—Ecury.

" No fighting unit of the IX Corps will move south of

the line Connantre—Euvy. Its rear-guards will be established on the line Aulnay-aux-Planches—Morains-le-Petit—Ecury.

" The 42nd Infantry Division will hold the exits of the Saint-Gond Marshes between Bannes and Oyes. No fighting unit of this Division must move south of the line Allemant—Fère-Champenoise.

" The 52nd and 60th Reserve Divisions, attached respectively to the IX and XI Corps will be disposed in rear.

" The 9th Cavalry Division will cover the right of the army, the front of which will extend along the general lines marked by the Saint-Gond Marshes and the river Somme, between Ecury and Sommesous."

If the continuation of the retreat originally planned for September 5th had been carried out, the Ninth Army would have found itself, on the 6th, in an unfavourable position for engaging in the battle, since it would have had at Sommesous, Fère-Champenoise and Sézanne, only its advanced guards, and it would have lost the advantages offered by the infrequent obstacles presented by the terrain in Champagne, namely the Somme, the Saint-Gond Marshes and the woods that prolong them. It was of prime importance for the Ninth Army, even at the risk of finding itself in advance of the Fourth and Fifth Armies (on its right and left), to be in a position to use these obstacles during the coming battle, and it was with this object in view that I issued the above orders. They were at once conveyed by liaison officers to the corps and divisional commanders.

My next task was to complete preparations for the following day's battle, keeping particularly in view the Commander-in-Chief's prescription for support of the

Fifth Army's attack. To this end it was important to seize the ridges north of the Saint-Gond Marshes in order to deny them to the enemy's artillery. For that artillery, once in possession of these ridges, would be in a position to prevent the Fifth Army's advance north of Sézanne.

Accordingly at 9.30 A.M., I gave the following order:

"The Fifth Army (X Corps) is to attack to-morrow in the general direction Sézanne—Montmirail and to the west. To cover the right of this attack, the 42nd Division will establish a strong advanced guard this evening on the line Villeneuve-lez-Charleville—Soizy-aux-Bois. The Division will take up positions that will enable it to operate to-morrow in the general direction Villeneuve-lez-Charleville—Vauxchamps (the X Corps advanced guards will reach Essarts-les-Sézanne in the evening). The IX Corps will similarly occupy Congy and Toulon-la-Montagne, being ready to operate to-morrow in the direction of Baye and Etoges."

After giving these orders in the morning at Fère-Champenoise, where I also saw the General Officer Commanding the IX Corps, I moved my Headquarters to Plancy.

My army was to cover the right of the Fifth Army in its attack the next day; to do this I was to hold the southern exits of the Saint-Gond Marshes and establish a part of my forces on the Sézanne plateau. These being my instructions I now proceeded to see how best I could carry them out.

The ground on which the Ninth Army was about to fight presents special features. The most noteworthy are the Saint-Gond Marshes, running from east to west, some ten miles long, and varying from half a mile to three or four in width. These marshes, except for the four roads which traverse them from north to south, are practically impassable. On the north bank the ground rises sharply to Congy (altitude 500 feet) and Toulon-la-Montagne (altitude 330 feet), which dominate the marshes.

On the southern bank it slopes up much more gradually, except for the isolated hill of Mont-Août, and to the west, in the vicinity of Mondement and Allemant. Here rise the cliffs of Sézanne, 250 feet high, dominating the plain and closing the western extremity of the marshes. The only stream flowing from the marshes in this direction is the Petit Morin. The country is rugged, densely wooded and with very limited fields of view, except at Mondement, which constitutes a strong point for defence and an excellent observation station.

The country to the east of the marshes, on the other hand, possesses all the well-known characteristics of the Champagne-Pouilly region; that is to say, vast chalky plains, slightly undulating and covered with thin crops of oats or scattered copses of pine trees, streams almost dry, and wooden villages, the houses of which were destined soon to be set ablaze by artillery fire. A country of easy passage, without obstacles, having no shelter or points for offering resistance; in short, one totally unsuited to defence.

The line of the Somme—Soude, on which our defensive operations were in the first place to be based, offers no variation from the weaknesses above described, while the town of Fère-Champenoise, though superior in extent and solidity of construction to the other villages in these parts, is of easy approach for an enemy. In the absence of anything better, we had to content ourselves with the little help that such ground afforded.

In the centre of the Ninth Army's front, however, the Saint-Gond Marshes provided ground favourable for defence. Here I assigned as small a portion of my forces as possible, namely a fraction only of the IX Corps for a line nine miles long between Oyes and Bannes. Since my left was expected to support vigorously the attack of the Fifth Army, I assigned to this task the 42nd Infantry Division, the advanced guards of the IX Corps (which, at 9.30 A.M., I directed to be pushed as rapidly as possible to the high ground north of the marshes) and the reserves which this Corps was to prepare with a view to operating along the Champaubert road.

To the eastern portion of my front, on the other hand, where, as has been seen, the terrain has no defensive value, I was obliged to detail a large number of troops. I therefore assigned the whole of the XI Corps to the line from Morains-le-Petit to Lenharrée, with instructions to take up at the beginning a defensive position along the Somme.

Such were the general arrangements for my Army. Its front covered something more than twenty-two miles. After they had been decided upon, I was still a prey to grave anxiety concerning my right, which extended only to Lenharrée, leaving between it and the left of the Fourth Army at Vitry-le-François, a gap of easily-traversed country, twenty-three miles wide. To fill this, I had available only the 9th Cavalry Division. Evidently this force could do nothing more than keep watch over such a wide stretch of country, possibly delaying any strong hostile bodies that might present themselves, but incapable of stopping them. This comparatively unprotected space exposed my right to being outflanked and enveloped.

That same evening, moreover, the Fourth Army informed me that it " would be unable to support the right of the Ninth Army against enemy attacks coming from Châlons in the direction of Arcis, as it had to co-ordinate its action with that of the Third Army." A yawning breach would therefore remain between the Ninth and the Fourth Armies.

Under these circumstances, it was impossible to shut my eyes to the gravity of the conditions under which we were about to engage a battle upon the outcome of which depended the fate of our country. If in the end we emerged victorious, it was due to the extraordinary individual skill of all, soldiers and officers alike, working in perfect harmony and rising in every emergency to a plane of magnificent heroism.

CHAPTER II

THE BATTLE OF THE MARNE

September 6th: The Battle develops along the whole front of the Ninth Army, which maintains its positions.
September 7th: Continuation of the enemy attacks—The left and centre stand firm, the XI Corps gives way on the right.
September 8th: The attacks become more violent—Serious repulse of the XI Corps—The remainder of the line holds fast—The left gains some ground.
September 9th: The 42nd Division is relieved by the Fifth Army—Repeated and violent German attacks—The Moroccan Division loses and retakes Mondement—Movements of the 42nd Division—The Battle ends in our victory.

AFTER having spent the night at Plancy, I established my Advanced Headquarters on the morning of the 6th at Pleurs.

My orders of the previous forenoon for placing posts at Toulon-la-Montagne and Vert-la-Gravelle, north of the Saint-Gond marshes, had been satisfactorily carried out by the 17th Division. The Moroccan Division, however, which should have occupied Congy, was not able to do so, as this place was already in the enemy's possession. When, at 3 A.M., General Blondlat's Brigade delivered an attack on the village, it found the enemy strongly entrenched and could make no headway. As a matter of fact, troops of another German army, in addition to the one that had been following me directly, had appeared on the scene. This was the Second Army, which, following closely on the heels of our Fifth Army, had reached by noon on the previous day, the line Montmirail-Vertus. In this forward movement, the enemy in passing had seized certain points, in particular

Congy, which I had ordered to be occupied. Moreover, this German Second Army, on the morning of the 6th, took the offensive and, supported by powerful artillery fire, launched a violent attack against the Ninth Army.

After its repulse at Congy, General Blondlat's Brigade tried to hold on to the northern edge of the marshes, but was soon forced to fall back and finally withdrew to the south bank.

The 135th Infantry Regiment of the 17th Division was more fortunate, and succeeded in occupying Toulon-la-Montagne. Its left flank, however, was soon exposed by the retirement of General Blondlat's Brigade, and, being violently attacked, it was in its turn forced back south of the marshes. A counter-attack launched by the 77th Regiment on Toulon had no success, being first met by a powerful artillery barrage and then assailed by its adversary from strongly held positions. Its situation soon became critical and it was forced to retire on Bannes.

By the end of the morning it was quite clear that the IX Corps would not be able to gain a footing north of the marshes. At midday, therefore, I issued the following instructions, recalling to that Corps the essential part of its task :

" It is imperative that the IX Corps take up by evening defensive positions of such indisputable strength as to prevent the enemy on its front from advancing further south.

" It must also maintain close and certain contact with the 42nd Division and the XI Corps.

" The location and distribution of troops of the IX Corps must be such as to obtain the above result without possibility of failure.

"This Corps is also reminded that a bombardment from the high ground near Toulon and Congy is to be anticipated this evening; measures must be taken to hold on in spite of this bombardment to the south bank of the Saint-Gond Marshes."

In execution of these instructions, the IX Corps established itself south of the marshes, but being subjected the whole afternoon to violent and repeated attacks, it was unable to prevent the enemy from reaching Bannes. The Germans pushed considerable forces, including the Guard, through the marshes, but the artillery of the 17th Division prevented them from debouching. For several days, in fact up to the end of the battle, all enemy attacks in this direction were broken up by the well-directed fire of our 75's.

Nightfall found the Germans on the south bank of the marshes with the 17th Division and the Moroccan Division entrenched in front of them. The French 52nd Reserve Division* in second line on the front Mont Août—Fère-Champenoise, kept the southern exits of the marshes under its fire.

While this was happening in the centre, the left and right of the Ninth Army were no less seriously engaged. On the left, the 42nd Division on the afternoon of the 5th had taken up its position around Mondemont; its advanced guards were pushed out to La Villeneuve-lez-Charleville—Soisy-aux-Bois—Saint-Prix, which line was occupied only after heavy fighting.

Early on the 6th, reconnaissances showed that Baye Saint-Prix and Corfélix were being held in strength by the enemy, who shortly after opened artillery fire on the Villeneuve plateau and the Bois des Grandes Garennes,

* General Battesti.

"ONE MUST EAT!" A PHOTOGRAPH TAKEN IN THE EARLY DAYS OF TRENCH WARFARE.

occupied since about 8 A.M., by the 162nd Regiment. The Germans then launched a general attack along the entire front of the 42nd Division.

Throughout the whole day desperate fighting took place around the Bois de la Branle and the village of Villeneuve, which was three times taken and retaken. In the evening, however, the X Corps, operating on the right of the Fifth Army, took Charleville, disengaged the left of the 42nd Division and ensured its possession of Villeneuve.

The struggle on the right of this Division went on with equal violence. After repulsing several German attacks on the Bois des Grandes Garennes, the 162nd Regiment about 11 A.M. was forced back with heavy losses; it withdrew to the northern edge of the Saint-Gond woods, which it set about to defend. In order to restore the situation in this direction, General Dubois, Commanding the IX Corps, ordered the Moroccan Division to deliver an immediate attack directed on Saint-Prix. Two battalions of Moroccans carried this out in conjunction with the 162nd. In the face of heavy artillery fire, they captured Montalard farm, but could advance no farther.

Towards 6.30 P.M., the fighting on the 42nd Division's front came to an end. This Division had suffered heavy losses, but by its stubborn resistance it had repulsed the repeated and violent attacks of the enemy and at nightfall was still holding its line.

On the right of the Army, the XI Corps had also been heavily engaged. Posted on the Somme, between Morains-le-Petit and Lenharrée (later on as far as Haussimont), it had the important task of covering the army's right flank, particularly against any German advance from the region of Châlons.

The 21st* and 22nd† Divisions had taken up positions on the river, the former between Morains-le-Petit and Normée, the latter above Normée. The 60th Reserve Division‡ was held in the region of Montepreux, Semoine and Herbisse in support.

Early in the morning the enemy made contact with our line of defence along the Somme and was evidently preparing to attack. At 10 A.M., the bombardment had become particularly violent in the direction of Morains and Ecury and it gradually spread south until, at 11 A.M., it embraced the whole front of the XI Corps. About midday the Germans launched their infantry attack. They succeeded in capturing Normée and Ecury, and our troops who were defending Morains, finding themselves isolated and in danger of being surrounded, were forced to retreat from that village.

On the right, the Germans captured Vassimont and Haussimont, so that at 5 P.M., with the exception of Lenharrée which still held, the whole line of the Somme was lost to us. The commander of the XI Corps ordered a general offensive to re-capture it. Vassimont and Haussimont were retaken, but on the left the 21st Division was so exhausted that it could not resume the attack. Normée, Ecury and Morains remained in the hands of the enemy, and all efforts were then directed to prevent his debouching from these villages.

We may sum up the events of the first day of the battle as follows :

The Ninth Army had been violently attacked on the whole of its front, the open ground to the east having favoured the enemy's advance. In spite of this, contact with the Fifth Army on the left had been fully maintained and the 42nd Division had held the enemy for the most

* General Radiguet.   † General Pambet.   ‡ General Joppé.

part in check. In the centre, the IX Corps had been forced back from its forward positions north of the Marshes, but south of them it had established a strong line of resistance.

On the right, while the XI Corps had given way only slightly, its situation was disquieting, since the ground here did not lend itself to defence and the right flank of the Corps was entirely in the air. To relieve this situation, the 18th Division, which upon detraining had been concentrated in the area Semoine—Villers—Herbisse, was placed at the disposition of the G.O.C. XI Corps. This was an important reinforcement and might enable this Corps not only to restore the situation, but also to fulfil an offensive mission which I contemplated assigning to it the following day.

As for the 9th Cavalry Division, it had been obliged to fall back during the evening towards Mailly.

The day's fighting had been very severe, but the Ninth Army had fulfilled its mission. It had withstood violent attacks from the greater portion of the German Second Army, in particular those of the German X Corps in the region of Saint-Prix and of the Guard Corps at Bannes, Morains-le-Petit and Normée. In addition, the German Third Army had brought the whole weight of its right wing against the line of the Somme from Normée to Lenharrée and Sommesous, whilst threatening with its left our junction with the French Fourth Army.

To offset this, the news from other parts of the front was fortunately reassuring. At 1.30 P.M., the X Corps (Fifth Army) reported that the front of this Army was clear of the enemy, who was retiring on Montmirail. In the evening we learned that the other corps of the Fifth Army were pushing forward with success, and that the battle engaged by the Sixth Army on the Ourcq was so far going in our favour.

For September 7th, I had in view for the Ninth Army the following tasks :

On the left, to support the forward movement of the Fifth Army by an offensive west of the Marshes ; to cover the right flank of the attack now being made by our armies to the west by checking the enemy forces operating in Champagne on the plains of Fère-Champenoise, Sommesous and Sompuis at any cost.

On the right, to keep touch with our armies to the east, whose nearest element, the Fourth Army, rested its left flank on Vitry-le-François.

Upon returning to my Headquarters at Plancy, I accordingly gave orders that the positions then held were to be maintained on the 7th at all hazard. The IX Corps was to cover the south of the Saint-Gond Marshes, the XI Corps, Morains-le-Petit and the valley of the Somme between Ecury-le-Repos and Haussimont. On the left of the Army, the 42nd Division, in conjunction with the X Corps, was to attack under the same conditions as on the previous day.

On the right, the XI Corps, after seizing Clamanges and the high ground south of that village, was to advance in the direction of Pierre-Morains—Colligny—Mont-Aimé. The IX Corps was to be ready to support the XI Corps in the direction of Aulnizeux and Vert-la-Gravelle. The 18th Division was to be held as army reserve in the vicinity of Euvy. The 9th Cavalry Division was to cover the right of the army, keeping watch in the direction of Vitry and Châlons and sending a detachment to endeavour to gain touch with the left of the Fourth Army at Camp Mailly.

Evidently, it was on this side that danger was most to

be expected. The Fourth Army was fighting fiercely on the defensive and a gap of twenty miles still existed between its left and the right of the Ninth Army. Moreover, de Langle de Cary informed me that only on September 8th could this space be partially filled by a new corps, the XXI* which would then come into line. We had to be ready therefore to meet unaided any blow coming from this direction.

Under these circumstances, I felt that the positions now held by the Ninth Army, however threatening the immediate outlook might be, must be maintained at all costs. The only way this could be accomplished was by the display of exceptional energy and activity on the part of every man, and I made a pressing appeal to my Army, " to maintain and extend the successes it had already gained over an enemy who had suffered heavy losses and whose situation was now extremely hazardous."

As the battle might last several days, I gave instructions for the attacks to be carried out methodically : infantry was to be economised, artillery freely used and every foot of ground gained was to be at once organized for defence. These were the tactics prescribed for commanders of all units.

The enemy, on his side, realized that his advance as a whole had been checked. His right wing being in difficulties on the Ourcq and his left indefinitely held up in Lorraine, he resolved to strike a decisive blow in the centre. This was his sole remaining chance of winning the victory on which he had counted, but the probability of which had been so singularly diminished during the last forty-eight hours. For this final effort he intended to put in every man he had left in the sector.

* General Legrand.

The main weight of his attack was to fall on the French Fourth and Ninth Armies. The plan was to put these Armies definitely out of action, or, failing this, to force them apart and dash through the resulting breach. The execution of the plan, in what concerned the front of the Ninth Army, was to be effected by launching violent attacks east and west of the Saint-Gond Marshes, that is to say in the very directions I had fixed for the attacks of my 42nd Division and XI Corps.

The fighting of September 7th, 8th and 9th was destined to be furious on both sides, but it was to end in the defeat of the German forces.

Early in the morning of the 7th the combat was renewed along the whole line. On the left, heavy attacks were pronounced against the Moroccan Division and the 42nd, the latter as it was in the act of advancing. La Villeneuve was lost but was retaken shortly afterwards by the 151st Regiment. By 10.15 A.M. the 162nd had been forced back from Soisy and the Saint-Gond Woods, as far as the Montgivroux road. The Moroccan Division having lost Oyes and Montalard Farm, fell back to the ridge north of Mondement.

The situation was serious and I felt it necessary to repeat my warnings to the XI Corps that its essential mission in this quarter, which was to maintain contact with the 42nd Division and at all costs prevent the enemy from debouching by Saint-Prix, remained unchanged. I also called its attention to the fact that the long ridge behind Mondement should by this time already be occupied by the division in reserve.

The G.O.C. Fifth Army, who had reported that the enemy was retiring on his front, ordered the X Corps to take measures to break up any attack the Germans might make on the left of the Ninth Army.

At about 5 P.M. the 42nd and the Moroccan Divisions, reinforced by the reserves of the IX Corps, launched a counter-attack with the object of recapturing Soisy, the Saint-Gond Wood and Saint-Prix. This attack was met by very heavy rifle-fire from trenches that the enemy had constructed between the Saint-Gond Woods and Montgivroux. Desperate fighting ensued, particularly in the Bois de la Branle, and though the situation was not entirely restored, the enemy's advance in this direction was in any case broken up.

Fighting came to an end about 6 P.M., with our troops holding the Montgivroux road and the southern portion of the Bois de la Branle. Small parties had even penetrated into the Saint-Gond Wood. As against this, the enemy, towards the end of the day, had once more retaken La Villeneuve.

In the centre of the army, on the southern bank of the Marshes, both sides had remained on the defensive, the action here having been confined to artillery fire.

On the right, the morning had started with heavy fighting. At 8 A.M. the XI Corps was attacked along the whole front, notably in the direction of Lenharrée. Shortly afterwards, strong forces debouching from Morains-le-Petit and Ecury-le-Repos fell on the 21st Division which, although well supported by the artillery of the 17th Division, only held its ground with difficulty.

The situation was already critical and might quickly become worse, for it was evident that the troops were on the verge of giving way. The consequences of any break at this point might be disastrous, for at this very moment the right wing of the German armies was yielding under the successful blows of our armies to the west.

Just as the attacks of the 42nd and Moroccan Divisions

had neutralized the enemy's efforts in the direction of Mondement, so it seemed that the only chance of stopping his advance on the XI Corps was by ourselves attacking him along the Somme. Convinced of this, and feeling sure that only a change of attitude on the part of the XI Corps could restore the situation, I issued the following orders:

"On the left wing of the Army, the enemy appears to be giving way. The XI Corps will ensure the defence of the Somme at Ecury, Normée and Lenharrée. A Brigade of the 18th Division is placed at its disposal. It will use this Brigade for delivering an immediate attack on Clamanges, from the direction of Normée. The 22nd Division will attack Pierre-Morains and the hill south-east of Pierre-Morains."

The necessity I felt for maintaining this situation at all costs, and also for blocking the enemy's advance into the gap between us and the Fourth Army, was entirely in accord with the Commander-in-Chief's views, which were telephoned to us at 5.15 P.M. It was deemed essential that we hold on until the right of the Ninth Army could be disengaged by the Fourth Army. General de Langle de Cary had been requested to ensure this as soon as a tactical success on his own front had been obtained.

The XI Corps meanwhile, had not been able to carry out the attack ordered, for the enemy, after severe fighting, had taken both Lenharrée and Vassimont. The XI Corps confined itself, therefore, to maintaining the 21st and 22nd Divisions on a line roughly following the woods south of Morains-le-Petit and the Sommesous—Fère-Champenoise railway.

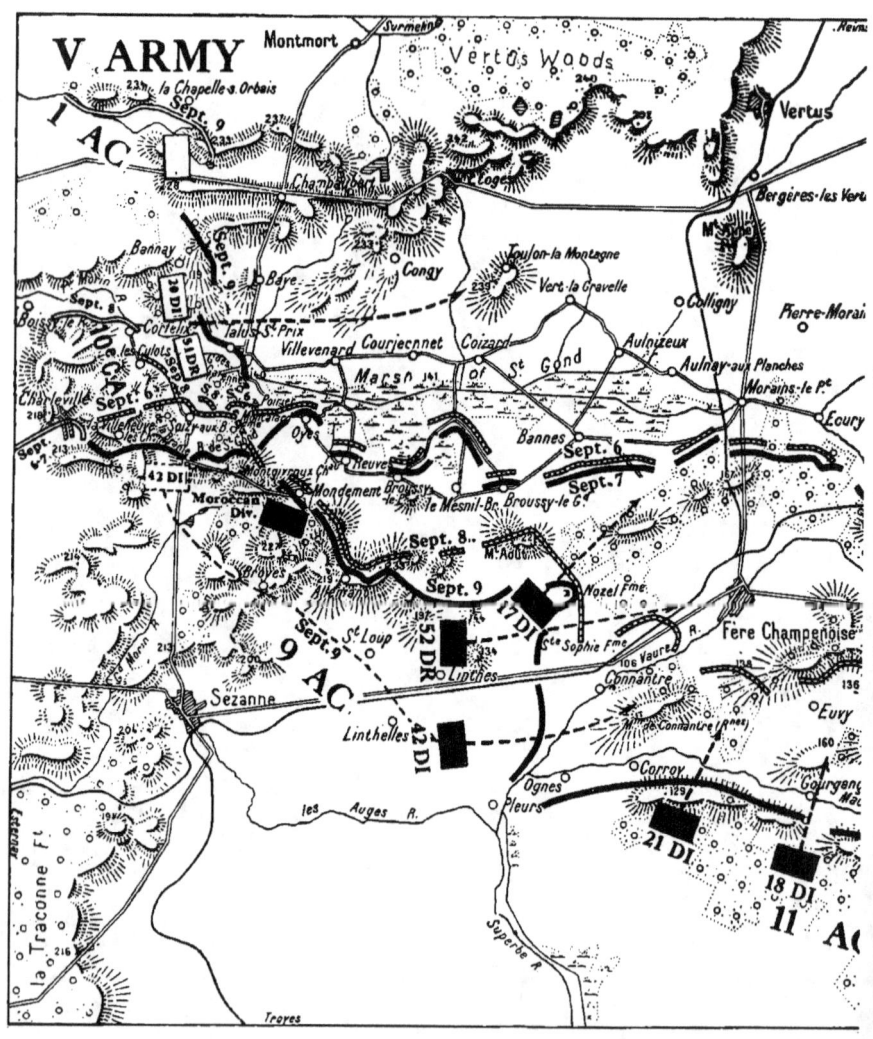

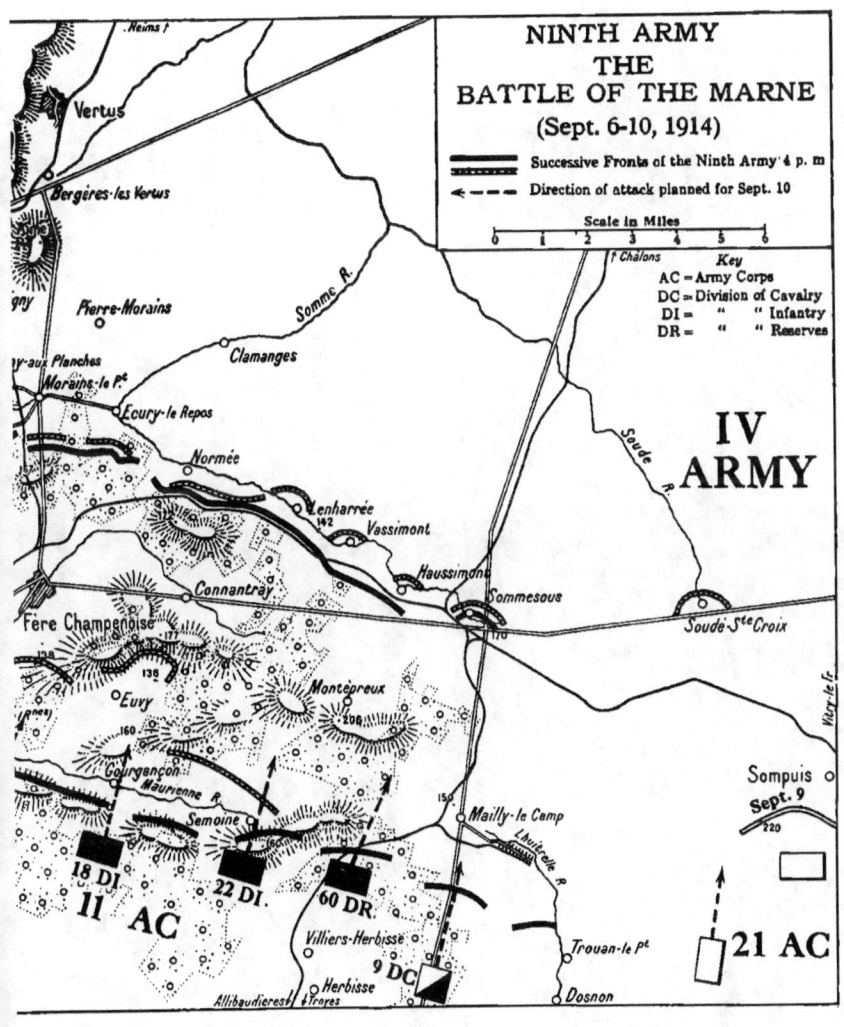

If the enemy had continued his advance, this failure of the XI Corps to make the prescribed attack might have had very serious results. Fortunately, he was checked by the opportune action of the IX Corps, which arrived just in time to disengage the left of the XI Corps. This occurred about 4.30 P.M., when the 90th Regiment of the 17th Division delivered a counter-attack in the direction of Aulnay-aux-Planches and Aulnizeux. It succeeded in gaining possession of the latter village, without however being able to hold it, for the Germans shortly afterwards retook it.

On my extreme right the 9th Cavalry Division, after having recaptured Sommesous which for a while had fallen into the possession of the enemy, succeeded in establishing its main body in the area Mailly—Villiers—Herbisse.

The 18th Division, including the Brigade placed at the disposition of the XI Corps, was still available in the second line. It occupied the woods on either side of the Normée—Fère-Champenoise highway.

The 60th Reserve Division was established in a defensive position on the Montepreux plateau.

The task of September 7th greatly resembled that of the previous day. The left of the Ninth Army, fighting with great obstinacy, had broken up the enemy's advance; the centre had held its ground; the right had again given way and definitely lost the defensive line of the Somme. It was in this state of uncertainty that we had to resume the battle the next morning, hoping that with the advance of the Fourth Army a decisive result would be obtained. That Army's left wing, however, was still a score of miles from our right.

The mission of the Ninth Army for September 8th

therefore remained unchanged. I merely repeated the instructions already given, but I added, " at dawn reconnaissances are to be pushed out along the whole front to ascertain definitely what points are still occupied by the enemy." For incoming Intelligence reports had shown that on the front of the left wing of the Allied Armies, including the greater portion of the Fifth Army's front, the Germans were in full retreat. It was now essential to ascertain whether this movement was spreading eastwards. In point of fact it was not, and September 8th and 9th were to mark the farthest limits of the enemy's drive against the Ninth Army.

Before daybreak on the 8th, he made an extremely violent attack against the XI Corps. Advancing under cover of darkness so as to approach our lines without coming under our artillery fire, he had succeeded in massing his infantry only a few hundred yards from our positions. Suddenly, at 4.30 A.M., while it was still dark and without any artillery preparation, these masses were launched to the attack, south of Morains-le-Petit and Ecury-le-Repos. The 21st Division on the left of the XI Corps was driven back on Fère-Champenoise, carrying with it in its disordered movement the 18th Division and a part of the 52nd Reserve Division. The 22nd Division also gave way in the neighbourhood of Lenharrée.

Notwithstanding all his efforts, the G.O.C. XI Corps succeeded in halting and rallying his troops only on the high ground south of Fère-Champenoise. The 18th Division reformed south of Connantray.

When news of these serious events reached me at my Advanced Headquarters at Pleurs, I ordered the XI Corps to re-occupy Fère-Champenoise and to hold on at all costs. It was the only point of resistance in this region, and with the idea of making sure of it, I placed the whole of the 18th Division at the disposal of the XI Corps.

On condition that the enemy be given no time to consolidate his position or organize it methodically, and provided that a body of unshaken reserves be employed for the operation, the place could be taken and used as a rallying point on which to reorganize the broken front of the XI Corps. I also directed the IX Corps to join hands with the XI Corps in this direction and then immediately make a common effort to drive back the enemy offensive coming from Morains-le-Petit.

In addition I asked for aid from the armies on my flanks. I hoped that the Fourth Army could come to the assistance of my left by putting in the XXI Corps, whose arrival on the battlefield had been announced for September 8th. General de Langle de Cary replied to this suggestion by saying that this corps was already attacking in a northerly direction, and that the interval between our armies was too great for him to be able to render any assistance.

I then turned to the Fifth Army, to whose commander I telephoned as follows:

"The right of the Ninth Army (XI Corps) is being heavily attacked by both the Guard Corps and the Saxon XII Corps* and I am unable to give it support, as my centre (IX Corps) is also heavily engaged. It is also impossible for the Fourth Army to render any direct assistance.

"In order to relieve the pressure on my right, the

---

* The Guard and XII Corps (Saxon) had been detached from the German Second Army to form a detachment operating on von Hausen's right.

Fifth Army is requested, if possible, to renew the attack on the plateau west of Champaubert, in conjunction with the 42nd Division and the left of the IX Corps."

General d'Esperey replied at once :

" The primary mission of the X Corps, as defined in operation orders, remains unchanged. This task is to support the left of the Ninth Army in driving back north of the Saint-Gond Marshes any enemy forces attempting to debouch from Saint-Prix and Soisy-aux-Bois."

I accordingly ordered the 42nd Division to continue its attacks vigorously, and to combine them closely with those of the IX and X Corps.

Having thus arranged for concerted and intensified action on the left, I turned my attention again to the right, where the situation, although appearing to be relieved, was still exceedingly serious. In addition to having sustained a heavy blow, my front here was threatened with envelopment. For the 9th Cavalry Division had been forced to abandon Sommesous, and in so doing had uncovered the approaches to Montepreux. The enemy was therefore in a position to outflank the XI Corps before the latter could launch the attack on Fère-Champenoise.

To meet this danger, I instructed the XI Corps to cover the retirement of the 9th Cavalry Division, if this had not already been done, by occupying Semoine with several Companies and thus close the gap at Montepreux. I also ordered the 9th Cavalry Division to operate along the Sommesous-Mailly road, so as to furnish a support on the flank of our Montepreux attack as well as to discover and delay the turning movement which I feared the enemy would make in that direction.

In addition to this, and with the object, if need be, of gaining sufficient time for the attack on Fère-Champenoise to be prepared, I ordered the 60th Reserve Division, which had withdrawn towards Semoine and Mailly, to be ready to launch counter-attacks against any hostile advance from the line of the Somme.

Finally, I appealed once more to the Fourth Army for the assistance of the XXI Corps :

" It is earnestly hoped that the Fourth Army will be able to order the XXI Corps to intervene to-day in the direction of Sommesous."

Unfortunately this hope could not be realized, for contrary to arrangements made by the Fourth Army, and due to unforeseen delays, the XXI Corps was not able to send any troops toward Sommesous before the 9th.

The enemy's success appeared to have cost him very dear, for while the XI Corps during the morning was proceeding to establish itself on the high ground south of Fère-Champenoise it met with little opposition.

The IX Corps took steps to strengthen its right, which had become exposed by the retirement of the XI Corps in the early hours of the morning. This was effected by sending the 52nd Reserve Division to Connontre, where it gained touch with the left of the XI Corps, and by posting the 17th Division on the line Mont-Août—Sainte Sophie farm, with orders to hold it at all costs.

On the left of the IX Corps, the Moroccan Division, operating in close touch with the 42nd Division, had renewed its attacks early in the morning. It took the Poirier ridge, and drove the Germans out of Oyes about 7 A.M. At the same time the 42nd Division advanced on

Saint-Prix, but was held up by heavy artillery fire from the high ground near Baye. News now came that the enemy was massing troops in the vicinity of Coizard, Courjeonnet and Villevenard.

In spite of all these difficulties and the menace of an attack on the west end of the Marshes, to meet which all the available troops of the IX Corps had been kept ready, I sent the Officer Commanding this Corps repeated warnings to the following effect :

" The vital point for your Corps to-day is its right, where you must give the XI Corps your full support.

" You will therefore move all your available troops in this direction, including those in the centre which are not at present engaged."

Thanks to the dispositions made in compliance with these instructions, both the right and centre of the Ninth Army found themselves towards noon standing on the defensive and preparing in comparative quiet their concerted attack on Fère-Champenoise.

During this time, the 42nd Division, which at dawn had begun an attack along its whole front, gained considerable ground. By 11 A.M. it had captured the wood Soizy-aux-Bois and the plateau north of Villeneuve. Keeping in touch with the X Corps, which advanced on Corfélix and Boissy, it had captured by eleven o'clock the wood of Soizy-au-Bois and the plateau north of Villeneuve. About midday, its left, supported by the 51st Reserve Division of the X Corps, reached Les Culets-Corfélix, but its right was now able to advance only with great difficulty.

At 2 P.M. the Germans opened a violent bombardment on the front Broussy-le-Petit—Ménil-Broussy—Reuves—

Oyes—Saint-Prix, following it half an hour later by an infantry attack along the whole of that front.

Debouching from the Saint-Gond Marshes, the enemy seized Broussy-le-Petit and Ménil-Broussy, and in spite of the heavy losses inflicted by our artillery, he forced the Moroccan Division to fall back to the line marked by the eastern edge of the Saint-Gond Wood—Montgivroux—Mondement—Allemant Wood and ridge. Here, at nightfall, it entrenched.

While this was taking place on the left, I was busy getting the attack on Fère-Champenoise launched as rapidly as possible. This action was essential, not only to check the envelopment with which the XI Corps was threatened, but also to bring relief to the hard-pressed Moroccan Division.

It was evident that the only way we could hope to frustrate the plans, which since the early hours of September 8th the enemy had been methodically executing, was to take the offensive ourselves. Favoured as he was by the wide stretches of open country, he might very well reach our weakest spot, the gap fifteen or twenty miles wide that lay between the right of the Ninth Army and the left of the Fourth, unless he were delayed by aggressive action on our part.

I therefore, at 3.30 P.M., urged the XI and IX Corps to deliver the attack on Fère-Champenoise without delay. Five groups of artillery prepared this operation. It was executed by two regiments of the 52nd Reserve Division, supported on the right by units of the 21st and 18th Divisions.*

Progress, although slow, was appreciable along the whole front. It was brought to a halt by darkness.

* A *group* in the French artillery organization consists as a rule of three batteries of Field Artillery, or two batteries of Heavy Artillery or Horse Artillery.—Translator.

Some small parties of the 52nd Reserve Division managed to get into Fère-Champenoise, but they could not remain there. The attack had not reached all its objectives, but by forcing the enemy to halt and even to fall back, it had fulfilled its purpose.

September 8th had been a particularly severe day for the Ninth Army. From dawn until dusk it had been called upon to sustain repeated and heavy assaults. It had lost some ground, but its front remained unbroken, and the threat of envelopment, that for many long hours had been hanging over us, appeared by evening less menacing. This was of prime importance.

Meanwhile the heads of columns of the XXI Corps were reported five miles south of Sompuis, and the 9th Cavalry Division, established near Mailly, was in contact with them.

After following the progress of our attack on Fère-Champenoise, I returned to my Headquarters at Plancy. From here I gave orders for the XI and IX Corps to entrench in the positions they had won. These preliminary arrangements made, I examined the general situation of my Army, and I could not disguise from myself the fact that it was still very serious, especially as regards my right wing.

The XI Corps had been repeatedly and heavily engaged. It was holding weak positions with worn-out troops. Touch with the Fourth Army, due to the enemy's having occupied Sompuis during the day, was most uncertain. It could only be definitely assured if the XXI Corps arrived in time. And that Corps was still far away.

The situation of the Fifth Army on our left was more favourable. Throughout the day, it had continued to make excellent progress, and in these results my 42nd

Division had had its share. Here at least we possessed some troops stimulated by victory; but above all it was the advantages afforded by the Champagne ridges upon which we could count to ensure our resistance in this quarter. It even seemed possible that, by using this high ground as a pivot and advancing in close touch with the X Corps, we might undertake to re-establish the situation. My right wing, broken as it was by repeated attacks as it advanced across an unsheltered plain, had to be reinforced immediately; perhaps this aid could be furnished by withdrawing reinforcements from the bluffs which its great strength might make it possible to spare.

Despite the fifteen miles separating these forces from the locality of Fère-Champenoise, where they had to march in order to restore the battle, no hesitation was possible. My left was now well placed; it must help my right in distress. The only question was whether it could arrive in time.

In any case, at 9 P.M. I telephoned General D'Esperey, G.O.C. Fifth Army, asking him to be good enough to order the X Corps on the 9th to relieve my 42nd Division, as I wished to move this Division to Linthes and Pleurs for employment on the right of the Ninth Army. In reply, he not only agreed to do this, but he placed the two Divisions and the Corps artillery of the X Corps at my disposal. Accordingly, on the evening of the 8th, I was able to issue the following orders for September 9th:

" The right of the Ninth Army is heavily engaged in the direction of Sommesous. The X Corps has been placed under the orders of the Ninth Army. The following operations will be carried out as early as possible on September 9th :

" The X Corps will relieve the 42nd Division about

5 A.M., and will continue the attacks begun by that Division on the line Bannay-Baye and especially along the road from Soizy-aux-Bois to Baye. Touch will be established at Baye with the Moroccan Division, which is holding the line Saint-Gond Wood—Montgivroux—Mondement. The X Corps will make sure beyond any possibility of miscarriage that the enemy does not get a footing on the plateau running from La Villeneuve-les-Charleville to Montgivroux, or on the northern approaches to this plateau.

"Units of the 42nd Division, as they are relieved by the X Corps, will move via Broyes—Saint-Loup to the line Linthes-Pleurs, where the Division will be formed in General Reserve. The 42nd Division will keep the Moroccan Division informed of its movements.

"My Command Post will be at Plancy."

Starting at daybreak on the 9th, the enemy's attacks, precisely as if he had divined my intentions, became more and more violent. First of all, advancing in force on our left, he overran the outposts of the Moroccan Division and pushed straight on to the village and the Château of Mondement, which he captured about 6 A.M. The Commander of the IX Corps at once placed his only remaining reserve, the 77th Infantry Regiment, at General Humbert's disposal; but this regiment was five miles away, at Saint-Loup, and it would be a long while before it could make itself felt.

To gain time for it to come up, General Humbert obtained from General Grossetti, whose troops had already been partly relieved by the X Corps, two battalions of chasseurs and part of the 42nd Division's artillery.

The aid of these comparatively fresh troops, small in

number though they were, was of great assistance to the Moroccan Division, which continued to put up a stout fight in the woods south of Mondement. The men held on under a terrific fire until the 77th Infantry Regiment was able to arrive.

This regiment reached the scene at about 11 A.M., and the danger was averted. At 2 P.M., aided by the remnants of a Regiment of Zouaves, it delivered an attack at Mondement. This attack withered under heavy machine-gun fire coming from the gate and windows of the Château. A 75 millimetre gun was run up to within 500 yards of the gate and a section of artillery pushed forward close to the southern end of the park. Then, at 6.30 P.M., in a dashing attack, the 77th Regiment drove out the enemy and, at 7 P.M., Colonel Lestoquoi, commanding the regiment, sent the following laconic report : " I hold the village and Château of Mondement and am establishing myself there for the night."

The gallant resistance of the Moroccan Division during the 9th had been essential to the success of our armies. It had enabled the 42nd Division to carry out that most delicate operation, a flank march in the face of the enemy and, when every moment counted, to arrive in the nick of time. Again, if we had lost the high ground about Mondement, we could not have held the spur of Allemant. This ground in the hands of the enemy would have opened up to him that portion of the plain of Champagne to which the Ninth Army had been clinging for dear life for four long days. And finally, this resistance on the part of the Moroccan Division was all the more precious in that the centre and right of the Army had continued to give way under the enemy's heavy blows.

Let us return now to the XI Corps, which on the

evening of September 8th was occupying the high ground south of Fère-Champenoise. Early on the 9th the Germans opened a heavy bombardment on our positions there; then, pursuing their plan of the day before, they launched infantry assaults against the centre and right of this Corps. The 18th and 22nd Divisions holding the line here were driven southwards, and by 10 A.M., they had retired to the left bank of the Maurienne, where they reformed. The 21st Division, placed on the left of the XI Corps, at first withstood the heavy bombardment, but being far in advance and isolated, it, too, was forced back to the other side of the Maurienne.

The situation on the right and centre of the IX Corps was not much better. At daybreak the 103rd Brigade (52nd Reserve Division), which had advanced the evening before half-way between Connantre and Fère-Champenoise, renewed its attack on the railway station at Fère. It could make no appreciable progress, and after a violent artillery duel, the enemy made a counter-attack and drove us back. We retreated under a murderous fire towards Connantre.

General Dubois had ordered the 17th Division to maintain itself at all costs along the front running from Mont-Août to Nozet farm and Sainte-Sophie farm, keeping touch on its right with the 52nd Reserve Division. But here also the enemy's pressure was increasing in its intensity. His artillery swept the whole plain, and unless the expected reinforcements arrived soon, the situation would become critical. With the object of encouraging our troops, I announced the imminent approach of the 42nd Division and the resumption of our offensive :

"The 42nd Division is coming up on the front

Linthes—Pleurs. The fact that the XI Corps has been obliged to yield ground will in no way prevent us from resuming the offensive with this Division, which will attack toward Connantre and Euvy. The IX Corps will co-operate by attacking the Morains—Fère-Champenoise road.

"The 42nd Division started at 8.30 A.M. It will be ready to attack about noon.

"The X Corps has relieved the 42nd Division and it is now at the disposal of the Ninth Army. This Corps has been ordered to support the Moroccan Division and at any price prevent the enemy from penetrating to the west of the Saint-Gond Marshes."

In their violent, repeated and—so far—not very profitable attacks, the Germans must certainly have used up a large number of their troops. Was it not likely that these losses would be felt at some other point of the front?

As has been seen, they had been attacking heavily ever since daybreak in the region of Saint-Prix and Mondement, and still more heavily in the direction of Fère-Champenoise. Meanwhile reports from French General Headquarters showed that our armies in the west were making notable progress. It was therefore essential for the issue of the battle that the Ninth Army hold out, at no matter what cost, until the advance made by our left wing became decisive.

The task of the Ninth Army was thus perfectly clear. However hard it might prove, this Army must contain the hostile forces on its front, prevent them from breaking through, and stop them where they were until victory was assured. I therefore once again called upon all ranks to put forth their best efforts and by informing them of the enemy's situation along the rest of the battle front, I tried to communicate to them my complete confidence in our ultimate success :

"Reports received at Ninth Army Headquarters show that the German Army, having been in movement without halt since the opening of the campaign, has reached the extreme limit of its endurance. In most of the units, officers and non-commissioned officers no longer exist. Regiments are marching mixed up together and General Officers have lost control.

"Convinced as he was that we were incapable of offering him any further resistance, our vigorous offensive has taken the enemy by surprise.

"It is impossible to exaggerate the importance of taking advantage of this situation, and I ask each one of you to draw upon that last spark of energy which in its moments of supreme trial has never been denied our race.

"The disorder in the enemy's ranks is the herald of our victory.

"If you fight on with undiminished spirit, you will stop him to-day, and to-morrow we will begin to drive him out of our country.

"Remember that success will come to the side that holds out longest. The honour and safety of France are in the balance. One more effort and you are certain to win. Reports from the entire front, moreover, are good."

Meanwhile, the attacks against the centre of the Ninth Army continued with redoubled intensity and our losses became heavier and heavier, until finally the G.O.C. the IX Corps had only one company left in reserve.

At 1.30 P.M. the troops of the 52nd Reserve Division

holding Mont-Août fell back, causing a withdrawal of the whole front of the 17th Division, which retired to a fresh position running from hill 344 (two miles from Linthes) to Sainte-Sophie farm. Here it stood fast and stopped the hostile advance.

On the front of the XI Corps the enemy's attacks extended beyond the Vaure, spread toward the Corroy rivulet and ended in gaining possession of Corroy and Ognes. Part of the 18th Division was driven back into the woods south of Gourgançon. Only the 22nd Division escaped assault, artillery fire alone being directed against it.

On the extreme right, the 9th Cavalry Division, finding itself threatened by the continued infiltration of hostile cavalry into the valley of the Huitrelle, fell back behind the Dosnon-Allibaudières road.

On the extreme left, fortunately, the Moroccan Division continued its gallant resistance on the high ground about Mondement. Beyond this division, the X Corps, stoutly supported by the I Corps (constituting the right of the Fifth Army), drove the enemy back and captured the Vannay-Baye position.

This situation on the left enabled us at Ninth Army Headquarters to devote our whole attention to Fère-Champenoise. After withstanding the heavy assaults launched by the enemy against this angle, the moment had now come for us to take decisive action. The arrival of the 42nd Division would give the signal.

This Division, after being relieved in the morning by the X Corps, had at once begun its march towards Linthes and Linthelles. Having been somewhat delayed by going to the aid of the Moroccan Division, it was only at 11.30 A.M., that it reached the main road leading to Sézanne; then, crossing the Champagne bluffs and descending into the plain, it marched across country, deployed in perfect order and at a good pace.

At 1.45 P.M., I again informed this Division what I expected of it:

" Starting from the general line Pleurs—Linthes, you will attack the spur running from Pleurs to the north of Euvy.

" You will be flanked on the north by the IX Corps, which will attack against the road running from Fère to Morains-le-Petit, and on the south by the XI Corps, which will attack the spur south of Euvy, hills 136 and 160, and along its whole front.

" Your attack will commence about 4 P.M."

I then repeated my previous orders to the other units. These orders embraced the following, which were to be carried out *under any and all circumstances :*

XI Corps—to attack the front Connantray—Montepreux in conjunction with the 42nd Division ;

IX Corps—to make ready to execute the order quoted above, attacking to the north of and in liaison with the 42nd Division ;

51st Reserve Division—to attack on the general line Saint-Prix—Baye ;

X Corps—to co-operate in the offensive prescribed for the 51st Reserve Division by attacking to the north of the Saint-Gond Marshes in a west-east direction.

I did not content myself with sending these orders. The action against Fère-Champenoise was so important and involved such a mass of detail that I sent Colonel Weygand to Linthelles to give decisions on the spot. At

4 P.M. a meeting took place in this village between the Chief of Staff of the Ninth Army and Generals Dubois and Grossetti, who settled between them the zones of action and the final details of the attack.

The objectives assigned to all the available troops of the 17th and 52nd Divisions of the IX Corps were, in the first place, Fère-Champenoise, then the line Morains-le-Petit—Normée. The 42nd Division was to take the Connantre ridge and Connantray, then the line Normée—Lenharrée. The XI Corps was to reach the line Lenharrée—Haussimont. The attack was to start at 5.15 P.M.

As it was of first importance that the right flank of the 42nd Division be firmly supported, and as the XI Corps seemed disposed to subordinate its action to that of this Division, Colonel Weygand, at 5 o'clock, dispatched the following order direct to the 21st Division at Linthelles:

" The 42nd Division is attacking at 5.15 P.M. from the line Linthes—Pleurs against Connantre—Connantre mill (north of Corroy).

" The XI Corps has been ordered to support the right of this advance by itself attacking along its whole front.

" The 21st Division will move at once against the ridge north-west of Euvy."

For my part I made a last appeal to the troops, urging them to put into this offensive all the strength they had left in them. Thus we were launching, on the evening of September 9th, from west to east, against Fère-Champenoise and its approaches, a vast counter-attack.

It is true that the men were nearly worn out, but by now resuming a general offensive we were showing our determination to win, and by timing it for the exact moment when the 42nd Division would bring its weight into the battle there was an excellent chance that we would succeed against an enemy undoubtedly exhausted by his violent efforts of the previous days. Moreover, his very success had carried him southwards so rapidly that the forces opposing us now found themselves in a precarious position at the exact moment when the German system to the west of the Saint-Gond Marshes was broken, indeed falling apart. For in that region the X Corps had gained ground rapidly, while farther to the north the I Corps had reached the road running from La Chapelle to Champaubert.

It was now 6 o'clock and the artillery bombardment was raging along our entire front. Every gun had been put into action. Night was approaching and the moment had come when, by spending the very last drop of our energy, we might break the unstable nervous equilibrium and incline the balance in our favour. For the nerves of all were worn to their extreme limit, Germans and French alike, officers and men.

The troops of the IX Corps moved to the attack on the left of the 42nd Division, advancing slowly and with difficulty through clumps of woods and bushes which had to be cleared with the bayonet. Large numbers of dead and wounded of the Prussian Guard testified to the efficiency of our fire, especially our 75's. Night soon fell, but the advance kept on. Small parties of the enemy continued to fire as they fell back from one bunch of woods to another. The 42nd Division, starting from Linthes-Linthelles, advanced astride of the high road from Connantre to Fère-Champenoise.

At midnight the G.O.C. the IX Corps reported that he had captured Nozet farm and the approaches of Sainte-Sophie farm, that his men were in **marvellous** spirits, and that his advance would be continued into the night. After a short halt, the troops pushed on and, by 5 o'clock on the morning of September 10th, the IX Corps was holding Morains-le-Petit and Fère-Champenoise.

By this time the 42nd Division had reached the Connantre ridge at Connantray. Further to the south, the XI Corps had followed the movement. On the Army's right, the 9th Cavalry Division had advanced toward Mailly and the XXI Corps of the Fourth Army was within less than three miles of Sompuis.

From this moment the whole of the Ninth Army was in march towards the Marne in the vicinity of Châlons.

The region around Fère-Champenoise and all the roads leading to it gave manifest proof of the heavy losses inflicted on the enemy. Large numbers of prisoners were captured and quantities of stores were gathered in. Signs of a precipitate retreat abounded.

CHAPTER III

THE END OF THE BATTLE, AND THE PURSUIT

(September 10th—12th)

Arrival of General Foch at Fère-Champenoise—The enemy's rear-guards make some resistance, September 10th.—The march to the Marne and the passage of that river, September 11th and 12th—Men and officers are worn out—General Foch enters Châlons, September 12th—Summing up of the Battle of the Marne—General Foch learns that members of his family have been killed in the battle.

FULL information as to the results of our attacks of September 9th, hidden as they were by the darkness, did not reach my Headquarters at Plancy during the evening; however, without waiting for details, I ordered that the offensive we had begun be pushed forward the next morning with the utmost vigour.

The units were to move as follows :

XI Corps—against the front Sommesous—Lenharrée ; 9th Cavalry Division—on Mailly ;

42nd Division—against the front Lenharrée—Normée ;

IX Corps—against the front Normée—Ecury—Morains-le-Petit ;

X Corps—to block the issues from Montfort and attack towards Etoges and Villevenard in the general direction of Colligny and Bergères-les-Vertus.

By 5 A.M. on the 10th, the hour ordered for these attacks to commence, the IX Corps had already reached most of its objectives. The XI Corps, the 42nd Division and the X Corps had also resumed their advance.

Their progress encountered few difficulties other than those presented by the mass of stores the enemy had abandoned and the obstacles that at some points he had constructed. The few German cavalry patrols which were met retired without offering resistance.

When at daybreak I was informed of the situation, and particularly as to the advance made in the region of Fère-Champenoise, I took steps to ensure that our success be exploited. To the X Corps I repeated my orders of the previous day :

" The X Corps, with the 51st Reserve Division attached, is directed to carry out as rapidly and as vigorously as possible the prescribed attacks on Etoges and Colligny, in order that the Ninth Army thus relieved of all anxiety concerning its left at the Saint-Gond Marshes, may be free to take the offensive with its centre and right, an operation which promises the most fruitful results."

The IX Corps I ordered " to gain touch with the X Corps, which is attacking north of the Marshes of Saint-Gond in the direction of Etoges and Colligny ; and as the X Corps advances, to withdraw from the southern exits of the marshes, in order to employ all its available forces in the attack which is to be pushed with the utmost violence along the whole front."

The entire Ninth Army, in execution of these orders, was thus launched in a march toward the north-east, its left following along the Champagne bluffs. The unbroken plain stretched before it for twenty-two miles, right up to the Marne, and it was imperative to push forward without halting and reach the river as soon as possible.

As I had no definite reports of the situation on the right of my army or the state of our liaison with the Fourth Army, I instructed the 9th Cavalry Division to send me immediate information as to the enemy, especially in the direction of Châlons and Sompuis. In addition, I ordered the Commander of this Division to unite his own unit with the 6th Cavalry Division* which had just arrived, forming the whole into a cavalry corps. My idea was thus to create a more efficient instrument of pursuit. The new formation was to be effected on the Archis—Châlons road.

At midday I moved my Headquarters to Fère-Champenoise.† The Germans had completely sacked the town and a characteristic sight was offered by the numberless broken bottles that littered the streets. It was difficult to pass on foot, on horseback, or even in a car. The Germans had taken care to empty all the cellars of this prosperous little champagne town. Numbers of their soldiers who had delayed too long were captured in the houses. At the still burning railway station, where I found the G.O.C. the IX Corps, I issued orders for the heads of columns to push during the day to the Soude.

The advance continued on the whole front, but towards the end of the afternoon actions here and there

* General de Mitry.

† During the five previous days my Headquarters had remained at Plancy, where the inhabitants were in a great state of excitement. They listened with anguish to the battle, the thunder of which they heard coming closer every day, fearing that it would end in a French defeat and they be swept away on the flood of the invasion. Although Plancy was not more than six miles from the battlefield, I spent every day at my advanced Headquarters at Pleurs or with the troops, thus leaving the village a prey to the greatest anxiety. The family in whose house I was quartered shared in all this emotion. Each day they made ready for their departure, and it was only when I returned in the evening and calmly went to bed, that the trunks were unpacked. But the following morning, as soon as I left, everything was packed up again. On September 10th joy reigned in Plancy—Headquarters had departed for Fère-Champenoise!

against enemy rear-guards slowed down our rate of progress from what it had been in the morning. For the enemy had been allotting to his rear-guard a high proportion of artillery, and this began to delay our pursuit.

At nightfall the Army had attained the general line Ecury-le-Repos—Lenharrée—Poivres—Sainte-Suzanné. On my left, the right of the Fifth Army had reached the Marne at Dormans, but had not yet gained contact with the Ninth Army. The left of the Fourth Army (XXI Corps) was still in the vicinity of Sompuis.

Instructions received from General Headquarters directed that on the following day the pursuit would be continued, the Ninth Army being assigned the zone west of the Sommesous—Châlons road inclusive.

We had now to arrange for crossing the Marne. This meant marching to it as quickly as possible, seizing such bridges as were still intact, reconnoitering those destroyed and arranging for their repair—in other words, to get over the river with the least delay, follow closely on the heels of the disorganized enemy and give him no time to pause and recuperate. These were the ideas I had in mind when I issued my orders on the evening of the 10th.

I added that time could be gained by trying to outflank and turn the enemy's rear-guards, rather than by attacking them in front. This was to be accomplished by using widely deployed formations and by the cooperation of adjacent columns, close contact between which should be maintained.

At 5 P.M. all the columns resumed the pursuit. The I Corps (Fifth Army) was to cross the Marne at Dormans, the X Corps, which had been retained for the day of September 11th under the orders of the Ninth Army, was to march on Epernay, keeping in close touch with the I Corps. The object was to explore and, by turning it, to clear up the wooded high ground which lay between the two armies ; likewise to reconnoitre and seize immediately the important crossing at Epernay. I also had in view the effect on the general course of the battle which might be obtained by the action of my army against the enemy corps facing the Fourth Army.

On the evening of the 10th, we again encountered the German rear-guards ; during the night those holding Clamanges and Trécon were driven back. On the morning of the 11th the road was at last clear and the Ninth Army was able to continue its advance with hardly any opposition. I urged the units under my orders to push on to the Marne as rapidly as possible and seize before night all points of crossing in their respective zones. The directions of march assigned were :

IX Corps—Aulnay-sur-Marne and downstream from that point ;

42nd Division—Matougues ;

XI Corps and the Cavalry Corps—Mairy, Sogny, Châlons.

Meanwhile, I collected at Fère-Champenoise all the lorries that were available, in order to rush infantry to such bridges as might be reported as still intact ; but no news came to enable us to profit by the precaution.

In fact, the march of our columns, notwithstanding the absence of any enemy reaction, had become rather slow ; the men were worn out, and their fatigue was further augmented by an unceasing rain that rendered the Champagne country almost impassable.

At the end of the day, the X Corps, on the left of the Army, got as far as Epernay and pushed small bodies north of the Marne ; the IX Corps reached the river

A LETTER WRITTEN BY MARSHAL FOCH TO HIS OLD FRIEND
GENERAL MILLET AFTER THE BATTLE OF THE MARNE.

valley at Plivot and Athis. The 42nd Division was in the wooded country north of Germinon and Velye, with advanced guards at Thibie. The XI Corps was on the line Thibie—Ecury-sur-Coole; its 18th Division having thrown small parties back as far as Châlons. These, however, fell back to the main body of the division at nightfall.

The Cavalry Corps had sent detachments to the bridges over the Marne at and above Châlons. Reconnaissances had found that the bridge at Châlons was intact and barricaded. The bridges at Sogny and Sarry were also found undamaged; these were each seized and occupied by a squadron. Along the remainder of the Ninth Army's front the bridges over the Marne had been destroyed.

Not until the following day did any reports reach my Headquarters, although the Cavalry Corps was in the region of Saint-Quentin-sur-Coole, while I myself, in my anxiety to have early news of the situation on the Marne, had spent the night in the Town Hall at Fère-Champenoise. I wanted to be as close as possible to all sources of information, in order to take immediate decisions. But nothing came in during the night.

Under these conditions, the passage of the Marne by the right of my Army could only be effected very slowly the next morning, September 12th.

During the day of September 11th, the enemy had retreated along the whole front of the Fourth Army, and the XXI Corps, on its left, had succeeded by nightfall in moving its advanced guards to the Marne near Mairy. The Fifth Army had continued its advance north of the Marne.

Meanwhile fresh instructions came from the Commander-in-Chief. He had received news on September

10th from the G.O.C. the Fifth Army that the Germans were in full retreat, a portion of their forces moving northward in the direction of Soissons, and a portion towards Epernay and to the east. The Fifth Army was therefore driving a wedge into the German front by forcing apart the two groups that seemed to be in process of formation, one to the east of Epernay and the other to the north-west of Soissons.

Seizing the idea, General Headquarters proposed for September 11th a combined action by our Ninth, Fourth and Third Armies against the eastern group of the enemy and by the Sixth and British armies against the north-western group, while the Fifth Army was to pursue its advance due north, holding itself ready to support either one or the other of our groups of armies. The operations of the Third, Fourth, Ninth and Fifth Armies were defined as follows :

" . . . The Ninth and Fourth Armies will concentrate their efforts against the centre and left wing of the enemy, seeking to force him back to the north-west. The Third Army, continuing its advance north, will make every effort to cut his communications. The Fifth Army will maintain a detachment on the right of the British Army and another on the left of the Ninth Army ; it will so dispose its main body that it can act against either the enemy's north-western group or against his north-eastern group, in accordance with the situation.

" The advance of the Allied Armies will be in a general north, north-easterly direction."

In addition, the Commander-in-Chief instructed General d'Esperey to use the X Corps for maintaining constant touch with the Ninth Army, and for assuring to that Army any needed support. Consequently the Fifth Army Commander on September 12th took the X Corps under his orders. In writing to me of this decision, General d'Esperey added : " You can count upon me, as I have already proved you could on September 8th and 9th."

In accordance with these instructions, the pursuit was resumed on the 12th at 5 A.M. along the entire Ninth Army front. The Army reached the Marne between Sarry and Condé.

With the idea of intercepting the enemy columns in retreat towards the Argonne, I had instructed the Cavalry Corps to move rapidly towards Auve. It was to be supported by an Infantry Division of the XI Corps heading towards L'Epine and Tilloy. I added to my orders : " The day's programme *remains unchanged:* attack everywhere, push forward everywhere."

At 9 A.M. my Command Post was established at Chaintrix-Bierges.* During the whole of the night the IX Corps had been repairing the bridges over the Marne at Condé, Tours and Bisseuil, and at 9 A.M. it began to cross the river.

The 42nd Division threw an infantry footbridge across the stream at Matougues, and used it for one Brigade. The other brigade and all wheeled traffic had to go to the bridge at Châlons, held by the left of the XI Corps. This considerably delayed this Division's advance.

* It was while I was at breakfast in this village that our sentries on the road stopped an American motor-car whose occupants bore a pass from the Military Governor of Paris. They wished to proceed up to the front-line troops ; but of course I could not permit that. They turned out to be two American officers, and both fought along side of us later on. One of them, General Allen, commanded the American Army of Occupation at Coblenz ; the other, General Frank Parker, in 1918 commanded the American 1st Division.

The XI Corps crossed via Châlons, its three Divisions moving in double column. The leading Division, the 18th, began to cross at 5 A.M. The demolition charges that had been prepared to destroy the bridge were found intact, but evidently the Germans had been too pressed for time to detonate them. The 60th Reserve Division had to use the bridges at Sogny and Sarry, but as the XXI Corps was ahead of it, this Division was not able to begin crossing until 9.30 A.M., which would have made it late in bringing its support to the Cavalry Corps, had such support been required. The Cavalry Corps had also crossed by the bridges at Sogny and Sarry, but not until after the troops of the XXI Corps, which had arrived before its turn, had passed over. The action prescribed for the Cavalry was thus considerably delayed. However, it pushed forward some units of the 9th Cavalry Division towards L'Epine, Tilloy and Auve, and of the 6th Cavalry Division towards Marson, Moivre and Herpont.

By evening, the 6th Cavalry Division, after bombarding a hostile column in the direction of Poix, reached Herpont and Dommartin-sur-Yèvre. The 9th Cavalry Division had difficulty in overcoming the resistance of an enemy rear-guard at L'Epine. Owing to this and other delays, the Division was not able to advance beyond Tilloy.

The Cavalry Corps thus failed to accomplish in full what we had hoped and expected of it, namely, to attack in flank the hostile columns moving north. But these had been able to retire in almost complete security, and the Cavalry had to limit itself merely to following the rear-guards which the columns left behind to cover their retreat.

As the Cavalry Corps might now interfere with the

advance of the Fourth Army, I ordered it to assemble its Divisions in the vicinity of Bussy-le-Château and La Cheppe, and be prepared to continue on the 13th its mission of pursuit in liaison with the XI Corps.

The fatigue of the men and the exhaustion of some of the officers following the trials of the retreat and the exigencies of a furious battle lasting several days was now more and more evident, notwithstanding the stimulation brought by their success. Nevertheless, in spite of their physical exhaustion, troops who have won a great victory perfectly understand the immense consequences which will ensue if their commanders, no longer depressed by defeat but now elated by triumph, refuse to content themselves with enjoying the turn of fortune, but on the contrary seek with new ardour, foresight and decision, to enlarge the results obtained. If the enemy is allowed a few days' respite, all the work must be done over again, and what might be accomplished to-day at the expense of exhausting, even cruel effort will have to be purchased to-morrow at the price of the soldier's blood.

When evening came, the heads of the Ninth Army's columns had arrived on the line Trépail—Les Grandes-Loges—Cuperly. On the left, the X Corps of the Fifth Army had reached the Vesle above Rheims. On the right, the XXI Corps of the Fourth Army was holding Bussy-le-Château and Saint-Rémy-sur-Bussy.

At 1 P.M., I entered Châlons and established my Headquarters at the Prefecture.

All day long there passed through the town in perfect order the numerous columns of the XI Corps, as well as the artillery and trains of the 42nd Division and the IX Corps. These, having found it dangerous to attempt to cross the Marne by the hastily repaired bridges on their front, came to Châlons where the bridge was intact. The Germans had swept the town of everything to eat, as well as of all the accessories to cleanliness, and for several days the Army had to supply such necessities to the inhabitants. Many of these had remained during the German occupation, others soon returned.

The Hotel Haute-Mère-Dieu, where we dined that evening (providing, by the way, our own food and cooks), had, on the previous night, served a sumptuous meal to a number of distinguished personages of the Saxon Army, headed by the Crown Prince of Saxony. We were certainly on the enemy's heels.

The Battle of the Marne was drawing to a close. It was undoubtedly a great victory. It was the work of the man who, as early as August 24th, had begun to plan it and who had carried it through to the end, the Commander-in-Chief, General Joffre. Immediately after our repulses on the frontier, he had clearly perceived wherein the game had been poorly played. He therefore broke off the action, with the idea of resuming it energetically as soon as he had repaired the weaknesses discovered. Clear as to the enemy's intentions, fully unveiled as they now were by his powerful manœuvre across Belgium, he did not hesitate to undertake a new distribution of his forces, as well as a reassignment of General Officers, made necessary by several proofs of incapacity. He created an army of manœuvre on the west and then continued his retreat until a favourable moment for halting his forces should present itself. When this moment arrived, he judiciously combined the offensive with the defensive, after executing an energetic "about turn." By a magnificently planned stroke he dealt the invasion a mortal blow.

From the Ourcq to Lorraine, all the armies had moved

to battle in perfect cohesion and with ferocious energy, knowing full well that the country could not survive the disaster which would follow defeat in such a vast encounter. The higher commanders and their staffs had vied with one another in carrying out their tasks, giving mutual help in the finest spirit of comradeship and discipline. The men had fought until they fell exhausted in their tracks, only to rise and fight more fiercely than before.

This battle proved once more that the spirit of an army in war is the reflection of the profoundest sentiments of the nation, and when these unseen forces are wisely directed by a capable Commander-in-Chief, a great historical event results. Such was the meaning of the Marne.

Paris, the heart of the country, had been saved by a victory in which her own immediate defenders had done their share. They had been sent to the battle by her Military Governor, who realized that by so doing he was deciding the fate of the capital.

The German plan had failed, the prestige of the German Army was broken. The swift and violent invasion which was to put France out of action had not only been stopped, but it had been driven back and partly disorganized.

Under these circumstances, it remained to be seen how the enemy was going to rearrange his forces and what new plan of operations he was going to adopt on the Western Front. During this time—and here were questions which concerned us deeply—would not the great Russian masses in the eastern theatre be able to make themselves felt? Again, was the High Command of the Central Powers equal to conducting upon two fronts an action henceforth sure to be separated, and which had already failed when concentrated upon only one?

On August 28th, when I took command of the Ninth Army, the communiqué ran, " from the Somme to the Vosges " . . . the invasion is triumphant. That of September 10th read, " the victory of the French is confirmed. . . ." I was happy that it had fallen to me to play a not unimportant part in this reversal of fortune for our arms.

The German forces that had attacked the Ninth Army with the object of breaking through the centre of the French front, were as follows :

German Second Army—X Corps (whose attack bore also in part against the French X Corps), X Reserve Corps and Guard Corps.

German Third Army—XIII Corps (32nd and 23rd Divisions) and XII Reserve Corps (23rd and 24th Reserve Divisions).

While engaged at Châlons in clearing up all sorts of matters, there arrived, at the same time as the happy confirmation of the greatness of our victory, news of the sad losses which my family had suffered at the front, beginning on August 22nd. This information was sent me by General Sarrail, commanding the Third Army. Engrossed as I was in pressing matters which concerned my country's interests, I had no time even to mourn for my dead. But I did feel that if these willing sacrifices were not to remain sterile, it was imperative to exploit with the greatest rapidity the success that had been gained.

While at Châlons, also, various notabilities of the district came to see me. First was Monsieur Chapron, Prefect of the Department of the Marne. I made him my apologies for having taken possession of his Prefecture and led him to hope that we would only have need of it for a short time. As a matter of fact, it was destined for many long months to house an Army Headquarters. Monsieur Chapron was followed by Monseigneur Tissier, Bishop of Châlons, who had remained at his post during the German invasion. He was recounting the events of the brief occupation. By his personal appeal to the Crown Prince of Saxony he had been able to save the town from certain heavy contributions. There also arrived Monsieur Bourgeois, a Senator of the Department, together with Monsieur Monfeuillard and Doctor Péchandre, two of its deputies. We all took a moment from our preoccupations to celebrate the greatness and the strength of our beloved France, which in utter forgetfulness of all party quarrels had united all of her sons to drive back the invader.

CHAPTER IV

THE HALT

The Ninth Army on the Suippe—Its movement towards the Aisne runs into strong resistance, September 13th and 14th—Methodical attacks, September 15th—The Germans hold fast; fruitless attempts to break through their fortified front, September 16th—25th—A violent enemy offensive is checked, September 26th—The dearth of munitions—End of the offensive operations in Champagne—General Foch is charged with a new mission, October 4th.

ON September 13th the Ninth Army continued the pursuit towards the line of the Py and the Suippe. The Cavalry Corps, in the van, reached the river Suippe about 9 A.M. It found Suippes and Somme-Suippe still occupied by the Germans.

At 2 P.M. the advanced guards of the 22nd Division (the right column of the Ninth Army) and the left column of the XXI Corps (Fourth Army) arrived and went into action. Suippes and Somme-Suippe were taken and the Cavalry Corps resumed its advance towards Souain. But it soon encountered fresh opposition on the edge of the woods between the Suippe and the Ain.

Resistance so frequent and so close showed that there was no room for the employment of a mass of cavalry on the front of the Army. I therefore broke up the Cavalry Corps, placing one brigade at the disposal of each Corps and holding the remainder of the 6th Cavalry Division on the east, and of the 9th Cavalry Division on the west; my object being to outflank points of resistance and maintain contact with the neighbouring armies.

Reconnaissances soon disclosed enemy entrenchments on the other side of the Suippe, along the Roman road which followed the high ground north of the river. After heavy fighting by the XI Corps along the Suippe and the IX Corps in the region of Prosnes and Les Marquises, the Ninth Army, on the evening of the 13th, found itself halted on the line Sillery—Suippes, abreast of the armies on its right and left, but without being able to determine whether the resistance encountered came from rear-guards or from the main body of the enemy forces. This could be ascertained only by further operations. Accordingly, the Commander-in-Chief, in his instructions for September 13th, ordered the pursuit to be vigorously continued in a general northerly direction. He also decided to assign the XXI Corps,* as from September 14th, to the Ninth Army, whose zone of action had been widened.

In obedience to these instructions and pursuant to my own orders, the Ninth Army resumed the pursuit on the 14th, with the object of gaining if possible the line of the Aisne. But barrage fire from the hostile artillery in position prevented any appreciable advance.

As a matter of fact, the Germans were strongly entrenched on a line marked approximately by the Roman Road—Souain—Pertes-les-Hurlus, and there was no longer any doubt that we were everywhere confronted by a powerfully organized defensive position. The question to determine was whether this position was taken up by the main body of the German Army with the intention of renewing the battle there, or only by strong rear-guards, whose mission was to put up a protracted resistance behind which the general retreat might be safely continued or preparations made for a

* General Maistre.

manœuvre in some other region.

In view of this uncertainty, the Commander-in-Chief issued the following orders :

" If the enemy continues to retire, the Fourth and Ninth Armies are to drive him back to the Meuse and into the difficult region of the Ardennes. If he attempts to stand fast, they are to contain him and prevent him from sending help to his right wing.

" The practical result may be that these two armies will find themselves effecting a movement of conversion toward the north-east which might carry them to the line Stenay—Rocroy . . . the Ninth Army being below Sedan."

At the same time the Commander-in-Chief emphasized the importance of not making frontal attacks on the prepared positions of the enemy rear-guards ; they should be turned. He also directed that the artillery of our advanced guards be strengthened. This would save the troops much fatigue, as the main bodies would be able to move more rapidly and in greater security. Finally, he prescribed that ammunition be husbanded, especially high-explosive shell. Shrapnel was to be used in preference, as in many cases it was more effective than high explosive.

In order to break through the entrenched line which had held up my troops the day before, I ordered methodical attacks to be carried out on the 15th. The enemy's strong points were to be captured one by one and all conquered ground was to be well consolidated, " whilst all the time maintaining a most aggressive attitude."

In compliance with these orders, the XXI Corps attacked the Souain position after a long artillery prepara-

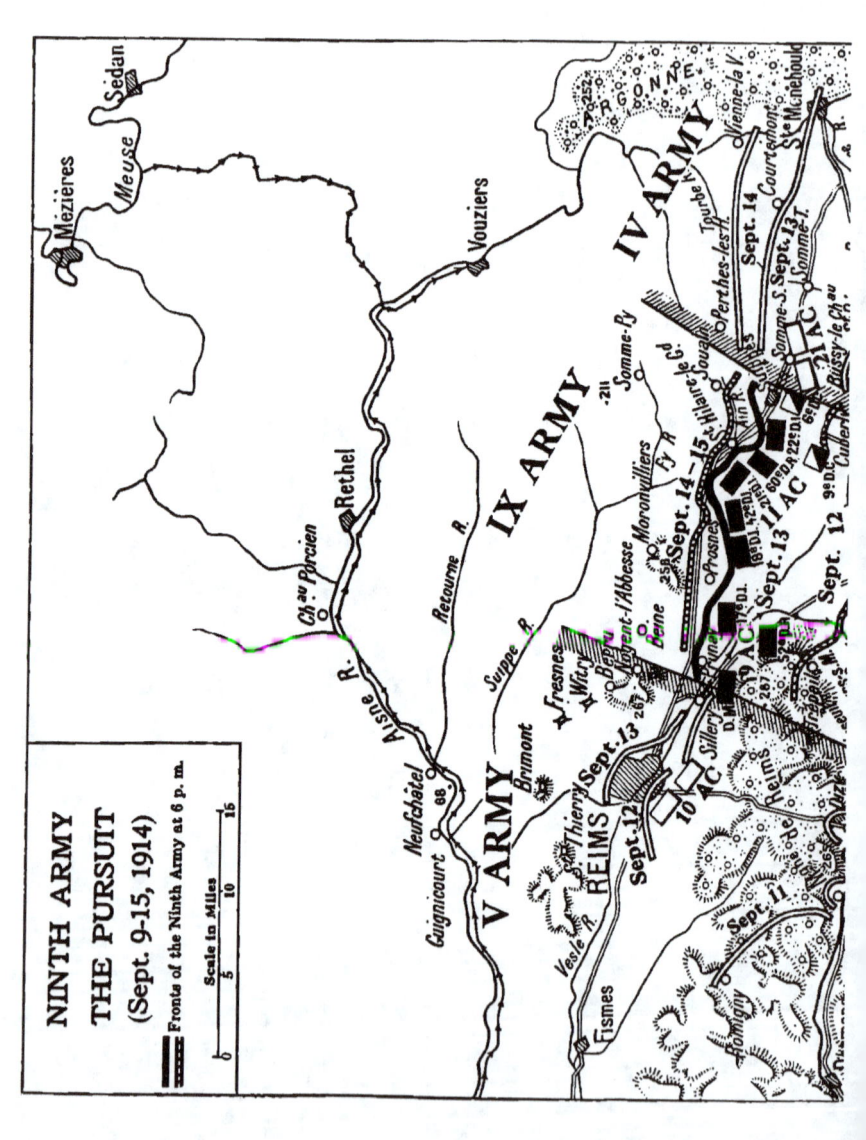

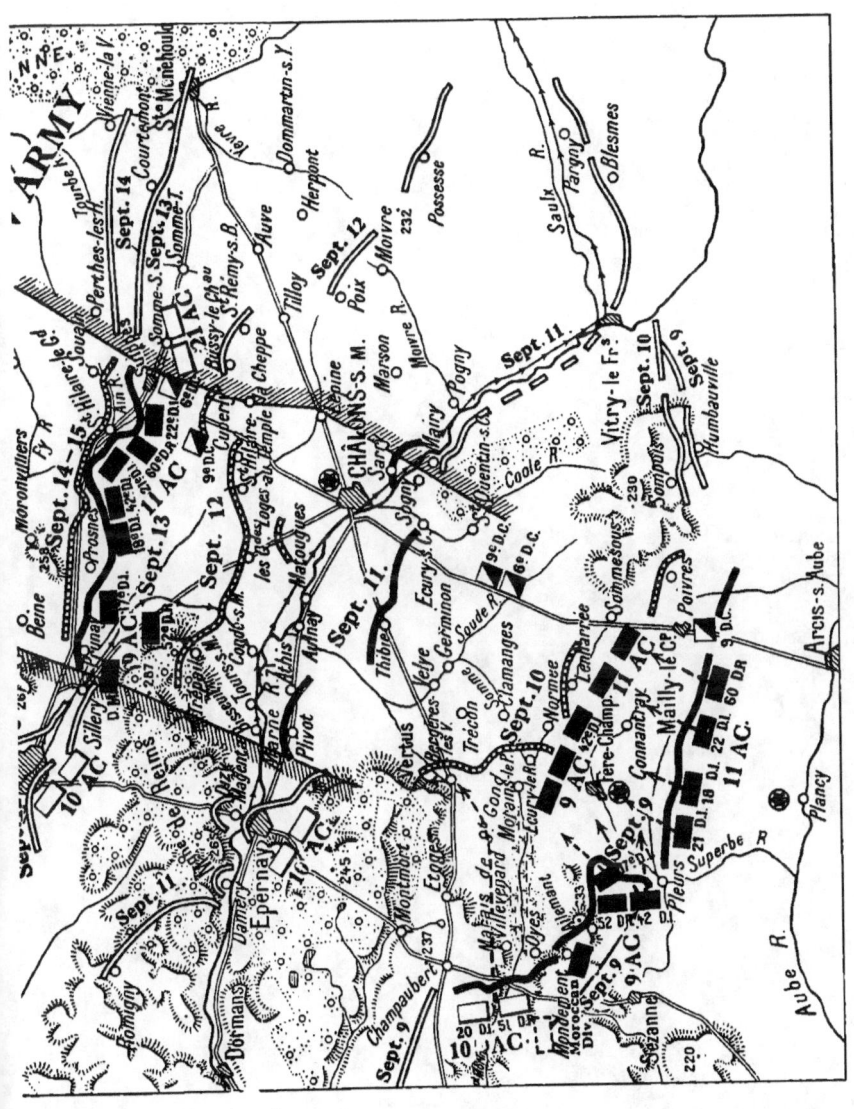

tion. By the end of the day it had gained possession of the village and ridge to the north-east ; further towards the east it took the woods south of the road from Souain to Perthes-les-Hurlus.

The remainder of the Army had not been able to make any progress on the whole of our front. The same was the case with the Fifth and Fourth Armies. We had come up against strong positions, defended by machine-guns and well concealed artillery ; in several places they were protected by barbed wire.

It was now quite clear that we were confronted by an adversary who was determined to resist. In consequence, the Commander-in-Chief telegraphed :

" The enemy seems to be disposed to accept a new battle on positions he has prepared north of the Aisne, the Vesle and the Suippe, where his rear-guards appear to have been strengthened.

" Consequently, measures applicable to a pursuit are no longer sufficient. Methodical attacks must be organized and all ground consolidated as it is won."

The pursuit had come to an end. The following days were to witness, first on one side and then on the other, attempts to break through the opposing lines. When all of these efforts had ended in failure, the front was to become stabilized for many long months.

In accordance with the Commander-in-Chief's instructions, the Ninth Army proceeded to prepare methodical attacks with the object of seizing the strong points of the enemy's line along its front. By making these without delay there was a possibility of finding him not yet completely organized and established and thus of overcoming him more easily. In any case, an aggressive and sustained activity would serve to keep him continually under the threat of penetration and prevent him from moving his reserves elsewhere. In this way, the French Commander-in-Chief would have time to prepare an operation in some new direction. By retaining the initiative and, with it, the mastery of events, he could combine a new and powerful manœuvre in some other theatre.

For it would be an error to suppose that a victory such as that of the Marne, however important it might be, would suffice to disorganize completely an Army as powerful as was that of Germany in 1914. The only way to achieve this end would be to strike one blow after another, and that without delay; then, taking advantage of the derangement of the enemy's plans and his resulting perturbation, surprise him by swift and unexpected movements which he was not yet ready to meet. Tactics of this description seemed no longer possible in Champagne, where the arrival of reinforcements and the time given them to fortify the ground, now enabled the Germans to put up a solid resistance and stop the exploitation of our victory in that region. But it was possible for our High Command to resume and pursue this exploitation by rapidly changing the point of our attacks into another and less defended region, that on the left of our armies. If, in this new theatre, we should take a strong initiative, the moral ascendancy which our success had brought us would give our Army the driving power necessary to push it home.

The determining factor was time, and it was essential to cut this down to the utmost.

In order to hold the hostile forces on its front, the Ninth Army, on September 16th and 17th, concentrated its efforts in an endeavour to seize the ridges of Moronvilliers. The attack was held up along our whole front by well-made trenches, the approaches to which were swept by artillery flanking fire and by heavy batteries posted in rear and well beyond the range of our guns. Under these conditions, our progress was almost nil.

As a matter of fact, the enemy had for several days been organizing the defence of this position with all the resources of modern science, and it now presented a resistance far superior, not only to the material means we had at our disposal, but to our conceptions of attack, based as the latter were solely upon the open warfare of the past.

Sheltered in trenches that grew deeper day by day, the Germans could defy our field artillery. Then, on the approach of our infantry, whose advance naturally caused this artillery to cease firing, they brought well-sheltered machine-guns into action. Against these, our infantry, however gallant and well-led they might be, could make no headway with rifle-fire alone. It was already evident that the defences of the German positions, dug-outs and machine-guns, would have to be demolished by heavy artillery fire before they could be taken by assault. We had no heavy artillery with our Army Corps as yet, and not much field artillery ammunition remained on hand.

On the afternoon of September 17th, the Commander-in-Chief instructed the Ninth Army to extend its front to the west, relieving the X Corps, which formed the right of the Fifth Army. The object of this move was to permit the eventual employment of that corps on General d'Esperey's left, where he seemed threatened by an enemy concentration in the direction of Laon. To compensate for this, I was given the XII Corps* from the Fourth Army.

* General Roques.

I at once issued the necessary orders, and September 18th was taken up in carrying out the exchange. During the process a heavy bombardment was directed upon us and strong attacks delivered on two of our divisions.

On the 19th, while my army was getting ready to resume its attack north with the idea of capturing the strong point of Moronvilliers, the enemy forestalled us. In the morning he seized Souain, which we counter-attacked and retook. On the IX Corps front a reconnaissance pushed out by the Moroccan Division north of Les Marquises, meeting only weak parties of the enemy, advanced about half a mile. Here a strongly organized second position was encountered and the reconnoitering detachment retired at nightfall to its point of departure.

The 52nd Reserve Division was obliged to withdraw from Bétheny, which artillery fire had made untenable. The enemy continued to bombard Rheims, and the Cathedral was in flames. In the meantime, violent attacks had been launched north and south of the Aisne against the Fifth Army. The Commander-in-Chief having instructed me to support this Army in every possible manner, I at once sent the following order to the XI Corps :

" While maintaining at all costs the line in front of and to the south-east of Rheims, where its action must be sharply aggressive, the XI Corps will make preparations to deliver an attack north-west of Rheims in support of the right of the Fifth Army. . . . Execution will be as rapid as possible."

In accordance with this order, the XI Corps organized an attack with three Brigades, but it could not be launched, as the zone of action assigned to it had not

JOFFRE AND FOCH, AS COMMANDER-IN-CHIEF AND ASSISTANT COMMANDER-IN-CHIEF, CONFER TOGETHER DURING THE AUTUMN OF 1914.

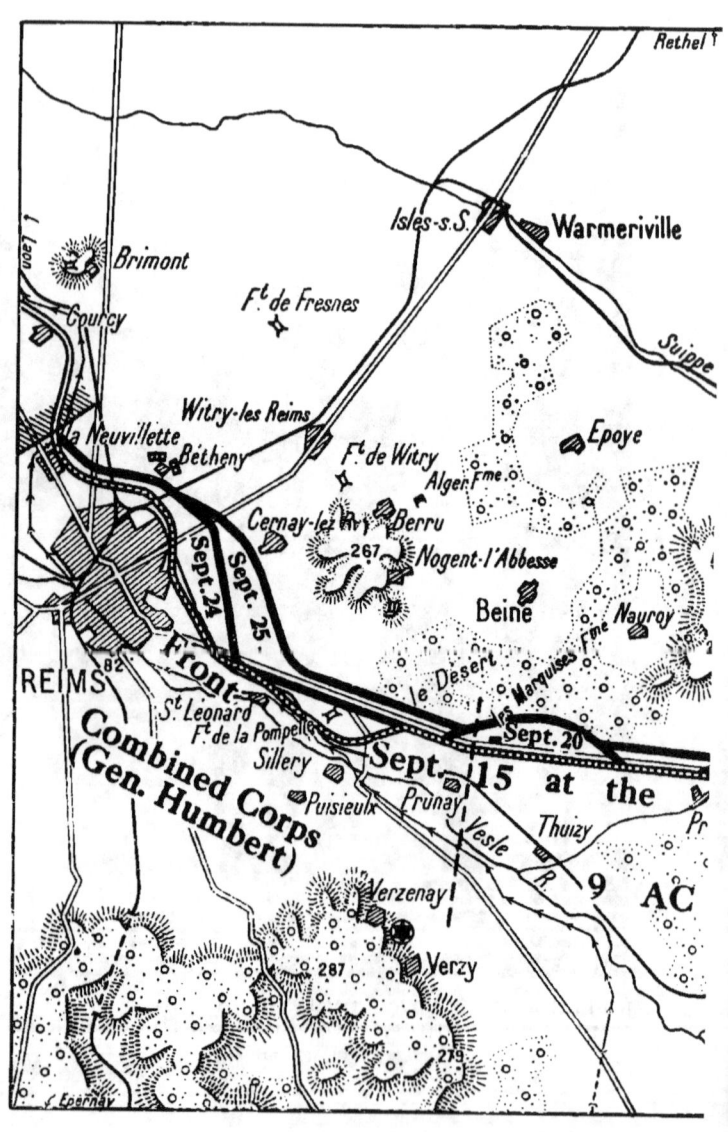

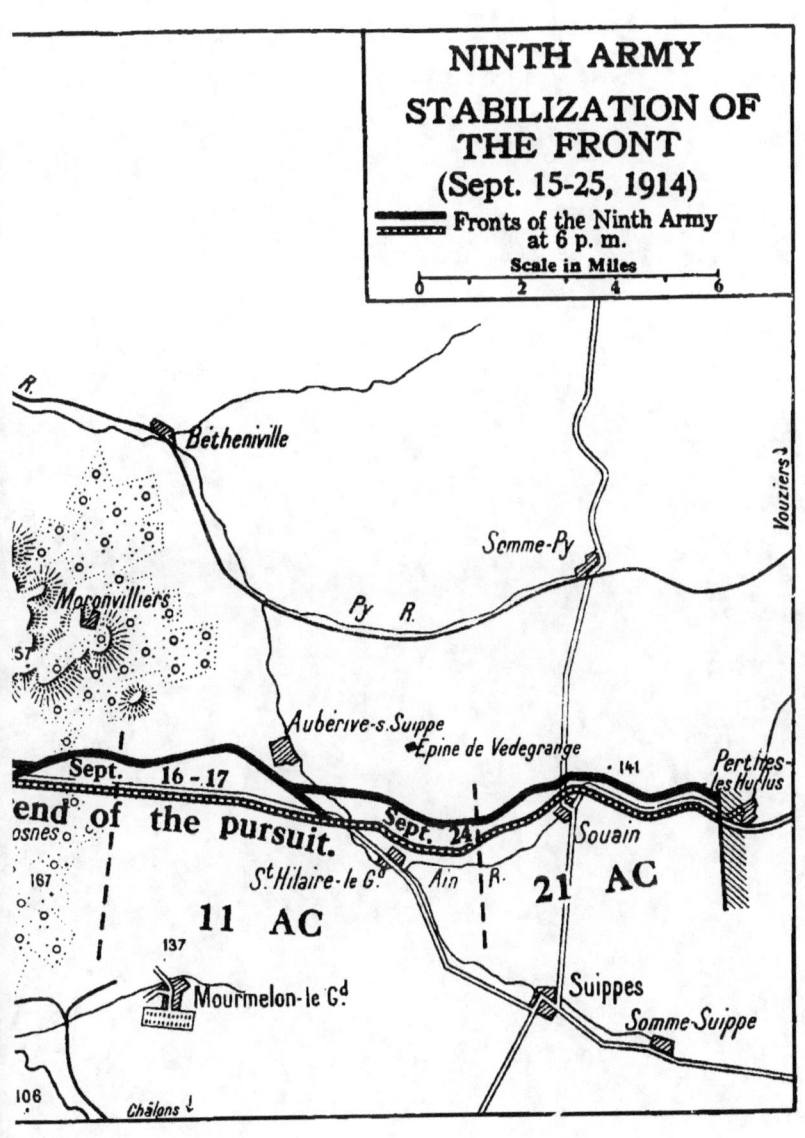

yet been vacated by the X Corps.

The Commander-in-Chief now emphasized once more the need of strict economy in the use of ammunition. He added that " neglect of this injunction might lead to very grave consequences."

The retirement of the enemy in front of the Moroccan Division, which had first been noticed on the 19th, induced me to clear up the situation ; I therefore ordered the IX Corps to resume its attacks early on the 20th in the direction of Nauroy and Beine.

The Moroccan Division succeeded in advancing about 1,300 yards north of Les Marquises, traversing the ground which the reconnaissance had covered the day before. The Division established itself there and held firm in spite of a sharp counter-attack, but it was unable to make any impression on the new German lines.

The attempts of the Ninth Army since September 16th to penetrate the enemy's front, and especially those made by the IX Corps against Moronvilliers, had demonstrated the strength of the German entrenchments which faced us. It was now evident that the only way to break through would be to launch an attack in force, powerfully supported by heavy artillery and directed against some vital point of the enemy's defence. A study both of the terrain and of the tactical situation indicated that the high ground between Nogent l'Abbesse and Berru best lent itself to this action. It was here therefore that I decided to make the attempt. In the meanwhile work on our defences would be pursued along the whole front, while the troops not employed in the first line could be rested and reorganized.

This was the situation when, at 11 A.M. on September 21st, a telephone message from the Commander-in-Chief reached Châlons, ordering the XI Corps to be transferred to the Sixth Army. It was to march that evening to the area south of Soissons. Upon receipt of this order, I at once constituted a new body of troops composed as follows :

The 23rd Division (XII Corps), which was in army reserve near Mourmelon ;
One brigade of the 42nd Division ;
The Moroccan Division ;
The 52nd Reserve Division ;
The 9th Cavalry Division.

This group, which I called the Combined Corps, was placed under the orders of General Humbert, commanding the Moroccan Division. Its mission was to ensure the defence of the front between Neuvillette and Prunay. It was also to make arrangements for the attack I contemplated for a later date on the Berru *massif*.

The relief of the XI Corps troops, then in the front line, was effected without difficulty during the night of the 21st—22nd, and about 7 A.M. on the 22nd the last units of that Corps left the Rheims area. By the morning of the 23rd the Combined Corps was entirely formed and was making preparations for the attack east of Rheims.

However, a movement of German forces toward the north-east was now reported by the Fifth Army. To oppose it, that Army attacked to the north and north-east on the morning of the 23rd. I therefore instructed General Humbert to support this attack with his artillery and then, towards 3 P.M., I directed him to act with all his available forces.

In execution of this last order, the Moroccan Division advanced against the line La Pompelle—Bois du Désort. Progress was slow and the ground gained was soon lost as the result of a heavy counter-attack. Our object, however, had been achieved, as General Humbert had drawn against himself all the hostile forces in his zone of attack. Indeed, air reconnaissances showed that German troops reported that very morning in close formation behind the line facing the Combined Corps had been brought up into the line.

During the four following days, September 24th, 25th, 26th and 27th, the Ninth Army concentrated all its efforts with a view to capturing the entrenched heights of Cernay-les-Rheims—Nogent l'Abbesse—Berru. The main operation was carried out by the Combined Corps, supported by the corps on its right. I established my Command Post on the 24th at Verzenay, and at 7 o'clock that morning the attack started.

On the left, the 52nd Reserve Division advanced for about half a mile in the direction of Cernay-les-Rheims; the 42nd Division captured the Fort de la Pompelle and the Alger farm, while the Moroccan Division gained a little ground towards the Bois du Désert and to the north of Les Marquises. In the centre, the IX Corps could make no progress. On the right, the XII Corps advanced about a quarter of a mile towards Aubérive and the Védegrange spur, while the XXI Corps gained a footing on hill 155 (west of Souain).

On the whole, fair progress had been made, and the situation seemed especially promising on the front of the Combined Corps. Consequently, at midday, I gave orders to accentuate the offensive and, after a careful artillery preparation, to resume the attack and continue it till nightfall. To the IX Corps, which was in an exceptionally good position to assist the Combined Corps, I gave the following instructions:

" . . . In order to support the attack now being made by General Humbert's forces, the infantry of the IX

Corps (in particular the 17th Division) will renew its attacks punctually at 4 P.M. Ground won during the day will be held and consolidated. Artillery will push batteries forward toward the front line."

In the afternoon, however, the enemy put up a strong resistance, and our troops, finding themselves faced by trenches defended with barbed-wire and flanked by artillery and machine-guns, made only insignificant progress. When fighting ended at nightfall, the 42nd Division alone could claim an advance, effected north and east of the Alger farm.

On the 25th, the attack was renewed on the left of the Army; the right was not to move without further orders. The Combined Corps progressed to the east of Rheims for about half a mile between the Linguet and the Jouissance. Nothing was reported from the rest of the front.

On the 26th, the Ninth Army was to continue the operations of the previous day, but its plans were upset by a serious offensive on the part of the enemy. Warning of this coming attack was received some hours before it took place, through an intercepted radio dispatch. I made this known to my troops in the following terms:

" It appears from an intercepted wireless message that the Kaiser has ordered the German Armies to attack to-day along the whole front.

" This order arrives at the very moment when the Allied Armies have completed their preparations for launching an offensive with their left wing. The circumstances, therefore, are greatly in our favour, and if we act energetically the enemy is certain to be defeated.

" The G.O.C. Ninth Army counts upon the exertions of all to maintain their positions intact and to seize every opportunity for taking the offensive."

The Germans began with an extremely violent artillery preparation and then delivered an attack along the whole front. Their efforts were first directed on Saint-Léonard, east of Rheims, where a Guards division succeeded in forcing our 23rd Division back to the bridge over the Canal.

General Humbert at once took the necessary measures, but his reserves were soon expended. He therefore asked that, " in view of the extent of the German attack, all available troops, if there are any remaining, be directed to my area."

Accordingly, I ordered the IX Corps to send at once one Brigade of its reserves to the Combined Corps. Four Battalions, the only troops available, were immediately dispatched from Thuisy towards the region south of Puisieulx. To replace these Battalions, a Brigade of the XXI Corps, not then in the line, was ordered to report to the IX Corps.

However, the IX Corps itself soon became heavily engaged about Prosnes, being attacked by a Saxon infantry division. The left of this attack completely failed, but north of Prosnes the enemy reached the Roman Road, and fighting there continued throughout the whole of the evening and well into the night.

In the direction of Saint-Hilaire and Souain, all the German efforts were blocked by the stubborn resistance of the XII and XXI Corps.

To sum up, it could be said, on the evening of the 26th, that the great German offensive on the Ninth Army's front had failed. And the little ground we had lost we recaptured the next day.

On the 27th, the IX Corps entirely re-established its

line. On its side, the Combined Corps, in conjunction with the 23rd and 42nd Divisions, carried out an attack on the enemy trenches north of the Saint-Léonard bridge. This action was skilfully supported by the few heavy guns we had, and it succeeded completely. By the evening of the 27th the situation on the whole front of the Ninth Army had been restored. This powerful offensive undertaken by the Germans was definitely arrested.

Such was not the case as regards the Fifth Army. Reports had come to me that the III Corps, on the right of that army, was heavily attacked, and I was directed to hold myself in readiness to intervene, if necessary, in order to disengage it.

At this moment, however, there arrived from the Commander-in-Chief an important dispatch which definitely prescribed the attitude we were to assume from now on. He informed his subordinates that the shortage in artillery ammunition had brought about a situation which, from being critical, might " even become tragic." I learned that I would receive no more 75 mm. shells for two or three weeks, and I was directed to regulate my operations accordingly. Moreover, the Commander-in-Chief's plans now contemplated a manœuvre north of the Oise which aimed at turning the German right. As a consequence, the Allied Armies from the Oise to the Swiss frontier would be obliged to stand on the defensive.

I immediately directed my Corps Commanders to organize their fronts defensively, to improve their positions, and seize this opportunity of giving the troops some rest. The reasons for our change of attitude was to be carefully explained to the men. In addition, I gave orders to restrict the expenditure of ammunition.

The period of big operations for the Ninth Army thus came to an end, since along its front the enemy also now assumed a defensive attitude. From September 28th to October 4th nothing of any importance affecting the general situation took place in this sector.

On October 1st the XXI Corps was relieved from the Ninth Army and transported to the north.

To meet the situation thus created, I drew up instructions prescribing the methods to be pursued in the defensive organization of an extended front. The basis of this organization was the establishment of a system of defence in depth which " would ensure both increased resistance and economy of force."

After October 4th, the operations on the front of the Ninth Army entered upon a period of stagnation that lasted some time. The enemy was established in commanding positions armed with powerful artillery of large calibre. He had constructed continuous lines of deep trenches protected by machine-guns and flanked by artillery, generally well concealed. It was not the moment to try to drive him out. On the other hand, his big offensive of September 26th had completely failed. Moreover, our own defences were getting stronger every day and gave us greater security against any attacks he might deliver. Under these conditions nothing decisive could be expected for a long time in the Champagne region.

What was happening on the rest of the front, and more especially in our armies constituting the left wing, I knew only vaguely through the daily communiqués. It was in this state of ignorance that on the afternoon of October 4th I received a message from the Commander-in-Chief calling me to his Headquarters at Romilly-sur-Seine. I reported there about 4 P.M.

General Joffre informed me that the primary object of the operations then being pursued on the western wing of the Allied Armies was to envelop the German Army's opposing wing. If this should prove impossible, the manœuvre would serve to prevent any corresponding attempt on the part of the enemy to envelop our left. With this object in view he had transported to the left of the Sixth Army, north of the Oise and Somme, General de Castelnau's Second Army, whose Headquarters were at Breteuil. An army detachment under the command of General de Maud'huy, with Headquarters at Saint-Pol, had also been constituted for the same purpose and was now moving on Arras. This detachment was being constantly reinforced and given a more and more independent rôle. On October 5th it would be transformed into the Tenth Army.

Liaison between these two Armies (the Second and the Tenth) was maintained by a group of Territorial Divisions under the command of General Brygère, with headquarters at Doullens.

In addition to this, the British Army had asked to be transferred from the Aisne to our left flank. This request had been granted, and the move would shortly take place. British Headquarters was to be established at Saint-Omer. Finally, arrangements would have to be made, sooner or later, for co-operation with the Belgian Army, now grouped in the vicinity of Antwerp.

In the presence of certain hesitance or lack of decision manifested by some of our commanders in this sector, and with a view to coming to satisfactory agreements with our Allies, the Commander-in-Chief had decided to send me immediately to the north, where I would take charge of our affairs and co-ordinate our operations with those of the Allied Armies. I was to have the title of Assistant to the Commander-in-Chief.

I returned at once to my Headquarters at Châlons.

arriving there at 7 P.M. I formed a staff, sent for General Humbert, then at the head of the Combined Corps, and handed over to him the command of the Ninth Army. Ever since the outbreak of the War, this young General had given the highest proofs of calmness and good judgment, coupled with energy and decision. I settled with him all outstanding matters, said good-bye with considerable emotion to good Monsieur Chapron, the Prefect of the Marne, and at 10 P.M. I left the town which had witnessed our victorious entry of September 12th, and started off to face new fortunes. The remainder of my staff was to rejoin me in the course of a few days.

The long night journey by motor-car lay along roads torn to pieces by artillery fire and still encumbered with convoys, across rivers where bridges had been destroyed and only summarily repaired, through villages disfigured by battle.

Our route took us at first across the battlefield of the Marne, through Montmirail and Meaux. Here we passed over the river and traversed the field of battle of the Ourcq, then through Senlis and then Creil, where we crossed the Oise. Next came Clermont, Saint-Just-en-Chaussée, and finally Breteuil, which place we reached on October 5th at half-past four in the morning.

I immediately sent word to General de Castelnau that I had arrived, and while waiting for him I lay down on a bench in the school house. He came in shortly afterwards, and I took over the direction of our affairs in the north.

PART III

THE BATTLE OF FLANDERS

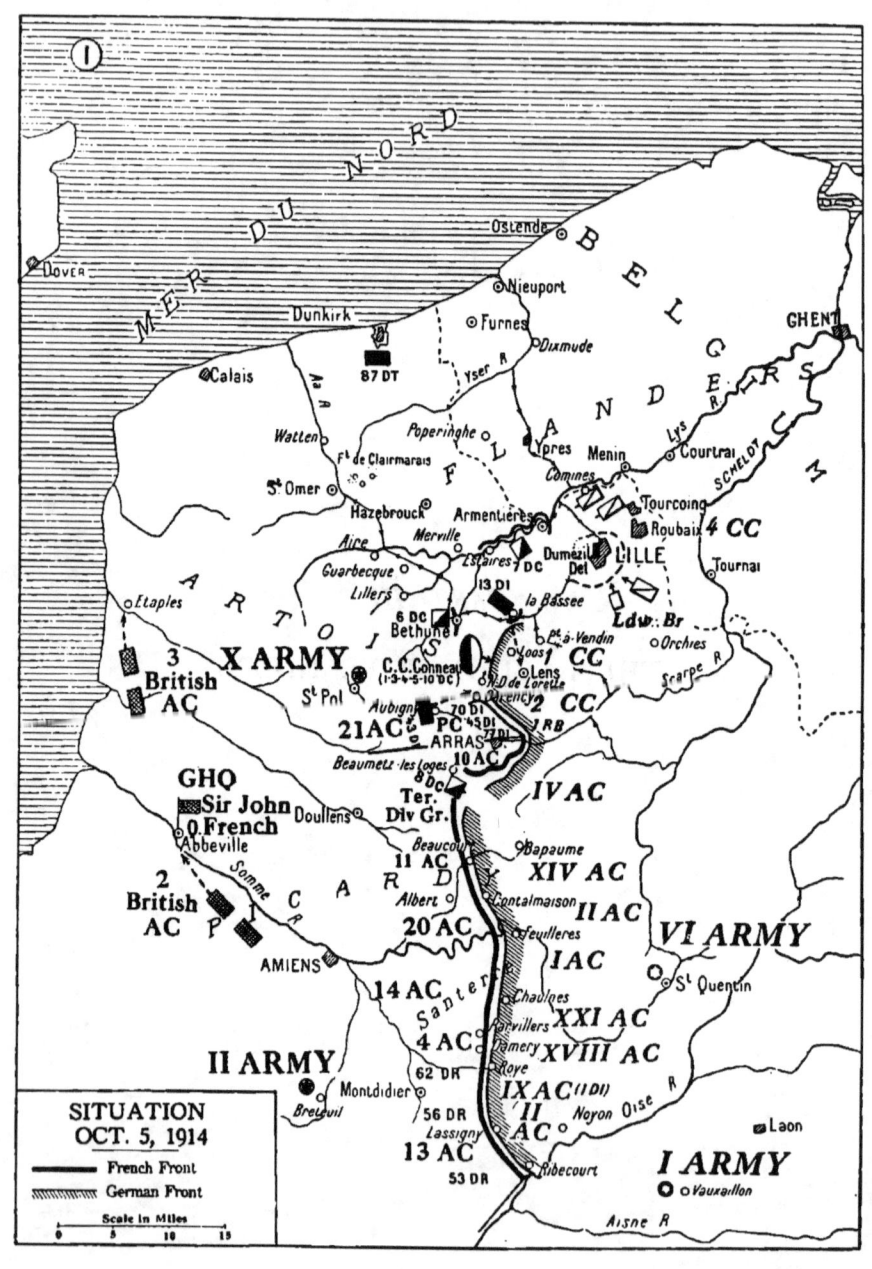

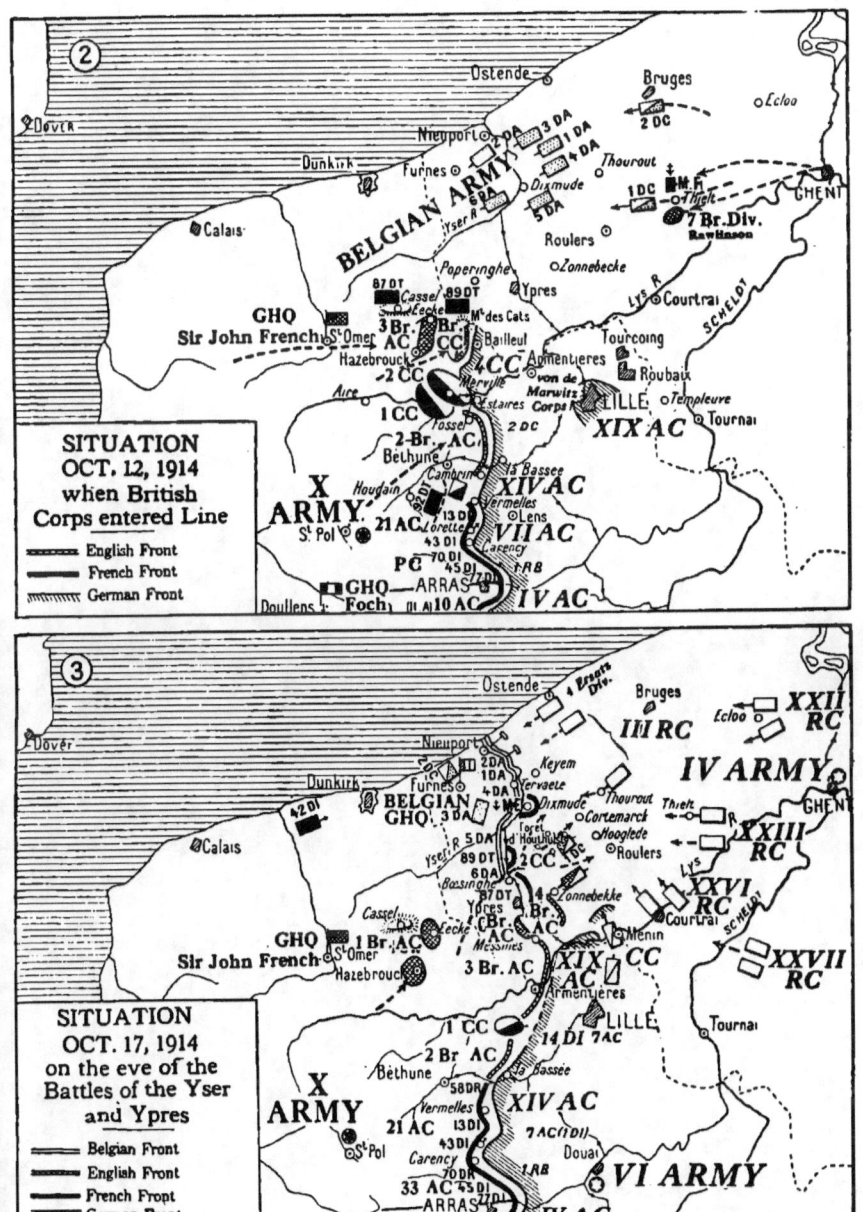

CHAPTER I

THE MOVEMENT NORTH

What the " race to the sea " really was—The situation of the French Second and Tenth Armies and their operations from October 5th to 7th—First dispositions north of the Lys—Fall of Antwerp, October 8th—The British Army enters the line—Its operations up to October 15th—Arrival of the Belgian Army on the Yser; the meeting at Furnes, October 16th—Forecast of the Battle of Flanders.

THE second period of the War which followed the Battle of the Marne was baptized " the Race to the Sea." The phrase sounds well, but it does not give a true conception of the operations ; nor does it really reflect the idea on which they were based. The race was towards the enemy. It was his right wing that we attempted to outflank and envelop. When he outstripped us, it was his effort to outflank us that we warded off. For he was trying by increased speed to envelop us in a manœuvre similar to our own. This produced on each side a race towards the northern wing of the opposing army. At the same time, we had to check the enemy's advance and immobilize him on the remainder of the front ; and this front was getting longer and longer. As a result of this symmetrical manœuvre, the northern wing moved at an ever-increasing speed through the Ile de France, Picardy, Artois and Flanders, up to the North Sea. In this way, the sea marked the end of the manœuvre, though it had never been its aim.

All along the road traversed, the efforts of each to outflank the other had ended in impacts of front against front, bringing no decisive result. When finally the sea put an end to further progress, there ensued the Battle of Ypres. Here both sides sought a decision in a supreme effort to break through hastily improvised defences.

After a race lasting a full month, the Allied forces which had shattered the enemy's invasion at the Marne again checked his march on the banks of the Yser, and by saving the Channel ports, strengthened the Coalition, and consolidated the Franco-British union. If they failed to overthrow the German Army in a decisive victory, they at least demolished all its plans by closing in its face the last possible door by which it could break through.

* * * * *

On arriving at Breteuil, my task was to co-ordinate the operations in the north, and I began with our Second Army.* Its Commander proceeded to explain to me the situation of our troops in that region. They stretched from the north of Arras to Ribécourt on the Oise, where the XIII Corps†, right wing of the Second Army, had been held up in its advance on Noyon. They faced the enemy on the line Lassigny—Roye—Chaulnes —Feuillères-sur-la Somme — Contalmaison—Beaucourt. Farther north, General Brugère's group of Territorial Divisions, falling back from the Bapaume region, were defending the approaches to the road from Amiens to Arras and were keeping up a most precarious connection with the Tenth Army,‡ in process of formation around Arras. For several days past, the Second Army had been engaged in heavy fighting, made all the more arduous

---

* General de Castelnau. † General Alix. ‡ General de Maud'huy.

by the length of front it had to defend. On the previous day alarming news from the Tenth Army had created fears of an envelopment of the Second Army. In the report which General de Castelnau made me, he had been led to consider the eventuality of having to withdraw part of his forces (especially those in action north of the Somme), in order to bring them south of that river, on the left bank.

Whatever might be the reasons for such a decision, it seemed to me that the results would have a most serious effect upon the whole conduct of the war; for a move would be initiated in a direction exactly contrary to our interests. In the first place, the outflanking operation which the French Commander-in-Chief had embarked upon would be held up; secondly, the road would be left open for the German enveloping movement against the left of our Second Army; finally, the Tenth Army would have to be abandoned to its fate, and this might very well mean its destruction. In any case, the withdrawal of the Second Army and its establishment in a stronger position, well protected by the Somme, would compromise the fate of our northern provinces and risk the loss of the Channel ports and our communications with Great Britain and Belgium.

In spite of the difficulties facing us at the present moment and the darkness of the picture as painted for me at Second Army Headquarters, it seemed to me imperative to avoid any such grave possibilities; to do so, we must stiffen our resolution, contend against the march of events, and in any case make no voluntary movement in retreat, especially as the pressure of the enemy did not as yet render this imperative. Instead of preparing for such a step, it could best be prevented by vigorously maintaining the troops in their positions and thus giving time for the development of the decisive operations then being pursued farther north. These operations, which were to be carried out by the British troops now coming up and those being sent forward daily by the French Commander-in-Chief, would in the end bring relief to the Second Army itself. It was in accordance with these ideas that I decided upon the line of conduct which the Second Army was to follow and that I demanded of it to hold on at all costs to the positions it was occupying.

Great wars, especially those in which several allied nations are engaged, as well as the important battles they involve, cannot be considered merely from the viewpoint of one particular participant in the fight. They constitute a whole, a combination of joint actions, which, although extending over large spaces and long periods of time, must necessarily be harmonized, if a favourable result is finally to be attained.

Even if one of these actions should come to a standstill, or one group of these forces be particularly tried, the commander of the whole must unflinchingly stand by his general plan, at the same time stimulating or sustaining the failing action; but without ever admitting that it can be wholly renounced or that its weakness cause the relinquishment or change of that plan. Losses suffered at any given moment by a group of forces even so great as an army cannot justify any such disturbance in the combined operations of the other armies, or in actions being pursued for the defence of the allied interests as a whole.

The moral to be drawn from this idea—and it is applicable to all degrees in the hierarchy of command—is that the more anxious and disquieting the situation of his own troops may be, and the more critical the moment then facing him appears, the more urgent it is for any commander to push forward with unshaken energy his share in the general operations. He must not let himself be influenced by the uncertainties and dangers of his own particular situation; this will always be restored by a general success. On the contrary, it is his duty to search his mind and call upon his imagination for means which will enable his troops to hold out until the crisis is over. In my opinion, the victory of the Marne had fully justified this doctrine; the moment had come to apply it once more.

On the morning of October 5th, it was agreed upon between me and the G.O.C. the Second Army that his troops would hold on to their present front, no matter what might be the difficulties encountered or the sacrifices entailed.

At 7 A.M. I left for Tenth Army Headquarters at Saint-Pol, after informing General de Castelnau that I would return to Breteuil in the evening. About 10 A.M. I met General de Maud'huy at his Command Post at Aubigny, not far from Arras, but a good sixty miles from Breteuil.

On the road we once more encountered the sad spectacle presented by dense columns of inhabitants fleeing before the enemy. At Aubigny I found General de Maud'huy in excellent spirits—the perfect type of a soldier in the full tide of battle. He had been dispatched with a strong force of cavalry in an endeavour to envelop the German northern wing, but he had been attacked by several army corps marching on Arras, and by October 5th, when I met him, his troops had been forced back to the approaches of that town. In fact, these corps had outstripped him, and their attacks forced him to close his forces in as soon as possible; for they were still spread out from the Lys, Merville and Armentières to the south of Arras.

In the meantime and while this junction was being effected, General de Maud'huy had to improvise a series of dispositions for opposing the enemy as well as to put an end to the state of doubt which existed in the minds of some of his commanders as to the attitude to be assumed. I arrived in the midst of this situation, and with him drew up the following plan of action :

I—Check forthwith the enemy's advance on Arras.

II—Maintain solidly in their positions the front line troops already engaged.

III—Concentrate as soon as possible the remaining troops in rear, seizing at the same time certain points of special tactical importance, such as Notre-Dame-de-Lorette.

IV—Continue the effort to envelop the enemy's flank by pursuing the offensive on our left wing with the XXI Corps.* The 43rd Division of this Corps was to advance from Aubigny on Carençy and the 13th Division from La Bassée to Loos and Lens.

Of the cavalry, a part would keep touch with the two Divisions just mentioned, while another fraction would cover them on the east.

The troops available were the X Corps,† the Provisional Corps‡ (70th and 77th Division), the XXI Corps, the 45th Division, General Conneau's Cavalry Corps (1st, 3rd and 10th Cavalry Divisions), and General de Mitry's Cavalry Corps (4th, 5th and 6th Cavalry Divisions).

Having made these decisions with General de Maud'huy, I left for Amiens in the afternoon and

* General Maistre.
† General Desforges.   ‡ General d'Urbal.

arrived that evening at Breteuil. Here reports I received from the Second Army indicated that the day had been devoid of any particular incident. I passed the evening with General de Castelnau and spent the night at Breteuil, not far from his headquarters. I left him the next morning, October 6th, after arranging with him that the line of action decided upon the previous day should remain unchanged. The enemy was to be vigorously opposed on the front of the Second Army and of the Territorial Divisions, while we pushed an outflanking offensive movement to the north of the Tenth Army. I then proceeded to join this Army.

Upon arriving at Aubigny on the morning of the 6th, I learned from General de Maud'huy that, in the face of the strong resistance it had encountered, the XXI Corps was making but slow progress in the direction of Lens. The cavalry however had occupied the plateau of Notre-Dame-de-Lorette. They were relieved there the next day by the XXI Corps, whose two Divisions, working in close conjunction, had pushed an advanced guard to Pont à Vendin.

Although the day had produced no important results, the operations of the Tenth Army on the whole had been well inaugurated. This was the situation when I returned to my Headquarters, which I had moved to Doullens, half-way between Aubigny and Breteuil. Immediately I arrived, the Chief of Staff of the Second Army telephoned me that his Army was being heavily attacked and it was greatly desired that I come to Breteuil that same evening. It appeared that in the face of attacks against the Santerre plateau, the IV Corps* had given way, losing Parvilliers, Damery,

* General Boëlle.

Andechy and Le Quesnoy. The G.O.C. the Second Army had the impression that his line was on the point of breaking somewhere.

This was the situation when I started off for Breteuil. Here, with General de Castelnau, I calculated the reserves remaining in his own hands, the reinforcements placed at his disposition by the Sixth Army, and the help which might be provided by the two Divisions of British Cavalry which, under General Allenby's command, were then passing through Montdidier bound for Flanders. Together we decided that if necessary the reinforcements would be employed, but that there was to be no alteration in the line of action laid down for the Second Army. It was to oppose a strong resistance to the enemy everywhere and check his advance. For this purpose a defensive front was to be organised as soon as possible and the men were to dig themselves in. It so turned out that October 6th was destined to be the last day of serious trouble for the Second Army for some time.

After having arranged matters at Breteuil, I returned at once to my Headquarters at Doullens where I arrived late at night. Since the evening of October 4th, that is to say, in fifty-seven hours, I had driven more than five hundred and thirty miles, hurrying from Châlons to the two battles that had just been fought, the one of the Second Army on the Somme and the one of the Tenth Army at Arras. Our quarters at Doullens lacked nothing in simplicity, for the town was already occupied, not to say filled to its limit, by the Headquarters of General Brugère's group of Territorial Divisions, with its two hundred comfortable motor-cars and numerous persons of note.

On October 7th, the fighting on the front of the Tenth

Army was continued under the same conditions as on the 6th.

*   *   *   *

Meanwhile, other operations required my attention in a quarter where the enemy was multiplying his attempts to break through. We had pushed our cavalry (two divisions) up to the Lys, which it was watching. But farther north, in that portion of Flanders which stretches to the sea, it was possible that the enemy might outflank our manœuvre in Artois, gain the Channel ports and cut us off from the Belgian Army, which was still concentrated around Antwerp. It was essential then to secure possession of this region as soon as possible. Accordingly, orders were at once given to put Dunkirk in a state of defence, start the fresh water inundations and make ready those from the sea.

Farther to the south of the Lys there was the city of Lille which had long since ceased to be classed as a fortified place, but which was a most important and thickly populated industrial centre. The town had been abandoned by our troops when our armies retired to the Marne. I got into telephonic communication with the Prefect, who confirmed the fact that no French troops were there and that the place would be an easy prey for enemy patrols; I therefore decided on the evening of the 9th to re-occupy it. This was effected by a detachment consisting of three Territorial Battalions, one battery and three squadrons. This force was attacked on the 11th and defended itself in the citadel. My expectation was that our enveloping movement would extend to Lille and thus join hands with this detachment.*

* As a matter of fact, we were unable to come to its aid, and the Lille garrison capitulated on October 13th.

The British Army, arriving from the Aisne front, was now ready to come into the line. The idea of the French Commander-in-Chief was that this Army should prolong the turning movement which he was carrying out on the northern wing of our armies. On the night of October 5th and 6th, two Cavalry Divisions arrived by road and two army corps began to detrain in the neighbourhood of Abbeville and Etaples. The British Army was to move as rapidly as possible to the left of the French, where it would regain contact with the British and Belgian forces operating in Belgium. To cover the debarkation, I sent a Territorial Brigade with some artillery from Dunkirk, with orders to take up a position on the line Watten Canal—St. Omer—Aire and defend the exits from the Clairmarais Forest.

At the same time I moved another Territorial Brigade from Dunkirk to Poperinghe, so that portions of the British Army could also detrain at Bethune and Saint-Pol.

*   *   *   *

On October 8th, after establishing his Headquarters at Abbeville, Field-Marshal Sir John French came to see me at Doullens. It was the first time I had met him since the beginning of the campaign. I was especially glad to see him once more. We had known each other for a long time, and the cordial reception he had always given me in former years, both in France and in England, left no doubt in my mind as to the frankness which would mark our relations now that we were both engaged in a great war.

Among other news he brought was that of the capitulation of Antwerp. To his question as to what we could do to counter an event which had made the

Germans masters of all Belgium, I replied that we were still far from having effected junction with the Belgian Army, and that our troops were a long way from the coast of the North Sea. To my mind the question was whether we would arrive in time to achieve this two-fold object. All that could be said at the present moment was that every effort must be directed to attaining it, supposing that, in the meantime, we did not succeed in turning the enemy's northern wing.

My old friend, Sir Henry Wilson (subsequently to become a Field-Marshal himself), was with Sir John French. I told him with a certain amount of emotion of the happiness I felt at seeing him again, and I added that I was convinced that the rapid and effective entry of the British Army into the war was due to the preparatory measures which he, as Director of Military Operations on the Imperial General Staff, had made for that contingency. General Wilson had already given evidence of possessing those qualities of patriotic vigilance and far-sighted intelligence which his later career was brilliantly to confirm.

For my part, I did not find the general situation bad, and I was full of confidence. I had seen the enemy fail in Lorraine and we had beaten him on the Marne. He was now attempting to restore his fortunes in the north, but we were holding our own. The lightning stroke by which he had expected to encompass France's destruction had been parried in victorious fashion, and Russia's weight could not now be long in making itself felt. Furthermore, the results already obtained by our Second and Tenth Armies and the imminent entry of the British forces into action justified the hope that we would be able to make our manœuvre to the north. Accordingly, on October 10th, I wrote to the Commander-in-Chief as follows :

"General :

"I consider our situation very satisfactory. Castelnau is not budging nor, barring some incidents, are his Territorials. Maud'huy is attacking around Arras. His success is slow but continued. Further north, our cavalry has just been driven back on to the line La Bassée—Béthune, but I do not attach great importance to that, because :

"At midday to-day the British II Corps will be at Béthune and Lillers, and the British Cavalry Corps at Aire and Guarbecque. More British are detraining to-day at and in the neighbourhood of St. Omer (which we hold) ; under these conditions, there seems little to fear from a German attack.

"The Second Army is recovering its confidence. Duchesne's arrival will have an excellent effect. There is no more talk of a retreat, which, in any case, I have expressly forbidden. The cavalry has not yet sufficient audacity.

"I will return to Romilly whenever you desire, but I think that I am needed here, inasmuch as our forces are still not lined up, the advance has not yet been resumed, and we have to consider a very extended territory, stretching as it does from Dunkirk through Lille to Noyon, and anything might happen.

"Please receive, General, the assurance of my respectful devotion.

"(Signed) Foch.

"P.S.—If you approve and if Sir John French agrees, I propose to advance our left (Tenth Army) by Lille to the Scheldt at Tournai or at Orchies, the British Army moving in the direction of Lille and to the north of that town, and forming line from Tournai through Courtrai.

In this way all the French, British and Belgian detachments would be united on the left banks of either the Scheldt or the Lys. After that we can see."

Since Sir John French expected to have, on October 10th, the II Corps and two Cavalry Divisions ready to come into action between Béthune and Aire, and on October 12th the III Corps and two Cavalry Divisions between Béthune and Saint-Omer, we made dispositions on the 10th for resuming the attack and clearing up the situation as soon as possible. These arrangements were set down in the following note:

" In the existing situation of the Allied Armies, the first thing to be done is, while acting with every precaution, to effect the union of the Belgian, British and French forces which, as a result of recent events, have become scattered.

" The area north and east of Lille, between the Scheldt and the Lys, seems to afford favourable ground for this operation.

" If to-morrow, the 11th, and the day after, the 12th, the left of the French Tenth Army is supported by the British Army (II Corps and Cavalry Corps) operating on the front Béthune—Merville, it is anticipated that the road to Lille will be cleared.

" On the other hand, the area north of the line Merville—Hazebrouck—Cassel (which we hold) appears to be occupied only by weak forces.

" Under these conditions, it is believed that on the morning of the 13th the left of the French Army could march towards Lille and, later on, towards Tournai, the right of the British Army towards the area north of Lille and, later on, towards Templeneuve, and the centre of the British Army, on Courtrai.

"With the Scheldt thus held at Tournai and the Lys held at Courtrai, the British, French and Belgian forces could be assembled behind those rivers.

"If the Field-Marshal Commanding-in-Chief the British Army is in agreement with these views, the French Army would be allotted for its movements the road Outreville—Houdain—Verquigneul—La Bassée—Lille—Tournai, and the roads to the south; the British Army would use all roads to the north of these.

"I have the honour to ask if the above is approved.

"(Signed) FOCH."

Sir John undertook to support the operations of the French troops as fully and as promptly as possible. Owing, however, to delays in detraining, the first Division of the British III Corps was not available till the afternoon of the 13th, and was not ready to move as a whole before the evening of the 15th.

In the meanwhile, the Second Army held fast to its positions, but the northern wing of the Tenth Army and the advanced troops of the British Army found their advance in the direction of Lille held up by repeated attacks which the enemy was developing in ever-increasing strength south of the Lys.

The arrival on the 15th of the British forces and their advance on the northern bank of the Lys marked our start in outflanking and enveloping the northern wing of the German armies operating in France. But a fresh storm was about to break.

* * * *

The hostile forces that had been operating in Belgium, having been freed by the surrender of Antwerp, were now moving to this same northern bank of the Lys. A new channel had been opened for the invasion we had managed to dam in Picardy, in Artois and in French Flanders, and which we were trying to encircle on the Lys, from Armentières to Menin. A new theatre of operations, namely in Belgium, henceforth had to be considered, and steps must be immediately taken to meet a military situation which revived the menace to the Channel ports and touch between the Allies.

It was now a question of blocking the march "*nach Calais*" and of saving at least a portion of Belgium, whose very existence was threatened. Where could we effect that junction of the scattered Allied forces which was forecast in the note of October 10th? The Lys and the Scheldt could no longer cover it. What was the real fighting value of these forces? To what extent could their co-operation be counted upon? Behind what barrier could they be united so as to form at least an obstacle to the enemy's advance?

Antwerp was occupied by the German Army on October 9th, and the Belgian Army began its retreat in the direction of Ecloo and Bruges. The British Admiralty had despatched the 7th Division and the 3rd Cavalry Division under General Rawlinson, and France a brigade of Marines under Admiral Ronarc'h, toward Antwerp for the purpose of supporting the Belgians. But these forces had been unable to proceed beyond Ghent, and were now falling back covering the right of the Belgian Army.

That Army first gained the region Ostend—Thourout —Dixmude—Furnes. Here General Pau, attached to the Belgians as representative of the French Supreme Command, joined it on the 10th. He found the troops worn out by the siege of Antwerp and the subsequent retreat. Their retirement was continuing on Calais and Saint-Omer, when General Joffre endeavoured (but without success) to divert them towards Ypres and Poperinghe, so that they might join the Allied Armies in the enveloping movement then in process.

When I learned of the Belgians' intentions, I asked General Pau to prevail upon them to fix Dunkirk as their base of operations rather than Calais, as this would place them nearer to Belgium at the very moment when the Allied Armies were about to advance into that country. It was decided, therefore, on the 11th at Ostend, that all the personnel of depôts and untrained men should be sent to Dunkirk, and that the six divisions constituting the Belgian Army would be assembled in the region Nieuport—Furnes—Dixmude. They would still be covered on the east by General Rawlinson's British Divisions and Admiral Ronarc'h's brigade of French Marines. The Belgians were not to retire unless attacked. In the event of being obliged to retreat, they were to take up a final defensive position behind the Yser and the canal from Dixmude to Ypres, keeping touch always with that last named town.

This retention of the Belgian Army along the coast isolated it to such a degree as might very well have proved fatal to it. Moreover, Ypres, that important centre of communications, would have to be abandoned, and this might deal a mortal blow to the entire Allied plan. Accordingly, on the 12th, I instructed General Bidon, the Military Governor of Dunkirk, to take under his orders the 87th and 89th Territorial Divisions. Then, having established himself in position on the Poperinghe—Ypres road, he was to endeavour to make contact in the direction of Zonnebeke and Roulers with the Allied forces to the east (Belgian, British and the

French Marines). He was to manœuvre so as to keep in touch with the British forces arriving that day on his right at Lecke ; in addition he was to organise a strong defensive position at Ypres, so as to check any hostile advance from the direction of Armentières, Comines or Menin.

Out of these heterogeneous, changing and unstable Allied elements, it was hoped and intended to create, at once, starting on October 14th, a safe place of contact and a centre of resistance upon which the Allies could base their future action.

The state of the Belgian Army also had to be taken into account. For two months it had been subjected to a succession of the hardest blows, (Liége, Namur and Antwerp), not to mention prolonged bombardments. For such trials this army was less prepared than any of the others. Up to 1914, it had known nothing but peace. The neutrality of Belgium, guaranteed by the Great Powers of Europe, had become an article of faith which not only removed all menace of serious war from her army, but brought about a limitation of its functions. From the point of view of home affairs, the Army was merely the guardian of public order. From the point of view of foreign affairs, its duty consisted in protecting the country from invasion until such time as the Guaranteeing Powers could come to her defence and take under the protection of their armies the maintenance of her independence. But the lofty sense of honour which animated the King and the nation caused the Belgians to throw themselves into a tremendous struggle which a formidable neighbour had carefully prepared. It was this reality, so different from anything it had ever had reason to expect, that the Belgian Army now had to face. And the nervous force of its soldiers was all that remained to replace the deficiencies of their equipment.

The uncertainty I felt regarding the situation on the North Sea coast, and the amount of resistance we could offer there to the progress of the invasion, decided me on the 16th to make a rapid visit to that region, with which as yet I was unacquainted. Accompanied by Major Desticker and Lieutenant Tardieu, I proceeded on the morning of the 16th first of all to Saint-Omer, whither Sir John French's Headquarters had been moved. I asked him to ensure the co-operation of the British Navy against the German right in the direction of Ostend; also to divert the enemy attacks from the Belgian Army by advancing General Rawlinson's corps from Ypres in the direction of Roulers.

I then went on to Dunkirk. A large stock of supplies had been collected there which it was essential to protect from a sudden raid, so I ordered up a Brigade of Territorials and, in conjunction with General Plantey, the new Military Governor, I assured myself that the defences were making good progress and that everything was in readiness for effecting the inundations. The fresh-water sluices had already been opened and the water was now spreading, whilst the salt-water inundations could be started whenever desired, as the canals had been filled to high water level.

At Dunkirk I met Monsieur de Brocqueville, the Belgian Prime Minister. After discussing with him the local military situation and the general political outlook, we decided to go together to the Belgian Army Headquarters at Furnes in order to see the King.

For it was now necessary to take a decision of paramount importance, namely, prevent the Belgian Army from entirely abandoning Belgium. Its retreat must be stopped and it must hold on to a portion of its native soil, however small the strip might be. Monsieur de Brocqueville was an able, far-seeing statesman, full of decision. He agreed with these views and undertook to support them.

On the road from Dunkirk to Furnes, once more we had to pass through a pitiful throng of inhabitants fleeing before the invasion. A dense mass, composed of women, children and young girls, of nuns, priests and old men, filled the roads, pressing onward in the confusion of a hurried flight, worn out by the fatigues of a ceaseless march and of nights passed in the open fields under a cold October rain. Furnes was crowded with Belgian troops, exhausted by the terrible bombardment of Antwerp and eight days of retreat. The King, Commander-in-Chief of the Belgian Army, had established his Headquarters in the Town Hall, a building of period architecture, situated in one corner of an artistic square, now the scene of a busy movement that contrasted strangely with its habitual solitude.

Accompanied by Lieutenant-Colonel Brécard, the head of our mission with the Belgian Army, and preceded by M. de Brocqueville, I made my way to Headquarters. Here I found General Hanotaux, the Belgian Chief of Staff, and General Wielemans, the Deputy-Chief. They were still suffering from the disturbing effects of the long and painful retreat.

I explained to them the reasons which justified the halting of this retreat and the means which could be employed to oppose the enemy. The German units on the Belgian front consisted of non-regular troops, army corps composed of reservists. The infantry undoubtedly was not as good as that which had just been stopped and driven back in France, but there could be no doubt that it would be accompanied by a large force of artillery.

By digging in, the Belgian Army could parry the enemy's blows and provide a barrier which French troops would soon reinforce. Dixmude was already held by a Brigade of French Marines, first class troops. This gave us a strong point on which to anchor the defence of the line.

A few moments later the King received me. He was in the Salle des Echevins, a large, finely decorated room, with a huge fireplace, whose heaped-up logs gave out a warmth most welcome on that cold, penetrating day. This was the first time I had met this illustrious personage, the very embodiment of honour and duty. I found a certain amount of embarrassment in approaching him, determined as I was to defend with all my might the common cause in which were bound up the safety of Belgium and the fate of the Allied battle then in progress.

His response to my sentiments was not long in coming. Belgium was now but a shred of territory to which its government and its army were clinging. If they retreated another twelve miles, their country would be lost completely. The enemy would have it entirely in his power to dispose of as he wished ; the country might even disappear from the map of Europe. For was it sure that it could be given a new birth in the treaty of peace ?

The King recognised that the Belgian Army was much exhausted, but he believed that, at the call of their Commander-in-Chief, the troops would find new energy with which to defend what remained of their native soil. They could be counted upon to hang on to the Yser and thus give time to the Allied forces to come to their aid.

Ample proof of the soundness of this reasoning was soon to come. Fresh decisions were taken, new dispositions made, and the reorganized Belgian Army proceeded to defend the Yser from Nieuport to Dixmude and Boesinghe ; and it was there that the French troops found them when they came up in support.

On the day following this interview, the King visited all his Divisions. He reminded them that the Belgian Army was now disputing the last parcel of their country's land and that they must die rather than give way. He informed the Divisional Commanders that if any one of them retreated without a formal order, he would be relieved of his command on the spot.

Thanks to these dispositions it now seemed possible to check the invasion which was moving down the coast. To this end we would defend the Yser from the North Sea to Dixmude with the reconstituted Belgian Army ; hold the position of Dixmude with the Brigade of Marines ; and farther south, on the Yperlé and up to Ypres, we could use the French Territorial troops which were already there, and which I was rapidly reinforcing with cavalry divisions. This would enable us to await the arrival of the French reinforcements which the Commander-in-Chief had promised.

In pursuance of these ideas, before leaving Furnes on the evening of the 16th, I dispatched a hurried message to Admiral Ronarc'h defining his rôle at Dixmude :

" Under the present circumstances, any idea of manœuvring is out of the question and your tactics must be confined purely and simply to resisting on your actual positions.

" With this end in view, every possible means should be used for providing shelter and defences for your troops.

" As to the line of conduct to be pursued, your mission is to stop the enemy in his tracks and above all by fire action. In view of the strength of your forces and the means at your disposal, which enable you to occupy a wide extent of front, you should find no difficulty in holding your ground.

" Nothing short of a formal order from your superiors or the capture of the whole of your position by the enemy will justify you in evacuating your position.

" Needless to say that I count upon you absolutely to fulfil this mission."

Let me add here that the Admiral and his sailors performed their task in a most glorious manner.

Finally, in order to provide for every contingency, I caused the defences of Dunkirk to be supplemented by inundations which stretched for seven or eight miles in front of the town, thus forming an obstacle along the coast behind which fresh resistance could be organized, should the Belgian line be broken.

Such was the defensive system we were able to throw rapidly together for the purpose of stopping the enemy's march " *nach Calais*," and frustrate his new plan, which no longer aimed at Paris, but at the Channel ports. This outcome was due to the King's quick understanding and his determination, as he himself affirmed on the 16th of October, to consecrate his entire Army to the task.

The hesitations of some of his subordinates were in marked contrast to this resolute attitude of the King, for at the very moment when our decisions were being made at Furnes, Monsieur Augagneur, then Secretary of the Navy, while returning to Belgian Headquarters, which he had left the evening before, stopped at Doullens and asked my Chief of Staff, Colonel Weygand, to have billets prepared in the neighbourhood of Calais where the Belgian Army might be housed and re-formed. For, according to its leaders, there was nothing it could do but retire from the struggle.

I returned in the evening to my Headquarters at Doullens, seventy-five miles from Furnes. Here I wrote a report of the day's doings to the Commander-in-Chief :

" I have just come from Furnes, General Headquarters of the Belgian Army. On my way there this morning, I stopped at Saint-Omer, Headquarters of Sir John French, and I have asked him :

" (1) To urge his government to order a naval squadron to operate off the coast at Ostend against the German right.

" (2) To advance Rawlinson's corps from Ypres in the direction of Roulers, in order to divert the German attack from the Belgian Army.

" I then proceeded to Dunkirk and saw the Governor. He informed me, and I believe it, that the place is in a good state of defence. The fresh-water inundations have been effected and the salt-water ones are ready.

" Belgian refugees of every description are now being taken care of without difficulty. The same conditions obtain at Calais.

" I then went to Furnes. The Belgian Army is established along the line of the Yser. It has been ordered to reorganise there, and to defend itself with the utmost energy. The King and the Prime Minister seem determined to adopt these tactics and to see that they are carried out. . . .

" The British Army is continuing its advance on Courtrai. To-day it has again made some progress.

" P.S.—All the same, whenever you have some really reliable troops available to send to the left of the Belgian Army, it would be well from every point of view to do so."

My day's journey in Flanders had made it clear to me that although our left, resting on the sea, was comparatively secure, there was still an open space some fifteen miles wide stretching from Boesinghe to the Lys, held only by a few regiments of territorials, some cavalry, and scattered British troops in the vicinity of Ypres. Fortunately, on my arrival at Doullens, I heard from General Joffre that the British I Corps would complete detraining at Hazebrouck on the 19th. It would be followed by the Lahore Division, sent to the same region, then by the French 42nd Division, directed on Dunkirk, and finally by the French IX Corps, which would proceed to a point not yet determined. It was my task to make the best use possible of these reinforcements, see that they arrived under the protection of troops already in the Ypres area and then co-ordinate their action.

As the battle in Picardy and Artois became more and more stabilised, a new era of events opened north of the Lys. Here was to be found the only ground now left where the Germans could seek to outstrip us, surprise us in the midst of our preparations and crush us with the weight of their powerfully armed masses. It was their last chance of winning the battle on the Western Front, which so far had gone against them, and of carrying out their original plan of bringing the war to a victorious conclusion in the west before proceeding to end it in the east. It was to be anticipated that, if left unhampered in their movements, the Germans would put forth an exceptionally powerful effort; accordingly, we once more tried to forestall them by seizing the initiative ourselves. As it turned out, we did not succeed, but we broke their plan completely and definitely, and thereby inflicted upon them a serious repulse.

On October 17th, I went to the Headquarters of the

Tenth Army at Saint-Pol to settle various details and more especially to meet Mr. Lloyd George, British Chancellor of the Exchequer, who was making a tour of our front with his friend Lord Reading. This occasion was my first meeting with this statesman, destined later on to become one of the leading actors in the war. The first impression he gave was that of a man of rare vivacity and a most uncommon quickness of mind; this impression was strengthened and prolonged by the breadth of his views, the diversity of the subjects he discussed and the fertility of the solutions he advanced. The French officer charged with accompanying him had lost sight of him that morning during a halt at Montdidier. When he found him, he was standing in front of the statue of Parmentier, and, as the officer approached, he exclaimed: "There was what you would call a great man!"

Our talk at Saint-Pol naturally dealt with the situation of the Allied armies and the barrier to the invasion which we had established up to the Lys and which we were trying to extend to the sea. I told him that I had decided to dig the troops in and by that means hold fast against the enemy's superior armament until such time as we ourselves should become just as powerfully equipped; then we would take the offensive, for in no other way could victory be won. On many occasions since that day Mr. Lloyd George has reminded me of this conversation, which he dubbed "The Saint-Pol programme," and of which he saw the fulfilment.

It was under these conditions that one of the most important encounters of the war was to take place. The Allies were still seeking to profit by the initiative and the freedom of action which their victory on the Marne had given them, to forestall the enemy's offensive and attack him before he could exploit his success at Antwerp by adding the forces there liberated to powerful reserves coming from Germany, thus preparing a gigantic offensive on the only ground where it remained possible to decide the war on the Western Front by manœuvre.

The question I had to ask myself was this : Would we have time to assemble the scattered and heterogeneous forces of three Allied Powers in sufficient numbers and well enough organized to make a combined effort to block the enemy's plan and retain that direction of events to which our victory entitled us ? If we could not expect this much, could we not at least arrest the full development of his plans ? This question would be answered by the terrific encounter known as the Battle of Flanders.

It comprised two distinct periods :

(1) The attack along the coast, or the battle of the Yser ; October 17th to November 1st.

(2) The Battle of Ypres, the principal centre of communications of the Flanders region ; October 21st to November 12th.

CHAPTER II

THE BATTLE OF THE YSER

The theatre of operations—The first German attacks on the Belgian Army and the French Marines, October 18th to 23rd—Arrival of the 42nd Division—The crisis of October 24th—The forcing of the Yser—Reorganization along the railway—The inundations—Final failure of the Germans.

SINCE October 17th, the Belgian Army had been established behind the Yser, covering a front of some twenty miles between Nieuport and the north of Boesinghe; it had four Divisions in line, two others in reserve or in course of reorganization. Our Brigade of Marines was occupying Dixmude, on the right bank of the river in advance of the centre; a Territorial Brigade (177th) was on its right at Boesinghe. To the south of Dixmude and still farther advanced, the Belgian Cavalry Division and the French II Cavalry Corps were holding the northern and eastern exits of the Forest of Houthulst and reconnoitering in the direction of Roulers.

The theatre of operations consisted of low-lying country, in large part reclaimed from the sea. Passage everywhere was easy, there being no natural obstacles or high ground of any importance. From time immemorial the invasions from Central Europe westwards have passed across this country. It was the battlefield where the destinies of the Old World, down to the time of Waterloo, had been fought out. Once more it was to serve as the arena where the fate and future of civilization would be decided.

157

In the part that we now occupied, the Yser had small value as an obstacle, being narrow and sluggish, with very low banks. The tides reached up to and above Dixmude. The river flowed through a country almost entirely flat, being mostly reclaimed land whose elevation was below sea-level at high tide.

A foot or two beneath the surface one comes to water, so that it was most difficult to construct trenches or provide any shelter for troops. Nevertheless this ground had to be held under powerful artillery fire.

*   *   *   *

On October 18th the German advanced guards delivered attacks on the Belgian outpost positions along the Yser, and against the Marine Brigade at Dixmude. These efforts failed everywhere, except at Keyem, which fell into the enemy's hands.

On the 19th the attacks were renewed between Nieuport and Dixmude, with no greater success. The British monitors and French destroyers at my request were operating off Nieuport, and they considerably hampered the development of the hostile manœuvre. On the 20th, the enemy's attacks became particularly violent; they extended south to the region of Boesinghe. Again they failed everywhere. On the 21st, they met with no greater success. The Belgian Army, however, in order to hold its own, had been obliged to reduce its frontage by closing in its right on Saint-Jacques-Capelle. It had also been obliged to employ all its reserves. Fortunately the French 42nd Division, commanded by General Grossetti, now arrived in the vicinity of Furnes. Here were troops and a leader whose great qualities I had seen tested in the Battle of the Marne. This

Division helped to parry the violent blows which fell upon us during the following days.

On the 22nd, the Marines and the 89th Territorial Division, at and to the south of Dixmude, were subjected to an exceptionally heavy bombardment, while the Belgians, attacked in the vicinity of Schorbake, were forced to give up the Tervaëte bend, thus providing the enemy with a place of assembly on the left bank of the river. On the 23rd the Marines, the Belgians and the 42nd Division, conforming to the offensive movement undertaken farther south, moved out to the attack. The 42nd Division succeeded in advancing between Lombartzyde and Westende, but our efforts on the Yser were checked, and the enemy continued to pass troops across the river and assemble them in the Tervaëte bend.

*   *   *   *

On the 24th, while General Grossetti, retaining one Brigade to occupy Nieuport, attempted with the other to retake the Tervaëte bend, the enemy launched a violent attack along the whole line of the Yser, pushing forward at the same time on the Saint-Georges bridge and road.

The line of the Yser was now definitely forced and was being crossed on a front of more than three miles. Between Nieuport and Dixmude, the river as an obstacle no longer existed. The question was where and how the Belgian Army could halt in order to organize and offer fresh resistance. It was in the midst of these tragic circumstances that I hurried again to Furnes.

The violence of the assaults showed clearly the importance the Germans attached to obtaining a decisive success immediately. They employed a most powerful artillery, reinforced by the heavy guns which had been used before Antwerp and by a large number of trench mortars. The latter were easy to transport and place in position, and at short range their effect was equal to heavy guns. This bombardment was directed against troops who were precluded by the nature of the ground from finding shelter in trenches.

And now behind this line of guns a new hostile army, the Fourth, was making its appearance. It was composed of Army Corps of recent formation, still entirely intact, trained by two months of instruction and recruited chiefly from the youth of the universities.

They felt absolutely certain of victory, for the German spirit reigned supreme among them and they were supported by a most powerful equipment. How could it be possible for the remnants of the Belgian Army to halt these troops on their march to Calais, where the victory of Germany was to be proclaimed?

On arriving at Furnes I again saw the King, and then examined with the Belgian Staff the extremely serious situation facing their Army. The effect of the terrible experience it had been through was evinced in the announcement of its retirement. Now that the Yser had been forced, it was first of all essential to find an obstacle which could be opposed to the invasion; for the troops had come to the end of their tether. Their numbers were seriously reduced, and their armament was greatly inferior to that of the enemy. Nor did the ground offer any protection. Only one French Division remained available, the 42nd. The flood of attack might at any moment roll impetuously over us, unless we succeeded in collecting and regrouping behind some obstacle those remnants of the worn-out Belgian forces which were still capable of resistance.

Now, in the direction of Dunkirk, the map showed not even any high ground, woods or localities susceptible of being used as points of support, much less any line or river capable of being organized and defended. But a decision had to be made without delay if too large a retirement with decisive consequences was to be prevented, and my thoughts centred on the line of the railway between Nieuport and Dixmude. This railway offered at least a continuous line actually traced on the ground, and one which the troops in their retreat would have to cross and where they might be halted. It was therefore an easy base on which to rally and form a new line of battle.

A railway often runs through cuts or on embankments; even on level ground the ballast alone affords some shelter to a firing line. I therefore assumed that this road would give a little protection to the troops forming up behind it. Moreover, its extremities rested firmly upon Nieuport and Dixmude at either end and, therefore, it might present a defensive line of considerable value.

Such were the brief but vital reflections which I exchanged—without knowing much more about the matter—with the Belgian Staff, and by virtue of which it was decided that the Belgian Army would bring its retreat to an end on this line and take up a defensive position behind it. On the north at Nieuport, it would be strongly held by a Brigade of the 42nd Division ; in the centre, towards Pervyse, by the other Brigade of this Division ; and at Dixmude by the Brigade of Marines.

It turned out that the railway lines ran along an embankment from three and a half to four and a half feet above the level of the plain. Why should we not, then, try to flood the shores of the Yser here as we had successfully managed to do in the west around Dunkirk ? If this were done, the strip of ground one or two miles wide which lay between the river and the railway would be denied to the enemy, while the water would be checked at the embankment; the latter, moreover, would afford some protection for the troops. At all events, in the confusion which always accompanies a withdrawal under heavy fire, the most essential point is to have a continuous line traced on the ground. This furnishes a front upon which the troops can rally and reorganize, and the men respond willingly if the terrain is ever so little favourable. The railway rendered us this service and the inundations completed it.

And so, when I left Furnes on the evening of the 24th, it had been arranged with the Belgian Staff that the retreat would be stopped and a defensive position established along the railway line. It was also agreed with the Belgian Staff that, notwithstanding the serious damage which the sea water would cause to this beautifully cultivated country for a long time to come, the inundation would be effected.

As for General Grossetti, he sent me from his Command Post at Pervyse, the following unequivocal message: "I don't know how much will be left to-morrow of the 42nd Division, but so long as one man remains the Germans will not cross the railroad."

Once more, we were about to offer battle with exhausted troops. This time it was along the Nieuport-Dixmude line. It is true that its defence was greatly strengthened at the two extremities by the presence of French detachments, as well as by General Grossetti's force in the centre, at Pervyse. It was also soon to be protected by flooding the approaches. The keys to the inundations were the locks at Nieuport, and these we firmly held. But the question was, how long would it take the water to spread and what extent of ground would it cover? There was nothing in previous

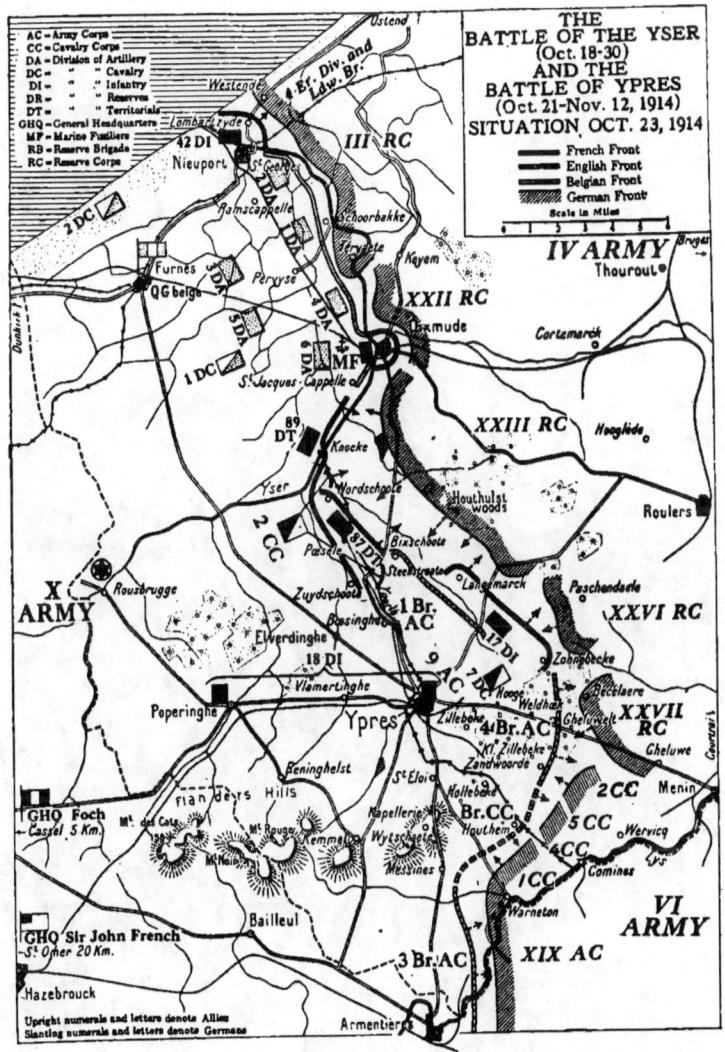

experience which could answer these questions, for the hydraulic system, which had been designed with the object of defending the country from the sea, was now about to be called upon to let that sea in upon the very ground it was devised to protect. Uncertainty on this point continued till the very end, with a corresponding effect upon the defence.

* * * *

On the 25th the Belgian Army was in line along the embankment. On the 26th the German bombardment was renewed with intense violence. It reached the railway and again spread anxiety among its defenders. However, they put much reliance upon the rising inundation. On the evening of the 25th the Belgian Staff informed Admiral Ronarc'h at Dixmude that all arrangements had been made " to flood the left bank of the Yser between the river and the line of the Dixmude-Nieuport railway." Special measures had to be taken to prevent the water from reaching our troops. The culverts passing under the track had to be damned and made water-tight, and the banks of certain canals had to be cut so as to let the sea-water in.

It was only on the evening of the 27th that all this work was finished. Then, at flood tide, the Nieuport locks were opened. They were shut again at low tide, and this manœuvre went on every day. On the 28th the water had reached the railway in the vicinity of Pervyse and spread southwards. This, however, did not stop the enemy's advance, nor cause him to modify his plan. Thus he delivered on the 29th a succession of violent attacks in the direction of Ramscapelle, but he did not succeed in entering the village. On the morning of the 30th, seeing that the water had gained his rear, he made a supreme effort, captured Ramscapelle and reached solid ground. If he could hold on to this place and succeed in debouching from it, the ground behind the inundations would lie open to him, the railway embankment and our whole system of defence would be turned. It was therefore necessary at all costs to recapture Ramscapelle. General Grossetti realized this immediately, and gave the necessary orders. The attack was carried out by Zouaves, Chasseurs-à-Pied and Senegalese, together with some Belgian units, and the village, before nightfall, was reoccupied.

On the following day, the 31st, the line of defence was completely reconstituted along the railway. The water in front of us continued to deepen and, except at a few points, the enemy retired beyond the Yser. The system of locks which controlled the inundations was at Nieuport, and we were in firm possession of this town. At the other end of the railway, at Dixmude, our Marines were putting up a stubborn resistance. From this moment on, that part of the left bank of the Yser, lying between these two places, was forbidden ground to the German Army. The route along the coast toward Dunkirk and Calais was closed.

The battle had lasted more than ten days. It had been characterized on the part of the Germans by an intensity of artillery fire of all calibres hitherto unheard of. Their infantry had shown itself full of enthusiasm. Leaving out of account his powerful artillery, the enemy had used in this attack the III Reserve Corps, XXII Reserve Corps, one Erzatz Division and one Landwehr Brigade.

The Belgian Army had put in its six Divisions; we had engaged our 42nd Division and our Brigade of Marines.

The German efforts had ended in complete failure.

CHAPTER III

THE BATTLE OF YPRES

Headquarters moved to Cassel—Formation of the French Eighth Army—The German Fourth Army makes its appearance ; Genesis of the Battle of Ypres—The Adversaries and the terrain—First phase of the battle, October 21st to 30th—The days of October 30th and 31st—The opening of November, the Dunkirk conference—Final German efforts against Ypres—The enemy settles down in his positions.

WHILE the invasion along the coast was thus being swamped in the mud of the Yser, a desperate struggle had already begun farther south, in the neighbourhood of Ypres and the Lys.

I moved my Headquarters on October 24th from Doullens to Cassel, that sentry-post of Flanders. Here I was nearer the front and also closer to British General Headquarters at Saint-Omer.

On the line of our Second Army, the German attack had been brought to a standstill ; but on our Tenth Army front, north of La Bassée, it had been renewed with vigour. However, on the left wing of the latter army, the British II and III Corps were engaged. The British I Corps, then in course of detraining at Hazebrouck joined them later, and also various troops which French General Headquarters was sending to Flanders by rail. As these Corps arrived they formed up under the protection of our Territorial Divisions, which had been pushed forward to Ypres on the 14th of October, and were later reinforced by the II Cavalry Corps. They were covered also by the British IV Corps (General Rawlinson), now reduced to the 7th Division and the

3rd Cavalry Division, which were returning from the Antwerp expedition.

On October 20th General d'Urbal, who had distinguished himself in command of a Corps at Arras, had been given command of the Army Detachment of Belgium, soon to be called the Eighth Army. He established his Headquarters at Roussbrughe, taking under his orders the French forces north of the Lys. Thus there came under my direction a new force whose action I had to co-ordinate as soon as possible with that of the other Allied troops arriving from different parts of the front.

By the fall of Antwerp, the adversary confronting us had gained complete liberty of action in Belgium. He had brought up important forces which as yet had suffered little loss, and he had formed a week before at Ghent an entirely new Army, the Fourth. In addition to this, he had created an Army Detachment (Fabek) at Lille.

It was with a view to facing the gateway of Ypres, and being nearer to British General Headquarters, that I had established myself at Cassel. Apart from affording splendid observation over the Flemish plain, Cassel was a point of junction of some most important roads. Our transports would soon be filling these to their utmost capacity, thereby transforming the peaceful little town into a scene of feverish activity.

* * * *

To understand the sequence of events which were to culminate at Ypres, it is necessary to go back to the middle of October. At that moment, all that was known of the enemy was that his XIX Corps was on the Lys between Armentières and Werwicq, while his III

GENERALS JOFFRE, FOCH, D'URBAL AND BALFOURIER INSPECTING TROOPS ON THE MARCH BEFORE THE FIRST BATTLE OF YPRES.

Reserve Corps and his 4th Erzatz Division were along the coast, engaged against the Belgian Army. Between the Lys and the country around Thourout stretched a region which was void of troops. This territory offered us conditions that were still favourable for the development of the movement then in course of evolution, namely the envelopment of the German right wing north of the Lys.

Accordingly, in the course of a meeting with Field-Marshal Sir John French at Anvin, on October 17th, it was decided to push the British forces up to the Lys at Menin and advance the four French Cavalry Divisions, supported by territorial infantry Divisions, from Ypres to Roulers. The British Corps made little progress; the French II Cavalry Corps pushed forward more boldly and, on the 18th, reached Roulers, Hooglede and Cortemark, only to be driven back on the 19th by very large forces. These turned out to be the XXII, XXIII, XXVI and XXVII Reserve Corps, all newly formed and just entering on the scene. They were advancing between Courtrai and Bruges in the direction of Ypres.

It was this important information that our cavalry gained by its reconnaissance towards Roulers. On October 20th a total of five and a half German corps (including the III Reserve Corps and the Erzatz Division which were operating on the lower Yser) were in the act of deploying between the Lys and the North Sea. Part of these forces, consisting of two and a half corps (III and XXII Reserve Corps and 4th Erzatz Division), attacked on the Nieuport—Dixmude front and took part up to the end of October in the Battle of the Yser, which, as has been seen, was brought to an end by the inundations. The other three Corps were preparing an attack on Ypres.

It can thus be seen that from this moment on, the German front stretched before us without break as far as the North Sea. Hence there could no longer be any question of our turning their right before we had pierced their front. The question was : Would we have the time, and did we possess the means of effecting a breakthrough before the enemy could complete defensive measures against which we would be more or less impotent ?

This was the effort we were about to make ; it was an attempt to exploit the last vestige of our victory on the Marne.

The idea dominating our tactics was that, in view of our feeble armament, notably in artillery and machine-guns, we were powerless to break through the front of an enemy who had had time to organize the ground, construct trenches and protect them with wire entanglements. Our plan, therefore, was to forestall him, assail him while he was in full manœuvre, assault him with troops full of dash before he could organize his defence and bring his powerful armament into play.

But our attacks undertaken with this idea encountered from the very start an offensive on the part of the enemy. His plan aimed at breaking through the Allied front at Ypres, the gateway to French Flanders and the starting point of many roads that lead from this region to the Channel ports. The clash of the two forces resulted in a shock of supreme violence and brutality as well as of amazing duration. The enemy was playing his last card and attempting his last manœuvre on the western theatre of operations.

In spite of a desperate struggle lasting more than a month, his efforts were destined to fail. No more success was to crown his march on Calais to crush

England, than attended his march on Paris to subdue France.

Not without reason this great battle has been called the Flanders mêlée. The diversity of the races, the intermingling of the various elements and units which took part in it, their arrival piecemeal upon the scene, all precluded up to the very last day any systematic direction of the struggle.

On their side, the Germans first sent against us intact bodies of troops, perfectly organized into new Army Corps and equipped with a formidable artillery. When, however, their initial efforts had been shattered, they drew on all their armies for divisions with which to feed the battle.

The nature of the ground was also the source of great confusion. Ypres is the centre of a rich, well-cultivated region, covered with comfortable houses, many surrounded by parks. From a military point of view, the terrain is enclosed and broken, consisting in its poorer parts of forests, while the low flat plain is cut up by fields bordered with high hedges that complete the obstruction of the view. In order to obtain an idea of the nature of the battlefield, I climbed the towers which surmounted the Cloth Hall of Ypres. In front of me stretched a sea of green, with little white islands marking the positions of the rich villages, with their fine churches and graceful steeples. To see open country in any direction was impossible. Three undulations slightly break the flatness of the plain; the first, north-west of Ypres, is from twelve to twenty-five feet high and about two and a half miles long; the second, from thirty to forty feet high, lies about six miles east of Ypres and runs from Passchendaele to Zandvorde, a length of some seven and a half miles; the third, and most accentuated, stretches to the south for about three miles, between Wyschaëte and Messines. The Yperlé canal, which joins the Yser to the Ypres-Comines canal, receives through a system of drainage canals (beekes and watergands), the surface waters of the region and makes communications, especially from west to east, very difficult.

As a protection from the water, the roads are paved and elevated; they are few in number and for the most part converge on Ypres.

Such a combination of circumstances resulted in offering a battlefield broken up into compartments with difficult communications and where all view is impossible. This necessarily entailed a parcelling out of the action, and slowed it down from the very start.

In order to comprehend the sequence of events, it is necessary to go back to what happened just after October 21st.

On that date, we assumed the offensive. The British I Corps,* supported on its left by our II Cavalry Corps, advanced on Roulers. The final objective assigned it by Field-Marshal Sir John French was Bruges. The British IV Corps advanced on Menin, while on its right the British III Corps† and the British Cavalry Corps were facing strong German forces from the Lys to the Ypres canal.

The British I Corps reached the line Langemark—Zonnebeke, but could make no further advance in the face of the German XXVI Reserve Corps. The other British Corps were heavily attacked by troops among which were identified four Cavalry Corps as well as the XXVII Reserve Corps. In this way the attention of the British Commander was drawn

* Lieutenant-General Sir Douglas Haig.
† Lieutenant-General Pulteney.

towards the Lys, and he requested that his I Corps might be relieved as soon as possible by French troops, so that he could move it from the direction of Roulers to a position astride the Menin road. In compliance with this request, I at once detailed the French IV Corps* to take over as it came up, from the British I Corps. The relief of the British troops under these conditions presented serious difficulties, the least of which was a slowing down of the action already begun. However it resulted in this advantage, that in a short time, each Allied Army had its own separate zone of action ; the British from La Bassée canal to the Ypres road at Menin ; the French from this road to Dixmude, the Belgian from Dixmude to the sea.

It was impossible for us to resume the offensive until the 25th. We were fighting along an immense semicircle, thirty miles in circumference, which jutted out to the east into a salient twelve miles deep. The forces we had at our disposal were unfortunately too small. All the British troops had arrived and the French reinforcements were coming up slowly. Consequently, our flanks were protected only by troops (mainly cavalry) extended over considerable distances.

The British I Corps did not succeed in breaking the German resistance in front of Becelaëre, and the French IX Corps, engaged against a reinforced and active adversary, advanced only with the greatest difficulty, making small headway towards Passchendaële.

Beginning with October 26th, the fighting became more and more desperate along the whole front. At several points the enemy had already erected barbed-wire defences. During the three following days the

* General Dubois.

battle reached its culminating point of violence. Imbued with the same offensive spirit, the two adversaries, night and day, hurled themselves unceasingly against one another in a succession of attacks and counter-attacks that produced no appreciable result. The German heavy artillery increased in numbers every day, and, through lack of suitable guns, we were unable to reply to it very effectively. On the other hand, the Germans were constantly held in check by the well-directed barrage fire of our 75's, though here we had to husband our ammunition. We had very little.

To sum up, after five days of continuous attacks, the Allied troops found their efforts nullified by an equal determination on the part of the enemy. The shock had been brutal but barren; the opposing forces were equally balanced. A break-through on our part could be effected only by bringing into play new and more powerful means of action.

The inundations along the Yser, which had put a stop to the fighting below Dixmude, now enabled us to throw the French XXXII Corps* into the battle of Ypres, while the French XVI Corps,† which was detraining, would soon arrive. But these reinforcements, however precious, were small in comparison with those which the Germans were concentrating on the Lys. These began to make themselves felt by the 30th on the British front, while those brought from the lower Yser, when the battle ended there, were directed against the French. This ever-increasing effort of the enemy had to be met with all our energy if we were to block his march on Ypres, Dunkirk and Calais.

Our offensive being now definitely arrested, we had to confine ourselves to consolidating the positions we had

* General Humbert. † General Taverna.

won. In the low ground around Ypres, however, the nearness of the water to the surface prevented trenches from being dug. Moreover, ever since the retreat from Charleroi a great number of our troops were without entrenching tools. The organization of a continuous line of defence, therefore, was out of the question, all the more so as its length alone would require more men than we had available. Finally, a merely passive resistance on our part would indicate to the enemy that we were abandoning the fight, and would be an acknowledgment of weakness that could only stimulate him to redouble his efforts. Our only recourse, therefore, was to maintain an offensive attitude and to defend ourselves by attacking. Profiting by the broken nature of the country, we could contest with repeated counter-attacks, all the enemy's gains, and by the rapid movement of reserves from the centre to the circumference of our semi-circular position, we could parry his efforts and minimize his advantages.

Nevertheless, we could not contemplate the future with anything but grave anxiety, for the poverty of our means and the duration of the battle might end by wearing out our troops' power of resistance and triumph over all our energy.

It was amidst this threatening outlook that the British made an examination into the possibility of organizing Boulogne for receiving a garrison of 100,000 men, in spite of the danger to French susceptibilities involved in such a solid installation.

The day of October 30th passed without serious incident for our IX and XXXII Corps, and our II Cavalry Corps, holding the northern face of the Ypres salient. On the southern face, however, the Germans launched a powerful attack on the right of the British I

Corps and on the left of the British Cavalry Corps, executed by their XV Corps, 48th Reserve and 26th Infantry Division, debouching from the Lys between Menin and Warneton.

Following upon an exceptionally heavy bombardment, the British Cavalry (2nd and 3rd Divisions), greatly exhausted and without any Infantry support, was thrown back from Zanworde and Hollebeke on Klein-Zillebeke and Saint-Eloi, two miles from Ypres. At the same time, the British 1st Cavalry Division lost a portion of Messines. The result was that the enemy's access to Ypres from the south-east was greatly facilitated, while at the same time this important centre of communication between the Allied Armies was brought within range of the German guns. Fortunately the G.O.C. the French IX Corps appreciated the seriousness of the situation thus created, and came at once to the aid of his neighbour. All his available forces, three infantry battalions, were directed upon Zillebeke, where they arrived in time to give their support that night to the British front.

Towards the end of the afternoon a first report of these events was brought to my Headquarters at Cassel by Captain Bertier de Sauvigny, liaison officer attached to Sir John French; but it was impossible for me to estimate their full significance. Generally speaking, during a modern battle where nothing is clearly seen, especially in an enclosed country, the results obtained are learned only through reports which show what localities are held by the troops at the end of the day. But when the line has been pierced, or even merely thrown back, these reports come in slowly and are not clear and definite, since the touch between units in the field has been weakened. In fact, it is precisely when the situation is gravest that a commander gets the least information from the front and runs the greatest risk of having no time in which to make dispositions to repair the harm.

I was awaiting the report of one of my staff officers, Captain Requin, whom I had sent up in the morning to get information on the spot. About 10 P.M. he informed me that there was certainly a gap in the British cavalry front, which they could not fill for want of men. If this breach was not rapidly closed, the road to Ypres would be open. I at once telephoned to British General Headquarters at Saint-Omer to ask if they had any fuller information regarding the situation at the end of the day, especially in the direction of Hollebeke and Saint-Eloi. Upon receiving the reply that nothing more definite was known, I telephoned that I was leaving at once for Saint-Omer to see Sir John French.

It was not far from midnight. If we waited any longer we ran the risk of seeing the enemy push through the gap the following morning, or at all events establish himself firmly a short distance from Ypres. This would prevent any movement through the town, and bring about a retreat under the fire of enemy guns of all our troops fighting east of the town ; that is to say, of the greatest portion of the army. This would amount almost to a complete disaster.

Arriving at Saint-Omer at 12.30 A.M., I saw my friend General Wilson, and had Sir John French awakened.

We studied the situation together. The British had no forces available for filling the gap. So far as I was concerned, I would have, on the morning of the 31st, eight battalions of the XVI Corps detrained at Alverdinghe, some of which had already arrived. I suggested to the Field-Marshal that I should send them without delay to close the breach in the British line, but there was not a moment to lose if the move was to be carried out before daylight.

Sir John expressed his gratitude in the warmest terms. On my return to Cassel at 2 A.M. I ordered the battalions of the 32nd Division which were being assembled at Elverdinghe to be dispatched by motor transport to Saint-Eloi as soon as they arrived. Here they would attack in touch with the British troops. In this way we repaired the effects of a surprise which might have had most serious results.

We were not, however, at the end of our troubles. At dawn on the 31st, the fighting was renewed along the whole front with the same violence as on the day before. Nothing of special importance happened on the northern face of the Ypres salient, held by the French corps, but a serious situation arose on the south face held by the British Army. The enemy had been reinforced here by a new corps, the II Bavarian, which, stimulated by success on the previous day, multiplied its attack from Gheluvelt to Messines.

The British 1st Division, in spite of a gallant resistance, was unable to hold Gheluvelt, which fell into the hands of the Germans. The British line was broken, and in the middle of the afternoon flowed back upon the woods between Vedhoek and Hooge.

The Château d'Hooge was heavily bombarded, and the General Officers Commanding the British 1st and 2nd Divisions, together with several officers of the staffs, were killed or wounded. The situation was critical. British Headquarters considered it to be of such gravity that it contemplated a retreat of the whole of the British I Corps. Such a decision would be the acknowledgment and the beginning of a defeat which might easily turn into a disaster, on account of the fact that the troops on the northern face of the salient would be in great part cut off from their communications. A providential piece of luck enabled us to forestall this disaster.

At the time when the British retreat started, I was in the Vlamertinghe Town Hall. General d'Urbal, the Army commander, and General Dubois, commanding the IX Corps, were with me. Here I was informed by Major Jamet, French liaison officer attached to General Haig, commanding the British I Corps, of the serious events which had taken place on the British front. At that moment (between 3 P.M. and 4.0 P.M.) Field-Marshal Sir J. French happened to arrive at Vlamertinghe, having just left his I Corps at the Château d'Hooge. Learning that I was in the Town Hall, he came to see me there. We at once discussed the situation and the proposed decision to retreat, which was on the point of being executed. The Field-Marshal painted a particularly black picture of the state of the I Corps. The troops were in full retreat towards Ypres, the heavy artillery was retiring at the trot towards the west, the roads were blocked by ammunition wagons and vehicles of every description, as well as by crowds of wounded streaming back towards Ypres. It was the beginning of a defeat. With troops as exhausted as these men were, and who could not be collected and reformed, the British line was definitely broken. If they were asked to continue the battle, Sir John French said, there was nothing left for him to do but go up and get killed with the British I Corps.

Without in any way under-estimating the gravity of the crisis which the British I Corps was facing, I had to consider above all else the critical situation which its retreat would entail for the Allied Armies fighting around Ypres, and indeed for the Allied cause itself. In face of the tremendous assault which all were sustaining, any voluntary withdrawal at any point would bring in its wake a great converging flood of attacks which we would be utterly unable to stem.

In rear of our front line nature offered no obstacle. For want of time we had not been able to organize a position to which we might withdraw. Under these conditions, a retreat carried out in full daylight by our comparatively weak effectives over open stretches of ground, wide indeed but cut up by battle, would be rapidly converted into a rout. Crippled and disorganized, we would be thrown back on the Flemish plain and rapidly swept to the coast. Moreover, it was only the British I Corps that was in retreat; our other troops were standing firm. The French IX Corps could furnish some help with its reserves, and more French reinforcements were due to arrive the following day. I therefore asked that for the moment the British I Corps be ordered to hold on at all costs, and I undertook to mount an attack as quickly as possible with the purpose of extricating it from the enemy's embrace.

While I was formulating these ideas in my mind, I wrote out on a piece of paper the general principles they involved. I did this as much to aid in fixing my own ideas as to furnish them in definite and precise form to my interlocutor. I there and then handed this informal scrawl to Sir John French. It read as follows:

"It is absolutely essential *not to retreat*; therefore the men must dig in wherever they find themselves and hold on to the ground they now occupy.

"This does not preclude organizing a position further in rear which could join up at Zonnebeke with our IX Corps.

"But any movement to the rear carried out by any considerable body of troops would lead to an assault on the part of the enemy and bring certain confusion among the troops. Such an idea must be utterly rejected.

"It seems particularly necessary that the 2nd British Division maintain itself in the vicinity of Zonnebeke, keeping in touch with the French IX Corps.

"The lateness of the day makes this organization feasible. It is useless to fall back, dangerous to do so in broad daylight."

The Field-Marshal had the good sense and straightforwardness to take the paper I handed him. He added on the back in his own hand a few words to the effect that he concurred entirely in my views. He then sent it by Major Barry, his A.D.C., accompanied by his private secretary, Fitzgerald, to General Haig for execution.

All movements in retreat of the British I Corps were countermanded and the battle was continued on the ground then held, without any retirement. And the valour of the British troops proved itself equal to this capital decision.

By evening the English line was once more established. The British I Corps, so seriously battered that day, was to be still more tried on the days following. But it never gave up the positions it had defended at the price of tremendous losses, and on November 15th, when the battle had been completely and happily ended, this Corps had every right to feel that its heroism had ensured to Great Britain results of the first importance.

On each side of the Ypres canal the rapid intervention of French troops during the day of the 31st re-established the situation, relieving the pressure on the right of Haig's Corps and the left of Allenby's cavalry.

Immediately north of the canal, General Moussy, who had made up a detachment from the French IX Corps and troops that had been coming up successively since the previous day to Zillebeke, launched an attack, in accordance with the orders he had received, on Hollebeke park and château.

After advancing a few hundred yards he encountered a powerful enemy offensive which stopped him dead. Any further advance was impossible; but he held gallantly on to his position, in spite of a heavy bombardment and very serious losses.

On the southern banks of the canal, the leading troops of the XVI Corps, preceded by cavalry, attacked under the orders of Colonel de Woillemont in the direction of Houthem. They soon encountered the 26th German Division which was advancing on Saint-Eloi, and like General Moussy's detachment, the most they could do was to hold their ground. This they did, beating off several assaults of the enemy. Further to the right, General Allenby's Cavalry Corps, which had been driven out of Messines in the morning, reoccupied that point of support in the evening.

To sum up, October 31st was characterized by a desperate and bloody struggle. The retreat of the British I Corps towards Gheluvelt marked the crisis. But in spite of all, we had succeeded in arresting every one of the enemy's efforts. Nevertheless they were to be redoubled during the next few days.

In order to thwart these efforts and relieve the pressure on the British I Corps, I directed General d'Urbal to make two attacks on November 1st, one on each flank of that Corps. They were to make an effort to outflank and envelop the German troops engaged in a frontal attack against the I Corps.

On my return in the evening to my Headquarters at Cassel, I drew up the following instructions which summarized this decision. These I sent to General d'Urbal and to British Headquarters :

"The British I Corps and General Rawlinson's Division should hold and consolidate the position from the right of the French IX Corps up to Klein-Zillibeke.

"On its left the French IX Corps will launch an attack in the general direction of Becelaëre and to the east.

"The French troops under the command of General d'Urbal will attack from the line Saint-Eloi—Wystchaëte on Hollebeke.

"Further French reinforcements will arrive in the course of the morning.

"The Battalions of the IX Corps which have been placed at the disposition of Lieut.-General Sir Douglas Haig should either be launched to the attack or restored to General d'Urbal."

This last paragraph emphasized once again the settled view of the French High Command that reinforcements sent to any threatened point were not to be used to feed the line of battle, but, on the contrary, their arrival should always be the signal for an offensive movement—this being the only way of producing any serious effect on the enemy.

The fighting was renewed at daybreak on November 1st and continued all day with the utmost violence. The crisis on our front reached its height on the Menin road and also towards Messines. The French troops on the northern face of the Ypres Salient continued their efforts to advance, but without success. The British I Corps held its position with difficulty, but repulsed all of the enemy's assaults; two Battalions of Zouaves from the French 42nd Division were sent to reinforce it.

The same failure attended the attacks of our IX Corps and of General Moussy's detachment at the two extremities of the British I Corps.

The Germans continued to direct heavy attacks on General Allenby's Cavalry Corps, which, for want of infantry support, was forced to abandon the strong point constituted by Messines. Troops of our 32nd Division, however, came up in time to check the enemy's attack on this side and enabled the British line to be re-established.

News of these events was brought to me in rapid succession during the early afternoon at Vlamertinghe. I immediately asked to see Sir John French, who was at his Command Post at Bailleul. He hastened to Vlamertinghe, and I once more urged upon him the necessity of maintaining the British positions at all costs, making use once more of the arguments I had employed the day before.

Sir John, however, continued to manifest great anxiety, pointing out the extreme fatigue of his troops. In order to restore the situation in the direction of Messines, I ordered the French Cavalry Corps to move to the south-west of Poperinghe, and to send with the utmost speed its nearest troops to reinforce General Allenby.

November 1st had been a particularly hard day, and it was not to be the last. The Germans had done everything possible to make it decisive, using various means to stimulate the morale of their troops. The Duke of Wurtemberg, commanding the Fourth Army, Prince Rupprecht of Bavaria, commanding the Sixth, and General von Deimling, commanding the XV Corps, all issued appeals to the men containing significant phrases

FIELD-MARSHAL SIR JOHN FRENCH, GENERAL FOCH AND GENERAL WILSON AT THE CHATEAU DE BRYAS, MAY 22ND, 1915.

JOFFRE AND FOCH AT AN INSTRUCTION CAMP BEHIND THE FRENCH FRONT.

such as : " The break-through at Ypres will have an importance which cannot be over-estimated."

The entrance of the Kaiser into Ypres was fixed for that day. He had arrived at Menin during the morning, coming from Thielt, and was due at Gheluvelt at 3 P.M.

The German soldiers fought furiously, never pausing to count their losses ; but the resistance of the Allied troops once more destroyed Germany's hopes.

Meanwhile, at 4 P.M., I had been summoned to Dunkirk to receive the President of the Republic and a number of political notabilities. They left Paris believing that the battle was nearly over and that our victory was assured. We were still far from that.

I was delayed by the incidents of the fighting and could not reach Dunkirk until about 6.30 P.M. ; but my Chief of Staff, Colonel Weygand, went there at 4 o'clock and explained the reasons of my absence.

With the President were M. Millerand, Minister of War, General Joffre, Monsieur Ribot, Minister of Finances, Lord Kitchener, Secretary of State for War and Monsieur Paul Cambon, the French Ambassador to Great Britain. The two last mentioned had just crossed the Channel.

The counter effects of the hard knocks we had received during the last few days had already been felt in England. Lord Kitchener, in particular, was very anxious. He accosted me with the words : " Well, so we are beaten !" I answered that we were not, and that I greatly hoped we would not be. I then related in detail the events of the last three days, which had brought such heavy losses to the Allied Armies. In finishing I asked him to send us reinforcements as soon as possible. On that first day of November, 1914, when each day seemed as long as a month, Lord Kitchener replied as follows :

"On July 1st, 1915, you will have one million trained English soldiers in France. Before that date you will get none, or practically none."

"We do not ask so many, but we would like to have them sooner—indeed at once," we all cried as if in preconcerted union.

"Before that date, do not count on anything," was all he vouchsafed in reply.

There was nothing, then, for us to do but to look forward to getting along through many a trying day as best we could without any further help.

During my conversation with Lord Kitchener I was struck by the accuracy of his conceptions in what concerned the war, which he already saw would last a very long time. Indeed, it was his conviction of that fact which had led this eminent organizer as early as September, immediately after the Marne, to begin to raise very considerable armies throughout the British Empire.

After finishing my report of events then in progress, and now feeling fully informed as to what reinforcements we could count upon, I took hasty leave of the President of the Republic and his entourage and returned to my Headquarters at Cassel. Here I could learn definitely what had happened during the day, and take the necessary decisions for the morrow.

* * * * *

After a night disturbed by bombardment and continuous rifle-fire, the struggle along the whole front was renewed on November 2nd.

On the northern face, nothing of importance happened : but south of the railroad from Ypres to Roulers, the Germans, now reinforced by a new Division, made desperate assaults at several places. In the vicinity of the railway line, towards Zonnebeke, they were stopped by a Brigade of the French 6th Cavalry Division and troops belonging to the French 18th Infantry Division. Further south they succeeded in driving back the British line east and south of Veldhoek to such an extent that the road to Ypres once more lay open. But this danger was averted by General Vidal, who launched all the available troops of the XVI Corps on Veldhoek, and thus halted the enemy's advance in that direction.

Meanwhile the situation south of the canal had become critical. Here a detachment under Colonel Olleris, which had been subjected to severe attacks since dawn, gave way and was thrown back as far as Saint-Eloi.

To extricate it, General Moussy's detachment tried in vain to debouch south of the canal, but could not succeed in developing its action. The situation remained exceedingly serious up to 5 P.M., when our artillery got the upper hand, mowed down the ranks of the enemy and stopped him in his tracks.

November 2nd was one more day of bloody and desperate fighting. The prompt action of our detachments interspersed along the front had prevented the enemy from reaping the fruits of his general assault, which in certain places had been unusually violent.

The exhaustion of the troops now began to reach its limit. This was especially the case with the British I Corps. Composed of three Divisions, it no longer could muster more than 9,000 rifles in the line. Everybody was praying for some respite in the tension, and fortunately there seemed good reason for believing that this day of November 2nd would mark the end of the assaults, at least on the British front. The persistent breaking up of their attacks during the last few days and the heavy losses they had suffered could not have failed to cripple the enemy forces.

During the early morning of the 2nd, the President of the Republic, accompanied by General Joffre and Monsieur Millerand, came to see me at my Headquarters at Cassel. He had just left the King of the Belgians at Furnes. The restricted hospitality which I was able to offer these distinguished guests at the Hotel du Sauvage, while doubtless giving evidence of the hard time through which we were passing, was nevertheless marked by the imprint of the confidence we felt, and above all of our determination to oppose the invasion with the utmost vigour and definitely arrest it.

The night of the 2nd–3rd passed in comparative quiet. On the 3rd, the Germans, feeling themselves reduced to impotence, opened a methodical bombardment upon Ypres, which was their habitual practice under such circumstances. For the rest, they undertook only partial attacks, with no result. On the 4th, the same proceeding.

It could now be said that their converging assault upon Ypres had failed. In spite of the troops and munitions they had massed, their efforts had broken against the stone wall which the Allied soldiers, though far inferior in numbers, had everywhere reared before them. The effort could be continued no longer, and the German General Staff found itself obliged to restrict the scope of its ambitions.

The enemy had found it impossible by mass attacks to overthrow along its whole length the barrier presented by the Allied Armies, seize the important centre of Ypres, and thus open a road to the coast. He therefore now proceeded to attempt to force the Salient, which was the form this barrier offered, by attacking its two pivots, the one to the north and the one to the south of Ypres.

The strategic success he had sought had eluded him, but he might at least terminate his adventure in Flanders by a tactical success which would consolidate his situation on the Western Front and thus leave him free to turn against Russia.

He could even achieve this result without capturing Ypres, since a pronounced advance at the two ends of the salient would enable him to move his artillery so close to the north and south faces as to interfere with our communications converging on that place, and force the withdrawal of our troops from the semi-circle. It was in this way that, following the violent struggle to the east of the town, the two opponents were once more about to join battle north and south of it.

Commencing on the 5th, the enemy, reinforced by a new Division, launched heavy attacks south of the Wyschaëte region, at the same time that we were advancing towards Messines. On the north, he successfully brought the III Reserve Corps into action against Bixschoote and Langemark. Everywhere else he remained inactive.

These assaults were continued on November 6th with the utmost violence. To the south they were concentrated upon the two banks of the Ypres canal and brought about a somewhat dangerous situation ; to the north, on the Bixschoote—Langemark front, they failed, with appalling losses to the enemy. These were costly days for the youth of Germany.

The battle was renewed with fury on the 7th, especially to the south, where the crisis became acute in the vicinity of the canal. We lost Klein-Zillibeke, and the situation was not restored until the 8th, when we drove the enemy back to the Ypres—Comines railway. The 9th passed without anything important happening; but the struggle was resumed in all its violence on the 10th, when the efforts of the enemy were directed mainly to the north of Ypres.

Definitely immobilized from Nieuport to Dixmude by the inundations, he was free to concentrate considerable forces on the lower Yser. These he engaged on ground which was still passable, at and below Dixmude. Beginning early in the morning, he launched a vigorous offensive along the whole front of the Yser, his plan evidently being to effect a crossing of the river. The main effort was directed on Dixmude and Steenstraate.

Our Marines here were forced back from Dixmude and obliged to withdraw to the left bank of the Yser, where they occupied a position which had been previously prepared. Part of our XXXII Corps was also driven to the other side of the river. We thus lost our points of egress to the right bank, and the neck of the bottle which Ypres presented became that much narrower.

What was more serious still, the enemy succeeded in crossing the Yser at Poesele and pushed some parties over to the left bank of the river. This constituted an extremely grave menace. We only succeeded in countering it and forcing him back to the right bank, by bringing into action the newly arrived troops of the XX Corps.*

On the 11th, however, the Germans, in pursuance of their plan, began to attack us heavily in the south. The bombardment of Ypres redoubled in violence during the night and was continued the following morning. The action now developed with fresh troops (amongst which was a Guards Division) all the way from La Kapellerie

* General Balfourier.

to Velehoek. At the same time, on the north they, attempted to extend their gains on the left bank of the Yser. Another day of violent battle ensued, but in spite of all his efforts the enemy was unable to record any important success. He was held along the whole front and, at certain points, even obliged to give ground.

On the 12th, the struggle continued without any results being obtained. On the 13th, there was no fighting except in the direction of Zonnebeke. This last effort marked the end of the series of violent combats in front of Ypres. There was still some fairly brisk fighting to come, but it was a matter of local actions only.

On the 13th the Battle of Ypres was over. The German attempts to smash the Salient by attacking its northern and southern pivots brought about two important battles which lasted several days. Neither accomplished any result. On November 18th, the situation of both armies became stabilized.

* * * * *

As soon as the battle ceased, we took advantage of the respite offered to reform the larger units and rest the men. This was greatly facilitated by the arrival of reinforcements sent by the Commander-in-Chief.

Most of our troops had come to the end of their tether and their relief was absolutely necessary. I now commenced negotiations with Field-Marshal Sir John French, with a view to a division of the front and its distribution among the Allied forces. After several days of close discussion, for both Armies were greatly exhausted, we reached an agreement as to the zones to be held by each.

On November 20th, the fronts held by the Allies in

the north of France were defined as follows :

(1) Behind the flooded Yser, the Belgian Army, flanked on the right by the 89th Territorial Division and on the left by the 81st Territorial Division, both of which Divisions had been reinforced by some regular troops.

(2) On the circumference of the Ypres Salient, from Knocke to Wyschaëte, the French Eighth Army, comprising, from north to south, the XXXII, XX, IX and XVI Corps, with troops amounting to a Division and a half in reserve.

In addition to these troops, I kept the Brigade of Marines, the 87th Territorial Division and the I and II Cavalry Corps under my own orders.

(3) From Wyschaëte to Festubert, the British Army. It had in the front line, from left to right, the II, III, IV and Indian Corps. The I Corps and Cavalry Corps were in reserve.

In the meantime, the organization of second line defensive positions had been actively pushed forward in the whole Ypres sector.

As we were still in doubt as to the enemy's situation, we carried out frequent air and cavalry reconnaissances, in order to discover whether he was making any movement in retreat. I also asked the naval authorities at Dunkirk to determine the positions of the German batteries on the coast north of Nieuport.

From these reconnaissances it appeared that the enemy trenches were strongly held. Rifle and gun fire abounded. The naval reconnaissance could not venture into the minefields which had been sown against submarines off the Belgian roadsteads.

On the whole, the enemy appeared to be solidly consolidating his positions.

CHAPTER IV

THE EVENTS ON THE REMAINDER OF THE FRONT OF THE ARMIES IN THE NORTH

(*From October 17th to November 20th*)

The fighting in front of the British II and III Corps, October 17th to November 9th—The struggle around Arras—The attack by the French Second Army—The Franco-Belgian offensive at Nieuport, November 7th to 12th.

THE fighting had not been confined to the battles in Flanders and around Ypres; it extended at the same time to the other parts of the front of the armies in the north. These actions included:

(1) Fighting on the British II and III Corps fronts from October 17th to November 9th.

(2) Fighting around Arras during the same period.

(3) An attack undertaken farther south by the French Second Army on October 8th and 30th.

(4) A Franco-Belgian offensive in front of Nieuport, from November 7th to 12th.

(1) *Fighting on the British II and III Corps fronts from October 17th to November 9th.*

Pursuing their offensive as originally planned, the British II and III Corps, in conjunction with Conneau's Cavalry Corps, had continued to attack between Givenchy and Messines from October 17th to 20th. The III Corps took Armentières, but the II failed at La Bassée.

Beginning with the 21st, the enemy, now reinforced, passed in his turn to the offensive. As the result of several days fighting he slightly forced back the French Cavalry Corps, and then, launching a heavy attack against the British, he drove them from their lines between Givenchy and Neuve-Chapelle, which he carried by assault. Everywhere else the Allied front held firm. He made a final attempt on November 2nd, in the vicinity of Neuve-Chapelle; but here the French XXI Corps came to the support of the British II Corps and stopped his advance. After this he gave up all further attempts south of the Lys, in order to concentrate his efforts north of that river, where he would be in closer touch with the operations going on against Ypres. This brought on heavy fighting near the eastern edge of the Ploegstreert Wood, on November 7th and 8th, but without any result being obtained.

(2) *Fighting around Arras (October 17th to November 9th).*
Meanwhile the struggle was continuing on the Arras—La Bassée front. In an effort to improve its positions, the French Tenth Army tried to capture several supporting points, such as Carency, Ablain-Saint-Nazaire, and Vermelles, where the enemy was solidly installed. These attacks continued during the second fortnight in October, without bringing any appreciable change in the situation.

On their side, the Germans concentrated their efforts more especially against the two wings of the Tenth Army, aiming in the south at the Ypres Salient near Saint-Laurent, and in the north endeavouring to advance along the Bassée Canal. After repeated and stubborn fighting which lasted from October 22nd until the beginning of November, they finally succeeded in capturing Saint-

Laurent, without being able, however, to extend their success.

The struggle then slowly died out on both sides, and from November 9th onwards the Artois front was the scene of no important event.

(3) *The attacks by the French Second Army (October 28th to 30th).*

Complying with the Commander-in-Chief's instructions, which prescribed offensives on various parts of the front with the idea of breaking through the enemy's lines, the Second Army, on October 28th, essayed attacks north and south of the Somme ; but very little ground was gained. By November 3rd these efforts had died out on both sides. On November 4th, the Second Army, by order of the Commander-in-Chief, passed from my control.

(4) *The Allied offensive in front of Nieuport (November 7th to 12th).*

As has been previously explained, the flooding of the Yser valley during the last few days of October had forced the Germans to withdraw to the right bank of the river, leaving on the left bank only some advanced posts in isolated farms. The roads being above water-level, access to these farms was still possible. On the other hand, as the inundations only extended a little way south of Nieuport, a slice of free ground remained between that town and the mouth of the Yser. The Belgians had even organized a strong bridgehead in front of Nieuport on the right bank of the river.

I decided to take advantage of this situation to deliver an attack against the German extreme right. This operation, apart from conforming to the Commander-in-Chief's intentions, was calculated to have a favourable effect on the battle being fought in front of Ypres. The Germans had withdrawn their best units from the Yser front and, under these conditions, we could very well make the attempt, even with troops still incompletely reorganized.

At a meeting at Cassel, on November 6th, with General Willemans, Chief of Staff of the Belgian Army, I drew up the details of the operation. It comprised an attack by the 81st Territorial Division debouching from Nieuport and moving on the line Lombartzyde—Westende, and an action by the Belgian Army, supported by the French heavy artillery, which aimed at driving the enemy detachments from the left bank of the Yser.

The operation was carried out between November 7th and 11th, but it was impossible to make any appreciable advance. The enemy brought into this fight a Marine Division which had recently detrained at Ostend. On the 12th the action was broken off.

It can be seen that while the struggle reached its height around Ypres, it was extended and maintained, with varying energy, it is true, on a front of more than ninety miles, reaching from Nieuport to Roye. This wide extension obliged us at first to put all our available forces into the trenches, thus leaving us without any reserves. We were constantly threatened, therefore, with the danger of having no troops except those in the line with which to oppose any effort at penetration which the enemy might make along this immense battle front.

CHAPTER V

A GENERAL SURVEY OF THE BATTLE OF FLANDERS

The essence of the Allied action was based on co-operation and activity—The professional value of the troops—The opposing forces—The results obtained—The strength of the defensive; the importance of matériel—Programme for the future—Visit of Lord Roberts; his death—Visit of King George — Exercising command in a coalition.

THE Allied operations in Flanders lasted a long time, covered a wide extent of territory, were carried on by a heterogeneous collection of troops, insufficient in number, always slow in arriving and rapidly intermingled. Under conditions as complicated as these, success would have been impossible without a unity of direction that enabled this confused and difficult battle to be seen in its general outlines with the real situation clearly in view. To this factor should be added the services rendered by a most efficient liaison between the allied combatants, as well as between the commanders of the units, which was only another manifestation of that spirit of co-operation and comradeship in arms which was long to constitute a bond of friendship between the Allied nations.

The Allied Commanders-in-Chief frequently saw each other in the course of the day. Each evening about eight o'clock, I sent for General d'Urbal, whose Headquarters were at Rousbrugge, to come to Wormoudt so as to discuss our affairs and prepare the orders for the following day. Then, about ten o'clock, Sir Henry Wilson usually arrived at my Headquarters at Cassel, bringing me news from British General Headquarters at

Saint-Omer and reports as to Sir John French's intentions for the following day. We also maintained a close co-ordination with Belgian Headquarters, which remained at Furnes.

Probably never before had the motto of our Belgian Allies, *L'Union fait la Force*, found a more happy and complete application than in this wholehearted co-operation. What a union of wills, each aiding and inspiring the other and all giving without stint, did this battle in common bring about! Here, without any doubt, is to be found the explanation of that marvellous improvised defence which resisted formidable attacks, powerfully mounted and doggedly repeated for nearly a month, and saw them to a triumphant conclusion.

I had, of course, remained in close touch with my Commander-in-Chief. Although I had not seen him since November 2nd, we had exchanged views daily. While he never failed to recognize the importance of the operations in Flanders, he was not able to give us all the forces we wanted. His armies were greatly fatigued by two months of heavy fighting, and they lacked ammunition. Moreover, he was forced to provide for the security of a front which was as yet only poorly organized, and whose length had rapidly increased until now it reached from the Vosges to the Lys, a distance of 375 miles.

On such a line, where both sides were everywhere in close contact, a surprise was possible practically anywhere. This fact explains the more or less piecemeal arrival of our reinforcements for the battle of Ypres; it also explains why the troops which had started the battle had to be kept in action for so long a time. The reason was simple—there were no others to take their place! But the men proved themselves equal to every call made upon their gallantry during the whole bitter struggle. Two examples out of many will serve as illustrations :

The British I Corps had suffered heavily since October 31st, and on that day it had begun to fall back. Nevertheless, it halted, returned to the battle with renewed ardour, sustained repeated heavy attacks, and finally left the battlefield only on November 18th, when the enemy had been definitely repulsed.

The French IX Corps, the 42nd Division and the Cavalry Corps were engaged without intermission from October 23rd to November 15th, and they were relieved only several days later.

What unshakable tenacity was required for efforts such as these, and what fatigue did such exertions entail !

The Battle of Ypres extended along a front of twenty-eight miles from Nordschoote to the Lys at Armentières. The Germans employed the equivalent of fifteen corps ;* the Allies ten.† On October 31st the French held about fifteen miles of the front, the British twelve. On November 5th, the French held eighteen miles and the British nine. It can be seen that the French troops, both as to length of front occupied and numbers engaged, had to sustain the major part of the battle. It would therefore be contrary to the truth to speak of the battle and victory of Ypres as exclusively British.

On both sides the losses were very heavy. In order to overcome our resistance, the Germans had brought into action heavy artillery much more powerful than any possessed by the Allies, comprising as it did many very

---

* III Reserve, II Bavarian, XXII, XXIII, XXVI, XXVII, XV and XIII Corps ; parts of II, VII, XIV, IV and III Bavarian Corps ; 4th Erzatz Division, 37th and 38th Landwehr Brigades, III Cavalry Corps.

† French—IX, XVI, XX, XXXII Corps ; II Cavalry Corps ; two Territorial Divisions. British—I Corps (three Divisions), III Corps, Cavalry Corps.

big guns, some even of 15 inch calibre. The German units composed of reservists were especially ardent, but they were surprised and bewildered by the tenacity shown by their opponents. These troops were thrust, amidst noise and shouting, into violent assaults in close formation, resulting in veritable hecatombs. Their morale thereby suffered greatly.

This produced a profound effect in Germany, and a year later the *Lokal Anzeiger* wrote : " The anniversary of Langemarck ! Never have the plains of Flanders been drenched with such rich blood, blood from the veins of our best and proudest youth. Never again will Germany shed such bitter tears as those which fell that day."

The *Frankfurter Zeitung* said : " Our regiments were hurled into the jaws of death. Enormous and irreparable sacrifices were made that day. These misty autumn mornings revive for many of us terrible memories and renew an inconsolable sorrow."

By November 13th I was able to forward to the Commander-in-Chief a general report in which I summed up the events and outlined the results of these battles. The following is the beginning and the end of this document :

" The enemy's attacks are dying down. He appears to have given up the idea of capturing Ypres and, consequently, his plan of outflanking our left.

" The reinforcements you have been good enough to send me have for the most part arrived ; detraining continues without pause. A certain number are already in the front line, relieving the troops until now engaged ; others are moving up. In the meantime, engineer companies aided by all available troops are organizing and strengthening the positions. Units which had become intermingled are being reorganized.

"Our situation is therefore improving steadily. The same applies to the British Army. Should the enemy renew his attacks, we are better placed to repulse them than ever before.

"The advantage of our situation for the moment stops there; for it will take time for us to prepare a new advance, and the defences in front of us seem to be very strong. But by carrying out small, well-planned actions we may hope to recapture certain points that constitute re-entrants in our line—in a word try to straighten out our front.

"I take advantage of the temporary calm to sum up what we have done and the results accomplished. . . .

"Although we have succeeded in uniting all the Allied forces and assuring the safety of our maritime bases, the tactical result we have obtained is as yet purely negative. We have prevented the enemy from accomplishing his plan, in spite of the sacrifices he made to that end. We shall continue to hold him.

"However, under the circumstances now existing, important decisions favourable to us may result from the powerlessness of the adversary.

"That is the point at which we have now arrived. The resistance of our troops has been equal to every demand made upon them. Our losses are serious; the enemy's must be heavier still, in view of his attacks in dense and deep formation.

"I shall shortly have the honour of submitting to you recommendations with a view to the recognition of the services rendered by certain of our Officers.

"Headquarters at Cassel.

"November 13th, 1914—10 P.M."

This document, written under the influence of facts

then very recent, shows that we had not gained a great victory over the enemy, but that we had prevented him from gaining one over us. In doing so we deprived him of the very considerable results which would have followed from his success.

By a continuous development of the outflanking manœuvre which we had undertaken a few days after the victory of the Marne, we had been led to extend our front from Switzerland to the North Sea. This was a distance of 425 miles—a line of battle hitherto unheard of in history. Moreover, six weeks after the Marne, we had been obliged to improvise a new battle—and a decisive one—on the northern extremity of this front. The outcome of such an encounter was, naturally, subject at first to the gravest misgiving, when one took into account the enormous reserves in men and material which the enemy had prepared and organized in time of peace, and which gave him from the start a redoubtable advantage. Faced by a shortage in men, a greater shortage in material and a still greater shortage in ammunition, obliged to create an organization for our own forces as well as one which would embrace those of our Allies—such were the conditions under which we approached this encounter. Every difficulty was surmounted by our united efforts ; but the result was mostly due to the vigilance and resolution of the French Commander-in-Chief, who did not hesitate to man with his own troops the greater portion of the Allied front.

The consequences were considerable. The definite repulse which the Allied Armies inflicted upon the enemy on the banks of the Yser and at Ypres frustrated his plan of defeating us first and attacking Russia afterwards. It rescued the particularly rich provinces of northern France from invasion and occupation; it saved the Channel ports and those of the North Sea, that is to say, the communications between France and England. It protected England from German attack; it preserved for Belgium a scrap of territory that maintained for her a place upon the map of Europe, and it established her Government beyond the reach of the enemy.

The Allied Armies had shared in a battle which had lasted for more than a month, and their close co-operation had brought about a victory. It was not possible that blood shed in common under such circumstances could fail to cement the friendship of the three nations. That alone constituted a big asset in the balance sheet of the Coalition.

The Germans had compensated themselves for their defeat by redoubling the violence of the bombardment of Ypres. On November 22nd they took St. Peter's Cathedral and the Cloth Hall as targets for their incendiary shells. These magnificent monuments soon became a mere pile of lamentable ruins.

The fighting around Ypres once more proved the strength which the defence had acquired through the development of fire-power, and especially that of machine-guns. The offensive had not gained in any similar proportion. Out of this situation there arose the long period of stagnation of the two opposing armies, during which a new sort of warfare came into existence, the war of position, as opposed to the so-called war of movement. It was really nothing but a temporary crisis in the business of war, an acknowledgment of helplessness which grew out of the fact that the offensive, armed with fairly satisfactory weapons, was powerless to get the better of the defensive, having at its disposal superior means of action. Some way had to be found which would enable the offensive to surmount the obstacle and break through the shield which the ground everywhere afforded the soldier—some way of dealing at close quarters with that unreachable weapon, the machine-gun, which, even when blindly directed, inexorably swept the battlefield with a rain of bullets. In other words, munitions had taken on a character of vital importance in war.

We had failed at Ypres when we tried the offensive, chiefly because our artillery was not heavy enough. The Germans had more powerful guns than ours, but they, in their turn, failed because they did not have enough of them and did not use them advantageously. As a matter of fact, the offensive never recovered its full power until we had increased more than ten-fold the number of our heavy pieces and the allowance of ammunition for all kinds. We next learned to regulate our artillery fire methodically, and finally we perfected armoured appliances which could seek out and destroy the hostile machine-guns.

Once an offensive was plentifully equipped in this fashion, it was no more restricted to a war of position than in the days of Napoleon. It could once more make full use of that power of movement of which it had been deprived by anæmia—by a sense of powerlessness in the face of obstacles.

Proof was thus again furnished that the aspects of war are ever a function of the engines placed at its disposal. Man alone, however gallant he may be, cannot change them; for without his machines he is helpless. And since in war machines change constantly and become ever more abundant, one of the first duties of the soldier at the front is to animate and serve them. These were things we had learned before the year 1914 closed.

There seems no limit to what may be expected in future struggles from the progress of aviation and the development of chemical warfare. Consequently, in making preparations for the next war, we must not fail to take fully into account the varied and formidable material which will be employed in battle, provide a part of it, at least, during peace time, and create a military organization which will ensure its proper use in time of war.

And so, at the close of 1914, it was quite clear that we should not be able to carry the struggle to its destination —Victory—unless we very greatly increased the number of our guns and our machine-guns, together with the supply of ammunition required for them. Production in the interior of the country alone could ensure the success of the army. The first duty of the High Command, therefore, was to make this condition perfectly clear to the Government. These considerations led me to send, on November 19th, a report to the Commander-in-Chief, which dealt with this subject. At the same time I gave him my views regarding the prospects which the war seemed to reveal :

" The situation remains unchanged ; the enemy is making no further serious attacks. We are refitting.

" A study of the situation here and on the Russian front leads me to the following conclusions :

" The Germans' fundamental plan included the destruction of the western adversary by turning his left flank from Ypres to the sea, before marching against the eastern adversary, the Russian Army. The first part of this programme has been brought to nought. The Germans were not able either to turn our left wing or to destroy us. Better still, we ourselves are in perfect condition, both materially and morally, for attacking them.

"On the whole, after three month's fighting, they have arrived at a grievous state of impotency in the west. On the east, their whole task still lies before them, and they have to undertake it with a greatly weakened army. Whatever solution they may apply to the problem—and there are many to choose from—they cannot help withdrawing troops from the western front and so reducing the length of that line. The first front on which they will make a serious resistance will doubtless stretch from Strasbourg through Metz, the Meuse at Mezières, Namur, Brussels and Antwerp.

"1. *Characteristics of the War.*

"Before arriving in front of this line, we will doubtless have other defensive positions to carry. In any case, the attack of fortified fronts is sure to become more and more our portion. It seems to me that the organization of this war has got to be carefully studied. What are its requirements? A large number of siege guns, *with plenty of ammunition*, heavy enough to break down the obstacles opposed to them. Naturally the attack of concrete fortifications requires a different weapon from earthworks.

"It is also evident that the existing phase of trench warfare requires the use of bombs. Therefore bomb-throwers or other apparatus must be provided; and again, ammunition in plenty.

"Apart from artillery of this description, provision must be made for *engineers* having special competence in sapping operations—mining warfare. On this subject I am not so well informed, but I have an idea. Has not the experience gained in boring artesian wells and constructing the Paris underground railway (Berlier tubes) brought to light mechanical means much more rapid than the old ones, for running mine-galleries and shoring them up, so that heavy charges could be exploded under certain points of the enemy's defences?

" 2. In regard to the *place* to choose for our attacks, I say this :

" The fate of Europe, up to the time of Waterloo, has always been decided in Belgium. It seems difficult to escape from this idea. In Belgium we can always count upon the collaboration of the British and Belgians, provided that we continue to stimulate them. Elsewhere, and without that stimulation, their collaboration may be unproductive. As far as the Meuse there is no serious natural obstacle, and the German defensive organizations in this region, being of more recent date, may prove less strong than those in other regions.

" All the above-mentioned considerations lead me to the conclusion that a strong attack should be carried out in the north, directed in the first place against the space between Antwerp and Namur (which will doubtless be supplemented by temporary fortifications around Brussels), and then against the Meuse between Namur and Liége. We would certainly encounter strong resistance there, as also along the Meuse from Namur to Mezières, Sedan, Mouzon. . . .

" We could probably overcome this resistance only by a manœuvre on the right bank, starting from Verdun and its approaches.

" A strong attack with our left to begin with, a strong attack with our right to finish—that is the sum and substance of my idea. Our centre would advance by taking advantage of the results obtained on the wings ; as closing in took place, this movement would be made first towards our left and subsequently towards our right.

"3. It may be argued that this plan would not at once give us possession of the territory we desire and need. I remain faithful to pure theory—that which asserts that it is the destruction of the enemy's forces which will settle everything. Hence I hold that our operations should be continued in a direction purely military, that it is this direction which will gain for us the greatest amount of territory and enable us best to support our claims, provided of course that we pursue our military efforts without respite or pity.

"4. Reverting to the beginning of my argument, I consider the German offensive as *definitely blocked in the West*. With troops of inferior quality, the Germans cannot resume the attempt on Ypres with the violence they displayed on November 1st. If they begin again, they will fail. They are necessarily condemned to the defensive on the Western Front. They can no longer manœuvre except on the Eastern Front; and even there, can they? Preparation for manœuvre requires considerable time and is sure to be preceded by much hesitation.

"After they had halted our pursuit along the line of the present front on September 15th, it was only on November 1st, *a month and a half afterwards*, that they launched the attack on Ypres. They would have made things very difficult for us if they had directed as great an effort by the 10th or 15th of October on Arras, when the British had not yet been moved up. The conclusion I arrive at is that we can anticipate their being very slow in turning to the East—in the withdrawal of their forces from this side, in modifying the façade they keep up in front of us. It seems to me, however, that they are withdrawing units from their rear, are sending up reinforcements to those they are keeping here, are moving good troops from places such as Metz and Strasbourg to garrison towns they now consider front line strongholds—Antwerp, Brussels, Namur.

" All this convinces me once more that our offensive has got to be organized with a view to operations against fortified positions—in other words siege-warfare on a vast scale.

" I have written down these ideas as they came into my head during moments of comparative leisure. Please pardon any incoherence they may present, and believe me to be, etc., etc.

" (sgd) FOCH."

On November 13th, the day following the serious events I have been relating, Field-Marshal Earl Roberts came to see me at my Headquarters at Cassel, accompanied by his daughter, Lady Aileen Roberts. He was a fine figure of a soldier and patriot, a great Englishman in the best sense of the word. Notwithstanding his age, which was more than eighty, he was still wonderfully active and in keen possession of all his faculties. He could not help but be interested both in the war on which was staked the existence of our two countries, and in the soldiers who were engaged in it. I had known him for several years and I had always been filled with admiration for the clearness of his vision and the greatness and uprightness of his character. I realized this in 1912 when, moved by a profound anxiety, he had made those speeches in which he urged upon his countrymen, then asleep and dreaming comfortable dreams of peace, the necessity of obligatory military service.

For over an hour we talked of the battle. I showed

him our maps, on which were marked up daily the successive moves of our troops and the positions won or lost. These maps constituted the only possible picture of this subterranean warfare in a country which was necessarily much enclosed. He was good enough to talk to the officers of my staff and to listen to their descriptions of the various events of the last few days. His keen way of looking at one and the vivacity of his observations made him seem younger perhaps than any of us.

This was the last time I was destined to see him. At two o'clock he left us and went over to visit the Indian troops, for whom he had always retained an especial attachment. They had just come out of a severe battle and were being given a rest. Confident in his seemingly inexhaustible youth and braving the rigours of the season, he took off his overcoat in order to pass them in review. In this way he caught a chill which obliged him to take to his bed on returning to Saint-Omer in the evening, and on the following day he died. But he had seen his faithful Indian troops in the moment of their victory, and he had walked over the battlefield where they had given freely of their blood to defend Great Britain from her enemy. It was an end well worthy of his glorious past.

Like Lord Kitchener, whose anxiety on November 1st I have described, the British people had followed with apprehension this long Battle of Ypres, which threatened to carry the war into their island. Its result had been for them a real relief, and the King crossed the Channel to express his satisfaction to his Army.

On December 2nd, accompanied by Generals d'Urbal, de Maud'huy, Conneau, de Mitry, Grossetti and Maistre, and by some of my staff, I went to meet him by appointment at Saint-Omer. Sir John French had fully explained to him the events which had taken place, and he took me apart to thank me. He expressed in the kindest way his appreciation of what I had done for his Army and the powerful and continual support I had given his troops, and which had ensured for us the great results of the Battle of Ypres. In my turn, I congratulated him upon the gallantry of his Army which, subjected to most violent assaults, had stubbornly held their ground for over three weeks.

The King terminated my visit by bestowing upon me the Grand Cross of the Order of the Bath, which he had desired to bring me, although—as he said—this dignity was of a higher grade than what was appropriate to my present functions. He then received and decorated the French Generals. He was good enough also to have the officers of my staff presented to him. These he decorated and honoured with most gracious words, in particular Colonel Weygand and Major Desticker.

Our relations with the British Army, which were already very frank and cordial, had grown even closer during the battle which we had fought together and won by our entire and perfect union. The stout friendship that reigned on the battle-field of Ypres had spread to the two nations, as the King had just made evident; in proportion as the War went on, it became stronger and stronger, until at last our common victory crowned it. Its maintenance will for a long time be a guarantee of world-peace.

* * * *

The two Battles of the Yser and Ypres had been won by the closely co-ordinated efforts of three severely tried Armies. The component parts of each national force had been suddenly and unexpectedly assembled. Each was commanded by its own chief: the King of the Belgians, Field-Marshal Sir John French and myself. And yet, in spite of this situation, no more perfect unity of will and of action was ever realized than in this improvised assemblage of units, hastily brought together to save the common cause from the assaults of a powerful adversary in the act of striking a decisive blow with fresh troops and very powerful accessories. If it had been my lot to play an important part in these two battles, to inspire certain decisions and stimulate a number of acts, together with two such commanders as a King and a Field-Marshal of England, both of proved capacity, my position did not depend in any degree on my having the right of command over Allied troops, but rather was it the result of the confidence in me manifested by these highly placed persons, and the authority accorded me in their councils.

This must necessarily be the attitude between allies in any coalition. Each army has its own spirit and tradition ; each has to satisfy the requirements of its own government, and the latter, in its turn, has its own particular needs and interests to consider. Moreover, each army has its own characteristic pride, and each rates very high the weight of the burden which the war has brought upon it and shows a corresponding hesitation in the face of new efforts and new sacrifices demanded of it by battle. It follows that common direction is created and maintained above all by the confidence which governments and allied Commanders-in-Chief bestow upon some chosen individual.

What later on was known by the term " unified command " gives a false idea of the powers exercised by the individual in question—that is, if it is meant that he commanded in the military sense of the word, as he would do, for example, in the French Army. His orders to Allied troops could not have the same characteristic of absolutism, for these troops were not his, especially in the sense that he could not inflict punishment in case this became necessary. But by persuasion he could stimulate or restrain their Commanders-in-Chief, decide upon the policy to follow, and thus bring about those concerted actions which result in victory, even when the armies concerned are utterly dissimilar.

If, at some appropriate moment, an official mandate is drawn up which clearly specifies for all the allies the functions of this person, nothing is more to be desired. But it must be on condition that the man thus designated can quickly justify the concession. For the greatness of a title will not long protect him from criticism, opposition or divergence of views and of efforts, on the part of armies which, in spite of everything, remain foreign armies for him. But they will willingly recognize his authority once they have seen and favourably judged his manner of exercising it.

Supreme command narrowly exercised divides the efforts of a coalition; confidence unites and strengthens them. Neither at the Yser nor at Ypres did I have any written authority to command.

CHAPTER VI

FIRST ALLIED ATTEMPTS AGAINST THE FORTIFIED GERMAN FRONT. REGROUPING OF THE ALLIED FORCES IN FLANDERS

December, 1914—April, 1915

The reason for attacking; plan of the offensive—Attack by the French Eighth Army in the region of Ypres—Attack by the French Tenth Army north of Arras—Deductions to be drawn—Attack by the II Cavalry Corps on Nieuport—General Joffre's motor-car accident—Relief of the Eighth Army by the British—General dispositions of the Allied forces in the North in April, 1915—The Belgian Army and its King.

WHILE the enemy offensive on the western front had been checked and the Allied armies given a chance to enjoy a comparative rest, the Germans would be obliged to launch an offensive on the Eastern Front, where the progress of the Russian Armies was very disquieting, if they were not to run most serious risks. To do this, they would have to take a considerable part of their forces from the West. This imposed upon the Allies the obligation of operating in such a way as to retain, on the Western Front, the greatest possible number of these forces.

The offensive to be undertaken by the French Armies to carry this out must be executed in those sectors which offered the greatest advantages both as to the area of attack and the possibilities of exploiting a success. In order to force the enemy to disperse his efforts, the offensive should also cover as wide a front as possible.

I had in view the following operations :—

(1) By the Eighth Army, an attack in the region south-east of Ypres, in conjunction with the British Army.

(2) By the Tenth Army, an important attack north of Arras, directed on La Folie ridge, between Souchez and Givenchy-en-Gohelle.

By the end of November these armies had begun to study the necessary problems actively. On December 6th, I went to General Headquarters at Chantilly to submit this programme to the Commander-in-Chief. On December 8th, General Joffre issued general instructions to the army of which the following is a summary :

The moment has arrived to resume the offensive " in order to throw the enemy back to the north-east and prepare further operations on our part against his communications."

With this end in view, the following main attacks will be carried out :

" (1) One, starting from the region of Arras, in the direction of Cambrai and Douai, to be executed by the Tenth Army reinforced.

" (2) The other in Champagne, in the direction of Attigny, by the Fourth Army."

In addition, secondary operations will be carried out on various parts of the front, more particularly :

By the Eighth Army and the left of the British Army, attacking in a convergent direction on Wervicq.

By the Second Army, attacking in the direction of Combles.

Etc., etc . . .

*   *   *   *

The attack of the Eighth Army

When the right of the Eighth Army was relieved by the

British, General d'Urbal was enabled to withdraw a considerable number of troops from his front. These were returned to the Tenth Army, from which they had been taken during the Battle of Ypres. Moreover, the Belgians had agreed to extend their line to the south, and this made it possible for General d'Urbal to relieve the whole of the XXXII Corps from that front and place it in reserve.

This being the situation, the G.O.C. the Eighth Army could start his preparations for executing during the first fortnight in December the prescribed offensive in conjunction with the British Army.

The attacks launched on December 14th, 15th and 16th failed as a whole or did not gain sufficient ground. Not only was the enemy discovered to be fully prepared and strongly organized, but still greater difficulties were created by the marshy state of the ground into which the men sank up to their thighs; wheeled vehicles could not leave the roads.

Our troops then undertook to run saps and mines under the front of our objectives, hoping in this way to reduce the vital points of the enemy's defence; but the work was greatly hampered by the almost insurmountable difficulties in the sodden ground.

In the northern part of the Ypres salient we encountered similar obstacles and effected very little progress. The same fate befell the British attempts in the south, where the results were confined to a few local advances.

The difficulties of the ground proving altogether too great, we halted our offensive on the 19th. On the 24th, seeing that there was nothing further to hope from the British attacks on the Lys, we reduced the density of the front line and built up our reserves. We thus resumed our defensive attitude in the region north of the Lys.

* * * *

The attack of the Tenth Army

As early as the end of November the Tenth Army had studied the possible advantages which attacks effected on both sides of Arras might bring. It was thought that if successful the very least result would be to straighten the salient at Arras and thereby render the defence of the town easier and less costly.

In order to concentrate our available resources, we limited our designs to the attack north of the town, which alone was capable of producing important and perhaps decisive results. The long ridge which, starting from Souchez, runs by La Folie and Thélus and rejoins the plateau of the Point du Jour east of Arras, constitutes an almost perpendicular cliff dominating the villages of Givenchy-en-Gohelle, Vimy, Farbus and Bailleul, and commanding the vast plain up to Douai.

If we seized this ridge and established artillery and observation posts there, the enemy would be prevented from maintaining any important organizations in the plain and he would be forced to make an extensive withdrawal up to the line of the Sensée and the upper Deule, thereby modifying the front to our advantage.

The ridge was the objective of our attack; we hoped to break through the German line at and to the south of Souchez, seize the high ground which commands Givenchy and Vimy, and exploit these results. The offensive was to be carried out by the XXXII Corps, commanded by General Pétain, and the XXI Corps commanded by General Maistre, operating concentrically on the objective.

The date was to be between December 16th and 20th. In the meantime, the ground from which the troops would take off was to be improved and several preliminary operations were to be carried out, namely, by the XXI Corps against Notre Dame de Lorette, by the XXXIII Corps against Carency and La Targette, and by the X Corps against Saint-Laurent and Blangy.

Experience had shown us the necessity of not attempting to go too fast, but rather to advance steadily from one result to another, and such a method precluded our drawing up a plan in which the final operations would be defined. For this reason, the main attack of the XXXII Corps could not be fixed at the start, for the time of its execution depended on the success of the secondary attacks and on a thorough artillery preparation.

In pursuance of these plans, the XXI Corps launched an attack on the 17th against the Lorette plateau, and succeeded in capturing the first German line, between the northern slopes of the plateau and the main road leading from Béthune to Arras. However, the rain soon rendered the ground impassable, holding up the advance of the infantry and interrupting the supply services. We could not even occupy the captured ground, for a sea of mud rendered its organization impossible. Only infantry as good as that of the XXI Corps could have retained possession of the position it had captured.

In the meantime the XXXIII Corps was encountering great difficulties. Its two attacks, to the north on Carency and to the south on La Targette, failed in the face of the well-made defences and sound dispositions of the adversary. For we had no means of destroying them. The main attack against the Vimy ridge was therefore postponed.

Thus on December 23rd our offensive operations in

the North had either failed, or yielded insignificant results. New methods of attack aided by powerful engines of destruction would have to be employed if formidable defences such as those now facing us were to be overcome.

The war of movement had already demonstrated the immense value of the machine-gun to the defence, especially when combined with entrenchments. The enemy had now time to reinforce the latter with barbed wire entanglements, with concrete shelters for machine-guns and with flanking guns, as well as underground or armoured communications. The quarters of the men were often veritable citadels which an opponent was obliged to destroy before launching any infantry attack. This destruction required artillery powerful enough to demolish these shelters, as well as the trenches and their fields of protecting wire. Lack of suitable *matériel* had already halted our offensive in the war of manœuvre; the want of it was even more strongly felt in this war of position which arose so suddenly.

Since man-power alone could not capture positions organised by modern methods, it was imperative that our factories be asked to furnish as quickly as possible machines capable of reducing them. The Commander-in-Chief had to turn his attention to the question of production. Here and here only could be found the means of pushing forward the War, at all events on the Western Front.

But during the time which must ensue before it was possible to realise this development in our tactics, we could not forget our Allies on the Eastern Front, the Russian Army, which, by its energetic intervention, had drawn upon itself a large portion of the enemy's forces, and had thus enabled us to achieve the victory of the

Marne. It was our duty, so far as was possible, to go to its assistance. Herein lay the reason for operations, however fruitless they may now seem, such as those we had already undertaken, and for continuing along the same lines with others. If we were not yet in a position to achieve victory, we could at least force the enemy to retain on the Western Front all the forces which he had accumulated there, and thus prevent him from moving them to the Eastern theatre. A decisive offensive on the latter front might be the prelude to his complete victory.

But in all that concerned the correlation to be established between the operations on the two fronts, I was entirely dependent upon the instructions of the Commander-in-Chief of the French Armies. It was not therefore my initiative which inspired our offensive operations in the north. My functions consisted in seeing that they were carried out in accordance with General Joffre's views and in the closest possible co-operation with our British and Belgian Allies. It must be remembered that toward the close of 1914, an offensive had been started in Champagne, and its beginning (December 20th) had been quite satisfactory.

My formula for the time being was this: activity in all the staffs and rest for the troops until an improvement in the weather might permit a resumption of operations with chances of success. The Commander-in-Chief approved this plan and issued instructions that all troops not absolutely needed in the trenches be rested. However, as the duration of the operations in Champagne necessitated the formation of large reserves, the armies in the north were instructed to furnish their share.

As time went on and these operations assumed still greater importance, the Commander-in-Chief, on

February 27th, directed that all enterprises contemplated by the Tenth Army be halted. Nevertheless, an active study of various operations was to be pursued, so that they might be set in motion without delay when the time came. In this way, the winter ended without any new moves being undertaken on our part, except at Nieuport.

Many of our troops were leaving the northern theatre, having been ordered to rest camps or placed at the disposal of the Commander-in-Chief. I had taken advantage of these circumstances to visit them in succession. I always assembled the officers and had a talk. I cannot say enough in praise of the splendid spirit which animated them all, officers and men alike, and that following a winter of unmitigated hardship. They fully realised the important results which they had obtained at Ypres and on the Yser, where they once more had brought the enemy's plans to nought. They had no doubts as to being able to get the better of him in the attacks that lay ahead. The confidence which filled them all was impressive.

* * * *

The attacks by the II Cavalry Corps east of Nieuport

The Belgian coast on the North Sea was of special interest to the enemy on account of the works which he could place there to support the submarine warfare against England and interrupt the Channel communications. Ostend was nearer to us than any other port he held, and its defence would certainly immobilise important German forces. This offered good reason for any attacks which we might be led to undertake in that direction. The coast itself consisted of fairly high sand dunes which had escaped the inundations along the Yser and thereby offered certain facilities for our action.

Early in December I had caused General de Mitry, commanding the II Cavalry Corps, to make a study of an offensive launched from Nieuport. The Military Governor of Dunkirk had prepared the necessary means for crossing the Yser above Nieuport, and a considerable naval equipment, including dorys and motor-boats, had been assembled and placed at General de Mitry's disposition. But we had no guns except field artillery.

On December 15th the attack was launched in the general direction of the line Westend-Ostend. We obtained a footing in the first houses of Lombartzyde and Le Polder but were unable to make any appreciable advance along the coast itself, on account of the powerful works which the enemy had constructed in the sand-dunes. We got to within 600 yards of Saint-Georges, while the French sailors and Belgian soldiers in dories took several farms to the south-west of it.

The operation was continued for the next few days. In vain the enemy launched vigorous counter-attacks; they were all repulsed. Indeed, on the 19th we captured and consolidated a strong bridge-head on the right bank of the Yser. We moreover made numerous crossings over the river.

When, on the 25th, we proceeded to resume the attack, all our efforts from Lombartzyde to the sea were broken by the enemy's defence and especially by his barbed-wire entanglements, which our poverty in artillery had made it impossible to demolish. On the 28th we captured Saint-Georges, while the Belgian 5th Division, after crossing the Yser south of Dixmude, established a small bridge-head on the right bank.

Before making further attacks in force, we had to

instal ourselves firmly where we stood. That required considerable time, for to organize ground such as this was a question not of days but of weeks, the atmospheric conditions alone constituting a most serious difficulty. Water and sand made inroads into our support and communication trenches, frequent storms damaged our telephone lines, and the bridge of casks we had thrown across the mouth of the Yser was continually being broken by German artillery fire.

In spite of all these difficulties, our troops displayed wonderful activity. For a whole month, from December 27th to January 27th, they toiled without pause, constructing works of approach for carrying out an offensive against Lombartzyde and Le Polder.

On January 28th this new attack was launched, and we captured the first German line. At nightfall, however, after having sustained heavy losses, and on account of the water which prevented any work of consolidation in the captured trenches, the troops withdrew to their original positions. Otherwise they would have been at the mercy of the slightest counterstroke.

While this operation was going on in front of Le Polder, a small reconnoitering patrol succeeded, by a sudden dash, in capturing a small fort in front of the Great Dune. But, caught by enfilade fire, and counter-attacked with the bayonet, the little detachment was almost wiped out. Six men and a non-commissioned officer resisted all day and part of the night; they were all killed at their posts.

These deeds showed clearly the excellent spirit and dash animating the troops of the French detachment at Nieuport. But no amount of courage and enterprise was sufficient to overcome the physical difficulties of every description which the elements piled up before them. It was not humanly possible to succeed, and it would have been madness to continue in the middle of winter an enterprise which obviously was destined to end in failure. January 28th really marked the end of this offensive.

It was during the month of January (on the 17th) that General Joffre was the victim of a motor-car accident which might have had serious results. We were travelling together in the same car along the road from Rousbrughe to Dunkirk, when the way was suddenly blocked by a heavy lorry, the steering gear of which had broken. A collision between the two vehicles resulted, in which the Commander-in-Chief received such serious contusions that he was obliged to give up the round of inspections he intended to make and return by rail to his Headquarters at Romilly. I emerged unhurt from the accident, but I was very anxious about my chief, and this feeling increased after I had left him at the Dunkirk station. Fortunately, he recovered completely in a few days.

A little while after this incident I wrote a letter to the Minister of War which I believed my functions as Assistant to the Commander-in-Chief justified. In it I asked him what course I should have taken if this accident had rendered General Joffre incapable of exercising command; also supposing such a case to occur, upon what officer at the front would devolve the duty of taking steps to meet an emergency which some action of the enemy might precipitate that very moment? In reply, I was informed that I need not concern myself about this contingency, since the Government had already provided for it.

As a matter of fact, during the month of August,

SAPPERS IN GAS MASKS LAY LINES TO THE TRENCHES.

FLOWERS FOR BRITISH SOLDIERS ALONG THE ROADS OF FRANCE.

A COUNTRY CHURCH BECOMES A HOSPITAL FOR THE FRENCH WOUNDED.

GENERALS JOFFRE, FOCH AND WIRBEL, IN 1915.

A FRENCH INFANTRY REGIMENT ADVANCING TO THE FIRING LINE.

General Gallieni had been nominated to command the French Armies in case of this happening. In spite of his great intelligence and undisputed ability, General Galliéni, at this date, had taken only a small part in the war and especially in the war of trenches. Politicians are too quick in forming opinions about soldiers. The only place where officers can be judged is on the field of battle, and here their ability may be measured by their accomplishments.

* * * *

The relief of the French Eighth Army by the British

At the beginning of December the British Government had indicated to the French Government its wish that the British forces in Flanders should be transferred further north. Here they could hold a part of the Allied front nearer to the coast, and, more especially, rest their left on the sea. It was thought that such a move would give great satisfaction to public opinion in England.

From Ostend to Zeebrugge on the Belgian coast, Great Britain was exposed continually to an enemy threat which could best be met by having the British Army attack along the coast toward the naval base at Ostend. This idea was especially dear to the British First Lord of the Admiralty, Mr. Winston Churchill. It was much less dear, however, to the Commander-in-Chief of the British Army, Field-Marshal Sir John French, and even less dear to the Commander-in-Chief of the French Armies, General Joffre.

Both these saw a serious disadvantage in devoting the main effort of the British Army to an object which concerned the naval struggle alone, and which diverted it from action against the most important factor in the enemy coalition, the German Army, at a spot which would determine the fate of the war. Under these conditions, and after much discussion, it was arranged during the latter part of December that the British Army, while maintaining its right on La Bassée, should successively relieve the corps of the French Eighth Army, availing itself for this purpose of reinforcements as they arrived from home. The French Army would keep in Nieuport the troops which were there, but would progressively evacuate the Ypres salient, retaining only a detachment at Elverdinghe, interspersed between the left of the British and the right of the Belgians.

As it turned out, the plan of relief thus arranged met with great delay in execution, due in the first place to the slow arrival of the British reinforcements. Lord Kitchener was anxious to dispatch to the Continent only troops which had been completely organized into Divisions or Army Corps, while Sir John French would have been glad to have received them by Battalions. Penury of munitions also proved a matter of embarrassment to the Field-Marshal in planning the extension of his front. Indeed, the slow progress being made for organizing their manufacture in England caused him considerable anxiety.

Meanwhile, the British First Lord of the Admiralty tried to have his plan for an attack on Ostend reconsidered by offering to provide a reinforcement of 3,000 marines for the French detachment at Nieuport. General Joffre maintained his opinion that a battle having land objectives was more important, insisting moreover that it was on the left of our Tenth Army, in the La Bassée region, that the efforts of the British Army could best be directed. He endeavoured therefore to obtain from Sir John French his agreement on two points, the extension of the British front and his active co-operation in the French attacks.

As has been seen, the progress of the war had been checked by the Allies' lack of munitions and war material. The prolongation of this inactivity and the anxiety it produced in public opinion, had led the Cabinet of a certain Government to intervene in the conduct of operations, push them into false channels, and thus render the task of the High Command more difficult. Once more our poverty in munitions was leading to serious consequences.

Troop, equipment and munition supply have become a question of capital importance in modern war, and they are bound to take a prominent place in the preoccupations of the High Command, not only in what concerns the prosecution of operations against the enemy, but in order that the continuance of these operations may be ensured at times when public opinion or the government is agitated.

As a result of these various complications, the British Army by the end of January had only relieved the French XVI Corps, which was less progress than had been jointly agreed upon. The French IX and XX Corps had not yet been replaced. This situation continued without any appreciable change up to the middle of March. But on that date the preparations of the British First Army for an attack in the La Bassée area were completed, and the negotiations then going on were interrupted and could not be resumed until the result of the enterprise was known.

The British First Army, commanded by General Sir Douglas Haig, was entrusted with this offensive. The troops were sent forward on March 10th. At the beginning they had some success, but this could not be extended or even wholly maintained during the following days.

On the night of March 12th–13th General Haig issued orders for the offensive to be stopped, but the troops were directed to establish themselves firmly in the positions they had captured on the 10th. The decision of the G.O.C. the British First Army is explained by his fear of running short of ammunition as well as by the losses his forces had suffered.

It was now possible to return to the plan of relieving the French Army corps around Ypres. At a conference held at Chantilly between Sir John French, Lord Kitchener, General Joffre and M. Millerand, it was decided that the British Second Army should relieve the French IX and XX Corps before April 20th, that two new British Divisions should be sent to France, and that the French offensive in Artois should take place at the end of April. These operations were carried out rapidly, and by April 7th the IX Corps had been withdrawn from the front, and directed toward the zone of the Tenth Army. Then, on April 19th, the XX Corps followed suit. Thus, by the end of April, a new distribution of Allied forces in the north had been effected.

The British forces stretched from La Bassée canal to the Ypres road at Poelcapelle. They were grouped into two armies. On the south, the First, under the command of Sir Douglas Haig ; on the north, the Second, under the command of General Smith-Dorrien.

The French Eighth Army, which, on April 4th, had been broken up, had been replaced in Flanders by " the Army Detachment of Belgium," under the command of General Pütz. This detachment consisted of two groups, one at Elverdinghe, between the Belgians and the British; the other at Nieuport, on the extreme left of the Allied line.

The Belgian Army which, at my request, had agreed to a fresh extension, from now on lay between Nieuport, which was held by a French force, and Steenstraaet. Its morale had continued to improve ever since its arrival on the Yser. The King was still animated by the same intentions, and if operations on a large scale were out of the question for his troops, they could at least be counted upon to display a profitable activity. And this they did from the beginning of March onward. The divisions in line prepared and carried out operations of detail almost without pause, taking a whole month, from March 11th to April 11th. Although these attacks did not achieve any results of great importance, they at least developed in the Belgian soldier a spirit of enterprise and proved the desire he had to do his part. This activity, moreover, did not fail to provoke quite sharp replies from the enemy.

We had established close and frequent relations with the Belgian Generals and Belgian Officers of all ranks. The consequence was that the two armies became one in spirit, and a comradeship in arms was created which was to have a most happy influence in the hour of need.

In January, Belgian General Headquarters evacuated Furnes. As this place was frequently and heavily bombarded by the enemy, it moved to Houthem, a very unpretentious locality. The King was quartered with the Queen and the Princes in La Panne, a town on the sea coast, not far from Houthem. He went to his Headquarters every day, staying at the Presbytery of Houthem, where some of his officers were billeted.

The Presbytery was not at all imposing. It was a solid square building, surrounded on all sides by water and reached by a narrow bridge. In this modest corner, the heart of Belgium continued to beat. Here burned the generating fires of that energy which for four long years unflinchingly faced a formidable enemy, and which went forth to reconquer the native land in 1918. This little house remains for me a monument that will testify to future generations more adequately than any other, the greatness of a little country, which, led by her chivalrous King and defended by her valiant children, triumphed over a most brutal and iniquitous aggression.

END OF BOOK I

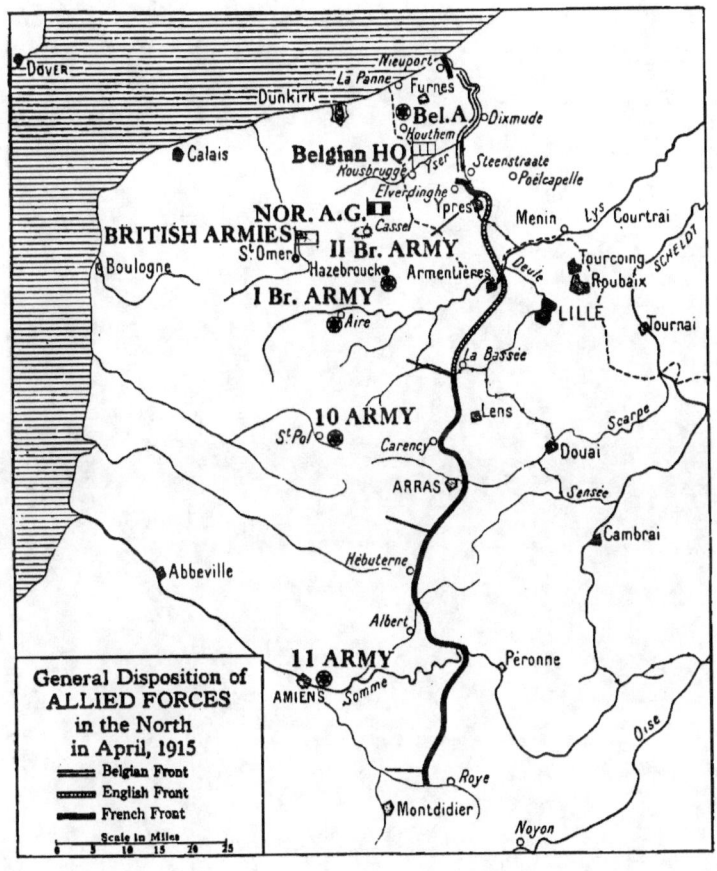

BOOK II

IN COMMAND OF THE ALLIED ARMIES

PREFACE TO BOOK II

MARSHAL FOCH did not have time to write all his recollections of the war and his observations on its conduct. He confined himself to reciting those events between 1914 and 1918 in which he took an active part. The events of 1914 are related in the first Book, those of 1918 in the second. In each case they comprise those acts which best illustrate the rôle played by the Marshal during the war, those concerning which his opinion has a special importance. Before resuming the Marshal's narrative, which now deals with the year 1918, it seems useful to give a brief account of his activities in 1915, 1916 and 1917. This recital will enable the reader to see by what successive and almost uninterrupted steps he rose to the supreme command of the Allied Armies, and how he prepared himself to meet this formidable task.

I

IN COMMAND OF THE ARMIES OF THE NORTH

(January 5th, 1915—December 27th, 1916)

ON January 5th, 1915, General Foch was assigned to the command of the Northern Group of Armies ; the order giving him these functions merely confirmed a state of fact which had existed for three months.*

Preparation of the Artois offensive.—The first task which fell to this group of armies was the preparation of the offensive for the spring of 1915.

The place chosen was the Vimy Ridge, north of Arras. "The wide extent of ground it commands," wrote General Foch on March 24th, 1915, " and the practicability of the ground it commands, as well as the impossibility for the enemy to make any addition to his defensive works, would give the occupation of the ridge an immense value and lead to the piercing of the enemy's line."

---

* For the non-military reader it may be useful to give the progression of units usually obtaining in a modern army : Battalion, Regiment (except in the British Army), Brigade, Division, Army Corps, Army, Group of Armies. All the groups taken together constitute the total national force at the front, whose head is the *Commander-in-Chief.* He and his staff constitute the *General Headquarters* of the army in question ; this collection is also referred to sometimes as the *High Command.*

The French terms *commandement, haut commandement, commandement unique,* are translated so as to avoid any confusion of ideas ; but suitable English terms seem not to exist, unless it be for *commandement unique.* This is usually rendered as *unified command* or *Supreme Allied Command,* meaning thereby the functions conferred upon Marshal Foch in April, 1918.

In writing of the Italian Army, the Marshal generally used the Italian term, *Comando Supremo* ; his terminology has been followed.—T. B. M.

The preparations were pushed forward with the greatest activity, and by the middle of April the movement of troops and munitions toward Arras was nearly completed—when suddenly a fresh alarm startled all Flanders.

First German Gas Attack.—On April 22nd, 1915, at 5.30 P.M., after a perfectly calm day, the Germans suddenly launched upon the northern part of the Ypres salient a dense cloud of suffocating gas, the effects of which were felt over a depth of more than a mile.

Surprised and partly asphyxiated, the French territorials and Algerian riflemen poured back in disorder and a part of our artillery fell into the enemy's hands. The British left (Canadian Division) retreated to Saint-Julien. The route to Ypres lay open.

In the midst of this general confusion, the enemy advanced without striking a blow. Ypres was at his mercy, since the few local reserves that could be thrown across his path were wholly inadequate to oppose him. Fortunately, after going two or three miles, he stopped at nightfall of his own accord. The fleeting opportunity passed; we were saved.

Informed by a brief report of what had taken place, General Foch once more gave proof of that quickness of decision and marvellous activity which never failed him in hours of peril. In order to get precise information, he sent a staff officer during the night to the spot where the surprise had taken place, ordered reinforcements to be sent from Nieuport, and aroused some of the numerous French units then assembled around Arras.

At 4.30 A.M., his liaison officer reported to him that the Yser had been crossed in several places by the enemy, that a breach two and a half miles wide had been made in our lines and that along this space the road to Ypres was wide open.

The danger called for immediate and extensive measures. First of all, the enemy must be halted, and to do this, the continuity of our front must be restored. Then, by counter-attacks, he must be thrown back from the positions he had conquered. Such was the programme which General Foch outlined during the night to General Pütz, commanding the French troops in Belgium. He completed these arrangements during the early hours of the 23rd by bringing from Artois a Division of infantry and by asking Sir John French to reinforce the British troops in the region of Arras. Thanks to these measures and to those taken on the spot by General Pütz, as well as to the aid furnished by the British and Belgians, the breach made by the Germans was closed during the morning of the 23rd and Ypres was once more saved.

Nevertheless, the tactical results obtained by the Germans were not negligible : one of the most important lay in the fact that the British, whose line was now advanced too far forward in a point, were obliged to evacuate a part of the Salient.

The attacks in Artois (May, June, September, 1915)

The Artois offensive was originally fixed to begin on May 7th, but unfavourable weather caused it to be postponed until the 9th. After a preparation by heavy artillery lasting six days, and by field artillery for two days, the new chief of the Tenth Army, General d'Urbal, launched the attack against the Vimy Ridge on May 9th at 10 A.M.

In the centre the success was immediate. In less than

an hour on a front of four miles and for a depth of two or three, the enemy's positions were captured. More than 6,000 prisoners, 20 guns, and 100 machine guns, remained in our hands. The crest at its culminating point, Hill 140, was reached and even passed. The German artillery ceased firing and we had the impression we had broken through. Unfortunately, this satisfaction was of short duration.

Our reserves were too far in rear to follow up our success or to widen the breach while there was yet time. The very slight progress accomplished on the right and left of this rapid advance also hindered it. Important points, such as the village of Carency on the left, and of Neuville-Saint-Vaast on the right, remained in the hands of the enemy. On the Lorette plateau and further along, toward Pont-à-Vendin, we had gained little or no ground, while to the north of La Bassée the British had all but completely failed.

Profiting by the fact that these places still held firm, the enemy concentrated upon Hill 140 all the troops he could assemble. Out of breath and unsupported, our men were driven from the crest and the German line reformed in front of them.

A new attack, which we undertook on the 11th, failed under flanking fire coming from the villages of Carency, Souchez and Neuville-Saint-Vaast, and it was evident that these points of resistance must be captured before trying to carry the ridge.

By minutely prepared operations, Carency was taken on May 12th, Ablain-Saint-Nazaire on the 13th, and Neuville on June 9th. Souchez alone resisted every effort, and it was decided to leave it to be cut off and enclosed in the general attack decided upon for June 16th at 12.15 P.M.

That day, as on May 9th, we succeeded in pushing some units to the top of the crest ; but being isolated in a narrow salient and subjected to cross fire as well as the counter-attacks of the enemy, they could not hold on very long, and on the 21st they were driven back. The enemy artillery and infantry fire was most severe along the whole front. Except on the Lorette plateau the ground gained was insignificant, and on the 24th General Foch, in obedience to the orders of the Commander-in-Chief, suspended the operations.

At this time General Joffre was planning another manœuvre, having for its object the combining of the Artois attacks with a large offensive in Champagne. A new grouping of French forces was therefore carried out in July, August and the first three weeks of September. During this period, army corps and divisions were rested, the training of troops resumed, and their equipment improved.

At this time, General Foch wrote a paper setting forth the conclusions he drew from the recent offensives. This he sent to the Commander-in-Chief on July 19th. We find in it the following observations :

" . . . Under the circumstances now prevailing and in the presence of an enemy defensive system long since established, it seems wise not to base all our hopes upon the possibility of breaking through, or risk all our available reserves in the attempt to effect a victorious and decisive piercing of the line by mere force of numbers. On the contrary, our plan should be directed toward the conquest of certain dominant points of the line ; each one of our attacks should have a distinct object, and one whose accomplishment would lead to some further result.

"In former times, the capture of such an objective was the necessary and sufficient condition of success. This condition remains necessary to-day; but while it is no longer sufficient to guarantee a complete success, it at least brings us a step nearer that end. Any other combination is likely to leave us with empty hands after a costly effort. . . .

"An attack merely launched forward without a definite and precise objective is incapable of producing a result, especially the result constituted by *penetration*, unless surprise has been effected.

"The greatness of the reward which any attack can bring depends upon the importance which the objective aimed at has in the *enemy's* system of defence or in his general situation.

"The assignment of forces to our various attacks should be based upon the following principles: make sure of taking this chief objective by assault; facilitate this main action by secondary ones."

In General Foch's eyes, the principal objective remained the Vimy Ridge and he considered that the principal effort should be directed to its conquest, since its loss would be a heavy blow to the enemy's defensive system. Attacks such as those then being prepared in Champagne were in no sense unimportant, but they should be considered solely as accessories, an aid offered to the Artois offensive.

In this opinion he differed from that held at General Headquarters, where it continued to be maintained, long after General Foch has ceased to believe in it, that a break-through was possible. But since General Headquarters was founding its hopes chiefly upon the Champagne offensive, where a large and decisive rupture of the enemy's front was counted upon, the Commander-in-Chief, logical with himself, assigned to this attack the major part of the French forces available. On September 25th the two attacks were launched simultaneously, one in Champagne and one in Artois.

In Artois, the Tenth Army had the benefit of a double extension of its field of action. On the one hand, to the south of Arras, where it put a new army corps in line; on the other, between the Lorette plateau and the La Bassée Canal, where the British First Army sent into action a mass of twelve divisions supported by eight hundred pieces of artillery.

After a powerful emission of gas, the British attack started at 6.30 A.M., advanced rapidly, took Loos and Hulluch, captured 1,400 prisoners and six guns. On its side, the Tenth Army assaulted the Vimy Ridge at 12.25 P.M. Its progress was not uniform; on the right it was checked; in the centre there was some success; on the left it gained ground distinctly.

The enemy now concentrated his efforts against the menace presented by the British advance. He re-took Hulluch and fought furiously in front of Loos, but without obtaining on this side appreciable results. He also multiplied his counter-attacks in the direction of Souchez in an effort to disengage this village, on which the French were closing in; but, checked everywhere, he was obliged to evacuate it on the morning of the 25th.

In spite of these results, and influenced by the success of the first day's fighting in Champagne, the Commander-in-Chief decided to restrict the amplitude of the operations in Artois; he notably ordered a severe economy in the expenditure of ammunition. General Foch then decided to concentrate the efforts of the Tenth Army upon the region where they had met with success, namely toward Givenchy. Moreover, in order to aid Sir John French, whose reserves were being rapidly used up in the face of the violent counter-attacks of the enemy, he decided to move the French Army Corps, which had failed in its attack south of Arras, towards Loos.

During the afternoon of September 28th, a French Division moved up the slopes of Hill 140 and reached its crest. This was a success which had not been repeated since May 9th and which General Foch wanted to exploit without hesitation. Early the next morning, therefore, he went to see Field-Marshal Sir John French and obtained his consent for a joint action of British and French troops to be launched on October 2nd against the front Pont-à-Vendin—Givenchy.

But, through a variety of circumstances which brought about a succession of delays, this joint attack was put off from day to day. Finally it was given up ; for, toward the middle of October, in order to aid the Serbian Army in the Balkans, the Allied Governments decided to send to Salonika an expeditionary force whose troops would be taken from the Western Front. Contributions to the formation of this army obliged both General Joffre and Sir John French to halt the Artois offensive.

The teachings to be drawn from the 1915 attacks in Artois

The offensives in 1915, those in Champagne as well as those in Artois, clearly demonstrated the insufficiency of our means of attack, above all in heavy artillery. On November 10th, 1915, General Foch set down his opinions in a report to the Commander-in-Chief. The following are some extracts from the memorandum :

" . . . Whatever may be the direction chosen for an

attack, what is more important than all else is to endow it with every means necessary for its success. The campaign of 1915 did not accomplish any results because we did not have enough heavy artillery ammunition. Our attacks were not sufficiently prepared and supported by the fire of heavy guns. . . .

" Trench artillery ought to be developed, made mobile and given more instruction.

" Our incendiary and asphyxiating shells yield but feeble results. Our gas projectors only emit substances whose effects are most uncertain. Up to the present our chemical laboratories have turned out very little that has proved useful.

" In what concerns gas, asphyxiating and incendiary shells, we must see that no more than a few months are taken to get a complete solution for problems already partially solved.

" In our attacks across ground fortified in depth, we must above all spare our infantry, in order that it may last through the time inevitably necessary for the battle to be finished.

" After artillery, call chemistry to our aid ; but it must not be allowed to take a whole year to evolve its products."

General Foch definitely condemned the conception of a break-through. He substituted for it the idea of successive efforts, made against a wide front, with the purpose of breaking up and separating the enemy's system of defence.

He wrote :

" . . . The succession of obstacles which an offensive encounters in its advance leads to an inevitable succession of attacks. This requires that the offensive, if it is to accomplish its purpose, must last and be continuous for a certain length of time. Instead of a short, sharp and violent action, we must prepare for a continuous action, that is, a series of efforts following each other as closely as possible.

" We must give up the idea of an assault undertaken with more or less deep and dense masses, the reserves following closely on the heels of the first line, with the idea of carrying in a single bound a whole series of obstacles and thus breaking through. This method has never succeeded.

" *It is a fact that the infantry attack always halts and fails at that point where the preparation has not been sufficient.*

" Once more we see that the power of organization is stronger than the bravery of troops. . . . We can launch infantry only against obstacles which we have with entire certainty prepared for this action."

On December 6th, he again wrote :

" The offensive draws its strength :

" 1. From its power of destruction (artillery, gas), increasing all the time, directed against each line for the benefit of the attacking troops.

" 2. From its ability promptly to renew its successive action against each succeeding line.

" Destruction, repetition ; these are its essential characteristics. The one, sought for and therefore to be reinforced ; the other forced upon us and therefore to be abridged.

" In any case, enterprises of long duration cannot at this time be avoided ; and yet they threaten to exceed our resources in men. Such efforts cannot be sustained to a conclusion, or even shortened, except by a new development of our destructive power through the use of *matériel*, which is the only way in which our infantry can be economised.

" The offensive we ought to prepare is one capable, as far as ground is concerned, of penetrating deeply ; and as far as time is concerned, of lasting longer than any so far undertaken."

On January 21st, 1916, he added :

" In short, it is a series of successive acts, each one necessitating a great deal of artillery and very little infantry. This form of attack applied in the battle of the future opens up the possibility of wide and repeated offensives, provided we have at our disposal many guns and much ammunition."

Preparations for a Franco-British offensive between Arras and the Oise in 1916.—The British effectives in France had so increased that, by the beginning of 1916, they constituted three Armies, deployed between the region around Ypres and the Somme. This increase of force made it possible for General Joffre to plan an Allied offensive on a scale hitherto never attempted. His idea was to attack along the whole front from Arras to the valley of the Oise. The operation would begin during the early days of July, 1916, the British advancing north of the Somme, the French south of that river. The general plans for the offensive were agreed upon in the course of an Inter-Allied Conference held at Chantilly on February 14th.

The French share in the attack, extending from the Somme to the Oise, was confided to the Northern

Group of Armies composed of fourteen Army Corps, divided into three Armies (the Second, the Third and the Sixth).

On March 16th, General Foch submitted to General Headquarters his plan for the employment of these forces, at the same time issuing his directions for the practical preparation of the attack. This done, he drew up for the use of his troops a " Note on the Offensive Battle," basing it upon the prescriptions of the Commander-in-Chief. In this note he set down the essential rules which should govern any attack against fortified positions.

During the preparation, the primary rôle belongs to the artillery. "The completeness of the artillery preparation is the measure of the success which the infantry can obtain. . . . The depth of ground that can be swept by the artillery determines the space which can be assigned for the infantry to conquer."

The execution consists of a series of efforts which must be estimated beforehand. The capture of a succession of fortified positions in echelon in depth is " an operation requiring much time. It should be methodically conducted until the enemy's power of resistance has been broken by his moral, material and physical disorganization, while at the same time our own offensive capacity has not been exhausted."

Successive actions should be undertaken against wide fronts, since these alone permit an important deployment of artillery, and General Foch concluded with these words : " When the enemy, his reserves exhausted, can no longer oppose us with organized and continuous defences, then only can we abandon the methodical mode of action. But this mode is the only one which will enable us first to destroy an organized front, and then to continue the combat by operations having the nature of a manœuvre in open country."

On April 13th, 1916, in a letter to the Commander-in-Chief, he again outlined the physiognomy of modern battle and the conditions it exacts. " The struggle will be long. The masses of artillery demanded for its support must be abundantly supplied with ammunition. If this can not be furnished, no military result can be attained on the Western Front."

While these preparations for the Battle of the Somme were being elaborated, grave events were taking place around Verdun. These obliged the Commander-in-Chief to modify his original plans. On April 26th he informed General Foch that the quantity of ammunition which could be placed at his disposal " is momentarily reduced by the consumption now going on around Verdun." The Northern Group of Armies could only count on nine Army Corps instead of fourteen ; thirty Divisions instead of thirty-nine ; its front of attack was reduced to twenty miles.

" We are a long way from that wide, powerful offensive which has in view an attainable objective and which can keep going," wrote General Foch. "And yet these are the sole conditions which permit an attack to reach a strategic result and not fade away into helplessness. After a few tactical successes at the start, we are likely to see our action halted—in other words, losses and sacrifices to no profitable end."

A month later, May 20th, there was a new reduction in his forces. Only seven Army Corps, and a maximum of twenty-six Divisions could now be counted upon for the initial attack. Under these conditions, the French effort would have to be limited to the front between Maricourt and the Amiens-Péronne road, and would be carried out by a single Army—the Sixth, operating astride the Somme. Its main function would be to support and cover on the south the British offensive, now to become the principal one. However, in order to be ready for some future eventuality, General Foch decided to continue the preparations already begun all along his front.

On June 3rd, the Corps of the Sixth Army which were to make the assault took over their sectors ; the placing of the heavy guns and their ammunition was over by the 15th. On July 1st the Franco-British offensive began.

The Somme Offensive (July 1st—November 15th, 1916)

The fortified system against which seventeen Allied Divisions were now launched consisted of two principal positions in echelon over a depth of from two to three miles. In some places there was an intermediate position. From the start the French Sixth Army and the right and centre of the British penetrated well into the German first position, in many places passing beyond the objectives assigned. The left of the British, running up against more powerful points of support, alone made little progress.

The advance was pursued during the days following. South of the Somme, in particular, it met with scarcely any resistance on the part of the enemy, being in reality only checked by the necessity of keeping within the general limits of the manœuvre. The principal action lay to the north of the Somme, where it was being pursued in conjunction with the British forces, the action south of the river having for its essential object to cover and support the one on the north. Its strength and objectives had been intentionally fixed as a part of this plan; it would have been a mistake therefore, to allow it to be pursued in a direction which would have prevented its fulfilling this duty. And, in the opinion of General Foch, all the more so, since the principal offensive north of the Somme was making but slow progress in the face of the increasing enemy resistance and violent counter-attacks.

However, between July 2nd and 20th, the Franco-British attacks managed to effect some progress in the sector which runs from the valley of the Somme to the Amiens-Bapaume high road. They captured all the intermediary positions established in this region and got within assaulting distance of the enemy's second position. The British centre even carried it for a length of four miles, during the attacks of July 14th, 15th and 16th.

Unfortunately, after the successes of July there followed a regrettable slowing up of operations. The British Commander-in-Chief was anxious to increase his artillery and his ammunition, put in the line new Divisions arrived from England and augment the number of his new offensive weapons, the tanks. Therefore, during the month of August, he limited himself to attacking a few special points, which resulted in but insignificant gains, or repulses. In vain the French Commander-in-Chief urged upon him the necessity of not delaying the resumption of attacks over an extended front. Sir Douglas, while declaring his agreement in principle, subordinated the undertaking of any large enterprise to first obtaining local results. This decision meant that the French Army would have to mark time, since its essential mission was to aid the British Army. Nevertheless, our Sixth Army distinguished itself by carrying the German second position from Maurepas to the Somme. The French Tenth Army, on the right of the

Sixth, made ready to prolong to the south of the Somme the Franco-British front of attack and to enter into action at the beginning of September.

On September 3rd the Allied attacks began again with an amplitude and a co-ordination which had been unknown in August. The results followed suit. On the left, the British, for the first time making use of tanks, captured powerful points of support such as Guillemont, Ginchy, Flers, Morval, Thiepval. While in the centre, the French Sixth Army, by a series of efforts, got as far as the Bapaume-Péronne road, which it reached at Bouchavesnes and Rancourt. The enemy tried to extricate himself by a powerful counter-attack launched against Bouchavesnes on September 20th. This failed, and six days later he was forced to evacuate the important centre of Combles.

South of the Somme, the Tenth Army captured villages whose defences the Germans had been improving for two years- Chilly, Soyécourt, Deniécourt, Vermandovillers. It was, unfortunately, limited in its efforts by the insufficiency of its offensive powers. Since the consequences of the Verdun battle continued to make themselves felt, it was not yet possible for the French command to feed at one and the same time the two fronts of attack north and south of the Somme. All available means were reserved for the Sixth Army, north of the river, which was acting in support of the British forces.

However that may be, the month of September was marked by undoubted success. On a front of nearly twenty miles the Franco-British forces had, in the course of this month, taken three successive enemy positions, advanced on a depth of more than three miles, and made impressive captures of stores and prisoners.

In order to arrive at this result, General Foch had been led to reinforce the three French Corps which were operating north of the Somme with two new Corps.

The presence of five Corps concentrated in this narrow space created an accumulation of troops whose movements and supply were effected with the greatest difficulty in the face of a numerous and watchful German artillery. It became essential to thin out this area and reduce the number of Divisions in the line.

Having in view the operations in progress at the Franco-British point of junction, this reduction could only be effected on the right of the Sixth Army. For this reason, General Foch decided to abandon provisionally any attack on the centre, between Bouchavesnes and the Amiens-Péronne road, and to pursue his attacks on the left and right in appropriate rhythm and with the necessary amplitude.

On the left, the efforts of the British Armies and the French Sixth Army were pursued in the direction of Bapaume-Bertincourt. On the right, the French Tenth Army, taking advantage of the rectangular shape of its front, continued its attacks southwards.

The month of October was employed in the development of this two-fold action.

On the 7th, a combined Franco-British attack was launched north of the Somme, on a twelve mile front. It obtained some success, but was unable to reach the objectives which had been assigned it. The enemy's means of defence had been remarkably strengthened. Nests of machine-guns, often established in shell-holes and other places hard to discover, checked the attacking troops, producing piece-meal attacks and slowing up any concerted advance—which alone could produce useful results. To these difficulties of a tactical order there were soon added unfavourable weather conditions. The rain, which began falling in the second half of October, soon rendered impassable the ground which had already been cut up by shells and trench-work. It brought in its wake all sorts of difficulties and increased the fatigue of the troops. On the 30th, for example, an exceptionally violent storm demolished the trench systems and put supplies and equipment temporarily out of use.

In spite of this precarious situation, our Sixth Army succeeded in capturing Sailly-Saillisel on October 18th, while the Tenth Army extended its positions appreciably in the direction of Pressoire and Ablaincourt.

The French High Command continued to stimulate the morale and encourage the ardour of the troops. It was determined to pursue its offensive plan in spite of everything, and it proceeded to prepare, for the beginning of November, a concerted attack by the Tenth and Sixth Armies between Chaulnes and Sailly-Saillisel.

On November 5th, the Sixth Army and the right of the British Armies advanced, but they gained no great success. November 7th, on the contrary, saw the Tenth Army reach all its objectives—Pressoire, Ablaincourt, Génermont. It was then in an excellent position for preparing the more important operation which General Foch's instructions considered should bring it to the railway line between Mazencourt and Happlincourt, and to the Somme above Péronne.

Unfortunately, after several days of fine, cold weather, the rain began again to fall heavily, destroying communications and trenches. It became impossible to attack, and it was decided to postpone the opening of the proposed offensive until the month of December.

On November 13th and 14th, the British Fifth Army gained another brilliant success on both sides of the Ancre valley. This success marked the end of the battle.

The French Commander-in-Chief had, in effect, drawn up his plan of action for 1917. He explained it on November 15th in the course of an inter-Allied meeting held at Chantilly.

The Northern Group, composed of four Armies, was to attack between the Somme and the Oise. At the same time, the British Armies were to carry out a combined operation between Bapaume and Vimy (north of Arras). The offensive was to be ready for February 1st. In order to organize these forces suitably, it was decided that, as from December 1st, the British should relieve the French up to the vicinity of Bouchavesnes.

On December 16th General Nivelle took command of the French Armies and adopted a new programme for the 1917 offensives.

The Northern Group of Armies was to take part in these operations under the orders of a leader other than General Foch. The latter, relieved of this command, quit the Headquarters of the Armies of the North at noon on December 27th, 1916, and took up his station at Senlis.

II

In disfavour (December 27th, 1916—May 17th, 1917)

The results obtained in the Battle of the Somme had been far from negligible. The number of prisoners and the quantity of *matériel* captured from the Germans, as also the amount of territory reconquered, exceeded by far anything that had been seen up to that time. On the enemy's side, to the disappointment caused by the check at Verdun there was added the uneasiness aroused by the unexpected strength in munitions which the Allies had just revealed, and which was certain to increase. This anxiety had already been manifested several times in the communiqués issued by the German staff during the battle. Other indications were seen in the replacement of Falkenhayn at General Headquarters by Hindenburg and Ludendorff, as well as in the peace offers made at the end of 1916 and the retreat towards the Hindenburg position effected in the spring of 1917.

However, these results were considered insufficient. Esteeming that the war munitions furnished had been amply sufficient both as regards quantity and quality, the French Government laid the blame upon the methods of attack prescribed and upon the generals who had devised them. There had to be victims, and General Foch was one of them. No account was taken of the warnings he had given at the time when, following on the events at Verdun, he was obliged to reduce his front of attack on the Somme to such a degree that any decisive success was rendered impossible. It was asserted that his methods of conducting a battle had seen their day and were now out of date. These methods were contrasted with the fruitful counter-offensives carried out in front of Verdun during October, 1916. But no account was taken of the fact that the success of the latter was, in great measure, due to the enemy's necessity of sending his reserves to the Somme battlefields and of keeping them there.

The chief command of the French Army, and that of the Armies of the North, therefore passed into other hands.

With splendid abnegation, General Foch withdrew. "To measure the greatness of his soul, one must have seen him in these sad moments. To the regrets, even to the indignation, he heard expressed around him, he contented himself with saying : 'Let them go ahead,' accompanying the words with that gesture we all knew so well and with which he dismissed everything that he did not wish to see or know. Never, during the whole of the period when his great faculties were left almost without employment, did he let fall a single word of recrimination or discontent."*

Senlis-Mirecourt

The new Commander-in-Chief, General Nivelle, having offered to retain him in the zone of the armies, General Foch established himself with a small group of officers at Senlis.

He was entrusted with the task of drawing up a plan of operations to meet the possible case of the violation of Swiss neutrality by the Germans. This plan was forwarded to the Commander-in-Chief on January 12th, 1917, and was approved by him.

Ten days later General Foch was sent to Mirecourt to assume temporary command of the Seventh and Eighth Armies, in the absence of the titular chief, General de Castelnau, who was then in Russia. This situation lasted until March 30th.

During these two months in the Vosges, he displayed the utmost energy in improving the defensive positions of the Armies under his command, and in perfecting certain plans of attack the preparation of which had been prescribed by General Headquarters.

He also occupied himself to a considerable extent with

* *Le Maréchal Foch*, by General Weygand. (Firmin-Didot. Paris, 1929.)

the practical realization of his plan of operations in Switzerland in case the Germans made them necessary. His Chief of Staff, General Weygand, was sent to Berne to concert measures with the Swiss Staff for this eventuality.

Shortly afterwards he received orders to proceed to Italy. On April 8th, 1917, he met General Cadorna at Vicenza and together they examined the conditions under which British and French units might best intervene in Italy in case of a very heavy attack by the enemy. The transport, concentration and employment of these units were the object of a prolonged study, whose excellence and usefulness were demonstrated by the events which occurred six months later on the Italian front.

On April 15th, General Foch found himself again at Senlis, in an atmosphere of almost complete calm. He suffered greatly from this heart-breaking inaction; but the period of rest was not without some value, for it enabled him to meditate upon the lessons and the future problems of the War, and thus prepare himself for the tasks awaiting him. These, growing constantly in importance, at last brought him to the chief command of the Allied Armies.

III

Chief of the General Staff

On May 15th, 1917, M. Painlevé, Minister of War, appointed General Foch Chief of the French General Staff.

As technical adviser to the French Government, he now entered into the councils of the Allied Governments; his field of action comprised not only the Western Front

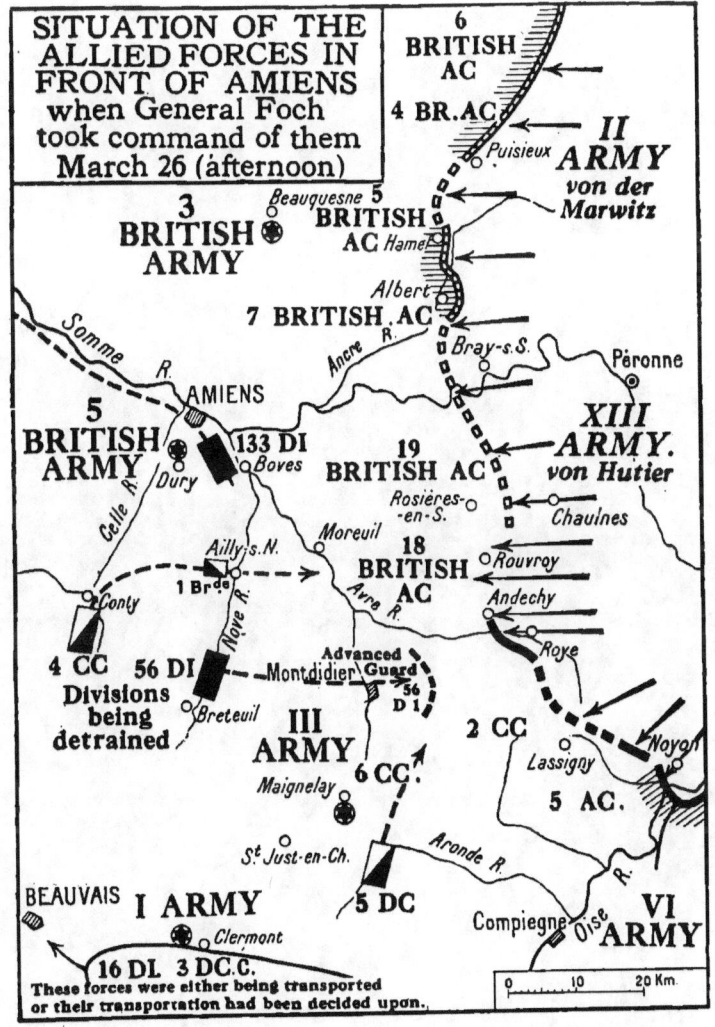

but that of the East as well.

At the moment he assumed this post, the cause of the Entente was passing through a critical period. On the West, the hopes founded on the plan of campaign for 1917 had just been crushed. The French Army, disappointed by the barren results of its efforts, was affected by a grave moral crisis which, for a considerable time, condemned it to a strict defensive. Deprived of its support, the British attacks could no longer hope for decisive results.

On the East, the Russian Army, fallen a prey to revolutionary propaganda, still held its ground, but seemed decided upon a purely passive attitude. Roumania was still in a period of convalescence, after the trials of the previous autumn. Greece, which had come in with us after Constantine's abdication, had a whole army to create. America was furnishing the Entente with large supplies of men and material, but the former would not be available for battle before the spring of 1918.

On the side of the Central Powers, although Austria and Turkey showed signs of weariness, Germany had regained a freedom of action of which the year 1916 had gradually deprived her. Her Army, liberated to a considerable extent on the East, would soon be able to concentrate with imposing magnitude on the West and thus take advantage of a superiority in numbers which she had not been able to realize in that theatre since the beginning of the war.

Plan of action for the second half of 1917

On June 8th, 1917, at Abbeville, General Foch met General Robertson, Chief of the Imperial General Staff, for the purpose of coming to an agreement as to the line of action to be followed in the second half of 1917. In view of the Russian default and the effect it would have upon the Western theatre, as well as the time it would take before the American Army could come into action, the two Generals decided that military operations in France must be limited to a policy of attrition, until such time as American aid, by re-establishing a superiority in our favour, would permit decisive results to be once more entertained.

In the meanwhile, the Italian Army, reinforced by heavy guns and ammunition supplied by France and England, and aided if possible by a concerted action of the Russians, was to attack the Austrian Army, with a view to putting it out of action. In this way it was hoped that, with the aid of diplomacy, Austria might be detached from her powerful ally.

But it soon became clear that no help could be expected from Russia, and that even her total defection must shortly be expected. General Foch's task, therefore, was now to study the arrangements which would enable the Entente to face the German armies in France when reinforced by the units coming from the Russian front. On July 27th, 1917, he drew up a memorandum which he communicated to the representatives of the Allied Governments assembled in Paris. The following were his conclusions :

" In case Russia's defection enables the enemy to transfer to the Western Front all the German and Austrian forces now employed on the Russian front, it would seem that the Coalition ought to be able to assemble the resources necessary to resist the enemy's onslaught until such moment as America can put into line enough troops to re-establish the balance to our advantage.

" But this relatively favourable military situation can only be obtained by the adoption of the following measures:

" (a) Confine ourselves to the simple defence of secondary fronts, and reduce the effectives on these fronts to a minimum consistent with this defensive attitude.

" (b) Hasten in every possible way the creation of an American Army and its transport to France.

" (c) Prepare the tonnage necessary for moving the forces to be taken from secondary fronts.

" (d) Obtain unity of action on the Western Front by means of a permanent inter-Allied military organ, whose function would be to prepare the rapid movement of troops from one theatre to another."

The solid foundation on which these conclusions reposed was proved by events a few months later; but they were received with little favour by the meeting. Mr. Lloyd George, in particular, declared that Russia's defection was not very probable, that military men lacked imagination, and that what must above all be sought was " to modify the situation to our advantage by detaching one of Germany's allies."

Assembled anew in London on August 7th, the heads of the Allied Governments requested their Chiefs of Staff to study the preparation of a powerful offensive in Italy for the beginning of 1918. General Foch, therefore, arranged with General Robertson and General Cadorna for the despatch to Italy, at the appropriate time, of ten Divisions and four hundred pieces of heavy artillery, half to be furnished by England and half by France.

The Russian Defection

Meantime, while making arrangements for sending future support to Italy, the Allied Governments exerted themselves to hold the Russians in the line. But the morale state of this Army, undermined by Bolshevist propaganda, was getting worse every day. On November 6th, Lenin's seizure of power marked the collapse of Russia and proved her desire to put an end to the War. On November 21st, Lenin ordered the Commander-in-Chief of the Russian Army to negotiate an armistice and draw up terms of peace with the enemy.

The French Government protested. General Foch telegraphed to General Niessel, Chief of the French Military Mission attached to the Russian Army, that France counted on the patriotism of the Russian High Command to repulse all criminal negotiations and keep the Russian Army facing the common enemy. He informed General Berthelot, our representative attached to the Roumanian staff, that the French Government appreciated the gravity of the situation which a total defection on the part of Russia would entail for Roumania, but there must be no thought of disbanding the Roumanian Army. If events necessitated the evacuation of Roumanian territory, the struggle must be pursued in Bessarabia and in the Donetz.

Thus, placing its reliance upon the Russian High Command and upon Roumania's fidelity, the Government in Paris endeavoured to thwart the politicians of Petrograd. This attempt did not succeed. Krylenko's nomination as Commander-in-Chief of the Russian Army deprived the Entente of the support on which it had counted.

However, the beginnings of national resistance now seemed to take form in Southern Russia. In agreement with the French Government, General Foch endeavoured to aid and encourage the movement. During the months of December, 1917, and January, 1918, his efforts were concentrated upon the organization of these anti-Bolshevist centres and the formation of Polish, Czecho-

Slovakian and Ukrainian Divisions. General Berthelot carried on the work in southern Russia, and General Niessel in central and northern Russia. The intervention of General Foch was in no way an effort to break up the newly-established government in Russia. What he sought was the continuation, under any form, of the struggle against the Central Empires and the maintenance of a war-front in the East.

Thus, having failed, in spite of all his efforts, to prevent the conclusion of the Russo-German peace, he endeavoured, by every possible means, to prevent its exploitation.

Accordingly, he made recommendations to the French Minister for Foreign Affairs for the immediate organization of inter-Allied action in eastern Siberia, where anarchy was making rapid progress, and where the Trans-Siberian railway was threatened. He requested that this action should be entrusted to the United States and Japan, and he indicated its objects. These were to prevent the despatch to Russia, and thence to the Central Powers, of munitions and raw material accumulated in Vladivostock; and also to enable the centres of resistance which might exist or be created in Russia to be encouraged and supplied. And, at all events, they could deny the enemy access to the Pacific, and thus deprive him of the possibility of developing submarine warfare in these waters.

The Austro-German attack in Italy

The grave events in Russia were not long in producing their effect on the Western theatre of war, through the freedom of action which in a large measure they procured for the Central Empires.

On October 24th, 1917, an Austro-German offensive on the Italian front, taking advantage of a very thick fog and a torrential rain which completely paralysed the active organs of the defence, broke through the Italian lines on the Upper Isonzo, in the region of Caporetto. The breach opened by the enemy on the front of the Italian Army forced the Commander-in-Chief, General Cadorna, to withdraw the whole of his forces towards the Tagliamento.

On October 26th, the French Government offered to send reinforcements to the Italians. The telegram crossed a message from General Cadorna, requesting the despatch of British and French Divisions in accordance with the agreements of 1915—1917. General Pétain at once made preparations to send a force of four Divisions and a corresponding proportion of heavy artillery.

The British Chief of Staff, General Robertson, at first displayed less eagerness to despatch British troops, and it was upon the formal advice of the French Chief of Staff that he decided to put in movement an Army Corps of two Divisions. " It is indisputable," wrote General Foch, " that General Cadorna has all that is necessary in the matter of munitions, troops and lines of resistance for repulsing the enemy. . . . But events are more powerful than arguments. It is to the Allies' interest to prevent the Italian disaster from growing larger at any cost. We must, therefore, without any delay, support the Italian Army both morally and materially."

It was possible, indeed, that the danger which hung over Italy might become serious. If the enemy penetrated far into the country, it would give him the possibility of considerably disturbing the Allies' communications with northern Africa, Egypt, Palestine and Greece. The matter was therefore of the highest importance. The French Government so well appreciated this fact that it did not hesitate to despatch its Chief of the General Staff across the Alps with full powers.

On the 28th, while the first French troops were entraining, General Foch left Paris. He arrived at Treviso on the 30th at daybreak, saw General Cadorna immediately, and learned the exact situation.

The Italian Army was retiring through the Frioul region towards the Tagliamento. Would it be able to establish itself behind this river? Cadorna dared not vouch for it. The Second Army had been so badly shaken at Caporetto that its powers of resistance seemed for the moment compromised, and it appeared probable that the retirement would have to be continued to the Piave.

Under this hypothesis, General Foch decided that the first French troops should detrain at Vicenza. But that very day, the 30th, information that was apparently reliable caused the Comando Supremo to apprehend a strong enemy offensive north of the Lake of Garda. General Foch, therefore, modified his original dispositions; he placed two French Divisions north of Brescia and two around Verona, in which place General Duchesne, commanding the French forces, established his Headquarters.

On the 31st, General Robertson in his turn arrived at Treviso and consulted with General Foch. Both Generals considered that the Italian Armies had not been beaten. One only, indeed, had been attacked. Provided that order was re-established, these Armies represented a force which should make it possible to dispute the line of the Tagliamento and establish a firm resistance on the Piave and in the Trentino.

On November 1st General Foch saw the Duke of Aosta, paid a visit to the King at Padua, and proceeded to Rome with the Italian Prime Minister, Signor Orlando. The latter took an intelligent and calm view of the situation. He was ready to fight to the bitter end, and if it were necessary, he declared, even to retreat to Sicily. " There is no question of retreating to Sicily," replied General Foch. " It is on the Piave that we must resist."

It was in similar terms that he had addressed Field-Marshal French under the walls of Ypres. Five months later he would be found repeating them as he paced up and down in front of the Town Hall of Doullens.

On November 2nd and 3rd he had numerous interviews in Rome with members of the Italian Government, and he emphasized the necessity of reorganizing the Comando Supremo with a view to making it more vigorous.

On the 5th the heads of the British, French and Italian Governments met at Rapallo. General Foch retraced for them the sequence of the recent events. The Italian Second Army was broken, the three others were intact ; all were withdrawing from the line of the Tagliamento to the line of the Piave, which was stronger and shorter. They should be able to hold it easily with their 700,000 men, provided the Comando Supremo clearly announced its determination and supervised the execution of its orders.

The conference was resumed on November 6th. The British Prime Minister, fortified by " the high authority of Generals Foch and Robertson," declared that he could not entrust Allied troops to the Comando Supremo as it then existed. M. Orlando replied that the reorganization of the Italian High Command and the appointments

GENERAL PERSHING ARRIVES IN FRANCE.

to be made in it were to be submitted at once to the King for his approval.

A further question was raised, that of effectives. The Italian Prime Minister requested the despatch of fifteen Allied Divisions to Italy. Generals Foch and Robertson considered that this number was exaggerated. " Moreover," added General Foch, " one of the noticeable events of this war is the strength of the defensive. In certain circumstances numerical superiority may ensure victory, but in others this may not be so. The best proof is the resistance of the Allied Armies behind the Yser against a vastly superior German strength. This same truth was demonstrated at Verdun, where the enemy, although he attacked many times, was repulsed by forces distinctly inferior. With the use of barbed wire and other obstacles, it is possible to establish a very effective resistance on the Piave. . . . Behind that river there stands an organized Army well commanded and well supplied with ammunition ; it can resist greatly superior forces."

The events in Italy also drew attention to a point which had occupied the minds of Allied statesmen and generals for several months. In face of the numerical superiority, of the liberty to manœuvre and ability to effect surprise which had been acquired by the adversary through the defection of Russia, the Allies could not fight under favourable conditions except by rapidly throwing in their reserves at any given point on their front. To effect this it was necessary in the first place to have information concerning the enemy's intentions, and in the second place to possess an organ which could immediately give the necessary orders for the movement of these reserves to the threatened quarter. This pointed to the creation of an inter-Allied body capable of exercising a comprehensive supervision over the conduct of operations in all the various war theatres. To speak plainly, a Commander-in-Chief of the Coalition was needed ; but general opinion, especially in England, was as yet little inclined to accept this view.

The solution which, in the month of November, 1917, carried the day, was the creation of a Supreme War Council, composed of the Prime Minister of each of the Allied Governments represented at Rapallo, assisted by one cabinet minister. This council had its seat at Versailles. It was assisted by a Staff which included a military representative of each Power. But this military representative was prohibited from exercising any other function. This provision was directed more particularly against France, whose selected representative, General Foch, was at the same time Chief of the General Staff. It was necessary, therefore, for the General, on his return from Italy, to resign one or the other of these posts.

The other members appointed to serve with General Foch were, for England, General Wilson ; and for Italy, General Cadorna. The latter was replaced at the Comando Supremo by General Diaz. Later on, the United States were represented by General Tasker Bliss.

As soon as they took up their work, the military representatives were requested to examine the general situation on all the fronts, and especially that existing in the Italian theatre.

On November 9th Generals Foch and Wilson met General Diaz, the new Italian Commander-in-Chief, at Padua. They found him quite resolved to defend the line of the Piave, but at the same time he expressed fear of being turned by an Austrian attack debouching from the Tonale Pass.

In order to allay this anxiety, General Foch once more

modified the dispositions of the French forces in Italy. One of the Divisions was moved to the Val Canonica, and the other to Brescia, where General Duchesne established his Headquarters. In addition, General Foch proposed, with the assent of the Comando Supremo, that General Duchesne be given command of the sector between the lake of Garda and the Swiss frontier.

Shortly afterwards, General Diaz regretted the decision which placed the French troops at such a distance. On November 11th he expressed considerable anxiety in regard to the Montello point of junction between the valley of the Piave and the mountain region. On this occasion he also informed General Foch that " public opinion in Italy was unfavourably impressed by the Allied Armies being kept so far from danger." He therefore requested that the French Divisions be directed successively to the Piave front.

General Foch refused to be induced by any matter of sentiment to move French troops along encumbered roads into a region already crowded with Italian troops, where conditions made their presence of little real help, and where they ran the risk of being involved in the Italian retreat. Moreover, ever since his arrival in Italy, he had always upheld the idea that it was essential to avoid a premature and piecemeal engagement of the Allied forces. They would have melted away in local operations and would have been wanting in the event of another penetration of the Italian front.

However, in order to give every possible satisfaction to the Comando Supremo, he decided to place the main body of the French forces between Valdagno and Vicenza, one Division being temporarily left west of the Lake of Garda. The British Army was to be concentrated on the French right, south of Vicenza.

On November 15th, General Foch found it possible to telegraph to Paris that " the situation on the positions now held by the Italian Army appears to have appreciably improved," and " morale seems to be getting generally better."

On the 16th he forwarded the report called for by the Supreme War Council as to the extent of the assistance to be furnished Italy. This report recommended that twelve Divisions, six French and six British, with a proportionate amount of heavy artillery, be sent immediately. After the first contingent arrived (presumably about December 12th), events would show whether it was necessary to increase these figures.

On the 18th, in spite of the fact that the situation was improving every day, the Italian General Staff sent General Foch a series of documents having to do with the organization of the retreat to the Mincio and the Adige. General Foch refused to contemplate any such eventuality.

Moreover, by November 20th, the Allied forces were in position to afford serious support to the Italian Army. On the 22nd and 23rd, heavy fighting took place on the Asiago plateau, as well as in the region of Monte Grappa and Monte Tomba. The Italian soldiers put up a splendid resistance everywhere.

On the 23rd General Foch was able to leave Italy ; the crisis was past. The first demoralization once over, the Comando Supremo rapidly recovered itself and, under its direction, the Italian Army re-established with its own forces a continuous front in the valley of the Piave, without the British and French units having to be engaged.

General Foch had aided and supported the Comando Supremo ; he had helped it to take the energetic decisions which the gravity of the situation exacted. Here, as in the Battle of Flanders three years earlier, he was listened to by reason of the clearness of his vision, his buoyancy, his promptness to act and his unreserved devotion to the common cause of all the Allies.

The events of Caporetto had justified the General's predictions, and they clearly proved the accuracy of his conclusions presented in the note of July 26th, 1917. These were, essentially, two : to expedite the arrival of the American Army in France so as to overcome the enemy's numerical superiority, and to create an inter-Allied military organ to direct Entente strategy.

Co-operation of the American Army

The general arrangements for the constitution of the American Army and its transport to France had been drawn up in the United States by agreement between Marshal Joffre and the American Government. When General Foch assumed the functions of Chief of the General Staff of the French Army, he, in accord with the French Government and the French Commander-in-Chief, proceeded to take the necessary measures for the debarkation of the American forces in France and their installation in camps. A section of his staff dealt especially with these matters. He was also charged with the question of the employment of the American contingents on the French front.

At the time America entered the war, everybody—in Europe as well as in the United States—was of one mind as to the utilization of the American Army, in large units under its own chiefs. It had been agreed that, once their period of instruction in France was terminated, the American Divisions would be progressively established in an American sector astride the Moselle.

But in November, 1917, following on the events in Russia and because of the delays foreseen in the matter of putting American Divisions in the line, the Allies modified their point of view. Preoccupied by their numerical inferiority and the crisis in man-power which menaced them on the eve of a German offensive, whose extent and duration no one could predict, they now envisaged, as the only remedy for a very grave situation, the employment of American troops one month after their arrival in France, that is to say, the moment their elementary instruction was finished. The idea was to place them by regiments or even by battalions in British or French Divisions.

This system of amalgamation in reality satisfied neither the United States, which saw in it a serious delay in the constitution of the self-contained army desired, nor General Foch, who considered that troops never fight so well as under their own flag. It was a passing necessity to which both parties would resign themselves.

To the propositions made in this sense, both President Wilson and General Pershing answered that, if necessary and because of the interests at stake, they would consent to the amalgamation. As a proof of their willingness, they immediately placed four negro Regiments at General Pétain's disposal.

As a matter of fact, it demanded a great effort to form, equip, instruct and transport the American Army to France.

" The problem presented," to quote Marshal Foch, " was of huge dimensions, since it was a question of putting on a war footing a country of over a hundred million inhabitants. Everything had to be created.

The Regular Army, maintained on a scale sufficient for the narrow requirements of peace time, could only furnish a small fraction of what was necessary for the mobilization of the numerous Divisions which America had decided to raise. These had to be constructed from the ground up—their staffs, their officers and non-commissioned officers, their troops, as well as the large supply of munitions without which nothing can be done in modern war. An entirely new instrument had to be forged. And not only was it necessary to forge on a vast scale, but to forge quickly. The war had been going on for three years ; no one could doubt that its very amplitude and intensity rendered its continuance for any great length of time impossible. If America was to make her weight felt in the final decision, she must hurry her forces to Europe with the utmost speed."*

But, however energetic had been the efforts made to place the American Army on the battle-fields of Europe, the results obtained so far were rather poor. Arrivals on the average did not exceed 30,000 men a month. In March, 1918, a year after America's entry into the War and at the moment the German offensive was launched, the American effectives in France did not reach more than 300,000 men ; of Divisions, there were only six.

The forecasts made at the end of 1917 showed that no useful help from the United States could be counted upon before the summer of 1918, and no powerful help before 1919.

The Allies' plan of action for 1918 ; the question of reserves and the inter-Allied High Command

These delays in putting the American forces into the

* Written by Marshal Foch a few months before his death : *The American Soldier.*

field had to be added to the many difficulties confronting the Allies at the end of 1917. It was certain that the Germans would exert every effort to bring the whole weight of their armies to bear in the Western theatre, so as to complete their victory before the arrival of the American Armies could decisively alter the situation. During the first half of 1918, the Allies would be reduced to opposing the adversary's masses with their own unaided resources. In face of the enemy's numerical superiority and the possibilities presented for his action, what was the line of conduct to follow?

On November 18th, 1917, General Pétain, in a statement before the French War Committee, declared himself in favour of a waiting policy on the Western Front.

Such tactics, he said, demanded a solid organization of the front, and the constitution of strong reserves ready to intervene at the point of danger. But it was also necessary that a Supreme Chief should be appointed for preparing plans and controlling the reserves. " Unity of command," he added, " is one of the conditions of success."

On January 1st, 1918, General Foch, in his turn, presented the following views on this subject to the Military Representatives at Versailles:

" We must prepare ourselves for a very serious offensive on the part of the Germans any moment after the beginning of this year. It will be combined as a function of *space* and of *time* ; that is to say, it will be directed upon different portions of the Anglo-French front, perhaps of the Italian front, at various intervals of time.

" We will meet this attack by defensive dispositions which at this moment are being carried out on the British and French fronts, and we have reason to hope that they will be sufficient to arrest the enemy before he can obtain decisive results.

" But we ought also to meet it by an attitude which, far from being passive, should be inspired by the determination of the Entente Armies to seize every opportunity to impose their will upon the adversary. This can only be achieved by assuming the offensive the moment it is possible ; for by no other means can victory be attained. . . .

" With this object in view, the Allied Armies should :

" (a) *In case of attack by the enemy :* Not only stop him and counter-attack on the ground he has used in attacking us, but also pronounce powerful counter-offensives by way of diversion. These should be prepared beforehand and launched against points chosen in advance and permitting rapid execution.

" (b) *If the adversary does not attack :* Be ready to take the initiative and operate against limited objectives, with the purpose of dominating the enemy, wearing him down and maintaining the combative spirit of our troops.

" (c) *In both of the above cases :* Be ready to develop these actions under the form of *a combined offensive with decisive objectives*, the moment the wearing down process, or any other favourable circumstance arising in the general situation, offers the hope of success."

This programme of January 1st, 1918, was the one which General Foch was to execute a few months later. In it can be seen the germ which he developed into ultimate victory : first, defensive action imposed by the situation ; then partial counter-offensives, and finally the general offensive which ended in victory. The General's sagacity was once more shown in this document.

However, in order to determine the conditions for undertaking a counter-offensive that would break the existing clinch, as recommended by General Foch, the General Staff stated in a note of January 6th, 1918 : " There must be a higher organ of command, which can at all times defend the general plan adopted as against personal inclinations and individual interests, and take rapid decisions and get them carried out without any loss of time. To make this possible, it is essential—at least in what concerns the front between the North Sea and Switzerland—that some military authority be appointed which, acting on behalf of the Coalition and in accordance with the views of the Supreme War Council, can exercise a directive action on the whole front, handle the common reserves, prepare the disengaging counterattack, and launch it at the proper moment."

Thus was brought up once more the question of inter-Allied reserves and the supreme command, for which General Foch had unsuccessfully pleaded at the hands of the Entente Governments on July 26th. But this time conditions were no longer the same ; serious events had occurred in Italy, the Rapallo agreement had been made and the Supreme War Council created.

Nevertheless, while this last institution represented a great improvement on the past, it was as yet far from meeting the requirements of the situation. A war council is an organ of consultation and study ; it is unfitted for rapid decision and execution ; it has no instrument of action at its disposal. With what could such a body oppose the approaching German attacks—in what way reply to them ? As soon as the action was engaged, would it not be reduced to accepting decisions already taken by others ? Would these decisions respond to the interests of the Coalition taken as a whole, or would they be dictated by individual interests and immediate necessities ?

The French and American Governments both desired a single supreme command. Mr. Lloyd George, personally, seemed to favour it, but public opinion in England and the British High Command were frankly hostile. England had adopted as her own the instructions given by Lord Kitchener to Sir John French at the outbreak of hostilities in August, 1914 : " I wish you to distinctly understand that your command is an entirely independent one, and that in no case will you place yourself under the orders of an Allied general."

Still more serious was the fact that the formation of a general reserve and its employment also encountered opposition. General Weygand, the French military representative at Versailles, as well as General Foch, did his utmost to overcome this.

On January 21st General Weygand submitted General Foch's plan of action for 1918 to his colleagues. Influenced by General Wilson, the British representative, they expressed the opinion that no advantage in the French theatre could be obtained by either of the opponents during the year 1918. Therefore, under these conditions, the Allies would be better advised to adopt the idea recommended by Mr. Lloyd George of an action against Turkey, " with a view to destroying the Turkish armies and crushing the resistance of that country." General Weygand's influence and sagacity fortunately brought his collaborators back to a more opportune examination of the situation on the West, and secured their adherence to General Foch's point of view.

On the other hand, the question of a provisional unity of command, proposed by the French staff, met with uncompromising opposition, and the military representatives confined themselves to the creation of a general reserve, " for all the Allied forces on the Western Front, both in France and in Italy."

In fact, faced by these vague aspirations which were substituted for practical action, General Weygand was obliged to write to the Prime Minister on January 22nd : " While we stand under the menace—and perhaps on the eve—of the most powerful effort which the enemy has so far attempted against us, there exists no general plan for the operations of the Coalition in 1918."

In fact, no preparations were made for mutual support, nor for common action on the part of the Allied Armies In the course of a conference held on January 24th at Compiègne, at which General Robertson (coming from London) and the Commanders-in-Chief were present, General Foch pointed out this situation. Taking his stand against a purely defensive attitude, he preached activity. Citing as an example the Battle of the Somme, which loosened the grip on Verdun, he demonstrated that the best way to stop a persistent enemy offensive was to pronounce in your own turn a powerful attack. But, he added, such an operation is only possible if it has been anticipated and prepared.

And with what should it be made up ? Of every British and French Division that could be mustered. Therefore, the whole of the Franco-British front must be kept in view ; and not merely the French front on one hand, or the British front on the other. We ought to have " a general plan envisaging an offensive action, and we ought to be prepared to launch it at any given moment on a common battlefield with every available man in the Allied forces."

The Commanders-in-Chief agreed with General Foch on the principle of a disengaging counter-offensive. But they held that the effectives they could oppose to the German masses (and which wastage must still further decrease) would not enable them to execute it.

" In that case," Foch replied, " we have only prepared palliatives to meet the enemy's offensive ; we have no ample, vigorous counter-stroke ready."

He again took up the question before the Prime Ministers of the Allied Governments when they met at Versailles, January 30th to February 2nd, 1918 :

" Circumstances oblige us to maintain a waiting attitude during the early part of 1918. From this fact there results the necessity of having a defensive plan for the whole line from Nieuport to Venice ; but this plan must be capable of being transformed, according to circumstances, into an offensive plan, partial or complete.

" Our offensive plan should be established with the idea of meeting the various enemy attacks which may be pronounced against the different Allied Armies ; from this there results the necessity, for these Armies, of combining amongst themselves the means of ensuring their common defence. Each Army must have its own defensive system ; also its own reserves ready to throw in at any menaced point of its front. But there should be, in addition, general reserves which can be transported from one part of the entire front or any other that may be in danger. These reserves must also be capable of being united and used in a counter-offensive launched as a diversion to relieve one of the Allies from a concentrated assault directed against his lines.

" It is therefore essential that at the same time we prepare for defensive action we also concert these offensive manœuvres."

The two questions of Allied reserves and a plan of

campaign were thus presented to the statesmen responsible for the general conduct of the war. General Foch's programme was examined and discussed; the Commanders-in-Chief offered the objections we have already cited, based on their weakness in men. But, defended by M. Clemenceau, the plan was finally adopted.

The matter of an inter-Allied reserve was then taken up. General Foch easily obtained agreement as to the necessity for it, and he proposed for its constitution, maintenance and employment, the creation of an organ which, after consulting the Commanders-in-Chief, would take the necessary decisions. He suggested that this organ be composed of the British, French and Italian Chiefs of the General Staff.

During the discussion General Bliss, the United States military representative, asserted the necessity of creating an inter-Allied reserve and urged that it be placed under the command of one man. Mr. Lloyd George emphasized the uselessness of a new organization, which would be doing the same work as the Supreme War Council; however, he expressed the desire that General Foch, by reason of his experience and past record, should form part of the already existing organization.

On his proposal, an Executive Committee was formed with General Foch as president, composed of the military representatives of America, England and Italy. Its task was to determine the size of the general reserve and the share to be contributed by each Army. It was also to fix the zones where the reserve was to be stationed, prepare its intervention in battle and, when the time came, decide on its employment.

The Versailles Conference thus marked a great step towards a rational organization of the Entente forces.

Failing a single supreme commander, which was the logical solution, but which remained the object of uncompromising opposition, the scheme offered the possibility of considerable unity of action in the grave moments of battle.

The new Executive Committee at once set to work. Having fixed the strength of the general reserve at some thirty Divisions, it asked the British Army on February 6th for nine or ten Divisions, to include the three then in Italy; the French Army was to furnish thirteen or fourteen Divisions, including the four in Italy; the Italian Army, seven.

This reserve represented one-seventh of the Allied forces. It was " a minimum which could not be reduced without abandoning the conception of a general reserve really capable of influencing the issue of battle." The Executive Committee decided, furthermore, that the units of the general reserve should, in principle, be stationed in the zones of their armies, within distance of rapid intervention, and it requested the Belgian Army to relieve the British up to the outskirts of Langemarck, in order that the latter's effectives might be increased.

These dispositions raised objections from those called upon to execute them. The French Commander-in-Chief considered that the number of Divisions required of him was too high and he proposed eight instead of ten, adding : " So far as regards the employment of the Infantry Divisions selected to form part of the general reserve, I trust that our common efforts will smooth out the practical difficulties which will be sure to arise as soon as a battle starts." General Foch accepted the proposed eight Divisions and replied to the Commander-in-Chief : " You may rest assured that the Executive Committee, for its part, will do its utmost to prevent all delay and remove all difficulties."

Thus, thanks to a mutual understanding, agreement was established between the Committee and French General Headquarters.

It was otherwise with the British. On March 2nd Sir Douglas Haig wrote to General Foch that he had already assigned all his troops for meeting an enemy offensive, that he was unable to modify their disposition or his plan, and that he regretted his inability to associate himself with the proposals of the Executive Committee.

The refusal of the British Commander-in-Chief made it impossible for the Executive Committee to accomplish its mission. On March 4th, seventeen days before the German offensive broke, the Committee placed on record the following conclusion :

" The Executive Committee finds it impossible to continue its task of organizing an inter-Allied general reserve in conformity with the instructions which it received on February 2nd from the Supreme War Council on this subject. The Executive Committee requests that each military representative inform his government of this decision and ask for its instructions."

The matter was then brought before the Supreme War Council on March 14th and 15th in London.

At the beginning of the meeting, Mr. Lloyd George, although once more proclaiming the necessity for an inter-Allied reserve, defended Sir Douglas Haig's point of view. The French Prime Minister ranged himself with Mr. Lloyd George. He declared that : " on account of the attack now imminent, it is impossible to withdraw Divisions from Sir Douglas Haig or General Pétain. Furthermore, a complete agreement, endorsed

DEEP TRENCHES AND DUG-OUTS, WITH SAND-BAG REVETMENTS.

by the two Governments, exists between Field-Marshal Haig and General Pétain, who have made all dispositions for affording each other mutual assistance in case of need."

The representatives of the United States and Italy were of a different opinion. In an effort to give them satisfaction, but without abandoning in any way the special arrangements made for the Franco-British front, it was decided that the British and French Divisions then in Italy, and a number of Italian Divisions to be fixed by the Executive Committee, should form the nucleus of the general reserve. As time went on, this reserve would be progressively increased by new Divisions coming from America.

General Foch protested against these decisions, the text of which, moreover, had not been communicated to him before the session. " The question before the meeting," he said, " was apparently to organize an Executive Committee ; but it looks as though the first thing done was to deprive that Committee of all power to execute."

To which M. Clemenceau replied that, in his view, the powers of the Executive Committee had not been decreased by the resolution adopted but, on the contrary, they had been extended.

General Foch reverted to the question the following day, March 15th. Lifting the debate above the simple matter of forming an inter-Allied reserve, he took up the general conduct of operations : " You say that there exists perfect agreement between the various Commanders-in-Chief ; that each army knows what to expect from its neighbour. Very well ; but if the Supreme War Council does not know exactly the situation of each Army or the magnitude of this mutual assistance, how can it take the decisions which events will doubtless demand,

and how will it get them executed? If the Supreme War Council is to render any service, its powers must be extended."

Mr. Lloyd George was impressed by General Foch's reasoning; but he did not touch the heart of the matter; he confined himself to having it decided that " the agreement arrived at between the Commanders-in-Chief of the Allied armies in France, with a view to mutual support, will form the subject of an official communication to the permanent military representatives at Versailles." With this, the London Conference broke up, having achieved practically nothing.

The solution found for the question of a general reserve was entirely inadequate, while that of the unified command was not even touched upon.

It required a disaster to retrieve the error committed in London on March 15th, 1918.

CHAPTER I

THE GERMAN OFFENSIVE OF MARCH 21ST, 1918, AND THE DOULLENS AGREEMENT

The German attack of March 21st; its leaders; its methods; its aims—Inadequacy of the Allied arrangements—The London Conference of March 15th—The British Fifth Army is driven in—Decisions adopted by the British and French Commanders-in-Chief—Efforts made by General Foch in Paris and by Field-Marshal Sir Douglas Haig in London—The conferences at Compiègne and Abbeville, March 25th—The Doullens Conference of March 26th.

ON March 21st, 1918, at 4 A.M., the German artillery suddenly opened a violent bombardment along the whole of the front included between the valleys of the Scarpe and the Oise. At 9 o'clock, under cover of a thick fog, the enemy's infantry reached the positions which the British Armies had occupied since the spring of 1917, namely, on the north, the Third Army (General Byng) between Arras and the region of Le Catelet, and on the south, the Fifth Army (General Gough) from the region of Le Catelet to Barisis-aux-Bois.

The Third Army, covering a front of twenty-five miles, had ten Divisions in the front line and six in reserve. The Fifth Army, on a front of thirty-seven miles, had eleven Divisions in the front line, with three infantry and three cavalry Divisions in reserve. Opposing these, the German attacking forces were grouped into three armies. On the north, in the Arras region, was the Seventeenth Army (Otto von Below), and in the centre, between Cambrai and Le Catelet, the Second Army (von der Marwitz). Both belonged to the Group of Armies of the Crown Prince of Bavaria. To the south, resting on the valley of the Oise, was the Eighteenth Army (von Hutier), forming part of the Group of Armies of the German Crown Prince.

At the time these Armies made their assault on the British positions, the Allies were unaware of their exact strength, but they had an approximate idea. A study made three months previously at French General Headquarters had shown that the Germans, now relieved of all menace coming from Russia, would have available on March 1st, 1918, for the Western Front, some two hundred Divisions. These could furnish an offensive mass of eighty Divisions with one thousand heavy batteries. It was to be presumed that at least fifty of these Divisions would be employed for the initial actions, thus giving the Germans in the zone chosen for attack a numerical superiority of two to one.

The ability of the generals who would direct these operations was equally well known, for it had been fully tested. General von Below had gained a high and well deserved reputation in the course of the attacks made on the Italian front in October 1917. General von Hutier, at about the same period, had achieved important results at Riga, in an attack which he had prepared with perfect secrecy and carried out suddenly and with the utmost vigour.

The methods which had succeeded at Caporetto and at Riga were employed without change on the French Front in the spring of 1918. They may be summarized as follows:

1. Effect a surprise by secretly transferring the manœuvring mass to the scene of action (movements conducted by night, absence of lights in billets and camps, concealment from hostile aircraft, etc. . . .), and

by placing the attacking units in position only at the last moment.

2. Short and violent artillery preparation throughout a depth of from two to three miles, with plentiful use of gas shell, then the assault by infantry which has been assembled during the artillery preparation to within two or three hundred yards of the first lines to be carried.

3. Rapidity of execution, obtained by a swift advance of the infantry, first preceded by a rolling barrage laid down by the artillery and then protected by accompanying guns, trench mortars in close support and above all light machine-guns.

4. The breach having been made, seek to widen it by attacks directed against the flanks.

5. Endeavour to secure a rapid penetration of the enemy's positions by means of a resolute advance of the troops on distant objectives fixed beforehand, so as to disorganize the hostile defence by seizing the points essential to it.

6. Initiative on the part of all leaders, the rôle of Commanding Officers in every arm and unit being the decisive factor; for, once the battle has begun, special orders no longer reach those to whom they are addressed and everyone must act upon his own responsibility.

7. Employ reserves, not against centres of resistance which entail useless losses, but at points where the attack is making progress and where its advance may be best facilitated.

Such were the general principles which were drilled into the German Divisions during weeks of practical exercises previous to the attack. In fact, the tool which Hindenburg and Ludendorff wielded in the spring of 1918 seemed to be, both from the point of view of munitions, *matériel* and of the training of the troops, of a condition and temper that left nothing to be desired. Every German soldier was convinced that he was about to win the great campaign which would bring peace. Confident in this excellent instrument, the German Supreme Command proceeded to employ it against a strategic objective from which it hoped to obtain results which would be not only swift but decisive.

To this end, the Germans selected one of the most sensitive parts of the Allied front, namely the junction between the British and French Armies. By aiming a well prepared and vigorously executed blow in the direction of Amiens, it might be possible to separate these Armies. Then, by exploiting the initial success and widening the breach, the British would be thrown back on the sea, the French on Paris, and the two principal adversaries would thus be put out of action and the Coalition broken before the American Army could effectively intervene. Such were the possibilities which presented themselves to the German Supreme Command.

In the north of France, moreover, special facilities for this manœuvre were already at hand, due to the existence there of a dense and conveniently oriented railway system which led to Amiens, one of the vital points of the Allied communications. On the greater part of the front of attack selected, the resistance would be in all probability less firmly organized than anywhere else ; for the Allies had only been in possession of these positions for a year, that is since they had been voluntarily abandoned by the Germans. Behind them and stretching up to Amiens, the ground was like a desert, having been devastated by the systematic destruction carried out by the enemy in the spring of 1917, or else churned to pieces during the Battle of the Somme in the summer of

1916. The German Supreme Command believed, therefore, that all the trumps were in its hands.

*   *   *   *

However, neither British nor French General Headquarters was unaware of the enemy's intentions. Ever since the month of February reports had indicated that the Germans had settled upon the region between the Oise and the Scarpe, and upon the Champagne country lying on either side of Rheims, as their principal zones of attack. But whereas the British judged that the enemy's main blow would fall in Champagne, General Pétain thought that it would be directed against the British front north of the Oise. In this latter case, the point of junction between the British and French forces seemed to him to be inevitably the point of least resistance, and one where it would be "more difficult to fight a battle than anywhere else."

The Chief of the French General Staff* and the military representatives at Versailles had done their best during the winter to remedy this weakness, but their endeavours had been practically fruitless. On March 13th, 14th and 15th, the Allied Governments had met in conference in London in order, more particularly, to decide the question of forming the Allied General Reserve, which fell to my charge as president of the Versailles Executive Committee. At the meeting on the 14th, Field-Marshal Sir Douglas Haig, who took part in the Conference, declared that he was unable to promise the help requested of him for the formation of this reserve, or to furnish the number of Divisions which it would require. In spite of my protest, the British

* General Foch.—Translator.

Government supported him in his stand and the French Government accepted the British view without qualification.

At the meeting on the 15th, since this solution on the part of the two governments was still causing me much anxiety, I asked to be heard, and I pointed out the defects existing in the organization of the Allied command at the very moment the Coalition was about to engage in a defensive battle of the utmost importance and which all were agreed could not be far off.

Experience justified me in saying what I did. From the beginning of the War we had fought numerous battles in which the various Allied armies had taken a share : in 1914, on the Marne and at Arras, French and British ; on the Yser and at Ypres, French, British and Belgians ; on the Piave in 1917, Italians, French and British. None of these battles could have succeeded without a centralizing organ which made it possible to obtain concerted action amongst the various Allied forces. Without it, our efforts, instead of being in concord, would have been dispersed and the common cause would have suffered.

Under the circumstances now existing, this organ would have been the Commander of the Allied General Reserve, had it been formed. In the absence, however, of this Allied instrument, it was much to be feared that the French and the British Armies, on which the enemy's blows were about to fall, would each be governed by the considerations of its own particular interests and dangers, and would each lose sight of the common weal, although that was more important than anything else. In a word, the Allied battle might be seriously compromised, under existing conditions, because unity of view and of action would be lacking.

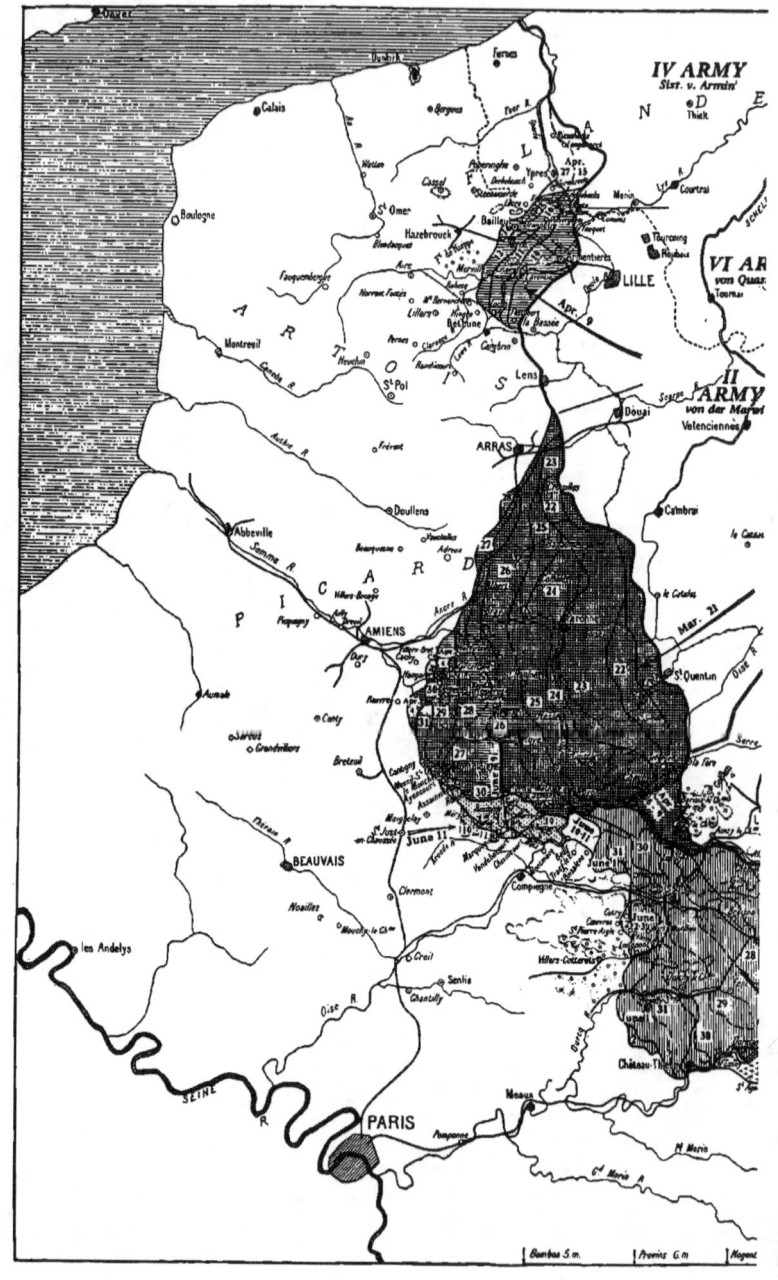

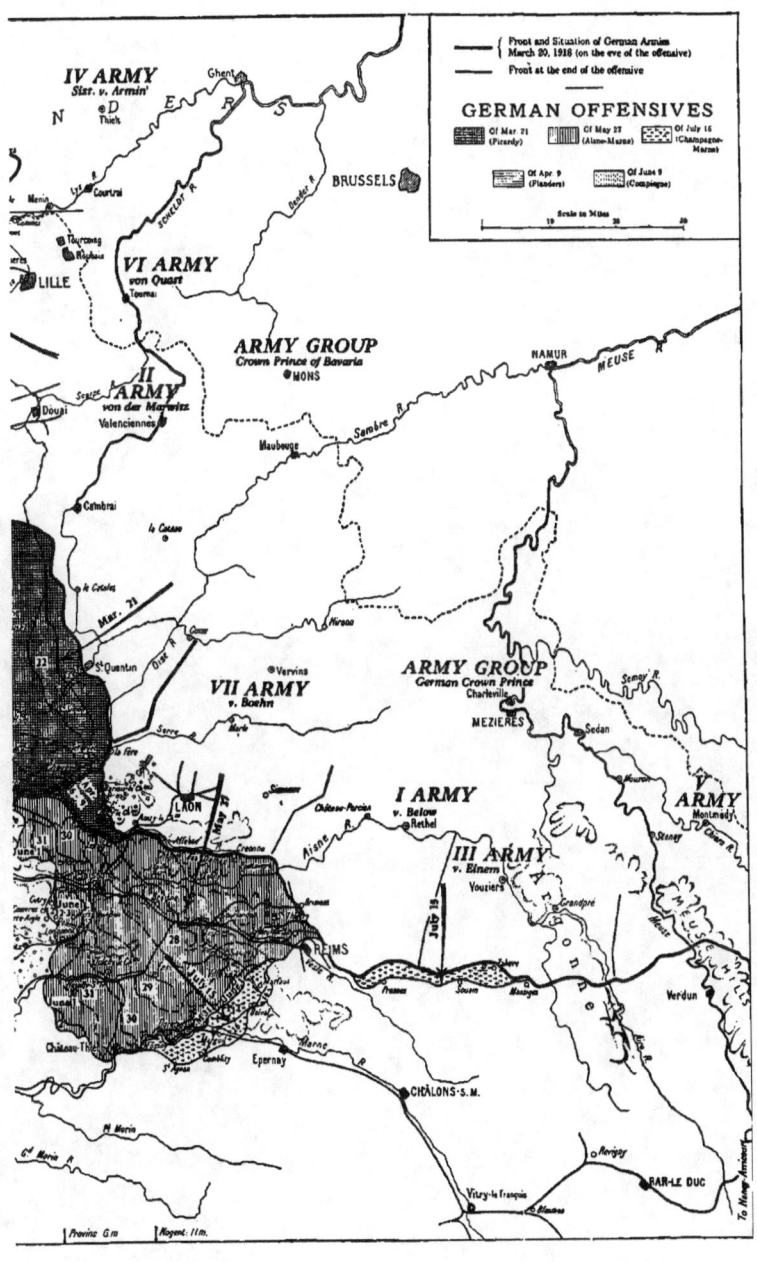

My remarks and predictions are contained in the minutes of the London Conference of March 13th. They greatly impressed the head of one government, Mr. Lloyd George, though without causing the Conference to modify the decision it had taken on the previous day. Six days later they were to receive ample justification on the field of battle.

Be that as it may, on the eve of the great German offensive, the Allied Governments had decided to depend solely upon the understanding between Sir Douglas Haig and General Pétain for meeting a situation which loomed dark with peril. As a matter of fact, the two Commanders-in-Chief had taken special measures to meet the threatening danger. General Pétain placed in reserve at Clermont the Third Army (General Humbert), composed of five Infantry Divisions, a Cavalry Corps and three Regiments of artillery, for action in the British zone, either between the Oise and the Somme, or to the north of the Somme. On the part of the British, their Commander-in-Chief engaging to send, in the event of an attack on the French front, a force of six to eight Divisions with from four to six groups of field artillery and two groups of heavy artillery, on the understanding, however, that this force would not be forthcoming if an extensive German offensive were directed against the British front.

These arrangements, however excellent they were, nevertheless presented grave imperfections and omissions, if they were to meet the threat of an offensive capable of striking at several points and of following up a success in some one direction previously fixed upon. The promises of mutual support by the two Commanders-in-Chief, moreover, were hedged about with reserves, avowed by Sir Douglas Haig, but equally present in the mind of General Pétain. The latter, although taking the British front into consideration, contemplated " the ever increasing possibility of a German offensive directed at one and the same time against our front in Champagne and against the British front."

Under these circumstances, when the thick and menacing fog of battle arose and spread across a limitless horizon, which of the two commanders would dare to part with the reserves he had promised? Of what value would such engagements be in the presence of those unforseeable happenings which inevitably accompany, in their form or in their execution, the development of a great hostile operation, and which might exceed or modify the conditions which dictated the arrangement between the two Allied Commanders?

Would either of them have the temerity to look beyond the limited field of action of his own Army, when each was responsible to his Government for the proper interests of his own country, bearing in mind the sacrifices entailed and the reinforcements he might be obliged to call for? When the time arrived to take vital decisions, would either be able to shake off this sense of responsibility, in order to bring to his threatened neighbour succour that would be appropriate, rapid and sufficient, and which might have to be sent a considerable distance?

Even if he should be willing to do all this—and it must be remembered that it was here a question of fighting a decisive battle whose violence was sure to be as great as its extent was undetermined—would he be able to bring his reinforcements into action rapidly, when staffs and regimental officers were still strangers to each other, ignorant each of the other's needs, means and methods, and whose intercourse was based on conventions and protocols, naturally rigid and inevitably slow?

For these reasons the agreement between the Commanders-in-Chief, when they were discussed in London, had seemed to me full of weaknesses and absolutely inadaquate. Events were soon to prove it. The Allied Governments assumed a heavy responsibility in so readily placing their trust and risking their tranquillity upon this simple agreement between two chiefs, each having his own interests to guard.

On March 21st, the plan of the German Staff was carried out in all its amplitude. The actual force of attack, fifty Divisions, and its extent, fifty miles, were far greater than anything seen since stabilization had taken place on the Western Front. The results obtained were not less.

On the north, the British Third Army maintained in general its positions, but it was quite otherwise with General Gough's Fifth Army. Along almost the whole of its front it was swept away, its right in particular being thrown back west of Saint-Quentin, up to the edge of the Crozat canal.

On the following day, the 22nd, this badly shaken Army retreated towards the Somme. An extraordinary incident here took place—one only to be explained by the contagion which spread from the confused and shaken troops, driven in by the heavy attacks on the front lines. The Somme, flowing several miles in rear, was captured by the enemy practically without a blow being struck. The same phenomenon occurred on the Aisne, two months later, during the attack of May 27th.

Despite the intervention of the British reserves, the general retirement of the Fifth Army proceeded at such a pace as to show that its power of resistance had been seriously weakened. Sir Douglas Haig, becoming anxious, requested General Pétain to relieve the British contingents distributed between the Oise and the Somme at Péronne as quickly as possible by French troops. But General Pétain was considerably preoccupied by his own front in Champagne, and for the moment he could do no more than adhere to the arrangements previously made, that is to say, dispatch the French Third Army to the British zone. However, in view of the time required to effect the move, the action of this Army could not be fully felt before the 27th. Until then, the British would have to be left more or less to themselves.

In order to lessen in part the gravity of their situation, the French Commander-in-Chief, in agreement with Sir Douglas, decided to entrust General Fayolle, commanding the Reserve Group of Armies, with the conduct of the battle between Barisis-aux-Bois and Péronne. General Fayolle therefore had under his command the British Divisions which were fighting in that area, the French Third Army on its arrival, and ultimately the French First Army, which was at that moment being withdrawn from the region of the Woëvre. He was instructed to establish at all costs a solid defensive front on the line Péronne—Guiscard—Chauny—Barisis-aux-Bois, or at the very least on the line Nesle—Noyon.

However, events marched with a rapidity that defied all calculations. On March 23rd, the Germans extended their front of attack to the east of Arras. The British Third Army, apart from a slight withdrawal west of Croisilles, successfully repulsed all the enemy's assaults, but in order to maintain contact with the Fifth Army, it was obliged to draw back its right in the direction of Bapaume.

The British Fifth Army continued its retreat without interruption. On the 23rd, it abandoned the bridgehead at Péronne and the next day the line of the Somme from Péronne to Ham. In vain the French V Corps (Third Army), hurrying into action, tried to defend Noyon and the Canal du Nord ; it was outflanked and, on the 25th, Noyon fell into the hands of the Germans.

What had happened was that General Gough's right, instead of retiring in the direction of Roye—Montdidier, which would have kept it in touch with the French left, retreated toward Nesle and Amiens, thus drawing away from the French and moving in the direction of the British bases. In this way there was created between the British right and the French left a gap some twelve miles in width. Our II Cavalry Corps, in spite of all its efforts, was unable to close this breach, and through it the enemy poured. General Fayolle counted on throwing into it the units of the Third Army as they detrained ; but the question was, would he have time to do so, and if the breaking up of Gough's Army continued, would not these arriving units themselves be carried away by the torrent before they could re-establish the continuity of the front ?

The French Commander-in-Chief, who had seen Field-Marshal Sir Douglas Haig at Duryon the 23rd, and had declared himself in accord with the latter as to the necessity of maintaining a close liaison between the British and French armies, now doubted whether this contact could be re-established. In view of the developments of the 24th, he despaired of the British resisting sufficiently to enable the French divisions to come into action under favourable conditions on the right of the British Fifth Army, and he considered that fresh dispositions were now required to meet the situation.

These views he communicated the same day, March 24th, to the Commanders of the various Army Groups, in the following instruction :

"It is above all essential," he wrote, "that the alignment of the French armies taken as a whole be solidly maintained ; in particular the Reserve Group of Armies must not be cut off from the remainder of our forces. This being assured, maintain contact with the British forces if possible . . ."

This was a grave decision, one which appeared to guard the interests of the Allies only imperfectly. Moreover, it threatened to deal a fresh blow at the morale of the British troops, already so gravely affected.

The following day, March 25th, Field-Marshal Sir Douglas Haig, at Abbeville, handed General Weygand a note in which he set forth his requests and his intentions. His requests had for their object the immediate concentration " astride the Somme, west of Amiens, of at least twenty French divisions for the purpose of acting against the flank of the German attack on the British Army." This was equivalent to a decision to transfer the British resistance to the west of Amiens. His intentions were expressed in this simple sentence : "The British Army will have to fight falling back slowly and covering the Channel ports."

As can be seen, the moment a violent and sustained crisis suddenly arose, each of the two Commanders-in-Chief found himself faced by the responsibility he owed his own country, and precisely what was to be feared, happened. Each was concerned most of all with preserving and maintaining his command ; he therefore moved it to cover its bases, the direction best calculated to protect his own nation's interests. For the British, this direction was the Channel ports ; for the French it was Paris and the interior of France ; and to each this appeared as the essential task. The result perhaps would be a divergent manœuvre, but to help his neighbour was no longer anything but a contingent duty to be fulfilled if possible.

As opposed to a single German battle, two distinct battles were being fought by the Allies : a British battle for the Ports, and a French battle for Paris. These were carried on separately, farther and farther away from one another. The Allied commanders thus tended to emphasize the separation of their Armies, which was the primary object of the German operations. And they risked making the separation absolute. Unless the Allied governments, upon whom rested most of the responsibility for what was happening, intervened quickly and energetically, we were marching towards certain defeat. It was their duty to make it quite clear that the interests of the Coalition came before everything else ; and the only way to do this was to create and place over their Armies in the field an organ which would take in hand the safeguarding of the common interests and direct the united resources of both partners.

On Sunday, March 24th, about 3 P.M., even before General Pétain had issued his orders which were to put the seal upon the divergence between his views and those of Sir Douglas Haig, I had, on my own responsibility, asked to see Monsieur Clemenceau, the Prime Minister, and had handed him a note in which I called his attention to the evolution of the battle then going on. I explained the military dispositions which should at once be taken and the necessity for " an organ to direct the war—one capable of giving orders and seeing that they were executed. Otherwise the risk remained for the Coalition of entering a battle entailing the gravest consequences, inadequately prepared, inadequately equipped, and inadequately directed."

His first words, when I gave him my note, were: "*You* are not going to desert me, you! I am in agreement with Haig and Pétain, what more can I do?"

"No, Mr. President," I answered, "I am not going to desert you; but each one of us must shoulder his own responsibilities and without delay. That is why I have handed you this note."

As Chief of Staff of the Army, I was military adviser to the French Government.* Grave events were happening and I could not remain passive when disaster was imminently threatening. The time had come for each man to shoulder his responsibilities, and it was most important for the French Government to understand that the patriotic fervour of its Prime Minister,† his unsurpassed activity and his frequent conversations with General Pétain or Field-Marshal Sir Douglas Haig were not sufficient *liaison* for the Allied Armies to fight an immensely long and difficult battle. To solve the problem it was essential to set up at once a directing organ, which would be wholly and solely concerned with the conduct of the Allied war, and which would be selected by and be responsible to the Allied Governments. It must be possessed of the necessary experience, prestige and ability, and be aided by an appropriate staff. Failing that, the struggle would end in division of efforts, impotence and disaster.

This organ could be neither the Versailles Executive

---

* General Foch was then Chief of the War Department Staff. The chief of staff of the armies in the field is known in France as "*le major-général*."—Translator.

† M. Clemenceau.—Translator.

Committee, which, on March 14th, had been deprived of all its means of action and therefore of all its authority, nor the Supreme War Council of the Allied governments, for its decisions would inevitably be always too late to meet an emergency.

Sir Douglas Haig that very day recognised the necessity. On March 24th, about 11 P.M., when he could no longer have any doubt as to the intentions of the French High Command, he telegraphed to the Chief of the Imperial General Staff in London to come at once to France, in order that a Supreme Command for the whole Western Front might be created as quickly as possible.

In response to this appeal, General Wilson* landed at Boulogne on the morning of the 25th. He had been preceded by Lord Milner, a member of the British War Cabinet, who had arrived at Versailles the day before, under orders from Mr. Lloyd George to "send the Cabinet a personal report on the situation."

Taking advantage of the presence in France of these two British officials, M. Clemenceau arranged a meeting for the afternoon of the 25th at Compiègne—French General Headquarters. Unfortunately, neither General Wilson nor Sir Douglas Haig were able to attend, both being detained at Abbeville. The result was there were really two meetings on that day : one at Compiègne, at which I assisted with the President of the Republic, M. Clemenceau, M. Loucheur, Lord Milner and General Pétain ; the other at Abbeville, where General Sir Henry Wilson, Field-Marshal Sir Douglas Haig and my Chief of Staff, General Weygand, were assembled.

At the Compiègne meeting, General Pétain described

---

* General Sir Henry Wilson had succeeded General Sir John Robertson as Chief of the Imperial General Staff.

the greatly disorganized condition of the British Fifth Army and the steps he had taken to come to its help, namely, the dispatch of fifteen Divisions, of which six were already heavily engaged. He asserted also that he could do no more for the present, in view of the necessity which faced him of defending the road to Paris, now threatened from the valley of the Oise, and perhaps from the direction of Champagne.

Being asked to give my views, I showed, as in my note of the previous day, that the urgent danger lay in the direction of Amiens, where the German offensive had broken through the Franco-British front, and produced a large gap, the first result of which was the separation of the British and French Armies. It was essential at all costs to re-establish this front and restore touch between the two Armies, even should that entail some risks elsewhere. Bring up the number of Divisions required to close the breach, and bring them up quickly! Such, in my opinion, was the line to pursue, the direction indicated for all our efforts.

To what extent were the British able to co-operate in this plan? In the absence of his military advisers, Lord Milner was unable to reply to this question put to him by Monsieur Clemenceau. He suggested, however, that another meeting be held the following day, the 26th, when the British generals could be present. We therefore separated at Compiègne about 5 P.M., having arranged the conference for 11 A.M. the following day at Dury.

At the moment this discussion at Compiègne was proceeding without any decision being taken, Sir Douglas Haig was holding a conference with General Wilson at Abbeville. Fully alive to the peril to which the Entente was exposed through the separation of the

British and French Armies, and convinced that it must at all costs be prevented, Sir Douglas proposed to the Chief of the Imperial General Staff that General Foch be immediately named Commander-in-Chief. His advice was as yet only partly heeded.

General Wilson reached Versailles that same evening, and after having a talk with Lord Milner, he came to see me in Paris about 11 o'clock. He suggested assigning to M. Clemenceau, whose technical adviser I would be, the task of "ensuring a closer co-operation between the Armies and a better utilization of all available reserves."

I had no difficulty in pointing out to him how little the realization of this plan was to be desired, since far from simplifying matters, it was likely to make them still more difficult. The arguments I developed at this meeting are clearly summarized in Lord Milner's memorandum: " Foch himself did not wish to command anything. All he wanted was to have the same sort of position which he had held once before at the time of the Battle of Ypres, when General Joffre sent him to try and get the British and the French to work more closely together—only he now wanted to be placed in that position with a more distinct and higher authority, that of both the Allied Governments."

Lord Milner and General Wilson agreed in thinking that, in the existing circumstances, this would be the best solution.

Such, roughly, was the situation on the morning of March 26th, as the Conference at Doullens opened.* When I arrived in that town, about 11.30 A.M., Field-Marshal Sir Douglas Haig, shortly joined by Lord

---

* Sir Douglas Haig was obliged to go to Doullens, as he had summoned his Army Commanders to meet him there. It was in accordance with his request that this Town was selected for the Conference instead of Dury, which had been named the previous day.

Milner, was receiving the reports of his Army Commanders in the Town Hall. The meeting was a protracted one, so that I had time to make a visit to the little schoolhouse in which I and my Staff had established ourselves on October 6th, 1914, when I arrived at Doullens to take part in the manœuvre which was then carrying the opposing armies northwards. This manœuvre, as we have seen, brought about the Battles of the Yser and of Ypres, with the definite repulse of the enemy. As my thoughts went back to this already distant period and I compared our numbers, organization, armament and supplies as they were in 1914 with what existed now, I could not permit myself for a moment to admit that, powerfully reinforced as we were, we could allow ourselves to be beaten in 1918 when, with means so relatively meagre, we had conquered in 1914.

The wise employment of our combined resources and an inflexible determination to win—here was still the formula for success. With the means at our disposal, the question of stopping the enemy was in the first place a matter of will power on the part of the High Command. There was no doubt in my mind as to the outcome of the enterprise, provided the Allied chiefs, with eyes wide open to each succeeding danger, should meet and dominate it in a spirit of close and energetic co-operation. That is what we had done on the Yser and at Ypres—and under what conditions !

I developed these fundamental ideas to the members of the French Government while we waited in the garden of the Town Hall of Doullens for the Allied Conference to begin. It opened at 12.45 P.M. in the Town Hall. There were present on the French side, the President of the Republic, MM. Clemenceau and Loucheur, and Generals Foch, Pétain and Weygand ; on the British side, Lord Milner, Field-Marshal Sir Douglas Haig and Generals Wilson, Lawrence and Montgomery.

From the outset all were unanimous in recognizing that Amiens had to be saved at all costs, and that the fate of the War depended on it. I made some strong remarks in this sense. Our front had already been driven back to Bray-sur-Somme, behind the lines of 1916. It was essential not to retreat any further, not to yield an inch of ground without fighting, to hold on at all costs where we were and with the utmost energy. Such was the first principle to be clearly defined and communicated to all ; then it must be put into execution without a moment's delay, especially by hurrying up reserves and using them to weld together the Allied Armies.

Now the British had no more troops available to send south of the Somme, unless they were taken from the Arras sector, which was being heavily attacked and which no one could think of weakening. Help therefore could come only from the French.

On being questioned, General Pétain explained his programme. He had decided to increase the number of Divisions to be sent into Picardy : instead of the fifteen specified the previous day at the Compiègne meeting he now proposed to move twenty-four on to Montdidier. In this way he hoped to prolong his front up to the Somme, but he could not guarantee it. This extension, however, would only be gradual and slow, because moving the divisions at the rate of two a day would require considerable time.

At this point of the proceedings, Lord Milner had a private interview with M. Clemenceau, in the course of which he proposed that I should be entrusted with the conduct of operations.

The French Prime Minister concurred in this idea and

at once drew up a text according to which I was charged with co-ordinating the operations of the Allied forces " around Amiens." Sir Douglas Haig, perceiving at once the narrowness and insufficiency of this combination, declared that it did not correspond with the end he was seeking. He then asked that the arrangement should be extended to include the British and French forces operating in France and Belgium. In the end, the formula was still further expanded so as to comprise all the Allied forces operating on the Western Front. Agreement was reached on the following text which was signed by Lord Milner and Monsieur Clemenceau.

" General Foch is charged by the British and French governments with co-ordinating the action of the Allied Armies on the Western Front. To this end he will come to an understanding with the Commanders-in-Chief, who are requested to furnish him with all necessary information."

At 2.30 P.M. the Doullens Conference came to a close and we went for a hurried lunch at the *Hôtel des Quatre Fils Aymon*, which I remembered from 1914. As we sat down, Monsieur Clemenceau turned to me with these words : " Well, you've got the job you so much wanted."

It was not difficult to answer him—and Monsieur Loucheur joined in my reply—that to assume the direction of a battle which during seven successive days had been largely lost, could hardly be the object of any great desire on my part, but rather constituted, by reason of its risks, an act of duty and sacrifice in the service of my country.

CHAPTER II

THE FIRST ACTS OF THE ALLIED COMMANDER-IN-CHIEF

General Foch goes to see the Allied Commanders engaged in the battle, March 26th and 27th—The fall of Montdidier, March 27th—Shortening of the German front of attack ; arrival of the French Divisions—The resistance of the Allies hardens—Assembling of French reserves in the Beauvais region—The American Army offers to take part in the battle, March 28th—Reconstitution of the British reserves—General Foch establishes himself at Beauvais—A general instruction is issued March 29th—Last efforts of the Germans on each side of Montdidier, March 30th—April 4th, and on the Ailette canal, April 6th.

March 26th.

IMMEDIATELY after being invested with the mission which the two Allied governments had confided to me, I fixed my plan of action along the lines which I had communicated to the French Prime Minister two days before. It can be summed up as follows :

(1) The French and British troops must keep close together in order to cover Amiens.

(2) With this object in view, the forces already in action must maintain their positions at all costs.

(3) Covered by them, the French Divisions sent as reinforcements will finish detraining and will then be used, first to consolidate the British Fifth Army, and second, to constitute a mass of manœuvre for employment under conditions to be fixed later on.

Instead of a British battle to cover the Channel ports and a French battle to cover Paris, we would fight an Anglo-French battle to cover Amiens, the connecting link between the two armies.

I drew up the detailed arrangements for carrying out

this general plan and, as time pressed, I went myself to explain them to those principally concerned. Accordingly, by 4 P.M., I was at Dury with General Gough, commanding the British Fifth Army. I instructed him to maintain himself at any cost on the front he then occupied. He must halt his troops where they were until the French forces arrived to relieve a part of his Army, starting from the south.

At Dury I also met General Barthélemy, Chief of Staff to General Fayolle, commanding the Reserve Army Group, and handed him similar instructions "with a view to ensuring the protection of Amiens at all costs."

I requested Major Moyrand, liaison officer from French Headquarters, to inform General Pétain of these orders. I then telephoned General Debeney, commanding the First Army, giving him my instructions as to what he was to do.

The rôle of this Army, which was still in course of formation facing Montdidier, was particularly important, for upon it depended, at that moment, the re-establishment of a continuous Franco-British front. I therefore followed up my telephone message by proceeding from Dury to Maignelay to see General Debeney personally and define his mission. This was to employ all the units he had available to relieve the troops of the British XVIII Corps on their actual positions, turning over the units of this corps, as they were relieved, to General Gough, who would employ them as reserves; also to hold his own line at all costs, joining up on the left with the British towards Rouvroy.

Before the close of this same day, the 26th, I had thus explained my intentions to all the commanders whose troops were in action. In the evening, moreover, General Pétain cancelled his instruction of March 24th, and ordered General Fayolle to cover Amiens and to maintain contact with Field-Marshal Sir Douglas Haig's forces. In addition, he directed that ten Divisions and four Regiments of artillery be withdrawn from other Army Groups and moved towards the Reserve Group.

March 27th.

After spending the night in Paris, I left again on the morning of the 27th for the front, still accompanied by General Weygand and Colonel Desticker. Before leaving, however, I wrote a private letter to General Pétain, insisting upon the line of action we should follow and asking him to explain its necessity to the French Army. It is superfluous to say that, on the part of General Pétain, as of all his subordinates, I found the fullest co-operation in framing our resistance along the lines I had indicated, and upon those which still remained to be organized.

I first went to Clermont, the headquarters of General Humbert, commanding the Third Army. Here I met General Fayolle. I repeated my instructions, always inspired by the same idea : " Hold on at all costs, organize our positions, relieve no unit until the first result is achieved."

At 12.30 P.M., I left for Dury to see General Gough. The liaison between the British right and French left seemed to be insecure, due to the too hasty retreat of certain units of the British XVIII Corps. I therefore prescribed new measures to General Mesple, commanding on the left of the French First Army, and I asked General Gough to make personally sure that the British XVIII Corps received my instructions and carried them out.

From there I went to Beauquesne to see General

Byng, commanding the British Third Army. He explained to me his situation. It did not cause him any anxiety for the moment, and he signified his entire agreement with me as to resisting on our present positions, employing for that purpose every means possible.

In the absence of a general reserve—whose intervention might have restored the situation from the very start—the first thing to do was to weld together as rapidly as possible the various fractions of the front that had been broken by the German attack and which had now necessarily become lengthened out. It was essential that all—whether troops in retreat, or reinforcements coming up, and whatever their nationality—co-operate in this task, since all idea of relieving any of them was, for the moment, laid aside. If this were not done, there could be no hope of repulsing the enemy for several days.

Under these conditions, a rapid re-establishment of the front, as well as a determined and simultaneous change of attitude on the part of the two Allied Armies, could only be brought about by the direct intervention of the Allied Supreme Command at the points still threatened.

On my return to Clermont in the evening, I learned that the Germans had debouched from Roye, and, slipping in between the French First and Third Armies, whose junction had not yet been firmly established, had seized Montdidier. Although serious, this unfortunate occurrence was offset by certain favourable events which gave reason to hope that March 27th would mark the culminating point of the crisis, and that the danger which for a week had so seriously threatened the Allies would soon be over.

The front of the German attack, far from extending,

became smaller every day, thanks to the firm stand of the British Third Army which, on the north, clung fast to Arras, and of the French Third Army, which, on the south, held the wooded heights of Ribécourt-Lassigny. Between these two dikes, the waves of the flood were steadily thinning out and growing more shallow each day.

The ground over which the enemy operated was the old Somme battlefield of 1916, a desolate and scarred wilderness whose few remaining roads had been completely destroyed by the last battle. This rendered difficult all support and supply coming from the rear. An offensive thus weakened was bound to die out the day the Allies re-established an organized system of resistance in front of it. This day was approaching.

The French Divisions which had been sent up as reinforcements were detraining without pause. The first of them were directed upon our First Army; the others were to form a mass of manœuvre in the region of Beauvais, to be at the disposal of the Supreme Command.

The command of the British Fifth Army was to be taken over by General Rawlinson, an energetic and able soldier who restored its confidence. A large number of men (75,000) were arriving from England. Three British Divisions, already refitted, had replaced fresh divisions in calm sectors, and the latter were now entering the battle.

A systematic organization was rapidly replacing the original confusion.

*   *   *   *

March 28th.

On March 28th the enemy's main effort was directed against the Santerre plateau, between the valleys of the

Somme and the Avre. The ground was easy to traverse, and the Germans succeeded in gaining ground in the direction of Amiens, forcing back the right of the British Fifth Army which was still shaky; moreover, General Debeney had not yet been able to bring up enough troops to support it properly. In fact, the deep drive of the enemy towards Montdidier had forced General Debeney to send his first available troops in that direction. These had thrown themselves into the action with great vigour and had even retaken several localities —Mesnil-St.-Georges, Le Monchel, and Assainvilliers. The fighting, however, was still fierce and the danger was not entirely past. In order to meet it, the G.O.C. the First Army had to postpone the relief of the British forces south of the Somme. For the time being, in any case, the British Fifth Army had to remain in line and reorganize on its positions.

But no matter what happened, the resistance along the whole front must be intensified, and I continued to impress upon everybody that there must be no exceptions to this inflexible principle.

General Pétain, renouncing all idea of a possible separation of the British forces from the Reserve Group of Armies, which would have brought about the loss of Amiens, instructed the latter to " hold on to your present positions at any price . . . drive the enemy back as soon as possible from in front of Montdidier and Amiens, and in every event maintain contact with the British Army."

General Fayolle moved his Headquarters from Verberie to Beauvais, so as to be nearer the danger point of the battle, the left of the French First Army, the place of junction with the British.

Meanwhile, the concentration of French reserves went

on in the Beauvais region. In order to provide for their organization and command, General Pétain had already withdrawn the staff of the Fifth Army from the Champagne front, and at a meeting held at Clermont on the afternoon of the 28th between General Pétain, M. Clemenceau, M. Loucheur and myself, it was also decided to recall the staff of the Tenth Army from Italy.

A few hours before this meeting, General Pershing had come to see me and, with magnificent spirit, spontaneously offered to throw immediately into the battle all the trained American divisions. General Bliss, the American representative on the Versailles Committee, animated by a similar sentiment, also arrived, exclaiming, " We have come over here to get ourselves killed; if you want to use us, what are you waiting for ? "

* * * *

March 29th.

On March 29th the range of the German attacks grew still narrower, embracing as they did only that part of the front between Montdidier and the Amiens—Péronne road. Although the attack failed almost entirely in the Montdidier region and only gained a little ground northwest of the town, a more appreciable advance was made between the Avre and the Amiens—Péronne road, where the British right wing and General Mesple's detachment were forced back to the line Marcelcave—Villers-sur-Erables.

In spite of this retirement, the situation of the Allies continued to improve. Five fresh Divisions had reached the First Army, and the latter had already been able to relieve the whole of the British XVIII Corps (the right of the Fifth Army). The units of the British III Corps attached to the French Third Army were now rejoining the British Army, except one Division (the 58th) which was temporarily kept south of the Oise.

Sir Douglas Haig was thus enabled to reconstitute his reserves, and thereby to reorganize his Fifth Army without withdrawing it from the line. We had a conversation at Abbeville as to the vital importance of this last point; as a result General Rawlinson was instructed to maintain his front south of the Somme at all costs which, in view of its reduced length, would not present any difficulty.

On the evening of the 29th, I established my Headquarters at Beauvais, where General Fayolle's Headquarters had been functioning since morning, and where General Pétain himself established a Command Post four days later.

The end of the Montdidier-Amiens Battle.

Ever since March 26th I had been attending to the most pressing needs, going from place to place, visiting the various Headquarters and laying down for all the immediate course of action which seemed indicated for reconstructing the broken front. But now that a systematic organization existed which could be counted upon to direct the resistance of the Allied forces, the time had come to lay down the general rules by which our battle should be conducted.

With this end in view, I forwarded to the Commanders-in-Chief a general instruction which constituted a summary of the detailed directions I had given since March 26th. The essential object to which the combined efforts of all were to be addressed remained " a close liaison between the British and French armies, to be ensured especially by keeping possession of Amiens and then by regaining the unhampered use of that centre."

This object was to be pursued firstly, by holding and organizing a strong defensive front on our present positions, and secondly, by the formation, north of Amiens for the British forces, and north-west of Beauvais for the French forces, of strong reserves *destined to counter an enemy attack, or undertake an offensive*.

In order to form this mass of manœuvre as rapidly and in as great strength as possible, fronts not under attack should be unhesitatingly drawn upon.

But at the moment this instruction reached its destinations, the enemy had begun to redouble his efforts. On March 30th he resumed and extended his attacks on both sides of Montdidier between the Amiens—Péronne highway and Lassigny. He was thus starting a second battle before we had become firmly established on our positions. However, in spite of his numbers and the munitions he put into play, the results he achieved were even less than those of the previous day. It was only in the valley of the Avre, towards Moreuil, and around Rollot and Roye-sur-Matz, east of Montdidier, that he gained any ground.

On the following day, March 31st, he renewed his attacks, but he was nailed to his ground by the resistance and counter-attacks of the Allies, and he was only able to mark a slight advance in the bend of the Luce, between Moreuil and Marcelcave. This, it is true, threatened a particularly sensitive point in the direction of Amiens itself, where the Franco-British touch was as yet by no means secure. The situation was met by sending the British Fifth Army enough reinforcements to make sure of its holding fast to the positions it occupied, and, in addition, by ordering the French First Army to extend its front up to Hangard.

The Battle of Montdidier—Amiens appeared to be coming to a close. On the evening of April 1st it was possible to write to the Prime Minister that: " the enemy's initiative seems now blocked and paralyzed."

But, as a matter of fact, after a short respite, on April 4th, the Germans again delivered violent attacks on the British Fourth Army* and the French First Army between the Somme and Montdidier. The centre of the British Fourth Army was forced back on Villers-Bretonneux, and the French First Army, on its part, was driven in for a considerable distance on the Rouvrel plateau. This loss was partly retrieved by counter-attacks carried out on the following day, April 5th.

But, the fact of vital importance was that the liaison between the two Armies in the region of Hangard had been firmly maintained, and in order to ensure it definitely, General Rawlinson was requested to employ all available reserves and artillery to support the French left. For the purpose of emphasizing our determination not to give ground, I asked Sir Douglas Haig to suggest to General Rawlinson that his Headquarters should not be moved further in rear as his predecessor had arranged.

In the course of this day, Clemenceau, Loucheur, Winston Churchill, and finally the President of the Republic, all came to see me at Beauvais. This shows some measure of the anxiety which reigned amongst the Allied governments.

From this time on the Germans could no longer hope for important results from the battle. In face of the

* The British Commander-in-Chief had decided that the Fifth Army, reorganized under the command of General Rawlinson, should be called the Fourth Army.

A HEAVY NAVAL BATTERY MOUNTED ON RAILS.

increased strength presented by the Allies, their attacks became more and more difficult and costly, and they finally found themselves forced to stop them without having been able to achieve the strategic results aimed at. The French Army had not been separated from the British Army.

In order to finish on a note of easy success, the Germans on April 6th undertook the capture of the strip of ground occupied by the French Sixth Army to the west of the St. Gobain Forest, between the Oise and the Ailette Canal. This action on the part of the enemy, however, had been so clearly foreseen that the Sixth Army, which was here very far advanced, had only maintained weak outposts north of the Canal. The German attack encountered merely scattered units which withdrew fighting. Nevertheless, the attack was made with great caution and took four days to reach the Ailette (April 6th—9th).

CHAPTER III

THE BEAUVAIS AGREEMENT

Inadequacy of the powers granted to General Foch by the Doullens agreement—The Beauvais agreement entrusts him with the strategical direction of the operations on the Western Front, April 3rd—Italy adheres to the Doullens agreement, May 2nd—The King of the Belgians, fettered by the constitution of his country, remains in theory outside the agreements, July 3rd—General Foch is named Commander-in-Chief of the Allied Armies, May 14th.

An examination of the situation which resulted from the temporary check given to the German offensive and from the reinforcement of the Allied troops south of the Somme, as well as a study of intelligence reports concerning the enemy, all led to conclusions having as their base the following facts :

(1) The enemy, held up between the Oise and Arras, might renew his attacks. He could do so with difficulty south of the Somme, more easily north. Between this river and Arras, therefore, a particularly strong defence should be provided. This was a matter for the British G.H.Q. to undertake. It was also important that the French reserves assembled in the Beauvais region should be able to come into action north of the Somme, and that means for their transport be prepared beforehand. This was a question concerning the French G.H.Q.

(2) No matter what attitude the Germans assumed, we should act as soon as possible south of the Somme, in order to drive the enemy away from the Paris—Amiens railway and the Amiens rail centre, both essential for our communications and supply. With this end in view,

the French troops should make an offensive in the Montdidier area, with the object of throwing the enemy back on Roye, and the British troops an attack on both sides of the Somme, in order to free Amiens.

This reasoning implied offensive action on the part of the Allied Armies. The purely passive attitude, and the work of consolidation to which events had condemned them since March 21st, would come to an end and be replaced by an active initiative.

Now to plan this offensive action, to inspire and direct it, to ensure its being carried out by the Commanders-in-Chief, and also to arrive at an equitable distribution of forces, the powers conferred upon me by the Doullens Agreement were plainly inadequate. They were insufficient to cover even the present defensive operations; they would necessarily be all the more inadequate when, in the not far distant future, it became my duty to decide upon the strategic employment of the Allied Armies, renewed and strengthened by the co-operation of the Americans; to determine, according to circumstances, the point against which these forces should be applied; to distribute the offensive and defensive tasks, and possibly to effect exchanges between the French and Italian fronts.

The simple rôle of *co-ordinator* was not sufficient for the larger programme which would certainly have to be undertaken shortly. It gave far too little play to the *initiative* of the officer who filled it, if he was to react rapidly and forcibly to contingencies brought about by a defensive battle, or to organize and launch important offensive operations. The rôle should be changed into one of *direction*. If the inter-Allied organ created at Doullens by an effort of mutual confidence was to produce all that was expected of it, its powers must at once be widened, and the strategic direction of the war on the Western Front entrusted to it. Its authority over the Allied Commanders-in-Chief should be affirmed, and this authority extended to include all the troops in line from the North Sea to the Adriatic.

A few days' experience had been sufficient to expose the inadequacy of the Doullens Agreement. The present as well as the future interests of the Coalition required that it be amended without delay. I placed the question before the French Prime Minister in this light and requested that the decision touching me, taken on March 26th by the British and French governments, be supplemented. Monsieur Clemenceau discussed the matter with me on April 1st and decided to assemble a new Conference. To this he invited the American representatives as well as the British and French. The meeting was held at the Beauvais Town Hall two days later, April 3rd, and the following resolution was adopted :

" General Foch is charged by the British, French and American Governments with the co-ordination of the action of the Allied Armies on the Western Front. To this end all powers necessary to secure effective realization are conferred on him. The British, French and American Governments for this purpose entrust to General Foch the strategic direction of military operations. The Commanders-in-Chief of the British, French and American Armies have full control of the tactical employment of their forces. Each Commander-in-Chief will have the right of appeal to his Government if, in his opinion, the safety of his Army is compromised by any order received from General Foch."

Mr. Lloyd George came from London for this Conference, landing at Boulogne and driving by motor-car to Beauvais, where M. Clemenceau had already arrived. He crossed the roads by which the British troops withdrawn from the battle were moving to the rear, and it seems evident that the order and morale of these units did not furnish him with a pleasant picture of the situation. For, apart from arriving very late, he seemed to bring with him a most gloomy impression.

He was not long, however, in shaking this off and recovering his characteristic animation and energy. While the session was in progress he made this statement regarding myself. " The English people have confidence in you. Your nomination as Commander-in-Chief of the Allied armies has nowhere been so well received as in my country." Then, as the meeting broke up and we left the room, he asked me, with his habitual gay manner : " And now which must I bet on, Ludendorff or Foch ? "

I answered him very calmly : " You can back me, and you will win. For Ludendorff has got to break through our lines, and this he can no longer do. As for us, our present business is to stop him, which we shall certainly accomplish. Later on, when our turn comes to break through his lines—that is another matter. Then it will be seen what we can do." With this exchange, our conversation came to an end.

The Beauvais agreement did not entirely meet my proposition, since it did not extend my authority over the whole of the Western Front from the North Sea to the Adriatic, or over all the Allied troops fighting there. Nevertheless, it did contain the essence of what was necessary for conducting the battle on the French front (which was the main theatre of operations) with the American, British and French Armies, the principal forces of the Entente. But as M. Clemenceau was now assured of the adherence of the British and American Governments to the new formula, he doubtless preferred, in order to gain time, first of all to limit the sphere of the inter-Allied Generalissimo's action to this theatre and to these Armies. Once such a result was obtained, he reserved to himself the possibility of seeking a future extension of the agreement so as to include the Italian theatre and Army on one hand, and the Belgian Army on the other.

The question of Italy's adherence was examined by the Supreme War Council on May 2nd at Abbeville. Signor Orlando and Signor Sonino declared, in the name of the Italian Government, that they could not unreservedly agree to the Beauvais text, but they proposed, by way of compromise, a formula which established a distinction between the Italian front and the command of the Italian Army. This formula, to which the other Governments agreed, was as follows:—

(1) The Italian front from now on is subject to General Foch's co-ordinating authority as defined in the Doullens agreement.

(2) The command of the Italian Army, on the other hand, will be accorded to that officer only when circumstances lead to the presence beyond the Alps of other Allied Armies fighting there subject to his orders under the same conditions as in France.

The restriction thus imposed by the Italian Government, none the less, left to the inter-Allied Commander the right of scrutiny over the Italian front, and furnished him with the power, if he esteemed it advisable, of using the trans-alpine theatre of operations for the realization of his strategic plans.

With regard to the Belgian Army, the question was discussed by the Supreme War Council at Versailles on

July 3rd, at the moment the Allied Armies were preparing to resume the offensive in France. As it was to be presumed that the Belgian Divisions would be called upon to participate in this action, it would have been preferable to have them placed at my disposal, the same as the other Allied Divisions. But no agreement could be arrived at in this sense, Lieutenant-General Gillain, the Chief of Staff of the Belgian Army, invoking the constitution of his country in formal opposition to the suggestion.

As a matter of fact, this uncompromising attitude, which arose more from a matter of principle than anything else, was not final; for a few weeks later the King of the Belgians accepted without hesitation the task of conducting in Flanders the operations of the united Belgian, French, British and American troops, in accordance with the directions of the Allied Commander-in-Chief.

In terminating this discussion of the Allied High Command, it may be well to add that a decision of the Allied governments, dated May 2nd, abolished the executive committee which had been created three months previously, and for which there was now no longer any necessity. On May 14th, I received the official title of Commander-in-Chief of the Allied Armies in France.

But all this was merely the formal proceeding which established my rights on paper; it remained to be seen how the Allied Command thus created would work in practice. I beg to repeat here what I said after Ypres, namely, that if this organ was to live, it must derive its strength solely from the confidence which the various Armies under its orders felt in it, and from the good understanding it maintained with and between these Armies. This understanding it must develop and strengthen at any price with a single object in view—the triumph of the common cause.

In any case, during the first days of April, 1918, there was no time to lose, if a situation still essentially precarious was to be improved by worn-out troops, and over a front considerably lengthened by the enemy's successes.

CHAPTER IV

THE RESTORATION OF THE ALLIED SITUATION ON THE SOMME AND THE GERMAN EFFORT IN FLANDERS

General Foch's instructions with a view to a Franco-British offensive to disengage Amiens, April 3rd—German attack in Flanders, April 9th ; French reserves move north—Extension and reinforcement of the enemy's front of attack, April 11th—French units are sent into Flanders, April 12th and 13th ; anxiety of the British staff, April 14th—The Belgians extend their line to the north of Ypres, April 18th—German attacks on the Flanders hills, capture of Bailleul, April 15th ; more French forces sent north, April 16th ; the British contemplate a retreat, General Foch intervenes, April 16th, 17th and 18th—Formation of a French army detachment in Flanders ; general movement of French reserves toward the north, April 17th to 23rd—Capture of Villers-Bretonneux, April 23rd ; successful counter-attack by the Australians —Fresh enemy efforts in Flanders ; capture of Mount Kemmel, April 25th ; important French forces moved up ; British withdrawal in the Ypres salient, April; 27th—Fresh intervention by General Foch and further despatch of French Divisions—End of the Battle, May 8th—General survey of the Battle and its consequences—Appeal made for American Divisions.

AFTER having obtained this first result by rapidly stopping up, with any means at hand, the serious breach in the Franco-British front which the German offensive of March 21st had brought about, the next thing to do was to consolidate the new front by systematically organizing its defence and forming a reserve. It then remained to ensure the needs of the troops and of the civil population by regaining certain portions of the ground which the enemy had seized and which, in his hands, threatened their safety.

To cover these points I drew up my instructions of April 3rd to Field-Marshal Haig and General Pétain. These prescribed, on the one hand, the organization of a strong defensive front north of the Somme, and on the other, an offensive south of that river, in order to disengage Amiens :

" The enemy is now held up from Arras to the Oise. On this front he may resume the offensive (*a*) with ease, north of the Somme, and particularly in the Arras region, where numerous railway lines are at his disposal ; (*b*) with greater difficulty on the south, since the railway lines which he has captured are here less numerous, are in bad order and lie partly within range of our guns."

We may then expect :
" On the front north of the Somme, an offensive, and even perhaps a strong offensive ; on the south front, a weaker or less early offensive."

Our own interests require that we push the enemy back as soon as possible :
" (1) From the Saint-Just—Breteuil—Amiens railway,
" (2) From the Amiens railway centre."

We must therefore :
" (1) Attack him south of the Somme in the Montdidier region.
" (2) Attack him astride the Somme, from the Luce to the Ancre."

By doing this, moreover, we would be furthering the realization of the fundamental ideas which had so far governed our operations ; namely, to strengthen the liaison between the French and British armies and cover Amiens. Again, while not anticipating decisive results, nevertheless, thanks to the right-angled formation of our front, we might cause the enemy a serious check by an offensive on and to the south of the Somme. This would be the best parry to his possible attack north of the river.

"These considerations lead me to fix as follows the task of the Allied Armies for the approaching operations :

"(1) As soon as possible, an offensive by the French Armies in the Montdidier region, with the object of clearing the Saint-Just—Amiens railway, while also taking advantage of the shape of our front to drive the enemy eastwards to the Avre, and northwards towards Roye.

"(2) An offensive by the British Armies, astride the Somme, in an easterly direction, from the Luce to the Ancre, with the object of disengaging Amiens.

"It would be of the greatest advantage if these two offensives, whose directions fortunately harmonize, could be carried out simultaneously.

"The Commanders-in-Chief are therefore requested to be good enough to communicate the date on which they judge it possible to undertake these operations ; it is important that they start with the least possible delay."

As it was essential also to guard against any new designs on the part of the enemy north of the Somme; measures touching both ground and reserves must be taken for their protection. I therefore requested the British and French Commanders-in-Chief to organize without delay the front between Arras and Albert. Similarly, General Pétain was asked to "maintain a French reserve in the region north of Beauvais and to make preparations for its move toward the north . . ."

I had already spoken to General Pétain about these matters on the afternoon of April 2nd, and we had examined together the conditions governing the realization of these instructions from the French point of view. On April 4th General Weygand went to Montreuil in order to go over with Sir Douglas Haig the measures which the British Staff proposed to employ in their turn. The most important task which, for the moment, demanded Sir Douglas' activity was surely the defence of the British front lying in the Arras region, in the neighbourhood of the Somme. I laid special stress on this point in a letter which I wrote to the Commander-in-Chief of the British Army. I pointed out to him that a certain time must elapse before the French reserves could intervene on the British front and that, consequently, the dispositions of the British Army should enable it to hold out, even in the face of a very heavy attack.

In view of the latest intelligence reports, the Field-Marshal was expecting a strong German offensive on the Béthune—Arras front, and he would have preferred immediate support from French troops, either in the form of a large offensive designed to draw off from him and engage the German forces which were threatening his front, or by replacing the British troops south of the Somme, or even by the formation of a French reserve in the British zone around Saint-Pol.

I discussed these various points with him on the afternoon of April 7th at Aumale. I was most anxious to give him the greatest possible satisfaction, but I was equally desirous not to disperse such French troops as were available or to use them up prematurely. As a result of our talk, it was decided that four French infantry and three French cavalry divisions, drawn from the Beauvais reserve, should be sent into the British zone west of Amiens. They would there be in a position to liberate British reserves in case of a heavy enemy attack in the Arras region.

In what concerned the preparation of the Franco-British offensive south of the Somme, its main lines were already decided upon. I merely laid down the immediate objective, namely, the recapture, at the earliest possible date, of the line Moreuil—Demuin—Aubencourt —Warfusée. I charged General Fayolle with establishing the necessary agreement to this end between the French First Army and the British Fourth Army.

On the following day, April 8th, General Fayolle saw Generals Debeney and Rawlinson at Breteuil, and drew up with them the plan of attack. This had to take into account the reduced resources at the disposal of the British Fourth Army. The attack was fixed, in principle, for April 12th; but we were forestalled and it did not take place. For, on the 9th, the Germans opened a powerful offensive in Flanders, and this absorbed the British reserves and a good portion of the French.

On the 10th, Sir Douglas Haig informed me that I must no longer count on the British Fourth Army for the attack south of the Somme; and General Pétain, on being requested to proceed with the preparation of a French attack on the Moreuil—Demuin front, prolonging it if necessary toward the north, reported that General Fayolle did not now have sufficient forces at his disposal to ensure a success. He was forced to confine himself to a local operation in the Moreuil region; this was carried out successfully on April 18th by the French First Army.

* * * *

The German offensive in Flanders (April 9th)

On April 9th, another big battle was begun in Flanders. That day, the German Fourth Army (von

Quast), nine Divisions strong, delivered an attack on the positions between La Bassée and Armentières, held by three British Divisions and a Portuguese Division belonging to the British First Army (General Horne).

Surprised at the moment when reliefs were being effected, the Portuguese Divisions was thrown back and a breach made in the British front. The enemy pushed straight through the centre towards Laventie, passed beyond that place and reached the Lys between Estaires and Sailly.

On the 10th he pursued his efforts and extended them northwards towards Messines by bringing in five new divisions. In this way he included the right of the Second British Army (General Plumer) in his attack. Armentières and Messines fell into his hands, and he crossed the Lys on a front of fifteen miles, from Le Touquet to Estaires, and advanced west in the direction of Hazebrouck—Saint-Omer.

On the first day of the German attack I made preparations to thrust the French reserve then being formed west of Amiens into the British sector. With this end in view, it had been decided with Sir Douglas Haig that the reserve should be allotted the bridges at Montières, Dreuil-les-Amiens, Ailly-sur-Somme and Picquigny, so that, if the necessity arose, it might debouch north of the Somme.

This decision did not wholly satisfy the Field-Marshal, who, being still under the influence of the blow he had received in Picardy, imagined the Germans already pouring in on top of his troops, and he counted upon more immediate and direct support from the French.

But however anxious I might be to restore confidence in the British, I could not, for all that, throw into action French divisions that were just being assembled, without being more certain than I was of the real intentions of the enemy. The attack in Flanders up to the present had accounted for only a small part of the forces he had available. The numbers he had engaged in the attack, its new direction and its extent, gave reason to suppose that, for the moment, he had in view not so much a decisive offensive as a diversion designed to draw away the Allied reserves and cover a more important action in another place. Our reserves must therefore be engaged sparingly. Sir Douglas for the moment would have to depend on his own resources.

These comprised nearly all the second line British Divisions which the British Commander-in-Chief had asked to have sent him. It was therefore permissible to believe that the German irruption would be quickly dammed and that, in any case, no territory not actually attacked by the enemy would be voluntarily given up. I drew the attention of General Headquarters at Montreuil most particularly to this latter point.

However, it was also to be anticipated that the enemy's effort in Flanders, in the direction of Saint-Omer and Dunkirk, might finish by absorbing all the troops the British had, and that then, reverting to their original plan, the Germans might develop a powerful offensive against Arras in the direction of Abbeville. In this case it was evident that the French reserves, at that time assembled south of the Somme, would be too distant from their ultimate field of action, and that they ought to be moved up without delay. Accordingly, after discussing this point with General Pétain at his Command Post on the afternoon of April 10th, I issued instructions for the Tenth Army* to be disposed astride

* Composed of four Divisions, assembled west of Amiens, under the command of General Maistre, who had returned from Italy.

the Somme, from Picquigny to Amiens, facing the line Doullens—Acheux, while the Fifth Army was to move up behind it to the line Beauvais—Breteuil.

This arrangement provided for a two-fold eventuality, in that it made it possible for the French reserves to intervene, as the case might be, on the Artois front in twenty-four hours, or on the Flanders front in forty-eight.

Sir Douglas Haig, however, impressed by the enemy's furious onslaughts against the British lines, considered these measures inadequate, and on the evening of the 10th he wrote to me asking urgently that the French take an active part in the battle by relieving a portion of the British front.

The anxiety which this letter revealed caused me to leave at once for Montreuil. In a conversation during the night with Sir Douglas, it was recognized that a relief of British troops would entail a delay which, in the circumstances, was not possible. On the other hand, it was agreed that a German attack was still to be feared in the Artois district, and that, to provide against this possibility, a French force should be assembled north of the Somme as soon as possible, so as to be within striking distance of Arras.

To accomplish this, General Pétain was requested to push the column heads of the Tenth Army as far as Villers-Bocage on April 10th, and, with a view to giving material support to the British in the north, he would send a French Division (the 133rd) by rail to Dunkirk.

*   *   *   *

The British Commander-in-Chief's fears were not without foundation. In order to exploit his success of

FOCH WITH HIS CHIEF OF STAFF, GENERAL WEYGAND, AT SARCUS, 1918.

the 9th immediately, the enemy had widened his front of action. On the 11th, the battle extended from La Bassée canal to Comines, on the Ypres canal, a distance of eighteen miles. The sector had, moreover, been reinforced by new enemy divisions. On April 14th, there were twenty-five German Divisions in action. This increase of strength was marked by an appreciable hostile advance in the direction of Hazebrouck.

After crossing the Lawe canal, General von Quast's troops seized Locon and Estaires, and, further north, Hollebeke. On the 12th, Merville and Merris fell into their hands and their advanced guards were already on the edge of the Nieppe Forest. In depth their gain thus amounted to eleven miles. Faced with this development of the battle, Field-Marshal Haig saw his resources being rapidly used up, and he deemed it more than ever essential that the French should co-operate in Flanders.

On the evening of the 11th, he sent General Davidson, the chief of the Operations branch of his staff, to see me at Sarcus. He bore a letter in which Sir Douglas described the exhaustion of the British forces and emphasized the necessity of " immediately concentrating a mass of at least four French Divisions between Saint-Omer and Dunkirk."

In the course of our conversation, General Davidson and I agreed that by using the whole of the British reserves, including those still on the right of the British Army, seventeen Divisions in all, plus the reinforcement furnished by the French units then moving north, the Field-Marshal would be able to restore the situation in front of Hazebrouck, provided :

(1) That the enemy be held by a minimum of forces in the first line.

(2) That he be definitely stopped on the line Mount Kemmel—Bailleul—Nieppe Forest—Valley of the Clarence—Mount Bernenchon—Hinges.

(3) That the troops be supported by a systematic organization of the artillery defence, directed more particularly against the flanks of the attack.

However, in calculating the number of units which would be at Sir Douglas Haig's disposal on the Lys, I had included the British Divisions which up to this time had been held in reserve in the Arras region. This made it necessary to entrust the defence of this region, in case it was attacked, to the French reserves. I was therefore led to move the Tenth Army up to the line Doullens—Vauchelles, which it reached on April 13th, thus passing into the British zone.

General Pétain, on his side, moved the Fifth Army further north, abreast of Amiens. This army was reinforced by taking troops from the Reserve Group of Armies, as no offensive task was contemplated for this force at the moment. He also moved the Oise Group to the westwards. This was composed of two Divisions, and part of this force proceeded to the right bank of the river. He also despatched the I Cavalry Corps from Les Andelys towards Aumale.

General Fayolle was requested to concentrate the reserves on his left wing in such manner as would best enable them, in case of need, to support the Fourth British Army in the Luce—Somme sector.

Finally General Maistre, commanding the Tenth Army, was given instructions regarding his mission on the Arras front. The principal line of resistance, which, in the event of a hostile attack, must be held at all costs, was prescribed for him as well as for the British Third Army. His initial dispositions and the method of his intervention in the battle were likewise indicated to him.

While making these general arrangements in preparation for the possible intervention of the French Divisions between Arras and the Somme, my intention was also to give as much support as possible to the British Commander-in-Chief, beset as he was by the material and moral difficulties of the Flanders battle. On the 12th, I decided to increase the direct support with which two days before I had already begun to furnish him.

To carry out this intention I ordered the II Cavalry Corps, which was in reserve in the Aumale region, to march to Saint-Omer, arriving on the 13th, and then to hold itself in readiness to co-operate with the French 133rd Division as a reinforcement to the British Second Army.

General Robillot, commanding the Corps, came to Sarcus* to receive my instructions. While indicating his mission in the general framework of the battle, I laid particular stress on the duty devolving upon him of ensuring the liaison between the First and Second British Armies.

As to the general trend of the manœuvre, I conceived it as follows:

(1) Hold the two flanks of the breach at all costs:

(a) On the north " by the successive occupation of the general line Mount Kemmel—Cassel, facing south."

(b) On the south " by the successive occupation of the general line Béthune—Saint-Omer, facing north-east."

(2) Between these two firmly-held flanks, to slow up and then stop the enemy squarely " by the occupation,

---

* My Headquarters had been at Sarcus (three miles north-west of Grandvilliers) since April 7th.

facing east, of the successive points of resistance offered by the ground."

Up to this time the British reserves, thrown into action at the most threatened points, had been put into line between La Bassée canal and the Lille—Hazebrouck railway, that is to say on the southern flank of the breach. It was now necessary to secure the northern flank, which was of the utmost importance to us. For if the enemy succeeded in capturing the Monts de Flandres and Mount Cassel, he would threaten the Allied troops established between Ypres and the sea. The defence of this flank was entrusted to General Plumer's British Second Army, and it was necessary to furnish it with means adequate to the task. With this object in view, I sent up the 133rd Division and French II Cavalry Corps. But as this help might soon become insufficient, I requested General Pétain to make preparations for moving to the north another French Division, taken if need be from units in course of reconstitution. The 28th Division was selected.

I also requested the Chief of Staff of the Belgian Army to place at General Plumer's disposal all the Belgian units which were not absolutely necessary to hold his front. Unfortunately, the Belgian High Command, for constitutional rather than military reasons, was not able to accede to this request. Finally, I sent Colonel Desticker, my assistant Chief of Staff, to convey instructions to General Plumer at Cassel, and co-ordinate the action of the French units that had been moved north to ensure the execution of my orders.

The defence of the southern side of the breach being assured and that of the northern side well on the way to improvement, the next question was to organize the resistance of the centre. Provision could be made for this, in the first instance, by moving the British Cavalry Corps to the vicinity of Aire, from which place it would be " in a position to help the troops in this sector to check the advance of the Germans in the direction of Hazebrouck."

Furthermore, in order to halt the enemy's advance towards Dunkirk and Calais, if it should become more pronounced, as well as to guard Dunkirk against any surprise, General Pauffin de Saint-Maurel, the Military Governor of the town, was requested to extend the freshwater inundations from Saint-Omer to the Dunkirk—Furnes road, including Watten and Bergues.

On the afternoon of the 13th, I went to Ranchicourt, Headquarters of the British First Army, and discussed with General Horne the measures taken (and about to be taken) to hold up the German advance in the direction of Hazebrouck and protect the Béthune mining district. On the following day, the 14th, in a note addressed to Colonel Desticker, I insisted that the defence of Hazebrouck be effected " as near as possible to the eastern edge of the Nieppe Forest."

In the presence of my cautious attitude, the British Staff was much preoccupied by the following question : " Supposing we are again driven back," they asked, " which base will you cover ? Are you going to protect Paris and France before everything else, and thereby abandon the defence of the Channel Ports, the bases of the British Army ? Or will you, in order to cover the Channel ports, sacrifice the protection of Paris ? "

My answer was this : " I do not intend to abandon or to uncover in any way either the road to Paris or the road to the Ports. The first is indispensable to the French Army, the second to the British Army and also to the safety of the Belgian Army."

"All very well," they replied, "but suppose you are forced to concentrate your forces in one or the other of these two divergent directions, which one will you sacrifice?"

I answered: "I count on sacrificing neither one nor the other direction, neither that of the Ports nor that of Paris. If either is lost, our men and our resources would be reduced by half. I am striving to save both, and I shall do my utmost to succeed. The thing seems to me possible, provided that we do not use up all our available troops to ward off the present attack, namely the one against the Ports."

There was no denying that very great difficulties confronted us, in view of the danger of engaging the last remaining French troops on a portion of the British front, when other hostile enterprises were to be feared on other parts of the line. In the course of a meeting on the morning of the 14th at Abbeville, at which Lord Milner was present, Sir Douglas Haig reverted once more to the exhausted state of the British Army and the poverty of reinforcements. He again asked that the French relieve the British on a portion of their front.

In reply I had to limit myself to repeating the arguments against this course: To relieve units while the battle was in progress would immobilize both the relieving troops and those relieved during the time required for the operation, and this at the very moment when the Allied reserves were scarcely sufficient to man the whole front. Furthermore, since a powerful German attack on some other part of the front might readily take place, we would be making a very bad use of the French reserves still available if we definitely condemned them to a more or less passive rôle. At present they were distributed and placed so as to be able to intervene actively and powerfully at any point which the vast battle might disclose as dangerous.

Nor could I as yet, in spite of the Field-Marshal's request, move the Tenth Army up to the line Béthune—Lillers and bring the Fifth Army up behind it. It would have been dangerous to strip the Artois region ; and, besides, it seemed that for the moment Sir Douglas was sufficiently strong in Flanders. In addition to the French units which had been sent him (two infantry and three cavalry Divisions), he had, as a matter of fact, two or three British Divisions just disengaged through the reduction of the front, following on the voluntary evacuation of the Ypres salient to the east of the line Bixschoote—Langemark—Hollebecke (April 13th—15th).

However, being anxious to support the British Commander-in-Chief, I made arrangements to shorten the time required for the French to intervene in the north, if this became necessary. The Tenth Army was instructed to echelon one of its Divisions to the north of Frévent, and to study a similar disposition for another Division, enabling it to support the British First Army rapidly, either on the front La Bassée Canal—Arras, or the front Béthune—Hazebrouck.

Besides this, in order to enable the Field-Marshal to increase his reserves, I requested Lieutenant-General Gillain to envisage and make preparations for an extension of the Belgian front towards Ypres. On April 18th a Belgian Division relieved a British Division and a British Brigade north of that town.

While we were strengthening the defence in Flanders by these dispositions, the enemy was making preparations to deal fresh blows.

After a respite of two days, during which his efforts

were appreciably relaxed, he renewed the attack in a new direction. He had doubtless seen that by continuing his advance west without having first captured the line of the Flanders hills, he would be exposing his right flank to serious risk. He therefore decided to attack that line before pursuing his march on Hazebrouck and Dunkirk. On the evening of April 13th, therefore, he launched heavy attacks in a northerly direction against the British Second Army and succeeded in capturing Bailleul and Wulverghem. On the 16th he continued his efforts on a still wider front, seized Wyschaete and Messines and arrived almost within assaulting distance of Mount Kemmel.

The Battle of Flanders was moving northwards, and this German offensive, by reason of its extent, its power and, above all, its new direction, now constituted, as we have already indicated, a serious threat to the Allied forces established north of Ypres. These, including as they did the whole of the Belgian Army, ran the risk of being cut off from their communications and reduced to helplessness. Danger threatened the Coalition and the northern extremity of its front, and no time must be lost in parrying it.

Our available railway lines had been reduced by the attack of March 21st, and the difficulty of moving troops was considerably increased. Nevertheless, French reserves must be hurried to Flanders. I therefore sent instructions to General Pétain to make ready the movement of a new Division to the region of Bergues, taken, if need be, from units in course of reconstitution; and to General Maistre (Tenth Army) to push the artillery and trains of the 34th Division to Norrent-Fontès, on the afternoon of the 16th, at the same time making ready to move the infantry of this Division by motor transport in the early hours of the 17th.

Once this move was carried out, the XVI Corps (at the head of the Fifth Army) was to cross the Somme and come under the orders of the Tenth Army, whose mission remained as previously defined.

Then, in order to examine for myself the situation in Flanders, after stopping to see General Wilson and Lord Milner at Abbeville, I proceeded to Blendeques, Headquarters of the British Second Army. I met General Plumer at Cappel near Cassel on the evening of the 16th. It was night, our lights were extinguished and the bombardment resounded with violence all around us. The enemy's activity in Flanders had become intense. Here I also found General Robillot, commanding the French II Cavalry Corps, and Colonel Desticker, whom I had sent on ahead to make an estimate of what troops the British had available. At ten o'clock we returned with General Plumer to his Headquarters at Blendeques, and from there I telephoned General Weygand at my Headquarters at Sarcus to issue orders for the 34th Division to move the following day by motor transport to Steenworde.

On the morning of the 17th, at a meeting with Lieutenant-General Sir Henry Wilson, Chief of the Imperial General Staff, who agreed with the opinion held by Field-Marshal Sir Douglas Haig and General Plumer in this respect, the British Staff proposed that the Allied Armies in Flanders should be withdrawn successively to the line of the inundations running from Aire to Saint-Omer and Furnes. I refused to adopt such a measure and I could not share Sir Douglas' fears in regard to the port of Dunkirk, the evacuation and destruction of which he already envisaged.

In my opinion, there was no course open for the

moment but to organize and maintain our resistance where we were, calling upon the French reserves as it became necessary, and making the best possible use of the Belgian forces in their own sector. This same point of view I expressed to the King of the Belgians and the Chief of Staff of the Belgian Army, whom I saw during the 17th. This spirit also inspired the instructions I left with General Plumer on the 18th, before leaving Blendecques to return to Sarcus. It was this way of looking at the matter which formed the basis of the letters I wrote some hours later to Lieutenant-General Gillain and to Sir Douglas Haig. For I wished to make clear to them again the line of conduct to be followed in the present circumstances by both the Belgian Army and the British Second Army. It was the same which was developed in the memorandum I had issued to the Allied Armies, treating of the general principles which should govern a defensive battle.

The idea of a vigorous resistance where they stood should not, however, relieve commanders from the duty of selecting and organizing one or more lines on which to retire in case of retreat, or of improving existing defences, such as those of the British First Army running from the neighbourhood of Arras to the vicinity of Saint-Omer.

At a meeting of the Belgian and British Staffs, held at this time, we arranged for a study to be made " of the measures necessary to adjust the successive British (defensive) dispositions with the existing or anticipated dispositions of the Belgian Army," as well as the best line of demarcation between the two Armies. Finally, in the case of an enemy offensive directed from Ypres on Poperinghe, the use to be made of Allied reserves, whatever their nationality—British, Belgian or French—

was prescribed in a general scheme fixed jointly by the Staffs concerned.

It was not long before all these precautions bore fruit.

From April 17th to 20th the enemy multiplied his efforts against the Allied front south of the Flanders hills in vain. He reaped nothing but sanguinary losses. But if the drain on the Germans was heavy, that on the British was no less so, and a letter from Sir Douglas Haig, dated April 18th, set forth its extent. Fortunately, other resources were about to become available for continuing the struggle ; these were the French reserves.

We have seen that the 34th Division was moved forward on April 17th. On the 18th, the 154th and 39th Divisions were brought up, and the 27th Division arrived on April 23rd. With the Divisions already assembled, they were formed into the " Army detachment of the North," under the command of General de Mitry. The size of these French forces, five infantry and three cavalry Divisions, taken with the extension of the Belgian front to the north of Ypres, enabled the British Second Army to withdraw seven Divisions and sixteen Brigades from the battle. It was thus placed in a position to fulfil its mission.

Nevertheless, in case the enemy continued his efforts without respite, it would be necessary to bring other French Divisions to Flanders. I therefore directed the Tenth Army to advance the column heads of the XVI Corps (31st and 32nd Divisions), up to the line Heuchin—Pernes without delay, and while remaining always ready to give support in the Arras region, to be prepared also to intervene with a part of its forces on the front Cambrin—Béthune—Robecq. At the same time, the 46th and 47th Divisions of the Fifth Army were to be brought up as far as Villers-Bocage.

Thus there was produced a general movement of extension of French reserves toward the north, justified by the threefold necessity of supporting the British in Flanders, of acting with them, if need arose, in the Arras region, and of being properly distributed for intervention on the Somme.

All menace in the latter directions was far from being removed, and the struggle might flare up there again at any moment. For according to the calculations of the French Staff, the enemy still had available some sixty Divisions with which to make another try at separating the French and British forces. So far he had failed to accomplish it.

*   *   *   *   *

For three weeks comparative calm had reigned on the front to the south of the Somme ; but on April 23rd the alarm was suddenly sounded. A German attack, carried out by eight Divisions advancing under cover of the fog, captured Villers-Bretonneux from the British Fourth Army and Hangard from the French First Army, and then pushed forward to the outskirts of Cachy.

The establishment of the enemy at Villers-Bretonneux was bound to have most unfortunate consequences for us. It provided him with observation posts and gun-positions which would enable him to bombard, attack and capture Amiens under excellent conditions. In other words, by following the line of the Somme, he could greatly advance his plan of cutting the communications of the Allied Armies, and he might even separate them.

Villers-Bretonneux was a fairly large place and would constitute a point of support of great value to the enemy if he were given time to organize it. It was necessary that we recapture it immediately and at all costs.

Accordingly, as soon as the news reached me, I wrote to General Rawlinson to make preparations to retake Villers-Bretonneux, the possession of which was vital to us, and to arrange with General Debeney for the counter-attack. General Rawlinson without hesitation fell in with these views.

The counter-attack, executed during the night of the 24th—25th was entrusted to some Australian Battalions. They carried the high ground and the village by assault, whilst, on the right, the Moroccan Division of the French First Army regained some ground north of Hangard. In order to consolidate the re-established situation, General Debeney continued his forward movement, while at the same time General Fayolle sent two Divisions northwards, so as to be in a position to intervene between the Somme and the Luce.

All the British reserves on their right had been engaged in the struggle around Villers-Bretonneux. They had suffered fresh losses there, an addition to a casualty list already enormous. Sir Douglas Haig drew my attention to this point on the evening of the 24th, and satisfaction was given him, not only by the assurance of the eventual co-operation of the French reserves, distributed as has just been explained, but also by the relief of the British III Corps, on General Rawlinson's right, by the French First Army.

At the same time I requested General Fayolle to make preparations as rapidly as possible for an attack by the Third Army in the Montdidier region. This attack, if it was pushed beyond the Avre, would have the effect of cutting the enemy's communications south of the Somme, and, subsequently, of clearing the ground in the direction of Amiens.

In fact, the German effort against Villers-Bretonneux

resulted in nothing. After the French and British had counter-attacked and recaptured the town, they in turn exhausted themselves in fruitless efforts during April 25th and 26th, and were definitely repulsed on the Villers-Bretonneux—Hangard road. This latter village remained in the hands of the enemy.

Everybody's attention was now once more drawn towards Flanders.

* * * * *

On April 25th the Crown Prince of Bavaria again attacked between Bailleul and Ypres, employing the right of his Sixth and the left of his Fourth Armies. The latter gained ground towards Ypres, while the former captured Dranoutre and threatened Locre on the Poperinghe road. In the centre, the Bavarian Alpine Corps assaulted and took Kemmel and Mount Kemmel, thus gaining a foothold on the eastern portion of the Flemish hills. On the following day, the 26th, the struggle was continued with fury on the Scherpenberg—Vormezeele front, but the enemy was unable this time to register any important advance, since Allied reinforcements came up continuously. On the 25th, the 31st Division of the XVI Corps arrived for the Army Detachment of the North; also the other Division of this Corps, the 32nd, reached Fauquemberges. At the same time I requested General Pétain to furnish two regiments of field artillery and twelve groups of heavy artillery for the Army Detachment of the North as well as one regiment of field artillery for the Belgian Army.

The importance of these reinforcements proved once more our willingness to support the British Commander-in-Chief to the utmost; it was also evidence of the determination to continue at any cost our defence of the ground whereon we stood.

Indeed, there was no more ground to lose in Flanders. Mount Kemmel is only twenty-five miles from Dunkirk, and it commands the whole plain stretching up to the town. If the enemy succeeded in establishing himself there with his heavy artillery, he would be able to crush any resistance we could oppose to his advance on the port. In other words, he would reach the shores of the Channel and threaten our communications with England, and at the same time he would place the whole Belgian Army in peril.

I did not succeed, however, in preventing the British front in the Ypres salient from being withdrawn, on April 27th, to the walls of the city, with, as a consequence, the withdrawal of the Belgian front to the Yperlée canal.

On the afternoon of the 27th, I again left for the North, I first saw General Plumer at Blendecques, and then General de Mitry at Esquelbecq. I explained to them the gravity of the situation and the fundamental principles upon which the existing circumstances required that the defence be based. I also emphasized the necessity of sending troops as they arrived straight into action with clearly defined missions, making all questions of cantonments yield to tactical requirements.

I was now struck with the enormous wastage among the Allied troops,* subjected as they had been to incessant attacks, and bombardment by a prodigious number of gas shells. In order to meet this situation, I ordered three more French Divisions (the 32nd, 129th and 168th) to be sent to Flanders ; a part of these would be used to relieve the British XXII Corps, which had reached the

* On April 23rd, in particular, Field-Marshal Sir Douglas Haig could count as reserves at his own disposal only two Divisions in course of being reorganized and one Division in process of detraining after its arrival from Italy.

extreme limit of endurance.

Furthermore, I requested General Pétain to make arrangements to keep three fresh French Divisions in rear of the front occupied by the Army Detachment of the North, as long as the violence of the German attacks made it necessary. At the same time, the Tenth Army was to be maintained at four Divisions and held in the region Doullens—Saint Pol, in order to meet unforeseen emergencies.

On April 29th the enemy attacked Mont Rouge and Mont Noir and the Scherpenberg, but was repulsed. On May 8th he carried out still another attack on a front of two miles south-east of Dickebusch; but this was an isolated action and was not followed up.

The Battle of Flanders had come to an end. It had occupied more than a month of violent and highly sustained efforts. That the German advance represented a less deep penetration than that effected on the Somme at the end of March, was due to two facts: His objective, the Channel coast, was in this case much closer, while we, by rapidly moving up troops, succeeded, as it was our duty to do, in repulsing his rush. The danger of being thrown back on the sea forced the Allied Armies to fight on their front lines, and resistance in depth was out of the question owing to lack of space to manœuvre. On account of the difficulty of reinforcing the northern extremity of the vast and seriously shaken Allied front, in time, it was more than once in grave danger.

However, while the battle had not obtained for the Germans the strategic results they had aimed at, nothing could prevent it from being begun again. The enemy might find it to his interest to resume his advance with the intention of gaining the Channel coast at any price, and by intensifying his submarine warfare in the adjoin-

GENERAL FOCH AND THE INTER-ALLIED STAFF AT SARCUS, IN APRIL, 1918.

ing waters, hamper communications with England and isolate the power of Great Britain. The battle had already produced tactical results which, on balance, were unquestionably against the Allies.

Our appreciable loss of ground left the Flanders hills (Rouge, Noir and Scherpenberg), those buttresses of the northern Allied line, under the close menace of the Germans, already masters as they were of Mount Kemmel. Our retention of these hills must be ensured at all cost, if the security of our front was not to be dangerously compromised. I therefore drew General de Mitry's attention to the necessity not only of strongly organizing the defence of the hills themselves, but of extending his works to the ground at the foot of the slopes, so as to prevent the enemy from surrounding the summits and penetrating to the saddles between them. Local operations, undertaken on May 4th by the Army Detachment of the North, enabled some progress to be made in this sense.

I continued to emphasize the necessity of holding on where the men stood and never making a voluntary retirement. I once more laid down the line of conduct to be followed, and gave instructions that, in the future, if any important withdrawal was contemplated, it must be submitted beforehand for my approval. I also drew up a note dealing with general principles, prescribing the guiding policy of a defensive battle, in order that unity of doctrine among the Allies might bring about unity of action.

Another result of the Battle of Flanders was to expose the Béthune coal basin to bombardment by German artillery. This produced a serious disturbance in the working of these mines and affected the output of the munition factories and railways which they supplied.

We were able to remedy this situation by certain measures whose execution was admirably assured by the British Army and the French Military Mission attached to British General Headquarters.

The Battle of Flanders had been a great drain upon Allied man-power. The British reserves had melted in the struggle and the calls upon the French reserves on behalf of our Allies amounted already to ten Divisions.

To enable General Pétain to reconstitute these reserves without weakening his front line, I had arranged with Sir Douglas Haig that the British Divisions which had been withdrawn from the battle should be placed in a quiet sector of the French front. In this way they set free a similar number of French units for reconstituting our reserves. But the movement could only be carried out slowly. At first General Pétain received four British Divisions, constituting the IX Corps. They were assigned to the French Sixth Army, and towards the middle of May they were put into the Craonne—Loivre front.

These battles, which had been waged incessantly for a month, brought about another result which has already been referred to—the equilibrium in the distribution of French forces had been upset. At the beginning of May, forty-seven French Divisions were north of the Oise (twenty-three in the front line and twenty-four in reserve). There remained only fifty-five Divisions to hold the front from the Oise to the Swiss frontier, namely, forty-three in line and twelve in reserve. General Pétain drew my attention to the danger presented by this situation.

The great wastage suffered by the British Army had to be taken into account ; but a renewal of the German attack between the Oise and the Lys was always possible and might have serious consequences for the Allies, on account of the proximity of decisive objectives. I therefore maintained a group of four Divisions north of the Somme, and another group of the same strength south of that river. This did not prevent the despatch of units to Flanders to feed the Army Detachment of the North.

At the same time, I did all that was possible to facilitate the task of the French Commander-in-Chief by making use of the American troops, requesting that their Divisions be put into action as soon as possible or assigned to quiet sectors. The American First Division had already been placed on the front of the French First Army, on April 26th, and it soon gave proof of its military qualities by taking the village of Cantigny by assault (May 28th). I asked General Pershing to send the 26th, 42nd and 2nd Divisions as soon as possible to the battle front, and to permit the infantry of the 32nd, 3rd and 5th American Divisions to be employed as reinforcements for the French Divisions which were coming out of battle much reduced in numbers. This would enable them to be rapidly employed again in quiet sectors. I also suggested to him that American pilots might be sent to French air squadrons, where they could pursue their training and, incidentally, lighten the work for their French comrades.

At the same time I reduced the requirements of the Army Detachment of the North, and diminished its field of action. The heavy losses which it was incurring seemed to be out of all proportion to the tactical results obtained. After making allowances for the severe conditions which obtained in the Flanders fighting, and especially the intense bombardments by gas shell, it was evident that these losses were in great part due to the inexperience of the men and a lack of vigilance on the part of those in command.

General de Mitry was therefore instructed to hasten the readjustment of his front, with the object of establishing a solid defensive situation, the general lines of which were traced for him.

Furthermore, General Pétain was requested to resume the training of the smaller infantry and artillery units, selecting for this work General and Field officers who were thoroughly familiar with war and had already practised, especially in the early days of the conflict, the sort of operations with which the troops should now be familiar.

Nevertheless, in spite of all the ingenuity displayed by the High Command to meet the exigencies of battle, one vital problem dominated the general situation of the Allied Armies in France in mid-spring of 1918—the problem of numerical strength.

CHAPTER V

THE QUESTION OF THE STRENGTH OF THE ALLIED ARMIES IN FRANCE

The losses of the British Army in the spring of 1918—Suppression of nine divisions—Intervention of General Foch and the French Government; the " B " divisions—The difficulties of reforming the French divisions—The only remedy lies in American help—The situation of the American Army in France in the middle of April; inadequacy of transports—The Conferences of Sarcus, April 25th, and Abbeville, May 1st and 2nd—Measures adopted by the Allies to expedite the arrival in France of the American forces—Co-operation of the British Navy; the results obtained—Organization and training in France of the American divisions.

1. *The British Army.*

SCARCELY recovered from the heavy losses brought about by its offensives in 1917, the British Army sustained, in the spring of 1918, two tremendous blows one after the other : the German attack on the Arras—Amiens front, begun on March 21st, and the German attack in Flanders, begun on April 9th. The first had cost the British Army 120,000 men, the second increased this figure to nearly 300,000, including 14,000 officers.

The reinforcements sent from England were far from making good these losses, especially among the officers and non-commissioned officers. It is true that by July and August the return of many men who had been wounded in the first battles could be counted upon. It was also possible to foresee that before the expiration of this time the military laws recently passed by the English Parliament would have borne effect. The question, however, was how to provide until then for the enormous shortage in British effectives.

Failing to find any other solution for the problem, Sir Douglas Haig resigned himself to abolishing the Divisions he was unable to keep up to strength ; namely, five after the German offensive on the Somme, and four after the Battle of Flanders. The British Army was thus reduced to fifty-one fighting Divisions.

The disappearance of so many Divisions caused, in addition to other serious consequences, a reduction in the Allied reserves at the very moment when the number of available German troops was augmented.* On May 11th, I intervened with the Field-Marshal in an effort to secure the retention of all the British Divisions, pointing out to him certain measures which, in my opinion, would enable this result to be achieved. He declared, however, that they were impossible of realization. I then requested him to reconstitute at least some of the Divisions it had been decided to suppress, if only to show his Government the importance attached to maintaining in France the highest possible number of British Divisions.

In face of this insistence, Sir Douglas urged the War Office to send him, in the absence of men capable of standing active operations, contingents of an inferior quality but capable of being employed in quiet sectors. In this way the general reserve would not be impaired.

Although I appreciated the value of this proposal, I at once pointed out the danger it presented if, instead of being considered as a temporary expedient, it established for the future a separation of the British Army into two classes of Divisions, one for battle and the other for holding the line. A like notion, it is true, was in considerable favour with the Germans ; but that did not

---

* According to the calculations of the French Staff, these amounted to 69 Divisions on April 25th, 70 Divisions on May 10th, and 81 on May 19th.

make it any the more sound. On the contrary, the thing to be desired was to have Divisions of approximately the same quality and equal fighting capability. By departing from this policy, certain governments would be encouraged not to put forth their best efforts. In order to bring the matter to a head, I requested the French Government to take it up immediately with Mr. Lloyd George.

I myself talked to General Wilson regarding the question on May 20th at Abbeville. I urged upon him the imperative, two-fold necessity of recompleting all the British Divisions and of excluding any definite distinction amongst them. General Wilson expressed himself as in entire agreement with me, and shortly afterwards he informed me that the British Government had decided to send to France 70,000 more men than had been previously provided for.

Meanwhile, the German attack of May 27th on the Chemin des Dames made a new hole in the British strength. Five British Divisions were involved in this attack and suffered heavy losses. I at once wrote a personal letter to General Wilson, asking him to hurry the filling up of the British units.

On his part, Sir Douglas Haig forwarded me, on June 10th, the programme for the reconstitution of his Divisions. In expressing my satisfaction at seeing now settled a question to which he himself attached so great an importance, I drew the Field-Marshal's attention both to the advisability of having it understood that the employment of the " B " contingents was a purely temporary measure, and to the necessity of supplying the Divisions which had been filled up by these contingents with large numbers of machine-guns and much artillery.

However, it would have been rash to count on the

British Army being put in proper condition again in the near future. Indeed, it took a good many weeks to reforge it as a fighting instrument and put it into proper shape. The last weeks of July arrived before it had regained its battle value, and it was not until the beginning of September that it got back all its units, excepting always two Divisions which were definitely skeletonized. Thus, from the middle of April to the middle of July, the situation of the British Army remained extremely precarious.

*   *   *   *   *

2. *The French Army.*

Without having suffered as much as the British, the French Army, which had hastened to the latter's aid, had undergone many ordeals since March 21st, which could not but have an influence upon its effectives. The front entrusted to it had been increased by seventy-five miles ; in all, its Divisions had been engaged ninety-six times and their losses had been considerable, especially during the Battle of Flanders.

Thus General Pétain was also confronted by great difficulty in filling up his ranks. The resources he had at his command for this purpose did not make it possible to wait for the incorporation of the conscripts of the 1919 class, as these recruits would only be ready during the month of October. He therefore requested the Government to return him 200,000 men employed in munition factories in the interior ; but only 40,000 were forthcoming.

Consequently, towards the close of the spring of 1918, France and England were finding the greatest difficulty in obtaining from their national resources the men necessary to make good the losses which their Armies had suffered.

However, there was one possible remedy for this trying situation, namely, an appeal to the United States, whose immense reservoir of men was still untapped. To what extent was America, at this period, capable of bringing to the Allies the *immediate* help of which they stood in need?

* * * * *

3. *The American Army.*

During the middle of April, at a time when the crisis in both French and British effectives was particularly acute, the American Army in France comprised only five fighting Divisions. One of these, the 1st, was about to join the French First Army, three others (2nd, 26th and 42nd) were holding quiet sectors of the front, and the remaining one (32nd) had temporarily distributed its infantry among French Divisions to complete its training.

This infantry force constituted, therefore, the only direct help which the American Army was furnishing to fill the gaps in the French Army. Counting the black troops which were serving with our Divisions, the total amounted to 23,000 infantrymen, which, as can be seen, was far from meeting such pressing needs as ours.

During the month of April, the infantry of two other American Divisions (3rd and 5th) was due to arrive in France, but these troops could not be incorporated in French units within less than from three to five weeks. In as far as the British Army was concerned, the help afforded by America was limited, for the moment, to the infantry of one Division (77th) then on the ocean.

We thus see that to replace their very heavy losses in infantry, the French and British Armies could not count on the immediate or early help of more than 70,000 American infantry.

The evident feebleness of this result demanded that the mistakes which up to the present had been made in the matter of transporting the American Army to France be corrected. What was needed above all was that for several months the United States should send the Allies only infantry, to the exclusion of all other arms. By this means only could the British and French Armies procure the 300,000 to 350,000 infantry which were needed to weather their existing crisis in effectives. In a detailed memorandum to the French Prime Minister, I presented these views and asked him to appeal to the American Government to put them into effect.

This Government, in fact, was already informed and seemed disposed to accept the proposition of the Commander-in-Chief of the Allied Armies. It remained to convince General Pershing, who was keen on the idea of commanding a great American Army as soon as possible, although he was not, it is true, fully aware of the urgency of our present necessities.

He and I readily fell into accord regarding this point, in the course of a Conference held at Sarcus on April 25th, which was also attended by General Bliss. After a close discussion, it was decided that the American troops to be brought over in May and June should, in principle, consist primarily of infantry. For the month of May, the question was settled there and then. For the month of June, it was agreed that a definite decision would be taken a little later. But from then on it was understood that the Government at Washington would prepare to send the infantry of at least six Divisions to France.

This meeting at the same time disclosed the urgent

necessity of directing and co-ordinating to the advantage of the Coalition the effort being put forth by the United States, of directing it so as to adapt it to necessities as they arose, of co-ordinating it so as to prevent personal arrangements, such as that concluded between General Pershing and Lord Milner, and revealed in the course of the Conference on April 25th, and which had the effect of frittering away that effort. In a word, what ought to be done was for the Allied Governments to study the question of American effectives as a whole and whatever decisions were taken, to take them together.

This was done at Abbeville, on May 1st and 2nd, when the following arrangements were agreed to :

1. The British Government undertook to furnish the tonnage necessary to transport from the United States to France 130,000 men in May, and 150,000 in June, consisting *solely of infantry and machine-gun detachments.*

2. The American tonnage would be used for the transport of artillery, engineers, services, etc.

3. A further examination of the situation would be made at the beginning of June and the programme for the future decided upon.

It can be seen that these decisions were of the highest importance. They proved to be perfectly satisfactory, for, thanks to the magnificent co-operation of British shipping, by July 1st nearly 450,000 American infantry and machine-gunners were landed in France to fill the gaps in the British and French Armies. On his side, General Pershing proceeded with the transport of the other arms and services, using for this purpose American tonnage. He was thereby enabled to constitute in a short time self-contained American Divisions in France. Special interests as well as those of the Coalition were thus safeguarded.

Confined to her own resources, America had transported only 60,000 men in March of 1918 and 93,000 men in April; with British help these figures rose to 240,000 in May and 280,000 in June.

However, the rapid arrival of these large contingents caused other problems to arise. Time had been lacking to complete the training and organization of troops in America, and it had to be continued and completed in France. Now, while the problem of training was comparatively easy to handle, that of organization and the supply of all the implements of war needed by a modern army—such as equipment, arms, horses, material of every description—was much more complicated. All this had to be closely watched if mistakes, omissions and loss of time were to be avoided.

To this end a section was created on my Staff in Paris, under the orders of an Assistant Chief of Staff, whose task it was to centralize and co-ordinate all questions relating to the completion of the organization of the American Divisions.

CHAPTER VI

THE GERMAN ATTACK FROM RHEIMS TO MONTDIDIER

(*May 27th—June 13th*)

1. *The Attack on the Chemin des Dames* (*May 27th—June 4th*)

A pause—The Allies make preparation for counter-attacks between the Oise and the Somme, and in the Lys region—German attack on the Chemin des Dames, May 27th ; the enemy captures Soissons and crosses the Vesle, May 28th ; measures taken by Generals Foch and Pétain—The Germans, continuing their offensive, reach the Marne ; General Foch sends the Tenth Army there, May 30th—Crisis brought about by want of confidence in the French ranks ; vigorous intervention on the part of General Foch and measures adopted by him to reinforce the troops in action, May 31st and June 1st—The enemy attacks are stopped on June 4th.

THE German attacks in Flanders came to an end on May 9th, and on the 18th, as we have seen, General de Mitry received orders to reduce his forces in the front line, so as to increase his reserves. The Military Governor of Dunkirk had also been instructed to lower the level of the inundations in order to lessen the inconveniences imposed upon the inhabitants.

To the battle period, the opening of which had been marked by the German guns on March 21st, there had succeeded a season of calm which we had not experienced for nearly two months. What was hidden behind this silence ? We knew that the enemy had large numbers of troops at his disposal. According to the Intelligence branch of General Headquarters the figures ran from seventy-five to eighty Divisions ; that is, more than what he had available for his first attack between the Scarpe and the Oise. Where would they suddenly appear? We searched the horizon, but the mystery remained unsolved.

Field-Marshal Sir Douglas Haig believed he was menaced with a new German offensive between Amiens and the sea, with its principal effort directed either on Albert or on Ypres. General Pétain likewise inclined to this view. Indeed, he no longer feared an enemy attack in Champagne, and, in the absence of confirmation from other sources, he put no faith in the tales of prisoners who, on May 19th and 22nd, declared that an important German offensive was in course of preparation between the Oise and Rheims.

While closely following the investigations of my subordinates, I did not propose that the activity of the Allied Armies should be limited to calculating and discussing the enemy's intentions. Another task, and an urgent one, imposed itself—that of preparing to pass in our turn to the offensive. "The offensive alone will enable us to bring the battle to a victorious close and, by seizing the initiative, assert our moral ascendancy."

But at a moment when we were obliged to husband our forces with the utmost care, this offensive must achieve results in proportion to the sacrifices entailed. Two fields of action fulfilled this condition :

(1) The ground between the Oise and the Somme. This offered the possibility of a combined attack by the French Third and First Armies and the right of the British Fourth Army, with the object of disengaging the Paris—Amiens railway line and the Amiens centre of communications.

(2) The Lys region. Here a combined action of the left of the British First Army, the British Second Army

and the Army Detachment of the North, would take as an objective the freeing of Ypres and the Béthune coal basin.

Having adopted these two fields of action, a programme for an offensive on the part of the Allied Armies was issued on May 20th to each Commander-in-Chief.

Preparations for the two offensives were to be made simultaneously and without delay. If the enemy did not attack, they would furnish the means of surprising him by a powerful blow. If he did attack, they would constitute, in the hands of the Supreme Command, a reply which might be invaluable. Of the two projects, the most important, from the point of view of numbers alone, was undoubtedly the former, between the Oise and the Somme. An examination of it had been commenced the moment I took over my functions at Doullens. General Pétain and General Fayolle had been associated in this study, to the end that the undertaking " might be prepared rapidly and powerfully."

The co-operation of the British Army was arranged for in a personal letter to Sir Douglas Haig.

The preparations for the Lys offensive were much less advanced. Sir Douglas, as we have seen, had already made his dispositions for an attack in the direction of Merville—Estaires. On the other hand, in the region of Kemmel and Ypres, nothing had as yet been done, and presumably the period of preparation would take considerable time. As a matter of fact, it was necessary to reorganize the troops, who had barely emerged from an arduous battle, and to prepare " jumping-off " places from positions which were only as yet indifferently established. It was also essential to carry out a re-grouping of the Allied forces in Flanders, where the exigencies of rapid intervention had entailed a mixing-up of French and British Divisions detrimental to the exercise of command.

*   *   *   *   *

Such was the situation when suddenly it was learned that a new German offensive was on the point of being launched, and that this time it would be directed against the French front. On the afternoon of May 26th, German prisoners declared that an attack on the Chemin-des-Dames would take place the following night after a short artillery preparation which would begin at 1 A.M. This information was correct.

At the hour named, the German artillery opened an extremely heavy bombardment, including an immense employment of gas-shells, along the front Rheims—Coucy-le-Château, and reaching to a depth of from seven to eight miles. In certain places more than thirty batteries to a thousand yards were counted.

At 3.40 A.M. the enemy's infantry advanced to the assault on a front of thirty-three miles between Brimont and Leuilly. Preceded by a dense creeping barrage and supported at various points by tanks, it penetrated by a single rush far into the French positions. The surprise had been practically complete and the results were most important.

Thirty German Divisions (Seventh Army, General von Boehn, and the right of the First Army, General von Below) had been concentrated and transported to the point of application without being observed by the adversary, and now hurled themselves against the Chemin-des-Dames. This mighty mass of attack found in front of it only seven Allied Divisions in the first line, four French and three British, supported in rear by one British and two French Divisions.

M. TARDIEU, GENERALS WEYGAND AND PERSHING, M. CLEMENCEAU AND MARSHAL FOCH AT PERSHING'S HEADQUARTERS IN CHAUMONT IN JUNE, 1918.

Their resistance was easily overcome. In the centre, more particularly, the French 22nd Division and the British 50th Division were literally submerged under the German flood. Rapidly gaining possession of the plateau along which runs the Chemin-des-Dames, the enemy pushed right up to the Aisne. At 10 A.M. he was in possession of the river, from Vailly to Oeuilly.

Unfortunately, the G.O.C. the Sixth Army, at the very beginning of the attack, sent almost the whole of the 157th Division, which was back on the Aisne, to the support of the first position, thus leaving along a wide front the important position of security offered by the Aisne almost wholly unguarded. By a fatal chance, the Germans made their main effort in this direction, and they thus reached the river without striking a blow. Here, thanks solely to the rapidity of their advance, they were able to seize all the bridges between Vailly and Pontavert before even the demolition charges could be prepared.

From that moment on, our situation was serious. At 11 A.M. no further illusion was possible. The three Divisions still available in reserve were employed against the two wings of the German attack, in an endeavour at least to dam it. In the centre, however, the enemy, moving freely in a breach ten miles wide, pressed on to the Vesle, which he reached in the evening between Courlandon and Braine. The possession of Fismes alone was still disputed by the leading units of a French Division (13th) which had been rushed up in motor lorries.

The error which we had already seen produced on the Somme on March 23rd was here repeated.

A river as wide as the Aisne or the Somme, lying some six or more miles from our original position, constitutes an obstacle which holds up any successful attack of the enemy and forces him to recommence a methodical artillery action, provided the defence has taken suitable measures for security on this line—such as leaving a company, or even a section or squad, at each bridge, whose sole duty it would be to cover and defend the passage.

Under cover of this standing protection, the first-line troops, thrown back in disorder by the violence of an attack, can move across the bridges and reorganize behind the obstacle which the river presents; and, since they are not being pursued, they can completely regain their order. The enemy, on arriving in front of the stream, is obliged to prepare a fresh artillery action in order to force it, which means for him a completely new operation.

It cannot be pretended that the absence of detachments maintained on a river will be felt by the troops in the front line during the battle. They are too small to constitute, of themselves, a perceptible weight whose influence in the struggle would be felt, even if unexpectedly engaged. On the other hand, in spite of their small strength, established as they are on the stream, they draw a special importance from their clearly defined rôle at these prepared points of the battlefield. They bring the enemy's pursuit to an end, and enable the troops which have been driven back to re-establish their resistance behind a clearly traced line.

For a commander who wishes to keep his freedom of action on the far side of a river or on its banks, it is an indispensable precaution that its bridges be guarded by a carefully organized system of defence, so that they may be always at his disposal. This precaution was lost sight of on the Aisne as it had been on the Somme.

During the afternoon of the 27th, General Pétain informed me of the measures he had taken to meet the grave situation. Headquarters of the Fifth Army, six infantry Divisions, the I Cavalry Corps, composed of three Divisions, four regiments of horse-drawn 75's, three regiments and six groups of tractor-drawn Heavy Artillery, as well as an Air Force detachment, were already on the move. One half of the infantry Divisions and two of the cavalry Divisions would be thrown into the battle the following morning.

On the 28th, the enemy brushed aside the isolated units opposing him in the vicinity of Fismes, crossed the Vesle on a wide front and established himself on the high ground south of the river, without, however, seeking to push further forward. Moreover, taking advantage of the breach in the centre, he combined frontal attacks with attacks in flank, and thus overcame the resistance encountered on the two wings. On the east, advancing rapidly along the valleys of the Vesle and the Ardre, he forced the British IX Corps back upon the heights of Château-Thierry and Savigny ; on the west he captured from our XI Corps the high ground commanding Soissons from the north-east, and at nightfall even penetrated into that town.

In vain did the G.O.C. the French Sixth Army fling infantry battalions, as they detrained, in front of the Germans. Four infantry Divisions and two cavalry Divisions brought into action in this way on the 28th were powerless to fill a breach which was hourly growing wider.

It was urgently necessary to bring up reinforcements, and General Pétain informed me on the 28th at Provins that, in addition to the reserves whose departure he had reported to me the previous day, he had given orders to send ten infantry Divisions, four regiments of Heavy Artillery and three regiments of horse-drawn 75's to the Northern Army Group. He had also instructed General Fayolle to withdraw four infantry Divisions from his front, and to send the II Cavalry Corps towards Creil and Chantilly.

In fact, nearly every available French unit was moving towards the battle.

The decision thus taken by General Pétain met the most urgent needs confronting him, and, at the outset, I could only give my approval. But from a general point of view, his action induced consequences which had to be provided against at once and as fully as possible.

For example, the whole of the Fifth Army, with its Staff and its four Divisions, had been sent south of the Oise. Consequently there disappeared one of the two French groups constituting the general reserve in the British zone. As a result of this, Sir Douglas Haig, being now obliged to rely almost wholly upon his own forces to parry a possible German offensive, had to form a British general reserve capable of being thrown in at any time and place, as required. This I requested him to do in a letter dated May 28th.

I also instructed the G.O.C. the Tenth Army to make preparations to ensure that, in case of need, the four Divisions to which his Army was now reduced could intervene on any part of the British front.

Finally, in order to facilitate General Pétain's task of getting together all the troops that could be made available, I ordered General de Mitry to place the Corps and Divisional troops of the XXXVI Corps as soon as possible at the disposal of General Headquarters, and to make arrangements for withdrawing one Division from his front by extending the others.

* * * * *

On the 28th the enemy deliberately halted on the high ground south of the Vesle, instead of further pursuing his advance across country ;* but on the 29th he resumed his attack even more violently than during the previous days. On that day his centre directed a powerful thrust toward Oulchy-le-Château, Fère-en-Tardenois, Ville-en-Tardenois. Encountering nothing but feeble French units which had already suffered heavily and were powerless to check him, he advanced rapidly on a front of from fifteen to twenty miles, and, in the evening, reached the heights commanding the northern bank of the Marne between Château-Thierry and Dormans.

Similarly, he made a vigorous effort in the region of Soissons with his right ; but here he encountered a much more solid resistance. He succeeded, nevertheless, in forcing back the French to the west of Soissons and to the high ground south of that town.

On their left, the German attacks were much less strongly organized. Profiting, however, by the advance effected in the direction of the Marne, they forced the Allied troops to retire towards the high road from Rheims to Ville-en-Tardenois.

* The explanation of this was furnished shortly afterwards. In the previous attacks against the British (March 21st to April 9th) the Germans, after an initial success, had each time found themselves held up by the intervention of French reserves. Before making another attack against the British front in Flanders, they decided to draw away and contain these reserves. Hence the attack of May 27th on the Chemin-des-Dames.

This attack was originally planned with a limited objective, namely, the high ground south of the Vesle. This explained the halt made on the afternoon of the 28th. In the evening of that day, in the presence of the unhoped-for success obtained in two days, the Supreme Command modified its plans and ordered the advance to be resumed, on the one hand, south-westwards so as to pass beyond Soissons and gain as much ground as possible toward Paris ; on the other, southwards, so as to reach the Marne rapidly, cut the Paris—Nancy railway and establish a strong bridge-head south of the river.

Thus ground was yielded along the whole of the line. The Divisions sent to the Sixth Army melted away as fast as they were flung into the battle, and this Army, consequently, remained in such a disquieting state of inferiority that General Pétain began to wonder if he would succeed in the object at which he now aimed, namely, to hold the Marne, the Montagne de Reims and the high ground south of Soissons. At mid-day on the 29th, in face of the ever-increasing development of the German offensive, he requested me to put the Tenth Army at his disposal and to arrange for the British and Belgians to relieve the Army Detachment of the North.

I was unable to comply entirely with this request. Notwithstanding the magnitude of the attack south of the Aisne, the enemy still had sufficient troops available* for another offensive in the Somme area and in the north. In view of this eventuality, it would have been premature to remove the Tenth Army from the British zone. But while maintaining the units of this Army in the regions where they then were, they were moved nearer to places where they could be quickly entrained.

Furthermore, I arranged with General Gillain that the Belgian Army would relieve the British left and extend its front to the immediate neighbourhood of Ypres, so as to increase the British reserves. To facilitate this arrangement, the British Second Army placed a certain number of batteries at General Gillain's disposal and undertook, in the event of need, to furnish him with strong support from its reserve.

Finally, I warned Sir Douglas Haig that the French Tenth Army might be called upon to leave the British zone. At the same time I notified him that, should the

* On May 29th it was estimated that the Crown Prince of Bavaria had some thirty fresh Divisions in reserve.

enemy bring all his available forces against the French front, I might have to call on the British general reserves which the Field-Marshal had just constituted.

Meanwhile, in order to provide the Northern Group of Armies with the necessary Divisions, General Pétain had been obliged to draw on the Reserve Army Group. In spite of the danger of such an expedient, he had ordered General Fayolle to place seven or eight Divisions in reserve. The latter could do this only by denuding his front and depriving himself of his own reserves—in a word, by weakening that particularly sensitive point, the junction between the British and French Armies. In order to remedy this source of weakness as far as possible, I confided to Field-Marshal Sir Douglas Haig the duty of supporting the right of the British Fourth Army south of the Somme, and of ensuring its junction with the French First Army.

It can thus be seen how strained was the situation and how the lack of effectives, already described, was so cruelly felt.

On May 30th, moreover, the German attacks continued with the same violence. Their main effort was still being aimed toward the centre; on the one hand, in the direction of the Marne, which they reached along the whole of the front from Château-Thierry to Dormans; on the other, in the direction of the Ourcq and the Forest of Villers-Cotterets, where the French Sixth Army marked a serious retreat.

Similarly, north of Soissons the Germans made progress, forcing the French back to the Nouvron plateau. It was only in the direction of Rheims that the situation tended to become stabilized, as a result of the entry into action of the French Fifth Army, and this success rendered the organization of the defence much easier.

The enemy's field of action appeared to be limited for the moment to the ground between Dormans on the Marne and Noyon on the Oise. But on this front, more than sixty-two miles long, the battle raged furiously. The German Supreme Command now put in its reserves. Six new Divisions from the Crown Prince of Bavaria's Army Group were identified on the 30th, and our air force reported heavy German columns moving west in the general direction of Paris.

Therefore, it was in this direction that General Pétain, after firmly organizing the defence of the southern bank of the Marne, decided to direct all his efforts. To further them, I ordered the Tenth Army with its four Divisions to be moved at once from the British zone towards the Marne.

This move was rendered all the more imperative in view of the numerous and detailed reports which reached French General Headquarters, foreshadowing an extension of the German attack to the west of the Oise, from Noyon to Montdidier. There remained no doubt that the Supreme Command intended to open up the road to Paris at all costs.

In fact, on May 31st, there had been desperate fighting between the Marne and the Oise. The French troops, still too few in numbers, retreated for a considerable distance in the Ourcq valley, and were driven back to the edge of the Villers-Cotterets Forest ; while north of Soissons they were obliged to abandon the Nouvron plateau.

General Pétain now urgently requested that there be placed at his disposal some of the Divisions belonging to the Army Detachment of the North, and some of the American Divisions undergoing training in the British zone. He also asked that a few of the available British

Divisions be moved to the rear of the Reserve Army Group. But immediate satisfaction could not be given to this request since the possibility of a German attack on the British front remained. The reported presence on the Marne of several units belonging to the Crown Prince of Bavaria's Army Group was not sufficient excuse for rejecting this hypothesis.

Moreover, the immediate addition of the Tenth Army and of two more trained American Divisions (3rd and 5th) to the Northern Army Group, added to the Divisions which General Pétain had withdrawn from the reserve and from the Eastern Army Group, enabled the situation in my opinion to be restored, provided always that a clear line of action was laid down for each and all, that orders in this sense be drawn up, and that they be executed with the greatest energy.

In my view, this was the predominating factor in the situation, and thus alone could the crisis be overcome. I stated it plainly to General Pétain and to General Duchesne* at Trilport, on the afternoon of the 31st.

However, it was not enough to invite the attention of commanders to an essential task ; it was necessary to continue to search for new resources with which to furnish them. In the course of the same day, the 31st, Sir Douglas Haig came to see me at Sarcus. I spoke to him regarding the possible employment in French sectors of the American Divisions undergoing training with the British Army, likewise of the possible withdrawal of two Divisions from the Army Detachment of the North, and the assistance which the British Army might be called upon to furnish in the event of a powerful offensive against the French front. I spoke of the preparations

---

* Commanding the Sixth Army which had been overwhelmed on the Chemin-des-Dames.—Translator.

which should now be made for sending this assistance if it became necessary.

On June 1st the enemy continued his attacks without a pause and made further important progress, both between the Marne and the Ourcq, and towards the Forest of Villers-Cotterets, whose eastern edges he reached.

General Pétain considered that urgent measures were more and more necessary, in view of the gravity of the situation. He wrote to me again, reiterated the difficulty he was experiencing in sustaining the battle, and renewed his requests of the previous day regarding the American and British Divisions.

He forwarded with this letter a report from General de Castelnau informing him that, if the Germans attacked in force on the front of the Eastern Group of Armies, at this moment denuded of all reserves, he would have no other course open to him but " to retire the Divisions which were not attacked as rapidly as possible, regroup them, and manœuvre to contain the enemy while awaiting a turn of fortune."

All this clearly showed a want of confidence, such as I had called attention to especially during my talk at Trilport on May 31st—the same symptoms I had already observed during the preceding weeks, and under similar circumstances, in the British. It once more became necessary for me to stimulate our energies.

On June 2nd after an interview with General Pétain at Pomponne, I left him the following note which summarized our conversation:

" (1) The line of conduct to be followed by the French Command is to stop the enemy's advance on Paris at all costs, especially in the region north of the Marne.

" (2) The means consists in a foot by foot defence of

the ground in this direction, pursued with the utmost energy.

" (3) To accomplish this it is essential that orders be drawn up saying exactly what the troops must do, and it is essential to see that *these orders are strictly carried out*, by removing any commander who shows signs of weakness."

And, in order to restore confidence, I added:

" (4) All the Allied troops are facing in the same direction and they will be put into the battle as resources of transport become available."

Moreover, I took important steps to carry out this promise.

In agreement with General Pershing, it was decided that five American Divisions, then in training with the British Army, should be sent to the French front to relieve French units in quiet sectors, thus making the latter available for the battle, while Field-Marshal Sir Douglas Haig was requested to move three Divisions of his general reserve by route march to the west of Amiens, where they would be in a position to act either in support of the British Army, or, if need be, in support of the French Army. Finally, in order to be nearer French General Headquarters, I established myself first at Mouchy-le-Châtel (June 1st); then at Bombon (June 5th).

In announcing these decisions, I once more emphasized the necessity of giving organization to the battle, and of making an immediate appeal to " the energy, activity and resolution of all commanders."

Moreover, the arrival of large French reinforcements,

a judicious redistribution of our command on the field of battle, added to the adversary's fatigue, tended more and more to stabilize the situation between the Oise and the Marne. As early as June 2nd and 3rd the Germans had been advancing only with difficulty south of Soissons, and on June 4th, upon encountering a solid front, they ceased their attacks.

Another battle was being prepared west of the Oise, between Noyon and Montdidier.

II.—*The German Attack between Noyon and Montdidier*
(June 9th)

German preparations west of the Oise—The preparatory measures to meet it, prescribed by General Foch, give rise to a protest from Field-Marshal Sir Douglas Haig—The Paris conference, June 7th—Dispositions taken by the Supreme Command on the eve of the enemy attack—the German attack on June 9th; its advance in the valley of the Matz—General Mangin's counter-offensive, June 11th; the German offensive stopped, June 13th.

The battle which the Germans were preparing was in reality part of a plan of operations, the execution of which had been begun on May 27th. Originally this aimed at a combined action along the whole front between Rheims and Montdidier. Lack of heavy artillery and trench mortars had prevented the Germans from carrying out this operation all at once, and they had been obliged to resign themselves to two successive operations : one, east of the Oise, effected on May 27th on the Chemin-des-Dames, and the other to be launched west of that river. The latter could not be begun until the artillery that had been used in the preparation of the first attack had been shifted.

But in the second operation the Germans no longer benefited by the same advantages as in the first. The necessity of making haste forced them to neglect the minute precautions that had enabled them to conceal their preparations with perfection for the attack of May 27th. Consequently their new intentions were quickly discovered by the French Aviation and Intelligence service. By May 30th, General Pétain knew the lines of the enemy's plan ; one point alone remained obscure, the strength of the forces that he would employ. In theory these might be very considerable, for, according to the calculations of the French Staff, the German Supreme Command had some sixty Divisions in reserve and could launch an offensive between the Oise and the Somme composed of forty-five Divisions, a stronger force consequently than he had used on May 27th against the Chemin-des-Dames, and in any case one greatly exceeding the total of everything we had available.

In reality, the German Eighteenth Army (General von Hutier), to which the operation was entrusted, placed only thirteen Divisions in the first line, on a front of twenty-one miles. This Army was confronted by, in the first line, the seven Divisions of the French Third Army (General Humbert), supported by five Divisions in second line or in reserve. Further support was possible by seven other infantry Divisions and three cavalry Divisions, assembled farther in rear, between Beauvais and Senlis.

As can be realized, this force was sufficient, certainly at the outset, to check the German assault. But, in view of the uncertainty prevailing during the days preceding the attack, as to its possible development, we were obliged to provide largely for the future.

Accordingly, on June 4th, I warned Sir Douglas Haig that if " the enemy pursued his manœuvre without pause in the direction of Paris between the Marne and the Oise, or if he developed it on a wider front—between Château-Thierry and Montdidier, for example—all the Allied forces in France would have to give their aid to a battle which, in all probability would decide the fate of the War." To provide for this eventuality, I requested him to make detailed preparations for moving towards the front all his available troops, general and local reserves, and also to prepare for a reduction of his forces in the front line in case of necessity.

This request caused a misunderstanding to arise with British General Headquarters.

Field-Marshal Sir Douglas Haig who, in accordance with previous instructions, had ordered three of his Divisions (XXII Corps) towards the Somme west of Amiens, and who, at the same time, was still apprehensive of an attack between the Lys and the Somme* formally protested against my withdrawing from his command any part whatsoever of the British Army, so long as the threat of an enemy attack hung over him, and he appealed to his Government in conformity with the Beauvais agreement.

A meeting was held in Paris on June 7th in the Prime Minister's office at which were present Monsieur Clemenceau, Lord Milner, Sir Douglas Haig, Generals Wilson, Lawrence, Weygand and myself.

Lord Milner stated that the British Government, as much disturbed as Field-Marshal Sir Douglas Haig had been by the call made on the British reserves, had requested the convening of this Conference. Nothing was more easy for me than to point out that I had in no way touched the British reserves, that all I had done so

---

* On June 4th the available troops of the Crown Prince of Bavaria were estimated at 49 Divisions, 26 of which were fresh ones.

far was to request the Field-Marshal to consider eventualities and make preparations for them, and that, moreover, I had not the slightest intention of depriving him of his reserves until the necessity for doing so should really be felt.

The incident was easily settled. But it illustrates the unexpected difficulties which the commander of the armies of a Coalition encounters at times, by reason of the difficulty one army has of understanding another. A great orchestra always takes a certain time to put its instruments in tune ; and when it is composed of diverse elements, a tuning-fork sometimes has to be employed to bring them into unison.

At the end of this same meeting, where other eventualities were discussed, General Wilson reverted to a question which had been raised at the time of the Battle of Flanders. He asked me, among other things, what my line of conduct would be in respect to the British Armies if the development of the German offensive should threaten Paris and the British sea bases at one and the same time.

I repeated what I had said once before, that it was my intention to ensure touch, at one and the same time, between the British and French Armies, the defence of Paris and the protection of the Ports, since each was essential to the success of the war.

Indeed, leaving out of consideration the uneasiness of the people, and consequently of their Governments, it was a fact that the enemy was very near to the attainment of one of his main objectives, Paris or the Channel ports. The Allies for the moment were condemned to the defensive, with all its perplexities, its more or less unexpected blows, the anxiety it causes to everybody and the uncertainty it brings to army commanders, who are either being attacked (or waiting to be attacked) and each of whom always thinks that the most ominous danger is the one directly threatening him !

All these were moral factors tending to weaken forces already worn down and shaken by nearly four years of violent war. Fortunately, the soldiers fighting under our colours were ready to sacrifice themselves in order that the world might be saved from a repetition of the abominations to which it had been subjected. Clemenceau and Lloyd George, at the head of their respective Governments, displayed a fine ardour in support of the struggle ; President Wilson, a long time coming into the war, now asked nothing better than to devote to it the immense resources of his country. It devolved on the Supreme Command to gather together every possible means that would shorten the crisis, watch over the weak spots, avoid fresh commotions and reverse the march of events as soon as possible.

Meanwhile, in anticipation of the impending attack between Montdidier and Noyon, on June 5th, I placed a Division from the Army Detachment of the North (the 14th) at General Pétain's disposal. I requested Field-Marshal Sir Douglas Haig to study the question of relieving another Division of this detachment by British troops, and proposed that I send him back in exchange the Staff of the VIII Corps and two British Divisions withdrawn from the Aisne battle.

I took every precaution to avoid being at the mercy of any partial attacks which the enemy might attempt as diversions in these regions, by moving into Lorraine and the Vosges the French Divisions which were to be refitted and the American Divisions which had come from the British Army, and by making preparations for sending if required a certain number of French Army Corps towards the British front, so as to be able, if the necessity arose, to meet a German offensive, which was always likely to occur in the Somme—Arras—Lens sector. I also ordered a study of possible small offensives north of the Somme, and on the front of the French Fifth Army, since it might become necessary to contain the enemy forces during the defensive battle on the Oise.

Finally, on the eve of a battle which might be decisive, I wrote a letter to the French Commander-in-Chief, reminding him of the strategic results to be pursued, the general line of conduct to be followed, the duties of commanders and the spirit which should be instilled into all the participants.

On June 9th, after a bombardment beginning at midnight, and to which our counter-batteries immediately replied, General von Hutier's infantry, at 3.45 A.M., reached our lines between Ayencourt and Thiescourt. At 6 A.M., the enemy's attack extended up to the Oise.

The German Divisions were not uniformly distributed over the front of attack. Spread out on the wings, they were heavily massed in the centre, between Rollot and Thiescourt, where nine of the thirteen Divisions took part in the attack.

It was here that the rupture occurred. The 58th and 125th French Divisions gave way under the shock, and shortly after 7 A.M. they were driven back beyond Gury. At 10 A.M. the enemy entered Ressons-sur-Matz and at 11 A.M. he was master of our second position on a front of seven and a half miles, from Méry to Mareuil-Lamothe. His rapid advance along the valley of the Matz then enabled him to turn the defences established between Ribécourt and Lassigny; the

Sainte-Claude plateau and the Thiescourt wood fell into his hands.

The intervention of six French Divisions which had been held in reserve, fortunately slowed up his advance in the course of the afternoon, and by the end of the day he was stopped along the line Méry—Belloy—Marquéglise—Vandelicourt.

In short, General von Hutier's attack, apart from the right wing which gained little ground, had made a fresh and important bulge in the French line. Compiègne was directly threatened.

In my opinion, however, the strength of the Reserve Army Group was still adequate to deal with the situation. Moreover, the fact that the Crown Prince of Bavaria's forces did not seem to have taken part in the fighting on June 9th, determined me to leave untouched all of Haig's forces. As a matter of precaution, however, I requested him to move the southern Division of the XXII Corps on the morning of the 10th to the neighbourhood of Conty, and to replace it south of the Somme by another Division. This was to enable General Pétain to bring down the whole of the French reserves which were then in rear of his First Army.

On the 10th, the enemy's attack was continued, but without his obtaining anything like the same success as on the previous day. Although he brought a new Division into action, he gained only a small amount of ground west of the Matz. His only important success was to the east of this place, where the retreat of a French Division (the 53rd) opened up the road to Ribécourt and enabled the Germans to establish themselves on the right bank of the Oise between Montmacq and Sempigny. The effect of this movement, however, was to force our troops on the left bank

(XXXVIII Corps) to withdraw to the old 1914 positions at Bailly, Tracy-le-Val and Puisaleine.

In spite of this unfortunate occurrence, the results of the 10th, taken as a whole, remained satisfactory. " The adversary had been unable to advance with the same facility as had marked all his attacks since the month of March. Our Divisions were defending their ground foot by foot ; the various echelons of command became rapidly organised ; reinforcements arriving were economically and methodically employed." The French defence, organized in depth in accordance with the latest instructions, had deadened the dash of the start, that is to say, the sudden and violent onrush of an attack prepared by powerful artillery.

Better still, General Fayolle was about to take advantage of this situation to deliver a counter-attack on the enemy's flank, using five fresh Divisions, four being in the first line.

General Mangin, who at that time was without a command, had been given the task of organizing and directing this attack. He took it in hand at once, and, on the afternoon of the 10th I found him at Noailles in the midst of a conference with General Fayolle, who commanded this Army Group. He explained to us the result of his reconnaissance, his intentions and the dispositions he had already made, with the most perfect clarity. Although the greater part of his troops, particularly the artillery, could not arrive before night, he undertook to carry out a properly concerted attack the following morning. To this end, before the day finished, he assembled his principal commanders on the ground, and allotted them their objectives and their lines of attack. The troops were to take up their allotted positions, during the night as they arrived.

In the evening and during the night General Mangin issued his orders to Divisional Commanders, fixing the hours for the artillery preparation and the " zero hour " of the attack.

Such rapidity in drawing up a general plan involving complete dispositions for the harmonious action of men and means still scattered and distant, was of a nature to astonish minds which several years of trench-warfare had accustomed to a much slower method of procedure. It engendered some doubts as to the result, for to certain methodical intellects, it did not seem possible that General Mangin could be ready to operate properly with his five Divisions before the 12th.

For my part, I emphasized the necessity of counter-attacking as soon as possible ; we should thus find the enemy's defences less well organized than if we allowed him more time. If the counter-attack should be launched on the 12th, it would find him better prepared than on the 11th.

This insistence of General Mangin and the clearness of his views finally convinced General Fayolle, and he drew up his orders, dated 4 P.M., the 10th, for the attack to be carried out as soon as possible on the 11th. These orders, which were communicated to the troops, concluded with these words : " To-morrow's operation should be the end of the defensive battle which we have been fighting for more than two months. It should mark the definite check of the Germans and the renewal of the offensive on our part. It must succeed. Let everyone understand this."

The attack did, in fact, begin the following day, the 11th, at 11 A.M. The effect was astonishing. The villages of Méry and Belloy were taken, the valley of the Aronde was cleared, and more than a thousand prisoners with several guns were captured.

On the 12th I met General Pétain at Chantilly and arranged with him for General Mangin's operation to be pushed only to the point where it would produce a definite effect, so as to avoid losses that brought no corresponding profit. Indeed, it was necessary to husband our available Divisions as much as possible. They might be useful elsewhere ; for example on the Somme, where the enemy threat remained undiminished.

Consequently, no more serious attacks were carried out. Further action was limited to the local actions of June 14th, undertaken to rectify the line to our advantage.

On his side, the enemy, after improving his position on the 11th, by seizing the left bank of the Matz below Chevincourt, definitely halted his offensive west of the Oise.

It might have been thought for a moment that this pause on the west of the river was only for the purpose of renewing the attack with greater intensity to the east, for on the following day, June 12th, two or three German Divisions delivered a vigorous assault north of the Villers-Cotteret Forest. Cutry and Dommiers were captured and the French troops driven back on Coeuvres and Saint-Pierre—Aigle. But this turned out to be a purely local operation and was not followed up.

On June 13th quiet once more reigned on the whole of the French front.

CHAPTER VII

THE PERIOD OF WAITING

(*June 13th—July 15th*)

FOLLOWING the third offensive executed by the Germans in the spring of 1918, an important duty devolved on me. This was to consolidate the existing situation, and in the light of what had been learned from recent events, to prepare the future operations of the Allied Armies.

I. *Teaching derived from the battles of the spring of* 1918.

Note by General Foch on the line of conduct to be pursued to meet the German methods of attack; his instructions regarding the occupation of second positions give rise to objections on the part of French General Headquarters.

In the three offensives which the Germans carried out between March 21st and June 12th, their methods of attack had not varied. Their characteristics were surprise, violence, rapidity of execution, manœuvring to widen the initial breach, and an effort from the start to penetrate deeply into the adversary's defensive system. To these methods it was essential for the defence to oppose appropriate measures. Its duty was to prevent surprise by obtaining information promptly from all possible sources; to counter the violence and rapidity of the hostile attack by occupying the first and second positions in sufficient strength before the launching of the attack (the sole task of the troops occupying these positions being to resist where they stood); to frustrate the opponent's manœuvre for widening the breach and effecting a deep penetration, by reinforcing the flanks of the pocket with the greater portion of the forces in reserve, and by employing the remainder to contain the enemy in front and check him. And this once achieved, to effect counter-attacks as soon as possible, more particularly on the flanks, by using all the troops that remained or had been rendered available on both sides of the breach.

Indeed, the sudden and violent method of attack used by the enemy could have been easily defeated if the commander on the defensive " had fixed beforehand upon a rational line of procedure, if he had drawn up a plan capable of an execution that was rapid and as certain as possible, and if he then had firmness enough to persevere in this plan and push the battle forward unremittingly."

These considerations were made the subject-matter of a note which I addressed on June 16th to Commanders-in-Chief under my orders, with the request that they communicate it to their armies unless they had observations to offer.

Following a battle in which, without striking a blow, we had lost the Aisne in May, and the Somme in March, it seemed appropriate to call the attention of Commanders and their staffs to the value of second lines, how they should be occupied and the use to be made of them.

My instructions gave rise to some objections in what concerned the simultaneous occupation of the first and second positions " in sufficient strength." French General Headquarters considered that it should not transmit these instructions and appealed to the Prime Minister.

It was not difficult for me to explain what a prudent Commander should understand by the occupation in advance of second positions. In no sense was it a question of a uniform and vague occupation along the whole extent of these lines. That would entail an exaggerated expenditure of men; what was meant was the occupation, in comparatively small numbers, of the most important and clearly indicated points of these positions. If these points were securely held, they would constitute a framework sufficient to ensure resistance until the arrival of reinforcements from troops held in reserve.

I took occasion to clear up this question, first in the course of an interview I had with General Pétain at Bombon on June 18th and again in a note which I forwarded to the Prime Minister at the latter's request.

Let us repeat that the most important lesson to be learned from the successes obtained by the German offensives of the spring of 1918 was the necessity for Allied Commanders of all grades to draw up judiciously prepared plans, persevere in their execution and insist that the men display the same energy and determination as was expected from themselves. Shortcomings in this respect had been noted in the course of the last enemy attacks, leading to disciplinary measures and changes amongst the French High Command.

But however great the interest attaching to past events might be, the exigencies of the present situation came first. It was evident that the enemy could not rest upon the check he had received on the Matz. He still had strong reserves available: fifty-four Divisions on June 15th, it was said; sixty-one Divisions on June 20th; seventy-five on June 30th, of which fifty-five were fresh.

On the Somme, in Flanders, in Champagne and on the

Oise, the efforts of the enemy had resulted in unquestionable gains of ground. He had inflicted heavy losses on his adversary, and it would seem that in his own interest he must employ these superior numbers without delay. For on the one hand, he could not doubt that America would soon bring a crushing weight to bear upon the struggle, and on the other hand, he must sense the approach for him of the same dangerous crisis in effectives which the British and French Armies were already feeling.*

A new offensive was therefore to be expected on his part. Where would it take place? While inclined to believe that it would be directed against the British front, it none the less had to be conceded that the German mass of manœuvre might be utilized in any part of the French theatre of operations. I therefore came to the conclusion that the Allied reserves ought to be ready to intervene anywhere on our front, from the North Sea to the Vosges, and in support of either the British or the French Army.

These considerations indicated the necessity of holding both armies in a state of complete readiness.

* * * *

II.—*Placing the Allied armies in a state of readiness.*

Reinforcing the British and French fronts; incident with French General Headquarters regarding certain measures of defence taken by General Foch. Regrouping of the Allied forces—General Foch again forbids any voluntary retreat; location of the French reserves on July 10th—General Foch's instructions in respect to the line of conduct to be followed in the event of an enemy attack, July 1st—The immediate defence of Paris; conference at Bombon, June 15th.

The first problem to solve was to arrange for the rapid intervention of French reserves in the British zone and of

* During the month of June, 1918, the German Supreme Command had been obliged to draw largely on the 1919 class. The 1920 class had been partially incorporated in May, and it was estimated that the men would arrive in the depots at the front during the month of July.

British reserves in the French zone. This had already been studied separately for a certain number of Divisions, by both Sir Douglas Haig and General Pétain. It was now time to resume this study in concert, having the whole of the Allied Reserves in consideration. The matter formed the subject of a letter from me to the two Commanders-in-Chief, dated June 13th. The work was completed by the 20th.

It was also important to strengthen the defence of both the British and French fronts. In what concerned the British front, independently of the occupation in advance of support positions, it was proposed to employ American Divisions as well as certain British Divisions for this purpose.

The XXII Corps was returned to Field-Marshal Sir Douglas Haig's command and he was authorized to move the whole of it as far up as the Somme, while General Pétain was instructed to secure the left of General Debeney's army south of that river, with French forces. Then General Pétain was requested to group the French Divisions destined to intervene in the British zone into Army Corps as soon as possible, taking first those which were already assembled close to that zone. Finally, French General Headquarters was requested to reinforce the Army Detachment of the North by two regiments of heavy artillery, one regiment of horse-drawn 75's, and a group of 11.2 inch mortars.

This last request gave rise on June 17th to a protest on the part of French General Headquarters, conceived as follows : " In view of the number of batteries at General de Mitry's disposal, the reinforcement in artillery of the Army Detachment of the North is not necessary. Moreover, it would be dangerous, since it would entail not only withdrawals from the battle-front south of the

Somme but would also commit our last mobile reserves..."
The Commander-in-Chief did not confine himself to this refusal, but he added :

" (1) . . . The French armies have been engaged in all of the four battles waged by the enemy since March 21st last. They have sustained the whole weight of two of these battles. Therefore, on the battle-fronts there are now a great many tired or worn-out Divisions which must be relieved very soon. This is *an undisputable fact* which will inevitably react for a long time upon the employment of our reserves.

" (2). . . The British armies have already had two months respite in which to recuperate and incorporate their reinforcements. On their front of ninety-four miles there exists a density of infantry and artillery such as it has never been possible to realize in any of my Armies that have been actively engaged. The British armies therefore are in a position to look after themselves, and to give the French Armies time in their turn to recuperate sufficiently to resist a new blow in the direction of Paris ; and this cannot fail to happen.

" Now at the present moment, the resources of the French Armies are scarcely sufficient to ensure the indispensable reliefs. They could not therefore now be diminished for the benefit of the British front without seriously compromising the future."

He concluded by informing me that, in view of the gravity of the question, he was forwarding a copy of his letter to the Prime Minister, and Secretary of State for War.

Thus, ten days after Field-Marshal Haig's protest, the French Commander-in-Chief in his turn appealed to his Government.

Fortunately the French Government understood that my task would rapidly become impossible if the important decisions I took in the common interest were liable to discussion every time that they disadvantageously affected individual interests. Determined to do all in its power to prevent fresh difficulties, the French Government decided that the clause in the Beauvais agreement giving Commanders-in-Chief the right to appeal to their governments would no longer apply to the Commander-in-Chief of the French Army.

Nevertheless, it was imperative to react against a state of mind which tended to make comparisons between the reciprocal efforts furnished by the various Allied Armies. This state of mind, which was to be explained, especially on the French side, by the nervous tension following the arduous weeks of the last battle, was none the less disturbing.

Accordingly, some changes were effected in the personnel, and—the German attack not taking place—a regrouping of the Allied forces was undertaken with a view to replacing them in their normal zones of action. Thus, I proposed to Sir Douglas Haig that British units should relieve the troops of the Army Detachment of the north, the latter being returned to General Pétain, while, in exchange, British General Headquarters would get back the British IX Corps and the four British Divisions employed on the French front. The Field-Marshal readily accepted the principle involved in this operation, but it was necessary to press him to expedite its execution, so as to have it completed during the first days of July.

Certain questions were at this time taken up concerning the defence of the French front; for a similar state of mind had prevailed there in anticipation of a defensive battle.

Instructions which French General Headquarters sent on June 23rd to the Headquarters of the Eastern Army Group contemplated, among other contingencies, " the partial or total withdrawal " of the forces of this group of armies in the event of an enemy offensive on its front or in a neighbouring region. I recalled, and with formal insistence, that in any eventuality " any part of our line which was not attacked was to be held by our troops whatever might happen."

Moreover, as the junction between the French and British Armies was always a point of great importance, I requested French General Headquarters to instruct General Debeney to prepare a fortified line in front of the Cachy plateau, including the village of Cachy, and joining up with the works constructed by the British south-west of Villers-Bretonneux.

As a consequence of these changes, French General Headquarters informed me about July 10th that its reserves would be constituted in two principal masses:

(1) North of the Oise (the Beauvais region): ten Infantry Divisions and a Cavalry Corps.

(2) Between the Oise and the Marne: eleven Infantry Divisions.

There would be in addition:

South of the Marne: ten Infantry Divisions and a Cavalry Corps.

Between Rheims and the Argonne: three Infantry Divisions.

Between the Argonne and the Meuse: two Infantry Divisions.

*   *   *   *

Under these conditions, it was to be anticipated that before July 15th the reorganization, regrouping and readiness for battle of the Allied Armies would be completely effected.

What was the line of conduct to follow if the enemy attacked about that date? I explained this in General Instruction No. 4, dated July 1st.

Should the Germans advance on Abbeville, from which they were not more than thirty-seven miles distant, or on Paris, from which they were separated by a similar distance, they would, in either case, obtain results more considerably affecting the fate of the War than they could achieve in any other direction. Their advance in these two directions therefore must be stopped at all costs and as quickly as possible. Now, to operate against Paris and Abbeville, the Germans were obliged to start from the front Château-Thierry—Lens. Consequently, it was facing this front, and in the greatest possible depth, that the Allied Armies should make their dispositions for defending the territory foot by foot. Solid *defensive positions* must be organized, duplicated and interlaced; battery positions must be strongly established and ranges carefully registered; clear and definite instructions must be given to all troops charged with holding positions or counter-attacking.

These dispositions once made, it was then essential when the time came for the Divisional and Corps commanders to act with energy, exercise their initiative to the full, and direct the battle on the ground itself.

Finally, the *Allied reserves* should be distributed and organized so as to be able to intervene where necessary. The French reserves would operate in support of the British Army if it were heavily attacked, and similarly, British reserves would support the French Armies, if the enemy concentrated his masses in the direction of Paris.

At the same time that the Allied Armies were placed in a position of readiness with a view more particularly to the distant defence of Paris, in order to provide for every eventuality, there was organized *the immediate defence of the Capital.* General Guillaumat, recalled from the East, was especially entrusted with this latter task.

On June 15th a conference was assembled at General Headquarters of the Allied Armies at Bombon. Monsieur Clemenceau presided, and the powers of each of the military authorities concerned were defined and delimited.*

The principle was first of all laid down that the defence of Paris was to be effected by the armies to which General Foch had entrusted the task of defending the territory and the Capital step by step and with the utmost energy. It was then decided that if the enemy advance on Paris reached the general line Meaux, Creil and Valley-of-the-Thérain, the Military Governor commanding the armies of Paris would, under the orders of the French Commander-in-Chief, assume command of the armies defending the valleys of the Oise and the Marne, as well as the country included between these valleys.

In the meanwhile, this officer was to prepare the immediate defence of the Capital throughout the whole extent of the entrenched camp, from Les Andelys to Nogent-sur-Seine, by constructing and arming trenches, by providing communications, and by establishing plans for the entry of the troops into line and their action on arrival.

In order to afford him every facility for the accom-

---

* There were present at the conference, Monsieur Paul Doumer, vice-president of the Defence Committee of Paris, René Renoult, president of the Committee on Military Affairs of the Chamber of Deputies, and Generals Foch, Pétain, Guillaumat, Roques, Herr, Mordacq and Weygand.

plishment of his task, it was further decided that Paris should be placed in the " Zone of the Armies," and that, by means of a liaison to be established and maintained with French General Headquarters, General Guillaumat should keep himself fully informed of their situation.

* * * *

III.—*Allied preparations for the counter-offensive.*

General Foch's plan of attack on Soissons, June 14th—Instructions issued to prepare the Allied troops for a renewal of the offensive.

These various measures, embracing as they did the zones of the front and of the rear, were intended as a reply on the part of the Allies to the enemy's new offensives and as a preparation for the great defensive battle which we were expecting to fight.

However, by drawing up plans by which it was hoped to arrest the German attack, I did not lose sight of the offensive task for which the Allied Armies must at once get ready and which ought to be undertaken as soon as possible ; since it was only by offensive action that they could bring the War to a victorious conclusion.

It has been seen that two fields had been originally selected with this object in view and that the essential preliminary work had been done by each of the armies concerned, the British in the Lys region, the French between the Oise and the Somme. But the profound penetration which had just brought the Germans from the Aisne to the Marne at Château-Thierry opened up a new perspective and suggested a new field of activity for the Allied arms.

In fact, it was easy to see that in this deep but comparatively narrow pocket where the enemy was operating the railways constituted the only suitable lines of supply for his troops, and these all passed through Soissons. Therefore, the day this vital centre of communications came under the fire of our artillery, " any German offensive in the direction of Château-Thierry would be deprived of its life-blood."

As the line of our front then lay, only very long-range guns could reach Soissons. While these might interfere with the enemy's supply services, they could not hope to interrupt them completely. This could only be accomplished by the fire of mobile heavy artillery and field artillery—the sole weapons capable of effecting and maintaining permanent results. It was therefore necessary to place this artillery within striking range. These considerations led me, on June 14th, to request General Pétain " to prepare an offensive action whose objective would be the capture of the high ground commanding Soissons on the west, in order definitely to deny the enemy possession of this place, so seriously important to him."

The Fifth Army, in conformity with a previous instruction dated June 7th, had already prepared an attack against the eastern flank of the Château-Thierry pocket; but the German attack on Compiègne had considerably reduced its scope. The enemy having been stopped on the Matz, this attack no longer presented an immediate profit, and, consequently, could be reduced or postponed. It was for this reason that, again explaining my idea, I requested General Pétain to direct all his efforts towards the preparation of an attack by the Tenth Army with a view to recapturing the Dommiers plateau up to the ravine of Missy-aux-Bois. This operation was to be executed as soon as possible, in order to profit by our adversary's lack of time to complete his defensive dispositions.

General Pétain at once issued the necessary orders, and fixed as a minimum advance for the Tenth Army, "the line marked by Pernant, Missy-aux-Bois, Longpont." A few days later, on June 20th, General Mangin, commanding this Army, drew up his plan of operations and the French Commander-in-Chief approved it.

Thus, by the end of June, the Allied Armies had at their disposal three localities in which an offensive was being prepared. They lay in very different regions—the Lys, the Somme and the Marne. It was in the last, as has been seen, that we proposed to direct the first effort, and that as soon as possible. But these plans did not prevent anticipating and studying a more general resumption of the offensive, and it was important that Higher Commanders and men alike should be prepared when the hour for it arrived.

The form to be given to this offensive and the time for launching it had to be chosen with considerable nicety. The fact could not be ignored that the Allied Armies, since March 21st, had been subjected to enemy blows of tremendous violence and strength. These, at the start, had been crowned with incontestable success and had been repulsed only at the cost of most serious sacrifices. This had resulted in very heavy losses on our part and a distinct appreciation of the enemy's power.

To overcome this impression, it was essential that our first initiative be crowned with success, and if checked in course of development, our attacks at least must not leave us in a perilous situation.

It was, moreover, in view of these considerations that

the projected attack on the line Soissons—Château-Thierry was to have its left flank continually covered by the Aisne. If it should be held up in course of execution, its advance would not constitute a " pocket " with dangerous flanks.

Finally, although we wished to attack at the outset at one point only, our successive enterprises ought to be prepared as a part of one and the same series, so that each of them could, without delay, take advantage of the moral ascendancy gained by the previous one and the disorder brought about in the enemy's dispositions. Also the direction to be given to each must be fixed in such a manner as to arrive finally at one single end. This would notably increase the effect of our operations taken as a whole.

After three years of trench warfare, it was likewise important to consider reviving in our Armies the notion of the power which lies in movement, as also in its practice and the physical aptitude it requires. It was desirable to disseminate these ideas in language which would be understood not only by the men who had been fighting since the beginning of the War, but by those which were now making their entry into the struggle.

Accordingly, on June 27th, General Pétain was requested to formulate, in a General Instruction for the use of all the Allied Armies, the main principles that should govern the organization and conduct of an offensive action. He was furthermore requested to arrange periods of instruction in camps which would complete the training of the larger French and American units intended to take part in the offensive.

Finally, it was pointed out to him that the offensive battle might at certain moments involve a mass of French, American and British forces and that their preparation for this task should be completed " in two months at the latest." Calculations could be based on a minimum of twelve American Divisions and about a dozen French Divisions, to which would be added seven or eight British Divisions ; in all, a total of some thirty units.

In this forecast, therefore, a whole-hearted co-operation on the part of the Americans was counted upon. This co-operation, indeed, though still in its opening phase, was beginning to weigh in the balance. The confidence which, from the start, the Allies had placed in its future efforts, found new reason each day for increasing. It was therefore all the more important that the Allied Commander-in-Chief, who had to utilize American forces on the battlefield, should take pains to see that those who were entrusted with the task of preparing them for their work were at all times in sympathy with his intentions and his plans. This he did.

* * * *

IV.—*Establishing a programme for American co-operation.*

Programme for the transport of American Divisions in July—The Allies request that one hundred Divisions be constituted by August 1st, 1919—Material difficulties encountered in the organization of the American Army—President Wilson states that in spite of any obstacles there will be one hundred Divisions in France on July 1st, 1919—It is the lack of artillery above all that delays the formation of an autonomous American Army—Plan for the intervention of American forces in Siberia—The field of action of the Allied Supreme Command becomes more and more extended.

At a meeting at Abbeville on May 1st and 2nd, the Allied governments had fixed a general programme for the transport of American troops to France during the months of May and June.

At a new meeting on June 2nd at Versailles, they requested Lord Milner, General Pershing and myself to submit a schedule for American transport during the month of July. An agreement was accordingly reached between us which confirmed the absolute priority to be given to the transport of infantry during the month of June and proposed that the same priority be observed for July. It was requested that 140,000 infantry and machine-guns units be conveyed to France in that month.

The Supreme War Council not only ratified this agreement, but expressed the further desire that the Government of the United States, in order to ensure the numerical superiority of the Entente and consequently its victory, should constitute an army of one hundred Divisions for August 1st, 1919, entailing a monthly levy of at least 300,000 men.

To this appeal of the Allies to America, General Pershing very shortly took occasion to respond in an indirect but particularly expressive manner. On June 9th, at the moment when the German Eighteenth Army was launching its attacks in the direction of Compiègne, the Commander of the American Expeditionary Forces, renewing his gesture of March 28th, came to see me at Bombon. He assured me that he associated himself entirely with the common cause and that more than ever he fervently desired to see all his Divisions taking part in the battle. At the same time he constituted himself the interpreter of the unanimous sentiment of the American nation which, he said, was absolutely determined to throw its whole force into the contest without counting the cost.

It can be understood how greatly the expression of such sentiments was calculated to facilitate the task of the Allied Governments. Indeed, material obstacles alone placed a limit on American co-operation. Unfortunately, these were serious, and I emphasized their importance in a note I addressed to the Prime Minister on June 14th.

In this note I discussed the basis on which should be established the programme for the transport of troops from America to France during the second half of 1918. I brought out, along with my legitimate desire to see the greatest possible number of men sent to France, the causes which might hinder its realization. I mentioned, among others, the amount of tonnage available, the possibility of finding in France, or near-by, horses necessary for the organization of the American units disembarked each month, the resources in the matter of armament to be procured in France or furnished by American factories, in short all the ever-increasing demands for supplying the American Expeditionary Forces. The complexity of the problem necessitated "careful preliminary studies in many different departments, as well as agreements to be arrived at between the Governments, in order that exact data might be established."

With the consent of the Prime Minister, I directed these studies and, in collaboration with Monsieur Tardieu who was at that moment in France, I framed a programme on the following basis :

To place the Entente in a position to make with certainty a decisive effort in 1919, it must have an undoubted numerical superiority over the 220 or 240 German Divisions ; *this means the presence of eighty American Divisions in the month of April and one hundred Divisions in the month of July*, 1919.

In order that these Divisions might have three months' training before embarkation, the last of those to arrive in April, 1919, must be composed of men called up in December 1918. The formation of each Division, taking into account the corresponding proportion assigned to services, army troops, corps troops, etc., entailed the incorporation of 41,060 men. Consequently, including reinforcements, a minimum of 300,000 men must be enrolled during each of the last six months of 1918 and the first four months of 1919.

This programme was approved by General Pershing at a conference held in Chaumont on June 23rd. It was then submitted on July 2nd to the members of the Supreme War Council at Versailles, who likewise adopted it and transmitted it to President Wilson. He replied immediately that there would be one hundred American Divisions in France on July 1st, 1919, and that other Divisions would follow if necessary.

The principal difficulty, that of tonnage, was next solved—thanks in the first place to the tremendous impetus given to the American merchant fleet*, and in the second to the help of the British Admiralty, which undertook to make good any unforeseen shortage.

However, the rapid growth of the American forces† rendered all the more pressing General Pershing's desire to form them into an autonomous army. On July 10th, he came to see me with a request to expedite as much as possible the formation into army corps of American Divisions then in the French zone; he also asked me to furnish artillery for those Divisions which had none, drawing it if need be, from French units.

I was emphatic on this occasion in once more assuring General Pershing that no one desired more fervently than myself the constitution of American corps, armies,

---

* At the end of the war, the American Army was employing 3,800,000 tons of shipping, against 94,000 at the beginning.

† In the middle of June 1918 the American Army numbered 42 Divisions, a total of 1,747,000 men, in the United States and in France.

and sectors in which American troops would fight an American battle, and that my best efforts were being directed to this end. I was, indeed, firmly convinced that the soldiers of any country only give of their best when fighting under their own leaders and under their own colours. National self-esteem is then engaged.

General Pershing's experience and character, moreover, were a guarantee that, whenever he might engage American troops, he would only halt when success had been achieved. Unfortunately, the lack of guns still prevented the furnishing of artillery to all the American Divisions or Army Corps which it might have been possible to form.

However, the object of the Entente was to obtain an indispensable superiority in numbers, and it would scarcely have accorded with its interests to deprive French units of their artillery for the benefit of American units. On the contrary, the American Divisions which had no artillery could be very advantageously used to relieve French Divisions in quiet sectors, and so make the latter available for battle.

The collaboration of the American Army was not confined solely to the Western Front.

On June 17th General Bliss came to Bombon to see me concerning Lord Milner's request, addressed to President Wilson, in regard to the despatch of an American contingent of 4,000 men (three Battalions and two Batteries) to Murmansk and Archangel.

President Wilson, as much for reasons of prudence as through his unwillingness to reduce the number of American troops and the corresponding transportation destined for the French front, was little inclined to accede to Lord Milner's suggestion.

However, six days later, having learned that the Germans had transferred a certain number of Divisions from Russia to France, I, in my turn telegraphed to President Wilson that this fact could be regarded as " a decisive military argument in favour of an intervention by the Allies in Siberia." On June 27th, in a second telegram to the President of the United States, I again stressed the point, and requested him to send two American regiments as soon as possible to Siberia.

On July 2nd the question was submitted to the Supreme War Council during its meeting at Versailles : the whole matter was taken in hand by the heads of the Allied Governments.

As can be seen, in order to ensure the formation or the maintenance of the troops under its direction, the Supreme Allied Command was called upon to extend its field of action more and more, until it reached the interior of each Allied country and embraced the whole theatre of operations in which Allied interests were at stake. The Doullens formula had been singularly enlarged.

But, while the War in all its aspects and on all its theatres claimed attention, it was still on the Western Front that the decisive game was being played; and the Western Front comprised all that vast territory which stretched from the mouth of the Yser to the mouth of the Piave. In spite of the preoccupation which the operations in France inspired, the importance and interest presented by the Italian theatre could not be lost sight of. For events on one side of the Alps necessarily had its effect upon the other.

In the first place, it was important that the Allied arms should suffer no harm in Italy, and then, as soon as possible, they must be given the possibility of achieving victory. It was with this end in view that, at the Abbeville conference, I had been entrusted with a mission of co-ordination in what concerned the Italian theatre of operations.

V.—*The operations on the Italian front.*

General Foch gets into touch with Italian Headquarters and follows its plans for an offensive, May 7th—The enemy's threatened attack causes these to be postponed—General Foch approves General Diaz's line of action; Monsieur Clemenceau is perturbed by it, May 28th to June 12th—The Austrian attack and its complete repulse, June 15th to June 23rd—General Foch then requests General Diaz to resume his projected offensive and to expand it, June 27th.

In virtue of this mission, I had written to General Diaz on May 7th, asking him to inform me as to the general lines of the offensive which Italian Headquarters contemplated in the Melettes region, the participation he contemplated on the part of Allied forces (French and British) in this action, and the date on which preparations for it would be completed.

The arduous battles engaged on the Franco-British front in France, the inaction and indecision displayed by the Austrian armies since the winter, and the superiority of the Allied forces in Italy constituted so many decisive factors in favour of beginning an important Italian offensive in the near future.

The object aimed at should be to shatter the resistance of the Austrians, or, in any case, to draw to their side a portion of the German forces which were then engaged on the French front.

With the idea of presenting these considerations more precisely to General Diaz, as also of being kept informed regarding his intentions, I sent an officer of my staff, Lieutenant-Colonel Lepetit, on a temporary mission to the Comando Supremo.

This was the situation when, on May 28th, General Graziani, commanding the French troops in Italy, reported by telegram that Italian Headquarters, fearing an enemy attack on the Piave, was postponing the execution of the offensive which had been planned in the Asiago region.

This decision was confirmed two days later by Colonel Cavallero, chief of the operations staff, whom General Diaz had sent to Sarcus with a personal letter for me. In this letter, the Chief of the General Staff of the Italian Army explained in detail the reasons which rendered it impossible for him, in face of the Austrian threat, to consider for the moment the execution of any offensive project.

Under these conditions, I was led to concur in his appreciation of the situation. While approving the decision he had taken under the circumstances, I expressed the hope that the Italian Army would be held in constant readiness to resume, at an appropriate time, the offensive operations, preparations for which had already commenced.

On June 9th Colonel-Brigadier Calcagno, who had been detailed by General Diaz as permanent liaison officer at my Headquarters, arrived at Bombon. He confirmed the information from the Comando Supremo regarding this Austrian attack, but gave no definite news as to its imminence. He added that the offensive programme of the Italian Staff was limited for the moment to a series of local operations which would be carried out shortly in the region of the Tonale.

Meanwhile, the Prime Minister, Monsieur Clemenceau, informed me of a conversation which Monsieur Camille Barrère, our Ambassador in Rome, had just had with Signor Orlando, and from which it appeared that

General Diaz had only postponed his offensive after having consulted me and obtained my agreement.

Monsieur Clemenceau, greatly perturbed, asked me to explain. Nothing was easier than to point out immediately that, although on May 30th I had indeed approved of General Diaz's attitude, I had at the same time advised him to attack as soon as conditions should alter. It seemed to me, moreover, that the Austrian indecision on the Italian front, combined with the persistence of the Germans on the Franco-British front, ought to justify an early change of attitude on the part of the Comando Supremo.

After again studying the situation with Colonel-Brigadier Calcagno, I wrote to General Diaz on June 12th asking him to proceed at once with the realization of his plans for an attack. In this letter I laid stress on the fact that an extensive and vigorous Italian offensive could well be expected to prove a powerful support for the troops on the Franco-British front in the heavy fighting they had been engaged in for more than two months.

In reporting to the Prime Minister the despatch of this letter, I requested Monsieur Clemenceau to notify Monsieur Barrère of its contents, so that the latter might be in a position, if necessary, to make representations in the same sense to the Italian Government. But I had hardly done this when the great Austrian offensive was launched.

On the 15th of June, the Sixth, Seventh and Third Italian Armies were attacked on a front extending from the headwaters of the Brenta to the mouth of the Piave. They held their positions firmly, however, and the enemy only succeeded in crossing the Piave at a few points. The battle continued for several days, without the Austrians being able to increase their small gains. On June 23rd they were even forced to retire to the left bank of the Piave. Their offensive had met with complete failure.

It was important for the Italians to take immediate advantage of the undoubtedly favourable opportunity thus presented.

Accordingly, on June 27th, I wrote again to General Diaz. After having congratulated him on the great success achieved by his Armies, I requested him to resume his offensive plans and execute them as soon as possible, at the same time extending them so as to capture the *massif* of Mélettes, and Mount Lisser. This advance would bring the Italian Army close to the Feltre road, and thus provide it with a favourable base from which to undertake further operations in the direction of Trente when the moment arrived for the Allies to make a general concerted offensive on all fronts—that is to say, in all probability during September next.

Lieutenant-Colonel Lepetit was directed to hand this letter to General Diaz and to develop its conclusions. Moreover, as the French Government, on July 11th, had declared itself ready to furnish the Comando Supremo with certain material of which it might stand in need, notably tanks and hyperite shells, there was reason to hope that the Italian offensive would begin very soon.

At this moment, however, our whole attention became again concentrated on the French front, where a fourth German offensive was on the eve of being launched.

CHAPTER VIII

THE SECOND BATTLE OF THE MARNE

Preparations for the German attack and for the Allied counter-offensive, first fortnight of July—The German attack in Champagne, July 15th—The Allied counter-offensive, July 18th—Halt is ordered on the Vesle, August 2nd.

THANKS to the activity of the Intelligence Service and to the successful raids carried out on various parts of the front during the early part of July, the Allied High Command had in its possession reliable indications of the enemy's intentions.

A new German offensive was in course of preparation on the seventy-five miles of front which lay between Château-Thierry and the Argonne. The Marne was to be crossed in the neighbourhood of Dormans. The attack was to take place some time in the first two weeks of July.

Another offensive was in preparation between Arras and Ypres. It was to be made in very great force.

The simultaneous organization of these two widely separated actions, one (in Champagne) directed to the south and the other (in Artois and Flanders) directed to the west (the two therefore divergent) was difficult for me to understand and justify. In any case, the number of German troops then available seemed to forbid for the moment the two attacks being executed simultaneously. It therefore remained for us to feel out the situation and decide which of them was to be given priority, and in no event lose sight of the second ; for we must be ready to deal with it also if necessary.

As time went on, certain indications enabled us to conclude that the first attack would come in Champagne. The enemy was actively pushing his preparations there, and in his haste he even neglected precautions which might have concealed them. The Allies, thus enlightened, made their dispositions and decided upon their line of action.

On July 3rd, I drew General Pétain's attention to the necessity, in a defensive action, of issuing precise orders, defining the tasks of each and all. On July 5th I requested him to reinforce the threatened front in aeroplanes, field artillery and infantry divisions. On the 11th, I again wrote : " The extension given to the enemy's preparations for an attack in Champagne reduces the likelihood of an action north of the Somme, or lessens the probable importance of this attack. Under these conditions, it would seem advisable to take preliminary steps for the rapid assembling behind our Champagne front of sufficient reserves to check a powerful enemy offensive quickly . . ." To this end, I requested him to take several divisions from amongst those then assembled on the French left with a view to ultimate intervention in the British zone.

Sir Douglas Haig was notified of this and at the same time requested to move two Divisions of his general reserve south of the Somme, so as to secure, in any event, the junction of the British and French Armies. He was asked to provide for the eventuality of the coming battle using up all the French reserves, in which case it would be necessary to call on British reinforcements to give aid.

It was also pointed out to him that a British attack on the line Festubert—Robecq might offer great possibilities in the event of the enemy offensive against the French Army developing to the extent of a threatened absorption of the greater part of the German reserves.

On the following day, July 13th, I drew on the British reserves by asking Field-Marshal Sir Douglas Haig to dispatch four of his Divisions at once toward the French front and to make preparations for sending four more in case of need. These moves were dictated by the wide development which the approaching battle in Champagne promised to assume.

In preparation for this battle we constantly made new dispositions for repulsing the enemy, while at the same time extensive measures were being prepared for launching the counter-offensive we contemplated to the south-west of Soissons. As the plans took shape, this latter action was given wider and wider development; it was to constitute a counter-thrust in the Tardenois answering the enemy's attack in Champagne.

Indeed circumstances seemed to favour the success of our enterprise. Between the Marne and the Aisne, it menaced the flank of the enemy, and this flank would grow longer and weaker if he should attack between Château-Thierry and the Argonne, and direct the mass of his forces towards the Marne, that is southwards.

In order to play this double game effectively, all the French units available had to be concentrated between the Oise and the Argonne. Rested and filled up to strength, they constituted, with the addition of some American and British Divisions, an imposing mass of thirty-eight Infantry Divisions and six Cavalry Divisions. This was enough to meet the requirements of our defensive front in Champagne, and of our offensive operations in the Soissons region.

Moreover, these reserves were certain to be increased in the near future, for the American Army, which already counted twenty-seven Divisions in France, was continually receiving reinforcements.

On the contrary, the Germans gave evidence of the difficulty they were encountering in maintaining the strength of their units, and it was clear that numerical superiority would very soon pass to the Allies.

By the middle of July it could be seen that the time was fast approaching when the opposing forces would be practically equal. If the enemy did not attack, the hour had come for us to take the offensive; if he did attack, to accompany our parry with a powerful counter-stroke.

In order to give still more force to this counter-blow, I instructed General Pétain on July 9th to combine the offensive of the Tenth Army with another one to be carried out at the same time between the Marne and Rheims. It was to be directed against the eastern flank of the " pocket," and executed by the French Fifth Army, under the command of General Berthelot.

Finally, on July 13th, I summarized these designs in a letter to the French Commander-in-Chief, who was tabulating the distribution of his forces for the coming battle.

The first operation—blocking the enemy's advance—required forces which, for the most part, were forthcoming, but which it was still possible to increase. In regard to the second—the counter-attack—which, " apart from its own inherent advantages, would constitute an extremely efficacious method of defence," it was essential to devote all the requisite forces to it without delay and to the fullest extent possible.

On the afternoon of July 14th I proceeded once more to General Pétain's Headquarters, where it was definitely decided that the French counter-offensive would be launched as a reply to the German attack in Champagne. The latter showed signs of being very near at hand.

The studies in preparation for this counter-attack had been going on for several weeks. The business would require four days, more especially for assembling and placing in position the various reinforcements coming from different parts of the front. If the sectors from which they were withdrawn were attacked during this period, these troops might be seriously missed. There was therefore a risk, perhaps a grave one, which must be run during the four days, when all useful action was out of the question.

Nevertheless, in order to hasten the march of events, I gave instructions for the preparations to be commenced on July 14th; and as, on this date, the German attack in Champagne appeared to be quite imminent, it was settled, in the course of an interview at Provins with General Pétain, that the counter-attack, the preparations for which would be completed on the 18th, should be launched as a reply to the enemy's offensive when it took place.

While our arrangements were proceeding, there occurred, in the course of a meeting of the Supreme War Council held at Versailles on July 4th, one of those displays of uneasiness which soldiers invested with wide authority excite in the breasts of certain politicians. Late that day, just as the afternoon session was about to close, Mr. Lloyd George presented a resolution, drafted in English, which was inserted in the minutes of the session and which Monsieur Clemenceau, President of the Council of Ministers, declared that he accepted in the name of the French Government. By the terms of this resolution the Versailles Committee made its re-appearance on the scene, and the military representatives who formed the Committee resumed their right of control, if not of initiative, over the plans for the operations of the Allied Armies. The result was to deprive the commander of these armies of all independence in laying plans for them and of all freedom in their execution.

As soon as the document could be translated and I could study its import, the gravity of which appeared to have escaped the notice of the members of the Council, I went to Paris to see Monsieur Clemenceau. I told him that I could not accept it or continue to command the Allied Armies if it were maintained in its existing form. We returned together to Versailles to find Mr. Lloyd George, who was preparing to dine with the representatives of the Dominions. In spite of the resulting inconvenience for this reunion, we immediately embarked upon a discussion with the British Prime Minister. A new draft was made, by the terms of which I retained entire latitude in the matter of drawing up plans of operations, being responsible for them to heads of Governments only. The military representatives, on their side, were under the obligation of coming to an agreement beforehand with me respecting any proposals they might wish to submit as to the conduct of the War.

Meanwhile the enemy had been pursuing his preparations and had greatly advanced them. On July 14th, a raid carried out by the French IV Corps brought in twenty-seven prisoners. Interrogated at once, they disclosed the fact that the German attack anticipated by the Allies would be launched that same night of July 14th–15th, and that the artillery preparation would begin ten minutes after midnight.

Before the German guns opened, our counter-preparation and counter-battery fire was begun along the whole front of the Central Army Group. The enemy was forestalled in opening fire and surprised by the number of our batteries, the majority of which were unmasked for the first time.

Nevertheless, he proceeded with the execution of his plan. At the hour fixed his artillery opened, and between 4.15 and 5.30 A.M. the German infantry moved to the assault along the whole front of fifty-six miles between Château-Thierry and Massiges, with the exception of the Rheims salient. East of Rheims, thanks to General Gouraud's careful dispositions, it sustained a complete check. Before the enemy's columns could reach the main line of resistance, where the French Fourth Army was solidly established, they were broken up by the dense and accurate fire of our batteries, as well as by the fire of machine-guns distributed along the line of our advanced posts. It was in vain that the Germans endeavoured several times during the day to take this position by assault; they did not succeed in encroaching upon it anywhere.

West of Rheims, the day did not go so favourably for us. On the front of the Fifth Army the enemy made rapid progress between the Marne and the Ardre in the general direction of Epernay, forcing the centre of this army (French V Corps and Italian II Corps) back up on its support lines. At the same time, he crossed the Marne east and west of Dormans, drove in the advanced posts holding the south bank of the river, and established a bridge-head following the general line Mareuil-le-Port—Comblizy—Saint-Agnan—Fossoy, where the left of the French Fifth Army and the right of the Sixth were posted.

In order to meet these attacks, the reserves of the various Armies and almost all the Divisions in general reserve had been engaged during the day of the 15th.

By evening General Pétain had only one Infantry and one Cavalry Division left in rear of the Fourth Army, and one Division in rear of the Fifth.

Thus the German offensive, though definitely repulsed along the front of our Fourth Army, had gained undoubted successes on the front of the Fifth Army, and at its junction with our Sixth Army. Here it had succeeded in breaking our front and even in crossing the Marne at Dormans. Was this partial advantage going to be the precursor of an advance sufficiently deep and executed rapidly enough to bring trouble to our adjacent lines of defence and prevent us from carrying out our programme? Was it going to divert us from our counter-offensive, whose preparation still required two more days? These were the burning questions of the hour on July 15th. However, indecision was no longer justified if one compared the paucity of the results obtained by the enemy with the magnitude of his effort and the mighty forces which his initiative had unchained—if the total extent of his check was considered.

He had failed in Champagne on a front of more than twenty-five miles. He had crossed the Marne at Dormans on a front of nearly twelve miles. The two fronts were some eighteen miles apart and separated by the powerful bastion presented by the town of Rheims and the adjoining Montagne de Rheims, both of which remained in our hands. In the forty-eight hours still required to complete the preparations for our counter-offensive, he would be unable to widen and augment his advantages on the Marne sufficiently to bring about a decision of the battle he had engaged.

On the other hand, once this delay was ended, we could attack him in flank from the Aisne to the Marne, on a front of twenty-five miles, in a new direction and on fresh ground, unexpectedly and in force ; in a word, under conditions calculated not only to neutralize his advantages, but even to render them disastrous. To effect this, we had only to maintain our plans inexorably and execute them in accordance with our previous intention of seizing the initiative and launching an offensive between the Aisne and the Marne. Without ceasing our efforts to penetrate the enemy's designs or guard ourselves against dangers which might be immediate, the wisest course was to pursue, and, if need be, intensify the line of action decided upon.

It was to this task that I devoted myself on the 15th.

Although he shared my confidence, the Commander-in-Chief of the French Armies, in more direct contact with the events of the battlefield, was especially preoccupied by the German advance south of the Marne in the direction of Epernay, and to cope with it, he contemplated drawing on the troops designated for the counter-attack and thereby postponing its preparation.

While on my way to Mouchy-le-Châtel, where I was to meet Sir Douglas Haig, I took occasion to stop at Noailles, the Headquarters of General Fayolle. Here I was informed of these dispositions. I at once sent a message to General Headquarters which ensured the necessary correction, and the preparations for the counter-attack were pursued without any delay being occasioned.

However, in view of the legitimate anxiety of the French Commander-in-Chief, I requested Sir Douglas Haig to dispatch the two British Divisions which, following the instructions contained in my letter of the 13th, would bring the number of British units on the French front up to four. Notwithstanding his fears of seeing a secondary offensive, similar to the one directed against the Champagne front, started in Flanders in conjunction with a main attack to be undertaken between Château-Thierry and Lens, the Field-Marshal yielded to my arguments, and two new British Divisions, the 13th and 34th, were moved to the French front.

Under these conditions, the two British Divisions constituting the British XII Corps, and already en route, were placed at General Pétain's disposal for reinforcing the front of the Central Group of Armies, which, for the time being, was on the defensive. The two Divisions just starting were to detrain in the Oise region and remain there at my disposal. They were to be employed ultimately either offensively to reinforce our Tenth or our Sixth Army, or defensively in support of our Third Army.

In this way immediate needs in the matter of defence were met, while the preparation of our counter-offensive was pursued and the forces assigned to it increased.

The 16th passed without fresh incident. The German attack, smitten with failure the previous day, did not now succeed in obtaining any better results. On the Champagne front it degenerated into unconnected and ineffectual local actions.

South of the Marne, the enemy tried in vain to widen his bridge-head. He encountered not only a stubborn defence, but vigorous counter-attacks on the part of the French Sixth Army, which stopped him everywhere; and certain points of support were even retaken. If it be added that " our artillery and air service bombarded the passages over the Marne unceasingly and rendered difficult the arrival of reinforcements, ammunition and supplies," it can be seen how precarious was the enemy's situation at the bottom of the Château-Thierry " pocket."

The sole progress he was able to register during the 16th was to the south-west of Rheims, between the Vesle and the Marne, particularly along the latter river. But these advances were so localized that they could have no influence on the situation as a whole, and so costly that they could not be renewed without serious prejudice.

After two days of fruitless efforts to improve the already precarious advantages gained on the Marne, it was only natural that the German Supreme Command should hesitate. What indeed had been the results of this " Friedensturm " which, it had been so loudly proclaimed, was to bring peace by one victorious rush ? Nothing but bitterness and deception, forerunners of defeat. The moral state of the whole army could not be otherwise than profoundly affected by this outcome.

On July 17th the Germans had been reduced to impotence ; on the 18th, the guns of the Allies were in turn to make their thunder heard at the time and place which had been fixed upon.

As already related, attention had been drawn as early as the month of June to the importance which Soissons had for the enemy, since it was here that railways converged which were absolutely indispensable for the adequate supply of his troops, engulfed in the deep but comparatively narrow pocket of Château-Thierry. The preparation of an offensive against this place, situated so short a distance from our lines, had been undertaken in accordance with my notes of June 14th and June 16th, and General Mangin's plans were all ready by June 20th. But since then I had been led to anticipate that an attack moving from west to east could achieve greater results than a simple disturbance of the enemy's communications, provided its base of departure was widened and the assault conducted with larger forces.

Accordingly, General Mangin had gradually extended his plan so as to embrace the fifteen miles which separated his positions on the Aisne from those on the Ourcq, where he joined up with the left of our Sixth Army. His forces had been correspondingly increased until, for the initial operation, he disposed of eighteen Infantry Divisions (among which were the American 1st and 2nd Divisions, forming the American III Corps), three Cavalry Divisions, 240 Batteries of 75's, 231 Heavy Batteries, 41 Air Squadrons and 375 Tanks.

General Degoutte, commanding the Sixth Army, had reported that he might be able to operate in a similar sense, prolong the Tenth Army to the right and extend the contemplated action beyond the Ourcq. He had drawn up a plan " for the resumption of the offensive " by the Sixth Army, which would continue along the front Ourcq-Clignon, the attack to be made on its left by the Tenth Army. He requested that a regiment of Tanks and one or two Infantry Divisions be placed at his disposal. With these additional troops, bringing his attacking force up to eight Divisions, he could extend the front of the offensive by sixteen miles.

On July 9th I had also contemplated a simultaneous attack by the Fifth Army on a front from Rheims to the Marne, moving in a westerly direction; but since then the situation of the Fifth Army had completely changed and its action could now be only secondary.

Meanwhile the Tenth and Sixth Armies had improved their base of departure by a number of successive operations. Thus, west of Soissons the Tenth Army established itself on the plateau from Cutry to Dommiers; further south it had captured the villages of Longpont and Corcy, adjoining the Forest of Villers-Cotterets, and pushed its advanced posts east of the Savières brook. On its side, the Sixth Army had recaptured several important positions west of Château-Thierry, such as the villages of Vaux, the Bois-des-Roches, and the Bois-Belleau, where the American 2nd Division had conducted itself brilliantly.

These local operations, prepared with the greatest care, had cost us very small losses, in comparison with the moral and tactical results obtained. In any case they had disclosed a certain decrease in the adversary's resistance in this region, indicated also by the large number of prisoners captured.

In order to meet the crisis in man power which now prevailed, the German Supreme Command had evidently divided its Divisions into two categories, those entrusted merely with the task of holding on to the ground facing west, and those charged with conquering new territory to the south. Their value appeared to be clearly unequal.

Such was the outlook and the point reached by our preparations, when the German attack fell with all its tremendous force—rapidly attenuated, it is true.

Whatever the uneasiness it had produced, I could not admit that this attack ought to prevent the completion of the preparations going on in our Tenth and Sixth Armies for an enterprise between the Aisne and the Marne, which seemed full of promise. The momentarily weakened situation in front of the Fifth Army and south of the Marne could, in the meantime, be met by fortuitous measures.

At daybreak on July 18th, the Tenth and Sixth Armies launched their offensive. At 4.35 A.M. on the front running from the valley of the Marne to the plateau of Nouvron, the heavily reinforced artillery of the two Armies suddenly opened, while the infantry, without further preparation, emerged from its trenches, and, preceded by tanks and accompanied by numerous aeroplanes, advanced against the enemy.

North of the Ourcq, the Tenth Army penetrated deeply into the enemy's main position ; by 10 A.M. it had captured Chaudun, Vierzy and Villers-Hélon. On the south, the Sixth Army first seized the line of German advanced posts, and then, conforming to its programme, carried out an artillery preparation of one and a half hours on the enemy's line of resistance. It then successfully resumed its advance, and by midday it had seized the line from Marizy-Saint-Mard to Torcy.

In view of the important results thus obtained, I sent the following instructions to General Pétain the same day :

" (1) The region north of the Marne at Château-Thierry appears the most favourable ground for a fruitful offensive. It is therefore advisable first of all to intensify the action undertaken to-day by our Sixth and Tenth Armies, and then to make preparations for its development northwards.

" (2) With this two-fold object in view, it is necessary to concentrate without delay all available fresh units that are now south of the line Château-Thierry—Rheims—Massiges, which line will doubtless become for us merely the scene of demonstrations.

" (3) The units to be considered, among others, are : The British XXII Corps, which should go to join the British 15th and 34th Divisions ; the American 42nd Division, also French or American units brought from the east.

" (4) This new distribution of forces must not in any way abate the offensive actively demanded of the Ninth,

Fifth and Fourth Armies. It is by the reorganization of the forces already engaged and not by the introduction of new forces that the action must be sustained."

At the same time I notified Sir Douglas Haig that " in order to be in a position to exploit the results already achieved," the British 15th and 34th Divisions had been moved to the region of Villers-Cotterets where, while remaining in reserve, they would be able to make preparations to enter the battle.

The results obtained on July 18th were, indeed, considerable. Apart from the ground gained, our advanced-guards had reached the line Pernant—Neuilly-Saint-Front—Torcy, and the Sixth and Tenth Armies had captured 10,000 prisoners and several hundred guns. The adversary had been surprised and in general he had not put up a very stout resistance. The use of the railway lines centering in Soissons was henceforth denied him.

On the 19th our advance was continued on the whole of the front without undue difficulty, while at the same time our air squadrons bombed the passages over the Marne and the enemy concentrations reported at Oulchy-le-Château and Fère-en-Tardenois. These concentrations seemed to indicate that the German Supreme Command had decided to defend the valley of the Ourcq ; for an Allied advance there would gravely compromise both the possession of the Soissons plateau and the bridge-head south of the Marne.

It was therefore to be anticipated that a big battle would take place in the Tardenois country. Accordingly, after seeing General Pétain on the morning of the 19th, I addressed to him the following Instruction :

" The battle now in progress should aim at the destruction of the enemy's forces south of the Aisne and the Vesle.

" It must be pursued with the utmost energy and without any loss of time, so as to exploit the surprise we have effected.

" It will be conducted by :

" The Tenth Army, covering itself by the Aisne and subsequently by the Vesle, and seeking to conquer the high ground north of Fère-en-Tardenois, its right on Fère-en-Tardenois.

" The Sixth Army, supporting the advance of the Tenth Army, and pushing its left to Fère-en-Tardenois.

" The Ninth and Fifth Armies, resuming a vigorous offensive as early as possible : the Ninth Army in order to drive the enemy to the north of the Marne ; the Fifth Army in order first to recapture the front Châtillon—Bligny, and subsequently the road from Ville-en-Tardenois to Verneuil."

On July 20th the enemy's resistance hardened. On that day the Tenth Army remained pinned to the high ground west and south-west of Soissons. Its right alone gained some ground in the direction of Oulchy-le-Château. The Sixth Army, likewise, encountered serious difficulties between the Ourcq and the Marne, and only effected a trifling advance. The Fifth Army, passing in its turn to the offensive, managed, with the support of two British Divisions, to move slightly forward between Marvaux and Belval.

The German Command, surprised at first, necessarily grasped at once the seriousness of the blow delivered on July 18th and 19th by our Tenth and Sixth Armies, and the danger to which their troops on and beyond the

Marne were exposed as a result of our drive along the Aisne and the Ourcq in the direction of Fère-en-Tardenois. The communications of the troops massed on the Marne for the attack of July 15th, as well as their supplies, were threatened to the point of being compromised. He realized that he must withdraw these troops as rapidly as possible and to do so he must at any cost halt or at least retard the march of our Tenth and Sixth Armies from the west, and the advance of our Fifth Army from the east, whatever the sacrifices to his flanks might be.

The Germans, therefore, on July 19th and 20th effected the withdrawal of all troops and *matériel* south of the Marne, and in the next few days, they abandoned on the line of the Ourcq the supplies of every sort which they had accumulated in the wooded regions north of the river.

From this moment the interest of our operations was transferred to the north of the Ourcq, and on July 21st I gave General Pétain instructions accordingly :

" . . . In order that the battle now in progress may yield all the results possible, the action of the Tenth Army on the high ground north of Fère-en-Tardenois must be intensified to the highest conceivable degree. To this end, all available resources should be furnished it, in addition to the constant support which the left of the Sixth Army must bring and the aid to be realized through continuing the offensive on the fronts of the Ninth and Fifth Armies. . . ."

Two days afterwards, on July 23rd, I again insisted :

" . . . It is important to resume the mastery of operations vigorously and without delay, if we are to obtain from this battle all possible results. . . .

" Everything available should be given to the Tenth Army. This Army should concentrate these resources on one part of its front so as to execute a powerful attack in a particularly important direction, viz. : the region of Fère-en-Tardenois.

" Supported on its right by the Sixth Army, and with all available troops concentrated on its left wing, this attack would force the enemy to evacuate the whole region south of Fère-en-Tardenois under difficult conditions.

" As a consequence of assigning all means now available to the Tenth Army, the Fifth Army will have only limited forces at its disposal. Therefore it should carry out a series of successive operations, concentrating all its available strength for each, and so arranging their sequence that each will create a favourable situation for the following one. For example, an advance on the high ground north of the Ardre will facilitate a subsequent attack south of that river, and this, in its turn, will force the enemy to evacuate the region north of the Marne. . ."

While thus occupied with directing and intensifying the battle in progress, I could not neglect the possibility of another German offensive in some other field. The Supreme Command of the Central Empires, in order to escape from the net which was now closing upon them, might be tempted to employ their reserves in a diversion north of the Oise, or against the British front. To be in a position to deal with such a move, I requested General Pétain to re-group in rear of the French left all worn-out Divisions withdrawn from the battle, and I restored to Field-Marshal Sir Douglas Haig's own command the two

British Divisions which on July 12th I had caused him to move south of the Somme.

The Sixth and Tenth Armies, having concentrated the greater portion of their strength on the two sides of the Ourcq, on July 25th launched an attack in the direction of Oulchy-le-Château. Oulchy-la-Ville and Oulchy-le-Château were captured by a brilliant assault, and a footing was obtained on the eastern slopes of the high Chalmont Hill that dominates the valley of the Ourcq. This was an important success which deprived the enemy of any hope or possibility of re-establishing himself on the line of the Ourcq.

On the following day the Germans carried out their retreat towards the high ground north of the river, and at such speed that in some places our advanced guards could not keep touch with them.

On the evening of the 29th, the French Tenth, Sixth and Fifth Armies were halted in front of these heights along the general line Grand Rozoy—Fère-en-Tardenois—Cierges—Ville-en-Tardenois—Vrigny.

Here the enemy resolutely opposed us. On July 30th and 31st, our efforts to dislodge him remained fruitless. The villages of Seringes, Sergy and Villers-Agron, furiously disputed, changed hands several times. The battle had once more reached a dead-lock.

But continuing the struggle in conformity with my directions of July 27th and General Pétain's instructions of July 29th, the Tenth Army resumed the attack on August 1st at 4.45 A.M. The French 25th, 41st and 68th Divisions and the British 34th Division, supported by tanks, assaulted the heights of Grand-Rozoy, and in spite of furious resistance on the part of the enemy, they carried the German position between Grand-Rozoy, the Signal de Servenay and the village of Cramaille at the point of the bayonet. Here they hung on in the face of numerous and powerful counter-attacks. This decisive action compelled the Germans to make a new withdrawal.

At day-break on August 2nd the Tenth, Sixth and Fifth Armies found there was nothing in front of them, and by evening they had reached the high ground south of the Vesle without striking a blow. Soissons was reoccupied.

On the 3rd the advance was continued. Reaching the left bank of the Vesle, our troops regained contact with the enemy, and at certain points even pushed units across the river.

However, on the 4th we found that the Germans were strongly entrenched along the line of the Vesle, and they seemed determined to defend it. To dislodge them, it would have been necessary to organize a new attack and bring up reinforcements; even then decisive results could not be expected for a long time. Moreover, at this moment, we were making preparations for another battle which might well produce very important results —the Battle of Picardy and the Santerre. The number of troops now available did not permit of our undertaking this battle and an attack against the Vesle at one and the same time. Accordingly, the Central and Reserve Groups of Armies were instructed " to establish themselves on their positions south of the Vesle, while continuing to give the enemy the impression that they were making preparations for a vigorous attack. . . ."

Thus, after three weeks of fighting, the second Battle of the Marne came to an end. After having been unprofitably started by the Germans on July 15th, it had been turned into success by the Allies on the 18th and continued ever since. A fortunate combination of circumstances had caused American, British, Italian and French Divisions to take part in it. Its results were important : 30,000 prisoners, more than 600 guns, 200 mine-throwers and 3,000 machine-guns captured ; the front shortened by twenty-eight miles ; the Paris—Châlons railway line re-established, and the menace against Paris removed.

But, above all, the morale of the German Army had been lowered, and that of the Allies raised. After four months on the defensive, imposed upon us by the enemy's numerical superiority, a victorious counter-offensive had once more placed in our hands the initiative of operations and the power to direct the progress of events in this long, vast war.

It was essential to retain this mastery by accelerating the phases of the struggle and developing our efforts in a series of well-ordered actions. We must therefore bring all the Allied resources into play as rapidly as possible, so as to prevent the enemy from recovering before we could effect his definite destruction.

CHAPTER IX

THE MEMORANDUM OF JULY 24TH

OBSESSED with these ideas, and especially so after the German offensive had been halted, the more our victory in the Tardenois assumed definite shape, the more I decided to apply them.

The immediate application would have to depend upon the means we now had at our disposal ; later on it could be based upon what had become available. It was essential not only to pursue tactical successes but to seek results such as might increase our resources and facilitate their employment. Finally, for the purpose of obtaining general approval, it was important that I set forth what I proposed to do in such fashion as to induce the conviction that our concerted efforts would bring decisive results, provided we gained time by hastening and co-ordinating them. With these purposes in view, I drew up the following memorandum :

" I. The fifth German offensive, halted at its very start, was a failure.

" The offensive taken by the French Tenth and Sixth Armies has turned it into a defeat.

" This defeat must first of all be exploited thoroughly on the field of battle itself. That is why we are pursuing our attacks without pause and with all our energy. But the consequences go far beyond the battle itself.

" II. The enemy's defeat forms a basis on which

should rest the general attitude to be adopted by the Allied Armies.

"As matters now stand :

"We have already attained equality in the number of Battalions at least, and, in a more general sense, in the number of combatants, though superiority in the total number of Divisions is not yet on our side.

"The Germans have been compelled to throw so many Divisions into action that, for the first time, we have a superiority in reserves ; also, owing to the large number of exhausted Divisions they will be compelled to relieve from the battle-front, we shall likewise have a superiority in the number of fresh reserves.

"Moreover, all available information is in agreement as to the enemy being reduced to the state of being compelled to have two armies : an army for occupying the line, reduced in strength and condemned to be sacrificed ; and a shock army, manœuvring behind the flimsy protection of the other. This shock army, though trained with the utmost care by the German Supreme Command, has been already greatly weakened.

"In addition, the Allies have a material superiority in aviation beyond dispute ; also in tanks. In artillery our advantage is bound to be increased when and as the American artillery arrives.

"Finally, in the rear of the Allied armies, the powerful reserve of the American forces pours 250,000 men every month upon the soil of France. While on the enemy's side, we know the urgent measures which he has been forced to take in order to meet the crisis in the supply of men for the month of May ; and it is apparent that, owing to the difficulty which the Germans find in keeping up the strength of their various units at the front, a new crisis is now asserting itself.

"In addition to all these indications that the factor of 'material force' is veering around in our favour, there can be added the moral ascendancy which has been maintained on our side from the beginning of the battle, owing to the fact that the enemy, despite his unprecedented efforts, has been unable to bring about the decisive result he needed to attain. And this moral ascendancy has been increased by the victory just won by the Allied armies.

"These armies, therefore, have arrived at the turning-point of the road. They have recovered in full tide of battle the initiative of operations; their numbers permit and the principles of war compel them to keep this initiative.

"*The moment has come to abandon the general defensive attitude forced upon us until now by numerical inferiority and to pass to the offensive.*

"III. This offensive—while not seeking a decision—should consist of a series of movements to be undertaken immediately, and having for their object results favourable to:

"1. The further development of the operations, and
"2. The economic life of the country.

"They will also serve to keep the fighting initiative on the side of the Allies.

"These movements should be executed with such rapidity as to inflict upon the enemy a succession of blows. This condition necessarily limits their extent, which will further be curtailed owing to the small number of units now at the disposal of the Allies for these offensives, after four months of battle.

"Keeping these considerations in mind, the programme of offensive actions to be executed without delay can be established as follows :

" 1. Operations having as their objective the clearing of the railway lines that are indispensable for the later operations of the Allied Armies, viz. :

" (a) The freeing of the Paris—Avricourt railway line in the Marne region. This is the minimum result to be obtained from the offensive movement now going on.

" (b) The freeing of the Paris—Amiens railway line by a concerted action of the British and French Armies.

" (c) The clearing of the Paris—Avricourt railroad in the region around Commercy, by reducing the Saint-Mihiel salient. This operation should be prepared without delay and executed by the American Army as soon as it has the necessary means.*

" 2. Operations with a view to clearing the mining region of the North and to driving to the enemy once and for all from the vicinity of Dunkirk and Calais.

" These operations pre-suppose two attacks, which may be carried out separately or conjointly.

" As previously stated, these actions must succeed each other at brief intervals, so as to embarrass the enemy in the utilization of his reserves and not allow him sufficient time to fill up his units.

" The attacks must be provided with everything necessary to make their success certain.

" Finally and above all, surprise must be effected. Recent operations show that this is a condition indispensable to success.

" IV. It is impossible to foretell at present where the different operations outlined above will lead us, either in

---

* In addition to shortening the front (to the advantage of both sides), this operation would bring us within striking distance of the Briey region and put us in a position to operate on a wide scale between the Meuse and the Moselle, which might one day become necessary.

the matter of time or space. Nevertheless, if the objects they have in view are attained before the season is too far advanced, there is reason for assuming now that an important offensive movement, such as will increase our advantages and leave no respite to the enemy, will be launched toward the end of the summer or during the autumn.

" It is still too early to be more precise in regard to this offensive.

" V. Finally, it must be borne in mind that, either for the purpose of freeing himself from our pressure or for economizing man-power, in the course of these operations the enemy may be compelled to execute a series of retrograde movements to shorter lines prepared in advance. If this should happen, the Allied Armies must not be taken by surprise.

" Therefore it is the duty of each Army :

" 1. To determine what retrograde movements are possible by studying the form presented by the enemy's organization in rear of his line.

" 2. To keep up a close observation in order to take note of any signs of contemplated retreat.

" 3. To make preparations which will prevent the enemy from executing such retrograde movements unmolested."

On July 24th, while the victorious battle of Tardenois was still in progress, the Commanders-in-Chief of the Allied Armies—Sir Douglas Haig, General Pétain and General Pershing—were assembled at my Headquarters at Bombon in order to examine with me the possibilities presented by the future. I requested my Chief of Staff, General Weygand, to read them the memorandum quoted above; and I must admit that it seemed to excite in them a considerable surprise, by reason of its ambitious nature, its magnitude and the number of operations it contemplated.

Each officer, looking at the matter from his own point of view—which, I acknowledge, did not lack justification—replied in turn:

Field-Marshal Haig: "The British Army, entirely disorganized by the events of March and April, is still far from being re-established."

General Pétain: "The French Army, after four years of war and the severest trials, is at present worn out, bled white, anæmic."

General Pershing: "The American Army asks nothing better than to fight, but it has not yet been formed."

How, then, under such conditions, were we to contemplate the possibility of carrying out a succession of offensives, each on a considerable scale?

While recognizing the justice of each of these observations, I insisted that I had given due weight to the temporary weaknesses mentioned, and I urged the fact that a proper combination of our forces would make the contemplated programme practicable, especially as we could carry it out at a pace which I would fix as circumstances arose—my idea being to hasten it or slow it up according to the success obtained as we went along.

The Commanders-in-Chief offered no formal objections. When they left me, they took with them the text of this note of July 24th, and the following day they gave it their full approval, accepting in principle the projected operations.

Another subject discussed at this conference was the

THE ALLIED COMMANDERS-IN-CHIEF ON THE FRENCH FRONT, WITH THEIR AUTOGRAPHS.

necessity for the Allies of finishing the War in 1919. In a letter to Monsieur Clemenceau, dated a short time before, I had asked him to call the class of 1920 to the colours, beginning with the month of October, 1919. I gave him the following reasons :

" The decisive year of the conflict will be 1919. By the spring of that year, America will have reached the climax of her effort. If it is desired to shorten the War, we must wage it with the greatest possible intensity from that moment on. Consequently, we must see that our Armies are given all the resources we can muster. And," I said in conclusion, " the stronger we are, the sooner we shall be victorious and the more we will be listened to." "

I wrote along the same lines to the Commanders-in-Chief on July 24th, asking them to draw up a statement of the resources upon which each of them could count at the beginning of 1919—in large units, in men, in artillery, in aircraft, in tanks and caterpillar transport.

I laid particular stress on the necessity not only of maintaining but of developing our superiority in tanks, and I requested the Commanders-in-Chief to bring the requisite pressure to bear on their respective Governments for speeding up the production of these engines of war which we so greatly needed.

On July 26th General Pétain sent me his written agreement to the contemplated programme of operations, adding that he was of the opinion that an attack on the Saint-Mihiel salient, taken " in conjunction with operations to clear the Armentières pocket, should be the main offensive envisaged for the end of the summer and the autumn. It will probably exhaust French resources for 1918, but in doing so, it will accomplish useful and definite results."

The other two Commanders-in-Chief sent no written answers to the memorandum laid before them, but they gave their acquiescence verbally.

CHAPTER X

PARTIAL ALLIED OFFENSIVES

(August—September, 1918)

I—The disengaging of Amiens and of the Paris-Amiens railway line—Preparations for the attack—The Battle of the Santerre, August 8th to 12th—Stiffening of the enemy's resistance; measures taken in consequence.

II—Extension of the Franco-British front of attack—The offensive from the Aisne to the Scarpe begins, August 20th to 21st—Results obtained since July 18th—The mining region of the north cleared of the enemy without a blow—Future prospect.

III—The freeing of the Paris-Avricourt railway line in the neighbourhood of Commercy—Autonomous American Armies are formed—First conception of the Battle of Saint-Mihiel—Changes made in it late in August owing to the combined programme of Allied offensive operations—Battle of St. Mihiel, September 12th.

I.—Disengaging Amiens and the Paris—Amiens Railway.

As a consequence of the decisions just related and the measures taken for carrying them out, we were now about to launch, starting on August 8th, a second great Franco-British offensive—the Battle of the Santerre. It started on August 8th and its consequences were destined to be of exceptional importance.

Ever since the 3rd of April I had entertained the idea of driving the enemy from the salient at Montdidier, as his proximity prevented our using the Paris—Amiens railway line. Later on the Germans got a foothold around Villers-Bretonneux, and they were now so close as to threaten the last rail communications between the French and the British. The enemy's cannon even reached the network of railroads centering at Amiens.

The region around Amiens and the Amiens—Paris railway must therefore be cleared as soon as possible.

This necessity had struck Sir Douglas Haig and on July 17th he had written :

" The most important operation, as I see it, and one which I suggest should be executed as soon as possible, is the advancing of the Allied front east and south-east of Amiens, so as to disengage this Town and the railway line. The best way of accomplishing it would be by a combined Franco-British operation, the French to attack south of Moreuil, the British north of the Luce."

This proposal was so perfectly in harmony with my previous instructions and with my way of looking at the matter—especially since our successes south of Soissons and in the Tardenois region—that I wished to follow it up immediately and increase its scope as much as possible. Therefore, on the 20th, I wrote to the Field-Marshal :

" Having reached the point where we now are, it is indispensable to seize the enemy and attack him wherever we can do so to our own advantage. I am extremely glad therefore to get your letter of the 17th, in which you inform me of the various plans which you have in view for operations on your front.

" The combined attack of the British Fourth and the French First Armies for the purpose of clearing Amiens and the railway should, it seems to me, be carried out at once, owing to the prospect it offers of most profitable results.

" I suggest that the generals commanding the British Fourth Army and of the French First Army be at once asked to arrange between them a plan regarding which we could come to a definite understanding later on."

And I said in conclusion :

" The enemy seems at present to be reduced to having two Armies. One, an Army for occupying the line, condemned to be sacrificed and consequently of no great value—as is proved by the complete success of the multiple minor operations recently undertaken by us and by the large number of prisoners captured in these operations ; and the second, a shock Army, trained with special care but already seriously weakened.

" This situation presents an element of weakness which we can exploit by carrying out immediately several attacks along those parts of the front held solely by inferior troops.

" The check administered to the last enemy offensive—a check whose importance each day confirms—offers an opportunity to be seized. We must not fail to grasp it."

This Franco-British offensive, having as an objective the disengaging of Amiens and the railway, formed part (as has been seen) of the plan outlined in the memorandum communicated to the Commanders-in-Chief at Bombon on July 24th.

On the 26th, during a conference at Sarcus with Field-Marshal Sir Douglas Haig, General Rawlinson and General Debeney, we drew up the general plan of the attack. It was to start from the line Somme—Hargicourt. The British Fourth Army,* twelve Divisions

* General Rawlinson.

strong, was to move in the direction of Chaulnes. The French First Army,* four to six Divisions strong, in the direction of Roye.

On July 28th the operation was prescribed in detail in the following instructions:

" I. The object of the operation is to clear Amiens and the Amiens—Paris railway as well as to defeat and throw back the enemy between the Somme and the Avre.

" II. For this purpose, the offensive, covered on the north by the Somme, is to be pushed forward as far as possible in the direction of Roye.

" III. It will be executed by:
" (1) The British Fourth Army, composed at the start of twelve Divisions of infantry and three Divisions of Cavalry supported by
" (2) The French First Army reinforced by four Divisions.
" The first will operate north, the second south, of the road to Roye, as soon as the possibility of debouching south of the Luce and east of the Avre is assured."

It could be assumed that by the time this operation took place our victory in the Soissons region would have yielded most of the results to be expected from it. Therefore good reasons existed for hurrying forward the offensive south of the Somme, so as not to allow the enemy any respite. Finally, for the purpose of ensuring perfect co-operation between the British Fourth Army and the French First Army, which were to act together, and of securing the greatest possible energy in execution, I asked Sir Douglas Haig to take personal command of

* General Debeney.

the two Armies. It was with this idea that I sent my second communication of the above date, handed by General Weygand to the Field-Marshal at Montreuil. It ran as follows :

" To-day, the 28th, our progress towards the Ardre and the Aisne is being rapidly accentuated. The enemy in the Marne region is retreating toward the north. There, beyond doubt, he will take up, behind some river, a defensive position which we shall not be able to attack immediately and which will probably enable him to reorganize his forces and in a short time restore his strength.

" Under these conditions, it seems in our interest to hasten the combined operation of your Fourth Army and our First Army. They would certainly be met by an enemy less able to cope with them.

" I ask you, therefore, to push forward as much as possible the date of these operations. I shall hasten proportionately the return of your XXII Army Corps.

" Finally, since this attack of two Allied Armies requires unified direction, I request you to take the command yourself."

On the 29th Sir Douglas sent his instructions to General Debeney, and on the 31st the latter in turn gave his orders to the three French Army Corps which were to operate to the southward of the British Fourth Army. To facilitate the outflanking of Montdidier, the left Corps of the Third Army, in position south of the town, was attached to the First Army.

Local operations that had been carried out during the preceding weeks had already secured for the Armies a better base of departure. Thus, on July 4th, the British

Fourth Army had captured the woods of Vaire and the village of Hamel, south of the Somme, while the French First Army, after taking the Anchin farm and Castel on July 12th, had, on the 23rd, gained possession of the villages and plateaux of Mailley-Raineval, Sauvillers and Aubvillers, capturing nearly 2,000 prisoners and several guns.

This last combat, in particular, had brought very advantageous results. Threatened in his positions on the left bank of the Avre, the enemy had withdrawn to the right bank, keeping only some outposts west of Montdidier (August 3rd and 5th). If in addition it be borne in mind that the Germans facing the British Third Army were crossing to the east of the Ancre, between Saint-Pierre and Dernancourt, and that in Flanders they were abandoning to the British Second Army a part of their positions south of the Lys, it will be realized what signs of exhaustion the enemy was showing in these first days of August, and under what favourable auspices the Franco-British attack in Picardy was being initiated.

*   *   *   *   *

On August 8th, at 4 A.M., hidden in a mist which continued to shroud the preparations of the preceding night, our artillery opened an intense fire which demolished the enemy's batteries. Immediately afterwards, the infantry and tanks of the British Fourth Army opened the attack; that of the French First Army, whose point of departure was at right angles to the British, was launched after an artillery preparation lasting forty-five minutes.

The enemy, wholly surprised by the violence and rapidity of the attack, fell back in great confusion, abandoning a large quantity of stores. Our advance during

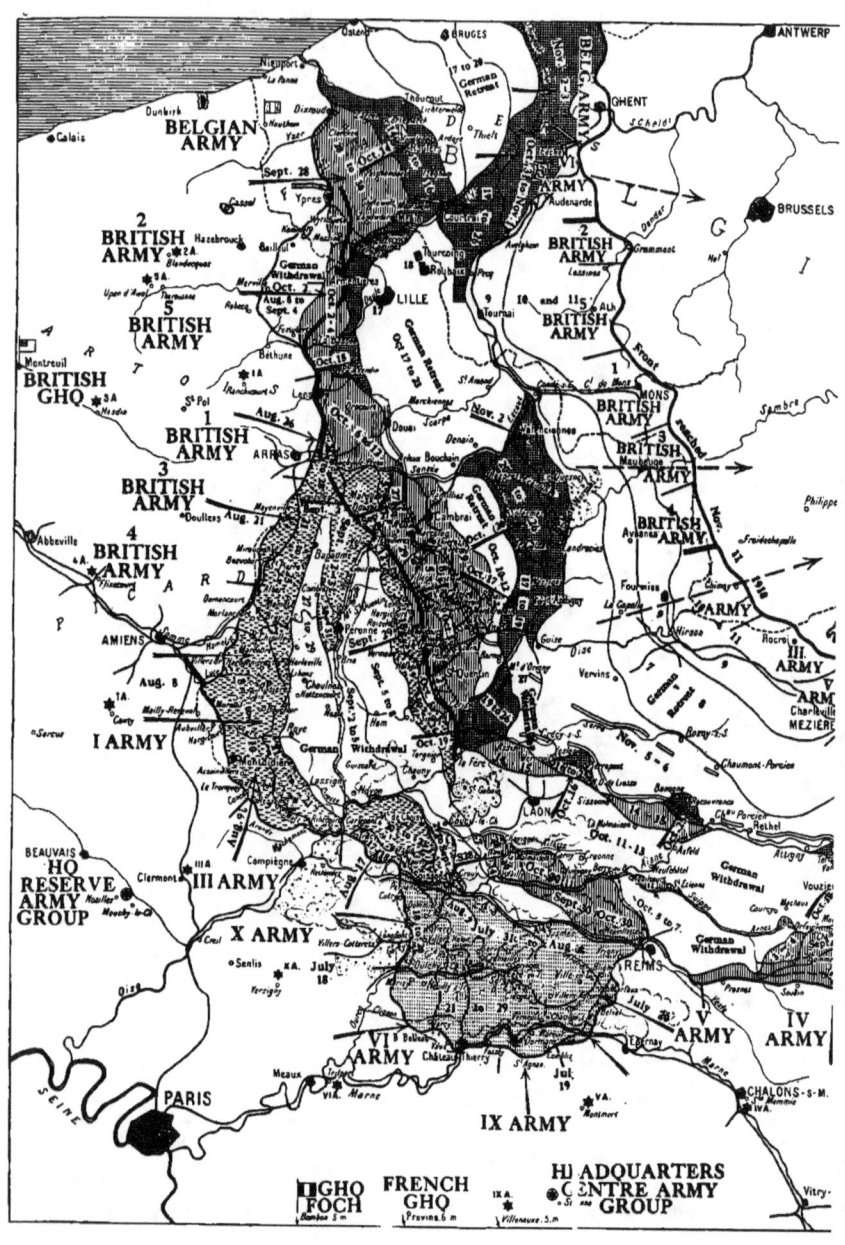

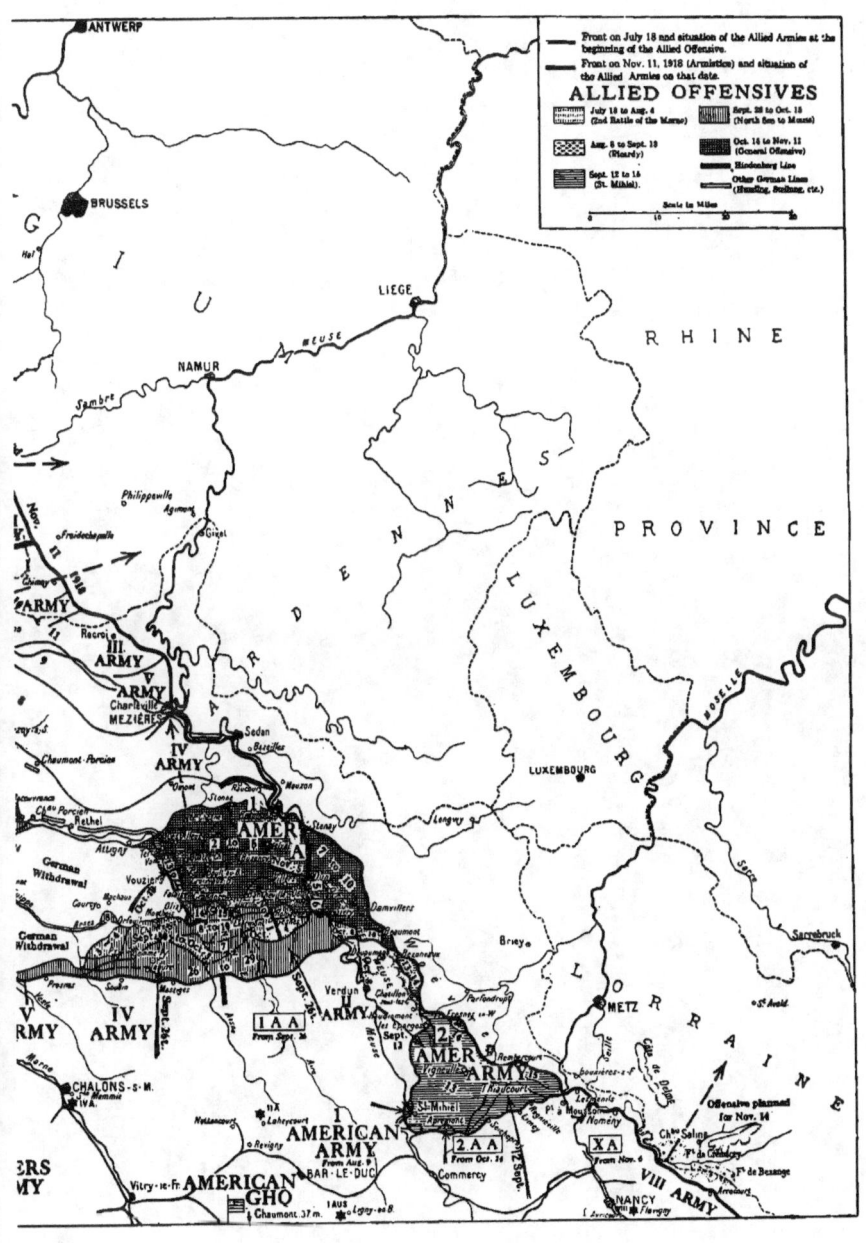

the day amounted to more than six miles on a front over twelve miles wide. We gained a firm foothold on the plateau of the Santerre, reaching the line Morlancourt —Morcourt—Harbonnières—Caix—Hargicourt. The capture of more than 13,000 prisoners and 300 guns gave evidence of the importance of the day's work. Now was the time to push our advantage vigorously by keeping up the action. It was with this end in view that Colonel Desticker, in compliance with my instructions, delivered the following note to General Debeney on the morning of the 9th :

" You understand, of course, that the French First Army should reach Roye *as quickly as possible*, and there make contact with the Third Army.

" When this result is obtained, the situation alone can indicate the next step, whether to halt or to continue to move forward.

" It is precisely because we cannot to-day determine exactly what is to be done that we must leave no possibility out of consideration.

" *With this in view, it is absolutely imperative that no Divisions should be sent to the rear*. Those that can advance no further are to be passed, relegated to the second line, and used as supports until the results expected have been accomplished.

" Therefore, *move fast*, march hard, manœuvre to the front, *reinforce firmly from the rear* with all the troops you have until the desired *result has been obtained*. If these three things are done, losses will be avoided a few days later."

Shortly afterwards, I sent another message to General Debeney, whose attention seemed to have become absorbed by the difficulties encountered by his right wing in crossing the Avre below Montdidier :

" Having assured the pivot of his manœuvre on the other side of Montdidier, General Debeney must not lose sight of the fact that his marching wing is on the right bank of the Avre along the Roye road, the point of contact with the British Army, the stronger force. It is here that he should take personal charge, especially with a view to pushing the XXXI Corps with the utmost vigour toward Roye, *without losing a minute*, beating down all hesitation and delay.

" It is here that the big decision will be obtained, and here must be his post and point of action."

During the 9th a considerable advance was again made on the Franco-British front, reaching as far as the line Morlancourt—Chipilly—Rosières-sur-Santerre —Bouchoir—Pierrepont—Assainvillers—Le Troquoy. Surrounded from the north and from the south, Montdidier was evacuated by the enemy during the following night.

On the 10th the attacks were continued; they gained considerable ground north of the Somme, in the direction of Bray, and southwards in the direction of Chaulnes and Roye.

The French Third Army in its turn now entered the action in obedience to the orders of General Fayolle. For, ever since August 5th, he had " foreseen the advantages to be obtained from the Franco-British offensive, and had made preparations for the Third Army to participate to the right of the First, with the idea of causing the entire Petite Suisse south of Noyon to fall as a secondary effect." The Third Army moved on Lassigny, and by the evening of the 10th had reached the line of Conchy-les-Pots—Ressons-sur-Matz—Machemont.

In view of this result, the Allied Supreme Command, on August 10th, addressed to its subordinates the following general instructions for the purpose of co-ordinating and orienting their efforts :

" I. The movements of the British Fourth Army and the French First Army will be continued eastward in the general direction of Ham—the object of the British Army being to reach the Somme below Ham, so as to prepare the passage of the Somme, while at the same time continuing its movement astride of this river from Bray to Péronne. The French First Army will support this advance, taking as an objective the Guiscard—Ham road.

" II. The French Third Army is now moving toward Lassigny—Noyon, for the purpose of exploiting the advance of the French First Army, clearing the region of Montdidier, and eventually that of Noyon.

" III. The attention of Field-Marshal Haig is invited to the unquestionable interest which attaches to preparing as soon as possible operations of the British Third Army in the general direction of Bapaume and Péronne, in order to shake the enemy's line and immediately exploit any break."

While our victorious advance was being pressed forward on the left bank of the Somme, it was to be foreseen that a time would arrive when it would be forced to halt for lack of breath, or because it found itself confronted by some serious obstacle strongly defended by the enemy.

When this moment came, an operation should be all ready for immediate execution on the right bank of the Somme and in Artois. This consideration inspired the third paragraph in my Instruction of the 10th.

On the morning of the 10th, I went to see Field-Marshal Sir Douglas Haig for the purpose of explaining to him this idea of preparing an extension of his attacks to the north of the Somme and in the direction of Arras. By doing so we should avoid any frittering away of our gains in local actions, we should profit by the confusion caused to the enemy's plans by our successive victories, and we should continue to shake his power of resistance by directing new blows at points where it could be assumed that this power had been weakened. And preparations for these operations should begin at once.

But now, after three days of incessant attack, the Franco-British Armies suddenly encountered serious resistance. The enemy had reached, at numerous points of the line, his old 1914 positions, and he seemed determined to make a stand there.

This is what happened, for on August 11th the British Fourth Army and the left wing of the French First Army were unable to advance, except with great difficulty, between the Avre and the Somme, although the French Third Army and the right wing of the First made considerable progress toward Lassigny.

I strongly urged Field-Marshal Sir Douglas Haig to push the advance toward Bray energetically. On the evening of the 11th I went to see him personally in order to ask him once more to put all possible force into his attacks. But on the day following it had to be admitted —as I set forth in a letter to the Commanders-in-Chief of the British and French Armies—that new tactics were required to ensure the results we were seeking between the Somme and the Oise, viz. : the repulse of the enemy on the Somme, and the seizure of all the passages of the river at (and below) Ham. My letter read :

" In the presence of the resistance offered by the enemy, we must not try to reach him by pushing forward simultaneously along the whole front. Such a course would result in our being weak at all points. Instead of this we must make concentrated and powerful attacks against the important points of the sector—in other words, against those whose capture by us will increase the disorganization in the enemy's ranks and will more especially jeopardize his lines of communication. These operations should be *prepared* promptly and in great strength, by assembling and putting rapidly into their places whatever means are at hand best suited for overcoming the resistance now being encountered—that is : Tanks, artillery and infantry in good condition. . . ."

Therefore, what should be undertaken was :

(a) *As quickly as possible*, a combined attack of the French First Army and the right wing of the British Fourth Army, having as objective the carrying of the network of roads around Roye. This attack should be supported towards the south by the French Third Army, with a view to clearing the Noyon region.

(b) *Without delay*, an attack to be carried out by the centre of the British Fourth Army, starting from the vicinity of Lihons—Herléville, and moving north-westwards, with a view to capturing, or at least bring within range of field guns, the high-road from Amiens to Brie. This attack should be combined with the left wing of the British Fourth Army in an easterly direction.

But, moved by the desire of giving our offensive greater scope, I added :

"These results can be enormously amplified by an extension of the attacks on the two flanks of the battle now in progress—north of the Somme, on the one hand, and east of the Oise on the other."

With this in view, I prescribed :
(*a*) North of the Somme, an attack of the British Third Army in the general direction of Bapaume—Péronne.
(*b*) East of the Oise, an attack of the French Tenth Army in the direction of Chauny and the Chauny—Soissons road.
In conclusion, I added :

"The results obtained by the French Third Army, unaided, show what may be expected from the extension of offensive actions on the flank of a victorious attack.
"Since July 15th the enemy has thrown one hundred and twenty Divisions into the battle. We now have an opportunity such as will not occur again for a long time, and that calls for an effort which the results in sight fully justify. Our interests demand that the attacks above outlined be executed as soon as possible and at the shortest possible intervals."

During the afternoon of this same 12th of August I met Sir Douglas Haig and General Pétain at Flixécourt, near Amiens, where they had been summoned, with myself, for an audience with H.M. the King of England. They both assured me of their complete agreement touching the Operation Orders just cited. We were therefore about to start on a new basis with a series of powerful attacks.

The re-grouping and concentration of forces in the various armies began on the 13th. On the 14th, the preliminary artillery preparation was begun by the British Fourth and the French First Armies. General Humbert (Third Army) and General Mangin (Tenth Army) were preparing to support the action on the south. The renewal of the combined offensive against Roye, Noyon and Chauny was fixed for August 16th.

During the afternoon of the 14th I repaired to Provins to discuss the projected operations with General Pétain. While on the way, about four o'clock in the afternoon, I was overtaken by an English officer, who arrived in an aeroplane bearing a letter from Sir Douglas Haig. The latter reported that during the preceding forty-eight hours the enemy's artillery fire along the front of the British Fourth and French First Armies had increased considerably, that the German positions on the Chaulnes —Roye line were solidly held, and that for these reasons he had decided to postpone the operation fixed for the 16th " until an adequate preparation enabled it to be undertaken in the best conditions." He added : " This attack might be made conjointly with the action on the front of the (British) Third Army, which is being made ready as rapidly as possible."

While fully realizing that troops must not be launched to the attack without an effective artillery preparation, I could not see the necessity for " subordinating the date of the attack by the British Fourth Army and the French First Army to that of the British Third Army," and I immediately replied in this sense. " On the contrary," I added, " there is good reason for hastening the action of the British Fourth and the French First Armies as much as possible, and having it speedily followed by an attack from the British Third Army."

As soon as I had returned to my Headquarters at Bombon, and had received information regarding the situation on the French side, I completed the expression of what was in my mind by another message to the British Commander-in-Chief, in which I stated that: " In view of the dispositions now taken by the French First Army and of the artillery preparation already under way, any postponement of the movement against Roye, decided upon for the 16th, would have the most serious consequences." Therefore, I stated, the date agreed upon should be adhered to and the British Fourth Army should " give its support to the French First Army on the 16th up to Hattencourt, unless this was utterly impossible on the part of the troops forming the right wing of the former Army." If this were impossible, Field-Marshal Sir Douglas Haig was requested to inform me without loss of time.

As can be seen, the enemy had pulled himself together west of the Somme, and had consolidated his resistance by using his old defensive lines of 1916. To what degree might this situation influence us?

On the morning of August 15th, I proceeded to Sarcus, where General Debeney came to see me. He told me that the projected attack on Roye would certainly be difficult, and he felt that even assuming his forces to be sufficient for making it, they would be too weak to keep it going. During the afternoon of the same day, I had still another conversation with Sir Douglas. He repeated his reasons for believing that the attack south of the Somme would be hard and success doubtful, even at the price of considerable losses. He thought that the result sought might be obtained through means which, though indirect, were more sure, that is by having the British Third Army attack north of the Ancre, on the front Miraumont—Monchy-le-Preux, in a south-easterly direction, thus turning the line of the Somme south of Péronne.

I definitely came around to the opinion of Field-Marshal Sir Douglas Haig, and I modified my orders of August 12th for the Somme operations. But I made it a condition that the impetus given to the attack of the British Third Army should be such as to ensure the resumption of the drive south of the river with a view to attaining the objectives previously assigned to it. I confirmed these various points in a letter which I sent Sir Douglas that same evening.

And now the time had come for considering an action of the British Fourth and Third Armies, working in conjunction, and an action of the French First Army combined with the attacks of the French Third and Tenth Armies. Therefore, on this day, August 15th, the First Army was returned to its Group Commander, General Fayolle, acting under the orders of the Commander-in-Chief, General Pétain.

At the same time, I informed the latter by telegraph that the attacks on Roye and Chaulnes had been postponed for the time being, that the British Armies were actively preparing the extension of their operations on the Ancre—Scarpe front, and that they expected these operations to reach their full development about August 20th. General Pétain was therefore requested to combine the operations of his First, Third and Tenth Armies with the object of clearing the region of Lassigny, Noyon and the forest of Carlepont, and preparing the eventual clearing of the country around Roye, Chauny and Noyon. As these operations, together with those of the British

Armies, were meant to force the withdrawal of German troops in position west of the Somme, it was important to maintain strong pressure in this region.

II.—*Extension of the Franco-British Front of Attack.*

Ever since the middle of the month of August I had been worried by the fear that the German Commander-in-Chief might extricate his Armies from our grip and abruptly break off the combat in order to resume it some distance in the rear. Here he could select better positions on a shorter front, behind obstacles and on ground more favourable to the defensive, and make a new distribution of his forces such as might enable him to launch an advantageous counter-attack. In short, I feared that he might attempt some manœuvre in this position similar to that by which General Joffre had prepared and won the first Battle of the Marne.

From a strictly military point of view such a solution would enable him to take and keep the initiative, and might give him a chance to restore the fortunes of his Army. The manœuvre might consist in slipping from our grasp as quickly as possible, breaking the close contact we were maintaining everywhere, and then re-forming on some line further back, such as that of Antwerp—Brussels—Namur—the Meuse—the Chiers—Metz-Strasbourg. He could do this by taking advantage of the necessary slowness which must mark our advance through the devastated regions.

On this new line the Germans might mass their forces and offer a fresh resistance, calling for most strenuous efforts on our part just as the winter was setting in. This line would be little more than half as long as the front extending from the North Sea to the Vosges, and most of it would run through country offering serious natural obstacles, while its two ends would rest upon fortifications providing the strongest kind of support. Such a line could not be assaulted by the Allied Armies under proper conditions in less than a fortnight, a period of time which would certainly be used to advantage by the German General Staff. And that would be for us the beginning of a hard battle, necessitating long and serious preparation. The battlefield would embrace Lorraine, already powerfully organized, the Ardennes region, most difficult to penetrate, and for a short distance, the plains of Belgium. We might even be compelled to spend the winter facing this line.

But the retreat necessitated by such a manœuvre—the only one offering the possibility of restoring the fortunes of the German Armies—would be tantamount to an acknowledgment by the German General Staff of an appreciable military defeat, and might dangerously influence German public opinion. It would mean the evacuation of a part of France, and most of Belgium, and of Upper Alsace. It would bring about a considerable modification of the War map at a moment when peace proposals were being thought of, and, finally, it would entail the immediate risk involved in removing or abandoning an enormous quantity of war material.

But whatever ideas on this subject the Germans may have had, the Allied General Staff, by unremittingly continuing its operations, proceeded to deprive them of all possibility of carrying out any such manœuvre.

* * * * *

As a consequence of the dispositions made, the Franco-British offensive was henceforth to reach from the valley of the Aisne to that of the Scarpe. The resumption of this offensive was set for August 20th.

On the right wing, the French Tenth Army had, on the 17th and 18th, prepared its principal operation by some local actions which gave it possession of the heights between Tracy-le-Val and Morsain, and enabled it to push forward a part of its artillery.

On the 20th it assaulted the enemy's main position, drove him from the Vouvron plateau and hurled him back toward the wooded region of Mont de Choisy and Carlepont. On the 21st we took those places and, pursuing the beaten Germans, reached the banks of the Oise and of the Ailette on the 22nd and 23rd. Simultaneously, the French Third Army occupied Lassigny and the right bank of the Divette.

Thus the first task entrusted to these Armies—the clearance of the neighbourhood of Lassigny, Noyon and the forest of Carlepont—had been successfully accomplished within three days.

On the left, the British Third Army, under General Byng, in its turn entered into action. Owing to delay in the arrival of certain units—which Field-Marshal Sir Douglas Haig reported—the attack had been postponed until the 21st. To avoid any further delay, on the 19th, following the successful results obtained by the Tenth Army, I addressed the following urgent appeal to Sir Douglas:

" The enemy has everywhere been shaken by the blows already dealt him. We must repeat these blows without losing any time, and to increase their effect we must use every Division that can be put into line without delay. Therefore I assume that the attack of your Third Army, postponed already until August 21st, will be launched on that day *with the utmost violence*, carrying along with it the Divisions of the First Army lying next to it and your Fourth Army in its entirety. After your brilliant successes of the 8th, 9th and 10th, any hesitation on their part would not accord with the situation of the enemy and the moral ascendancy we have obtained over him."

The British Third Army did not fail to do all that was expected of it. On August 21st, after a rapid penetration of the German lines, it threw the enemy back to beyond the Arras—Albert railway, between Moyenneville and Beaucourt. It resumed its advance on the 23rd, and on the 25th, reaping the fruit of its efforts, arrived at the gates of Croisilles and Bapaume.

Profiting by this advance, the British Fourth Army pushed forward north of the Somme and arrived on the plateau of Mametz and the heights of Bray.

But while perfect success was attending the attacks of the two wings north of the Somme and on the Oise, the Franco-British centre was fighting hard between the Somme and the Oise, in the direction of Roye, without obtaining any appreciable results.

It seemed more and more certain that German resistance in this central region could be broken only by the action of our wings, which were being constantly extended and reinforced. I had no difficulty in bringing the Commanders-in-Chief into agreement with me on this point. As early as the 22nd of August, Sir Douglas Haig, in particular, with accuracy of vision and admirable ardour, informed me in the course of an interview at Mouchy-le-Châtel that the attack of the British Third Army would be pushed with the utmost energy, supported to the north of the Somme by the British Fourth Army. The commanders of these two Armies,

Generals Byng and Rawlinson, were given the mission to reach as quickly as possible the line Quéant—Velu—Péronne. At the same time, the British First Army, in its turn, was to attack about the 26th beyond the Scarpe and try to pierce the Drocourt—Quéant line.

These dispositions, prescribed in a general Operations Order from British Headquarters, dated August 24th, corresponded entirely with my way of looking at the situation and my wish to precipitate events and widen the front of our attacks. Therefore, on the 26th, I wrote to Field-Marshal Sir Douglas Haig :

" Things are going very well with you. I can only admire the resolute manner in which you press the business forward, giving no respite to the enemy and constantly increasing the scope of your action. It is this persistent widening and intensifying of the offensive—this pushing vigorously forward on carefully chosen objectives without over-preoccupation as to alignment or close liaison—that will give us the best results with the smallest losses, as you have so perfectly comprehended. No need to tell you that the Armies of General Pétain are about to recommence their attacks, using similar methods."

The combative ardour animating Sir Douglas even led him to desire to take along the American Divisions in his victorious career. On August 27th he wrote :

" I am convinced that it is desirable for the American Divisions to take an active part in the fighting without delay, and I have the honour to submit to your consideration the suggestion that the distribution of these Divisions be arranged in such a way as to make possible the launching of a concentric movement against Cambrai and, starting from the southwards, against Mézières.

" The actual direction taken by my attacks will bring me to Cambrai, provided the pressure exerted against the rest of the enemy's front be constantly maintained."

The hour was thus approaching for the " important offensive " envisaged in my memorandum of July 24th.

The clearing operations north of the Oise had thoroughly succeeded. Before it was possible to pass to a concentric advance on Cambrai—Mézières, it was important to undertake first the operations already planned for the Meuse region and reserve for them a large force of American troops. Therefore, in answering Sir Douglas, I observed :

" . . . The final objectives which you mention to me in your letter are exactly those I have in mind and toward which I am directing the operations of the Allied Armies.

" These operations are now being conducted in several different regions, each in its own style, and at short intervals one from the other. So all that is needed now is to develop them as actively as possible. That is what I am doing.

" Approaching events, with their results, can alone form the basis for a new distribution of the forces now available. They must also decide whether additional American Divisions should be assigned to the British Army. For the time being, all we have to do is to push hard and get forward as far as possible."

And we *were* pushing hard. On August 26th the British right wing, under General Horne, attacking east of Arras, brilliantly carried the heights of Monchy-le-Preux, and seized the crossing of the Sensée below Croisilles next day. But after capturing this place on the 28th, the British ran against the fortified line Drocourt—Quéant, which proved a serious obstacle to its further advance as well as a strong base for the enemy. The latter availed himself of this position for launching, on the 29th, violent counter-attacks against the British First Army. Although these failed to shake the British, they gained for the enemy the time needed for the retrograde movement being carried out further south.

For the Germans, menaced by General Horne's rapid advance, and under constant pressure from the British Third and Fourth Armies and the French First Army, now proceeded to retreat along a wide front between the Sensée and the Oise, during the whole of August 27th, 28th and 29th. They established themselves on the heights east of Bapaume, behind the Somme above Péronne, and behind the Canal du Nord, thus abandoning to the Allies important centres such as Combles, Chaulnes, Roye and Noyon. West of the Somme they now held only one bridge-head, established in front of Péronne, and from it they had to be dislodged by main force.

On August 30th the British Fourth Army captured the railway bridge south of the town, and during the night of August 31st—September 1st it stormed the hill of Saint-Quentin, key to the defence of Péronne. At dawn next day the old city was free from Germans.

While the British First Army, continuing its advance on the extreme left of the battle-line, was preparing to attack the Drocourt-Quéant line, and the Franco-British centre (British Third and Fourth Armies, French First and Third Armies) was turning and carrying the

A CAPTURED GERMAN BATTERY.

line of the Somme, the French Tenth Army, on the right of the battle-line, was engaged in very hard fighting between the Aisne and the Ailette, on the plateaux north of Soissons. Here the enemy, strongly entrenched, offered a desperate resistance. For the Germans must at all costs prevent the turning from the south of the Saint-Gobain *massif*, which for four years had been the buttress of their defensive system. Despite this resistance, the French Tenth Army, fighting foot by foot, was gaining ground daily, and to such an extent that on September 2nd it had surmounted the heights of Crouy and reached the high-road from Soissons to Coucy-le-Château.

At the other end of the battle-line, the British First Army, continuing its broadly conceived operations, recommenced its attacks. On September 2nd, after violent and stubborn fighting, it broke through the Drocourt—Quéant line and passed on for several miles in the direction of Marquion. After this smashing blow, the enemy began to retreat along the whole front between the Somme and the Sensée, reaching new positions behind the Tortille and the Nord Canal, in front of the Hindenburg Line. Thus, at the beginning of September, victory had passed to the Allied banners, thanks to the rapid and sustained development of the operations following the German offensive of July 15th. The results envisaged in the memorandum of July 24th were being attained.

On July 18th the Reserve Group of Armies (Sixth and Tenth) attacked between the Aisne and the Marne, followed shortly by the Centre Group of Armies (Ninth and Fifth), advancing between the Marne and the Vesle. In three weeks the enemy had been pushed back to the latter river and the Paris—Châlons railway cleared.

On August 8th the Franco-British attack was launched between the Ancre and the Avre and soon extended to the Oise. In three days the enemy was relegated for the most part to his 1914 positions. Amiens and the Paris—Amiens railway line were entirely relieved of danger.

These results being obtained, the offensive was continued by three British Armies (First, Third, Fourth) and three French Armies (First, Third, Tenth) operating simultaneously along the whole front between Arras and Soissons. After two weeks' fighting the enemy, badly shaken, fell back towards the Hindenburg line.

Now, the incessant attacks which the Germans had been obliged to meet since July 18th, the serious losses which these attacks had occasioned them in men and stores and munitions, the necessity of feeding a battle which widened out each day—perhaps also worry as to whether they ought to expose themselves any longer in a salient where they ran the risk of being attacked under unfavourable conditions—all combined to decide them to shorten their front in the north and voluntarily give up the gains they had made in April in the direction of Hazebrouck. Between August 8th and September 4th, the German Supreme Command withdrew its troops from the salient south of Ypres, and placed them on the line of Wytschaete—Armentières—La Bassée, abandoning important positions like Mount Kemmel and raising the heavy hand which for four months had weighed upon the coal basin of Béthune. This was one of the advantages—and not the least—obtained by the Allies from a victory which, despite its extent, was still only at its beginning.

To sum up, in six weeks the enemy had lost all the gains he had made in the spring. He had lost heavily in men, munitions and stores. Most important of all, he had lost the initiative of operations—he had lost his moral ascendancy. Material and moral confusion must inevitably reign within his ranks. All we now needed to do was to continue the execution of our programme— push forward the disengagement of the Paris-Avricourt railway line in the vicinity of Commercy by using the American Army, just as we had cleared the Paris-Amiens and the Paris-Châlons lines by using the French and British Armies. In short, the time had come to extend further eastward the scope of the general operations in which we were engaged and—as had been provided for in the memorandum of July 24th—bring into the battle as soon as possible the Army which had been the last to enter the struggle, that of the United States.

Furthermore, in view of the retrograde movements of the enemy, giving evidence as they did of exhaustion and lack of reserves, I called the attention of Field-Marshal Sir Douglas Haig and of Lieutenant-General Gillain to the fact that the situation in the north offered favourable opportunities for exploitation. " What particularly strikes me," I wrote on September 2nd, " is that it might be possible to undertake an operation by the Belgian Army and the British Second Army which could at small cost, seize the heights of Clercken, the forest of Houthulst, the Passchendaële ridge, the heights of Gheluvelt and Zandworde, and Comines. Besides the immediate advantages which such an action would bring to our present offensive by the unexpected extension of our front of attack to the north of the Lys, the attainment of the objectives mentioned would give an excellent base of departure for subsequent operations toward Roulers and Courtrai."

In asking the Commander-in-Chief of the British

Army and the Chief of Staff of the Belgian Army to make an immediate study of these projects, I was furthering the preparation of the general offensive which I now had in view for the Allied Armies—an offensive made possible by the success of all the partial operations carried out since July 18th, the finishing touch to which was to be furnished by the American First Army in the Saint-Mihiel salient.

*   *   *   *

III.—Disengaging the Paris-Avricourt railway in the neighbourhood of Commercy.

As will have been noted, the Memorandum of July 24th included a plan for an American attack in the Woëvre region.

With this in view, it had been decided on July 22nd to form, in addition to the American First Army on the Marne, an American Second Army on the Meuse which, as the troops composing it arrived, was to take possession of the sector from Nomény to the region north of Saint-Mihiel.

The possibility of creating these two large units by the end of July showed clearly the importance which American assistance was assuming on the French front. It was proof also of the ardent desire of American soldiers, so often expressed by General Pershing, to have the American Expeditionary Forces united as soon as possible under his orders, and given an autonomy similar to that of the other Allied Armies ; they wished to see the Stars and Stripes waving over a battlefield at the earliest moment.

I was convinced more than anybody else of the necessity of forming with the least delay a great American Army under the orders of its commander, since I knew perfectly well that soldiers of a national army never fight so well as under the orders of the officers their country has given them—who speak the same tongue, fight for the same cause, have the same sort of ideas, and act in a manner familiar to the men under them. I greatly desired to satisfy General Pershing's wish as soon as possible ; but to do so it did not seem advisable to stop or slow down, at the end of July, operations so successfully begun and then being continued in the Tardenois country, and in which Divisions of the American First Army were participating. It was also necessary to consider the possibility of unforeseen emergencies arising, which might necessitate engaging American troops under some command other than that of their own Commander-in-Chief. That is what I wrote General Pershing on July 28th. So well did he seize the meaning of my letter in its application to the French front, that, on July 29th, he informed me of his anxiety in connection with the sending of American reinforcements to Italy. He asked me to adhere to my opinion in the matter (of which he was fully cognizant), viz : " That it was necessary to concentrate our military effort on the Western Front and impossible to deflect to some other territory any part whatsoever of the American forces."

It was to this same effect that I answered our Minister of War* when, shortly afterwards, he transmitted to me a message from M. Noulens† suggesting that American reinforcements be sent to the Allied contingents operating in northern Russia. I declined to see the necessity

* Monsieur Clemenceau.—Translator.
† French Ambassador to Russia.—Translator.

of increasing these forces beyond the total fixed by the Supreme War Council, and I added that, in any case, no troops should be taken from the French front.

At this moment I was pushing forward as rapidly as possible the preliminaries for the Woëvre attack. With this object I asked General Pétain, on August 4th at my Headquarters at Bombon, to finish these preparations by the end of the month, and I urged General Pershing to speed up the formation of the American Army of the Woëvre. On August 9th, in view of the magnificent development of the operations on the Somme, it seemed advisable to make the Woëvre attack as soon as possible. Therefore, to gain time, it was decided, at a meeting at Sarcus between General Pétain, General Pershing and myself, to form the American First Army in this region instead of in the Aisne territory as had been previously contemplated, since the front along the Aisne was now stabilized. For the time being, as will be noted, we were confining ourselves to the formation of only one American Army.

On August 17th General Pershing received my general instructions for the projected attack. After reminding him of its purpose, the disengaging of the Paris—Avricourt railway line by the reduction of the Saint-Mihiel salient, I described for him the objectives to be attained, viz : the line running roughly through Bouxières-sous-Froidmont (four miles north-east of Pont-à-Mousson)—Mars-la-Tour—Parfondrupt—Bezonvaux. I also indicated the general procedure of the action, which was to consist of three attacks : One, on the east of the Saint-Mihiel salient, starting from the Lesménils—Seicheprey front and moving in a northerly direction ; the second, on the north of the salient, starting from the entrenched front of Calonne—Haudimont, and moving in an easterly direction; the third, flanking the second on the left and starting from the front Châtillon-sous-les-Côtes—Bezonvaux.

A total of eighteen or nineteen Divisions would be necessary.

If the objectives thus defined were attained, the result would be to clear far more thoroughly than was essential the railway from Paris to Avricourt. These operations in the Woëvre would, moreover, have other results besides the one immediately sought—such as hitting the enemy as hard a blow as possible, obtaining the maximum benefits to be expected from a major operation, conquering an advantageous base of departure for subsequent offensives.

General Pershing was given all material aid possible. At his request, three American Divisions (33rd, 78th, 80th), drawn from those under Field-Marshal Sir Douglas Haig, were transferred from the British zone of operations to the Meuse. The American First Army received from the French Army a certain amount of supplementary artillery, ammunition trains, tanks, aviation, etc., and finally the French forces (three Army Corps) which were to co-operate in the American attack, were placed under General Pershing's command.

On August 24th, the Commander-in-Chief of the American Expeditionary Forces came to Bombon and explained to me the general plan and the command organization for the Woëvre operation. We also reached an agreement regarding the employment of certain American Divisions in the Allied Armies. Two Divisions (27th and 30th) were to remain under the orders of Sir Douglas Haig and take part in the operations in the British zone; dating from September 8th, two other Divisions of General Pershing's reserve (over and above the fourteen American Divisions earmarked for the Woëvre operation) were to be held in readiness to participate, as circumstances might dictate, either in the attacks of the French Armies or in the American Army's attack.

*   *   *   *

These matters being arranged, I decided (as we shall see later) that, in view of the successful development of the Allied offensives since July 18th and the increasing disorganization of the enemy, I would now begin the grand offensive operation foreshadowed in the Memorandum of July 24th for the end of the summer or for the autumn.

At the end of August our series of victories made it possible to contemplate a far more important result than the mere disengaging of the Commercy railway line by the capture of the Saint-Mihiel pocket. We were now justified in contemplating the Battle of Mézières, provided we brought all the Allied Armies into the battle, and provided especially that we did not permit the American Army to get carried too far in an offensive of its own, and headed in a wrong direction—which might well happen if it made too great an advance in the Woëvre region.

Therefore, on August 30th, after apprising General Pétain in the morning of this new programme, I repaired to Ligny-en-Barrois and saw General Pershing that same day. I explained to him the broad lines of the projected manœuvre which would consist of combining with the Franco-British attack, already under way around Cambrai and Saint-Quentin, a Franco-American attack towards Mézières, along both banks of the Meuse. This attack was to be entrusted to an American Army disposed astride the Meuse, with the French Fourth Army on its left, and later on the French Second Army on its right, the two latter being reinforced by from twelve to sixteen American Divisions. It was to begin between the 15th and 20th of September.

In the meantime, both in order to deny respite to the enemy and also to facilitate the withdrawal and transfer of the American troops destined for the attack on Mézières, the Woëvre operations were to be begun about September 10th by forces reduced to some nine Divisions and with their objective limited to the mere clearing of the Paris—Avricourt railway line—that is to say, to the conquest of the line Vigneulles—Thiaucourt—Régnéville. In other words, to enable me to direct against Mézières an offensive from which I expected very great results, I was led to reduce the Woëvre operation to a far smaller scope than I had had in mind when I wrote my instructions of August 17th; and in addition I was led to ask General Pershing to undertake a new offensive.

Before quitting Ligny, I left the General a note summarizing and explaining in detail the various points touched upon in our conversation. This note elicited from the Commander-in-Chief of the American Army some observations which he developed in a letter he sent me on August 31st.

To smooth out any difficulty and avoid loss of time, General Pershing, General Pétain and I assembled on September 2nd at my Headquarters. We took as a basis for our conference the answer to the letter which I had sent General Pershing the day before. It was as follows :

" My note of August 30th and my verbal explanations of the same date contemplated organizing immediately a

general battle of the Allied Armies :
" (1) In a predetermined direction,
" (2) With the maximun of Allied forces,
" (3) In the shortest possible time,
" (4) Under the best conditions of supply and hence of communications.

" To accomplish this, I had in view as the American Army's part :
" (a) An operation against Saint-Mihiel, on a more or less reduced scale.
" (b) An attack west of the Meuse.

" The attack west of the Meuse will be maintained at all costs
" as regards direction,
" as regards the importance of the forces engaged,
" as regards considerations of time.

" If you think, as you state in your letter of August 31st, that you cannot undertake the Saint-Mihiel operation previously or simultaneously, even if its scale be reduced, I consider that this operation should be abandoned.

" In any case, with a view to organizing at once and without any loss of time the operations west of the Meuse, I request you to meet General Pétain and me to-morrow, September 2nd, at 2 P.M. at my Headquarters, in order that the broad lines of these operations may be then and there definitely drawn up."

In the course of this meeting which took place under the conditions stated, General Pershing, after going over the list of American Divisions then in a condition to undertake an offensive, admitted that the Saint-Mihiel operation and the offensive against Mézières did not, by any means, each cancel the other's importance, provided they followed in rapid succession and that the dates were arranged with this end in view.

Under these conditions, it was decided:

(1) That the attack on Saint-Mihiel, limited to the occupation of the line Vigneulles—Thiaucourt—Régnéville, would be prepared for execution on September 10th, using from eight to ten Divisions.

(2) That the attack west of the Meuse would be made between September 20th and 25th by the American Army (twelve to fourteen Divisions, not counting those which had refitted after the previous battle) between the river and the Argonne, supported on the left by an attack of the French Fourth Army, the whole under the command of General Pétain.

The decisions thus arrived at were incorporated in a note which was handed immediately to the two Commanders-in-Chief as a preliminary to the General Instruction sent them on the next day, September 3rd.

And so, after the changes and negotiations just explained, the Saint-Mihiel operation was at last got under way. But even then it had to be put off forty-eight hours after the time first arranged, owing to " the extreme complexity of the movements of concentration."

On September 12th, after an artillery preparation by nearly 3,000 guns lasting four hours, the principal attack (American IV and I Army Corps), starting from the front of Seicheprey—Limey, was launched at 5 A.M. in the direction of Vigneulles—Thiaucourt. This attack was so violent and was carried out with such resolution that the enemy succeeded nowhere in stopping it. The thick wire entanglements were crossed, the centres of resistance were overwhelmed and passed over, and by evening all the objectives had been reached.

Meanwhile, the secondary attack (American V Corps), having debouched at 8 o'clock from the Eparges front, moved forward with the same rapidity as the main attack, and, pursuing its advance throughout the day, reached Vigneulles-les-Hattonchâtel in the course of that same night. There, on the morning of the 13th, touch was established between the secondary and the principal attacks.

A few hours had sufficed for disengaging this Saint-Mihiel salient, where the enemy had been established for four years. The Germans did not have time to evacuate the pocket completely, and 13,250 prisoners with 460 guns were taken.

It was a splendid success, and I hastened to send my congratulations to General Pershing. To complete it, all that had to be done on the days following—September 13th, 14th and 15th—was for the troops to install themselves in front of the new positions occupied by the enemy and build a solid defensive line to face him.

For the American First Army would now be called upon to withdraw a considerable part of its forces and send them to the west of the Meuse. Here new tasks and new fortunes awaited them.

CHAPTER XI

THE GENERAL OFFENSIVE OF THE ALLIED ARMIES, SEPTEMBER 26TH TO OCTOBER 15TH. BREAKING OF THE HINDENBURG LINE

Instructions given by the Commander-in-Chief of the Allied Armies for carrying out the general offensive from the Meuse to the North Sea—Fighting around the advanced works of the Hindenburg Line—Franco-American offensive between the Suippe and the Meuse—Franco-British offensive against the Saint-Quentin—Cambrai front—Offensive of the Flanders Group of Armies north of the Lys.

WHILE the American Army was preparing and fighting in the Woëvre region a battle whose usefulness for the future development of operations was evident to all, the advance of the Franco-British armies between the Aisne and the Scarpe continued without pause.

Shaken by the piercing of the Drocourt—Quéant line, driven from the valley of the Somme by the loss of Péronne, and hard-pressed on the plateaux north of Soissons, the enemy, as we have already seen, had been compelled to fall back toward the Hindenburg line. This retreat, begun on September 2nd, was continued until the 9th, and brought the Allies to the general line Arleux—Marquion — Vermand — Tergnier — Vailly. On this enormous front we had advanced from twelve to thirty miles in a month.

We now had to attack the formidable defensive system erected by the enemy during the winter of 1916-1917 on the front Cambrai—Saint-Quentin—La

Fère—Saint-Gobain. This system was prolonged both northward and southward by the positions (since constantly strengthened) in front of which we had been halted at the end of 1914.

To drive the enemy from this fortified line, to break down this obstacle, we must assail it by continuing and maintaining the attacks of our already victorious armies. But there was a chance that this method might not suffice; for, should we confine ourselves to it alone, we ran the risk of finding all the enemy reserves massed to meet the onslaught of our Armies, and, aided by a powerful system of fortification, in a position to frustrate our efforts.

If we were to continue our plan of rapidly exploiting the enemy's disorganization, we must launch as soon as possible fresh attacks in new directions, adding to the attacks already under way—and which must be maintained—other attacks capable of absorbing a part of his forces, and, by their convergent directions, make them concord their effects with those produced by our already successful enterprises. In short, we must extend the front of our offensive while keeping it always headed in the same general direction. This was to be the task of the American Army on the right, and of the Belgian Army on the left.

Having settled, on September 2nd, as has been stated, that the Saint-Mihiel operation would take place with limited objectives, I sent the Commanders-in-Chief on September 3rd a General Instruction urging them to hurl the mass of their forces against the line Cambrai—Saint-Quentin—Mézières, where they would reach the principal German lateral railway line. This meant the launching, west of the Meuse, of a new and powerful American attack. The Instruction stated:

"At present the Allied offensive is being developed successfully from the Scarpe to the Aisne and is forcing the enemy to fall back all along that front.

"In order to develop and increase the scope of this offensive, all the Allied forces are being thrown into the battle. They are following converging directions along those positions of the front promising favourable results.

"With this in view and while :

"(1) The British Armies, supported on the left by French Armies, continue to attack in the general direction of Cambrai—Saint-Quentin, and

"(2) The central units of the French Armies continue their efforts to throw the enemy across the Aisne and the Ailette,

"The American Army will carry out the following operations :

"(a) The offensive decided upon for the Woëvre region, reduced to occupying the line of Vigneulles—Thiaucourt—Régnéville, which suffices for ensuring the results in view, viz : disengaging the Paris—Avricourt railway line and securing a satisfactory base of departure for subsequent operations.

"This attack is to start as soon as possible—on September 10th at the latest—in order to allow the enemy no respite.

"(b) An offensive in the general direction of Mézières, as powerful and violent as possible, covered on the east by the Meuse and supported on the left by an attack of the French Fourth Army.

"The last named offensive will be prepared with the greatest rapidity in order that it may be launched, at the latest, between the 20th and 25th of September.

"Its first objective will be to force back the enemy, by

operations on each side of the Argonne, to the line of Stenay—Le Chesne—Attigny, and afterwards to occupy the region of Mézières, manœuvring to the eastwards, so as to overcome the resistance of the Aisne.

" The successive stages of this operation are marked by the lines : Dun, Granpré, Challerange, Somme-Py, Stenay, Le Chesne, Attigny."

In tracing this outline of operations, I by no means gave up the idea of urging vigorous and direct action by the British Armies against the Hindenburg line. On September 8th I wrote asking Sir Douglas Haig " to undertake at once the preparation of an offensive having for its purpose the capture of this line and the advance beyond it towards certain indicated objectives (Valenciennes, Solesmes, Le Câteau, Wassigny). In order to catch the enemy as ill-prepared as possible, it is advisable to launch this offensive without delay."

With the object of increasing to its extreme limit the scope of the operations, I went next day, September 9th, to La Panne, the residence of the King of the Belgians. I pointed out to His Majesty how, owing to the fact that the Germans were shaken and exhausted and that their forces were largely concentrated in France, a most favourable opportunity was presented for defeating them in Belgium and reconquering the province north of the Lys. We discussed the general lines of an operation which might be undertaken with this end in view by the Belgian Army, aided by the British and French armies.

King Albert was in full accord with these views and gave them his approval in principle. I then went to Cassel for a conference with Field-Marshal Sir Douglas Haig, General Plumer and Lieutenant-General Gillain.

FOCH AND H.M. KING ALBERT OF THE BELGIANS.

Here I discussed the project more in detail, and we worked out a plan of operations suitable for giving it effect.

The first requirement was to prepare a base of departure for the capture of the following line : Clercken ridge—Houthulst wood—Passchendaële ridge—Gheluvelt heights—Zandworde—Comines canal ; then march resolutely on the one hand towards Bruges, in order to liberate the Belgian coast, and, on the other, in the direction of Thielt and Ghent. The first operation would require nine Belgian and two British Divisions ; the second would be executed by the bulk of the Belgian Army, the British Second Army, three French Infantry Divisions and three French Cavalry Divisions.

At the close of our conference I handed those participating in it a written note setting forth the decisions arrived at.

Naturally, General Pétain was kept informed of these plans, as also of my intention of placing General Degoutte in charge of them, if occasion arose.

The King of the Belgians having come to Bombon on the morning of September 11th, I requested him to take the command, not only of the Belgian Army, but of the British and French forces designated for these operations. He agreed to do this and personally asked that a formal order to this effect be made out. Since His Majesty also requested that a French General be assigned to him, General Degoutte was definitely detailed for this service and immediately assumed his duties as Chief of Staff of the Allied Army in Flanders, under the orders of King Albert. Lieutenant-General Gillain, Sir Douglas Haig and General Pétain were notified of these decisions. At the same time I asked that pains be taken to see that they were kept absolutely secret.

Sir Douglas had thoroughly entered into my views, for, on the 14th, he answered my letter of September 8th by stating that it was his intention shortly to launch a heavy attack between Vermand and Gouzeaucourt, so as to capture the enemy's defences west of the Saint-Quentin canal and the river Scheldt, thus bringing the British Fourth Army within assaulting distance of the Hindenburg Line.

To aid this action, I ordered General Debeney to support with his left the right wing of the British Fourth Army—this to be henceforth his essential and permanent task. The order stated that " during the period now approaching, the left wing of the French First Army must constantly support the right wing of the British Fourth Army and remain in close liaison with it . . ."

On September 18th, the British Fourth Army, supported by the left of the French First Army and the right of the British Third Army, successfully attacked the line Holnon—Fresnoy-le-Petit—Hargicourt—Lempire—Gouzeaucourt. Every objective was taken : more than 10,000 prisoners and 150 guns fell into its hands. Above all, we achieved our principal object, for our troops were now within attacking distance of the Hindenburg Line. This became all the more important in that Field-Marshal Sir Douglas Haig's intention was to direct his main attack precisely against that portion of the line which lay between Saint-Quentin and Cambrai.

Preparations were at once made with this in view. On September 22nd, Sir Douglas gave orders to his First, Third and Fourth Armies for a general attack on the Hindenburg Line, and, though he still refrained from communicating the date for this attack to his subordinates, he decided in his own mind to launch it on about the 25th.

Meanwhile, General Pétain had been apprised of the intentions of the British Commander-in-Chief, and was asked to reinforce the French First Army without delay, especially with artillery. For this purpose he was instructed to obtain what was necessary, chiefly from the centre of the Reserve Army Group, " where no operations of importance were contemplated for the time being." It was easy for General Pétain to comply with this request, for the front of the Reserve Army Group, as a result of the advance made during the last two months, had become considerably shortened—to such an extent, indeed, that during the first half of September, two of the Armies composing it, the Sixth and Third, had been placed in reserve.

While the Allied forces designated to make the breach in the German fortress were being concentrated (and in order to conceal these movements as much as possible by turning the enemy's attention away from the storm preparing on our left), I made a tour of inspection, from the 19th to the 22nd of September, along the Lorraine and Vosges front. I stopped successively at Chaumont, Saint-Mihiel, Nancy, Lure, Massevaux and Belfort, inspecting our advanced positions and prescribing the immediate preparation of important attacks along this front, as well as the execution of movements preparatory to them.

I returned to my Headquarters at Bombon, and after a conference with the Commanders-in-Chief, I definitely fixed the time schedule for the general offensive from the Meuse to the North Sea, viz:

September 26*th*.—A Franco-American attack between the Suippe and the Meuse.

September 27*th*.—An attack by the British First and Third Armies in the general direction of Cambrai.

September 28th.—An attack by the Flanders Group of Armies between the sea and the Lys, under the command of the King of the Belgians.

September 29th.—An attack by the British Fourth Army, supported by the French First Army, in the direction of Busigny.

The plan for this offensive comprised :

(1) An operation, named " B," to be carried out between the Meuse and the Argonne by the American First Army in the general direction of Buzancy—Stonne.*

(2) An operation, named " C," to be carried out between the Aisne and the Suippe by the French Fourth Army, taking as a general axis the Chalons—Mézières road.

A mixed Franco-American detachment was to manœuvre on the right bank of the Aisne, to ensure liaison between the two operations.

Meanwhile, General Pétain had decided to extend the front of attack of the Central Army Group. This was to be effected by " Operation D "—prescribed for the Fifth Army—" for the purpose of capturing the Rheims forts and the Monts de Champagne in conjunction with the lateral exploitation of the first successes of the Fourth Army."

Operations " B " and " C " were scheduled for September 26th ; operation " D " was to be ready for noon of the 28th.

Finally, in order to profit by the eventual success of the last named operation and to dislodge the enemy from the Chemin-des-Dames, where he might decide to re-establish himself, the Tenth Army had received orders to

* The Woëvre operation (reduction of the Saint-Mihiel Salient) had been denominated " Operation A."

" prepare an action on its right wing in the direction of Chavignon and La Malmaison."

Thus, the Franco-American manœuvre was so prepared that it could be extended, according to the march of events, from the Meuse to the Ailette. These orders, as now perfectly worked out, satisfied me, except for the parts which limited the advance of each Army with the purpose of assuring better liaison between them. This restriction offered the risk of preventing *a priori* the favourable exploitation of opportunities that might arise, and of damping the ardour of the troops, which must at any cost and under all circumstances be upheld.

My preoccupation over this point led me on September 25th to draw up the following note:

" The nature and importance of the operation undertaken for the 26th requires that all its advantages be followed up without the slightest delay; that the rupture of the line of resistance be exploited uninterruptedly to as great a depth as possible. For this reason, halts in the development of the action must be avoided. This applies especially to the advance of the American Army between the Meuse and the French Fourth Army. As the strength of this Army relieves it from all risks, it must, *without further instructions*, and upon the initiative of its Commander, push its advance forward as far as possible.

" The American Army therefore must endeavour before all else to press its advantage as far and as promptly as possible in the direction of Buzancy.

" The French Fourth Army is to cover the American Army by an advance toward the Aisne near Rethel, and this must be executed with similar speed, resolution and initiative. The Fourth Army must in all cases endeavour to maintain liaison with the American Army, *but under no circumstances must it retard the latter's advance, which remains the deciding factor.*

" Hence there must be no question of determining limited objectives for these Armies which they are to reach but not pass unless they get further orders. Such restrictive instructions would tend to prevent full exploitation in the favourable circumstances which may arise, and impair the enthusiasm of the attack—a thing to be maintained above all else.

" Under the conditions now existing, the main thing is to develop before anything the shock power of the Allied Armies.

" The Marshal Commanding-in-Chief the Allied Armies counts upon a spirit of decision and initiative in each of these Armies.

" The General Officers Commanding-in-Chief the Armies of the North and North-east will please make the strongest possible appeal to this spirit."

This message was followed by a second, dated the 27th, dealing with the principles which, under the conditions then existing, should guide the decisions of all responsible executive officers :

" At the point which our affairs have now reached, surprise and extensive attacks launched by us on the enemy compel him to parry our blows immediately when and as he can, in order to support his troops occupying the line. They prevent him from bringing up units in proper form, capable of waging a well-ordered battle, and from assembling artillery and infantry in a defensive position of any considerable extent and prepared in advance—in short, they prevent him from conducting any battle on a large scale, even a defensive one.

" Hence, if we do not give him time enough to pull himself together we shall be confronted everywhere with nothing but disorganized units, mixed-up together, or in any event, improvisations hastily made.

" The use of numerous machine-guns can undoubtedly retard or cover the enemy's retreat. But they do not suffice to create a solid defensive system. And at all events, small units properly manœuvring can get the better of any such methods.

" This being the situation, our attacks must constantly seek to break through. For this purpose attacking groups composed of infantry and artillery should be formed for advancing against objectives the capture of which will break down the enemy's front.

" Therefore, it is important :

" *In Army Corps*, to decide upon and point out distant objectives of capital importance ;

" *In Divisions*, to chose intermediate objectives ;

" *In smaller bodies of troops*, to manœuvre with precision and rapidity against points which hold up their advance, especially machine-gun nests.

" From now on, the progress of the battle depends upon the spirit of decision evinced by Corps Commanders and the initiative and energy shown by Divisional Commanders.

" The issue once more hinges upon the activity of Commanders and the endurance of the troops ; the latter is never found wanting whenever an appeal is made to it."

The Allied offensive operations " B " and " C " were started by the American First Army at 5.30 A.M. on September 26th, and by the French Fourth Army at

5.25 A.M., following a violent artillery preparation. Appreciable gains were at once obtained between the Meuse and the Suippe; along the entire front of attack the enemy's first line was captured, and at several points passed. The average advance of our troops was from two to three miles.

In order to follow more closely the development of the operations, I had installed myself, on the afternoon of the 26th, at the Château de Trois-Fontaines (north of Saint-Didier), and remained there throughout the 27th. In the course of the day I paid visits to General Pétain, who was temporarily at Nettancourt, and to the Headquarters of General Gouraud at Châlons-Sainte-Memmie.

During the 27th and 28th the enemy's resistance stiffened and became more active. The Fourth Army soon came up against defences which the Germans had erected in the valley of the Py, while the American First Army, hampered by flanking fire in the Argonne, was brought to a standstill around Apremont.

However, on September 29th, the French Fourth Army, concentrating its efforts on the centre, succeeded in over-running the line of the Py and driving the enemy back upon a second position between Somme-Py and Monthois. But on its side, the American Army, squeezed into the narrow corridor between the Meuse and the Argonne, opposed by a resistance which was all the stronger because favoured by difficult and broken country, and hampered in its advance by flanking fire both from the Argonne and from the east bank of the Meuse, continued to mark time. It tried to overcome these difficulties by increasing its forces in the front line; but this only intensified these difficulties, and resulted in a complete blocking of its rear and the bottling up of its communications.

To remedy this situation, I decided, in agreement with General Pétain, to withdraw a certain number of Divisions from the American sector of attack, and to use them in part east of the Meuse, and in part west of the Argonne. To avoid all loss of time, it was proposed to incorporate them in French Army Corps already in line. General Pershing was then to take under his orders the Franco-American forces operating on both banks of the Meuse, while a new French Army Commander (Second Army) would take command of the Allied forces operating on each side of the Argonne.

General Weygand was instructed to communicate these measures to General Pershing, who accepted them as a whole, but refused to agree to the placing of another French Army in the Argonne region. In order to satisfy him, I agreed to maintain the organization of the command as it was, " provided the American attacks should be resumed, and, once started, continued without pause . . ."

While the American First Army was restoring order in its units before recommencing operations in the direction of Mézières, the centre and left of the French Fourth Army added the efforts of its centre and left to the attacks of the Fifth Army, aiming at the reduction of the Monts de Champagne and the *massif* of Rheims (Operation " D "). On September 30th the Fifth Army made a surprise attack between the Vesle and the Aisne and, despite strong enemy resistance, forced the Germans back. Continuing its offensive on October 1st, it obtained even more valuable results than the day before, compelling its adversary to cross to the east bank of the Aisne-Marne canal, from Berry-au-Bac to La Neuvilette, leaving behind 2,500 prisoners and some thirty guns. Simultaneously, the Fourth Army aided by the American 2nd Division, attacked and carried the strong German positions on the heights south of Orfeuil, capturing such solid points of support as Notre-Dame-des-Champs and Blanc-Mont, and between October 1st and 3rd taking 18,000 prisoners with 200 guns.

This double success was not long in bearing fruit. During October 5th, 6th and 7th, the Germans carried out an extensive retrograde movement north-east of Rheims, establishing themselves behind the Suippe and the line of the Arnes.

Meanwhile, on October 4th, the American First Army resumed its attacks. Its left and centre, advancing through the Argonne, reached Apremont, Exermont and Gesnes. Its right, hampered by the German flanking positions on the heights east of the Meuse, advanced only slightly. It became absolutely necessary to suppress these flanking positions by capturing the ridge from Dun-sur-Meuse to Damvillers. During the days October 8th to 10th, the French XVII Corps, aided by two American Divisions (33rd and 39th), began operations on the right bank of the river, and, after heavy fighting, got possession of the line Sivry-sur-Meuse—Beaumont.

However considerable the results obtained by the Franco-American offensive, they seemed, nevertheless, " inferior to what it was permissible to expect against an adversary assailed everywhere and resisting at certain points with only worn-out, heterogeneous and hastily-assembled troops, and in a region where his defensive positions had already been captured." Through not having been adequately conducted the battle under way presented some confusion. Those in command,* too

---

* The French words are " le commandement," which is here translated by "those in command."—Translator.

distant from the action, did not seem "to push it personally with the utmost energy, themselves supervising the execution of their orders."

Therefore, General Pétain was asked to give to the High Command (Armies and Groups of Armies) instructions "with a view to ensuring, at the present stage of the war of movement, a personal and active direction of the battle upon the field itself. *To encourage, inspire, and supervise, still remains a chief's principal task.*"

In issuing these instructions, General Pétain again specified the objectives to be attained :

"*By the Fourth Army, march straight to the Aisne in the direction of Rethel.*

"*By the Fifth Army, push towards Neufchâtel and Soissons, in order to aid the movement of the Tenth Army upon Laon.*"

Thus placed, the attacks along the whole front were resumed on October 8th. While the American First Army, having cleared the Argonne, reached the defiles south of Grandpré and captured the heights of Romagne and of Cunel, the French Fourth Army, attacking in force in the direction of Cauroy—Machault, gained a footing on the north bank of the Arnes and on the heights of Monthois. On its left, the Fifth Army assaulted and forced the passage of the Suippe between Aguilcourt and Saint-Etienne, while north of the Aisne, the Tenth Army, pushing forward in its turn, carried the line of the Ailette and gained the heights of Cerny-en-Laonnois and of Jumigny.

These threatening advances struck the enemy a heavy blow. On October 11th, 12th and 13th he found himself obliged to execute a wide movement in retreat along the entire front included between the Aisne at Vouziers and the Oise at La Fère, and to fall back on the strong position (*Hunding Stellung* and *Brünnhilde*

Stellung) established along the general line La Fère—Crécy-sur-Serre—Sissonne—Château-Porcien, and the valley of the Aisne below Grandpré.

On October 15th the Franco-American Armies established touch with this position and made immediate dispositions for assaulting it.

* * * *

Franco-British offensive against the Cambrai—Saint-Quentin front.

On September 27th the British First and Third Armies (Generals Horne and Byng) moved in the direction of Cambrai and attacked the German positions between the Sensée and Villers-Guislain at dawn. They crossed the Canal du Nord and with magnificent dash captured the celebrated points of support of Marquion, Bois-Bourlon and Flesquières, piercing the enemy's lines to a depth of four miles and taking over 8,000 prisoners and 100 guns. On the 28th they followed up their advance, seized Fontaine-Notre-Dame and Marcoing, crossed the Scheldt north of the last-named place, and, the next day, September the 29th, they reached the very gates of Cambrai. The whole of the Hindenburg line that lay in their sector of attack was in their hands.

The British Fourth Army (General Rawlinson) responded to this brilliant victory by an equally successful advance farther south. On September 29th, in its turn, it attacked the Hindenburg position between Vendhuille and Holnon, carried the front lines and, advancing resolutely upon Bohain, crossed the Saint-Quentin canal between Ballicourt and Lahaucourt.

On its right, the French First Army (General Debeney) attacked south of Saint-Quentin, and, after heavy

THE FIRST BRITISH PATROL ENTERS THE STREETS OF CAMBRAI CLOSE ON THE HEELS OF A RETREATING ENEMY, THIRTY-THREE DAYS BEFORE THE ARMISTICE.

fighting, captured the strong point of Cérizy.

The Franco-British offensive was furiously pursued during the next few days. On October 3rd the British Armies, following the Scheldt above Masnières, reached the outskirts of Le Catelet and the ridges east of the Saint-Quentin canal. At the same time the French First Army, having extended its front of attack north of Saint-Quentin, crossed the canal near Le Tronquoy, surrounded the town from the north and from the south, and reoccupied it.

There was nothing left to capture in this region but the last strongholds of the Hindenburg Line. On October 5th, these were assaulted. The British Fourth Army, crossing the Scheldt between Crèvecoeur and Le Catelet, captured the plateau of Beaurevoir—Montbréhain and thereby completed for its sector of attack the conquest of the renowned German position. In contrast to this success, the French First Army, closely held to its mission of " supporting at all costs the right of the British Army," encountered the strongest sort of resistance east and north-east of Saint-Quentin. Renewing its attacks on the following days, it captured Lesdin (October 6th) and advanced upon Fontaine—Uterte. On the 8th it captured the latter, and turned the German defences north-east of Saint-Quentin. Seconded by the progress of the British Fourth Army, it was soon to reap the fruits of its tenacity.

The day the entire Hindenburg Line fell into the hands of his Armies, Sir Douglas Haig had given instructions for exploiting the success without the least delay. Rapid movement must prevent the enemy from having time to re-establish himself solidly on his second line, the *Hunding Stellung*, which, being south of Cambrai, was nearer to the Hindenburg Line than anywhere else. The Field-Marshal therefore ordered his Third and Fourth Armies, still covered on the right by the French First Army, to make a general attack, on October 8th, in the direction of Bohain—Busigny and capture the heights south of Cambrai. This object having been achieved, the British First Army was to try to force the passage of the Scheldt north of the latter town in the vicinity of Ramillies.

In execution of these orders, the assault of the British Third and Fourth Armies was made on October 8th between Cambrai and Sequéhart. It met with complete success, carrying at one blow the *Hunding Stellung* along the whole front prescribed. General Debeney's Army, having seized (as already noted) the high plateau of Fontaine—Uterte, extended and effectively supported the British advance. On October 9th the British First Army, in its turn, forced the passages of the Scheldt at Ramillies and further south.

This victory, succeeding those of the preceding days, was a serious disaster to the Germans, obliging them to effect a wide movement in retreat between the Sensée and the Oise. On October 12th, the Allied advanced guards, pressing the enemy hard, reached the left bank of the Selle between Haspres and Le Câteau, the western edge of the forest of Andigny, and the northern bank of the Oise below Bernot.

Their left now came in contact with a third position which the enemy had erected along the general line of Bouchain—La Capelle—Le Câteau—Hirson—Mézières, while their right faced that part of the *Hunding Stellung* which runs along the western bank of the Oise between Mont d'Origny and the mouth of the Serre.

* * * *

Offensive of the Flanders Group of Armies north of the Lys.

The Flanders Group of Armies was ordered to be formed, as we have seen, on September 11th. The work was pursued with the greatest rapidity. Haste was essential, for here in the low-lands of Flanders, wholly devastated by the war, if the bad season should overtake us while we were still engaged in mere preparations, it would be well nigh impossible to withdraw the Belgian Army from the ground it occupied, or had consolidated, on the left bank of the Yser, and throw it across to the right bank. For both banks of the river were nothing but quagmires, and four years of battle and bombardment had transformed the adjacent land into an almost continuous marsh, which bad weather would make absolutely impassable.

After ensuring a suitable direction for the Flanders Group of Armies (H.M. the King of the Belgians, assisted by General Degoutte and his staff), it became necessary to provide it with the troops necessary to accomplish the mission which fell to it as part of the general Allied offensive. Besides the Belgian Army, there was the British Second Army (General Plumer), the French Second Cavalry Corps and two French Army Corps (VII and XXXIV). In order to furnish them with the necessary equipment, munitions and transport, appeals were made to the British Army, the French Army and even to the Military Governor of Paris. The British Navy promised the co-operation by day and by night of an Air Force detachment.

I insisted that all the means thus placed at the disposal of the King of the Belgians should be used in such a way as to obtain results of the widest possible scope from the start. With this in view, I asked Sir Douglas Haig to take the necessary steps with General Plumer ; and, in order to avoid any mistaken interpretation, I requested him to specify that the entire British Second Army was placed at the disposal of its Commander from the very first day. Its attacks to the north-east of the Comines canal aimed at reaching Zandworde and the heights of Kruisecke as soon as possible.

It was under these conditions that, after an artillery attack lasting three hours, the offensive of the Flanders Army Group was launched on September 28th at 5.30 A.M., in the gap between Dixmude and the Lys. It immediately obtained a great success, capturing the entire German first line and greatly weakening the second.

Next morning, I was in Flanders. I saw in turn General Plumer at Cassel, King Albert at La Panne, and Lieutenant-General Gillain at Houthem. I urged them to push forward rapidly toward Roulers and Thourout. Not that enthusiasm was lacking ! On the 29th Dixmude was reoccupied, and the whole Passchendaële ridge, as well as the strong position of Messines—Wytschaete, fell into the hands of the Allies. In two days nearly 10,000 prisoners and 200 guns were taken.

The advance was continued on the 30th, but hampered by bad weather, progress became slower. The British Second Army, nevertheless, drew nearer to Menin and reached the left bank of the Lys from Warneton to Wervicq.

On October 1st and 2nd, after some unimportant progress had been made, it was decided to call a halt in order to prepare a new and powerful attack, after re-establishing communications with the rear.

For the difficulties of the ground had become only too apparent. While the troops had rapidly pushed forward

M. POINCARÉ SALUTES FOCH AFTER PRESENTING HIM WITH THE BATON OF A MARSHAL OF FRANCE.

across this country—which presented nothing but a succession of more or less continuous shell-holes filled with water—and had come to solid soil, farther to the rear, communications on the right bank of the Yser had been cut in many places and it became clear that it would be impossible to make repairs with earth taken from neighbouring ground, since the place was little more than a marsh.

To supply the troops in battle, both in the matter of food and ammunition, was becoming impossible in certain zones. For a time we were reduced to having thousands of rations transported by air. To make it possible for the convoys to move, it was necessary first of all to repair our lines of communication thoroughly. This required the construction at certain places of miles of roadway supported on piles.

Notwithstanding these difficulties, the result of our incontestable success in Flanders was already becoming noticeable. Menaced by the advance of the Flanders Army Group north of the Lys and by the simultaneous advance of the English Armies south of the Sensée, the Germans again fell back before the British Fifth Army (General Birdwood), operating to the right of the British Second Army, and also in touch with the First.

On October 2nd La Bassée and Lens were reoccupied. On the 3rd, Armentières; on the 4th, the advanced guards of General Birdwood were on the railway from Armentières to Lens and had reached the Haute-Deule canal. Here they established contact with the advanced guards of General Horne, whose left wing likewise was following up the retreating enemy.

Since the 18th of July, we had dealt the Germans blow after blow, and now he was being shaken in Flanders as well as along the rest of the front. This process had prevented him from re-establishing his resistance at any point, and the favourable situation resulting for our Armies could be maintained or even enlarged, provided we exploited it immediately and left him no time for recuperation.

This seemed the more certain since, according to all information received, the Germans had no line of defence in Belgium further back than Douai, to which they might withdraw. Therefore, in letters dated October 6th and 9th, I urged the Flanders Army Group to hurry the resumption of its attacks as much as possible by expediting the repair of its lines of communication.

" The defeat which the enemy has just suffered on the British front," said the last of these letters, " as well as the development of our attacks on the Franco-American front, create at present an exceptionally advantageous situation for the continuation of the offensive in Belgium.

" This state of affairs makes it particularly desirable for you to hasten your attack, and consequently it is most urgently suggested that you push forward your preparations to the utmost."

Nevertheless, despite the good will of everybody, the Flanders Army Group could not be got ready for another attack until October 14th. But on that date, with its troops operating on territory that had not been devastated, and with communications now assured across a region torn by four years of conflict, it was able to resume the battle. If material resources of sufficient power were forthcoming, it would now be in a position to continue its attacks, in no matter what season, until the enemy's resistance was entirely overcome.

CHAPTER XII

THE PROBLEM OF EFFECTIVES, COMMUNICATIONS AND MANUFACTURE OF MUNITIONS IN THE AUTUMN OF 1918

WOULD it indeed be possible to keep up this uninterrupted effort, daily becoming more extensive, which the Allied Armies had furnished since July? This grave question presented itself to the Allied High Command and to the Entente Governments as the autumn of 1918 opened. The problem particularly involved these three points : The maintenance of the strength of the armies in the field, the assurance of the ammunition supply and the restoring of means of communication in reconquered territory.

It must be added that upon the solution given to these problems, both as to extent and time, depended the possibility of the Allied Armies following up their successes and attaining a definite victory by means of an offensive pursued without pause. Delay in meeting material requirements might render our success in part sterile, and might impose upon our forces severe and bloody fighting to overcome a recuperated enemy.

The fact of having mapped out a scheme of operations on July 24th was not sufficient ; it was necessary to provide means for keeping them going.

(1) *Effectives.*

From July 1st to September 15th the *French Army* had lost 7,000 officers and nearly 272,000 men. At the beginning of October most of its Divisions were something between 1,000 to 2,500 men below full strength, all available reinforcements having been incorporated. The situation became even worse during the subsequent weeks, because it was now necessary to add to our losses in battle those occasioned by having to divert men for the repair of communications in the rear.

Nevertheless, we were maintaining the same number of Divisions, the momentary deficits in their strength were being met by various devices adopted in the internal structure of the component units. It was for that reason that General Pétain had decreased the theoretical strength of the Divisional centres of instruction, reduced the strength of infantry companies to 175 men and ordered the General Officer Commanding the Tank Corps to rectify his deficiencies in men, munitions, material and stores by similar methods.

To replace our losses in the matter of horses also presented serious difficulties. France's resources having been almost exhausted, we were obliged, in and after September, to import from America some 10,000 horses monthly, and this had the disadvantage of absorbing part of the tonnage required for transporting American troops. Moreover, long delays ensued before these horses were ready for service. To meet the emergency, General Pétain was obliged to adopt certain temporary expedients, such as ordering those responsible Generals to send forward only a number of units or batteries proportional to the available horses ; or else to decrease by one gun per battery all horse-drawn formations.

The *British Army* had lost, from July 1st to September 15th, 7,700 officers and 166,000 men ; and, as with the French army, it was unable to fill the gaps in the ranks. The Government in London, being inclined to give aviation and tanks a perhaps exaggerated importance in relation to the combatant forces as a whole, favoured the suppression of some infantry Divisions. At a conference held on October 7th at Versailles, with Mr. Lloyd George presiding, I was compelled to protest against this intention, and I succeeded in obtaining a decision that the number of British Divisions would be maintained intact, even if it should become necessary to reduce temporarily the number of men in each. I also suggested to General Sir Henry Wilson that some of the fresh British Divisions in Italy be substituted for some of the exhausted Divisions in France, sending the latter for recuperation across the Alps.

The *Italian II Corps* was 13,000 men short, following the attacks in which it participated during the summer on the French front, and the Government in Rome wanted to make good the reconstitution of this Corps by having all the labourers lent to France by the agreement of January 13th, 1918, sent back to Italy.

Fortunately, M. Clemenceau arranged that this repatriation should be discussed by the Commanders-in-Chief concerned. I succeeded in convincing General Diaz that the recall of all the Italian labourers would be a great hindrance to the French Army; it was therefore agreed that only 4,000 of the labourers should return. Moreover, in order to justify the retention in France of the Italian auxiliaries, General Pétain was asked to establish an organization " guaranteeing the rational and full-time employment of the labourers under his orders," and to exercise a rigid control over the work performed.

Finally, the Italian II Corps was brought up to strength by drafting a certain number of men from among the best of the labourers and by reinforcements arriving from Italy.

Even the *American Army* showed a deficit in men. For

a total of thirty Divisions at the front on October 10th, 90,000 were lacking. This shrinkage, it must be admitted, was merely temporary, since the transport of men from America to France was being pushed forward most energetically. Nevertheless, it might have somewhat hampered the projected operations for the moment. General Pershing thought it his duty to inform me of the situation, and he asked me whether there did not seem cause to change my programme. Naturally, I maintained the full programme of attack decided upon.

Another difficulty was presented by the necessity of furnishing the American Army with the numerous horses required for the organization of its Divisions. The policy of sending at first only infantry and machine-gun units had caused the postponement of shipment of the necessary horses from the United States to France. This particularly affected artillery units. Purchases of horses in Spain and some drafts on the French and British stocks had made it possible to meet the first requirements, but, from September onwards, reliance had to be placed solely on importations from America. This—as we have already stated with regard to the French army—was attended with considerable inconvenience.

These few points show the efforts which, during the autumn of 1918, were demanded of commanders of the various armies and their staffs to keep up the strength of the Allied forces. Though it was found impossible to obtain the complete solution desired, nevertheless the emergency measures I was obliged to adopt were always inspired by the two-fold purpose of seeing that the progress of the operations was not retarded, and that the number of Allied Divisions was at all costs maintained.

Arms and munitions. Though not quite so difficult a

problem as keeping up the strength of the various armies, that of munitions also caused a certain degree of worry.

Towards the end of July, Monsieur Loucheur, Minister of Munitions, told me that the average consumption of shells for the 75 mm. gun amounted, in the French army, to 280,000 a day, whereas only 220,000 were being manufactured. Therefore he was being forced to draw the surplus needed from stocks on hand. During August the situation became actually critical, owing to the delays in receiving steel from America. I had to ask General Pershing to take action with his Government in order to hasten the shipments.

On his side, General Pétain gave orders on several occasions and in very severe terms to his subordinates, demanding the exercise of a close supervision over the expenditure of ammunition.

The crisis was not entirely overcome until October, when the United States began sending completely finished shells to France.

The French war munition service had to make a considerable effort to construct and keep in order the numerous machines needed for fighting—guns, aircraft and tanks, to mention only a few. But we had not only our own needs to meet, but also most of those of the American Army, since American factories were not yet able to supply all the material required. I often received visits at my Headquarters from officials occupied with these questions—MM Clemenceau, Loucheur, Tardieu, General Bourgeois, General Le Rond, etc. I discussed with them the progress being made in manufacture, both in France and America ; what supplies were to be turned over to the Americans ; how much metal was to be asked from them in exchange ; what purchases were to be made in England, and so forth.

In order to decrease our importations of coal and thus increase the ocean tonnage available, I discussed with Sir Douglas Haig, at the request of M. Loucheur, the possibility of getting the British Army to turn over 4,000 prisoners of war for labour in the mines in central France. Sir Douglas, however, found it impossible to accede to this request.

Communications. The systematic devastation effected by the Germans in the areas which their defeat forced them to evacuate is well known. Much of the destruction was in no way justified by the exigencies of war, but was due solely to that "joy in wreaking damage" (*Schadenfreude*) which our enemy had made into a veritable dogma, and which he employed as a war instrument.

On September 6th I asked M. Clemenceau to demand of the Germans that they " refrain from these barbaric acts, under pain of incurring the gravest responsibilities and the severest reprisals." In spite of this threat, they continued their acts of wilful damage in northern France and in Belgium, up to the very day of the Armistice.

In addition to this destruction which nothing could justify, there was also more which conformed to the necessities of war, such as damaging railways, navigable waterways and roads. This seriously retarded the advance of the Allied Armies. The restoration of these lines of communication was one of the most important problems which I and my staff had to solve during the autumn of 1918. It required simultaneously active direction, experienced personnel and a considerable amount of material.

The management of this work was reorganized in August, 1918, and turned over to the Commander of the Allied Armies. At its head was placed a French

General Officer* charged primarily with the duty of meeting the general necessities of the Allied Armies in what concerned supplies and communications, more especially in reconquered territory. Hence his title : Director General of Army Supplies and Communications.

To recruit the necessary personnel for restoring and maintaining the lines of communication destroyed by the enemy was no easy matter. Despite the diminished effectives from which the Allied Armies were already suffering, they were obliged to furnish a large part of this special labour force. For instance, the French Army supplied nearly 100,000 men for railway work. For the remainder, we were forced to take anything we could find : civilians who had been held by the Germans, workmen replaced in factories by prisoners of war, civilian prisoners, etc. At one time, Belgium furnished personnel for service in Northern France.

The material required for repairing railways was supplied partly from French, partly from British or American mills. From the United States 70,000 tons of rails arrived each month, making it possible to repair about 120 miles of lines. Most of the engines were repaired by the efforts of the Ministry of Munitions.

I also had to devote my attention to the organization on the liberated Belgian coast, of harbour and marine services, concerning which I gave instructions to General Degoutte.

The hasty sketch just given of the problem presented by munitions, communications and man power is made with the sole purpose of showing how it weighed upon the development of operations during the autumn of 1918, and of indicating, in a general way, its magnitude, the difficulties attending its solution, and the efforts made to that end.

* General Payot.

CHAPTER XIII

GENERAL OFFENSIVE OF THE ALLIED ARMIES FROM OCTOBER 15TH TO NOVEMBER 11TH, 1918

Combined manœuvre of the British Armies and the Flanders Group of Armies between the Oise and the North Sea—Combined manœuvre of French Armies and of the American First Army between the Oise and the Meuse—Manœuvre prepared east of the Meuse—General retreat of the German Armies on the whole line from the Meuse to the sea.

IN their advance along a front 200 miles wide, from the North Sea to the Meuse, the Allied Armies, each launched in its own direction, were destined to meet various enemy positions more or less strongly organized and more or less strongly manned. It was difficult to estimate beforehand what degree of resistance these various positions were capable of offering, except by taking into consideration the nature of the ground lying in front of each Army, and the rate of progress it had already attained. But speaking generally, the ground became lower and flatter as we moved from the right to the left of the Allied line—from the hilly banks of the Meuse to the great plains of Flanders, where, from the earliest days to Waterloo, the destines of Europe had been so often decided.

It was in the region north of the Oise that it was easiest for us to accumulate and employ our superiority of numbers, a superiority which in our day consists chiefly of having more stores and larger supplies of ammunition than the enemy. The marked advance made in this region by the British Armies was an illustration of this. The advantage of pushing it was already apparent. Moreover, by reason of the convergent direction of our movements, the blows successfully delivered on one part of the enemy's defensive system must be made to react upon neighbouring parts, turning them and thus causing their fall, even though they were still capable of offering resistance.

On October 10th I invited Sir Douglas Haig's attention to this situation and at the same time I instructed General Pétain to reinforce the French First Army operating on the right of the British. My letter was as follows :

" To day, October 10th, operations are being pursued in three converging directions :

" (1) In Belgium.

" (2) Along the Solesmes—Wassigny front.

" (3) Along the Aisne—Meuse front.

" Of these, the one most advantageous to exploit— thanks to the success obtained by the British Armies—is that of Solesmes—Wassigny. Therefore operations along this direction must be pursued in the greatest possible strength, in order not only to advance towards Mons and Avesnes, but also to develop :

" (a) A manœuvre in combination with the Belgian offensive, having as its objective the clearing of the Lille region ; to be executed by the British forces in a north-easterly direction, between the Scheldt and the Sambre.

" In order to make possible this extension of the British attacks northward, the limit of the zones of action between the British and French Armies is hereby prolonged to the General line, south of Wassigny— south of Avesnes.

" (b) A manœuvre in combination with the Aisne— Meuse offensive, with a view to turning the line of the Serre ; to be executed by the French First Army.

" Therefore, the first available French reinforcements

are to be given to the First Army, in order that it may carry out this manœuvre. Forces which may later become available are to be used for feeding either the attack in Belgium or that of the Aisne—Meuse."

On October 15th the Franco-American Armies between the Oise and the Argonne, headed toward Mézières, came into contact with a strong German position (*Hunding Stellung* and *Brünnhilde Stellung*) established along the general line La Fère—Crécy-sur-Serre —Sissonne—Château-Porcien—Vouziers—Grand-pré.

North of the Oise, the British Armies, marching on Mons and Avesnes, reached that same day the front Wassigny—Le Câteau—Solesmes—Douai. They had thus, from the south, turned the region of Lille, which was likewise threatened from the north by the Flanders Group of Armies between the Lys and the sea.

For, on October 14th, this Army Group arrived on firm ground and, free from all worry as to its lines of communications (now completely restored), had resumed the offensive between Zarren and Werwicq under excellent conditions. Two American Divisions, taken from those which had already participated in attacks, had been sent to support its action. In addition, for the purpose of assuring to the Flanders command an organization commensurate with the increase of French forces in that region, General de Boissoudy was placed at the head of the Sixth Army, while General Degoutte, under the direction of the King of the Belgians, devoted himself exclusively to conducting the operations.

Thus reinforced, the Flanders Army Group uninterruptedly continued its movement toward Thourout, Courtrai and Menin, gaining ground rapidly. On the 14th, it took possession of Hooglede, Roulers and Moorseele ; on the 15th it marched beyond Cortemarck, reached the gates of Courtrai, and entered Menin and Werwicq. On the 16th, Thourout, Lichterwelde, Ardoye and Iseghem fell into its hands.

Then the enemy gave way. He evacuated the entire Belgian coast, including his armoured batteries and submarine bases, which, for months and years, had threatened England and the English lines of communication with France.

On the 17th the Belgian Army re-occupied Ostend, and on the 19th, Blankenberghe and Zeebrugge. On the 20th it reached the Dutch frontier and the Shipdonk canal, at the moment King Albert was making his triumphal entry into liberated Bruges.

The Flanders Army Group had accomplished the task prescribed for it five weeks before by the Commander-in-Chief of the Allied Armies, viz: "To defeat the enemy in Belgium and reconquer the province north of the Lys."

On October 22nd I came in person to congratulate those who had won this victory, and, making a new appeal to them, I asked them to resume their forward march at once, as soon as they had reorganized their units, and had put their communications in order, especially the port and marine services along the liberated Belgian coast.

During this advance of the Flanders Army Group between the North Sea and the Lys, the right of the British Armies continued its attacks toward Wassigny and Solesmes, according to plan. On October 17th, the British Fourth Army took Le Câteau in the face of very strong resistance from the enemy. On the 18th and 19th, having captured Wassigny and the Andigny woods, it threw the Germans back to the eastern bank of the Sambre—Oise canal. Then, pushing its left wing beyond the Selle, in conjunction with the British Third Army, it gained possession of Solesmes (October 20th) and advanced to the edge of Landrecies and the Mormal Forest (October 24th).

On its left, the British Third Army, clearing the ground south of the Sensée, forced the passages of the Ecaillon and reached the gates of Le Quesnoy and Valenciennes (October 24th and 26th).

While the double manœuvre in the north was thus being developed by the Flanders Group of Armies on the left and by the left wing of the British Armies on the right, the centre, composed of the British First and Fifth Armies, pressing the enemy in front, gave the finishing touch which compelled him to execute a general retreat. This retirement, begun on October 17th on the front between the Lys and the Scarpe, lasted ten days. On October 17th, Lille and Douai were reoccupied ; on the 18th, Tourcoing and Roubaix ; on the 19th, Marchiennes and Bouchain ; on the 20th, Denain ; on the 21st, Saint-Amand. By the 27th, the British lined the left bank of the Scheldt from Tournai to Valenciennes.

The right wing of the Flanders Group of Armies, thrown anew into the attack, crossed the Lys between Courtrai and the Roulers—Audenarde railway line, captured Courtrai on October 19th, and pressed forward immediately towards the Scheldt, which it reached between Avelghem and Tournai (October 20th-26th).

Profiting from this success, the left and centre of the Flanders Army Group attacked again on October 31st, and after four days of battle threw the enemy back to the right bank of the Scheldt.

Thus the manœuvre prescribed in my order of October 10th was being developed north of the Oise under the best possible conditions.

Indeed, by the 19th of October I was able to direct the efforts of our Armies on this part of the battlefield towards fresh objectives, while constantly pushing those on the right wing toward their common goal, Mézières.

I therefore ordered :

" For the purpose of exploiting the advantages already gained, the operations of the Allied Armies will be continued as follows :

" (1) *The Flanders Group of Armies* will march in the general direction of Brussels, its right towards Hal, reaching the Scheldt at Pecq, the Dender at Lessines.

" During this march, important waterways such as the Scheldt and the Dender will be forced by combining, if need be, with a flank movement on the part of the British Armies, so as to turn these streams.

" (2) *The British Armies* (Fifth, Third, First, Fourth) will advance south of the line Pecq—Lessines—Hal, their right marching via Froidchapelle and Philippeville, upon Agimont, north of Givet.

" The mission of the British Armies continues to be to throw the enemy back upon the almost impenetrable *massif* of the Ardennes at the point where this obstacle cuts his principal transversal line. At the same time, the advance of the Flanders Army Group must be aided in effecting a crossing of the various water courses (Scheldt, Dender), which might lie across its march.

" The British Armies will be supported by the French First Army.

" (3) *The French Armies* (First, Tenth, Fifth, Fourth) and the American First Army will operate south of the above-mentioned line.

" Their rôles will be as follows :

" For the French First Army, to support the attack of the British Armies by marching towards La Capelle, Chimay, Givet, and to manœuvre by its right in order to turn the enemy resistance presented on the line Serre—Sissonne.

"For the French Fifth and Sixth Armies and the American First Army, to reach the region Mézières, Sedan and the Meuse above that place, causing the line of the Aisne to fall, through a manœuvre on both wings—the left (French Fifth Army) directed towards Château-Porcien, the right (French Fourth Army and American First Army), towards Busancy—Le Chesne."

As will have been noted, the French First Army was to continue in support of the British Armies, and at the same time turn the enemy resistance on the Serre—Sissonne line. It is this second part of its task which will now be examined by giving it its place in the general plan of the Franco-American offensive under way between the Oise and the Meuse.

Attacking in liaison with the British right, and profiting by the latter's advance on Wassigny, the French First Army captured, between October 18th and 26th, the entrenchments of the *Hunding Stellung* between the Oise at Mont d'Origny, and the Serre below Assis. This success gave the Tenth Army an opportunity to outflank the lines of the Serre and the Aisne. Attacking with its right north-east of Laon, it captured Verneuil-sur-Serre and Notre-Dame-de-Liesse and crossed the drainage canal between Vesle and Pierrepont.

Under the pressure of this double action, the Germans, on the 27th, evacuated a wide band of territory between Guise on the Oise and Crécy-sur-Serre.

The French Fifth Army, conforming to its orders, attacked at the same time west of Chaumont—Porcien, and succeeded, on the 25th, in capturing, together with the heights of Banogne—Recouvrance, the last portion of the *Hunding Stellung* remaining in German hands—that lying between Saint-Quentin and the Aisne.

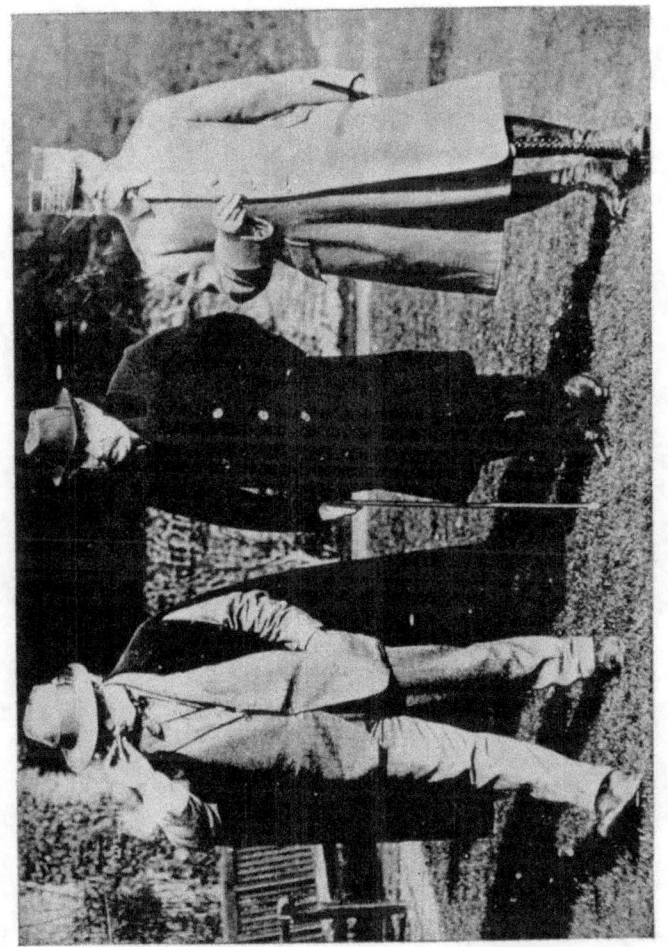

MR. LLOYD GEORGE, M. BRIAND AND MARSHAL FOCH.

Thus, at the end of October, the manœuvre prescribed for the left wing of the French Armies on October 19th, and having for its object the capture of the line of the Aisne, was moving as smoothly as possible.

Let us turn now to the right wing and see what the French Fourth Army and the American First Army were doing at this same moment.

By the middle of October, after three weeks of bitter and costly fighting, the American First Army had reached the defile of Grandpré on its left, and, on its centre, the heights of Romagne-sous-Montfaucon.

The advance through the Argonne from south to north had presented undeniable difficulties to the American Staffs. Most of the roads in this region run from west to east, and the hilly nature of the country makes easy organization of new lines of communication impossible. Hence the varied difficulties encountered in supplying the numerous American troops engaged in the battle ; and yet their enthusiasm had to be kept up at any price, and their violent efforts sustained.

Instead of supplying the aid of French direction, which might surely have smoothed over some of the difficulties, it seemed to me that the most efficacious way of facilitating the American task was to rely upon the spirit of initiative of the American High Command itself and, for that purpose, to establish direct relations—on the same footing as those existing with the Commander-in-Chief of the French Armies, the Commander-in-Chief of the British Armies and the King Commanding the Belgian Army—between the Allied High Command and General Pershing, Commander-in-Chief of the American Armies, of which the First was operating on the Argonne front, and the Second in the Woëvre region, not to mention the other American troops distributed along the front. At the point which American cooperation had now reached, I believed that this was the arrangement which would enable the Americans, working side by side with the other Allied Armies engaged in the battle to strike the heaviest blows at the enemy. The American Armies would be fighting with the Stars and Stripes floating over them, under a leadership which had always given evidence of magnificent authority, and with Staffs bringing their talents to the aid of soldiers animated by an incontestable ardour.

In order to augment the effort demanded of the American Army, I did not hesitate to increase the scope of its command. The autonomy of this force had been fully established, and now, in order to effect a concordance between operations in the Argonne and those in Champagne, as well as a close union of efforts, General Maistre, who commanded the Central French Army Group, was charged with assuring co-ordination between the operations of the French troops on the right of his group, and those of the American First Army.

The delay in the Argonne operations had been otherwise interpreted in certain quarters less acquainted with the difficulties encountered by commanders in handling the masses of modern armies. It was thus that M. Clemenceau, impressed by the " marking time " of the American Army, wrote me on October 21st the letter which I quote below, and which had in view nothing less than to effect a change in the chief command of the American Army :

" I have postponed from day to day writing you about the crisis existing in the American Army. It is not that I have anything to tell you regarding a state of affairs which assuredly you know better than anybody else, since, as Commander-in-Chief of the Allied Armies, you are necessarily the first to suffer from its consequences. We have talked too often and at too great a length concerning the employment of the American troops for it to be necessary to revert to the subject to-day, even in the most summary fashion.

" You have watched at close range the development of General Pershing's exactions. Unfortunately, thanks to his invincible obstinacy, he has won out against you as well as against your immediate subordinates. To go over all this again can only lead to useless regrets.

" You are in the midst of the action, so that past events and mere words are out of place here. What matters is the immense battle now going on, a battle which you have conducted in such a way as to place you in the front rank of great captains. It is this battle in its present stage that I am now thinking of, in the hope of furnishing you with the military means of bringing to a magnificent conclusion the succession of glorious feats of arms with which your name will be for ever associated.

" Constitutionally, I am the head of the French Army.

" The interests of this Army lie only too obviously in the parallel organization of all the troops under your command.

" I would be a criminal if I allowed the French Army to wear itself out indefinitely in battle, without doing everything in my power to ensure that an Allied Army which has hurried to its aid was rendered capable of fulfilling the military rôle for which it is destined.

" The French Army and the British Army, without a moment's respite, have been daily fighting, for the last three months, battles which are using them up at a time when it is impossible for us to reinforce them immediately with fresh effectives. These two Armies are pressing back the enemy with an ardour that excites world-wide admiration; but our worthy American Allies, who thirst to get into action and who are unanimously acknowledged to be great soldiers, have been marking time ever since their forward jump on the first day; and in spite of heavy losses, they have failed to conquer the ground assigned them as their objective. Nobody can maintain that these fine troops are unusable; they are merely unused.

"One does not have to be a technician in order to understand that the immobility of your right wing cannot possibly be a part of your plan and that we have lost—no matter how favourably other things may have turned out—the benefit of movements which, through lack of organization, have not been effected. I am aware of all the efforts you have made to overcome the resistance of General Pershing; indeed, it is because you have omitted nothing in the way of persuasion that I cannot shirk the duty of asking myself whether, after the failure of fruitless conversations, the time has not come for changing methods.

"When General Pershing refused to obey your orders, you could have appealed to President Wilson. For reasons which you considered more important, you put off this solution of the conflict, fearing that it would bring reactions of a magnitude which you thought it difficult to gauge.

"I took the liberty of differing with you. You had a right to think that I was resorting too hastily to a radical solution of the problem. You wished to prolong the experience.

"Now that I have learned, however, that you have taken in hand the direct command of General Pershing's troops, I cannot refrain from feeling that this trial should be the last of those we have been compelled to undergo.

I ardently wish you success, and it may come, provided it is possible for you, through some miracle, to combine the separate direction of one Army with the general conduct along comprehensive lines of the Allied Armies as a whole.

" I think that it will not take long for you to make up your mind on this subject. If General Pershing finally resigns himself to obedience, if he accepts the advice of capable Generals, whose presence at his side he has until now permitted only that he might reject their counsels, I shall be wholly delighted.

" But if this new attempt to reconcile two contrary points of view should not bring the advantageous results you anticipate, I must say to you that, in my opinion, any further hesitation should be out of the question. For it would then be certainly high time to tell President Wilson the truth and the whole truth concerning the situation of the American troops. Indeed, neither you nor I have the right to conceal it from him.

" The President of the United States has frequently declared that he was ready to conform to your judgment in all military questions. He will undoubtedly appraise at their true value, as he ought to do, both the patience you have so long shown and the decision to which you have finally been led.

" Whether you share my opinion or form a different one, you will certainly agree with me in recognizing that this state of affairs cannot continue any longer. For this reason, I would be glad if you could find it possible to send me an early answer.

" The reason why I have deemed it my duty to offer you these observations is that, in the present circumstance, the responsibility of the French Government and of the constitutional head of the French Armies is no less directly involved than is your own. I feel sure that you cannot misinterpret the sentiment which inspires me and I hope you will do justice to my motives, as I do to yours.

"(Signed) CLEMENCEAU."

Having a more comprehensive knowledge of the difficulties encountered by the American Army, I could not acquiesce in the radical solution contemplated by Monsieur Clemenceau. Not wishing, however, to start a discussion of this subject with the French Prime Minister, I confined myself to maintaining my orders and to answering him, on October 23rd, as follows:

"The American Divisions, on October 20th, were thus distributed:

	INFANTRY DIVISIONS FIT FOR BATTLE.		
	In the French and British Armies	Under the orders of Gen. Pershing.	
On the French front:			
In the Vosges	3		
With the French Fourth Army	2		
With the French Army in Flanders	2		
Distributed among various French Divisions	1		
On the British front:		2	
Under the orders of General Pershing:			
In the Argonne and Lorraine:			
In the first line		14	
In the second line		6	
TOTAL	10	20	30
	30		
At bases		9	
Being disembarked		4	13
GRAND TOTAL			43

508

"As shown by the above table, of the thirty Divisions fit for battle, ten are distributed among the Allied Armies (French and British) and twenty are under General Pershing's orders, constituting the self-contained American Army.

"I count upon maintaining these two categories, differing in their nature and the existence of which I consider necessary for various reasons.

"I also contemplate varying the proportion between the two according to circumstances, increasing the ten and diminishing the twenty, whenever operations being prepared permit it.

"It is by manipulation of this sort that I expect to diminish the weaknesses of the High Command, rather than by orders. These I shall give, to be sure, but the High Command may not perhaps be in a position to have them executed, since to do so would require Corps and Divisional Commanders and Staffs having the necessary experience. Moreover, this crisis is of the sort from which all improvised Armies suffer, and which always considerably impairs their effectiveness at the start.

"But there is no denying the magnitude of the effort made by the American Army. After attacking at Saint-Mihiel on September 12th, it attacked in the Argonne on the 26th. From September 26th to October 20th its losses in battle were 54,158 men—in exchange for small gains on a narrow front, it is true, but over particularly difficult country and in the face of serious resistance by the enemy."

In the meantime, with a view to hastening as much as possible the resumption of the combined offensive of the French Fourth Army and the American First Army, and in order to render their progress easier, I drew up, on

October 21st, a General Instruction, setting forth the objectives to be attained and the methods to be employed in reaching them :

"For the purpose of assuring close co-operation between the American First Army and the French Fourth Army, it is advisable to observe the following :
"The general aim of the combined operations of the American First Army and the right wing of the French Fourth Army is to reach the region of Buzancy (for the American First Army), and Le Chesne (for the French Fourth Army), in order to liberate the line of the Aisne from the east.

"The operations which these Armies have been conducting up to the present in the region of Olizy—Grandpré, north of Saint-Juvin, have resulted in assuring complete liaison between them through the defile of Grandpré and permitting the American Army to debouch from the wooded region which had hampered its first movements.

"Now that this first indispensable result has been obtained, the combined attacks of these Armies should have as their object the capture of the goal fixed for them (Buzancy—Le Chesne) by turning, from the west and from the east, the wooded heights of the Argonne, by movements of wider scope ; this will obviate exhausting the troops by fighting in the woods, which is costly, and of little value.

"To accomplish this, the following is necessary :
"(1) That the American First Army prepare and execute *without the least delay* a powerful attack in the direction of Boult-aux-Bois, Buzancy and the Bois-de-la-Folie, and thus take advantage of the wide opening so gained by it north of the Bois-des-Loges and of

Romagne, while avoiding direct engagements in actions in the woods of the Argonne and of the Bantheville region.

"Nothing but an attack of this amplitude will enable it to reach its objectives.

"(2) That the French Fourth Army, maintaining through Grandpré its touch with the American Army, should act *rapidly* and in strong force through Vouziers against Quatre Champs, and, by way of Vandy and Terron and farther north, against Les Alleux; likewise towards Le Chesne, resolutely widening its attacks.

"The attention of the G.O.C.-in-C. the American Army and of the G.O.C. the Centre Group of Armies is invited to the above instructions, which have as their purpose both to enlarge the sphere of action of each of these Armies and to assure the convergence of their efforts upon the objectives assigned.

"They are requested to be good enough to inform me as to the measures they each intend to take to carry out these orders, as well as the arrangements they arrive at for co-ordinating their efforts."

My intention was thus to launch an enlarged Franco-American offensive on both sides of the Argonne, over territory for the most part easy to traverse.

The preliminary plans drawn up by the French Fourth Army and the American First Army for the execution of this manœuvre did not entirely correspond with my conception of its conduct. The movements they presented gave evidence of a rigidity which might conceivably hamper the rapid exploitation of any success achieved. They indicated a return to the method of attack which consisted in marking beforehand on the map successive lines to be reached, and betrayed an exaggerated solicitude in the matter of alignment.

In my opinion, this was by no means the style which should characterize operations at this moment, because :

"Important results such as we are pursuing in the present stage of the war, when we are confronted by an enemy whose exhaustion increases every day, can only be achieved by progress as rapid and as deep as possible.

"Troops launched upon an attack need not think of anything except *the direction of their attack*. In that direction they must go as far as they can, attacking and manœuvring against the resisting enemy with no preoccupation as to alignment; units which have got the farthest forward working for the advantage of those temporarily delayed. They must operate not against lines indicated *a priori*, and suggested by the nature of the ground, but against the enemy; and once they have seized him, they must never let go their grip."

Though he shared this point of view in principle, as regards "direction of exploitation along which the advance is to be resolutely pushed, with no preconceived notions and without thinking about alignment," General Pétain thought that in practice it was impossible to escape from fixing successive objectives to be attained. In his opinion, "whether one is breaking through a fortified zone or attacking in open country, this procedure is indicated. For, in the face of an opponent who defends himself, it is always necessary that efforts succeed each other as a function of: (1) The amount of support which this or that fortified point, this or that peculiarity of the ground, may give or seem to give to the enemy; and (2) the possibility of bringing to bear fire action (artillery or infantry).

However, on November 1st, General Pétain sent out

to his troops a General Instruction reconciling the two points of view:

"The designation of successive lines of objectives," he wrote, "must never be allowed to hamper the dash of attacking troops nor diminish the chances of pushing forward as far as possible. . . .

"It follows that to lay down such objectives is justified as a general procedure only during the phase when the rupture of a fortified line is being effected.

"As soon as pursuit begins, speed becomes the principal factor of success, and the idea of direction must take precedence over everything else in the mind of a Commander. Once the enemy has been seized, the hold on him must not be relaxed. . . .

"When this moment arrives, the only thing which need concern any unit is the direction of exploitation assigned to it, and along which it must boldly push forward, without stopping to regulate its advance with that of its neighbours. . . ."

Complete identity of views thus existed between the Commander-in-Chief of the Allied Armies and the Commander-in-Chief of the French Armies.

It was now important to pass from theory to action. For that reason General Pershing was urged to hasten the launching of his offensive west of the Meuse:

"It is of the highest importance," the Allied Commander-in-Chief wrote him on October 27th, "that the American First Army be ready to begin operations on the date decided upon, namely November 1st, and that it be able to continue them until important and certain results have been attained."

I therefore prescribed that the attacks to be undertaken by the American First Army on November 1st should be pushed forward and continued without any pause until this Army was in possession of Boult-aux-Bois—Buzancy, and the ground further to the east, and had assured the occupation of this region, as a first result to be obtained.

These attacks were facilitated by successive actions which the French Fourth Army had been developing since October 13th east of Vouziers. These attacks, having assured a bridge-head on the right bank of the Aisne between Vandy and Falaise, now enabled it to draw upon itself a considerable part of the German troops in the Argonne, thus relieving the pressure on the American Army.

It was under these conditions that the American offensive was carried out on November 1st. From the beginning it achieved brilliant success, capturing the first day the enemy positions as far as the Buzancy—Stenay road, while on the left the French Fourth Army extended its foothold east of the Aisne.

Orders were now given to develop the advantages obtained without delay by continuing the combined Franco-American operations in the direction of Sedan and Mézières.

Severely shaken, the enemy, between the Aisne and the Meuse, was not long in beginning a retreat. On November 2nd, Croix-aux-Bois, Buzancy, Villers-devant-Dun and Doulcon fell into our hands. On the 3rd the entire northern part of the Argonne was cleared, the heights of Belval were occupied and our troops lined the left bank of the Meuse as far as Dun. On the 4th, the Franco-American advance was continued beyond Stenay and Le Chesne, penetrating into the wooded region south of Beaumont and progressing along the Meuse almost to Stenay.

I warmly congratulated General Pershing on the very important results obtained, " thanks to the ability shown by Commanders and the energy and bravery of the troops." I urged him to continue his operations " in the direction of the Meuse around Bazeilles and up-stream from there," and to extend them as much as possible on the right bank of that river.

In view of the withdrawal of the Austrian Divisions from France, as a consequence of the Armistice concluded with Austria, General Pershing had been asked a few days before to have the American Second Army execute, with the means at its disposal, " local operations sufficiently vigorous to reconnoitre the enemy positions and develop whatever partial success may be obtained."

But what was now happening east of the Meuse?

*   *   *   *   *

Mention has already been made of the action of the French XVII Corps, reinforced by two American Divisions (33rd and 29th), in prolonging, from October 8th to 10th, along the right bank of the Meuse, the offensive being conducted on the left bank by the main body of the American Army, and how, after hard fighting, this force had reached the line Sivry-sur-Meuse—Beaumont.

Continuing these operations on the ensuing days, it had met with constantly increasing resistance from the enemy, and the means at its disposal were insufficient to overcome the obstacles which its advance encountered. Its gains became more and more modest. The enemy seemed firmly resolved to hold the right bank of the Meuse at all costs—an assumption which was all the more plausible since this was his sole chance of covering and assuring the retreat of his beaten Armies on his right wing and centre.

With the idea of frustrating this scheme, by taking the Meuse defences in rear, the Allied High Command decided that the time had come to make an attack along both banks of the Moselle in the general direction of Longwy—Luxembourg on one hand, and of the Sarre on the other.

On October 20th, the following instructions were given General Pétain :

"The operations now under way are intended to throw the enemy back on the Meuse at Stenay and below that place. To overcome his resistance on this river, by turning the position, attacks should be prepared west and east of the Moselle, moving in the general direction of Longwy—Luxembourg on one side, and of the Sarre on the other.

"The chance of a rapid success for these attacks will be in proportion to the promptness with which they are made, since the enemy has at present in line 127 Divisions west of the Meuse and only thirty-two Divisions east of that river.

"Their chances are also increased by the fact that the enemy will soon be deprived of his principal lateral railway line from Mézières to Sedan.

"Therefore, it would be well to utilize French troops released by the shortening of our line, in those parts of the Lorraine front, west and east of the Moselle, where our accumulation of munitions and the nature of the ground permit immediate action.

"It would also be useful to examine in what way the American forces available, or rendered in part available by the advance being made on the left bank of the Meuse, might best participate in these operations as soon as they can be directed in a new direction."

This decision to attack in the Moselle region seemed all the more justified in view of the fact that a survey recently made by the Intelligence Branch of French General Headquarters had shown not only the lack of equilibrium existing between the German effectives on the two sides of the Ardennes, but also the impossibility which would exist for the German Supreme Command to re-establish this equilibrium the moment it lost possession of the railway between Hirson and Mézières.

The decision mentioned above was not such as to surprise those whom it concerned, who, having been stationary on this part of the front for a long time, were fully prepared for the chance of a march forward.

I had taken up this matter personally with the G.O.C. the French Eighth Army (General Gérard) during my trip to the east on September 20th, and on his side General Pétain, more than a month before, had charged General de Castelnau with the elaboration of a plan for an attack along the front of the Eastern Group of Armies.

It was thus possible to draw up rapid plans for the action.

On October 21st, the Commander-in-Chief of the French Armies sent me his proposals covering the general organization of the projected attacks in Lorraine. Though judiciously conceived, this study nevertheless had the drawback of making a sufficiently rapid execution difficult. The action proposed west of the Moselle was such as to require, for various reasons, a delay that was imcompatible with the need of quickly seizing the favourable opportunity presented by the weakness of the enemy and his lack of reserves in this region. East of the Moselle, on the other hand, conditions seemed better, and it was for this reason that I decided to utilize in that quarter first, and without delay, such forces as were immediately available.

I therefore gave up for the moment the action against Luxembourg, and restricted the scope of the original plan. But I still counted upon obtaining, even with relatively reduced resources, important results. " . . . From the military standpoint," I wrote, " by penetrating at small cost the entire depth of the defensive zone through a wide exploitation of our attacks ; and from the moral standpoint, by making our first entry upon territory considered by the enemy as part of his own country and which we therefore ought to conquer."

General Pétain was asked to prepare an attack which, starting from the line Nomény—Arracourt and covered on the side of Metz, would move in the general direction of Saint-Avold—Sarrebrück. On October 25th he reported that this attack could be made on about November 15th, and he explained from what sources he expected to draw the Divisions required.

On the 27th he sent General de Castelnau, commanding the Eastern Army Group, instructions fixing the objectives of the offensive and designating the resources on which he could count for making it. The execution was to be entrusted to two Armies—the Eighth (General Gérard), already in position, and the Tenth (General Mangin), which would be removed from the Aisne front, transported eastward and placed between the American Second Army and the French Eighth Army. Twenty Divisions (of which four or five were American), ten or twelve Brigades of field artillery, 180 to 200 Heavy Batteries, three regiments of light tanks and two groups of medium-sized tanks, one Cavalry Corps and an Air Force detachment, were to constitute the attacking forces. As explained in General Pétain's orders, these operations were to constitute " not an assault delivered without pause against a fortified line, but a manœuvre."

In addition, the Commander-in-Chief of the French Armies asked that " a certain number of American Divisions " be placed at his disposal. Even under the most favourable circumstances he could not count upon the co-operation of more than six or eight American Divisions, over and above the forces to be employed in covering Metz. This was to be entrusted to the American Second Army.

On October 30th, General de Castelnau issued his orders. He assigned similar missions of rupture and exploitation to the Tenth and Eighth Armies, one to operate north of the Grémecey Forest and the slopes of Delme, the other south of the Bezange Forest. In making this arrangement, General de Castelnau supposed that these two Armies would be nearly equal in strength; but the High Command made certain modifications in his plan, induced by the belief that exploitation would probably be much easier for the Tenth Army, and that this Army, in addition, would be obliged to cover itself on the sensitive flank towards Metz. Therefore it was deemed wiser to assign to this Army the major part of the troops available.

On November 5th General Pétain transmitted these observations to the G.O.C. the Eastern Army Group and asked him to make the required changes in his original arrangements. This was done on the next day.

Meanwhile, the Allied forces were being concentrated in Lorraine, and on November 6th General Mangin and his Staff arrived on the scene of preparations.

In spite of the desire expressed by General Pétain to have ten or twelve American Divisions assigned to him (four to cover the Tenth Army from the direction of Metz and six or eight for the attack itself), it turned out that such a large American participation could not be hoped for. Moreover, it was added : " There is an obvious interest in beginning the Lorraine offensive as soon as possible, since the size of the force is less important than the moment chosen for action."

However, efforts to provide General Pétain with the greatest possible number of American units went on actively. Some were obtained by reducing the length of the American First Army's front as soon as it arrived on the Meuse. I also wrote to General Pershing asking the co-operation of six of his reserve Divisions, and I wrote him again a few days later to reassure him : " The G.O.C. the French Tenth Army, who will have these Divisions under his orders, will take measures to see that they operate as much as possible on his left, and, on my side, I will give orders to have them promptly replaced under American command. It is a case before everything else of moving quickly. That is why I again insist."

I also asked General J. Haller, Commander-in-Chief of the Polish Army, to authorise the participation in the approaching offensive of the Polish 1st Division which, after serving on the front in a quiet sector, was now capable of taking an active part in the battle.

Thus, thanks to everybody's activity, the Lorraine attack was quickly prepared. It was to start on November 14th with " twenty-eight Infantry Divisions and three Cavalry Divisions, supported by a considerable mass of artillery and by about 600 tanks. It was to cover a front of twenty miles, which would be added to a battle already being victoriously pursued along a 200 mile front. It was to be launched in a new direction, where there was no possibility of its encountering strong enemy forces. For this reason it was permissible to expect from it a brilliant start, and a rapid conquest of a dozen or so miles. After this, it would undoubtedly encounter devastations such as were already retarding elsewhere the progress of our other Armies. It would add its efforts to theirs, augment them, reinforce their effect, without changing their nature.

It was the march toward the Rhine, in the direction of Berlin, once more confirmed for the ensemble of the Allied forces by a convergence of repeated efforts growing greater every day. Such a march along such a route could not fail to bring about the definite decision of the War.

At the beginning of November the line of the Scheldt below Valenciennes and as far as Ghent constituted an obstacle in front of the left wing of the Allied Armies, while in Champagne the strong defences of the Serre were soon to confront a portion of our centre.

By pushing forward the actions confided to the American First Army and the French Fourth Army on the left bank of the Meuse, we would be outflanking the line of the Serre from the east. On the west we were turning it by advancing the French First Army and the British right north of the Oise. This last movement would also turn the line of the Scheldt from the south, while the Flanders Army Group would soon be facing it further north in front of Ghent. All that was needed, then, was to intensify these various movements.

Foreseeing the important events destined to occur in

the north, I had transferred my Headquarters on October 18th from Bombon to Senlis.

It was in accordance with the manœuvres just described that I intended to push without interruption the advance of the Allied Armies. The halt we had been forced to accept toward the end of October had ended.

From November 1st to the 5th, the American First Army and the French Fourth Army, by continuous wide attacks, had successfully pursued their outflanking manœuvre, and on the last-named date had reached the line Le Chesne—Beaumont—Stenay.

Similarly, the British right, supported by Debeney's Army, had advanced towards Avesnes—Philippeville. Thanks to this double effort, we were masters of the line of the Serre on November 5th and 6th.

To make this possible, it had been necessary to arrive at a new arrangement with Sir Douglas Haig. As I had asked him especially to push his right wing forward, he sought to have restored to him the British Second Army, which had been temporarily attached to the Flanders Army Group. This Army would have formed his left wing and, at the same time, would have enabled him to make a new distribution of his forces. I had no trouble in showing Sir Douglas that, if the Flanders Group was to do the work expected of it, the British Second Army must remain with it until it had conquered Belgium as far as the Scheldt.

As a matter of fact, the Flanders Army Group reached the Scheldt above Ghent on November 1st, and the British Second Army, on November 4th, was restored to the direct command of Field-Marshal Sir Douglas Haig. This was effected by a note dated November 2nd:

" The Flanders Group of Armies, by a series of successful operations, has now reached the Scheldt above Ghent.

"Since the principal manœuvre for effecting the fall of the Scheldt defences must now be executed by the bulk of the British Armies south of Valenciennes, it is necessary that all his British forces be placed at the disposal of the British Commander-in-Chief.

"Marshal Foch, therefore, has the honour to request H.M. the King of the Belgians to be good enough to consider the British Second Army as under the direct command of Field-Marshal Haig from noon of November 4th."

Meanwhile, the success achieved by the French First Army between October 24th and 27th prompted me to write as follows to Sir Douglas on the 27th:

"The advance made by General Debeney makes it possible to resume, under most favourable conditions, the offensive of the main force of the British Armies, in touch with the French First Army, in the direction of Mons, Avesnes and La Capelle, the objectives designated for the Allied Armies in this region."

On October 29th, the Field-Marshal, in conformity with these directions, ordered his Fourth, Third and First Armies to be ready to resume their attacks beginning on November 3rd.

As a matter of fact, they resumed them on the 4th—and with complete success—strongly supported by the French First Army's movement on Guise. This was another *coup de grace* for the German Army.

Reeling under this blow and shaken by the uninterrupted advance of the Franco-American Armies on his left, the enemy, on the 5th, began a vast movement in retreat between the Mons canal and the Aisne at Rethel ; during the following days the retreat extended to the Meuse.

On the 8th the Franco-Belgian troops of the Flanders Army Group captured the passages of the Scheldt between Ecke and Audenarde, accelerating the retirement of the enemy, who now, from the Dutch frontier to the Côtes-de-Meuse, was in full retreat.

CHAPTER XIV

THE ARMISTICE

Germany asks for an Armistice, October 6th—First pourparlers—The High Command is commissioned to study the matter and propose the conditions of an Armistice, October 25th—Examination of these conditions by the Supreme War Council—Adoption of the final text, October 31st to November 4th—Arrival of the German plenipotentiaries, November 8th—Negotiations at Rethondes—Signing of the Armistice, November 8th to 11th—Cessation of hostilities—Orders given to the Allied Armies.

By the beginning of October the Belgian Army had crossed the marshy country of the Yser and reached firm ground, and the Allied Armies were in a position to pursue into the winter season the series of attacks they had begun. They had been waging a victorious battle since July 18th, and now, to increase its power and scope, they were preparing to extend it first to the Moselle and afterwards to the Vosges.

The direction of their operations was plainly marked, for their objectives could only be the main body of the German Army, and this they were already pressing hard. The base of this Army was in North Germany, the head in Berlin. By attacking uninterruptedly in this direction, we were certain to shake, dislocate and finally destroy the enemy's military power, and, by depriving the German Government of its Armies, force it to beg for terms.

On the other hand, without counting the destruction which the enemy could operate along our obligatory lines of communication, and the resulting delays to our march, if he continued the struggle, a serious obstacle would soon confront our advance in this direction—the Rhine. Here the Germans would be in a position to stop our progress for a long time, and, under the protection of the river, they could reconstitute their Army.

It was to prevent this contingency that the Allies sought to reach and cross the Rhine as soon as possible, by pushing forward the battle and exploiting without a moment's halt the enemy's increasing demoralization.

Once the barrier of the Rhine was conquered, Germany would be at the mercy of the Allies, even should they have to go as far as Berlin to prove it. These were the higher considerations which dictated the movements of the Allied Armies as long as political action did not intervene to retard or modify the course of operations.

Already on October 6th, 1918, through the intermediary of the German Minister at Berne and the Swiss Government, the Government of Germany had addressed a note to the President of the United States. It requested Mr. Wilson " to take into his hands the cause of peace, to inform all the belligerent nations that he had done so, and to ask them to send plenipotentiaries to open negotiations." It declared itself ready to enter into these negotiations on the basis of the programme announced by President Wilson in his message to Congress of January 8th, 1918, and in his subsequent utterances, particularly that of September 27th, 1918. Finally, urged by its state of pressing necessity, the German Government asked for " the immediate conclusion of a general Armistice on land, on sea and in the air."

President Wilson replied to this note on October 8th, stipulating as a condition preliminary to the conclusion of an armistice that the German Armies be withdrawn immediately from all invaded territory.

The same day (October 8th) I took the initiative of sending M. Clemenceau a résumé of the obligations which, in my opinion, should be imposed upon our foe " in case the question arose of stopping hostilities, even momentarily." These obligations were based on three essential principles :

There must be no question of halting hostilities in what concerns the armies operating in France and Belgium unless the following conditions are fulfilled :
1. *Liberation of the countries* which, in violation of all law, have been invaded, viz. : Belgium, France, Alsace-Lorraine, Luxemburg, with the return of their inhabitants.
Therefore, the enemy should evacuate these territories within fifteen days and repatriate their inhabitants immediately.
First condition of the Armistice.

2. *Assure a suitable military base of departure* permitting us to pursue the war until the enemy's forces are destroyed in case peace negotiations fail.
For this we need two or three bridge-heads on the Rhine : Rastadt, Strasbourg and Neu-Brisach. (The bridge-head would be a semi-circle traced on the right bank, with a radius of eighteen and three-quarter miles, taking the edge of the right bank as a centre.) This also to be effected within fifteen days.
Second condition of the Armistice.

3. *Take securities for reparations,* to be exacted for damage done in the Allied countries, the bill for which to be presented at the time of the peace negotiations.
For this purpose the territory on the left bank of the

Rhine must be evacuated by the enemy's troops in not more than thirty days; this territory will be occupied and administered by Allied troops in concert with the local authorities until such time as peace shall have been signed.

Third condition of the Armistice.

In addition, the following supplementary conditions should be exacted:

4. All the war material and supplies of every kind that cannot be removed by the German Armies within the time-limit prescribed, must be left on the spot; their destruction is forbidden.

5. Troops which have not evacuated the territory specified within the time-limit fixed shall be disarmed and made prisoners of war.

6. All railway material, including track and operation equipment, must be left where it is, and none of it destroyed. All seized Belgian and French material (or its numerical equivalent) shall be immediately returned.

7. Military establishments of all sorts intended for the use of troops—camps, barracks, ammunition dumps, arsenals—must be left intact, it being forbidden to take away or destroy anything therein.

8. The same applies to industrial establishments and factories of all sorts.

9. Hostilities will cease twenty-four hours from the day on which these conditions shall have been approved by the contracting parties.

During the first two weeks of October, to be sure, we were still too far from the northern Rhine to consider its occupation under the terms of an immediate Armistice; but we could assure to ourselves the possession of the southern Rhine, which was much nearer to our Armies. This would guarantee for us the certainty of manœuvring the obstacle, should hostilities be resumed. Therefore, in the note of October 8th, I demanded the bridge-heads of Neu-Brisach, Strasbourg and Rastadt, which gave us the possibility of turning the defences afforded by the central portion of the Rhine, in case it should become necessary to take up arms again after a suspension of operations at this moment.

As will be noted, there was considerable difference between these proposals and the sole condition of evacuation announced up to that time by the President of the United States. To be sure, it was apparent that President Wilson, in fixing a minimum without which there could be no Armistice, had not thereby excluded such other stipulations as might seem necessary to the Allies. It was this additional set of conditions that I developed before the representatives of the Allied Governments, assembled in Paris at the Ministry of Foreign Affairs on the afternoon of October 9th.

In spite of the opinion held by M. Clemenceau, who preferred to take no part in the debate begun between Berlin and Washington, Mr. Lloyd George, in order to avoid any subsequent misunderstanding, convinced his colleagues of the urgent necessity of sending President Wilson a message calling his attention to the insufficiency of his conditions. These, said the British Prime Minister, would not prevent the Germans " from drawing such advantages from a suspension of the fighting as to be in a better military situation at the expiration of an Armistice not followed by peace, than they were at the moment when hostilities had been interrupted. The chance would be given them to extricate themselves from a critical situation, save their war material, re-form their units, shorten their front and retreat without loss of men to new positions which they would have time to select and fortify."

And he added: "The conditions of an Armistice cannot be fixed until consultation has been held among the military experts and after consideration of the military situation at the moment when negotiations are begun. . . ."

Mr. Lloyd George was well advised in urgently demanding that this message be sent; for the Germans, as might be expected, did not fail to seize the unhoped-for opportunity offered them to extricate themselves honourably from their dilemma.

On October 12th Prince Max of Baden hastened to inform Washington that he was ready " to conclude an Armistice in conformity with the *evacuation proposals* presented by the President."

But Mr. Wilson, warned meanwhile by the Allies of the danger into which he risked being dragged, brought the pourparlers back to firmer ground. On October 14th, he telegraphed the German Chancellor:

" . . . It should be clearly understood that the conditions of the Armistice are matters that must be left to the judgment and advice of the military counsellors of the United States and the Allied Governments, and that no arrangement could be accepted by the Government of the United States which did not secure, by means of absolutely satisfactory safeguards and guarantees, the maintenance of the present superiority of the Armies of the United States and of the Allies on the battlefield."

It would have been presumptuous to suppose that a German Government, whatever its complexion, would accept with good grace these new exactions coming from the White House. The conditions imposed for the conclusion of an Armistice having suddenly struck it as too severe, it proceeded to ignore them. The Government of Berlin had been referred to the Allied Generals. It could not object; but what it could do was to endeavour to lead them on to ground which it hoped might prove more favourable. Why speak of military advantages, it asked? These are difficult to estimate; would it not be better, for casting up the balance sheet of the War's profit and loss, to take a basis, figures easy to establish—for instance, the total number of troops now confronting each other on the battlefield? . . .

" The German Government," wrote the Chancellor on October 20th, " in accepting the proposals relating to the evacuation of occupied territories, assumed that the methods to be pursued in this evacuation, as well as the conditions of the Armistice, were to be left to the judgment of military advisers, and that the proportion now existing between the troops at the front would serve as a basis for the arrangements which would assure and guarantee these conditions. The German Government leaves it to the President to draw up the conditions necessary for regulating details. It is confident that the President of the United States will countenance no demand that would be irreconcilable with the honour of the German nation and the making of a just peace. . . ."

The trap set by the Prince of Baden could not fool the Allied Governments. It was high time, nevertheless, that the conversations which for two weeks had been under way between Berlin and Washington should come to an end.

All they could accomplish would be to create confusion. Moreover, it was undesirable that the Germans should come to consider President Wilson as a sort of arbitrator between the Entente Governments and the Central Powers. In such a game the Entente had everything to lose and nothing to gain. It was advisable, therefore, that without delay the military counsellors be given the floor.

When the Supreme War Council was created in 1917, the heads of the Allied Governments had at their disposal as technical advisers their military representatives installed at Versailles. The creation, four months later, of a Commander-in-Chief for the Allied Armies had somewhat diminished the importance of these advisers, but theoretically they remained none the less the normal counsellors of their Governments. It was in their capacity as such that they were called upon, on October 8th, to draw up a project for an Armistice with Germany.

However, while it was natural that the Allied Governments should seek the advice of their military representatives, it was still more appropriate that, first of all, the Generals in command of their Armies should be consulted. They knew better than anybody else the state of the troops, the efforts of which they were still capable, and the conditions under which they could halt their operations without losing the benefit of the victories gained, and be assured of an advantageous situation in case hostilities were resumed. Their responsibility, therefore, was as much involved in granting an Armistice as it was in conducting the fighting ; and this I brought out in a letter to the French Prime Minister dated October 16th. It was as follows :

"In my letter of October 8th I had the honour of informing you concerning the principal conditions under which, in my opinion, we might consider a cessation of hostilities at that date.

"The first and second conditions named are those imposed by military exigencies; and in his answer of October 14th to the German proposals, President Wilson states that the matter of fixing the terms of an Armistice should be referred to the military counsellors of the Governments.

"This phrase 'military counsellors,' already frequently employed in the course of previous conversations, is ambiguous and demands elucidation. As a matter of fact, the only military counsellors qualified to deal with the conditions of an armistice are the Commanders-in-Chief. They alone are responsible to their Governments for the safety of their armies and the conditions under which hostilities should be resumed in case of rupture. They alone are thoroughly informed as to the state of their armies and of the enemy forces confronting them.

"In what concerns the French and Belgian theatres, I consider that the Marshal Commanding-in-Chief the Allied Armies, after agreement with the Commanders-in-Chief of the French, British and American Armies, and the Chief of Staff of the Belgian Army, should be the Governments' counsellors.

"The third condition deals with taking guarantees for obtaining reparation for damage done in Allied countries, which is to be demanded at the time the peace treaty is negotiated. This guarantee consists in the occupation of the territory on the left bank of the Rhine, to be evacuated by the troops of the enemy within a specified time, and to be occupied and administered by

Allied troops in concert with the local authorities until the treaty of peace is signed.

" Will these guarantees suffice for ensuring the reparation to be demanded by France and her Allies, especially Belgium ?

" If so, after reparations shall have been paid, what is to be the fate of these territories ? Are we to continue in occupation ? Are we going to annex a part of this territory, or to favour the creation of neutral, autonomous, or independent states, forming a buffer ?

" Should the Armistice make complete reservations at this time as to the fate of these territories ?

" These are questions concerning which it is important that the military commander, whose duty it will be to sign the Armistice, and discuss its terms when a request for it has been presented, be informed, after a study of them made beforehand with the Governments concerned. For it is certain that the Armistice should give us full guarantees for obtaining, in the course of the peace negotiations, the terms that we wish to impose upon the enemy ; and it is evident that only the advantages secured to us by the Armistice will remain to us ; that only the sacrifices of territory agreed to by the enemy at the time of signing the Armistice will be final.

" For these reasons, it seems necessary that I be placed in close and continuous touch with a prominent member of the Ministry of Foreign Affairs, whose duty it would be to keep me informed as to your views and those of the Allied Governments regarding the terms of the Armistice. In this way, it would be possible for me to determine what conditions would secure, in addition to military guarantees, the necessary diplomatic guarantees, reconcile these conditions with the military situation of the moment, and, consequently, be always in a position to meet without loss of time my responsibilities, not only to the French Government but to the Governments which have entrusted me with the command of their Armies.

"If you share this point of view, I request you to inform me with which member of the Ministry of Foreign Affairs I am to collaborate."

In this letter, as will be noted, I emphasized the matter of territory to be held as security for reparations due to the Allies, and the situation which was expected to arise for these territories. In short, I brought up a series of questions of a political nature, demanding immediate study, and concerning which the Government ought to make up its mind and announce its decision to the military commander upon whom would devolve the duty of communicating it to the enemy.

What was obviously needed was a careful preliminary examination of the political terms to be put in the Armistice, as a guard against being surprised by future events. The Armistice involved halting the operations of enormous armies, and it ought to contain within itself the germ of the principal conditions of the definitive treaty of peace in such a way that whatever was decided upon later could involve no serious modification of the situation established at the moment hostilities were arrested.

The Prime Minister, however, wishing to preserve the Government's freedom of action, in a letter dated October 23rd, rejected the suggestion that some important official of the Foreign Affairs be placed at my disposal.

The conditions of the Armistice were, in fact, to be established by the Allied Governments. This meant that the preparation of the terms would naturally be conducted by the most active of these Governments.

The question had just been placed before them by President Wilson. Cutting short his correspondence with Berlin, he referred the German Government to the tribunal composed of the Allies, leaving to the latter, however, full latitude to conclude (or not conclude) an Armistice, and to dictate to the enemy conditions such as " would fully protect the interests of the peoples concerned and assure to the associated Governments unlimited power for the purpose of safeguarding the peace to which the German Government has consented and of causing its details to be executed."

The Allied Governments had no reason to reject the principle of the Fourteen Points as a basis of peace, except that, if deemed advisable, they might ask that some of them be modified or elucidated. They also had no reasons for objecting to a cessation of hostilities, provided the conditions which they intended to impose were accepted by the enemy.

They asked me, therefore, to prepare a detailed proposal from the military standpoint. M. Clemenceau, their spokesman, made an appointment with General Pétain and myself on October 24th in Paris. We agreed verbally upon the conditions which would assure full security to the Allied Armies and the guarantees to be exacted to that end. The blockade was to be maintained and the duration of the Armistice was to be short. The progress made by our Armies since October 8th permitted us to reinforce and make more definite certain points in the note drawn up on that date.

With a view to learning their opinion, on the afternoon of the next day I called together at my Headquarters at Senlis the Commanders-in-Chief of the American,

British and French Armies ; also the Chief of Staff of the French Navy, Vice-Admiral de Bon.* I requested them, in turn, to state what they thought should be the Armistice conditions.

Sir Douglas Haig, speaking first, declared that, in his opinion, the German Army as a whole was not so broken that it could not still offer serious resistance ; that it was capable of retiring to the German frontier and of defending it against equal or even superior forces. On the other hand, the British Army was under strength to the extent of 50,000 infantry, the French Army was exhausted and the American Army incompletely organized. Therefore he thought that the conditions to be imposed upon Germany should be moderate and demand nothing further than :

1. Evacuation of Belgium and the occupied portions of France.
2. Evacuation of Alsace-Lorraine ; Metz and Strasbourg being delivered to the Allies.
3. Return of rolling-stock taken from France and Belgium and the repatriation of their citizens.

Without going into a discussion of these conditions, it did not seem that the reasons supporting them were well founded. In the course of a few months the German Army had lost an enormous amount of ground, prisoners and war material. It was a beaten Army and must assuredly be badly shaken and greatly demoralized. In what concerned the Allied Armies, it had to be recognized that victorious forces are never fresh. Ours had just emerged from a successful battle, but a battle of the sort in which the victor often loses as heavily

* The Chief of Staff of the Belgian Army was unable to arrive in time on account of the distance that he had to cover. He came to Senlis the next day and gave his approval to the text which I presented to him.

as the vanquished. This, however, did not imply that the Germans were anything but thoroughly disorganized. Hence there was no reason to anticipate serious resistance from them.

Questioned in his turn, General Pétain declared that it must be made impossible for the Germans to resume hostilities. To ensure this he proposed :

1. Allied occupation of the left bank of the Rhine from the Dutch to the Swiss frontiers, including bridge-heads on the right bank. Limit to be fixed at fifteen days.
2. Surrender by the Germans of 5,000 locomotives and 100,000 railway trucks in perfect condition.

When asked for his opinion, General Pershing stated that he considered the military situation most favourable for the Allies, and that it justified imposing upon Germany severe conditions.

He therefore proposed :

1. Immediate evacuation of all territory occupied by the enemy.
2. Occupation of Alsace-Lorraine by the Allies.
3. Withdrawal of the German Armies to the right bank of the Rhine and occupation by the Allies of bridge-heads on that bank.
4. Transportation by sea of the American Army and its supplies not to be interfered with.
5. Immediate repatriation of all the inhabitants of territory occupied by the Germans.
6. Delivery of all submarines and submarine bases to the Allies, or to some neutral power.
7. Return of all rolling-stock seized in Belgium and France.

At the close of this meeting to which the Commanders-in-Chief had thus been summoned for the purpose of giving their views on the subject of the Armistice, a draft was made of the military conditions to be submitted to the Allied Governments. They were in substance :

1. The immediate evacuation of lands unlawfully invaded—Belgium, France, Alsace-Lorraine and Luxembourg—and the immediate repatriation of their inhabitants.

2. Surrender by the enemy of 5,000 guns, 30,000 machine-guns and 3,000 minenwerfer.

3. Evacuation by the German Army of all territory on the left bank of the Rhine ; occupation by the Allies of bridge-heads on the right bank, drawn with a radius of eighteen and three-quarter miles, at Mayence, Coblence, Cologne and Strasbourg, and the creation on the right bank of a neutral zone twenty-five miles wide running east of the river.

4. Prohibition of any destruction or damage by the enemy in the area evacuated.

5. Delivery of 5,000 locomotives and 150,000 railway trucks in good condition.

6. Delivery of 150 submarines, withdrawal of the surface fleet to Baltic ports, occupation by the Allied fleets of Cuxhaven and Heligoland.

7. Maintenance of the blockade during the period fixed for the fulfilment of the above conditions.

I took this paper myself to Paris on the afternoon of October 26th, and I handed the text to both the President of the Republic and the Prime Minister. During my conversation with M. Poincaré, when he remarked that these conditions might be judged inacceptable and refused by the Germans, I replied : " Then we will continue the War ; for at the point the Allied Armies have now reached, their victorious march must not be halted until they have rendered all German resistance impossible and seized guarantees fully ensuring peace—a peace we will have obtained at the price of inestimable sacrifices ! "

The prosecution of our march toward Berlin ought not to be interrupted until we were masters of the obstacle presented by the Rhine, for it barred the road to Berlin along the space between Cologne and Mayence.

On the other hand, in a letter dated October 29th, I warned M. Clemenceau against the tendency of some of our Allies to show too great a severity in the matter of naval terms they might wish inserted in the Armistice :

" I had the honour of sending you, on October 26th, the military conditions of the Armistice.

" It seems probable that naval conditions will be added. These cannot be accepted without examination ; for if they are too exacting, it would result in the continuance by the land forces of a costly struggle for the purpose of obtaining advantages of doubtful value.

"I ask you therefore to give me a hearing before the final draft of the terms of the Armistice is agreed upon."

On the morning of October 31st the heads of the Allied Governments held their first meeting. It took place at the Paris residence of Colonel House, who had been sent expressly to France by President Wilson. At the opening of the meeting it was learned that Turkey had just signed the Mudros Armistice, and that Austria had collapsed. This news made it all the easier for me, when asked to give my opinion as to the general military situation, to point out how distinctly favourable events were for the Allies.

During more than three months the Germans had been steadily beaten in France and Belgium and forced continuously to retreat. They had lost over 260,000 prisoners and 4,000 guns. The military situation of their country was seriously disorganized, whereas we were in a position to keep up the fighting all winter, if need be, and along the whole 250 mile front. We could readily go on fighting until the enemy was destroyed, if that became necessary.

After I had concluded my statement, Colonel House asked if I considered it preferable to continue the War against Germany or conclude an Armistice with her.

I answered : " I am not waging war for the sake of waging war. If I obtain through the Armistice the conditions that we wish to impose upon Germany, I am satisfied. Once this object is attained, nobody has the right to shed one more drop of blood."

During the afternoon of the same day (October 31st), a plenary session of the Supreme War Council was held at Versailles. At the opening of the meeting, which was to be devoted to examining the terms of the Austro-Hungarian Armistice, I was again asked to express my opinion and I repeated my statements of the morning, to the effect that the Allied military situation was becoming more and more favourable.

On November 1st the detailed examination of the terms to be imposed upon Germany commenced.

In the morning a first meeting of the heads of the Allied Governments was held in Paris at the Ministry of War. The conditions I had proposed concerning the occupation of the left bank of the Rhine were read. A discussion was then begun in order to give Sir Douglas Haig an opportunity to develop his point of view once more and to repeat his statements of October 25th, which evidently expressed the opinion of Mr. Lloyd George and his colleagues.

This proposal which, for the purpose of suspending hostilities, would halt the Allied Armies at the frontiers of Belgium, Luxemburg and Alsace-Lorraine, that is to say, on the left bank of the Rhine and some distance from the river—in other words, with this obstacle in front of our very noses—was militarily inacceptable. It would leave to Germany, protected as she would be by the Rhine, the possibility of re-forming her Armies while the conditions of peace were being discussed and the possibility, if she refused those terms, of resuming the fighting under conditions disadvantageous to the Allies. The latter might thereby lose much of the benefit of their hard-won victories. If the Armistice did not give the Rhine to the Allied Governments, there would be a risk of jeopardizing the peace they were seeking. My thesis was accepted.

The reading and examination of the document continued at Versailles that afternoon. It was decided that clauses concerning the Russian front should be added to the convention and that my Staff should draft them.

On the afternoon of November 2nd there was another session at Versailles, during which the naval conditions and those dealing with the Russian front were discussed.

At that very hour the Austrian High Command was receiving from General Diaz the text of the Armistice terms offered by the Entente. What was the Vienna Government going to do? Would it accept or not? And if it accepted, would not the disruption of the Dual Monarchy render it incapable of fulfilling its promises? All these questions preoccupied the thoughts of the Allied leaders, and so heavily did they weigh upon the discussion of the afternoon, that Mr. Lloyd George abandoned his naval experts and a considerable part of their demands relative to the delivery of the German war fleet.

But as soon as Vienna's capitulation was known, he resumed these exigencies in their entirety. They demanded more especially the disarmament of the German war fleet, the surrender of many ships, both submarine and surface, along with considerable naval material—in short, terms so heavy that they might prove inacceptable to Germany, and thus prevent the signing of an Armistice convention which, in the matter of land conditions, would be entirely satisfactory to us.

Faced with the fact that these naval clauses might be so severe as to make Germany reject our Armistice, thus necessitating the continuation of the War on land for the purpose of acquiring at the cost of much blood naval material of no value for our operations, I called the attention of the Allied Governments to the responsibility they would be incurring if more of our men had to be killed for so little profit to the common cause. In reply to this, I was told to insert the naval clauses in the Armistice conditions. Then, if the enemy found them inacceptable, the matter of what modifications to admit would be taken into consideration. As a matter of fact the Germans accepted everything.

The propositions regarding the Russian and Roumanian fronts were approved without discussion. In connection with this point, Monsieur Pichon, the French Minister of Foreign Affairs, raised the question of Poland's restoration, which was one of the Allied aims in the War; but it was decided that this matter lay outside the scope of the Armistice and that for the moment it was sufficient to make Germany withdraw to her eastern boundaries as they existed in 1914.

Finally, on November 4th, after a last reading, the

definitive text of the Armistice was agreed to by the heads of the Allied Governments and immediately cabled to President Wilson. In addition, it was decided that, aided by a British Admiral, I should be charged with the duty of communicating this text to envoys duly accredited by the German Government and of treating with them on the basis of its terms.

In transmitting to Washington the conditions they had just agreed upon, the Allied Governments, at the special request of Great Britain, made all due reservations as to the principle of the freedom of the seas, which figured amongst the Fourteen Points of President Wilson. The latter was careful to point this out in the message he sent Berlin on November 5th, referring the Germans to Allied Headquarters. This was sufficient proof that the Allied Governments, however little they seemed to think so, were free to set aside at this moment all formulas that might embarrass them in the coming negotiations.

I immediately gave orders for receiving any German envoys who presented themselves at our front lines. And, as I intended, if warned beforehand of their coming, to direct them along the line Givet—La Capelle—Guise, I sent special instructions to General Debeney. At the same time I warned all the armies against false rumours which the enemy might circulate prematurely regarding the conclusion of an armistice.

It was the night of November 6th–7th, at half past twelve, that I received the first wireless message from the German Supreme Command. It gave the names of the plenipotentiaries designated by the Berlin Government and asked me to fix a place of meeting. It added: " The German Government would be glad if, in the interest of humanity, the arrival of the German delegation before the Allied front might cause a provisional suspension of hostilities."

I replied at once in these simple words: " If the German plenipotentiaries wish to meet Marshal Foch to ask him for an armistice, they should present themselves at the French outposts on the road Chimay—Fourmies—La Capelle—Guise. Orders have been given to receive and conduct them to the place selected for the meeting."

On the morning of the 7th, I was informed that the German plenipotentiaries would leave Spa at noon and arrive before the French lines between 4 and 5 o'clock in the afternoon. Measures were taken, both by the French and German commanders, to stop the firing on each side during the passage of the enemy delegation.

Accompanied by General Weygand, three officers of my staff* and the British naval delegation headed by Admiral Wemyss, First Sea Lord of the Admiralty, I left Senlis at 5 o'clock in the afternoon and went by special train to the place chosen for meeting the German plenipotentiaries—a spot in the Compiègne Forest, north of and near the station of Rethondes. My train was there run on to a siding built for railroad artillery.

The German delegation, having been constantly halted by the blocked condition of the roads behind the German front, reached the French lines only at 9 P.M., and arrived at their destination twelve hours late. It was not until seven in the morning of November 8th that the train bringing them drew up near mine.

Two hours afterwards, at 9 o'clock, the first meeting took place in the office-car of the French train.

The report reproduced below, sent by me to the

* Major Riedinger, Captain de Mierry, Interpreter-Officer Laperche.

French Prime Minister and to the President of the Republic after the signing of the Armistice, gives in detail what occurred at Rethondes between the Allied and German plenipotentiaries.

Let me add that, on the 9th, in order to show the determination of the Allies to put an end to all German resistance, I sent the following telegram to the Commanders-in-Chief:

" The enemy, disorganized by our repeated attacks, is giving way all along the front.
" It is urgent to hasten and intensify our efforts.
" I appeal to the energy and initiative of Commanders-in-Chief and their Armies to make the result achieved decisive."

And all of them, feeling the wind of victory that played upon their standards, sent word in answer : " Count upon us to keep on as long as need be."

Report

The pourparlers leading up to the conclusion of the Armistice with Germany took place in the office-car of Marshal Foch's special train. The Marshal's train, and the one which the German plenipotentiaries had taken at Tergniers were lying on sidings built for heavy railway artillery in the Forêt de l'Aigle, near the station of Rethondes.

November 8th.—The special train bearing the German plenipotentiaries arrived on November 8th at 7 A.M.

The Marshal informed the German delegates that he would receive them on or after 9 o'clock. They asked to be received at 9, and at that hour they proceeded to the Marshal's train.

Marshal Foch, accompanied by Admiral Sir Rosslyn Wemyss, General Weygand and Admiral Hope, asked the delegates to show him their credentials. These were produced and handed to the Marshal. They read as follows :

" (1) FULL POWER :
" The undersigned, Chancellor of the German Empire, Max, Prince of Baden, hereby gives full power :
" To Imperial Secretary of State, Matthias Erzberger, (as President of the delegation),
" To Imperial Envoy Extraordinary and Minister Plenipotentiary, Count Alfred Oberndorff, and
" To Major-General Detlev von Winterfeldt, Royal Prussian Army, to conduct in the name of the German Government with the plenipotentiaries of the Powers allied against Germany, negotiations for an armistice and to conclude an agreement to that effect, provided the same be approved by the German government.
" Berlin, November 6th, 1918.
" (signed) Max, Prince of Baden."

" (2) FULL POWER :
" The undersigned, Chancellor of the German Empire, Max, Prince of Baden, hereby appoints as additional plenipotentiary for the armistice negotiations with the Powers allied against Germany,
" Captain Vanselow, Imperial Navy.
" General Erich von Gundell, Royal Infantry, has been relieved of his post as plenipotentiary ; consequently his name has been stricken from the power enclosed herewith.
" Berlin, November 6th, 1918.
" (signed) Max, Prince of Baden."

After withdrawing with Admiral Wemyss and General Weygand to examine the above credentials, the Marshal returned to the place of conference and asked the head of the German delegation to announce the names of its members. They were :

> Secretary of State Erzberger,
> Major-General von Winterfeldt,
> Minister-Plenipotentiary Count Oberndorff,
> Naval Captain Vanselow,
> Staff Captain Geyer,
> Cavalry Captain von Helldorff.

The Marshal then announced the members of the Allied delegation, viz :

> Admiral Wemyss,
> General Weygand,
> Admiral Hope,
> Captain Mariott, R.N.

And, as interpreters :

> Commander Bagot,
> Interpreter-Officer Laperche.

Places were now taken at the conference table.

Marshal Foch asked the German delegates the purpose of their visit.

Herr Erzberger replied that the German delegation had come to receive the proposals of the Allied Powers looking to an armistice on land, on sea and in the air, on all the fronts, and in the colonies.

Marshal Foch replied that he had no proposals to make.

Count Oberndorff asked the Marshal in what form he desired that they should express themselves. He did not stand on form ; he was ready to say that the German delegation asked the conditions of the armistice.

Marshal Foch replied that he had no conditions to offer.

Herr Erzberger read the text of President Wilson's last note, stating that Marshal Foch is authorized to make known the armistice conditions.

Marshal Foch replied that he was authorized to make these known if the German delegates asked for an armistice.

"Do you ask for an armistice? If you do, I can inform you of the conditions subject to which it can be obtained."

Herr Erzberger and Count Oberndorff declared that they asked for an armistice.

Marshal Foch then announced that the armistice conditions would be read ; as the text was rather long, only the principal paragraphs would be read for the present ; later on the complete text would be communicated to the plenipotentiaries.

General Weygand read the principal clauses of the armistice conditions (text agreed upon at Versailles on November 4th).

The reading terminated, and Herr Erzberger requested that military operations be immediately suspended. He gave as a reason the disorganization and lack of discipline which reigned in the German Army, and the spirit of revolution that was spreading through Germany as a consequence of the people's sufferings. He described the difficulties which he and his fellow delegates had encountered in passing through the German Armies and in crossing their lines, where even the order to cease fire was executed only after considerable trouble. All these circumstances led him to fear that Germany might soon fall into the grip of Bolshevism, and once Central Europe was invaded by this scourge, Western Europe, he said, would find the greatest difficulty in escaping it. Nothing but the cessation of Allied attacks would make it possible to re-establish discipline in the German Army, and, through the restoration of order, save the country.

I immediately answered :* " At the moment when negotiations for the signing of an armistice are just being opened, it is impossible to stop military operations, until the German delegation has accepted and signed the conditions which are the very consequence of those operations. As for the situation described by Herr Erzberger as existing among the German troops and the danger he fears of Bolshevism spreading in Germany, the one is the usual disease prevailing in beaten armies, the other is symptomatic of a nation completely worn out by war. Western Europe will find means of defending itself against the danger."

When I had finished my statement regarding the impossibility of my acquiescence to the verbal request of Herr Erzberger, General von Winterfeldt asked to be heard. He had a special mission to fulfil on behalf of the German Supreme Command and the German Government.

He read the following statement, prepared in advance :

" The armistice terms which have just been brought to our knowledge require careful examination by us. As it is our intention to come to a decision, this examination will be made as promptly as possible.

---

* It will be observed that this report is written partly in the third person and partly in the first. No attempt has been made to change the Marshal's method of dealing with the subject.—T. B. M.

Nevertheless, it will require a certain amount of time, especially as it will be necessary to consult our Government and the military Supreme Command.

"During this time the struggle between our Armies will continue and it will result, both among soldiers and civilians, in numerous victims who will die in vain at the last minute, and who might be preserved to their families.

"Therefore, the German Government and the German Supreme Command have the honour to revert to the proposal made by them in their wireless message of the day before yesterday, viz: that Marshal Foch be kind enough to consent to an immediate suspension of hostilities on the entire front, to begin to-day at a certain fixed hour, the very simple details of which could be decided upon without loss of time."

To this, Marshal Foch replied:

"I am the Commander-in-Chief of the Allied Armies and representative of the Allied Governments. These Governments have decided upon their terms. Hostilities cannot cease before the signing of the Armistice. I am likewise desirous of reaching a conclusion and therefore I shall help you as far as is possible toward this end. But hostilities cannot cease before the signing of the Armistice."

At the end of the session the German delegates asked the Marshal if it would be possible to extend the time-limit for a reply by 24 hours, on account of the time required for informing their Government of the terms. The Marshal replied that, in view of the fact that the limit set had been fixed by the Allied and Associated

Governments, it was impossible for him to change it.

After conferring amongst themselves, the German delegates asked that the following message be sent by wireless:

"German armistice Plenipotentiaries to the Imperial Chancellor and to the German Military and Naval High Commands:

"The plenipotentiaries received the armistice conditions on Friday morning at Allied General Headquarters; also the ultimatum that they be accepted or refused within seventy-two hours, expiring on Monday morning at 11 o'clock (French time).

"The German proposal for an immediate agreement to suspend hostilities provisionally was rejected by Marshal Foch.

"A German courier bearing the text of the armistice conditions has been sent to Spa, there being no other practical mode of communication. Please acknowledge receipt and send back the courier as soon as possible with your final instructions.

"It is not necessary for the time being to send new delegates.

"(signed) Erzberger."

This message was forwarded at 11.30 A.M.

The German delegation decided to send Captain von Helldorf as courier, in order to transmit the text of the terms to German General Headquarters.

The Marshal's Staff took measures to assure the safe-conduct and passage through the lines of this courier, who left at 1 P.M.

Count Oberndorff, General von Winterfeldt, and

Captain Vanselow then requested that personal conferences between them and General Weygand and Admiral Hope might be held in order to obtain certain explanations desired by the German delegates.

These conversations took place in the afternoon. Count Oberndorff and General von Winterfeldt with General Weygand ; Captain Vanselow with Admiral Hope.

Below is a resumé of these conversations :

Count Oberndorff first asked whether the Allies had drawn up such severe terms with the object of having Germany refuse them.

The answer was that the Allies were making known the conditions under which they would grant an armistice, and that there was nothing hidden in their intentions.

Count Oberndorff then asked whether the Allies did not intend to cause the armistice to fail in order to proceed immediately with peace negotiations.

The answer was that Marshal Foch had come here to negotiate—and he wished to negotiate—nothing except the conditions governing an armistice.

Later on in the conversation with Count Oberndorff, as well as in the subsequent one with General von Winterfeldt, questions were asked concerning the various armistice conditions. During these conversations the principal ideas or arguments advanced by the German delegates for the purpose of softening the terms may be summarized thus :

Germany wishes for an armistice. The fact that her delegates were here proved that no other course was open to her. Hence, it might be assumed that the delegates were sincere.

The German Army was beset by unimaginable

difficulties : exhaustion among the troops who have been fighting without pause for four months ; the consequent relaxation of discipline ; the blocking of roads and railways, which paralyzed all movement. To enforce upon this Army any rapid movement would prevent it from being put in order.

Even should it so desire, the German Army would be incapable of recommencing the fight, once the Armistice was signed. Hence there was no point in imposing too severe terms.

No protest was made against the military clauses concerning the surrender of arms, except as to delivering 30,000 machine-guns. If this were done there would not be enough left to fire on the German people, should this become necessary.

Germany's internal situation was extremely serious. The country was in revolt, infected with Bolshevism. Order must be maintained. This was to the interest of the Allies, so as to prevent Bolshevist infection and assure the solvency of their debtors—for very heavy demands for reparation were expected.

Consequently it was to the advantage of everybody that the German Army should march back to Germany in orderly fashion. To do this the time-limit fixed for the evacuation must be extended. It is not a case of allowing merely additional days, but weeks.

Moreover, Germany was threatened with famine. The Armistice clauses touching blockade and railway material were inhuman, because they would paralyze the work of feeding the population and would cause the death of women and children.

To sum up, Germany must be left with an Army in good order, so that she might suppress revolts ; and she must be provided with food.

The answer given was, in general terms, this : The state of disorganization in the German Army was the result of the victorious advance of the Allied Armies during the last four months. It was the duty of the Allied High Command to secure by the terms of the Armistice, as a minimum, the continued possession of all advantages won.

In terminating these conversations General Weygand clearly specified :

(1) That private conversations such as those that have just taken place are merely exchanges of opinion implying no engagements whatever for those participating. Their sole object is to give the German delegates the explanations which will enable them to make their requests with full knowledge of the situation.

(2) That questions or requests from the German delegates must be made in writing.

This was agreed to ; likewise that a confidential note would be sent to General Weygand so that he could study whatever questions it was desired to have submitted to Marshal Foch (this to avoid examining these questions for the first time in plenary session).

November 9th.—At 3.45 P.M. on the 9th the German delegation handed General Weygand a text entitled " *Observations on the Conditions of an Armistice with Germany.*"

This text was brought by Count Oberndorff and General von Winterfeldt, who reverted to the arguments of the day before, without saying anything new worth recording.

November 10th.—A paper headed " *Answer to the Observations on the Conditions of an Armistice with Germany*" was handed to the German delegates on November 10th at 9.30 P.M.

That same day at 6.30 P.M., Marshal Foch had the following note delivered to the German plenipotentiaries:

Headquarters of the Allied Armies,
November 10th, 1918.
General Staff

" According to the terms of the text handed to Marshal Foch, the powers of the German plenipotentiaries for concluding an armistice are limited by the fact that the approval of the Chancellor is necessary.

" As the time allowed for coming to an agreement expires at 11 A.M. to-morrow, I have the honour to ask whether the German Plenipotentiaries have received the acceptance by the German Chancellor of the terms communicated to him, and if not, whether it would not be advisable to solicit without delay an answer from him.

" By order :
" (signed) Weygand
" Major-General, Chief of Staff."

In reply, the German delegates sent the following note at 9.30 P.M. :

"November 10th, 1918.
" The German Plenipotentiaries have the honour to inform the Allied High Command, in reply to the question asked them on November 10th, that no decision from the Imperial Chancellor has as yet reached them.

" The plenipotentiaries have already taken steps to

have instructions sent them as promptly as possible.
"(signed) Erzberger
"Secretary of State."

Meanwhile, between 7 and 8 P.M., the following two messages arrived by wireless:

"I. The German Government to the plenipotentiaries at Headquarters of the Allied High Command:
"The German Government accepts the conditions of the Armistice communicated to it on November 8th.
"The Chancellor of the Empire—3,084."

"II. The German Supreme Command to the Plenipotentiaries at Headquarters of the Allied High Command:
"The Government of the Empire transmits to the High Command the following for Under-Secretary of State Erzberger:
"Your Excellency is authorized to sign the Armistice. You will please, at the same time, have inserted in the record the following:
"The German Government will do all in its power to fulfil the terms agreed upon. However, the undersigned deems it his duty to point out that the execution of some of the conditions will bring famine to the population of that part of the German Empire which is not to be occupied.
"If all the provisions which had been accumulated for feeding the troops are left in the regions to be evacuated, and if the limitation (equivalent to complete suppression) of our means of transportation is maintained and the blockade continued, to feed the population and organize a food service will be impossible.

"The undersigned requests, therefore, to be authorized to negotiate with a view to modifying certain points, in order that supplies may be assured.

"(signed) The Chancellor of the Empire.

"P.S.—The Supreme Command likewise draws attention to the points transmitted at noon to-day to General von Winterfeldt. Advise by wireless when the Armistice is signed."

Then, about 9 P.M., a very long telegram in cipher from Marshal von Hindenburg began to arrive.

When he handed these telegrams to the German delegates, General Weygand asked Herr Erzberger whether he considered that they gave sufficient authenticity to the expected acceptance, from the Chancellor. Herr Erzberger replied in the affirmative, pointing out that the number 3,084 added to the signature of the first of these telegrams was the number agreed upon to vouch for authenticity.

The German delegates were then asked at what time they would be ready to assist at a plenary session for drawing up and signing the definitive text of the Armistice. The delegates asked to be given the time to decipher the Hindenburg telegram and to examine the Allied High Command's answer to their observations.

They were requested to state as soon as possible the hour at which this plenary session could be held, so that bloodshed might be stopped as soon as possible, now that the signing of the Armistice has been decided upon.

November 11th.—On November 11th at 2.5 A.M., the German delegates stated that they were ready for the session. It was opened at 2.15 A.M.

F. DURÉE DE L'ARMISTICE.

XXXIV.- La durée de l'armistice est fixée à 36 jours avec faculté de prolongation.

Au cours de cette durée, l'armistice peut, si les clauses ne sont pas exécutées être dénoncé par l'une des parties contractantes qui devra, en donner le préavis 48 heures à l'avance. - Il est entendu que l'exécution des articles III et XVIII ne donnera lieu à dénonciation de l'armistice pour insuffisance d'exécution dans les délais voulus, que dans le cas d'une exécution mal intentionnée.

Pour assurer dans les meilleures conditions l'exécution de la présente Convention, le principe d'une Commission d'Armistice Internationale Permanente est admis. - Cette Commission fonctionnera sous la seule autorité du Commandement en Chef Militaire et Naval des Armées Alliées.

Le présent armistice a été signé le 11 Novembre 1918 à 5 heures (cinq heures) heure française.

THE LAST PAGE OF THE ARMISTICE AGREEMENT

FOCH'S OFFICE IN HIS HEADQUARTERS AT SENLIS IN OCTOBER, 1918.

THE TABLE AT WHICH THE ARMISTICE WAS SIGNED IN MARSHAL FOCH'S CAR.

MARSHAL FOCH HOLDS IN HIS HAND THE SIGNED COPY OF THE ARMISTICE, AS HE LEAVES HIS TRAIN AT 7 A.M. ON NOVEMBER 11TH, 1918.

LORRAINE WELCOMES THE FRENCH ARMIES,
NOVEMBER 10TH, 1918.

Marshal Foch declared that the definitive text of the Armistice would now be approved and he asked General Weygand to read it, substituting the new text set down in the " Answer to Observations " for the text of November 8th, wherever the latter had been changed.

The text was read, discussed and adopted, article by article. It reads as follows :

Between Marshal FOCH, Commander-in-Chief of the Allied Armies, representing the Allied and Associated Powers, assisted by Admiral WEMYSS, First Sea Lord, parties of the first part ;

and Secretary of State ERZBERGER, President of the German delegation ; Envoy Extraordinary and Minister Plenipotentiary Count von Oberndorff ; Major-General von Winterfeldt, and Naval Captain Vanselow, duly empowered and acting with the approval of the German Chancellor, parties of the second part ;

an Armistice has been concluded, embodying the following conditions :

CONDITIONS OF THE ARMISTICE CONCLUDED WITH GERMANY

A—Clauses Relating to the Western Front

1. Cessation of hostilities by land and in the air six hours after the signing of the Armistice.

2. Immediate evacuation of the invaded countries—Belgium, France, Luxembourg as well as Alsace-Lorraine—so ordered as to be completed within fifteen days from the signature of the Armistice.

German troops which have not left the above-mentioned territories within the period fixed will be made prisoners of war.

Occupation by the Allied and United States Forces jointly will keep pace with the evacuation in these areas.

All movements of evacuation and occupation will be regulated in accordance with a Note (Annexe 1) determined at the time of the signing of the Armistice.

3. Repatriation, beginning at once, to be completed within fifteen days, of all inhabitants of the countries above enumerated (including hostages, persons under trial, or condemned).

4. Surrender in good condition by the German Armies of the following equipment :—

 5,000 guns (2,500 heavy, 2,500 field)
 25,000 machine-guns
 3,000 Minenwerfer,
 1,700 aeroplanes (fighters, bombers—firstly
   D 7's—and night-bombing machines).

The above to be delivered *in situ* to the Allied and United States troops in accordance with the detailed conditions laid down in the Note (Annexe 1) determined at the time of the signing of the Armistice.

5. Evacuation by the German Armies of the districts on the left bank of the Rhine. These districts on the left bank of the Rhine shall be administered by the local authorities under the control of the Allied and United States Armies of occupation.

The occupation of these territories by Allied and United States troops will be assured by garrisons holding the principal crossings of the Rhine, (Mayence, Coblence, Cologne) together with bridge-heads at these points of a thirty kilometre (about nineteen miles) radius on the right bank, and by garrisons similarly holding the strategic points of the area.

A neutral zone shall be reserved on the right bank of the Rhine, between the river and a line drawn parallel to the bridge-heads and to the river and ten kilometres (six and a quarter miles), distant from them between the Dutch frontier and the Swiss frontier.

The evacuation by the enemy of the Rhine districts (right and left bank) shall be so ordered as to be completed within a further period of sixteen days, in all thirty-one days after the signing of the Armistice.

All movements of evacuation and occupation will be regulated according to the Note (Annexe 1) determined at the time of the signing of the Armistice.

6. In all territories evacuated by the enemy, evacuation of the inhabitants shall be forbidden ; no damage or harm shall be done to the persons or property of the inhabitants.

In the case of inhabitants no person shall be prosecuted for having taken part in any military measures previous to the signing of the Armistice.

No destruction of any kind shall be committed.

Military establishments of all kinds shall be delivered intact, as well as military stores of foods, munitions and equipment, which shall not have been removed during the periods fixed for evacuation.

Stores of food of all kinds for the civil population, cattle, etc., shall be left *in situ*.

No measure of a general or official character shall be taken which would have, as a consequence, the depreciation of industrial establishments or a reduction of their personnel.

7. Roads and means of communication of every kind, railroads, waterways, roads, bridges, telegraphs, telephones, shall be in no manner impaired.

All civil and military personnel at present employed on them shall remain.

5,000 locomotives and 150,000 wagons in good working

order, with all necessary spare parts and fittings, shall be delivered to the Associated Powers within the period fixed in Annexe II (not exceeding thirty-one days in all).

5,000 motor lorries are also to be delivered in good order within thirty-six days.

The railways of Alsace-Lorraine shall be handed over within thirty-one days together with all personnel and material belonging to the organization of the system.

Further, working material in the territories on the left bank of the Rhine shall be left *in situ*.

All stores of coal and material for upkeep of permanent way, signals and repair shops shall be left *in situ* and kept in an efficient state by Germany, so far as the means of communication on the left bank of the Rhine are concerned.

All lighters taken from the Allies shall be restored to them. The Note attached as Annexe II, defines the details of these measures.

8. The German Command shall be responsible for revealing within forty-eight hours of the signing of the Armistice, all mines or delay-action fuses disposed on territories evacuated by the German troops and shall assist in their discovery and destruction.

The German Command shall also reveal all destructive measures that may have been taken (such as poisoning or pollution of wells, springs, etc.) under penalty of reprisals.

9. The right of requisition shall be exercised by the Allied and United States armies in all occupied territories, save for settlement of accounts with authorized persons.

The upkeep of the troops of occupation in the Rhine districts (excluding Alsace-Lorraine) shall be charged to the German Government.

10. The immediate repatriation, without reciprocity, according to detailed conditions which shall be fixed, of all Allied and United States prisoners of war, including those under trial and condemned. The Allied Powers and the United States of America shall be able to dispose of these prisoners of war as they think fit. This condition annuls all other conventions regarding prisoners of war, including that of July, 1918, now being ratified. However, the return of German prisoners of war interned in Holland and Switzerland shall continue as heretofore. The return of German prisoners of war shall be settled at the conclusion of the Peace preliminaries.

11. Sick and wounded who cannot be removed from territory evacuated by the German forces, will be cared for by German personnel, who will be left on the spot with the material required.

B—Clauses relating to the Eastern Frontiers of Germany

12. All German troops at present in any territory which before the War formed part of Austria-Hungary, Roumania or Turkey, shall withdraw within the frontiers of Germany as they existed on 1st August, 1914, and all German troops at present in territories which before the War formed part of Russia must likewise return to within the frontiers of Germany as above defined, as soon as the Allies shall think the moment suitable, having regard to the internal situation of these territories.

13. Evacuation by German troops to begin at once, and all German instructors, prisoners and civilians, as well as military agents now on the territory of Russia (frontier as defined on 1st August, 1914) to be recalled.

14. German troops to cease at once all requisitions and

seizures and any other coercive measures with a view to obtaining supplies intended for Germany in Roumania and Russia (frontier as defined on 1st August, 1914).

15. Annulment of the treaties of Bucharest and Brest-Litovsk and of the supplementary treaties.

16. The Allies shall have free access to the territories evacuated by the Germans on their Eastern frontier, either through Danzig or by the Vistula, in order to convey supplies to the populations of these territories or for the purpose of maintaining order.

C—Clause Relating to East Africa

17. Evacuation of all German forces operating in East Africa within a period specified by the Allies.

D—General Clauses

18. Repatriation, without reciprocity, within a maximum period of one month, in accordance with detailed conditions hereafter to be fixed, of all interned civilians, including hostages and persons under trial and condemned, who may be subjects of other Allied or Associated States than those mentioned in Clause 3.

Financial Clause

19. With the reservation that any future concessions and claims by the Allies and United States of America remain unaffected, the following financial conditions are imposed :—

Reparation for damage done.

While the Armistice lasts, no public security shall be removed by the enemy which can serve as a pledge to the Allies to cover reparation of war losses.

Immediate restitution of the cash deposit in the National Bank of Belgium, and, in general, immediate return of all documents, specie, stock, shares, paper money, together with plant for the issue thereof, affecting public or private interests in the invaded countries.

Restitution of the Russian and Roumanian gold yielded to Germany or taken by that Power.

This gold to be delivered in trust to the Allies until peace is concluded.

E—*Naval Conditions*

20. Immediate cessation of all hostilities at sea, and definite information to be given as to the position and movements of all German ships.

Notification to be given to neutrals that freedom of navigation in all territorial waters is given to the Navies and Mercantile Marines of the Allied and Associated Powers, all questions of neutrality being waived.

21. All Naval and Mercantile Marine prisoners of war of the Allied and Associated Powers in German hands to be returned, without reciprocity.

22. To surrender at the ports specified by the Allies and the United States all submarines at present in existence (including all submarine cruisers and minelayers) with armament and equipment complete. Those that cannot put to sea shall be deprived of armament and equipment and shall remain under the supervision of the Allies and the United States. Submarines ready to put to sea shall be prepared to leave German ports immediately on receipt of wireless order to sail to the port of surrender, the remainder to follow as early as possible. The conditions of this Article shall be completed within fourteen days of the signing of the Armistice.

23. The following German surface warships, which shall be designated by the Allies and the United States of America, shall forthwith be disarmed and thereafter interned in neutral ports, or failing them, Allied ports, to be designated by the Allies and the United States of America, and placed under the surveillance of the Allies and the United States of America, only care and maintenance parties being left on board, namely :

    6 battle cruisers
    10 battleships
    8 light cruisers, including two minelayers
    50 destroyers of the most modern type.

All other surface warships (including river craft) are to be concentrated in German Naval bases, to be designated by the Allies and the United States of America, completely disarmed and placed under the supervision of the Allies and the United States of America. All vessels of the Auxiliary Fleet are to be disarmed. All vessels specified for internment shall be ready to leave German ports seven days after the signing of the Armistice. Directions for the voyage shall be given by wireless.

24. The Allies and the United States of America shall have the right to sweep up all minefields and destroy all obstructions laid by Germany outside German territorial waters, and the positions of these are to be indicated.

25. Freedom of access to and from the Baltic to be given to the Navies and Mercantile Marines of the Allied and Associated Powers. This to be secured by the occupation of all German forts, fortifications, batteries and defence works of all kinds in all the routes from the Cattegat into the Baltic, and by the sweeping up and destruction of all mines and obstructions within and without German territorial waters without any questions

FOCH'S ARRIVAL AT JULIERS, IN THE RHINELAND, MAY, 1919.

FOCH LEADING THE FRENCH TROOPS PAST THE ROYAL STAND IN THE LONDON "VICTORY PARADE" OF JULY 19TH, 1919.

of neutrality being raised, and the positions of all such mines and obstructions are to be indicated by the Germans.

26. The existing blockade conditions set up by the Allied and Associated Powers are to remain unchanged, and all German merchant ships found at sea are to remain liable to capture. The Allies and United States contemplate the provisioning of Germany during the Armistice as shall be found necessary.

27. All Aerial forces are to be concentrated and immobilized in German bases to be specified by the Allies and the United States of America.

28. In evacuating the Belgian coasts and ports, Germany shall abandon *in situ* and intact, the port material and material for inland waterways, also all merchant ships, tugs and lighters, all Naval aircraft and air materials and stores, all arms and armaments and all stores and apparatus of all kinds.

29. All Black Sea ports are to be evacuated by Germany; all Russian warships of all descriptions seized by Germany in the Black Sea are to be handed over to the Allies and the United States of America; all neutral merchant ships seized in the Black Sea are to be released; all warlike and other material of all kinds seized in those ports are to be returned, and German materials as specified in Clause 28 are to be abandoned.

30. All merchant ships at present in German hands belonging to the Allied and Associated Powers are to be restored to ports to be specified by the Allies and the United States of America without reciprocity.

31. No destruction of ships or of materials is to be permitted before evacuation, surrender or restoration.

32. The German Government shall formally notify the neutral Governments, and particularly the Govern-

ments of Norway, Sweden, Denmark and Holland, that all restrictions placed on the trading of their vessels with the Allied and Associated countries, whether by the German Government or by private German interests, and whether in return for special concessions, such as the export of shipbuilding materials or not, are immediately cancelled.

33. No transfers of German merchant shipping of any description to any neutral flag are to take place after signature of the Armistice.

F—Duration of Armistice

34. The duration of the Armistice is to be thirty-six days, with option to extend. During this period, on failure of execution of any of the above clauses, the Armistice may be repudiated by one of the contracting parties on forty-eight hours' previous notice.

It is understood that failure to execute Articles 3 and 18 completely in the periods specified is not to give reason for a repudiation of the Armistice, save where such failure is due to malice aforethought.

To ensure the execution of the present convention under the most favourable conditions, the principle of a permanent International Armistice Commission is recognized. This Commission will act under the supreme authority of the High Command, Military and Naval, of the Allied Armies.

The present Armistice was signed on the 11th day of November, 1918, at 5 o'clock A.M. (French time).

Signed :

F. Foch   Erzberger
R. E. Wemyss   Oberndorff
                   Winterfeldt
                   Vanselow

At 5.5 A.M., agreement was reached as to the final text. In order that hostilities might cease as soon as possible, it was decided to have the last page of the text typed immediately and the signatures attached thereto.

At 5.10 A.M., the Allied and German plenipotentiaries affixed their signatures. Five o'clock was agreed upon as the time of signing.

The Allied High Command, in view of political events in Germany, asked to have added to the text the following clause (at the end of "Answer to Observations") :

"In case the German vessels are not delivered within the periods agreed upon, the Governments of the Allies and the United States will have the right to occupy Heligoland in order to assure such delivery."

The German delegates stated that they could not sign this clause, but they agreed to urge its acceptance by the German Government. These matters were embodied in a separate document.

Herr Erzberger then asked to be heard. He read the following declaration, the text of which, signed by the four German plenipotentiaries, he handed to Marshal Foch :

"November 11th, 1918.
"*Statement of the German Plenipotentiaries on the occasion of signing the Armistice*

"The German Government will naturally make every effort within its power to see that the terms imposed are fulfilled.

"The undersigned Plenipotentiaries acknowledge that

on some points, upon their representation, a certain degree of benevolence has been shown. Therefore they feel that they can consider that the observations made by them on November 9th regarding the Armistice terms with Germany, and the answer made them on November 10th, constitute an integral part of the agreement as a whole.

" But they cannot allow any doubt to exist as to the fact that the shortness of the time allowed for evacuation, and the surrender of indispensable transport equipment, threaten to create a situation such as may render it impossible for them to continue the fulfilment of the terms, through no fault of the German Government and people.

" Referring to their repeated oral and written statements, the undersigned plenipotentiaries also deem it their duty to insist strongly on the fact that the carrying out of this agreement may plunge the German people into anarchy and famine.

" In view of the discussions which brought about the Armistice, we might have expected terms which, while assuring our adversary complete and entire military security, would have terminated the sufferings of non-combatants, of women and children.

" The German nation, which for fifty months has defied a world of enemies, will preserve, in spite of every kind of violence, its liberty and unity.

" A nation of seventy millions suffers but does not die.
" (signed) ERZBERGER, OBERNDORFF,
" WINTERFELDT, VANSELOW."

Marshal Foch then declared the meeting closed and the German delegates withdrew.

The following telegram was immediately sent along

the whole front by radio and by telephone to the Commanders-in-Chief:

" 1. Hostilities will cease on the entire front on *November* 11*th* at 11 A.M. French time.
" 2. Allied troops are not to pass until further orders beyond the line reached on that day at that hour.
" Exact report must be made as to this line.
" 3. All communication with the enemy is forbidden until receipt of instructions by Army Commanders."

(signed) WEYGAND
Major-General, Chief of Staff.

In the course of the morning the various documents were handed to the German plenipotentiaries. Their train left the Rethondes station at 11.30 A.M. for Tergnier, where they were to take their automobiles.

At their request every facility was afforded Captain Geyer of the German Army for his journey by air to German Headquarters bearing the texts and maps.

This officer left the Tergnier landing-field at about 12.30 P.M.

On November 11th at 11 A.M., firing ceased along the whole front of the Allied armies. An impressive silence followed upon fifty-three months of battle. The nations could now look forward to seeing a world once more restored to peace.

The next day I issued the following General Order:

" Officers, non-commissioned officers and soldiers of the Allied Armies :
" After resolutely repulsing the enemy for months, you confidently attacked him with an untiring energy.

"You have won the greatest battle in History and rescued the most sacred of all causes, the Liberty of the World.

"You have full right to be proud, for you have crowned your standards with immortal glory and won the gratitude of posterity.

"F. Foch
"Marshal of France
"Commander-in-Chief of the Allied Armies."

CHAPTER XV

THE MARCH TO THE RHINE

Did the Allied Armies completely fulfil their duty toward their respective countries on November 11th?—The March to the Rhine—The renewals of the Armistice.

In accordance with the protocol which accompanied the Armistice, the Allied Armies a few days later were put in movement towards the Rhine for the purpose of taking possession of the three bridge-heads at Cologne, Coblence and Mayence, and occupying the German territory on the left bank of the river.

Before following them on this victorious march, it may be well to ask whether, in accepting the Armistice of November 11th, they had entirely done their duty toward their countries.

The Armistice signed by the Commander-in-Chief of the Allied Armies did not constitute a peace treaty or even the preliminaries of peace. It was a suspension of hostilities which intervened in the course of a conflict for the purpose of stopping bloodshed and giving the belligerent countries the time required for drawing up a treaty of peace. Though its text embodied certain political and financial clauses calling for immediate fulfilment, it did not determine the situation of the belligerent states at the close of the war; the Allied Governments had reserved to themselves the important task of drafting the treaty which would fix this situation.

To guarantee to these Governments the possibility of

fully carrying out this task, the Allied Armies and their commanders agreed to halt their operations under conditions which rendered the military situation sufficiently advantageous to prevent any resistance on the part of the enemy to the intentions of the Allied Governments and to the peace terms they might dictate.

The Rhine was an obstacle under the protection of which Germany might have jeopardized the victories of our Armies, reconstituted her forces and then proceeded to discuss conditions of peace. But now the Allied Armies were going to hold the Rhine. They were even going to hold both banks. Here they were in a position, if need arose, to resume their advance and put a stop to any difficulties which the German Government might seek to create. Proof of this fact was furnished later when, on June 28th, 1919, at Versailles, the treaty of peace, in the exact form which the Allied and Associated Governments had decided to give it, was signed by the Germans without demur.

In addition, the occupation of the Rhineland by virtue of the Armistice constituted a mortgage in the hands of the Allies such as would guarantee the payment of the indemnities they had decided to claim.

By making it possible, if necessity arose, to resume the War from dominating positions, and by exacting this mortgage—both assured in the very text of the Armistice and thus representing a consolidation of our victory—the Allied High Command had placed in the hands of the Allied Governments the means of making whatever terms of peace they might decide to be desirable, and of ensuring their execution by the enemy.

Moreover, it must not be imagined that the signing of the Armistice was premature on our part, or that we might have derived advantage from delaying it some

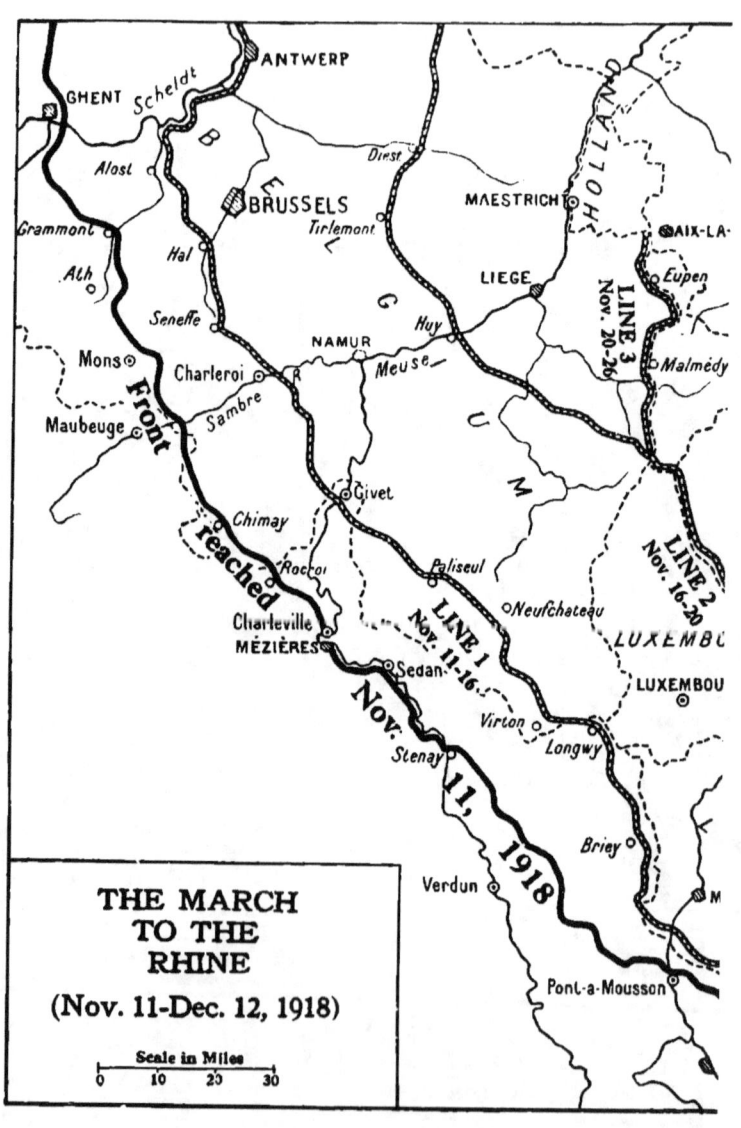

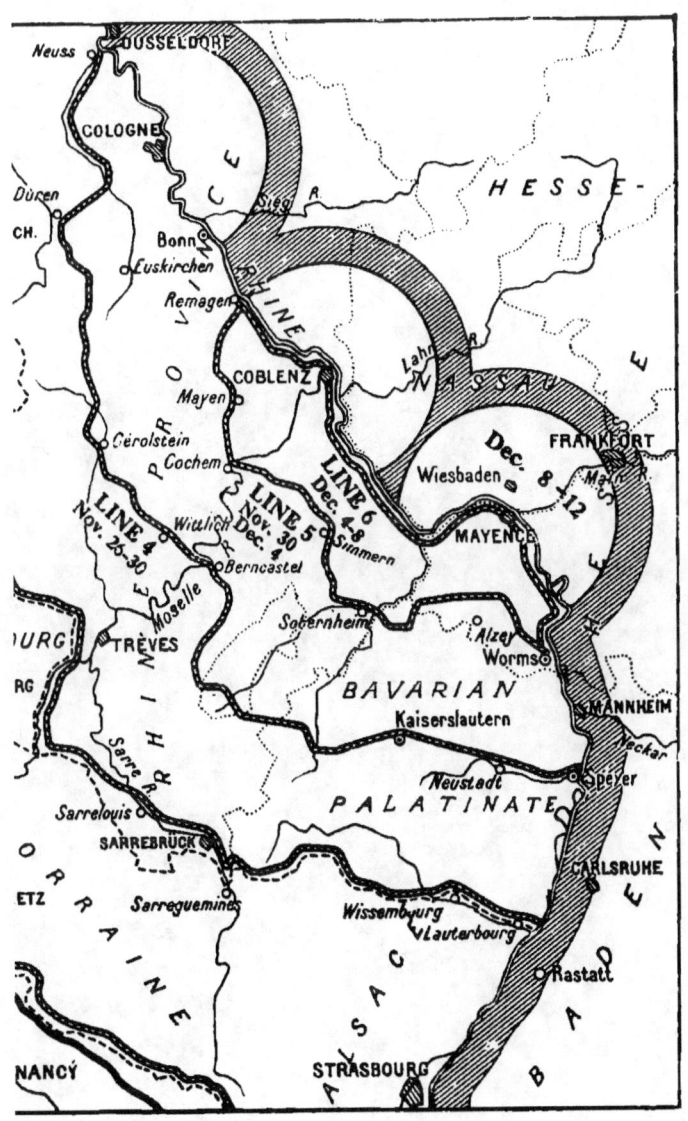

days or even some weeks, until such time as the German defeat had been finally sealed by a military disaster equivalent to a new Sedan. In what concerns this point, I have described in the preceding pages the results we had a right to expect from the attack all ready to be launched east of the Moselle on November 14th, the execution of which we halted as a consequence of the suspension of hostilities ordered on November 11th. These results would have been, after a victorious start, to extend our battle front by yet another twenty miles, already stretching for 200 miles, and along which, up to that moment, we had been waging a successful battle from the North Sea to Lorraine. But the nature of this frontal assault could in no way have modified the situation to our ultimate profit.

Ever since the middle of July the Allied Armies, in a series of encounters, had beaten and driven back the Germans; 7,990 officers, 355,000 men, 6,215 guns, 38,622 machine-guns, had been taken—figures surpassing anything history had recorded up to then, and equivalent to several Sedans. By their constant pounding they had sown among the enemy troops a demoralization bordering on insurrection. If hostilities had been continued, the Allies would have been able to accentuate and augment these emphatic results, but without changing their nature. Several millions of German soldiers, armed with rapid-fire guns and still disposing of vast quantities of war material, retreating across a relatively restricted area, would have preserved to the struggle all its former characteristics.

Disordered masses of men, the débris of more than 200 German Divisions, were falling back in confusion, filling the whole countryside like a swarm of ants on the march. But they were armed with guns, machine-guns and rifles, and, thanks to these rapid-fire weapons, they were unapproachable and impenetrable until such time as we could bring up more guns and more machine-guns than they had. These armed hordes, moving like a great scourge, left behind them a devastated land. On all sides there was nothing but destruction. Roads and bridges were made impassable and abandoned war material littered every practicable line of advance.

Hence it was most difficult for the heads of columns launched in pursuit to bring up forces with sufficient speed to throw this retreating mob into even greater confusion, and break through or surround it. Only with the aid of powerful artillery could they move successfully.

But as the victorious columns advanced, they had to be supplied with food and munitions. This again greatly retarded their rate of march, owing to the lack of railways and the condition of the roads. In short, it was a case of well-ordered armies pushing before them troops in ever increasing disorder, gathering in prisoners and material as they went, the daily proof of a steadily growing success.

We could have continued the campaign along these lines up to the Rhine, where we should have started anew after having established a strong base on the river and repaired the indispensable lines of communication—if, meanwhile, some cataclysm had not taken place among the German masses. But the disorder our Armies had created in the ranks of the enemy, and the cruel suffering they had inflicted upon him, rapidly increased and finally brought on insurrection. This feeling was spreading through the country, where the sufferings of the people and the conviction that further resistance was impossible developed into revolution.

Famished by four years of war, there remained to Germany nothing but a disorganized army, incapable of staying the victorious rush of the Allies, and in revolt against its commanders. The country lay at the mercy of the victors. Germany signed the Armistice without discussion in order to save from the destruction of war what remained of her institutions.

On November 11th, I sent the Commanders-in-Chief general instructions prescribing the conditions under which Allied territory evacuated by the enemy was to be occupied by their troops.

On November 17th, the Allied Armies crossed the lines they held at the moment hostilities ceased. On the 30th, all the invaded territories (in France, Belgium, Luxembourg and Alsace-Lorraine) had been entirely re-occupied. On the 25th I entered Metz and on the 26th Strasbourg.

During this time I was making ready the approaching occupation of the Rhineland. It was to be divided in four zones, Mayence, Coblence, Cologne, Aix-la-Chapelle, placed respectively under a French, American, British and Belgian command. In each zone, the troops were, in principle, to be of the same nationality. At the bridge-heads, however, as well as in the territory on the left bank of the Rhine lying between the Cologne bridge-head and the Dutch frontier, it was stipulated that the garrisons would be composed of troops belonging to several Allied nations. This was done in order to maintain the Allied character of the occupation.

The total force of the Allied Armies initially holding the Rhineland, including those in the first line and those in reserve, consisted of sixteen Army Corps, composed of forty Divisions, plus five Divisions of cavalry. The maintenance of these troops was to be at the expense of the German Government.

In practice, the inter-Allied character of the occupation of the bridge-heads could not be entirely maintained. Thus, the one at Cologne was handed over wholly to the British, since the French Division which was to have been assigned to it was, through needs of the moment, attached to the Belgian zone around Aix-la-Chapelle.

On December 1st, the march of the Allied Armies brought them into Germany; on the 9th, they were on the Rhine; on the 13th, they crossed it; on the 17th, the bridge-heads were completely occupied.

From that date onwards the Entente Armies mounted guard on the Rhine. From its shores they beheld vanquished Germany at their feet; at the slightest attempt on her part to lift her head and cause trouble, they had but to make a move to stop it. Posted there, they enabled the Allied Governments to dictate to the Central Powers whatever conditions of peace they might consider it proper to impose. The Allied Armies had accomplished their task.

However impatient the world might be to see the definite conclusion of this peace for which it thirsted, the negotiations leading up to it were destined to be long-drawn-out. The tardy arrival of President Wilson in France, the scope of the problems demanding solution, the necessity of reaching a preliminary agreement among the Allies, who often held divergent opinions on almost all of the questions, all required such a long time, that, despite the good will and arduous labour of the treaty's architects, four months were required to shape it, and five to obtain Germany's acceptance.

Now, the Armistice signed at Rethondes was only valid for thirty-six days. It expired on December 17th, and on this date the Allied plenipotentiaries were only beginning to reach Paris. The convention of November 11th, therefore, had to be renewed. The negotiations for this purpose took place on December 12th and 13th, 1918. The same delegates as at Rethondes met in the same railway car, the office car of my train. It is unnecessary to go into the details of these negotiations which ended in the following agreement :

1. The duration of the Armistice was prolonged one month, viz : until January 17th, 1919.
2. The Allied High Command reserved the right to occupy the neutral zone on the right bank of the Rhine, north of the Cologne bridge-head and up to the Dutch frontier, whenever it might consider this additional guarantee was required.

It was hoped that the new convention would cover the time necessary for handing the preliminaries of peace to the Germans—a result desired by them as much as by ourselves ; and, indeed, this would have been the natural solution if the large armies still existing were to be cut down.

Unfortunately, the Council of Four could not solve its problems in time. Therefore, I again went to Trèves and, on January 15th and 16th, negotiated with the German delegates a second extension of the Armistice. The principal clauses covered the following points :

1. Extension of the Armistice for one month—until February 17th.

2. Germany to furnish agricultural machines and implements.

3. Establishment at Berlin of an Allied Commission for supervising Russian prisoners of war in Germany.

4. Details for executing clauses of the agreement of November 11th regarding the surrender of German vessels and the restitution of material taken out of France and Belgium.

5. The entire merchant fleet of Germany to be placed under the control and under the flag of the Allies for the duration of the Armistice; this measure was intended to assure the feeding of Germany and the rest of Europe.

6. The Allied High Command reserved the right to occupy the sector of the fortified zone of Strasbourg, consisting of the forts on the right bank of the Rhine, together with a strip of land in front of these forts from three to six miles deep, whenever it might consider this additional guarantee to be required.

The second extension of the Armistice, like the first, was concluded in the hope that it might cover the time required for the conclusion of the preliminary terms of peace. But these remained unformulated—in fact, the Allied Governments gave up the idea of formulating them; therefore the Armistice was renewed a third time. But it was now understood that this extension was to be the last and that no date was to be fixed for its expiration. The Allied Powers merely reserved the right of terminating it on three days' notice. No new dispositions were made. Supervision of the execution of clauses incompletely carried out was confided to the permanent Armistice commission.

However, the Germans were at once required to give up all offensive operations against the Poles in the

Posen region and everywhere else, and a line of demarcation was drawn beyond which their troops were not to advance.

On June 28th, 1919, peace was concluded and signed in the Hall of Mirrors in the Palace of Versailles.

THE END

FOCH AT HIS COUNTRY PLACE, "TREUFEUNTINIOU," IN BRITTANY, WITH HIS GRANDCHILDREN.

THE FUNERAL OF MARSHAL FOCH, AN IMPOSING PAGEANT WATCHED BY THOUSANDS IN THE CHAMPS ELYSEE.

THE PAPAL NUNCIO, CARDINAL DUBOIS AND CARDINAL BINET IN FOCH'S FUNERAL PROCESSION.

INDEX

ABBEVILLE, 140 (French's H.Q.), 255, 292, 316 (War Council), 332 (Allied Meeting), 335, 349, 353, 388, 394
Agadir, xlii
Air Transport, 487
Aire, 142 (British Cavalry)
Aisne, 48 (Fourth Army), 53 (Foch attacks), 54 (enemy attack), 56 (French danger), 113 (Foch advances), 118 (Fifth Army attacked), 140 (British Army), 359 (enemy success), 406, 411, 415, 454, 460, 467, 479, 502, 503, 514 (Allied success), 524
Aix-la-Chapelle, 577
Albert of Belgium, 149, 150, 151, 152, 160, 186, 227, 317 (in Flanders), 336, 470, 471, 485, 486, 498, 499 (enters Bruges), 523 (British troops)
Allemant, 89 (Importance)
Allen, General, 105
Allenby, General, 138 (Flanders), 179, 180 (at Messines), 182 (reinforced)
Allied Armies, 274 (no mutual action)
American Army, 255, 259, 267, 269 (only 300,000 men), 279, 345, 351 (general survey), 367, 368, 369, 394, 396 (its strength), 406, 415, 417, 452, 457, 458, 460, 466 (initial success), 468 (on Meuse), 477 (new offensive), 491 (shortage of men), 503 (reach Grandpré), 508 (present distribution), 510 (Foch's orders), 514 (offensive starts)
Amiens, 48 (Sixth Army), 49 (to attack), 284 (enemy attack), 296 (grave danger), 299, 301, 303, 306, 309, 313 (British attack), 320, 325, 339, 433, 456 (now free)
Ammunition, 489 (still short), 493, (critical situation). *See also* Artillery
Ancre, 251 (British success), 456
Antwerp, 126 (Belgian Army), 139, 140 (capitulation), 144, 145, 204, 205

Anvin, 167 (Foch and Sir John French)
Aosta, Duke of, 262
Archangel, 398
Ardennes, 53 (Fourth Army), 449, 517
Argonne, 406, 470, 478, 481, 498, 503, 511 (American Army), 514 (North cleared)
Armentières, 324 (enemy capture), 456, 487 (occupied by Allies)
Armistice, 526 (German plea), 527 (Foch's suggestions), 529 (obvious danger), 531 (Foch's views), 537 (Haig's conditions), 538 (Pétain's views), 538 (Pershing's proposals), 559 (final conditions), 568 (duration), 568 (International Commission)
Arnes, 57 (French retreat)
Aroude, 378 (French success)
Arras, 135 (attack), 138 (Tenth Army), 142 (attacked), 191 (heavy fighting), 192, 213, 215 (Tenth Army), 235 (British troops), 239, 281 (German offensive), 290 (enemy attack), 305, 320, 322, 325 (attack expected), 328, 333, 336, 404, 451 (enemy retreat), 454
Artillery, 16 (Importance), 39 (attack delayed), 41 (German superiority), 69 (attack on Ninth Army), 117 (French retreat), 168 (French weakness), 172 (enemy attack), 197 (enemy superiority), 202 (vital importance), 217 (shortage), 225 (serious position), 240 (shortage persists), 398 (American shortage). *See also* Ammunition
Artois, xx, 193, 226, 235, 238, 239, 326 (attack feared), 331, 442
Asiago, 266 (heavy fighting), 401
Attigny, 53 (Foch's H.Q.)
Aubigny, 135 (Foch arrives), 137
Augagneur, M., 152 (Belgian Secretary of Navy)
Aumale, 322
Australians, 339
Austria, xliii (Ultimatum), xliv

583   RR

INDEX

(War), 255, 256, 515 (Armistice concluded), 542 (Terms)
Austrian Armies, 400, 401, 402 (new offensive)
Auve, 105 (French Cavalry)
Avelghem, 500
Avesnes, 498, 522 (British advance), 523
Avre, 309, 321, 339, 438, 440, 456
Avricourt, 15

BADEN, Prince Max, 530 (peace terms), 547
Balfourier, General, 5, 41 (Command of XX Corps), 188
Bannes, 70 (taken by enemy)
Bapaume, 132 (French retreat), 248, 249, 251, 290 (Haig withdraws), 451 (Byng's success), 454
Baronville, 21, 22 (hostile forces)
Barrère, M., 401 (Ambassador in Rome)
Barthelemy, General, 302
Bavaria, Crown Prince, 282, 340, 366, 367, 376
Baye, 88, 93
Beauvais, 306 (Fayolle's H.Q.), 308 (Foch's H.Q.), 314 (Allied Conference), 321, 325
Belfort, 473
Belgian Army, 139, 146 (at Nieuport), 146 (Ypres), 147 (deplorable state), 150, 151 (King Albert), 157 (at Yser), 158 (German attack), 160, 161, 163, 171, 194, 214, 227, 317, 330, 334 (in danger), 341, 470, 471, 485
Belgium, xlv (German menace), 8 (invasion), 47 (in German possession), 126 (Army at Antwerp), 141 (held by Germans), 145, 147 (neutrality), 219 (North Sea), 495 (liberated coast), 499 (Germans driven back), 524 (in full retreat)
Belgrade, xliv (bombarded)
Belval, 514 (occupied by Allies)
Berlin, 521, 526, 540 (Foch's objective)
Berlioncourt, 23
Bernhardi, xxxiii
Berru, 119, 121 (attacked by Foch)
Berthelot, General, 258, 259, 407
Bétheniville, 55 (Foch's H.Q.)
Béthune, 142 (British II Corps), 143, 322, 331, 333, 343
Bezange Forest, 32
Bidon, General, 146 (Dunkirk)
Birdwood, General, 487 (advances)
Blankenberghe, 499 (occupied by Belgians)

Blendeques, 335 (Foch), 341
Bliss, General, 264 (U.S.A.), 276, 307, 352, 398
Blondlat, General, 68
Boelle, General, 137 (gives way)
Boissoudy, General, 498
Bombon, xiii, xvi, 369 (Foch's H.Q.), 389 (Conference), 395, 401, 429 (Conference), 446, 460, 471 (King Albert)
Bon, Admiral de, 537
Bontemps, Major, xiv
Boulogne, 173, 295
Boult-aux-Bois, 514
Bourgeois, General, 493
Boutal, Captain, xvi
Bray, 442, 451
Breteuil, 126 (Castelnau's H.Q.), 127 (Foch arrives), 137 (Foch), 138, 323, 325
Bretons, 54 (XI Corps), 59 (heavy losses)
Brimont, 358 (enemy success)
Britain, Great, xliv (Protest), 48 (Army on the Somme), 49 (at Guise), 104 (to attack in N.W.), 126 (Army moved from Aisne), 126 (H.Q. at St. Omer), 133 (Channel Ports). *See also* British Army
British Army (*see also* Britain, Great), 138 (Flanders), 140, 142, 143 (Bethune), 144 (delayed), 165 (La Bassée), 166, 171 (at Menin), 173 (Boulogne), 176 (serious position), 184 (no further troops), 191 (continued attack), 223 (Flanders), 225 (Haig advances), 239 (advance), 251 (Ancre), 265 (in Italy), 281 (enemy offensive), 289, 291, 303 (hasty retreat), 306 (still shaken), 313 (Amiens), 315 (Lloyd George), 321 (Somme), 324 (lost confidence), 326 (Haig's anxiety), 334 (heavily attacked), 340 (French support), 347 (heavy losses), 349 (further fighting), 350 (situation precarious), 394, 417, 483 (on Scheldt), 496 (advance at Oise), 499 (strong advance)
British Navy, 148, 485
Brocqueville, M. de, 148 (Belgian Prime Minister), 149 (visits Furnes)
Broussy-le-petit, 84 (enemy attack), 85
Brugère, General, 138 (Territorials)
Bruges, 145 (Belgian retreat), 170, 471, 499 (King Albert's entry)
Brunnhilde Stellung, 498

INDEX

Bulow, General von, 281, 282, 358
Buzancy, 475, 514 (American success)
Byng, General, 281, 304 (visited by Foch), 305 (good work), 450 (enemy retreat), 482

CACHY, 338 (enemy advance)
Cadorna, General, 254 (meets Foch), 257 (in London), 260, 261 (with Foch), 264 (War Council)
Calais, 145 (German hopes), 146, 152, 172, 331, 428
Calcagno, Colonel, 401, 402
Cambon, M., 183 (at Dunkirk)
Cambrai, 213, 453, 462, 467, 472, 482, 484
Canadians, 234
Cane, Du, Sir John, xiii
Caporetto, 260, 261, 267
Carlepont, 450
Cardot, xxix
Carency, 236
Cary, General de, 51 (and Foch), 52 (at Machault), 78 (and Foch)
Cassel, 165 (Foch's H.Q.), 166, 174, 181, 184, 186 (Joffre), 194, 195 (Sir Henry Wilson), 207 (Lord Roberts), 330, 335, 470, 486
Castelnau, General de, 8 (Second Army), 36 (at Meurthe), 38 (orders advance), 40 (troops rest), 126 (at Breteuil), 127 (and Foch), 137, 138, 142, 253, (in Russia), 368, 517, 518, 519
Casualties, 489 (French), 490 (British), 509 (American)
Causson, Father, xxiv
Cavallero, Colonel, 401
Cérizy, 483
Chacemont, 397
Châlons, 71 (German advance), 103 (French advance), 105, 107 (Foch's H.Q.), 110, 111 (Bishop of)
Champagne, 87 (advantages), 89 (in danger), 99, 102 (heavy rains), 125 (at a standstill), 213, 238, 285, 288, 290, 296, 382, 404, 406, 411 (German failure), 413, 521
Channel Ports, 133, 139, 145, 152, 168, 201, 219, 292, 301, 341
Chantilly, 213 (French G.H.Q.), 226 (Allied Conference), 243, 251, (Allied Conference)
Chapron, M., 110, 127
Charleroi, 173 (French retreat)
Charleville, 71 (X Corps)
Charmes, 42 (forced by enemy), 44 (enemy held)

Château Chalins, 23 (Foch's H.Q.), 26 (retreat), 29 (bridgehead)
Château-Thierry, 365, 391, 406, 410, 413, 416, 417
Chaumont, xiii, 473, 502
Chemical Warfare, 203
Chemin des Dames, 358 (enemy attack), 359, 474
Cherfils, xxix
Churchill, Winston, 223, 224, 310
Clamanges, 78 (attacked)
Clemenceau, M., xvi, 276 (supports Foch), 293 (Foch visits), 295, 297, 298, 299, 300, 307, 310, 314, 372, 374, 389, 401, 408, 431, 459, 491, 493, 504 (and American troops), 505 (Pershing's obstinacy), 527 (Foch and the Armistice), 529, 536 (consults Foch)
Clermont, 303 (Foch's visit), 304
Coblenz, 573, 577
Cologne, 573, 577
Combles, 248 (French success)
Comines, 327
Compiègne, 274 (Allied Conference), 295 (French G.H.Q.), 376 (threatened), 391, 395, 545 (German peace envoys)
Congy, 68 (held by enemy)
Conneau, General, 9
Couchil, 26 (lost)
Coucy-le-Château, 455
Couronné, Grand, 5, 43 (French success)
Courtacon, 62 (Fifth Army)
Courtrai, 498 (Allied advance), 499, 500 (captured)
Craonne, 48 (Fifth Army)
Crévic Woods, 39 (11th Div.)
Croix-aux-Bois, 514 (Allied capture)
Crozat Canal, 289 (enemy attack)

DAMVILLERS, 480
Dantant, General, 5
Davidson, General, 327
Debeney, General, xxxiv, 302, 306, 323, 339, 384, 439, 446, 471, 482, 484, 522, 523 (rapid advance), 544 (peace envoys)
Degoutte, General, 415, 471, 485, 498 (with Belgians)
Delme Hill, 13, 22 (German withdrawal)
Denain, 500 (occupied by Allies)
d'Esperey, General, 82 (Fifth Army), 87, 104 (to support Foch), 117 (threatened on left)
Desticker, Major, 209 (decorated by King George), 303, 330, 331, 335, 439

585

INDEX

Destruction, Wanton, by Germans, 494
Devaux, Colonel, 47
Diaz, General, 264 (Italian C.I.C.), 400, 401, 402, 403, 491, 542 (Armistice terms)
Dieuze, 18 (German withdrawal)
Dixmude, 150 (held by Marines), 157, 158 (German attack), 159, 161, 162, 163, 164 (Stubborn fight), 171 (French troops), 188, 486 (reoccupied)
Donnelay, 15 (advance), 17 (attack), 18
Dormans, 365, 366, 404, 410
Douai, 213, 488, 498, 500 (occupied by Allies)
Doulcon, 514 (American success)
Doullens, 137 (Foch's H.Q.), 138 (Territorial H.Q.), 140 (Sir John French), 152, 153 (Foch's report), 297 (Allied Conference), 325, 328, 342
Drocourt, 455, 467
Dubois, General, 10, 51 (with Foch), 71 (IX Corps), 90, 95, 171, 177
Duchesne, General, 142, 265 (in Italy), 358, 359, 367
Dun, 514 (occupied by Allies)
Dunkirk, 139 (defended), 146 (concentration), 148 (Foch arrives), 152 (defences inundated), 172 (danger here), 183 (French President), 325, 327, 331, 335 (Haig suggests destruction), 428
Durand, General, 15
d'Urbal, General, 166, 177, 180, 195, 208 (King George), 214, 235

ECOLE de Guerre, xxix, xxxiv, xxxv
Eparges, 466
Epernay, 10? (French advance), 104 (German forces), 410 (enemy attack), 412
Erzberger, Herr, 547 (peace envoy)
Espinasse, General, 16
Eydoux, General, 51 (with Foch)

FALKENHAUSEN, xxxiii
Falkenhayn, 252 (replaced)
Fayolle, Marshal, xxi, xxxiv, 290, 291, 302, 303 (at Clermont), 306, 323, 328, 339, 362, 365, 377, 378, 412 (visit of Foch), 440, 447
Fère-Champenoise, 80 (in danger), 82, 83, 84, 85, 86, 87, 90 (bombarded), 91 (heavy fire), 94 (Colonel Weygand), 95 (a counter attack), 97 (heavy enemy losses), 100 (Foch's H.Q.), 100 (German "attack" on cellars)
Fère-en-Tardenois, 421
Ferry, General, 35
Flainval Heights, 35 (enemy attain), 37 (Foch advances)
Flanders, 138 (Allenby), 139, 154 (dangerous gap), 156 (Battle of), 169 (desperate struggle), 195 (general survey), 233 (British troops), 323 (enemy offensive), 329 (difficult position), 333, 340 (new attack), 341 (more French troops), 343 (German menace), 382, 404, 438, 485, 486 (Foch arrives), 487 (French advance), 496, 498, 499
Flixecourt, 444 (King George)
Foch, Marshal, xiii, xvi, xxi (birth), xxi (his father), xxvi (enlists), xxxv (Chief of Staff), xxxvii (visits Russia), lvi (outbreak of war), 3 (recalled from leave), 21 (a dangerous advance), 21 (XX Corps moves), 27 (communications threatened), 28 (at the Seille), 31 (ordered to fall back), 37 (attacks at Lunéville), 38 (XX Corps in hard fighting), 39 (advance on Friscati), 40 (new command), 41 (farewell to XX Corps), 41 (in Lorraine), 48 (and Joffre), 50 (not yet employed), 51 (new command), 53 (H.Q. at Attigny), 54 (pressed at Mézières), 56 (in danger on the Aisne), 61 (Ninth Army), 66 (plans for attack), 67 (dangerous situation), 72 (on the Somme), 78 (enemy held back), 80 (XI Corps attacked), 92 (hopeful of success), 94 (new plan of attack), 100 (enemy retreat), 106 (crosses Marne), 107 (H.Q. at Châlons), 110 (family losses), 123 (attacked at Berru), 125 (goes to Joffre), 126 (assistant to C.I.C.), 137, (at Breteuil, 140 (Sir John French), 142 (report to Joffre), 149 (King of Belgians), 153 (report on Belgian Army), 155 (meets Lloyd George), 159 (returns to Furnes), 160 (sees King), 169 (at Ypres), 175 (hurries to St. Omer), 182 (sees Sir John French), 183 goes to Dunkirk), 183 (and Kitchener), 186 (and Joffre), 189 (with Sir John French 194 (Belgian Chief of Staff), 196 (and Joffre), 203 (Report to H.Q.), 207 (Lord Roberts), 208 (King George), 209 (Grand Cross of the Bath), 222 (motor accident), 233 (command of

586

INDEX

Northern Armies), 233 (Vimy Ridge), 237 (Lorette), 238 (importance of Vimy), 239 (Tenth Army), 240 (comments on artillery shortage), 241 (gas attacks), 249 (the Somme), 251 (transferred to Senlis), 253 (in command at Mirecourt), 254 (sent to Italy), 254 (returns to Senlis), 254 (Chief of General Staff), 257 (in London), 260 (support for Italy), 261 (goes to Treviso), 262 (visits Rome), 263 (Italy), 264 (Supreme War Council), 264 (at Padua), 267 (American troops), 268 (new problem), 270 (his programme), 274 (at Compiègne 276 (Clemenceau's support), 278 (opposition from Haig), 279 (his protests), 288 (vital need of a Supreme Command), 293 (visits Clemenceau), 297 (at Doullens), 300 (Allied Commander-in-Chief), 304 (rapid action), 315 (Lloyd George), 316 (Generalissimo), 327 (H.Q. at Sarcus), 343 (forbids withdrawals), 360 (dangerous situation on Aisne), 368 (interview with Pétain), 372 (Paris Conference), 378 (Mangin's good work), 383 (fresh plans), 385 (support from French Government), 392 (plans for the new offensive), 408 (interference of Lloyd George), 409 (Foch threatens to resign), 416 (German counter attack), 422 (German retreat), 423 (Soissons recaptured), 444 (meets King George), 455 (enemy retreat on whole front), 476 (now Marshal), 486 (in Flanders), 494 (prisoner labour), 506 (trouble with Pershing), 520 (American troops for big offensive), 527 (the Armistice), 531 (German tricks), 536 (consulted by Clemenceau), 540 (Naval conditions), 541 (war or no war), 542 (fight for the Rhine), 548 (stern attitude), 551 (refuses to cease hostilities), 559 (final conditions), 571 (Foch's final General Order), 577 (Foch enters Metz and Strasbourg), 581 (Peace signed at Versailles)

France, xlii, xlvi (her Army), liii (strength of Army), lv (General Staff), lvii (Mobilization), 6 (Frontier violated), 8 (Germans declare war), 24 (battle along whole front), 31 (Second Army withdraws), 39 (Foch advances), 42 (Lorraine), 43 (success at Couronné), 43 (checked at Morhange), 47 (invasion from Somme to Vosges), 47 (advance on Paris), 48 (retreat), 49 (Fifth Army retires), 57 (Fourth Army retires), 59 (no hope of offensive), 60 (retreat continues), 61 (retreat ended), 75 (enemy checked), 80 (German retreat), 119 (short of ammunition), 124 (Fifth Army heavily attacked). *See also* French Army

French, Sir John, 140, 153, 167, 170, 173 (Boulogne), 174 (Captain de Sauvigny), 175 (British danger), 176 (considers retreat), 177 (with Foch), 179, 182, 189 (with Foch), 196, 223, 224 (troops wanted), 226, 240 (Givenchy attack), 273

French Army, 189 (reinforcements), 190 (Ypres), 253 (Nivelle in command), 350 (general survey). *See also* France

Friscati, 39 (citadel position), 40 (11th Div.)

Fugitives, 135, 149

Furnes, 148 (Belgian H.Q.), 149 (Foch meets the King), 158 (General Grossetti), 159 (Foch returns), 186 (King Albert)

GALLIENI, General, 223
Garda, Lake, 265
Gas attack, 234, 239, 241, 341, 358
Géline Wood, 30 (Foch's H.Q.)
George, King, 208 (visit to troops), 444 (meets Foch)
George, Lloyd, 155 (Tour of France), 257 (on Russia), 273 (favours Supreme Command), 273 (Turkey), 278, 280, 287, 314 (at Beauvais), 349 (weak British Reserves), 374, 408 (interference with Foch), 409, 491, 529, 542 (peace terms)
Gérard, General, 517, 518
German Army, 166 (strong position), 255 (superiority in numbers), 281 (new offensive), 309 (fresh efforts), 322 (threat to British), 323 (Flanders), 327 (rapid advance), 358 (quick success), 366 (furious fighting), 378 (heavy defeat), 414 (standstill), 416 (heavy counter attack), 419 (surprised), 448 (a lost chance), 455 (retreat on whole front), 481 (further retreat), 487 (retreat), 523 (shattered at Guise), 526 (demoralised), 526 (sue for peace). *See also* Germany
German Crown Prince, 282

INDEX

Germany, xxxix, xliv (French Gov.), xliv (war on Russia), liii (strength of Army), 7 (Metz), 8 (Luxemburg and Belgium), 8 (war with France), 16 (long range guns), 49 (big advance), 53 (success at Rethel), 58 (Third Army) 62, (First Army in danger), 91 (expensive attacks), 100 (driven back), 103 (retreat from Fourth Army), 109 (failure of attempt on Paris), 116 (her strength), 118 (bombarded Rheims), 578 (Allied Armies enter). *See also* German Army

Geyer, Captain, 548 (peace envoy), 571

Ghent, 145 (Allies retire), 166 (German forces), 471, 521, 522

Gillain, General, 317 (Belgian Chief of Staff), 333, 336, 364 (to relieve British), 457, 470, 486

Ginchy, 248

Givenchy, 240 (Allied success)

Gough, General, 281, 289 (heavy defeat), 291 (faulty retreat), 302 (visited by Foch), 303, 305 (replaced by Rawlinson)

Gourand, General, 410

Grandpré, 481, 482, 503 (reached by Americans)

Graziani, General, 401 (commanding French troops in Italy)

Greece, 255

Grossetti, General, 51 (with Foch), 95, 158 (at Furnes), 159, 162, (his curt message), 164 (attacked on Ramscapelle), 208 (King George)

Guillavmat, General, 389 (returns from East)

Guillemont, 248

Guise, 49 (British Army), 502 (abandoned by Germans), 523 (Allied advance)

HAIG, Sir Douglas, 170, 177, 179 (retreat stopped by Foch), 181, 225, 226, 247, 278 (refuses Foch's plan), 285, 287, 290 (defeated on Somme), 292, 295 (need for action), 297, 299, 308, 319, 322, 324, 326 (anxiety), 327 (rapid enemy advance), 332 (anxiety), 335 (suggests destruction of Dunkirk), 344, 349, 364 (hard pressed), 367 (visits Foch), 372, 405, 406, 412, 429 (at Bombon), 435, 442, 444, 445 (advises delay), 452 (American troops), 470 (at Cassel), 483 (forces Hindenburg Line), 494 (Prisoner labour), 522

(Flanders Army), 537 (Peace terms)

Haller, General, 520 (Polish troops)

Hamell, 438

Hangard, 310, 340 (held by enemy)

Hanotaux, General, 149 (Belgian Chief of Staff)

Haut de Koking, 22 (11th Division)

Hazebrouck, 154 (British troops), 327 (enemy advance), 331, 333

Helldorff, Captain, 548 (peace envoy)

Herpont, 106 (French Cavalry)

Hindenburg, 252 (in command German Armies), 283, 558 (peace terms)

Hindenburg Line, 455, 456, 467, 470, 472, 483 (final assault)

Hollebeke, 175 (British danger), 180 (French attack), 181, 327 (enemy capture)

Hooge, 176 (shelled)

Hope, Admiral, 547 (peace envoy)

Horne, General, 324 (attacked), 331, 453, 454 (rapid advance), 482, 487

Horses, 490

Hostilities Cease, 571

House, Colonel, 540 (representing President Wilson)

Houthem, 227 (Belgian H.Q.), 486

Humbert, General, liv, 58 (Moroccan Div.), 88 (attacked), 120 (increased command), 120 (in action), 127 (in command Ninth Army), 172 (Ypres), 287, 303, 371, 445

Hunding Stellung, 483, 484 (carried by British), 498, 502 (captured by Allies)

Hutier, General von, 282, 371, 375, 376

IMPERIAL, Prince, xxiv

Indian Troops, 208 (Lord Roberts)

Italian Army, 263, 266 (heavy fighting), 279, 316, 399, 402 (heavily attacked), *see also* Italy

Italy, 254 (Foch's visit), 256, 260 (enemy assault), 261 (army retiring), 491 (British troops). *See also* Italian Army

Italy, King of, 262 (Foch visits)

JAPAN, 259

Jesuit College, St. Etienne, xxi

Joffre, 41 (Foch meets J.), 48 (high praise), 78 (attack approved), 103 (German retreat), 108 (great victory on Marne), 114 (orders for the Aisne attack), 119 (shortage of

INDEX

ammunition), 124 (tragic shortage), 125 (sends for Foch), 140 (and British Army), 153 (Belgian Army), 154 (and British troops), 167 (Sir John French), 181 (reinforcements), 183 (at Dunkirk), 186 (at Cassel), 196 (and Foch), 203 (Foch's report), 213 (at Chantilly, 217 (shortage of artillery), 222 (motor accident), 223, 236, 238 (Foch's opinion), 243 (Allied offensive), 253 (retired from command), 267 (now Marshal), 267 (American Army)
Joppé, General, 72 (on Somme)

KEMMEL, Mount, 334, 340, 456
King of Belgians, see Albert, King of Belgians
Kitchener, Lord, 183 (at Dunkirk), 224 (recruits), 226, 273
Kleinzillebeke, 181, 187 (lost and retaken)
Koking Forest, 24, 26 (ground lost), 27 (powerful offensive)
Krylenko, 258 (Russian C.I.C.)

LA BASSEE, 171 (British Army), 191 (fighting), 192, 224 (British Army), 226, 236, 239, 324, 327, 333, 456, 487 (Allied success)
La Capelle, 523
Landrecies, 500 (British advance)
Langlois, xxix
Laon, 502 (Allied attack)
La Panne, 470 (residence King Albert), 486
Lassigny, 442
Lawrence, General, 299 (at Doullens), 372
Le Chesne, 514 (Allied advance), 522
Lefèvre, General, 61 (with Foch)
Lenharrée, 77 (attacked), 78, 80 (French retreat)
Lenin, 258 (seizes power)
Lens, 137 (slow progress), 388, 487 (occupied by Allies)
Le Petit, Colonel, 400 (Italy), 403
Le Polder, 221
Le Quesnay, 500
Le Rond, General, 493
Lescot, General, 5
L'Espée, General de, 51 (with Foch)
Liège, 205
Ligny, 463
Lille, 139 (French occupation), 143 (favourable for attack), 166 (German troops), 498, 500 (occupied by Allies)
Lindre, Lake, 9 (dam cut)

Linguet, 122 (slight advance)
Lissen, 403
Lloyd George, see George, Lloyd
London, 257 (allied conference), 278 (Supreme War Council), 285, 287
Loos, 239 (taken by British)
Lorette, 216 (enemy line captured), 236, 237, 239
Lorraine, xxiii, 13 (importance to Germany), 32 (danger of French Army), 41 (Foch's views), 42 (German hesitancy), 75 (Germans held), 108 (French advance), 374, 449, 473, 516, 519
Loucheur, M., 298 (at Doullens), 300 (supports Foch), 307-310, 493 (Minister of Munitions)
Ludendorff, 252 (in command German Armies), 283
Lunéville, 37 (enemy advance), 39 (Foch advances), 40 (XX Corps)
Lure, 473
Luxemburg, xlv (violation), 8 (German invasion), 516, 518
Lys, 139 (French cavalry), 145 (German advance), 154 (German repulse), 155, 165 (heavy fighting), 172 (enemy in force), 197, 324, (enemy reach), 328, 356, 392, 438, 470, 486, 487, 498, 499, 500 (crossed by Allies)

MAILLARD, xxix
Mailly, 73 (Ninth Cavalry), 79, 86, 97
Mairy, 103
Maissin, 59 (heavy fighting)
Maistre, General, xxxiv, 113, 136 (XXI Corps), 208 (King George), 215, 325, 328 (at Arras), 334
Maizières, 17 (advance), 28 (retreat), 52 (IX Corps forced back)
Mangin, General, 377, 378 (striking success), 392, 414, 445, 518, 519
Manteuffel, General, xxvii
Marion, Captain R.N., 548 (British peace delegation)
Marne, 97 (Ninth Army), 101 (to be crossed), 106 (crossed by Foch), 108 (Joffre's great victory), 363, 364 (in danger), 365, 366, 368 (enemy progress), 392, 404, (second big battle), 406, 410, 413, 414, 416, 419, 421, 424, (German disaster)
Marsal, 19 (XX Corps), 20, 28 (XV Corps)
Marthil, 23 (occupied)
Marwitz, General von, 281
Massevaux, 473
Massiges, 410

INDEX

Matz, 375 (enemy success), 376, 379, 382, 391
Maud'Huy, General de, xxxiv, 126, 132, 135, 142, 208 (King George)
Maurienne, 90 (retreat)
Mayence, 573, 577
Mélettes, 400, 403
Menin, 171, 181, 183 (Kaiser present), 486, 498, 499
Mesple, General, 303, 307
Messines, 174 (British losses), 180 (lost and retaken), 181 (heavy fighting), 182 (abandoned), 187 (French advance), 191 (fighting by British), 324 (enemy capture), 334 (fresh attack), 486
Metz, xxiii, xxiv, 4 (mobilized), 7 (German force, 12, 25 (dangerous advance), 204, 518, 519, 577 (Foch enters)
Meurthe, 7, 34 (French retreat), 35 (bridges blown up) 36 (enemy advance), 40 (French held up)
Meuse, 49 (French retreat), 55 (attack planned), 204, 205, 453, 461, 462, 473 (new offensive), 478, 496, 502, 513 (American offensive), 514 (enemy in retreat), 520, 521, 524 (full enemy retreat)
Mézières, 54 (French danger), 462, 470, 479, 498 (French advance), 514, 516, 517 (importance of railway)
Millerand, M., 50 (Minister of War), 183 (at Dunkirk), 186, 226
Millet, Major, xxix
Milner, Lord, 295 (at Versailles), 297, 299, 300, 332, 335, 353 (and U.S.A.), 372, 394, 398
Mirecourt, 253 (Foch in Command)
Miribel, General de, xxxi
Mitry, General de, 220, 337, 341, 343 (important work)
Mondemont, 70 (Ninth Army), 76 (Moroccans), 78, 85 (enemy attack), 88 (captured by enemy), 89 (recaptured), 91 (heavy fire)
Mons, 498, 523 (Allied advance), 524 (Canal)
Montdidier, 299, 302, 304 (enemy attack), 306, 309, 310 (close of battle), 321, 339, 366, 370, 374, 433, 437, 440 (abandoned by Germans)
Montgomery, General, 299 (at Doullens)
Monthois, 481 (French success)
Montreuil, 322, 325 (French G.H.Q.), 326 (Foch arrives)
Morains, 72 (abandoned), 80 (attacked), 81
Moreuil, 323 (French success)
Morhaye, 43 (important fighting)
Moroccan Division, 339
Moroccan Infantry, 51, 58, 68, 70, 71, 76, 77, 83, 85, 88, 89, 91, 93, 118, 119, 120, 121
Moronvilliers, 116 (attacked by Foch), 118
Morval, 248
Moselle, 12, 15 (advance), 40 (enemy advance), 44 (enemy advance), 516 (new Allied offensive), 518, 525
Mouchy-le-Châtel, 412
Mount Cassel, see Cassel
Mount Kemmel, see Kemmel
Mount Lissen, see Lissen
Mount Noir, see Noir
Mount Rouge, see Rouge
Moussy, General, 180, 182, 185
Mouthois, 56 (Foch's visit)
Moy, 48 (Fifth Army)
Murmausk, 398

NANCY, xxvii, xxxvi, lvi (outbreak of war), 3 (Foch returns), 6 (strategic points), 31 (Army H.Q.), 35 (Foch goes to H.Q.), 39 (further advance), 473
Napoleon, xxiv
Naulin, Major, 50 (Foch's staff)
Naval Conditions of Peace, 542, 543 (German Fleet)
Negro Regiments, 268
Neufchâteau, 8 (Second Army)
Neuve-Chapelle, 192 (enemy success)
Nicholas, Emperor, xxxvii
Nieppe, 327 (enemy advance)
Niessel, General, 258 (attached to Russian Army), 259
Nieuport, 146 (Belgian Army), 157, 158 (German attack), 158 (French destroyers), 159, 161, 162, 163 (locks opened), 164, 188, 191 (Belgian attack), 193 (Allied offensive), 219 (cavalry attacks), 224 (French troops), 227 (Belgian troops), 275
Ninth Army, 61 (under Foch), 62 (to hold Sézanne), 70 (at Mondemont), 72 (violent attack on Somme), 75 (dangerous gap), 79 (enemy held) 81 (heavily attacked), 85 (wide gap) 86 (heavy assaults), 89 (holding Champagne), 92 (heavy losses), 93 (forced back), 96 (successful advance), 97 (at the Marne), 98 (further advance), 103 (bridges destroyed), 104 (to attack German

INDEX

centre), 110 (details of German forces), 112 (on the Suippe), 113 (at Suippes), 113 (XXI Corps added), 113 (towards the Aisne), 115 (pursuit held up), 116 (attacks enemy), 117 (XII Corps added), 119 (strong German entrenchments) 121 (strong attack on Berru), 122 (attacked by enemy), 123 (Herman offensive fails), 124 (on the defensive), 127 (General Humbert in command)
Nivelle, General, 251 (in command French armies)
Noir, Mount, 342
Nomény, 8 (serious alarm), 79 (18th Div.)
Nordschoote, 197
Normée, 72 (positions held)
North Sea, 148, 168, 201, 219, 496, 499
Noulens, M., 459 (French Ambassador to Russia)
Nouvron, 366 (abandoned), 416
Novion Porcien, 54 (enemy advance)
Noyou, 132 (French held up), 291 (enemy capture), 366, 374, 445, 450, 454 (enemy abandon)

OBERNDORFF, Count, 547 (peace envoy)
Officers and Politics, xlix
Oise, 48 (Fifth Army), 49 (retreat), 54 (retreat), 124, (French attack planned), 281 (German offensive), 285, 311, 320, 344, 356, 366, 375 (fresh enemy attack), 376, 383, 450 (French success), 453, 496, 498, 499 (German retreat), 500 (Allied success)
Orfeuil, 480 (captured by Americans)
Orlando, Signor, 262 (Italian Prime Minister), 316 (War Council), 401
Ostend, 146, 148 (British Navy), 219 223, 224, 499 (occupied by Belgians)
Oulchy-le-Château, 419, 422 (French success)
Ourcq, 75 (Germans held), 108 (French advance), 365, 366, 368 (enemy progress), 415, 417, 419, 420
Oyes, 83 (enemy retreat)

PADUA, 264 (Foch arrives)
Painlevé, M., 254
Pambet, General, 72 (on Somme)
Paris, xxvi, 47 (German advance), 109 (saved), 293, 296, 301, 366, 372 (Allied conference), 388, 389,
428, 456, 529 (meeting of Allies), 540 (Peace terms)
Parker, General, 105
Passchendaele, 169, 171, 486
Pau, General, 145 (attached to Belgians)
Payot, General, 495
Peace Signed, 581
Péronne, 290, 291 (abandoned), 307, 309, 454 (free from Germans), 467
Pershing, General, xiii, xvi, 268 (U.S.A.) 307, 345, 352, 353, 369, 394, 397, 429 (at Bombon), 458, 462, 463, 479, 492, 505 (Clemenceau complains of his obstinacy), 515, 518, 538 (Peace conditions)
Pervyse, 162 (General Grossetti), 163 (flooded)
Pétain, General, xiii, xxxiv, 215, 260, 268, 270, 285, 287, 290, 291, 293, 295, 298, 302, 306, 307, 319, 321, 325, 326, 328, 334, 340, 344, 361, 362 (hasty action), 366, 368, 371, 382, 393, 405, 407, 411, 429 (at Bombon) 444 (meets King George), 460, 463 (American troops), 474, 479, 490, 512, 518, 536 (Peace terms), 538 (his conditions)
Piave, 263, 264 (to be defended), 265, 266, 401, 402
Picardy, 299, 324 (British attacked), 423, 438
Pierre-Morains, 78 (attacked)
Pierrepont, 502
Plancy, 64 (Foch's H.Q.), 74, 86, 88, 98
Plantey, General, 148 (Dunkirk)
Pleurs, 80 (advanced H.Q.)
Plumer, General, 324, 330, 335, 341, 470, 485
Poesele, 188 (enemy advance)
Poincaré, M., 539 (Peace terms)
Poison Gas. *See* Gas.
Poland, 543 (peace conditions)
Polignan, xxi
Polish Troops, 520
Pont à Vendin, 137 (held)
Poperinghe, 182
Portuguese Troops, 324
Pressoire, 250
Prisoner Labour, 494 (British refusal)
Prosnes, 123 (Foch is attacked)
Prussia, xl
Pulteney, General, 170
Py, 478 (enemy resistance)
Putz, General, 226, 235

" RACE TO THE SEA," 131

INDEX

Radiguet, General, 72 (on Somme)
Rambétant, 3
Ramscapelle, 164 (held by Germans), 164 (captured by Grossetti)
Rapallo, 262 (Allied conference), 272 (Agreement)
Rawlinson, General, 145, 146, 148, 165, 181, 305 (succeeds Gough), 308, 309 (reinforcements), 310 (another attack), 323, 339, 435, 452, 402 (further advance)
Reading, Lord, 155 (tour of Front)
Rechicourt, 371 (British H.Q.)
Refugees, 61, 135, 149
Reparations, 535
Requin, Captain, 175 (with Foch)
Rethel, 52 (bridges lost), 53 (Foch retreats), 524
Rethondes, 579 (where Armistice was signed)
Retreat, French, 48
Révange, 22 (11th Division)
Rheims, 118 (bombarded by enemy), 118 (Cathedral in flames), 123, 285, 356, 358, 363, 365, 370, 407, 410, 411, 414, 474, 480 (German retreat)
Rhine, 521, 526, 541, 573, 574, 577 (occupied)
Ribot, M., 183 (at Dunkirk)
Roberts, F. M. Lord, 207 (at Cassel), 208 (Indian Troops), 208 (his death at St. Omer)
Robertson, General, 255, 257 (in London), 260, 261 (visits Treviso), 263, 274 (at Compiègne)
Robillot, General, 329 (at Sarcus), 335
Rocroy, 51 (enemy movements), 51 (Foch in charge)
Rodez, xxi
Romagne, 503
Rome, 262 (Foch arrives)
Ronarc'h, Admiral, 145, 146, 151 (at Dixmude), 163
Roques, General, 117
Roubaix, 500 (occupied by Allies)
Rouge, Mount, 342
Roulers, 167 (French advance), 170 (Haig advances), 486, 498 (Allied advance), 500
Roumania, 255, 258 (danger from Russia), 543 (peace terms)
Roussebrughe, 166
Rouvroy, 302
Roye, 439, 440, 445, 446, 451, 454 (enemy retreat)
Rupprecht, Prince, 182
Russia, xxxviii, xliv (War declared), 109, 459, 542 (peace terms). See

also Russian Armies
Russian Armies, 212 (slow progress), 217, 255 (passive), 255 (default), 257 (morale undermined), 258 (Armistice required), 259 (Russo-German peace). *See also* Russia

SAINT-AMAND, 500
Saint-Eloi, 176 (French troops), 181
Saint-Georges, 220
Saint-Gobain, 455
Saint-Gond, 64 (to be seized), 66 (favourable for defence), 70 (to be held), 71 (fighting), 74 (to be held), 76 (German defeat), 85 (fresh advance)
Saint-Maurel, General de, 331 (Military Governor Dunkirk)
Saint-Mihiel, 431, 458, 460, 462, 465, 473
Saint-Omer, 142, 148 (French's H.Q.), 165, 175 (Foch arrives), 196, 208 (death of Lord Roberts), 208 (King George), 324, 325, 327, 329, 336
Saint-Pol, 135, 155 (Foch)
Saint-Prix, 71 (attacked), 77
Saint-Quentin, 462, 467, 472, 482, 483
Salines Canal, 20
Salonika, 240
Sambre, 499 (German retreat)
Sanon, 37 (French attack), 39 (further advance)
Santerre, 137 (ground lost)
Sarcus, xiii, 327 (Foch's H.Q.), 335, 352 (Foch and U.S.A.), 367 (Haig visits Foch), 401, 435, 446
Sarrail, General, 110
Sarre, 12, 516
Sarrebruck, 21, 518
Saussié, Father, xxiv, xxvii
Sauterre, 305, 423, 439
Sauvigny, Captain de, 174 (Sir John French)
Saverne, xlii
Saxony, Crown Prince, 106, 111
Scarpe, 281 (German Offensive), 285, 452, 467, 500 (enemy retreat)
Scheldt, 144 (French advance), 472, 482, 483, 500, 521, 522 (reached by Allies), 524 (Germany in full retreat)
Schnoebele, xlii
Schorbake, 159 (Belgians attacked)
Second Army, 40 (heavy fighting)
Sedan, 514, 516
Seille, 9 (Cavalry advance), 9 (flooded) 18 (held), 28 (XX Corps), 32 (Foch retires)

592

INDEX

Selle, 499
Semoine, 82 (Ninth Cavalry)
Senlis, vii, 251 (Foch in command), 253, 254, 522 (Foch's H.Q.), 536
Sensée, 482, 484, 487 (British advance), 500
Serbia, xliii (Ultimatum), xliv (War)
Serbian Army, 240
Serres, 16 (XX Corps)
Serre, 502, 521, 522 (Allied success)
Sézanne, 62 (Foch to hold), 64 (attack), 93 (42nd Div.)
Siberia, 259, 399
Signy L'Abbaye, 53 (French attacked)
Sillery, 58 (Foch's H.Q.)
Sissonne, 502
Smith-Dorrien, General, 226
Soissons, 104 (German forces), 361, 363, 365 (enemy progress), 370, 391, 406, 414, 418, 423 (recaptured by Foch)
Soisy, 77 (attacked)
Solesmes, 497, 498 (British capture)
Somme, xx, 47 (enemy advance), 49 (crossed by Germans), 71 (heavy fighting), 72 (enemy attack), 72 (line lost), 78 (further attack), 138 (Second Army), 193 (more fighting), 243 (British troops), 245 (Foch to attack), 246 (attack starts), 247 (four mile advance), 249 (Allied attack), 289 (Gough's retreat), 305 (further fighting), 310, 319, 321, 338 (3 weeks quiet), 364, 382, 392, 405, 438 (French advance), 440, 446
Sommesous, 82 (abandoned), 87
Sompuis, 86 (XXI Corps), 97, 101 (Fourth Army)
Sonino, 316 (War Council)
Souain, 114 (captured by Foch), 118 (seized by enemy)
Souchez, 215, 236, 239
Strasbourg, 12, 204, 577 (Foch enters)
Submarines, 342
Suippe, 57 (positions prepared), 112 (Ninth Army), 113 (heavy fighting), 478, 480, 481
Swiss Neutrality, 253
Switzerland, 526

TAGLIAMENTO, 260, 261
Tangier, xlii
Tanks, 248, 358 (German), 415 (French), 417, 422, 438, 461, 490, 519
Tarbes, xxi

Tardieu, M., 50 (interpreter to Foch), 396, 493
Taverna, General, 10, 172
Tcherbatcheff, General, xxxvii
Territorials, 138 (at Doullens), 157 (at Yser)
Thiancourt, 465
Thielt, 471
Thiepval, 248
Thiescourt, 376
Thionville, 12
Thourout, 498 (Allied advance), 499 (captured)
Tilloy, 106 (French Cavalry)
Torcy, 417 (French success)
Toul, xliv
Toulon-la-Montagne, 69 (held by Foch)
Tourcoing, 500 (occupied by Allies)
Tournai, 500 (held by British)
Tours, 61 (Army H.Q.)
Trèves, 579 (Foch's arrival)
Treviso, 261 (Foch arrives), 261 (Robertson arrives)
Turkey, 255, 273, 540 (signs armistice)

UNITED STATES. See America

VAIRE, 438
Valdagno, 265 (French Forces)
Valenciennes, 500 (held by British), 521, 523
Vannay, 93 (enemy retreat)
Vanselow, Captain, 547 (peace envoy)
Vassimont, 78 (enemy capture)
Vaure, 93 (enemy attack)
Velehoek, 189
Verdun, xliv, 48 (Third Army), 205, 245 (grave events), 263
Versailles, 264, (Allied War Council), 270, 275 (Conference), 295, 316, 394, 397, 399, 408, 409, 491 (Conference), 541 (Allied meeting), 574 (Treaty of Peace), 591 (Peace signed)
Vesle, 359, 361, 363 (enemy halt), 414, 419, 423, 479, 502
Vertus, 61 (refugees)
Vicenza, 265 (British Army)
Vidal, General, 185
Villeneuve, La, 70 (attacked), 71 (taken and retaken), 76, 77, 84
Villers-Bretonneux, 338 (held by enemy), 339 (retaken)
Vimy, 215, 216, 233, 235, 238, 239, 251
Vitrimont, 39 (passed)
Vitry-le-François, 7 (G.H.Q.), 41,

INDEX

(Foch arrives), 47 (serious news), 50 (Millerand's visit), 74 (Fourth Army)
Viviers Wood, 27 (enemy penetration)
Vlamertinghe, 177 (Foch arrives), 182
Vosges, 47 (German invasion), 253 (Foch's work), 374, 473, 525
Vouvron, 450
Vouziers, 514

WAR COUNCIL, Supreme (Allied), 264, 273, 278, 280 (a grave error), 285, 294, 316 (Italy), 395, 397, 399, 408, 460, 541 (peace terms)
Wassigny, 499 (British advance), 502
Wemyss, Admiral, 545 (peace envoys)
Werwicq, 498, 499
Weygand, General, xiii, xiv, 41 (Chief of Staff to Foch), 52 (at Machault), 94 (in charge at Fère-Champenoise), 152 (Foch's Chief of Staff), 183 (at Dunkirk), 209 (decorated by King George), 254 (visits Berne), 273 (at Versailles), 274 (his protest), 292 (at Abbeville), 295, 298, 303, 322, 335, 372, 429 (at Bombon), 479, 545 (peace envoy)
Willemans, General, 194 (Belgian Chief of Staff)
Wilson, Sir Henry, xxxvii, 141, 175 (and Foch), 195 (at Cassel), 264 (War Council), 264 (at Padua), 273 (supports Foch), 295, 297 (at Versailles), 299, 335, 349, 372, 491
Wilson, President, 268, 374, 397, 398, 526 (Germany asks for peace), 529, 532 (not arbitrator), 536, 544, 578 (arrival in France)
Winterfeldt, General, 547 (peace envoy)
Wirbel, General, 15 (advance), 21 (covers flank), 22 (beyond Château Salins), 25 (attacked), 27 (outflanked)
Woevre, 458, 460, 503

Wurtemberg, Duke of, 182
Wyshcaete, 187 (heavy assault), 190 (British Army), 334 (enemy seize), 456, 486 (captured by Allies)

XX CORPS, 21 (advance), 38 (hard fighting), 40 (at Lunéville), 40 (Foch's new command), 41 (Farewell Order)

YPERLE CANAL, 170
Ypres, xx, 132, 146 (Belgian Army), 147, 151 (French Territorials), 156 (Battle of), 165, 166, 168 (German attack), 169 (Foch present), 172, 173, 174 (British driven back), 177 (British retreat), 179 (French troops), 183 (Kaiser appears), 184 (fresh assaults), 185 (British driven back), 186 (now safe), 188 (attacked again), 189 (battle over), 197, 201 (German vandalism), 234 (poison gas), 243 (British troops), 327 (further fighting), 330, 333 (Belgian Front), 334 (threatened), 340, 404, 456 (enemy withdraw)
Yser, xx, 132 (enemy checked), 146 (defensive position), 150 (defended), 157 (Battle of), 158 (German attack), 159 (crossed by Germany), 163 (to be flooded), 164 (enemy retired), 172, 188 (fresh attack), 190 (Belgian army), 193 (Foch attacks), 220 (crossed by Allies), 234 (river crossed by enemy), 485, 525

ZARREN, 498
Zeebrugge, 223, 499 (occupied by Belgians)
Zillebeke, 174 (attacked)
Zonnebeke, 179 (critical situation), 185, 189
Zouaves, 182

www.ingramcontent.com/pod-product-compliance
Lightning Source LLC
Chambersburg PA
CBHW071351300426
44114CB00016B/2027